Contents

PART 3
Text, discourse and ideology

PART 4
The voice of authority: institutional settings and alliances

PART 5
Individual voice and positionality

In Memory of John Sinclair
1933–2007

Acknowledgements

The articles appearing in this volume are a subset of those I selected for a much larger, four-volume reader that is also being published by Routledge, entitled *Critical Concepts: Translation Studies*. I am grateful to a number of colleagues for advice and support in preparing both readers. In particular, I would like to acknowledge my debt to Luis Pérez Gonzalez, Vicki Flippance, Iris Bachmann, Martha Cheung, Chunshen Zhu, Loredana Polezzi, Kate Sturge, Francesca Billiani, James St. André, Aleka Lianeri, Patricia Willson and Dirk Delabastita. I am also grateful to Siobhan Brownlie for translating the article by Pascale Casanova, and to Sue-Ann Harding for compiling both indexes.

My thanks also to the staff at Routledge, especially Louisa Semlyen, Andrew Watts, Ursula Mallows and Eloise Cook for their assistance throughout.

The editor and publishers would like to thank the following people for permission to reprint material:

Baker, Mona (2007) 'Reframing Conflict in Translation', *Social Semiotics* 17(1): 151–69. © 2007 Taylor & Francis Ltd, http://www.informaworld.com, reprinted by permission of the publisher.

Pascale Casanova, 'Consécration et accumulation de capital littéraire. La traduction comme échange inégal', *Actes de la recherche en sciences sociales*, 144, 2002, pp. 7–20; translated by Siobhan Brownlie. With permission from *Actes de la recherche en sciences sociales*.

Eric Cazdyn, 'A New Line in the Geometry' from Atom Egoyan and Ian Balfour, 'Subtitles on the Foreignness of Film', Alphabet City Media Book, © 2004. Reproduced by permission of MIT Press

Coldiron, A. E. B., 'Translation's Challenge to Critical Categories: Verses from the French in the Early English Renaissance'. *Yale Journal of Criticism* 16: 2 (2003), excerpt from pp. 315–344. © 2003 Yale University and The Johns Hopkins University Press. Reprinted with permission of The Johns Hopkins University Press

Michael Cronin, 'The Cracked Looking Glass of Servants', in *The Translator*, vol. 4, no. 2, 1998, pp. 145–62. Reproduced by permission of St Jerome Publishing

Brad Davidson, "The Interpreter as Institutional Gatekeeper: The Socio-linguistic role of Interpreters in Spanish-English Medical Discourse", in *Journal of Sociolinguistics*, vol. 4, no. 3, August 2000, pp. 379–405 (27)

Douce Fragm. D. 10, p. 2+4 – *The Kalendayr of Shyppars* (Paris: Verard, 1502). Reprinted by permission of Bodleian Library, University of Oxford

Johan Helibron, European Journal of Social Theory, vol 2, no. 4, pp. 195–212, copyright © 1999 by Sage Publications Ltd. Reprinted by permission of SAGE

Theo Hermans, 'The Translator's Voice in Translated Narrative' in *Target* 8:1, 1996, pp. 23–48. With kind permission of John Benjamins Publishing Company, Amsterdam/Philadelphia. www.benjamins.com

Moira Inghilleri, 'National Sovereignty versus Universal Rights: Interpreting Justice in a Global Context', *Social Semiotics* 17(2): 195–212, 2007, Taylor & Francis Ltd, http://www.informaworld.com, reprinted by permission of the publisher

Hephzibah Israel, 'Translating the Bible in Nineteenth Century India', from *Translating Others*, vol. 2, ed. Theo Hermans, 2006, pp 441–459. Reproduced by permission of St Jerome Publishing

Marco Jacquemet, 'The Registration Interview: Restricting Refugees' Narrative Performance', from Mike Baynham and Ana De Fina (eds) *Dislocations and Relocations: Narratives of Displacement*, pp. 197–200. Reproduced by permission of St Jerome Publishing

Alexandra Jaffe, 'Locating Power: Corsican Translators and their Critics', in Blommaert, *Language Ideological Debates*, 1999. pp. 39–67. Reproduced by permission of Walter de Gruyter

Kahf, Mohja (2000) 'Packaging "Huda": Sha'rawi's Memoirs in the United States Reception Environment', in Amal Amireh and Lisa Suhair Majaj (eds) *Going Global: The Transnational Reception of Third World Women Writers*, New York and London: Garland Publishing, 148–172. Reproduced by permission of Garland Publishing

Indra Levy, 'Engendered by Translation: Modern Japanese Literature, Vernacular Style, and the Westernesque Femme Fatale'. Reworked extract based on chapters 1 and 2 of *Sirens of the Western Shore: The Westernesque Femme Fatale, Translation, and Vernacular Style in Modern Japanese Literature* (New York: Columbia University Press, 2006). Copyright © 2006 Columbia University Press. With permission from Columbia University Press

Karin Littau, 'Translation in the Age of Postmodern Production: from Text to Interntext to Hypertext', *Forum for Modern Language Studies*, 1997, XXXIII (1), pp. 81–96, by permission of Oxford University Press

Ian Mason, "Discourse, ideology, and translation" in R. de Beaugrande et al. *Language, Discourse and Translation in the West and Middle East,* 1994, pp. 23 – 34. With kind permission of John Benjamins Publishing Company, Amsterdam/Philadelphia. www.benjamins.com.

'Pôru Rûta/Paul Rotha and the Politics of Translation', by Abé Mark Nornes, from *Cinema Journal* Volume 38 Issue 3, pp. 91–108. © University of Texas Press

Vicente L. Rafael, "Translation in Wartime," in *Public Culture*, volume 19, no.2, pp. 239–246. Copyright 2007, Duke University Press. All rights reserved. Used by permission of the publisher

Raley, Rita, "Machine Translation and Global English." *Yale Journal of Criticism* 16: 2 (2003), Excerpt from pp. 291–313. © 2003 Yale University and The Johns Hopkins University Press. Reprinted with permission of The Johns Hopkins University Press

Selim, Samah (2009) 'Pharaoh's Revenge: Translation, Literary History and Colonial Ambivalence', in *The Making of the Arab Intellectual*, Dyala Hamzah. © 2009 Routledge. Reproduced by permission of Taylor and Francis Books UK.

John Sturrock, Consulting Editor of the *London Review of Books*, for kind permission to reprint 'Writing Between the Lines: The Language of Translation', first published in *New Literary History*, 1990, 21: 993–1013, The Johns Hopkins University Press

Talal Asad, 'The Concept of Cultural Translation in British Social Anthropology' in James Clifford and George E. Marcus (eds) *Writing Culture: The Poetics and Politics of Ethnography*, 1986. Reproduced by permission of the University of California Press

Maria Tymoczko, 'Ideology and the Position of the Translator In What Sense is a Translator "In Between"?', from *Apropos of Ideology*, Maria Calzada Perez, ed., 2003, pp. 181–201. Reproduced by permission of St Jerome Publishing

Lawrence Venuti, 'Translation as cultural politics: regimes of domestication in English', *Textual Practice* 7(2): 208–23, 1993. © 1993 Routledge. Reproduced by permission of Taylor and Francis Books UK

Sources

Asad, Talal (1986) 'The Concept of Cultural Translation in British Social Anthropology', in James Clifford and George E. Marcus (eds) *Writing Culture: The Poetics and Politics of Ethnography*, Berkeley, CA: The University of California Press, 141–64.

Baker, Mona (2007) 'Reframing Conflict in Translation', *Social Semiotics* 17(1): 151–69.

Casanova, Pascale (2002) 'Consécration et accumulation de capital littéraire. La traduction comme échange inégal', *Actes de la recherche en sciences sociales* 144: 7–20.

Cazdyn, Eric (2004) 'A New Line in the Geometry', in Atom Egoyan and Ian Balfour (eds) *Subtitles: On the Foreignness of Film*, Cambridge, MA: Massachussetts Institute of Technology (MIT) Press & Alphabet City Media Inc., 403–419.

Coldiron, A. E. B. (2003) 'Translation's Challenge to Critical Categories: Verses from French in the Early English Renaissance', *The Yale Journal of Criticism* 16(2): 315–44.

Cronin, Michael (1998) 'The Cracked Looking Glass of Servants: Translation and Minority Languages in a Global Age', *The Translator* 4(2): 145–62.

Davidson, Brad (2000) 'The Interpreter as Institutional Gatekeeper: The Social-linguistic Role of Interpreters in Spanish–English Medical Discourse', *Journal of Sociolinguistics* 4(3): 379–405.

Heilbron, Johan (1999) 'Towards a Sociology of Translation: Book Translations as a Cultural World-System', *European Journal of Social Theory* 2(4): 429–44.

Hermans, Theo (1996) 'The Translator's Voice in Translated Narrative', *Target* 8(1): 23–48.

Inghilleri, Moira (2007) 'National Sovereignty versus Universal Rights: Interpreting Justice in a Global Context', *Social Semiotics* 17(2): 195–212.

Israel, Hephzibah (2006) 'Translating the Bible in Nineteenth-Century India: Protestant Missionary Translation and the Standard Tamil Version', in Theo Hermans (ed.) *Translating Others* (Volume 2), Manchester: St. Jerome, 441–59.

Jacquemet, Marco (2005) 'The Registration Interview: Restricting Refugees' Narrative Performance', in Mike Baynham and Anna De Fina (eds) *Dislocations/Relocations: Narratives of Displacement*, Manchester: St. Jerome, 197–220.

Jaffe, Alexandra (1999) 'Locating Power: Corsican Translators and Their Critics', in Jan Blommaert (ed.) *Language Ideological Debates*, Berlin & New York: Mouton de Gruyter, 39–66.

Kahf, Mohja (2000) 'Packaging "Huda": Sha'rawi's Memoirs in the United States Reception Environment', in Amal Amireh and Lisa Suhair Majaj (eds) *Going Global: The Transnational Reception of Third World Women Writers*, New York & London: Garland Publishing, 148–72.

Levy, Indra (2006/2009) 'Engendered by Translation: Modern Japanese Literature, Vernacular Style, and the Westernesque Femme Fatale', reworked extract based on chapters 1 and 2 of *Sirens of the Western Shore: The Westernesque Femme Fatale, Translation, and Vernacular Style in Modern Japanese Literature*, New York: Columbia University Press.

Littau, Karin (1997) 'Translation in the Age of Postmodern Production: From Text to Intertext to Hypertext', *Forum for Modern Language Studies* 33(1): 81–96.

Mason, Ian (1994) 'Discourse, Ideology and Translation', in Robert de Beaugrande, Abdulla Shunnaq and Mohamed H. Heliel (eds) *Language, Discourse and Translation in the West and Middle East*, Amsterdam: John Benjamins, 23–34.

Nornes, Abé Mark (1999) ' "Poru Ruta"/Paul Rotha and the Politics of Translation', *Cinema Journal* 38(3): 91–108.

Rafael, Vicente L. (2007) 'Translation in Wartime', *Public Culture* 19(2): 239–46.

Raley, Rita (2003) 'Machine Translation and Global English', *The Yale Journal of Criticism* 16(2): 291–313.

Selim, Samah (2009) 'Pharoah's Revenge: Translation, Literary History and Colonial Ambivalence', in Dyala Hamzah (ed.) *The Making of the Arab Intellectual: Empire, Public Sphere and the Colonial Coordinates of Selfhood*, London: Routledge.

Stahuljak, Zrinka (2009) 'War, Translation, Transnationalism: Interpreters in and of the War (Croatia, 1991–1992)'. Paper written for this reader.

Sturrock, John (1990) 'Writing Between the Lines: The Language of Translation', *New Literary History* 21(4): 993–1013.

Tymoczko, Maria (2003) 'Ideology and the Position of the Translator: In What Sense is a Translator "In Between"?', in María Calzada Pérez (ed.) *Apropos of Ideology – Translation Studies on Ideology – Ideologies in Translation Studies*, Manchester: St. Jerome, 181–205.

Venuti, Lawrence (1993) 'Translation as Cultural Politics: Regimes of Domestication in English', *Textual Practice* 7: 208–223.

INTRODUCTION

The literature in translation studies has traditionally been preoccupied with elaborating various types of dichotomies and taxonomies, and to some extent much of it still is. This volume attempts to orient the discipline away from dichotomies and taxonomies as much as possible, while recognizing that some may be embedded within a sophisticated and enriching discourse that is worth engaging with. On the whole, the work represented here assumes, implicitly or explicitly, that human behaviour is too complex and too dynamic to be streamlined into stable sets of choices that can be tied to specific textual or non-textual features. As a form of human behaviour, translation cannot be productively explained as a consistent choice between two or more discrete sets of strategies or options, however nuanced.[1]

Translation studies has come of age. So much so, I would argue, that we are now in a position to move safely and confidently not only beyond dichotomies and taxonomies, but also beyond the foundational literature and scholarly canon, and beyond reiterating and reasserting core assumptions, revisiting our institutional history, and defending our disciplinary agendas. While holding on to earlier achievements, we can now engage with innovative new research that is not necessarily indebted to the theories with which we are most familiar. We can afford to think outside the box. This collection is therefore deliberately prospective rather than retrospective in orientation. The material included in it has been selected to help us move on, to explore new ground, rather than pay tribute to and consolidate past achievements. It is meant to provide pointers towards the future and open up the field to innovative concepts and theoretical approaches, as well as to voices and perspectives from a wide range of traditions, beyond the dominant Anglo-Saxon world. Some of the material will already be familiar, but even there what is familiar has been combined with less familiar contributions in order to explore a range of themes that I see as key to moving the discipline forward. To this end, the emphasis throughout is on contemporary critical material culled from a broad range of sources, including but not restricted to sources in mainstream translation studies. Translation and interpreting being pervasive phenomena that have attracted the attention of scholars working in a variety of disciplines, some of which have a much longer history and stronger disciplinary base than translation studies, it would have been odd – given the nature of this project – to ignore the wealth of innovative, critical thinking in these areas. Some of the articles included here are written by scholars of anthropology, literature, linguistics, pragmatics, sociology and film studies, among other fields. One (Casanova's) is translated from French specifically for this reader, and many of the rest, though written in English, deal with translation and interpreting in a variety of non-Western and minority cultures, including Japanese, Corsican, Arabic, Tamil, Croatian and Albanian.

Themes and divisions

This reader consists of 25 articles, each preceded by a detailed summary, follow-up questions for discussion, and recommended further reading. It is divided into ten sections, as follows:

1   Politics and dynamics of representation
2   Modes and strategies: the language(s) of translation
3   Text, discourse and ideology
4   The voice of authority: institutional settings and alliances
5   Individual voice and positionality
6   Minority issues: cultural identity and survival
7   Translation in world systems
8   The making of literary traditions
9   Translation and war
10 Changing landscapes: new media and technologies

These divisions, and the order in which they appear, are based on thematic rather than chronological groupings and, importantly, they cut across modes and genres. In other words, the divisions are not based on the type of material being analyzed in each article. Some of the articles focus on literary translation, others on screen translation, machine translation, bible translation or the translation of official documents, and others still on one or other form of interpreting. Some engage with several genres simultaneously. This reader thus attempts to move not only beyond disciplinary divisions, but also beyond internal divisions within translation studies, the priority being to identify and give prominence to a number of pressing themes that merit our attention and that I believe we would do well to engage with in a sustained fashion. Most of these themes are reflected in the titles of the relevant sections and discussed in the introductory summaries of the articles in each section. But some cut across several sections and are worth highlighting here. They include the following:

● The relationship – past and present – between dominant European and Western societies and their many 'Others'. A number of articles explore and critique aspects of this relationship, including the type of representations that are generated through translation and that travel back to less dominant societies and influence their own processes of self representation, as well as the way in which translation is implicated in characterizing various rich literary traditions outside Europe in terms of what Selim (this volume) calls 'historical collapse and critical dystopia' by posing European literary genres and techniques as the 'standard' against which they must be measured. Articles that address this issue include those by Asad, Kahf, Jaffe and Selim.

- The intricate negotiation of dominance and resistance in many acts of translation and interpreting, and the many (textual and non-textual) forms that resistance can take. Domination is never absolute, and some of the articles in this reader redress the emphasis on power and hegemony by exploring the dynamics that force power itself to generate modes of resistance which undermine and question it. They suggest that streamlined accounts of unidirectional influence and absolute dominance – whether in postcolonial contexts or in the context of modern war – are unsatisfactory and fail to reflect the full complexity of the encounters they examine. See articles by Baker, Israel and Selim.

- The shifting and ongoingly negotiable positioning of translators and interpreters, and the unease to which it can give rise among those who rely on their services, as discussed in several articles, especially those by Tymoczko, Stahuljak and Rafael.

- The relationship between power, ideology and mediation. Mason (this volume), defines mediation as 'the extent to which one feeds one's current beliefs and goals into processing a text'. Mediation, as defined here, can be conscious or subconscious, and several of the articles included in this volume discuss instances of both. See especially Kahf, Mason, Baker, Nornes, Inghilleri and Stahuljak.

- The relationship between minority, globalization and the power of English, and the role that translation plays in suppressing or resisting this power. This is an extremely pressing issue that concerns practically all languages, rather than just those we might normally think of as marginalized. As Cronin (this volume) puts it, 'the hegemony of English in the fastest-growing area of technological development means that all other languages become, in this context, "minority languages" '. The articles by Cronin, Raley, Asad and Venuti address different aspects of this theme.

- The role played by translators and interpreters in suppressing or authorizing the 'voice of the lifeworld', i.e. the voice and narrative of the individual, as opposed to the voice of authority, of the dominant institution, be that an organization such as the United Nations, a medical establishment, the asylum system, a religious society, or a powerful discipline such as anthropology. The articles by Jaquemet, Davidson, Israel, Inghilleri and Asad all address this theme, to a greater or lesser extent.

- The growing importance of the role played by translators and interpreters in the context of armed conflict, and in dealing with the aftermath of conflict. For reasons to do with the spread and intensity of armed conflicts since the early 1990s and the increased visibility of translators and interpreters that accompanied this development, scholars both within and outside translation studies have begun to engage with various aspects of this issue in a sustained manner. For example, the Languages at War Project launched in May 2008 by two universities (Reading and Southampton) and the Imperial War Museum in London is headed by a scholar of French history, rather than translation studies, and devotes much attention to language policies and practices and to the role played by translators and interpreters in the liberation/occupation of Western Europe (1944–47) and in peacekeeping in Bosnia (1995–98). Articles that address aspects of this theme here include Baker, Rafael, Stahuljak, Jaquemet and Inghilleri.

- The ethics of translation and interpreting, and the moral dilemmas involved in attempting to 'do right' by various parties in the interaction: the source author and culture, the target reader and culture, various parties in an interpreted encounter, or a particular political or social cause. This theme runs through most of the articles included in this volume but is addressed explicitly in the articles by Asad, Sturrock, Venuti, Inghilleri and Cronin.

Many more themes can be traced across several articles in this volume. I have tried to alert the reader to these where appropriate, and to link them to other relevant issues raised in material not included in this reader.

Finally, this collection may be prospective in orientation today, but it is bound to appear dated in a few years. As I have argued elsewhere, no object of study, including translation and interpreting, stands still while we elaborate 'better' theories of it; 'it changes because the world changes, and our theories have to follow that dynamic' (Baker 2008:26). Perspectives and issues prioritized here are thus not better or more important, in absolute terms, than those prioritized in other readers and contexts, but it is my hope that, at least for the time being, this collection might succeed in relating meaningfully and productively to the way in which translation and interpreting function in our societies today.

Mona Baker
February 2009

Note

1   As I have argued elsewhere (Baker, 2009), scholarly research cannot completely avoid drawing on some form of categorization. This is therefore a question of the extent to which we rely on discrete categories in analyzing acts of translation, and to which we recognize and highlight the unstable nature and shifting boundaries of such categories.

PART 1

Politics and dynamics of representation

Chapter 1

Talal Asad

THE CONCEPT OF CULTURAL TRANSLATION IN BRITISH SOCIAL ANTHROPOLOGY

EDITOR'S INTRODUCTION

> . . . the process of 'cultural translation' is inevitably enmeshed in conditions of power – professional, national, international. And among these conditions is the authority of ethnographers to uncover the implicit meanings of subordinate societies. Given that that is so, the interesting question for enquiry is not whether, and if so to what extent, anthropologists should be relativists or rationalists, critical or charitable, toward other cultures, but how power enters into the process of 'cultural translation', seen both as a discursive and as a non-discursive practice.

IN AN ESSAY THAT HAS BECOME A STANDARD reference in several disciplines, Asad explores the concept of cultural translation as a metaphor that anthropologists have long used to describe their work and critiques the tendency to understand translation as reading implicit meanings in the utterances of natives, where the translator is assumed to be able to reveal meanings that are hidden from the native informants themselves. The discussion is based on an extended critique of Ernest Gellner's essay 'Concepts and Society' (Gellner 1970). Asad argues that Gellner fails to consider the impact of cultural translation as an *institutionalized* practice within the wider relationship of unequal societies, to acknowledge that it is not the abstract logical status of concepts that is relevant but the way in which specific political discourses mobilize or direct the behaviour of people within given cultural situations. Despite its highly questionable assumptions and methods of analysis, Gellner's essay remains extremely popular with academics because, Asad suggests, it adopts a style that facilitates the *textualization* of other cultures and encourages students to seek simple answers to complex cultural questions.

The process of cultural translation – however understood and defined – is inevitably enmeshed in conditions of power. One of these conditions is precisely the authority accorded to ethnographers to uncover the implicit meanings of subordinate societies. Different understandings of the concept of cultural translation reflect the inequality between the anthropologist, who typically belongs to a powerful culture and writes for a largely English-speaking academic audience, and those he or she writes about and 'translates', who are typically illiterate or at least belong to less powerful cultures than the anthropologist's. Within this context, the anthropologist behaves somewhat like the psychoanalyst in that he or she assumes final authority in determining the subject's meanings and as such becomes the 'real author' of those meanings. Here, Asad explains, ' "cultural translation" is a matter of determining implicit meanings – not the meanings the native speaker actually acknowledges in his speech, not even the meanings the native listener necessarily accepts, but those he is "potentially capable of sharing" with scientific authority "in some ideal situation" '.

The representation/translation that the ethnographer as 'cultural translator' produces of a particular culture is inevitably a textual construct and, importantly, one that cannot normally be contested by those the ethnographer writes about. And because of the powerful status of the ethnographer, and the fact that the 'translation' he or she produces has the status of a 'scientific text', this textual construct becomes a privileged element in the potential store of historical memory. As such, the anthropologist's monograph may return, retranslated, into a 'weaker' Third World language and influence mechanisms of self representation within that language/culture. Asad thus argues that ultimately, 'it is not the personal authority of the ethnographer, but the social authority of his ethnography that matters. And that authority is inscribed in the institutionalized forces of industrial capitalist society, which are constantly *tending* to push the meanings of various Third World societies in a single direction'.

Asad insists that society is not a text that the skilled anthropologist can 'read' in order to uncover meanings. Anthropologists like Gellner assume that translating other cultures is a matter of matching a sentence produced by a native informant with an equivalent sentence produced by the anthropologist, one that encodes the 'real meaning' of the first, with the anthropologist alone controlling this operation. This is the privileged position of someone who does not have to engage in a genuine dialogue with those he or she presumes to represent.

Follow-up questions for discussion

●   Asad is ultimately concerned with the way power shapes the process of 'cultural translation', and seems to suggest that most if not all of this power resides in institutions. In the case of anthropology as an institution, for instance, anthropologists must 'write up their people' using 'the conventions of representation already circumscribed . . . by their discipline, institutional life, and wider society'. Sturge (2007:6) similarly argues that the 'production of "cultural translations" is not the individual business of the ethnographer but a process strongly constrained by the context of institutional power'. To what extent and how do institutions in general constrain and orient the choices of individual translators (and interpreters)? What levels and forms of resistance might individuals adopt in the face of institutional power – see, for example, Gentzler (1996), Baer (2006)?

●   Asad draws a distinction between *contesting* and *translating*: criticizing people in an ethnographic monograph they cannot read is not the same as taking a critical stance towards a peer member of one's own community. In other words, responsible criticism must be addressed to someone who can contest it. It must also be clearly presented as such: 'In taking up a critical stance toward his [Gellner's] text', Asad states, 'I am *contesting* what he says, not *translating* it, and the radical difference between these two activities is precisely what I insist on'. Consider the implications of this distinction for strategies and practices of translation in different genres – anthropological, literary, academic, religious, etc. At what points, in or around the text, might an ethically responsible translator *contest* what the author says? How might he or she ensure that this contestation is sufficiently signalled as his or her own rather than presented as a position that the author or readers are surreptitiously co-opted into? And how might an *interpreter*, rather than translator, negotiate the difference between *translating* and *contesting*, especially in emotionally charged situations such as those described by Stahuljak and Inghilleri (both in this volume)?

● Asad argues that 'the good translator does not immediately assume that unusual difficulty in conveying the sense of an alien discourse denotes a fault in the latter, but instead critically examines the normal state of his or her *own* language. The relevant question is not how tolerant an *attitude* the translator ought to display toward the original author (an abstract ethical dilemma), but how she can test the tolerance of her own language for assuming unaccustomed forms'. How does this argument compare with those elaborated by Sturrock and Venuti (in this volume)?

Recommended further reading

Polezzi, Loredana (2000) 'Reflections of Things Past: Building Italy through the Mirror of Translation', *New Comparison* 29: 27–47.

Said, Edward (1989) 'Representing the Colonized: Anthropology's Interlocutors', *Critical Inquiry* 15: 205–25.

Sturge, Kate (1997) 'Translation Strategies in Ethnography', *The Translator* 3(1): 21–38.

Sturge, Kate (2007) *Representing Others: Translation, Ethnography and the Museum*, Manchester: St. Jerome.

Sturge, Kate (2008) 'Cultural Translation', in Mona Baker and Gabriela Saldanha (eds) *Routledge Encyclopedia of Translation Studies*, London & New York: Routledge, 2nd edn, 67–70.

A LL ANTHROPOLOGISTS ARE FAMILIAR with E. B. Tylor's famous definition of culture: 'Culture or Civilization, taken in its wide ethnographic sense, is that complex whole which includes knowledge, belief, art, morals, law, custom, and any other capabilities and habits acquired by man as a member of society'. It would be interesting to trace how and when this notion of culture, with its enumeration of 'capabilities and habits' and its emphasis on what Linton called *social heredity* (focusing on the process of learning), was transformed into the notion of a *text* – that is, into something resembling an inscribed discourse. One obvious clue to this change is to be found in the way that a notion of *language* as the precondition of historical continuity and social learning ('cultivation') came to dominate the perspective of social anthropologists. In a general way, of course, such an interest in language predates Tylor, but in the nineteenth and early twentieth centuries it tended to be central to varieties of nationalist literary theory and education (cf. Eagleton 1983:ch. 2) rather than to the other human sciences. When and in what ways did it become crucial for British social anthropology? I do not intend to attempt such a history here, but merely to remind ourselves that the phrase 'the translation of culture', which increasingly since the 1950s has become an almost banal description of the distinctive task of social anthropology, was not always so much in evidence. I want to stress that this apparent shift is not identical with the old pre-Functionalism/ Functionalism periodization. Nor is it simply a matter of a direct interest in language and meaning that was previously lacking (Crick 1976b). Bronislaw Malinowski, one of the founders of the so-called Functionalist school, wrote much on 'primitive language' and collected enormous quantities of linguistic material (proverbs, kinship terminology, magical spells, and so on) for anthropological analysis. But he never thought of his work in terms of the translation of cultures.

Godfrey Lienhardt's paper 'Modes of Thought' (1954) is possibly one of the earliest – certainly one of the most subtle – examples of the use of this notion of translation explicitly to describe a central task of social anthropology. 'The problem of describing to others how members of a remote tribe think then begins to appear largely as one of translation, of making the coherence primitive thought has in the languages it really lives in, as clear as possible in our own' (ibid.:97). This statement is quoted and criticized in the article by Ernest Gellner that I analyze in the next section, and I shall return to it in the context of Gellner's argument. Here I draw attention briefly to Lienhardt's use of the word 'translation' to refer not to linguistic matter per se, but to 'modes of thought' that are embodied in such matter. It may not be without significance, incidentally, that Lienhardt has a background in English literature, that he was a pupil of F. R. Leavis's at Cambridge before he became a pupil and collaborator of E. E. Evans-Pritchard's at Oxford.

Oxford is, of course, famous as the anthropological centre in Britain most self-conscious about its concern with 'the translation of cultures'. The best-known introductory textbook to emerge from that centre, John Beattie's Other Cultures (1964), emphasized the centrality of the 'problem of translation' for social anthropology and distinguished (but did not separate) 'culture' from 'language' in a way that was becoming familiar to anthropologists – though not necessarily therefore entirely clear (see pp. 89–90).

It is interesting to find Edmund Leach, who has never been associated with Oxford, employing the same notion in his conclusion to a historical sketch of social anthropology a decade later (1973:772):

> Let me recapitulate. We started by emphasizing how different are 'the others' – and made them not only different but remote and inferior. Sentimentally we then took the opposite track and argued that all human beings are alike; we can understand Trobrianders or the Barotse because their motivations are just the same as our own; but that didn't work either, 'the others' remained obstinately other. But now we have come to see that the essential problem is one of translation. The linguists have shown us that all translation is difficult, and that perfect translation is usually impossible. And yet we know that for practical purposes a tolerably satisfactory translation is always possible even when the original 'text' is highly abstruse. Languages are different but not so different as all that. Looked at in this way social anthropologists are engaged in establishing a methodology for the translation of cultural language.

Even Max Gluckman (1973:905), responding shortly afterward to Leach, accepts the centrality of 'cultural translation', while proposing a very different genealogy for that anthropological practice.

Yet despite the general agreement with which this notion has been accepted as part of the self-definition of British social anthropology, it has received little systematic examination from within the profession. One partial exception is Rodney Needham's *Belief, Language, and Experience* (1972). This is a complex, scholarly work that deserves extended treatment. Here, however, I wish to concentrate on a shorter text, Ernest Gellner's 'Concepts and Society' (Gellner 1970), which appears to be fairly widely used in undergraduate courses at British universities and is still available in several popular collections. I propose, therefore, to devote the next section to a detailed examination of that essay and then to take up some points that emerge from my discussion in the sections that follow.

A theoretical text

Gellner's 'Concepts and Society' is concerned with the way in which Functionalist anthropologists deal with problems of interpreting and translating the discourse of alien societies. His basic argument is that (a) contemporary anthropologists insist on interpreting exotic concepts and beliefs within a social context, but that (b) in doing so they ensure that apparently absurd or incoherent assertions are always given an acceptable meaning, and that (c) while the contextual method of interpretation is in principle valid, the 'excessive charity' that usually goes with it is not. The paper contains several diagrams intended to fix and clarify the relevant cultural processes visually.

Gellner introduces the problem of interpretation by reference to Kurt Samuelsson's *Religion and Economic Action* (1961), which is an economic historian's attack on the Weberian Protestant-ethic thesis. Samuelsson takes issue with the fact that Weber and his supporters have reinterpreted religious texts in a way that enables them to extract meanings that confirm the thesis. Gellner presents this example merely to bring out more sharply the contrasting position of the Functionalist anthropologist (1970:20):

> I am not concerned, nor competent, to argue whether Samuelsson's employment, in this particular case, of his tacit principle that one must not re-interpret the assertions one actually finds, is valid. What is relevant here is that if such a principle is made explicit and generalized, it would make nonsense of most sociological studies of the relationship of belief and conduct. We shall find anthropologists driven to employ the very opposite principle, the insistence rather than refusal of contextual re-interpretation.

But this modest disclaimer of competence allows too many interesting questions to drift by. To begin with, it calls for no great competence to note that Samuelsson does not hold to the principle that one must *never* reinterpret. Nor does he insist that there is *never* a significant connection between a religious text and its social context, but only that the conclusion the Weber thesis seeks to make cannot be established (see, for example, Samuelsson 1961:69). There is, furthermore, a real contrast that Gellner might have picked up between the Samuelsson example and the typical anthropologist's predicament. For economic historians and sociologists involved in the Weber debate, historical texts are a primary datum in relation to which the social contexts must be reconstructed. The anthropological fieldworker begins with a social situation within which something is said, and it is the cultural significance of these enunciations that must be reconstructed. This is not to say, of course, that the historian can ever approach his archival material without some conception of its historical context, or that the fieldworker can define the social situation independently of what was said within it. The contrast, such as it is, is one of orientation, which follows from the fact that the historian is *given a text* and the ethnographer has *to construct one*.

Instead of investigating this important contrast, Gellner rushes along to define and commend what he calls 'moderate Functionalism' as a method, which

> consists of the insistence on the fact that concepts and beliefs do not exist
> in isolation, in texts or in individual minds, but in the life of men and
> societies. The activities and institutions, in the context of which a word or
> phrase or set of phrases is used, must be known before that word or those
> phrases can be understood, before we can really speak of a *concept* or a *belief*.
> (ibid.:22)

This is well put and, even if it has been said before, it is worth restating. At this point the reader might expect a discussion of the different ways in which language is encountered by the ethnographer in the field, how utterances are produced, verbal meanings organized, rhetorical effects attained, and culturally appropriate responses elicited. After all, Wittgenstein had already sensitized British philosophers to the complexity of language-in-use, and J. L. Austin had set up distinctions between the different levels of speech production and reception in a way that foreshadowed what anthropologists would later call the ethnography of speaking. But Gellner had previously rejected the suggestion that this philosophical movement had anything of value to teach (see his polemic in *Words and Things* 1959), and like other critics, he always insisted that its concern with understanding everyday language was merely a disguise for defending established ways of speaking about the world, for denying that it was possible for such speech-ways to be illogical or absurd. Gellner has always been determined to maintain the distinction between defending and explaining 'concepts and beliefs' and to warn against the kind of anthropological translation that rules out *a priori* the critical distance necessary for explaining how concepts actually function, for 'to understand the *working* of the concepts of a society', he writes, 'is to understand its institutions' (1970:18; see also note 1 on the same page).

This is why Gellner's brief statement about moderate Functionalism quoted above leads him immediately to a discussion of Durkheim's *Elementary Forms of the Religious Life* which, besides being 'one of the fountainheads of Functionalism in general' (ibid.:22), is concerned to explain rather than to defend concepts – to explain, more precisely, 'the compulsive nature of our categorial concepts' (ibid.) in terms of certain collective processes. Thus:

> Our contemporary invocations of the functional, social-context approach
> to the study and interpretation of concepts is in various ways very differ-
> ent from Durkheim's. Durkheim was not so much concerned to defend
> the concepts of primitive societies: in their setting, they did not need a
> defence, and in the setting of modern and changing societies he was not
> anxious to defend what was archaic, nor loath to suggest that some
> intellectual luggage might well be archaic. He was really concerned to
> explain the compulsiveness of what in practice did not seem to need
> any defence (and in so doing, he claimed he was solving the problem of
> knowledge whose solution had in his view evaded Kant and others, and

to be solving it without falling into either empiricism or apriorism). Whether he was successful I do not propose to discuss: for a variety of reasons it seems to me that he was not. (ibid.:23)

It is clear that Gellner has recognized the basic project of *Elementary Forms* – namely, its attempt to explain the compulsive nature of socially defined concepts – but he moves too hastily from a consideration of what might be involved in such a problem to a dismissal of Durkheim's attempt at explanation. The possibility that *a priori denunciation* may not further the purposes of explanation any better than *defence* does not seem to be envisaged in 'Concepts and Society'. Instead, the reader is reminded, by way of quotation from Lienhardt, that the contemporary anthropologist typically 'appears to make it a condition of a good translation that it conveys the coherence which he assumes is there to be found in primitive thought' (ibid.:26). So we have here what I think is a misleading contrast – Durkheim's attempt to explain versus the contemporary anthropologist's attempt to defend. I shall return to this point later, but here I want to insist that to argue for a form of coherence by which a discourse is held together is not *ipso facto* to justify or defend that discourse; it is merely to take an essential step in the problem of explaining its *compulsiveness*. Anyone familiar with psychoanalysis would take this point quite easily. We might put it another way: the criterion of abstract 'coherence' or 'logicality' (Gellner tends to use these and other terms interchangeably) is not always, and in every case, decisive for accepting or rejecting discourse. This is because, as Gellner himself correctly observes: 'Language functions in a variety of ways other than "referring to objects" ' (ibid.:25). Not every utterance is an *assertion*. There are many things that language-in-use does, *and is intended to do*, which explains why we may respond positively to discourse that may seem inadequate from a narrow 'logical' point of view. The functions of a particular language, the intentions of a particular discourse, are of course part of what every competent ethnographer tries to grasp before he can attempt an adequate translation into his own language.

Gellner does seem half-aware of this point, but quickly brushes it aside in his eagerness to display to Functionalist anthropologists their 'excessive charity' in cultural translation.

> The situation, facing a social anthropologist who wishes to interpret a concept, assertion or doctrine in an alien culture, is basically simple. He is, say, faced with an assertion S in the local language. He has at his disposal the large or infinite set of possible sentences in his own language . . .
>
> He may not be wholly happy about this situation, but he cannot avoid it. There is no third language which could mediate between the native language and his own, in which equivalences could be stated and which would avoid the pitfalls arising from the fact that his own language has its own way of handling the world, which may not be those of the native language studied, and which consequently are liable to distort that which is being translated.
>
> Naïvely, people sometimes think that *reality* itself could be this kind of mediator and 'third language.' . . . For a variety of powerful reasons, this is of course no good. (ibid.:24–25)

Again, this sensible statement might seem to some readers to support the demand that the ethnographer must try to reconstruct the various ways in which the 'native language' handles the world, conveys information, and constitutes experience, before translating an alien discourse into the language of his ethnographic text. But Gellner's account proceeds in a different, and very dubious, direction.

Having located an equivalent English sentence, he continues, the anthropologist notices that it inevitably carries a value connotation – that it is, in other words, either Good or Bad. 'I do not say "true" or "false", for this only arises with regard to some types of assertion. With regard to others, other dichotomies, such as "meaningful" and "absurd" or "sensible" or "silly" might apply. I deliberately use the "Good" and "Bad" so as to cover all such possible polar alternatives, whichever might best apply to the equivalent of S' (*ibid.*:27).

Have we not got here some very curious assumptions, which no practised translator would ever make? The first is that evaluative discrimination is always a matter of choosing between polar alternatives, and second, that evaluative distinctions are finally reducible to 'Good' and 'Bad'. Clearly neither of these assumptions is acceptable when stated as a general rule. And then there is the suggestion that the translator's task necessarily involves matching sentence for sentence. But if the skilled translator looks first for any principle of coherence in the discourse to be translated, and then tries to reproduce that coherence as nearly as he can in his own language, there cannot be a general rule as to what units the translator will employ – sentences, paragraphs, or even larger units of discourse. To turn my point around: the appropriateness of the unit employed itself depends on the principle of coherence.

But Gellner's parable of the anthropologist-translator requires the assumption that it is sentences that the latter matches, because that makes it easier to display how the sin of excessive charity occurs. Having made an initial equivalence between a sentence in the local language and one in his own, the anthropologist notices that the English sentence carries a 'Bad' impression. This worries the anthropologist because, so runs Gellner's parable, an ethnographic account giving such an impression might be thought to be disparaging the natives he has studied, and to disparage other cultures is a sign of ethnocentrism, and ethnocentrism in turn is a symptom of poor anthropology according to the doctrines of Functionalist anthropology. Functionalist method requires that sentences always be evaluated in terms of their own social context. So the worried anthropologist reinterprets the original sentence, with a more flexible and careful use of the contextual method, in order to produce a 'Good' translation.

The sin of excessive charity, and the contextual method itself, are together linked, Gellner writes, to the relativistic-functionalist view of thought that goes back to the Enlightenment:

> The (unresolved) dilemma, which the thought of the Enlightenment faced, was between a relativistic-functionalist view of thought, and the absolutist claims of enlightened Reason. Viewing man as part of nature, as enlightened Reason requires, it wished to see his cognitive and evaluative activities as parts of nature too, and hence as varying, legitimately, from organism to organism and context to context. (This is the relativistic-functionalist view.) But at the same time in recommending life according to Reason and Nature, it wished at the very least to exempt this view itself (and, in practice, some others) from such a relativism. (*ibid.*:31)

Typically, Gellner's philosophical formulation presents this 'unresolved dilemma' as an abstract opposition between two concepts – 'a relativistic-functionalist view of thought' and 'the absolutist claims of enlightened Reason'. But how do these two 'concepts' work as 'correlates of . . . the institutions of [Western] society' (ibid.:18)? It would not be difficult to argue that the claims of 'enlightened Reason' are *materially* more successful in Third World countries than many relativistic views, that they have exerted greater *authority* than the latter in the development of industrial economies and the formation of nation states. We shall have occasion to discuss this further when examining translation as a process of power. The point is that 'the absolutist claims of enlightened Reason' are in effect *an institutionalized force*, and that as such it is by definition committed to *advancing* into and appropriating alien territory, and that its opponents (whether explicitly relativistic or not) are by definition *defensive*. Thus when Gellner continues on the same page to characterize this abstract dilemma in the attitudes of anthropologists, he fails to consider what 'cultural translation' might involve when it is considered as institutionalized *practice* given the wider relationship of unequal societies. For it is not the abstract logic of what individual Western anthropologists *say* in their ethnographies, but the concrete logic of what their countries (and perhaps they themselves) *do* in their relations with the Third World that should form the starting point for this particular discussion. The dilemmas of 'relativism' appear differently depending on whether we think of abstracted understanding or of historically situated practices.

However, Gellner says he is not in principle against anthropological relativism. 'My main point about tolerance-engendering contextual interpretation', he writes, 'is that it calls for caution' (ibid.:32). But why such caution is reserved for 'tolerance-engendering' as opposed to intolerance-engendering contextual interpretations is not explained. After all, Gellner insisted earlier that all translated sentences are bound to be received either as 'Good' or as 'Bad'. Why should we be suspicious only of those that appear 'Good'? If 'it is the *prior* determination that S, the indigenous affirmation, be interpreted favourably, which determines just how much context will be taken into consideration' (ibid.:33), can we perhaps escape this vicious circularity by adopting an *unsympathetic* attitude? Gellner does not address himself directly to this possibility here, but one must assume that it cannot be a solution, especially in view of the claim that 'there is nothing [*sic*] in the nature of things or societies to dictate visibly just how much context is relevant to any given utterance, or how the context should be described' (ibid.).

Yet can this last remark be meant seriously? *Nothing*?! How, then, is communication even between individuals in the same society ever possible? Why does one ever say to foreigners that they have misunderstood something they heard or saw? Does social learning produce no skills in the discrimination of relevant contexts? The answers to these questions should be obvious, and they are connected with the fact that the anthropologist's translation is not merely a matter of matching sentences in the abstract, but of *learning to live another form of life* and to speak another kind of language. Which contexts are relevant in different discursive events is something one learns in the course of living, and even though it is often very difficult to verbalize that knowledge, it is still knowledge about something 'in the nature of society', about some aspect of living, that indicates (although it does not 'dictate') just how much context is relevant to any given utterance. The point, of course, is not that the ethnographer cannot know what context is appropriate for giving sense to typical statements, or that he is induced to be more charitable than he should be in translating them, but that his attempts at translation may meet with problems rooted in the linguistic materials he works with *and* the social conditions he works in – both in the field and in his own society. More on this later.

The latter half of Gellner's essay is devoted to examples from ethnographic studies in order to display, first, excessive charity in translation, and then, the explanatory advantages of taking a critical look at the logic of alien religious discourse.

The first set of examples comes from Evans-Pritchard's *Nuer Religion* (1956), in which odd-sounding initial translations of Nuer religious discourse, such as the notorious statement that 'a twin is a bird', are reinterpreted. 'This kind of statement', Gellner observes, 'appears to be in conflict with the principle of identity or noncontradiction, or with common sense, or with manifest observable fact: human twins are *not* birds, and vice versa' (1970:34). According to Gellner, Evans-Pritchard's reinterpretation absolves Nuer thought from the charge of 'pre-logical mentality' by an arbitrary use of the contextual method. The apparent absurdity is reinterpreted to deny that Nuer beliefs conflict with manifest fact by relating the meaning of the 'absurd' statement to 'logical' behaviour. Gellner indicates how this is done by quoting (with the deliberate omission of one significant sentence) from Evans-Pritchard:

> no contradiction is involved in the statement which, on the contrary, appears quite sensible and even true, to one who presents the idea to himself in the Nuer language and within their system of religious thought. [He does not then take their statements about twins any more literally than they make and understand them themselves.] *They are not saying that a twin has a beak, feathers, and so forth. Nor in their everyday relations as twins do Nuers speak of them as birds or act towards them as though they were birds.* (1970:35. Sentence in brackets omitted by Gellner; emphasis supplied by Gellner.)

At this point Gellner breaks off the quotation and interjects in mock despair: 'But what, then, *would* count as pre-logical thought? Only, presumably, the behaviour of a totally demented person, suffering from permanent hallucinations, who *would* treat something which is perceptibly a human being as though it had all the attributes of a bird' (*ibid.*). So eager is Gellner to nail utterances that must count as expressions of 'pre-logical thought' (why *is* he so eager?) that he does not pause to consider carefully what Evans-Pritchard is trying to do. In fact, Evans-Pritchard devotes several pages to explaining this strange sentence. It is plain that he is concerned to *explain* (in terms of Nuer social life), not to *justify* (in terms of Western commonsense, or Western values). The aim of this kind of exegesis is certainly not to persuade Western readers to adopt Nuer religious practices. Nor does it rule out the possibility that individual speakers make mistakes or utter absurdities in their religious discourse when employing their traditional ways of thinking. It is not clear, therefore, why Gellner should point to this example from *Nuer Religion* to substantiate his charge of excessive charity on the part of Functionalist anthropologists. Evans-Pritchard is trying to explain the coherence that gives Nuer religious discourse its sense, not to defend that sense as having a universal status – after all, Evans-Pritchard himself was a Catholic both before and after his monograph on Nuer religion was written.

Now whether Evans-Pritchard succeeds in explaining the basic coherence of Nuer religious discourse is, of course, another question. Several British anthropologists – for example, Raymond Firth (1966) – (though not, to my knowledge, any Nuer themselves) have disputed aspects of Evans-Pritchard's interpretation. But such disagreements are still about different ways of making sense of Nuer religious discourse, not about too much or too little 'charity' in translation. In fact contrary to Gellner's allegations, Evans-Pritchard's exegesis *does* make quite explicit apparent 'contradictions', or at least ambiguities, in Nuer concepts – for example, between the notion of 'a supreme and omnipresent being' and that of 'lesser spirits', both of which are categorized as kwoth. And it is precisely because Evans-Pritchard insists on keeping the different senses of kwoth together as parts of 'one concept' and does not treat them as homonyms (as Malinowski might have done by relating the word to different contexts of use) that the Nuer concept of spirit might be said to be 'contradictory'. But whether the identification of ambiguities and 'contradictions' in the basic conceptual repertoire of a language provides obvious evidence of 'pre-logical thought' is, of course, a different issue – I would suggest that only someone with a very naïve understanding of what was involved in translation could think that it does.

Yet Gellner's discourse typically evades the issues it seems to be raising, in a style that seeks to hurry the reader along over a series of archly phrased disclaimers:

> I do not wish to be misunderstood: I am not arguing that Evans-Pritchard's account of Nuer concepts is a bad one. (Nor am I anxious to revive a doctrine of pre-logical mentality a la Lévy-Bruhl.) On the contrary, I have the greatest admiration for it. What I am anxious to argue is that contextual interpretation, which offers an account of what assertions 'really mean' in opposition to what they seem to mean in isolation, does not by itself clinch matters. (1970:38)

Now who would have claimed it did? Certainly Evans-Pritchard does not. In any case the opposition between a 'contextual interpretation' and one that is not contextual is entirely spurious. Nothing has meaning 'in isolation'. The problem is always, what kind of context?

But that is something Gellner never discusses, except by suggesting that the answer must involve a vicious circularity – or by uttering repeated warnings against 'excessive' charity (when is charity not 'excessive'?). He appears unaware that for the translator the problem of determining the relevant kind of context in each case is solved by skill in the use of the languages concerned, not by an a priori 'attitude' of intolerance or tolerance. And skill is something that is learned – that is, something that is necessarily circular, but not viciously so. We are dealing not with an abstract matching of two sets of sentences, but with a social practice rooted in modes of life. A translator may make mistakes, or he may knowingly misrepresent something – much as people make mistakes or lie in everyday life. But we cannot produce a general principle for identifying such things, particularly not through warnings to be careful of 'the contextual method of interpretation'.

And so to another of Gellner's charming disclaimers: 'To say all this is not to argue for a scepticism or agnosticism concerning what members of alien languages mean, still less to argue for an abstention from the contextual method of interpretation. (On the contrary, I shall argue for a fuller use of it, fuller in the sense of allowing for the possibility that what people mean is sometimes absurd.)' (ibid.:39). The charm of this statement consists in Gellner's cheeky appropriation of his opponent's method to strengthen his own distinctive position.

But before that is done, we are given further examples of the tolerance-engendering contextual method at work in Leach's Political Systems of Highland Burma (1954). Thus according to Leach, Kachin statements about the supernatural world are 'in the last analysis, nothing more than ways of describing the formal relationships that exist between real persons and real groups in ordinary Kachin society' (cited in

Gellner *ibid.*:40). At this point Gellner intervenes: 'It is possible to discern what has happened. Leach's exegetic procedures have also saved the Kachins from being credited with what they *appear* to be saying' and thus made it possible 'to attribute meaning to assertions which might otherwise be found to lack it' (*ibid.*:41). Gellner goes on to insist that he is not concerned to dispute Leach's interpretations, but merely 'to show how the range of context, and the manner in which the context is seen, necessarily affect the interpretation' (*ibid.*). This is a significant remark, because it is indeed not Leach's reductionism to which Gellner objects (we shall find him insisting on it himself later in connection with Berber religious ideology) but to the fact that this example of reductionism – which Gellner misleadingly calls 'contextualism' – seems to defend, rather than to attack, the cultural discourse concerned.

Gellner's demonstration of how 'the *uncharitable* may be "contextualist" in the second, deeper and better sense' (*ibid.*:42) begins by presenting a fictitious word in a fictitious society – the word 'boble', used in a way remarkably like the English word 'noble'. Thus we are told that it can be applied to people who actually display certain habitual forms of conduct, as well as to people who occupy a particular social status irrespective of their behaviour. 'But the point is: the society in question does not distinguish *two concepts*, boble (a) and boble (b). It only uses the word boble *tout court*' (*ibid.*). The logic of bobility is then analyzed further to show how

> bobility is a conceptual device by which the privileged class of the society
> in question acquires some of the prestige of certain virtues respected in
> that society, without the inconvenience of needing to practice it, thanks
> to the fact that the same word is applied either to practitioners of those
> virtues or to occupiers of favoured positions. It is, at the same time, a
> manner of reinforcing the appeal of those virtues, by associating them,
> through the use of the same appellation, with prestige and power. But all
> this needs to be said, and to say it is to bring out the internal logical
> incoherence of the concept – an incoherence which, indeed, is socially
> functional. (*ibid.*)

In fact the concept of 'bobility' is not shown to be *incoherent* – even if it be accepted that the ambiguity of the word allows it to be used in political discourse to consolidate the legitimacy of a ruling class (and therefore, in principle, also to undermine that legitimacy). Gellner's satisfied conclusion to his fictional example is surely far too hasty: 'What this shows, however, is that the over-charitable interpreter, determined to defend the concepts he is investigating from the charge of logical incoherence, is bound to misdescribe the social situation. *To make sense of the concept is to make nonsense of the society*' (*ibid.*, emphasis added). Clearly the word 'bobility' makes sense to its users in particular statements (or they would not use it), and it makes sense also, although of a different kind, to Gellner, who states that by deceiving its users it somehow upholds a social structure. Sense or nonsense, like truth or falsehood, applies to *statements* and not to abstract concepts. There seems to me no evidence here of a 'nonsensical' concept, because there is no analysis of socially situated statements.

But there is also a more important failure evident in this example: the lack of any attempt to explore its *coherence* – that which makes its social effect such a powerful possibility. Of course, political discourse employs lies, half-truths, logical trickery, and so on. Yet that is not what gives it its *compulsive* character, any more than the use of true or clear statements does, and compulsiveness is precisely what is involved in Gellner's example. It is not the abstract logical status of concepts that is relevant here, but the way in which specific political discourses seem to mobilize or direct the behaviour of people within given cultural situations. The compulsiveness of 'bobility' as a political concept is a feature not of gullible minds but of coherent discourses and practices. That is why it is essential for a translator of powerful political ideologies to attempt to convey something of this coherence. To make non-sense of the concept is to make nonsense of the society.

Gellner's final example comes from his own fieldwork among the central Moroccan Berbers, and is intended to clinch the argument that an uncharitable contextualist makes better sense of the society he describes by emphasizing the incoherence of its concepts: 'Two concepts are relevant', he writes, 'baraka and agurram (pl. igurramen). Baraka is a word which can mean simply "enough", but it also means plenitude, and above all blessedness manifested amongst other things in prosperity and the power to cause prosperity in others by supernatural means. An agurram is a possessor of baraka' (ibid.:43).

Igurramen – translated as 'saints' in Gellner's later writings (e.g. 1969) – are a fairly privileged and influential minority in the tribal society of central Moroccan Berbers who act as foci of religious values and also as mediators and arbitrators amongst the tribal population with whom they live. 'The local belief is that they are selected by God. Moreover, God makes his choice manifest by endowing those whom he has selected with certain characteristics, including magical powers, and great generosity, prosperity, a consider-the-lilies attitude, pacifism, and so forth' (ibid.).

This is Gellner's 'translation'. But his too-fluent use of a religious vocabulary with strong, and perhaps irrelevant, Christian overtones must prompt doubts and questions at this point. What precisely are the behaviour and discourses translated here as 'a consider-the-lilies attitude', 'makes his choice manifest', and 'endowing', for instance? Do the Berbers believe that God *endows* their 'saints' with dispositional characteristics such as great generosity and pacifism, or do they take it rather that these characteristics are *conditions* of saintliness, of the closeness of igurramen to God? Do the Berbers really behave as though religious and moral *virtues* were 'manifestations' of divine choice? What do they say and how do they behave when people fail to display the virtues they *ought* to have? By whom is an agurram's behaviour conceptualized as a 'consider-the-lilies attitude', given that he has both family and property, and that this fact is taken by the Berbers to be perfectly in order? Gellner does not give the reader the relevant evidence for answering these important questions, whose significance for his translation will emerge in a moment.

> The reality of the situation is, however, that the igurramen are in fact selected by the surrounding ordinary tribesmen who use their services, by being called to perform those services and being preferred to the rival candidates for their performance. What appears to be vox Dei is in reality vox populi. Moreover, the matter of the blessed characteristics, the stigmata [sic] of agurram-hood is more complicated. It is essential that successful candidates to agurram status be credited with these characteristics, but it is equally essential, at any rate with regard to some of them, that they should not really possess them. For instance, an agurram who was extremely generous in a consider-the-lilies spirit would soon be impoverished and, as such, fail by another crucial test, that of prosperity.
>
> There is here a crucial divergence between concept and reality, a divergence which moreover is quite essential for the working of the social system. (ibid.:43–44)

It is not at all clear from the account given by Gellner what is meant by the statement 'The local belief is that they are selected by God' – 'selected' for what exactly? For being arbitrators? But arbitration must be initiated by one or other member of the tribal society, and that fact can hardly be unknown to the tribesmen. For being pacific? But pacifism is a virtue, not a reward. For worldly success and prosperity? But that cannot be a local definition of saintliness, or the French colonial rulers would have been regarded as more saintly than any agurram.

It is really no great explanatory achievement for a European anthropologist to inform his agnostic and/or modern European readers that the Berbers believe in a particular kind of direct intervention of the deity in their affairs, that they are of course mistaken in this belief, and that this mistaken belief can have social consequences. In this kind of exercise we do not learn what they believe, but only that what they believe is quite wrong: thus, the Berbers believe that God 'selects' igurramen; we know God does not exist (or if some of us still 'believe' he does, we 'know' he does not intervene directly in secular history); ergo the 'selector' must be another agent whom the tribesmen do not know as the agent – in fact, the surrounding tribesmen themselves. The igurramen are 'selected' (for a particular social role? for a moral virtue? for a religious destiny?) by the people. The 'selection' appears to be vox Dei and is in reality vox populi. Or is it?

In reality the social process described by the anthropologist as 'selection' is the locus of a vox only if it is pretended that that process constitutes a cultural text. For a text must have an author – the one who makes his voice heard through it. And if that voice cannot be God's, it must be someone else's – the people's. Thus Gellner the atheist insists on answering a theological question: who speaks through history, through society? In this particular case, the answer depends on the text containing at once the 'real', unconscious meaning and its appropriate translation. This fusion of signifier and signified is especially evident in the way in which the Islamic concept of baraka is made to sound remarkably like the Christian concept of grace as portrayed by an eighteenth-century skeptic, so that the conditions defining the agurram's baraka are referred to with a knowing Gibbonian smile as 'stigmata' – and by that deft sign, a portion of the Berber cultural text is at once constructed (made up) and designated (shown up) within Gellner's text, as exquisite a union of word and thing as any to be found in all his writings.

But society is not a text that communicates itself to the skilled reader. It is people who speak. And the ultimate meaning of what they say does not reside in society – society is the cultural condition in which speakers act and are acted upon. The privileged position that Gellner accords himself for decoding the real meaning of what the Berbers say (regardless of what they think they say) can be maintained only by someone who supposes that translating other cultures is essentially a matter of matching written sentences in two languages, such that the second set of sentences becomes the 'real meaning' of the first – an operation the anthropologist alone controls, from field notebook to printed ethnography. In other words, it is the privileged position of someone who does not, and can afford not to, engage in a genuine dialogue with those he or she once lived with and now writes about (cf. Asad 1973:17).

In the middle of his article, when discussing anthropological relativism, Gellner complains that 'anthropologists were relativistic, tolerant, contextually-comprehending vis-à-vis the savages who are after all some distance away, but absolutistic, intolerant vis-à-vis their immediate neighbours or predecessors, the members of our own society who do not share their comprehending outlook and are themselves "ethnocentric" . . .' (ibid.:31).

Why have I tried to insist in this paper that anyone concerned with translating from other cultures must look for coherence in discourses, and yet devoted so many pages to showing that Gellner's text is largely incoherent? The reason is quite simple: Gellner and I speak the same language, belong to the same academic profession, live in the same society. In taking up a critical stance toward his text I am *contesting* what he says, not *translating* it, and the radical difference between these two activities is precisely what I insist on. Still, the purpose of my argument is not to express an attitude of 'intolerance' toward an 'immediate neighbour', but to try and identify incoherences in his text that call for remedy, because the anthropological task of translation deserves to be made more coherent. The purpose of this criticism, there-fore, is to further a collective endeavour. Criticizing 'savages who are after all some distance away', in an ethnographic monograph they cannot read, does not seem to me to have the same kind of purpose. In order for criticism to be responsible, it must always be addressed to someone who can contest it.

The inequality of languages

A careful reading of Gellner's paper shows that although he raises a number of important questions, he not only fails to answer them, but misses some of the most crucial aspects of the problem with which the ethnographer is engaged. The most interesting of these, it seems to me, is the problem of what one might call 'unequal languages' – and it is this I want now to discuss in some detail.

All good translation seeks to reproduce the structure of an alien discourse within the translator's own language. How that structure (or 'coherence') is reproduced will, of course, depend on the genre concerned ('poetry', 'scientific analysis', 'narra-tive', etc.), on the resources of the translator's language, as well as on the interests of the translator and/or his readership. All successful translation is premised on the fact that it is addressed within a specific language, and therefore also to a specific set of practices, a specific form of life. The further that form of life is from the original, the less mechanical is the reproduction. As Walter Benjamin wrote: 'The language of a translation can – in fact must – let itself go, so that it gives voice to the *intentio* of the original not as reproduction but as harmony, as a supplement to the language in which it expresses itself, as its own kind of *intentio*' (1969:79). It is, incidentally, for the reader to evaluate that *intentio*, not for the translator to preempt the evaluation. A good translation should always precede a critique. And we can turn this around by saying that a good critique is always an 'internal' critique – that is, one based on some shared understanding, on a joint life, which it aims to enlarge and make more coherent. Such a critique – no less than the object of criticism – is a point of view, a (*contra*) *version*, having only provisional and limited authority.

What happens when the languages concerned are so remote that it is very dif-ficult to rewrite a harmonious *intentio*? Rudolf Pannwitz, quoted in the Benjamin essay on which I have just drawn, makes the following observation:

> Our translations, even the best ones, proceed from a wrong premise. They want to turn Hindi, Greek, English into German instead of turning German into Hindi, Greek, English. Our translators have a far greater reverence for the usage of their own language than for the spirit of the foreign works . . . The basic error of the translator is that he preserves the state in which his own language happens to be instead of allowing his language

to be powerfully affected by the foreign tongue. Particularly when translating from a language very remote from his own he must go back to the
primal elements of language itself and penetrate to the point where work,
image, and tone converge. He must expand and deepen his language by
means of the foreign language. (1969: 80–81)

This call to transform a language in order to translate the coherence of the
original poses an interesting challenge to the person satisfied with an absurd-
sounding translation on the assumption that the original must have been equally
absurd: the good translator does not immediately assume that unusual difficulty in
conveying the sense of an alien discourse denotes a fault in the latter, but instead
critically examines the normal state of his or her own language. The relevant question
therefore is not how tolerant an attitude the translator ought to display toward the
original author (an abstract ethical dilemma), but how she can test the tolerance of
her own language for assuming unaccustomed forms.

But this pushing beyond the limits of one's habitual usages, this breaking down
and reshaping of one's own language through the process of translation, is never an
easy business, in part because (if I may be allowed a hypostatization) it depends on
the willingness of the translator's language to subject itself to this transforming power. I
attribute, somewhat fictitiously, volition to the language because I want to emphasize
that the matter is largely something the translator cannot determine by individual
activity (any more than the individual speaker can affect the evolution of his or her
language) – that it is governed by institutionally defined power relations between the
languages/modes of life concerned. To put it crudely: because the languages of Third
World societies – including, of course, the societies that social anthropologists have
traditionally studied – are 'weaker' in relation to Western languages (and today,
especially to English), they are more likely to submit to forcible transformation in
the translation process than the other way around. The reason for this is, first, that
in their political-economic relations with Third World countries, Western nations
have the greater ability to manipulate the latter. And, second, Western languages
produce and deploy desired knowledge more readily than Third World languages do.
(The knowledge that Third World languages deploy more easily is not sought by
Western societies in quite the same way, or for the same reason.)

Take modern Arabic as an example. Since the early nineteenth century there has
been a growing volume of material translated from European languages – especially
French and English – into Arabic. This includes scientific texts as well as 'social
science', 'history', 'philosophy' and 'literature'. And from the nineteenth century,
Arabic as a language has begun as a result to undergo a transformation (lexical,
grammatical, semantic) that is far more radical than anything to be identified in
European languages – a transformation that has pushed it to approximate to the latter
more closely than in the past. Such transformations signal inequalities in the power
(i.e., in the capacities) of the respective languages in relation to the dominant forms of
discourse that have been and are still being translated. There are varieties of knowledge to be learnt, but also a host of models to be imitated and reproduced. In some
cases knowledge of these models is a precondition for the production of more knowledge; in other cases it is an end in itself, a mimetic gesture of power, an expression
of desire for transformation. A recognition of this well-known fact reminds us that
industrial capitalism transforms not only modes of production but also kinds of
knowledge and styles of life in the Third World. And with them, forms of language.
The result of half-transformed styles of life will make for ambiguities, which an

unskillful Western translator may simplify in the direction of his own 'strong' language.

What does this argument imply for the anthropological concept of cultural translation? That perhaps there is a greater stiffness in ethnographic linguistic conventions, a greater intrinsic resistance than can be overcome by individual experiments in modes of ethnographic representation.

In his perceptive essay 'Modes of Thought', which Gellner criticizes for making over-charitable assumptions about the coherence of 'primitive thought', Lienhardt has this to say:

> When we live with savages and speak their languages, learning to repre-
> sent their experience to ourselves in their way, we come as near to think-
> ing like them as we can without ceasing to be ourselves. Eventually, we
> try to represent their conceptions systematically in the logical constructs
> we have been brought up to use; and we hope, at best, thus to reconcile
> what can be expressed in their languages, with what can be expressed
> in ours. We mediate between their habits of thought, which we have
> acquired with them, and those of our own society; in doing so, it is not
> finally some mysterious 'primitive philosophy' that we are exploring,
> but the further potentialities of our thought and language. (1954: 96–97)

In the field, as Lienhardt rightly suggests, the process of translation takes place at the very moment the ethnographer engages with a specific mode of life – just as a child does in learning to grow up within a specific culture. He learns to find his way in a new environment, and a new language. And like a child he needs to verbalize explicitly what the proper way of doing things is, because that is how learning proceeds. (Cf. A. R. Luria on 'synpraxic speech' in Luria and Yudovich 1971:50.) When the child/anthropologist becomes adept at adult ways, what he has learnt becomes implicit – as assumptions informing a shared mode of life, with all its resonances and areas of unclarity.

But learning to live a new mode of life is not the same as learning about another mode of life. When anthropologists return to their countries, they must write up 'their people', and they must do so in the conventions of representation already circumscribed (already 'written around', 'bounded') by their discipline, institutional life, and wider society. 'Cultural translation' must accommodate itself to a different language not only in the sense of English as opposed to Dinka, or English as opposed to Kabbashi Arabic, but also in the sense of a British, middle class, academic game as opposed to the modes of life of the 'tribal' Sudan. The stiffness of a powerful estab-lished structure of life, with its own discursive games, its own 'strong' languages, is what among other things finally determines the effectiveness of the translation. The translation is addressed to a very specific audience, which is waiting to read about another mode of life and to manipulate the text it reads according to established rules, not to learn to live a new mode of life.

If Benjamin was right in proposing that translation may require not a mechanical reproduction of the original but a harmonization with its intentio, it follows that there is no reason why this should be done only in the same mode. Indeed, it could be argued that 'translating' an alien form of life, another culture, is not always done best through the representational discourse of ethnography, that under certain condi-tions a dramatic performance, the execution of a dance, or the playing of a piece of music might be more apt. These would all be productions of the original and not mere

interpretations: transformed instances of the original, not authoritative textual representations of it (cf. Hollander 1959). But would they be thought of by most social
anthropologists as valid exercises in the 'translation of culture'? I think not, because
they all raise an entirely different dimension of the relationship between the anthropological 'work' and its audience, the question of different *uses* (practices), as
opposed merely to different *writings and readings* (meanings) of that work. And as social
anthropologists we are trained to translate other cultural languages as texts, not to
introduce or enlarge cultural capacities, learnt from other ways of living, into our
own. It seems to me very likely that the notion of culture as *text* has reinforced this
view of our task, because it facilitates the assumption that translation is *essentially* a
matter of verbal representation.

Reading other cultures

This inequality in the power of languages, together with the fact that the anthropologist typically writes about an illiterate (or at any rate non-English-speaking) population for a largely academic, English-speaking audience, encourages a tendency I
would now like to discuss: the tendency to read the *implicit* in alien cultures.

   According to many social anthropologists, the object of ethnographic translation
is not the historically situated speech (that is the task of the folklorist or the linguist),
but 'culture', and to translate culture the anthropologist must first read and then
reinscribe the implicit meanings that lie beneath/within/beyond situated speech.
Mary Douglas puts this nicely:

> The anthropologist who draws out the whole scheme of the cosmos
> which is implied in [the observed] practices does the primitive culture
> great violence if he seems to present the cosmology as a systematic
> philosophy subscribed to consciously by individuals . . . So the primitive
> world view which I have defined above is rarely itself an object of
> contemplation and speculation in the primitive culture. It has evolved as
> the appanage of other social institutions. To this extent it is produced
> indirectly, and to this extent the primitive culture must be taken to be
> unaware of itself, unconscious of its own conditions. (1966:91)

   One difference between the anthropologist and the linguist in the matter of
translation is perhaps this: that whereas the latter is immediately faced with a specific
piece of discourse produced within the society studied, a discourse that is *then* textualized, the former must construct the discourse *as* a cultural text in terms of meanings
implicit in a range of practices. The construction of cultural discourse and its translation
thus seem to be facets of a single act. This point is brought out in Douglas's comments on her own translations of the meanings of the pangolin cult among the Lele:

> There are no Lele books of theology or philosophy to state the meaning of
> the cult. The metaphysical implications have not been expressed to me in
> so many words by Lele, nor did I even eavesdrop a conversation between
> diviners covering this ground . . .
>   What kind of evidence for the meaning of this cult, or of any cult, can
> be sensibly demanded? It can have many different levels and kinds of
> meaning. But the one on which I ground my argument is the meaning

which emerges out of a pattern in which the parts can incontestably be shown to be regularly related. No one member of the society is necessarily aware of the whole pattern, any more than speakers are able to be explicit about the linguistic patterns they employ. (ibid.:173–74)

I've suggested elsewhere (Asad 1983) that the attribution of implicit meanings to an alien practice *regardless of whether they are acknowledged by its agents* is a characteristic form of theological exercise, with an ancient history. Here I want to note that reference to the linguistic patterns produced by speakers does not make a good analogy because linguistic *patterns* are not meanings to be translated, they are rules to be systematically described and analyzed. A native speaker is aware of how such patterns should be produced even when he cannot verbalize that knowledge explicitly in the form of rules. The apparent lack of ability to verbalize such social knowledge does not necessarily constitute evidence of unconscious meanings (cf. Dummett 1981). The concept of 'unconscious meaning' belongs to a theory of the repressive unconscious, such as Freud's, in which a person may be said to 'know' something unconsciously.

The business of identifying unconscious meanings in the task of 'cultural translation' is therefore perhaps better compared to the activity of the psychoanalyst than to that of the linguist. Indeed British anthropologists have sometimes presented their work in precisely these terms. Thus David Pocock, a pupil of Evans-Pritchard's, writes:

In short, the work of the social anthropologist may be regarded as a highly complex act of translation in which author and translator collaborate. A more precise analogy is that of the relation between the psychoanalyst and his subject. The analyst enters the private world of his subject in order to learn the grammar of his private language. If the analysis goes no further it is no different in kind from the understanding which may exist between any two people who know each other well.[!] It becomes scientific to the extent that the private language of intimate understanding is translated into a public language, however specialized from the layman's point of view, which in this case is the language of psychologists. But the particular act of translation does not distort the private experience of the subject and ideally it is, at least potentially, acceptable to him as a scientific representation of it. Similarly, the model of Nuer political life which emerges in Professor Evans-Pritchard's work is a scientific model meaningful to his fellow-sociologists as sociologists, and it is effective because it is *potentially acceptable to the Nuer in some ideal situation in which they could be supposed to be interested in themselves as men living in society*. The collaboration of natural scientists may from this point of view be seen as developing language enabling certain people to communicate with increasing subtlety about a distinct area of natural phenomena which is defined by the name of the particular science. Their science is, in the literal meaning of the term, their commonsense, their common meaning. To move from this common sense to the 'common sense' of the wider public involves again an act of translation. The situation of social anthropology, or sociology in general, is not at this level so very different. The difference lies in the fact that sociological phenomena are objectively studied only to the extent that their subjective meaning is taken into account and that the people studied are potentially capable of sharing the sociological consciousness that the sociologist has of them. (1961:88–89; emphasis added)

I have quoted this remarkable passage in full because it states very lucidly a position that is, I think, broadly acceptable to many anthropologists who would otherwise consider themselves to be engaged in very different kinds of enterprise. I have quoted it also because the nature of the collaboration between 'author and translator' is neatly brought out in the subsequent reference to the psychoanalyst as scientist: if the anthropological translator, like the analyst, has final authority in determining the subject's meanings – it is then the former who becomes *the real author* of the latter. In this view, 'cultural translation' is a matter of determining implicit meanings – not the meanings the native speaker actually acknowledges in his speech, not even the meanings the native listener necessarily accepts, but those he is 'potentially capable of sharing' with scientific authority 'in some ideal situation': it is when he can say, for example, with Gellner, that *vox Dei* is in reality *vox populi*, that he utters the true meaning of his traditional discourse, an essential meaning of his culture. The fact that in that 'ideal situation' he would no longer be a Muslim Berber tribesman, but something coming to resemble Professor Gellner, does not appear to worry such cultural translators.

This power to create meanings for a subject through the notion of the 'implicit' or the 'unconscious', *to authorize them*, has of course been discussed for the analyst-analysand relationship (e.g., recently in Malcolm 1982). It has not, to my knowledge, been considered with regard to what the cultural translator does. There are, of course, important differences in the case of the anthropologist. It may be pointed out that the latter does not *impose* his translation on the members of the society whose cultural discourse he unravels, that his ethnography is therefore not authoritative in the way the analyst's case study is. The analysand comes to the analyst, or is referred to the latter by those with authority over him, as a patient in need of help. The anthropologist, by contrast, comes to the society he wants to read, he sees himself as a learner, not as a guide, and he withdraws from the society when he has adequate information to inscribe its culture. He does not consider the society, and neither do its members consider themselves to be, sick: the society is never subject to the anthropologist's authority.

But this argument is not quite as conclusive as it may seem at first sight. It remains the case that the ethnographer's translation/representation of a particular culture is inevitably a textual construct, that as representation it cannot normally be contested by the people to whom it is attributed, and that as a 'scientific text' it eventually becomes a privileged element in the potential store of historical memory for the nonliterate society concerned. In modern and modernizing societies, inscribed records have a greater power to shape, to reform, selves and institutions than folk memories do. They even construct folk memories. The anthropologist's monograph may return, retranslated, into a 'weaker' Third World language. In the long run, therefore, it is not the personal authority of the ethnographer, but the social authority of his ethnography that matters. And that authority is inscribed in the institutionalized forces of industrial capitalist society, which are constantly tending to push the meanings of various Third World societies in a single direction. This is not to say that there are no resistances to this tendency. But 'resistance' in itself indicates the presence of a dominant force.

I must stress I am not arguing that ethnography plays any great role in the reformation of other cultures. In this respect the effects of ethnography cannot be compared with some other forms of representing societies – for example, television films produced in the West that are sold to Third World countries. (That anthropologists recognize the power of television is reflected, incidentally, in the increasing number of anthropological films being made for the medium in Britain.) Still less can the effects of ethnography compare with the political, economic and military constraints of the world system. My point is only that the process of 'cultural translation' is inevitably enmeshed in conditions of power – professional, national, international. And among these conditions is the authority of ethnographers to uncover the implicit meanings of subordinate societies. Given that that is so, the interesting question for enquiry is not whether, and if so to what extent, anthropologists should be relativists or rationalists, critical or charitable, toward other cultures, but how power enters into the process of 'cultural translation', seen both as a discursive and as a non-discursive practice.

Conclusion

For some years I have been exercised by this puzzle. How is it that the approach exemplified by Gellner's paper remains attractive to so many academics in spite of its being demonstrably faulty? Is it perhaps because they are intimidated by a *style*? We know, of course, that anthropologists, like other academics, learn not merely to use a scholarly language, but to fear it, to admire it, to be captivated by it. Yet this does not quite answer the question because it does not tell us *why* such a scholarly style should capture so many intelligent people. I now put forward this tentative solution. What we have here is a style easy to teach, to learn and to reproduce (in examination answers, assessment essays and dissertations). It is a style that facilitates the textualization of other cultures, that encourages the construction of diagrammatic answers to complex cultural questions, and that is well suited to arranging foreign cultural concepts in clearly marked heaps of 'sense' or 'nonsense'. Apart from being easy to teach and to imitate, this style promises visible results that can readily be graded. Such a style must surely be at a premium in an established university discipline that aspires to *standards* of scientific objectivity. Is the popularity of this style, then, not a reflection of the kind of pedagogic institution we inhabit?

Although it is now many years since Gellner's paper was first published, it represents a doctrinal position that is still popular today. I have in mind the sociologism according to which religious ideologies are said to get their real meaning from the political or economic structure, and the self-confirming methodology according to which this reductive semantic principle is evident to the (authoritative) anthropologist and not to the people being written about. This position therefore assumes that it is not only possible but necessary for the anthropologist to act as translator and critic at one and the same time. I regard this position as untenable, and think that it is relations and practices of power that give it a measure of viability. (For a critical discussion of this position as it relates to Islamic history, see Asad 1980.)

The positive point I have tried to make in the course of my interrogation of Gellner's text has to do with what I have called the inequality of languages. I have proposed that the anthropological enterprise of cultural translation may be vitiated by the fact that there are asymmetrical tendencies and pressures in the languages of dominated and dominant societies. And I have suggested that anthropologists need to explore these processes in order to determine how far they go in defining the possibilities and the limits of effective translation.

Chapter 2

Mohja Kahf

PACKAGING 'HUDA': SHA' RAWI'S MEMOIRS IN THE UNITED STATES RECEPTION ENVIRONMENT

EDITOR'S INTRODUCTION

A 'First World' feminist exercise of discursive power over 'Third World' subjects is not an inescapable given determined by the identity or physical location or education of the writer or reader.

THE QUESTION OF REPRESENTATION is closely linked to the environ-ment(s) of reception, and Kahf's study demonstrates the interdependence between the two. She examines a series of subtle but cumulatively meaningful shifts in Margot Badran's 1986 English translation of the Egyptian writer Huda Sha'rawi's *Mudhakkirati* (My Memoirs, 1981) to demonstrate how the politics of reception can constrain our reading of a text by an Arab woman. The translation, entitled *Harem Years: The Memoirs of an Egyptian Feminist*, was undertaken and published within a specific reception environment, that of the United States, which is shaped by a certain horizon of expectations for writing by and about Arab and Muslim women. In engaging with Arab and Muslim women, the United States reading public largely draws on a long history of Western stereotypes about Arabs and Islam. Kahf discusses three such stereotypes: the Arab or Muslim woman as a victim of gender oppression; as an escapee of her intrinsically oppressive culture; and as the pawn of Arab male power. She traces the historical development of these stereotypes, noting, for example, that the image of Palestinian women as fighters and Iranian women as supporters of the Islamic Revolution in more recent years complicated the picture of Arab and Muslim women as having to be either victims or escapees, and that the stereotype of a fanatic Arab or Muslim woman who is a pawn of (male members of) her culture emerged as a resolution to this contradiction.

Kahf argues that Western writers are not all inevitably guilty of generating such represen-tations and, equally, Arab women and men are not all automatically innocent of this distorting representational practice. The stereotypes that underpin representations of Arab and Muslim women can be challenged by publishers and translators in both communities. Kahf's detailed analysis demonstrates that the pressures of the United States reception environment work in four ways in transforming the Arabic *Mudhakkirati* into the English *Harem Years* – that is, in 'haremizing' the narrative. Sha'rawi's engagement with Arab men in relationships that she saw as satisfying and enriching is minimized; her orientation toward Europe is exaggerated; her command of class privilege is camouflaged; and her story as a much respected and influential public figure is recentred in *Harem Years* around private life and the 'harem'.

Follow-up questions for discussion

- Kahf refers to a 'process by which Western feminist discourse "colonizes" an entity called "Third World woman", casting her as silent victim in need of discursive succour from her more liberated "Western" sisters'. How does this statement compare with Asad's description of the type of cultural translation exercised by anthropologists such as Gellner? And what role might feminist translators play in this context?
- Stereotyping, as Kahf explains, is not necessarily restricted to focusing on negative features but can also involve idealizing certain aspects of those being stereotyped. Translators of a writer like Sha'rawi should therefore resist softening the élitist elements in her legacy, because '[i]t is [her] record of accomplishment, even with its flaws intact, which will serve Sha'rawi; there is no need to render her politically correct in our terms today'. Kadish and Massardier-Kenney raise similar issues in *Translating Slavery* (1994). Consider the implications of this position and the potential effects of different representational strategies within a context of unequal power relations.
- Kahf's argument seems to rest heavily on the environment of reception as the sole 'culprit' in generating distorted representations of Arab and Muslim women. For example, she argues that 'to describe the process by which the Arabic text of the memoirs is transformed by being cast toward this set of expectations is to shift from blaming the translator toward seeing the translation of a text as part of a process larger than one individual will'. Likewise, her formulation in 'Let us see how the relationship with the brother *is transformed by the reception process*' (my emphasis) could be said to diminish the agency and responsibility of the translator. Fawcett (1997) similarly reveals racist elements in Stuart Gilbert's translation of André Malraux's *La Voile royale* but concludes that Gilbert was not necessarily a racist: he was simply 'living and writing in times when the pressure of the dominant discourse made such language almost inescapable, since it was part of the wallpaper, so to speak' (*ibid.*:264). What arguments might be presented for or against this view of the balance between the environment of reception and the translator's individual role in generating negative representations?

Recommended further reading

Amireh, Amal (1996) 'Writing the Difference: Feminists' Invention of the Arab Woman', in Bishnupriya Ghosh and Brinda Bose (eds) *Interventions: Feminist Dialogues on Third World Women's Literature and Film*, New York: Garland, 185–211.

Damrosch, David (2005) 'Death in Translation', in Sandra Bermann and Michael Wood (eds) *Nation, Language, and the Ethics of Translation*, Princeton & Oxford: Princeton University Press, 380–98.

Kadish, Doris and Françoise Massardier-Kenney (eds) (1994) *Translating Slavery. Gender and Race in French Women's Writing, 1783–1823*, Kent, Ohio: Kent State University Press.

Schaffer, Kay and Xianlin Song (2006) 'Writing beyond the Wall: Translation, Cross-cultural Exchange, and Chan Ran's *A Private Life*', *Journal of Multidisciplinary International Studies* 3(2). Available online at http://epress.lib.uts.edu.au/ojs/index.php/portal/article/view/155/341.

St. André, James (2004) ' "But do they have a notion of Justice?": Staunton's 1810 Translation of the Great Qing Code', *The Translator* 10(1): 1–31.

THE MEMOIRS OF HUDA SHA'RAWI (Mudhakkirati, Cairo: Dar al-Hilal, 1981) have been abridged, translated, and transformed into a text widely available to the English-reading public and frequently taught in US college courses in disciplines such as history and literature, and in interdisciplinary programmes such as women's studies and Middle Eastern Studies. The translation endeavour that produced Margot Badran's *Harem Years: The Memoirs of an Egyptian Feminist* (New York: The Feminist Press, 1986) is a valuable one and alerts Anglophonic readers worldwide to the work of this woman of achievement and influence. *Harem Years* was what led me to deeper study of Huda Sha'rawi's life and work and to the research for this article. However, the translation and publication of *Harem Years* occurs within a specific reception environment – the 'First World' Anglophonic market, which is shaped by a 'horizon of expectations' (Jauss 1982) for writing by and about Arab and Muslim women. The process of this reception restricts the range of meaning made possible in the Arabic text. Knowing these distortions will help educators use the English translation more effectively, not only in teaching about Egyptian feminism but also in explaining how the politics of reception can constrain our reading of a text from an Arab woman.

Hans Robert Jauss's work provides the insight that a reading public's 'horizon of expectations' is formed by 'what the public already understands about a genre and its conventions' (Guerin 1992:338) and by 'a reader's knowledge and assumptions about the text and literature in general' (Childers and Hentzi 1995:258). The United States reading public, despite promising resistances here and there, takes in data about women from the Arab world mainly by using conventions emergent from a long history of Western stereotypes about the Arab peoples and the Islamic religion. I find that these conventions take shape today in three stereotypes about the Arab woman: One is that she is a victim of gender oppression; the second portrays her as an escapee of her intrinsically oppressive culture; and the third represents her as the pawn of Arab male power. To describe the process by which the Arabic text of the memoirs is transformed by being cast toward this set of expectations is to shift from blaming the translator toward seeing the translation of a text as part of a process larger than one individual will.

The pressures of the United States reception environment work in four ways in the transformation of the Arabic text, Mudhakkirati, into the English text, Harem Years. Sha'rawi's engagement with Arab men in relationships that she saw as satisfying and enriching is minimized; her orientation toward Europe is exaggerated; and her command of class privilege is camouflaged. Finally, her story, which, in Mudhakkirati, is the story of a public figure, is recentred in Harem Years around private life and the 'harem'. In these ways, Sha'rawi can be accommodated within the United States reading environment as a victim and an escapee and shielded from the negative category of pawn.

Packagings: victim, escapee or pawn

Western literature has not always represented women from the Arabo-Islamic world in this threefold typology that I outline here. My study of the earliest representations of the Muslim woman in European literature suggests that medieval and Renaissance representations differed considerably from those of later periods and do not construct her as victim. Rather, the opposite — in these early texts, the Muslim woman is a virago (Kahf 1999). Over the course of the past four hundred years, however, against the changing material and ideological grounds of the relationship between Western Europe and the Islamic world, a very different discourse emerged. The new discourse, Orientalism, expanded most during the nineteenth century and depended on a 'positional superiority, which puts the Westerner in a whole series of possible relationships with the Orient without ever losing him the relative upper hand' (Said 1979:7). One of its constants has been the representation of Islam as innately oppressive to women. Drawing on the late nineteenth-century relations between Britain and Egypt, Leila Ahmed shows that 'the thesis of the new colonial discourse of Islam centred on women — was that Islam was innately and immutably oppressive to women, that the veil and segregation epitomized that oppression' (1994:151–52). The twentieth-century US reception environment is heir to this discourse. Decolonization, the Cold War, the post-1967 emergence of independent Palestinian movements, the 1979 Iranian Revolution, and the current climate of preoccupation with an 'Islamic threat' have shifted the material conditions and the ideological climate for 'the Western narrative of women in Islam' (Ahmed's phrase, 1994:149). For example, the image of Palestinian women as fighters and Iranian women as supporters of the Islamic Revolution complicated the picture of Arab and Muslim women as having to be either victims or escapees. The idea of a fanatic Arab or Muslim woman who is a pawn of her culture is related to these developments.

Second-wave United States feminism of the 1960s and 1970s and the ensuing critique of its limitations by women of colour have opened spaces where these stereotypes are reiterated on one hand and subjected to new challenges on the other hand. Chandra Talpade Mohanty points out that Arab women are specifically included in the process by which Western feminist discourse 'colonizes' an entity called 'Third World woman', casting her as silent victim in need of discursive succour from her more liberated 'Western' sisters. This process creates an irreducible 'Third World women's difference'. With this useful term, Mohanty gives a name to the assumption that the women of the 'Third World' are somehow inherently oppressed and that this always already oppressed state is defined by their gender and their being 'Third World'. Therese Saliba, Marsha J. Hamilton, and others detail the ways this 'third worlding' continues to happen with regard to Arab women in United States academic and popular settings, feminist and otherwise.[1]

The concept of the Arab woman as 'escapee' was given to me by Barbara Nimri Aziz, a journalist with a disciplinary grounding in anthropology whose work intersects with academic discourse but occurs primarily in radio and print mass media (see Aziz 1994, 1997). Aziz, from her years of work between the East Coast of the United States and the Arab east or mashreq (Syria, Iraq, Palestine, Lebanon and Jordan) interviewing people and documenting lives, garnered the insight that United States audiences, when faced with an Arab woman who did not fit the victim mould, tried to understand the woman as an 'escapee' from her culture. 'How brave,' they seemed to be saying, 'she has been able to escape from that terribly oppressive world' of Islam and Arabness.[2]

Marnia Lazreg's 'Feminism and Difference: The Perils of Writing as a Woman on Women in Algeria' suggested to me the third concept in this typology describing the range of contemporary United States representations of 'the Arab woman'. Lazreg, in the course of a larger argument, says that one of the implications of United States feminist discourse 'is that an Arab woman cannot be a feminist (whatever the term means) prior to disassociating herself from Arab men and the culture that supports them!' (1990:332). Citing Elly Bulkin's work, she notes that if Arab women do not separate from common causes with Arab men, they 'are accused of being "pawns of Arab men" ' (ibid.). An Arab woman who seems to wield some degree of power in her society and/or does not divest herself of Arab culture and attachments to Arab men must be operating under a false consciousness and is a 'pawn'. The concept of the Arab woman as 'pawn' is a useful refuge when a system of representation whose range for Arab women extends from 'victim' to 'escapee' is confronted with data that does not fit either of those categories. Like the other two concepts, it is an evasion of an alternative, if difficult, path: the deconstruction or demystifying of the irreducible difference attached (in Western discourse) to women in the Arabo-Islamic world and the approach to them and their texts with as much nuance, rigour and openness of paradigm as is applied to the study of European and American women's literature and literary history.

Here, despite all my recourse to depersonalized processes, I wish to find succour in Lazreg's appeal to some late humanism and assert that none of this is inexorable. A 'First World' feminist exercise of discursive power over 'Third World' subjects is not an inescapable given determined by the identity or physical location or education of the writer or reader. In other words, all Western writers are not a priori guilty of colonizing Arab women, nor are all women and men of Arab origin automatically innocent of this distorting representational practice. The 'victim, escapee or pawn' triad is a frame of reference ready to bog anyone. I agree with Lazreg that 'the misrepresentation of "different" women is a form of self-misrepresentation' (1990:338). Uncritical acceptance of these three stale categories for Arab women is a quagmire of unoriginal thinking that readers, as well as publishers and translators, can understand and resist. Responsible scholarship is still possible in the age of the postmodern.

Comparing Mudhakkirati to Harem Years

Sha'rawi (1879–1947) was a pioneer in the women's rights movement in the twentieth century and was as much in the vanguard of the Egyptian nationalist movement as a woman of her era could be. She was among those public figures who left us a written record of their lives as makers of modern Egypt, in such company as Sa'd Zaghloul and Muhammad Hassanein Haykal. After a coming-of-age section, which takes up thirteen of the forty-five chapters comprising the Arabic text, Mudhakkirati, her memoirs leave aside her personal life to tell mainly of her life as a public figure in Egypt's coming-of-age as a nation. This story includes the public debates taking place in Egypt in the early decades of the twentieth century, not only debates over women's roles, but debates over the type of government Egypt would have, its relationship with Sudan, the role of the king, relations with Turkey and Britain, and so forth. Her sweep of experience includes observations of nationalist leader and occasional Sha'rawi nemesis Sa'd Zaghloul, glimpses of Taha Hussain and other intellectuals, milestone events in Egypt's educational institutions, the emergence of international feminism, the emergence of inter-Arab feminism, the growth of Egyptian newspapers, and more.

The Arabic version tells the story by interspersing her narrative with reports, letters and documents; approximately one hundred in all. About a fourth are penned by Sha'rawi; most of the other articles were written to or about her during the course of her life. The Arabic book consists of a one-page publisher's preface, a short introduction by Dr. Amina Sa'id, and 450-some pages of text, which end abruptly in *medias res* since Sha'rawi did not live to complete the task. *Harem Years* contains eighty pages of translation proper, preceded by a chronology, preface and introduction and followed by an epilogue, appendix and notes. It is a translation, with some rearrangement and abridgement, of the first thirteen chapters that are present in *Mudhakkirati*. The epilogue in *Harem Years* summarizes material corresponding approximately to the next dozen chapters of *Mudhakkirati*.

It is important to note that the person finally responsible for editing the manuscript resulting in *Mudhakkirati* was her secretary, Abd al-Hamid Fahmy Mursi. Amina Sa'id describes Mursi's role in her introduction to the memoirs: 'He gave it to us without any compensation. He absolutely refused to allow us to recompense him even for a little of what he was burdened with in putting these memoirs in order and preparing them for printing and publication. He did this in fulfillment of his duty to execute the testament which his spiritual mother Huda Sha'rawi left for him. She chose him out of all her disciples, male and female, to order them and publish them at an appropriate time' (Sha'rawi 1981:9).[3] This appears to be an effort to confirm the legitimacy of Mursi's editorial work and establishes *Mudhakkirati*'s line of descent, so to speak, from Sha'rawi. We see a parallel effort in *Harem Years* when the translator recounts that Sha'rawi's niece Hawa Idris granted Badran access to a copy or portion of the manuscript and gave her permission to translate and publish it. The manuscript Badran worked with and the manuscript Mursi worked with may not have been the same; apparently Mursi's manuscript was more complete. In any case, the Arabic version, in its arrangement and selection of documents, enacts the voice of a public figure who, like all public figures, utilized the services of a committed, expert staff in producing her public voice. Thus, there is no need to continue the debate that occurred between Badran and Mervat Hatem on the pages of the Association for Middle East Women's Studies newsletter over whether or not there was one 'pure', originary Arabic document embodying the intent of its author without mediation of any sort (see Badran 1988a, 1988b, Hatem 1988). My purpose here is simply to compare the two published books to see what we can learn from the transfiguration of Sha'rawi's memoirs from one readerly context to another.

Banishing beloved bashas

Sha'rawi's memoirs begin with her memory of the death of her father. Much has already been said about the importance of Sha'rawi's vindication of her father, Sultan Basha, in the second chapter of her memoirs and the inclusion of documents authored by his contemporaries to substantiate Sha'rawi's defence. Badran has been duly criticized for relegating it to an appendix and overriding the primacy of Sha'rawi's concern with this issue. Badran's response points out that much of the chapter is composed of documents authored by others, inserted into Sha'rawi's text by her secretary-editor. This rendering of the apologia for the father as an appendix has been criticized by Mervat Hatem (1988) and Leila Ahmed (1987), and responded to by the translator (Badran 1988a, 1988b). My interest in the shift in the placement of the father between the Arabic and the English versions of the memoirs is that it is part of a pattern in which the English version minimizes the presence of male figures whom Sha'rawi describes with affection and pride. Huda Hanim's paternal grandfather, al-Haj Sultan, does not appear in the English version. The narrative about the father, aside from the apologia section, has been modified in specific ways. The brother, who is at least retained in the English translation, is nevertheless affected by the pressures of the reception process.

Sha'rawi's concern to establish her ancestral roots, very understandable in the Arabic context given the importance of genealogy in the Arabic tradition, does not appear in the English version. She writes in Mudhakkirati:

> I have heard from some of our relatives who have heard from their fathers and grandfathers that my father was of Arab [i.e., Arab bedouin] origin. His ancestors settled in the land of Hijaz and a group of them migrated to Egypt before the era of Ali Basha and took it as their land and married Egyptian women. Based on what I have been told, my grandfather al-Haj Sultan was the head of the fifth generation of his family in Egypt ... He was famous for generosity and kindheartedness and goodnaturedness. So involved was he in benevolent and charitable deeds and so overflowing was his piety that his contemporaries used to say: He is a saint who embodies all the blessings of his family and all those around him. (1981:14)

Sha'rawi goes on to relate, with dramatic panache, several anecdotes illuminating her grandfather's generosity, charity and kindliness. He was, she says, a man who even allowed his tenant farmers to cheat him out of money rather than embarrass them by calling their bluffs.

Aside from the issue of the apologia for her father, there are some other differences between the English and Arabic versions in the way Sha'rawi describes her father. In Harem Years we do not find Sha'rawi's praise of her father's virtues (e.g. 'generosity, loyalty, elevation, attachment to the symbols of religion', 1981:12). Adjectives such as 'beloved' that Sha'rawi frequently uses when speaking about her father do not make it through the translation process (1981:32). The translator says in her preface that she has made 'some minor deletions to remove repetitions or the occasional over-elaboration' (Badran 1986:). It is true that Sha'rawi's praises of family and friends are repetitious and indulge in Arabic conventions that might be tiresome for the Anglophonic reader. Still, Sha'rawi's gracious curtsies to these conventions of generous praise are part of her narrative persona.

While the tedious historical detail of Sha'rawi's apologia for her father might raise budgetary and marketing worries for a publisher, the omission of the charming stories about her grandfather and the adjective 'beloved' modifying the father is puzzling. It can only be explained by the pressures of the reception environment that I have described. The excision of the paternal grandfather encourages the tendency of the Anglophonic reader to see Sha'rawi as a woman severed from her roots, a victim-turned-escapee. A kindly Arab paterfamilias does not fit the expectations of United States readership. A story of an Arab woman's escape from the gender oppression of the 'harem' requires rather less glowing portraits of the Arab men who lived in those 'harem years'. If Badran were to translate Sha'rawi's warmth of tone toward her father and grandfather, the reception apparatus would veer toward labelling Sha'rawi a pawn of Arab men. The pawn stereotype is something Badran, as a sincere advocate for Sha'rawi before the United States readership, swerves to avoid. Whether this protective instinct is articulated and conscious or not, it is an observable example of the reception environment shaping the way the material emerges in English.

Sha'rawi's beginning her account with a recital of her lineage and the virtues of her father is a rhetorical move embedded in the traditions of Arabic literature. In Arabic poetry, for example, *fakhr* (the boast) and *nasab* (genealogy) are important initiatory elements. Sha'rawi's opening words in the Arabic version are: 'When I stand before the memories of my childhood . . .'. In this metaphor, memory is a site. She does not simply remember; she stands before the memory site. She goes on to remember and lament the way that knowledge of her father's death was kept from his children by 'the kindred' and 'the servants', and the sheltering customs of the upperclass in those days. The whole passage, then, is a circumspect way to lead into her father's death.

Where does Sha'rawi's language come from in this opening passage of her memoirs? Sha'rawi's opening alludes to a conceit that permeates all of Arabic culture from high poetry to folksong, the *waqf 'ala al-atlal* (standing at the deserted site). The classical Arab poet always stands figuratively before the old campsite in order to begin speaking. A renowned example is 'Let us stand, you two, and weep, at the remembrance of loved one and home', the opening line of the best-known ode of pre-Islamic poet Imra'ul Qais.[4] In this conceit, remembering is a 'standing before' and a calling up of the presences who used to inhabit the now-abandoned ruins. Sha'rawi activates this conceit at several points in a narrative that is also about the structure of memory and knowledge ('And today I close my eyes and I retrieve memories of those empty rooms one by one. I see my mother . . .'; 1981:57). Thus, not only the priority of place granted the father and grandfather in the memoirs, but the language of the narrative itself invests Sha'rawi in her Arabo-Islamic heritage. These enriching relationships of an Arab feminist with her own culture are difficult to portray given the poverty of a reception environment that wants to imagine Arab women only as victims, escapees or pawns. *Mudhakkirati* evinces a woman who, far from desiring escape from her people, saw women's liberation as something nourished by love for her family and rooted in her own culture.

In the Arabic version, Sha'rawi describes her close and loving relationship with her brother as a mainstay in her life, so much so that when he died suddenly, as a young man, she wanted to kill herself, reconsidering only when she remembered that she had two small children counting on her as a mother. Let us see how the relationship with the brother is transformed by the reception process. Here is a key passage about the brother from the Arabic version: 'I loved my brother with an endless love, despite my jealousy of him. And my affection for him was increased by his delicate health. Knowing that he would keep alive the name of my beloved father also increased my love for him, love buoyed by the praiseworthy qualities with which he was graced. My attachment to my brother multiplied after a certain incident' (1981:65). Sha'rawi goes on to describe a story Badran also includes, in which her brother refuses to snitch on her to their mother. Here is the translator's treatment of this passage: 'Despite my jealousy I loved my brother very much. My attachment to him was strengthened still more by an incident that occurred one day' (1986:37). The translator changes the order, skips the praise, and leaves out the name of the father binding the siblings together, but does keep the general sense of the relationship and does include the incident narrated as evidence of her brother's loyalty to her. We may regard this as a good faith rendering of the Arabic version despite the reordering and excisions. From here, however, let us go to a blurb on the back cover of the English paperback edition, where reviewer Hanna Papanek characterizes Sha'rawi as expressing 'bitter jealousy of the brother whom all favored over her'. How far this is from what the Arabophonic reader is given to understand about the brother–sister relationship. This is an excellent example of how the process of reception is larger than the will of the individual translator. The translator has included the passages related to the brother Umar, passages that place young Huda's moments of jealousy in context as part of a relationship of mutual trust, intense loyalty, and tender, protective love. It is true that the translator has subtly shifted Sha'rawi's emphasis. However, it is quite a leap from there to Papanek's complete mis-characterization of the brother–sister relationship. I believe we must turn to the victim part of my threefold typology to understand this leap. The workings of a larger grid of reception, which insists on Sha'rawi as unidimensional victim of gender oppression, overcome, in this case, even the efforts of the translator to relay the textual evidence to the contrary. The Papanek blurb, in turn, becomes a frame of expectation influencing any reader who picks up the paperback edition.

Exaggerating Europe

Albert Hourani's blurb on the back cover of the English book reads, 'Harem Years shows how a gifted and sensitive woman, brought up in seclusion but with a knowledge of French that opened a window onto European culture, gradually became aware of her own predicament and that of her sex and society'. There is no doubt that Sha'rawi, as a member of the sophisticated Egyptian upper class under the Turkish khedive (ruler), was exposed to a wide variety of cultures, European cultures being significant among them. It is also clear that Europe was slowly replacing Turkey as a preferred focus for her class during the early decades of the century. However, the English version exaggerates the European element in Sha'rawi's memoirs.[5]

On the first page of her preface to the translation, Badran reverses the order in which Sha'rawi learned languages, emphasizing first the chronologically last of the three: 'As an upper-class woman, Huda Shaarawi's social language was French. She also knew Turkish, the language of her mother and the Turco-Circassian élites and royal family. But Huda [sic] had a special fondness for Arabic, her father's tongue and the national language' (1986:1). By contrast, we learn from Sha'rawi's narrative that French lessons did not begin until after she had finished her courses in Arabic, religion and the Qur'an at age nine, and that she was eagerly buying cheap Arabic tales from the peddlers as well as reciting Turkish and Persian poetry, long before she could read a word of French (1981:47). The Arabophonic reader would understand that Sha'rawi suffered from the common problem of diglossia resulting from the large gap between formal standard Arabic and the vernacular, a problem more pronounced for those with restricted access to education, and therefore very much connected to gender. The Anglophonic reader may not, however, understand that Sha'rawi's primary language of daily interaction was Egyptian Arabic, even with the multilingualism common to her class. Sha'rawi's style of narration (inasmuch as it can be assumed to be basically hers, after editing by her secretary) shows the imprint of her early education in the occasional echo of Qur'anic diction (for example, the phrase 'when war had put away its garments', 1981:38, comes straight from the Qur'an, Surat Muhammad, verse 5).

Many of the Arab, Turkish and African characters who people the Arabic narrative are eliminated or reduced in the English version. For example, Sha'rawi describes how her mother always observed the Night of Mid-Sha'ban by inviting a *sheikha* (religious female elder) to assemble everyone in the heart of the house and lead the family in a prayer recital: 'After we finished feeding the poor, we would gather in a large room. Sheikha Jalsan would then come and sit in the middle of the room and recite for us the prayer of mid-Sha'ban and we would repeat after her in upraised voices. This prayer had an affect upon us of great awe and reverence' (1981:54). The story of Fatanat, a feisty lower-class woman who leaves her husband and seeks refuge with Huda Hanim's mother, is left out of the English version. The intrigues of the lively lower-class peddler women – Sha'rawi goes on indignantly for pages about them – are given only a few lines. The Circassian cousin Huriya gets a whole page in *Mudhakkirati*, where Sha'rawi describes Cousin Huriya's adventures as a soldier and includes an interpolated story narrated by the warrior woman herself (1981:37–38). This cousin only gets an aside in a subordinate clause in *Harem Years* (1986:25). These omissions reduce the number of indigenous women who do not fit the victim mould and who provide the reader with non-European models that may have excited the imagination of young Huda Hanim. At the same time, almost every single mention of Mme Richard and Mme Rushdi, European friends of the family, is retained in the English version, which abridges so much else.

The way in which some European characters are cited is also relevant. The *Harem Years* text frequently uses the given name of Rushdi Basha's wife, Eugenie Le Brun, which has the effect of highlighting her Europeanness rather than the fact that she was the wife of a prominent Egyptian. In *Mudhakkirati*, Sha'rawi never calls her friend anything but 'Haram Rushdi Basha'. This is a reflection of Sha'rawi's respect for propriety, titles and seniority, but it also draws the reader's attention to Mrs. Rushdi's investiture in her Egyptian context. Sha'rawi's memoirs certainly draw a picture of a close friendship with Mme Rushdi, and Badran transmits Sha'rawi's sense that her friend had a deep and lasting effect on her: 'even after [Mme Rushdi's] death I felt her spirit light the way before me' (1986:82). The significance of this passage, with its emphasis on Sha'rawi's friendship with the European woman, is granted more weight in the English version than in the Arabic by its positioning. The passage closes Part Three of the English text, whereas in the Arabic text it is embedded within a chapter. In contrast, the English text omits a similar sensation that Sha'rawi recounts after the death of another friend, Egyptian feminist Malak Nasef: 'After that, I used to search for her during the critical days that we traversed during the Revolution and after it, and I used to call to her in my soul, but her voice did not reverberate except within my conscience' (1981:160).[6] In *Mudhakkirati*, Sha'rawi mentions her love and admiration for the Princess Amina, wife of the Khedive Tawfiq, before her mention of Mme Richard, a European friend of her mother; the translated text reverses the order in which they are mentioned. The English text also leaves out an incident in which Mme Richard seeks refuge in the Egyptian customs of gender segregation to evade sexual harassment from a European man, her husband's boss (1981:68). In the Arabic memoir, European culture appears to be one influence among several present in Sha'rawi's world, without overshadowing the others. European friends and mentors are important in Sha'rawi's social circle, but there are Egyptian and Turkish friends and mentors who have comparable places in her life.

The Arabic narrative does not allow the impression that the European women are all liberated while Arab women are all oppressed. Sha'rawi in Arabic does tell the story of Eastern women who suffer from oppressive conditions, such as Atiyya Hanim, but also describes the case of a Frenchwoman condemned for murdering a man who slandered her sexual honour in the newspaper (1981:139–40). Sha'rawi is shocked that no one in Paris seems to sympathize with the woman, who is, in her view, a victim of male exploitation of women's vulnerability when sexual purity is the issue. This story does not make it into the English text. Atiyya Hanim's story of Eastern women's oppression, however, is translated in full as 'Portrait of the Hard Life of a Woman'.

The reader of Sha'rawi's memoirs in Arabic will be struck by the energy with which she decries Western stereotypes of Egyptian women and by Sha'rawi's refreshing assumption that women in Europe and the United States are as much in need of Arab feminists' succour as the reverse. When she is wrapping up the Rome conference in 1923, she and the other attendees are granted an audience with Mussolini. Sha'rawi does not miss the opportunity to put in a good word for the Italian woman: 'I repeated my personal appeal that the Italian woman be granted political rights' (1981:260). The reader never gets the sense that Sha'rawi thought of herself on inferior ground with European women. A similar confident tone informs Sha'rawi's United States tour and her lectures to Americans in various venues, reminding the reader that American women were not that much further along in their struggle than Egyptian women at that time. Moreover, Sha'rawi narrates several incidents that highlight her insistence on Egypt's place among nations, as when the Egyptian delegation at the Rome conference notices the absence of an Egyptian flag among the other flags and quickly produces a large flag to be given pride of place next to the Italian flag.

The Anglophonic reader would naturally have an interest in knowing about the European people in Sharawi's life. But the overall effect of this pattern of excisions and inclusions is to exaggerate the European element in the English text. This effect is shaped by the readerly expectation of Arab woman as escapee. The back cover blurb from the prominent Middle East Studies scholar Hourani reinforces the idea that Sha'rawi could only have been rescued from her narrow straits as an Eastern woman through a European 'window' of rescue.

Camouflaging class

The English version of Mudhakkirati softens Sha'rawi's class biases, very evident in the Arabic publication, in keeping with the pressures of the United States reception environment to see Sha'rawi as an idealized victim and a heroic rebel against her society. Harem Years does give the reader information about class in the front and end matter of the book, but does not reveal or analyze Sha'rawi's elegant dodging of class issues in her narrative.

Sha'rawi's nostalgia for the days when families such as hers were served by a small army of slaves, employees and peasant farmers might temper the sympathy a United States readership would have toward the ostensible victim of harem life. She looks back on those years with happiness, she says, 'especially when I am confronted with some of the modern customs, which make me long to return to the past, and all it contains of custom and memories' (1981:56). What are these customs that she longs to revive? She continues (1981:56–57):

> I recall, for example, our grand house with its spacious apartments
> and vast parlour, and how it used to teem with slavegirls and bondsmen.
> They were well-trained to work, sincere in performing their duties, sensi-
> tive to the responsibilities placed on their shoulders, respectful of their

employers, careful with the things in their hands, and loving toward the children of their employers who were born under their hands. Each one would rise to his task in the best manner and would accompany us for better or for worse, and would never reach his hand toward anything, no matter how costly, and would not covet a single thing but the good pleasure of those who had authority over him. And we reciprocated this love with them, and appreciated in them this loyalty.

Sha'rawi never baldly calls the eunuchs 'eunuchs'; the translation does (1986:39). Nor does Sha'rawi nakedly term her husband's first consort a 'slave-concubine', as Badran does; rather she uses the decorous term *um awladuhu* (mother of his children), which underlines the legal rights and improved status (she could no longer be sold) the woman had gained by virtue of bearing the children of a free man (1981:82). This evasion on Sha'rawi's part might be clarified by a translator's note. To eliminate Sha'rawi's evasion in the translation of the text itself, however, disables the reader from learning something from the narrator's delicate circumlocutions.

When the Revolution of 1919 excites the masses to do more than just support the transfer of power from élite Britons to élite Egyptians, and to revolt against the landowning system itself, Sha'rawi is quick to censure the 'excesses' of the crowds. These excesses are attacks on the houses of English gentry in Sha'rawi's village, whose privileges strikingly resemble the privileges of Sha'rawi's own family. She reports that her nephew risked his life to prevent this destruction of English residential property (1981:171). This passage is not in *Harem Years'* section summarizing the Revolution.

Details in the Arabic text that allow the reader to see Sha'rawi's class bias in play are more often than not absent from the English version. One example is the story of Sha'rawi's first shopping trip. In *Mudhakkirati*, Sha'rawi goes on for pages about the intrigues of the door-to-door peddlers, lower-class women who, she says, ruined 'great families' with their intrigues, even attempting to fall between herself and her husband. These entrepreneurs were also loansharks (1981:61). Her fierce 'I hated those women (*niswa*)' (1981:61) is translated as 'I didn't like most of these peddlers' in *Harem Years* (1986:48). In *Mudhakkirati*, when Sha'rawi recounts how she gained her mother's approval for her novel first shopping trip to a department store in the city, she says that what finally persuaded her mother is the prospect of cutting out the profits of these meddlesome peddler middlewomen with 'their evils and malignities' (1981:89). In *Harem Years*, the class antagonism of this passage is blunted. The desire to eliminate the peddlerwomen is not mentioned; that part of the passage seems to have been abridged into the phrase 'wise spending': 'I finally persuaded my mother to accompany me. She was then quick to see the advantages of shopping in person. Not only was there a wide range of goods to choose from but there was money to be saved through wise spending' (1986:69). *Mudhakkirati* allows us to see, perhaps in spite of Sha'rawi, that feminist consciousness conceived in privileged terms of personal autonomy was played out against a colonial economy in which modernization profited Western business and certain affluent sectors of Egyptian society at the expense of vast numbers of local distributors and small producers (Ahmed 1994:146).

The English text changes Sha'rawi's use of the word 'ladies' (*sayyidat*), which though it may be an unconscious reflex on Sha'rawi's part is accurate, to 'women' (*nisa'*). The title of the Wafd Central *Ladies* Committee is rendered 'Wafd Central *Women's* Committee' in English. It was really composed of ladies, women of high status and great privilege in their society. (The high point of Sha'rawi's naïveté about class is when she – still very young – and Mme Rushdi decide that women's struggle in Egypt would best be furthered by building a tennis court; 1981:99.) Softening the élitism of the committee's title in English translation makes invisible to the Anglo-phonic reader the most salient drawback of early feminism in Egypt. This is the will of élite women to 'appear on the feminist stage as representatives of the millions of women in their own societies. To what extent they do violence to the women they claim authority to write and speak about is a question that is seldom raised' (Lazreg 1990:332). Leila Ahmed's reading of Sha'rawi is a critique of this violence, a mark-edly different reading from the naiveté about class that *Harem Years* asks its readers to have (Ahmed 1994:176–79). Badran's second book shows that she does understand the complex of class issues in which the nationalist and feminist activities began. It is the vulnerability of *Harem Years* to the pressures of reception reserved for Arab women's writing that obscures the issue of class.

To her immense credit, of course, Sha'rawi went on to found institutions that addressed women's health, education and poverty. She generously opened her house and her patrimony to enable future generations of Egyptian women to reach the highest levels of a formal education denied to Sha'rawi, and generally to gain more access to the resources of their society. Her work netted a minimum marriage age for both sexes, pushed for limits on polygamy, and strove for women's inclusion in political rights. As Amina Sa'id puts it in her introduction to the Dar al-Hilal publica-tion, Sha'rawi may have been 'born in a golden cradle, but she rejected amusement and chose to spend her life in struggle and strife for the sake of the most noble and lofty of goals' (Sha'rawi 1981:7). It is that record of accomplishment, even with its flaws intact, which will serve Sha'rawi; there is no need to render her politically correct in our terms today. However, showing Sha'rawi's aristocratic bent would go against the grain of United States readerly expectations that an Arab feminist be an idealized victim rather than a grand and regal lady.

Haremizing the narrative

Mudhakkirati means 'My Memoirs'. Amal Amireh points out that 'Shaarawi's title puts her at the center of her own narrative, emphasizes her subjectivity and agency, and identifies her as the source of enunciation' (1996:23). The Feminist Press book *Harem Years*, on the other hand, 'identifies Shaarawi with an institution and locates the narrative in a harem' (ibid.). *Harem Years* targets for translation, with rearrangement and abridgement, only the early chapters, which are about Sha'rawi's girlhood and coming-of-age. The translator's division of the material is structured around the notion of 'harem': 'The Family', 'Childhood in the Harem 1884–92', 'A Separate Life 1892–1900', and 'A Wife in the Harem 1900–18'. An epilogue summarizes the events of several more chapters, which cover the beginning of Sha'rawi's work as a nationalist and feminist public figure. Badran explains: 'After Part Four, Huda's [sic] account changes in tone and content. She begins to speak about how she and other women became nationalist activists and started the feminist movement. This portion of her memoirs becomes fragmentary' (1986:3). It is this portion that represents the bulk of the Arabic version. Its 'fragmentary' nature consists of the back-and-forth between direct narration and interpolated documents. The meaning of Sha'rawi's story in the Arabic version lies, I believe, in the weaving between her narration and the documents, and in the relationship between the personal story and the much more expansive political story. The transformation of Sha'rawi's account into a harem memoir makes the English version a radically different reading experience from the Arabic version. The English version permits the reader to relegate Sha'rawi's writings to a harem of 'First World' creation, a ghetto where Arab women's writing is put by the United States reception process, there to languish behind the mystique of 'Third World woman's difference'. Perhaps a full translation of the portion summarized in the epilogue would have counterbalanced this haremizing effect.

Every text creates its ideal reader by implying the body of knowledge and the expectations the reader is presumed to possess.[7] The readers toward whom the book *Harem Years* gestures in its title, prefatory and end matter, covers and the texture of the text itself are expected to approach the book with the harem genre in mind. The translator says that the text 'will appeal to anyone eager to know about life in the harem – a word highly charged in the Western popular imagination . . . Firsthand accounts by women who lived in harems are rare'. Here is the translator's explanation of the memoirs' importance: 'The *Memoirs* of Huda Shaarawi have dual significance. They give insight into harem experience in Egypt in its final decades. At the same time they reveal how the roots of upper-class women's feminism in Egypt are found in the nexus of their harem experience and growing change around the turn of the century' (1986:20). The Egyptian publisher's preface asserts the significance of the memoirs on very different grounds: 'This book is considered among the most important and most valuable to appear in the Kitab al-Hilal series from its inception, because it treats the most monumental political events of the first half of our modern history. The immortal leader recounts these events within her memoirs, which she wrote herself, aiming at the utmost probity in every word which her pen inscribed' (Sha'rawi 1981:2). The Arabic version of Sha'rawi's memoirs calls for a reader with knowledge of certain conventions, too; the knowledge demanded is of the topography and society of pre-WWII Cairo, its old buildings, bridges and streets, its customs, protocols and niceties.

The translator seems to offer a critique of the Western harem genre, saying that it mystifies what was 'simply the portion of the house where women and children conducted their daily lives' (1986:7). Amal Amireh argues that 'this critique of "harem writing" turns out to be an empty gesture' (1996:23), because so many other elements of the English text are cast toward the conventions of the harem literature genre. The diction and syntax of the English book's front matter, for example, calls into play the rhetorical affects of the Western harem literature genre: 'The harem or household where Huda [sic] grew up in Cairo was in the then new and fashionable area of Ismailiya . . . Here the mature Sultan Pasha kept his Cairo harem – Huda's [sic] mother and his wife, (who figures in the memoirs) and their children'. Sultan Basha's wives were not 'kept' any more than Lady Cromer or Mme Rushdi or women of the upper classes in the United States were 'kept' anywhere by anyone. Rather, they negotiate places for themselves among the choices made available to them in ways tempered by their degree of access to resources and privileges. The grammatical subordination of the Eastern women in this clause is a rhetorical trigger alluding to the Western heritage of harem stories about subordinated Eastern women and makes little sense if separated from this reception environment.

The placement and captioning of photographs in *Harem Years* refer the reader to knowledge gained elsewhere about 'the harem'. One photo placed in the section on holidays is captioned, 'Huda [sic] and friend pose in Egyptian peasant dresses. Dressing up was a favourite pastime in the harem' (1986:47). The second sentence reminds the reader of the framing notion 'harem', although the word is not in the accompanying text at all. What the caption alludes to is the convention that *ennui* was a defining characteristic of 'harem life' and required special effort at amusement to relieve. This notion of 'the harem' as a site of trivial amusements infantilized the women who were the objects of observation.[8]

The translator explains that she uses the English word *harem* because the 'standard transliteration "harim" would be unfamiliar to the general reader' (1986:3). Perhaps the use of something unfamiliar to the general reader, with an explanation, might have jolted the reader out of the comfortable pattern of expectations and created a more challenging and transformative reading experience. In any case, there is barely any use of the word *harim* in the entire Arabic text to worry about. Sha'rawi only uses the word once in 457 pages.[9] The English version uses the word *harem* twenty-five times in the Introduction alone and numerous more times in endnotes and captions. By contrast, the only time Sha'rawi uses a special term to refer to a household location is when she mentions the *salamlik*, a room to which men were restricted when they came to visit (1986:33). In Arabic, Sha'rawi does use *haram* for 'missus', so that, just as Lady Cromer is the woman whose name is subordinated to Cromer's by marriage, 'Haram Rushdi Basha' is Rushdi's wife. *Harem* is not an operative term in the Arabic memoirs because it does not delineate a meaningful category for Sha'rawi. *Harem* is the word of the outside looking in. Sha'rawi's terms represent the narrative perspective of the writerly self looking out and moving about the world in ways that seem natural to her (and which are hardly more restrictive than the orbits of the average Victorian or Edwardian woman of the same class). When Sha'rawi does write specifically about the household site, her description does not have that oppressed victim tone. Rather, she writes in glowing terms that 'Our house was guided by regularity and was the epitome of calm. Tranquility was settled upon it, as a result of accord between the servants and concord and cooperation between all who were in it' (1981:58).

Not only is the word *harim* missing, but the issue of seclusion as a problem is not an organizing principle in *Mudhakkirati*. If Huda Hanim and her contemporaries seem to live in seclusion to Western observers, there is nothing secluded about her life as she describes it. Her mother's house is awhirl with guests, visitors, sojourners, petitioners, to the extent that young Huda Hanim finds the openness of the household taxing (1981:33). The poor teem at the door for alms; the relatives come and go summer and winter; the upper-class men and women make the rounds of social calls; Mother plays cards with friends, does charitable affairs, keeps up with court life; Huda Hanim enjoys visiting friends, neighbours, kin, the palace, Jabaliya, and vacationing in Helwan, Ramleh, Alexandria and Minya. A young woman of quality in turn-of-the-century London or Paris could not have led a less 'secluded' life, except that she would have been permitted to sit, under close supervision, with gentlemen callers. By contrast, the problem of seclusion seems to the English reader a central issue defining Sha'rawi's lifestyle (see Ahmed 1987, Amireh 1996).

Even the editorial mistakes in the text suggest that the editing process is not free from the pressures of the reception environment. One phrase in the Arabic version refers to Mme Sha'rawi and Mme Rushdi conversing about 'offspring and *immortality*'. This slips past the editors of the English version as 'offspring and *immorality*', a strange association that caused me to do a double take. It could, of course, be a simple typographical error. On the other hand, the harem, in the conventions of Western discourse about the harem, was, in fact, considered a place of both excessive offspring and excessive immorality. Could this have contributed to this error getting past an editorial eye embedded in the United States horizon of expectations that I have described?

A final issue, albeit minor, that reinforces the packaging of Sha'rawi as a victim in the English version is the treatment of Sha'rawi's mother. *Harem Years* introduces Sha'rawi's mother by explaining that mother, though Circassian, was not a slave (1981:16). Separated from a reception environment built for Muslim-women-as-victim stories, such an observation adds strangely little. Migration from the Caucasus to the Arab world was not unusual during this period of Czarist conquest, and free Circassians did live in Egypt. Introducing the mother as not-a-slave, then rearranging the material so that the memoir begins with the mother instead of the father, heightens the perception of the reader that this is the story of a victim, the subjugated daughter of supine 'harem women' (a Badran term, 1986:19). Sha'rawi's narrative preserves enough indeterminacy and complexity in drawing the mother figure to allow the reader to wonder if she might have had more influence on her famous daughter than is assumed, as Leila Ahmed's invaluable work on Sha'rawi points out. It is the mother's angry stance against Sha'rawi's husband, for example, that enabled Sha'rawi to defy him and live apart because his polygamy was unacceptable to her. Here is a woman who could not read or write, and yet extracted from her daughter's suitor a pre-nuptial agreement preserving her rights – and insisted on enforcing it. The daughter later will lead a campaign that works within Islamic legal traditions to limit polygamy. Perhaps Iqbal Hanim had an unacknowledged influence on the work of her daughter.

Reopening Sha'rawi's memoirs

Let me say here, as I have maintained throughout, that this is not a criticism of particular translating individuals or editing individuals for anything so nebulous and B-movie conspiratorial as harbouring neoimperialist sentiments or practising neo-colonial feminism. 'The most I can say', to draw upon Spivak, 'is that it is possible to read these texts . . . in a politically useful way. Such an approach presupposes that a "disinterested" reading attempts to render transparent the interests of the hegemonic readership' (1989:191). Amireh adds a moral motivation for examining this issue: 'The emphasis on difference, unfortunately, undermines the book's ability to build bridges of solidarity and understanding among women from different cultures' (1996:22).[10] There are also aesthetic reasons to call for the challenging of reader expectations in translating texts across culture. Wolfgang Iser says,

> . . . expectations are scarcely ever fulfilled in truly literary texts. If they were, then such texts would be confined to the individualization of a given expectation, and one would inevitably ask what such an intention was supposed to achieve . . . For the more a text individualizes or confirms an expectation it has initially aroused, the more aware we become of its didactic purpose, so that at best we can only accept or reject the thesis forced upon us. More often than not, the very clarity of such texts will make us want to free ourselves from their clutches. (1980:53)

This calls for texts that make reading less smooth. It calls for publishers, translators, authors and readers to become conscious of comfortable patterns of reception of the sort that restrict Arab women's writings to the ghetto of victims, escapees and pawns. If we are to continue discussing Huda Sha'rawi in English through the medium of *Harem Years*, it is important to be aware of the limitations put on the text by its Anglophonic reception environment. It may be desirable, in addition, to let multiple translations abound so that one English version does not become the only funnel through which the Anglophonic reader knows Sha'rawi.

Looking forward, more study of the Sha'rawi phenomenon using reception theory may be able to make sense of the stridently conflicting views held about Huda Sha'rawi in Arab countries. In that contest, some on the Left who are in blithe ignorance of the woman and her work invoke her name willy-nilly. In one instance, she is invoked in support of change in the superstructure and the relations of production,[11] which might have perturbed her as much as did the attacks on propertied classes during the Revolution of 1919. Sha'rawi's moderate, reformist approach, which justified improving the education and position of women mainly in terms of women's roles as mothers in the new nation and which opposed a change in Islamic inheritance laws, was hardly radical feminism. Meanwhile, some people on the right consider her name anathema and her work a blasphemy against God, country and family.[12] Sha'rawi's personal decorum and concern to observe propriety in all her actions can hardly have been studied by these opponents, with whom she actually may have more in common than some of her modern-day supporters. Happily, there are also more measured voices in the Arab reception of Sha'rawi. But a survey of that reading environment requires another politics of reception study.

Sha'rawi is a figure who merits careful rereading. What is the meaning of Sha'rawi's life and work – for Egypt in her own period, first of all? How has Sha'rawi's meaning changed since she became an icon for women's liberation and how is she read by contesting ideological groups? What local and regional meanings does her example hold for women's movements in Egypt, the Arab world, and the world? How can our 'global' age benefit from the discursive record of her work in the international feminist arena? These are questions that take Sha'rawi's significance out of the harem of Third World women's difference and into relevance for women and men everywhere.

Notes

1   See their articles and also those by Azizah al-Hibri and Mona Fayad in Kadi (1994).
2   Personal communication from Barbara Nimri Aziz, May 1993.
3   All translations from the Sha'rawi text are my own.
4   The first hemistich of Imra ul-Qais's famous 'hanging ode' or mu'allaqa, a pre-Islamic poem whose opening lines are almost universally memorized in the Arab world (translation mine).
5   Even a short account of Sha'rawi's earliest political and organizational experience, her membership in a ladies' committee supporting the Turks in their war against the Greeks in 1895, which in the Arabic account occurs in her early married life before separation, does not appear in Harem Years.
6   Badran includes this passage in her book, Feminists, Islam, and Nation: Gender and the Making of Modern Egypt (1995).
7   Walker Gibson calls this 'the mock reader'; Gerald Prince, 'the narratee'; others, 'the implied reader'.
8   Some of the earliest examples of this convention occur in Samuel Johnson's Rasselas and Mary Wollstonecraft's A Vindication of the Rights of Women.
9   Sha'rawi uses the word harim once, when she explains that she chose a man to tutor her in Arabic who was elderly enough to enter the harim of their house without offending the conservative sensibilities of her family (1981:83).
10   She is speaking here of Nayra Atiya's Khul-khal: Five Egyptian Women Tell Their Stories but in an essay that also analyzes Harem Years, beginning with her next sentence.
11   Abd al-Azim Ramadan does this in his introduction to Nabil Raghib, Huda Sha'rawi wa 'Asr al Tanwir, Tarikh al Masriyun (Cairo: al-Hay'a al-Masriya al-'Amma lil Kutub, 1988). Raghib

himself shows he has read the memoirs only hastily by making obvious reading mistakes, such as when he assumes Sha'rawi is referring to her own mother instead of her father's other wife when she says, 'I loved this woman with a great love' (in fact, she very pointedly does *not* say this about her mother) and goes on to explain how that 'great love' was so formative an influence on the psychological preparation of the leader (Raghib 1988:55).

12   One such attack is carried out by Muhammad Fahmy Abd al-Wahhab in a booklet entitled 'Women's movements in the east and their links to imperialism and international Zionism' – *Al-Harakat al-Nisa'iya fi al-Sharq wa Silataha bi al-Isti'mar wa al-Suhyuniya al-Alamiya* (Abd al-Wahab, n.d.). Another example of this is Ghawaji (1982:148–53).

PART 2

Modes and strategies: the language(s) of translation

Chapter 3

John Sturrock

WRITING BETWEEN THE LINES: THE LANGUAGE OF TRANSLATION

EDITOR'S INTRODUCTION

> Languages may converge but not merge: it is in the act of translation that their apartness manifests itself. Or it is there that it should do so. And yet we hold that act of translation the most successful which contains no evidence at all of the apartness of languages, but only of a source text flawlessly naturalized, which is to say finally occluded.

STARTING WITH A DETAILED DISCUSSION of different types of *en face* translations (those printed side by side with their originals), Sturrock suggests that *en face* translations of verse into prose in particular – as opposed to *en face* translations of verse into verse, for instance – aim at literalism. The *en face* format has two advantages: it brings the source of a translation back materially into view, and it enforces a certain separateness between source and target text that ensures we are less tempted to conflate the two. However, *en face* translation is an end product; it shows no trace of the activity of translation. The interlinear format, by contrast, presents translation completely and dramatically as a process. The translation here appears *between the lines*. Interlinear translation is translation at its most explicit, and at its most provisional: whatever is written or printed *between* the lines on the page, and normally in a different typeface, is not granted the definitive status of what appears *on* the lines. The interlinear format thus complicates matters by drawing our attention to the between-ness of any act of translation and by denying us the illusion of its immediacy.

In arguing for literalism as an ethical practice, Sturrock distinguishes the kind of interlinear translation he advocates from pedagogic and some ethnographic uses of word-for-word translation. Whereas Asad (this volume) focuses on the shortcomings of Gellner's version of cultural translation, it is Malinowski's reflections on and practice of word-for-word translation that are specifically critiqued at length here. Malinowski's version of interlinear translation is designed to make his natives sound not only strange but, relative to his readers' linguistic expectations, naïve. Sturrock analyzes his methods to demonstrate how decontextualization works, what Malinowski gets up to between the lines in order to show us how badly we need him as an expert. The interlinear translation Sturrock advocates could represent, if intelligently used, a reflexive and responsible refusal on the part of the translator to naturalize his or her source without showing any trace of the original; it could make visible the between-ness in which the translator is trapped. Sturrock insists that an interlinear language does not have to be as patronizingly primitive as that employed by Malinowski; instead, it need only allow certain untranslatable characteristics of the syntax and lexicon of the source to show through in the translation. Interlinear English, for example, will always be English but not an *altogether* familiar English, its departure from readers' expectations being designed specifically to acknowledge the derivative nature of what they are reading.

Follow-up questions for discussion

- Sturrock states that '[t]ranslators know how much their sources lose on their passage into another language' and that 'a greater tolerance of literalism in translation would bring some ease to their consciences and restore the lost balance between the claims to ultimate respect of the source and the brazen imperatives of the market'. Consider the ethical implications of the specific form of interlinear translation he advocates in this essay and compare it with the kind of foreignizing translation advocated by Venuti (this volume and elsewhere).
- Shamma (2009:47) argues that 'the exhibitionary effect that literal translation assumes in situations of radical power disparity is far from encouraging respect for the difference of foreign cultures. For the power to put on display, to dissect and analyze to the smallest detail, is the symbol – indeed, the actual realization – of the power to control and subjugate'. Shamma (*ibid*.:48) thus concludes that 'literalism *per se* cannot be advanced as an ideology; nor can one make assumptions about its desired effect in isolation from its political and social environment'. How might Sturrock and other advocates of literalism such as Spivak and Nabokov respond to this argument?
- In critiquing the term 'target language' (endnote 3), Sturrock states that '[t]he notion of having a "target" at which to aim in translating implies that the right form of words is already "there" if only one can find it. Only where is "there"?'. How might a functionalist like Christiane Nord or Hans Vermeer respond to this criticism?

Recommended further reading

Benjamin, Walter (1968) 'The Task of the Translator: An Introduction to the Translation of Baudelaire's *Tableaux Parisiens*', in Hannah Arendt (ed.), *Illuminations*, New York: Schocken Books.

Berman, Antoine (1992) *The Experience of the Foreign: Culture and Translation in Romantic Germany*, trans. S. Heyvaert, Albany: State University of New York Press.

Coates, Jennifer (1999) 'Changing Horses: Nabakov and Translation', in Jean Boase-Beier and Michael Holman (eds) *The Practices of Literary Translation: Constraints and Creativity*, Manchester: St. Jerome, 91–108.

Lianeri, Aleka (2002) 'Translation and the Ideology of Culture: Reappraising Schleiermacher's Theory of Translation', *Current Writing: Text and Reception in Southern Africa* 14(2): 2–18.

Spivak, Gayatri (1993) 'The Politics of Translation', *Outside in the Teaching Machine*, New York: Methuen, 179–200.

A TRANSLATION IS A SUBSTITUTED text which keeps no further company with its source once it has been published; after that it stands alone, patently derivative but a text in its own right. As books, translations differ from original texts only on the title page, where it is advertised that this work is a translation, made from language *x* by translator *y*.[1] Its status of translation may or may not be borne in mind by readers as they read. Generally, it is not; readers hope not to be reminded as they go that what they are reading is (only) a translation. The translator whose prose is not sufficiently smooth to pass for indigenous will be faulted, and accused of writing 'translationese', which counts against him as a professional failure. In complaining of the awkwardness or 'unnatural' phrasing distinctive of 'translationese', we take as a premise that in good translation the source must not show through. What follows here is an extended questioning of the soundness of this premise.

Because published translations exist in physical independence of their source, they are only ever collocated with it by rare individuals on rare occasions: when there is a translation prize to be given, perhaps, or when a translated author checks the foreign version of his work for gross infidelity. At most other times, the translator's work is taken on trust, the source from which he has been working having been definitively shelved so far as its new audience is concerned. There are interesting exceptions, however, when the convention of independence is broken and a translation is published in the presence of its source, in order to make metalinguistic points about the technique or the theory of translation. A treatise on translating, for instance, will quote or make up specimen sentences from at least two languages, through the intelligent examination of which degrees of bilingual synonymy or equivalence may be established.

But beyond the banal and fragmentary instances such as manuals of translation provide, more elaborate juxtapositions can be made: in the form of *en face* translations of longer, continuous texts. *En face* translations differ markedly according to whether they are of prose or verse. In the case of prose their use is narrowly illustrative; they are merely fuller, more palatable versions of the textbook, teaching random or recurrent lessons in how best to translate between the languages involved. In their format they tend toward literature inasmuch as they are of complete texts and not broken sentences; but they remain anonymous, the translator himself claiming to be nothing more than a pedagogue or the impersonal conduit through which one language has been turned (has turned itself?) into another.

En face translations of verse are very different. They come in two kinds: translations of verse into prose and of verse into verse. *En face* translations of verse into prose aim at literalism and since literalism is my main theme in this essay I shall for now withhold further reference to them. *En face* translations of verse into verse by no means display the exemplary correspondence with their originals that the modest teacher of prose translation looks for. On the contrary; the translation of verse into verse is undertaken by poets and is therefore a less self-effacing activity than the translation of prose. The poetic translator wishes to identify himself by the virtuosity of his translations, and in order to do that must take the risk of printing the original poems alongside his own versions of them. If we know something of the language he is translating from we can compare the two poems and admire his talent, or not (though the comparison is not made directly between source and version, only indirectly between the translator's version and our own hypothetical alternative to it). I have implied that the *en face* translator-poet prints his source out of vanity, in order to prove his skill; in fairness, let me concede that he may also supply it out of guilt, since the peculiarly high standing we accord to poetry as a literary genre means that in translation a greater guilt attaches to the occlusion of a poetic source than of a prose one, so the *en face* format may also be taken as a public confession on the part of the translator that he is engaged on an inescapably damaging literary exercise, and that to print his source is the least he can do if he is to reassure us that originals may be supplanted by their translations but never finally erased.

The *en face* translation is not a *method* of translation, it is merely an unusual format for it. The format will have effects on the translator who adopts it, who knows that he is for once being invigilated and may find this either inspiring or inhibiting, a spur either to pedantry or ostentation. When source and translation are printed together *en face*, the source comes first: that is, it is given the formal precedence of the lefthand page of a spread, whether or not we choose to read it before reading the poet's version on the page opposite. The degree of symmetry between the two texts will depend on whether the translator has attempted to keep to the line lengths, stanza scheme, and so on, of his original, but one might in general say that the facing layout, or confrontation of two typographically distinctive texts, *represents* iconically the act of translation, conceived of as the matching of one text to another. Source and translation are in apposition, but they do not meet or mingle. Between them is the 'gutter,' or the empty space that runs down the center of any page spread, and this wordless hiatus I shall take also to be valuably representative of the radical grammatical and semantic divide between any two natural languages. The *en face* format does us then a twofold service, first in bringing the source of a translation back materially into view, and second in enforcing a certain separateness so that we are not tempted rashly to conflate them.

In an *en face* translation, however, finished text confronts finished text; the translation that we are given to read is an end product, it shows no trace of the activity of translation, in the difficult course of which the translator can be assumed to have tried out and abandoned other versions of words and sentences before settling on his final version. The *en face* format represents the achievement of translation, not its process, and in it the translator's fumblings show no more than do those of the author of his source. In this respect source and translation keep their distance from one another too decorously, as if it were no business of the reader to be allowed to see anything of the work which requires to be done in the turning of one text into another. The blank space of the 'gutter' is a little too blank.

There is another format for translation which represents it more completely and dramatically as a process: the interlinear format, in which source and translation appear one above the other, a line at a time. This is an exceedingly uncommon format actually to meet with in print. The paired sentences of translation textbooks do not rank as interlinear translations because unless they extend over several lines they have no effect on the eye of interlinearity. Interlinearity requires verse or prose sequences long enough for the format to be appreciated for the typographically eccentric thing it is, with a deeper than usual space inserted between successive lines of print to make room for the translation. Whether the translation appears above or below the source hardly matters, though the 'natural' setting for the translation, as coming after the source, would surely be in superscript, like the changes or insertions we make to what we write. But what is important is that the translation should be understood as appearing *between* the lines. We all of us know how to *read* between the lines; the practice of interlinear translation is one of *writing between the* lines. It might seem that reading and writing between the lines must somehow be alike, but paradoxically they are practices leading in opposite directions. When we 'read between the lines' we take what we read in other than a literal sense, in compliance with certain conventions of the language which enable us to decode the text's deliberately 'hidden' or secondary meaning; literalism is specifically bypassed. But the whole purpose of 'writing between the lines' is, on the contrary, to display literalism, to translate with a rare fidelity to the word-forms of the source; it is translation at its most explicit: 'the more literal translation is seen as more literally a translation', as Quine (1959:169) aphoristically has it.

It is translation also at its most provisional, for whatever is written or printed *between* the lines on the page, and normally in a different typeface, is not granted the definitive status of what appears *on* the lines. The interlinear translation is asking to be, if not expunged, then certainly transcended before it is held worthy of taking up a dignified position on the line; its subordinate place is in part determined by our ineradicable prejudice against literalism. But whether it be actually realized, in the pages of a book, or whether it remain as a concept, interlinear translation exemplifies the most familiar and deep-rooted model of translation, as a linguistic process divisible into two stages: a first stage in which the translator travels from his source to a 'literal' translation of it, and a second stage in which this first, temporary version is suitably edited so as to make a finished, publishable one. This is not an empirical model, in the sense of being descriptive of what must occur in any given act of translation; but it does square with the experience known to translators, of passing from a first, quickly found translation of a word or phrase, deemed to be inadequate because of its literalism or formal proximity to a too-influential original, to a revision judged on reflection to be more 'natural'. To revert for a moment to the *en face* translation of verse: the two-stage model is perfectly illustrated by the occasional practice of offering *successive* versions of poems in translation, the first made in prose or at best blank verse by a translator without literary ambitions but expert in the foreign language and striving to be literal, the second a finished poem, made by a poet who may not even know the source language but has based himself on the prose 'crib', rather as if this were his dictionary. In all such flights from literalism, the translator relegates his source to one more remove from himself, since the revised version of his translation is just that: a revision of what he (or his helper) has already thought of or written down. The translator in fact has shifted his stance, from a source-oriented to a reader-oriented practice of translation, and this is a shift which frequently leads to a remarkable libertarianism among those theorists of the subject who take the reception of a translation to be of more importance than its fidelity. Eugene Nida and Charles Taber, for example, who approach translation from the standpoint of Bible translators engaged in an apostolic endeavour, are so firmly wedded to the two-stage model as to envisage the doctrinally qualified Bible translator producing his literal version and then if need be calling in a 'stylist' to 'fix it up' (1969:157). This general sequence, of an ultraclose translation being handed over for cosmetic surgery, is one followed daily in publishing houses across the world, where translations are subject to the same editorial procedures as other texts, and are freely 'naturalized' with little or no consultation with either their source or their translator. As a way of redirecting the heathen into the paths of a Protestant godliness Nida and Taber's method may work miracles, but as a general recipe for translation its pragmatism is offensive; it is surprising, what is more, to find it coming from translators who have for their source the peculiarly authoritative word of God, which surely deserves better than to be so casually 'fixed up'.

But then sustaining the assumption that as a process translation advances beyond an unprintable literalism into a successful literariness is a second assumption: that in the course of this advance the meaning of the source has been preserved intact. The commonest defence of 'freedom' in translation has always been that nothing is lost by way of meaning in the revision of the literal version but that something has been gained by way of style. When Nida and Taber and their collaborators 'fix up' the scriptures for missionary use the word of God is assumed to survive unscathed; it has merely been made more easily intelligible and more appropriate to its new audience than had the translation process been arrested at its more primitive stage. (That 'intelligibility' is a virtue Nida takes for granted; he is modernist in these matters, who would have the Bible sound as unambiguous as is compatible with its unusual textual prestige.)

Traditionally, the arguments against literalism in translation have been far more vigorous and effective than those we find for literalism. It is only in the later twentieth century, with the intrusion into the theory of translation of philosophers of language, that literalism has acquired a new standing, not as yet as a characteristic considered to be desirable in the translator's finished product, but as a uniquely revealing index to the problematic nature of translation itself. The translator who is adjudged a literalist remains an incompetent, just like the computers with which experiments in translation have been going on for many years and around which there has grown up a corpus of contemptuous anecdotes, all of them celebrating the machines' inability to disambiguate and hence to avoid grotesque 'literalisms' that a human translator would intuitively reject. But the literary world's easy confusion of literalism with a presumptuous machine's failure to distinguish between homonyms is one more sign of the prejudice against it as a mode of translation.

It is essential, in fact, to step outside any merely literary context when starting to theorize about translation, since literary translation has a vested interest in ignoring the philosophical problems that underlie its practice. The high service which the inter-linear format does us is to complicate matters, by drawing our attention to the between-ness of any act of translation and by denying us the illusion of its immediacy; translation is a process, even though not one that should be so simplistically divided as it has been into the two distinct, hierarchical stages of literalism and fluency. For an example of interlinear translation in use I go to the academic discipline that has done more than any other in recent years to fix attention on the question of translation: to ethnography. In some quarters ethnography has come to be seen as specifically con-cerned, no longer with the disingenuous description of other cultures, but with their 'translation' into a form comprehensible to ourselves. An explicit 'translation' of an alien society's customs, rites, and beliefs is no longer mistakeable for the 'real' thing, it is a version or account of another culture familiarized for us through the agency of a translator, himself now more fully sensitive to his own inescapable ethnocentrism.

Or perhaps we should say glotto-centrism, because what is at stake here is eth-nography's dependence for its data on linguistic contact between the ethnographer and those users of the local language picked out as his 'informants'. It is paradoxical that a discipline which has done so much to increase knowledge in the West of the world's languages and their structure should so often have presented its findings about other societies and cultures without any serious analysis of the means by which these had been gathered. Informants must inform and do so either in their own language or in that of the visiting ethnographer or in whatever third, common tongue is available to the two parties. Ethnography as published hinges on the fullness, intelligibility and truthfulness of a whole series of verbal exchanges in the course of which the ethnographer is initiated into a language not his own. When the time comes for this process to be reversed, and for his enquiries to be reformulated as a 'translation', the ethnographer cannot be granted the same degree of licence in respect of his source as we grant to literary translators; his professional name is to be made otherwise than the poet's, by the closest conceivable approximation to the source rather than by florid departures from it. Here then is the best imaginable setting in which to look more closely at the actual process of translation.

Happily, one of the great masters of twentieth-century ethnography was unusually conscious of the language problem: Bronislaw Malinowski. Malinowski was himself a Pole who had had to learn to speak and to write in English, no bad preparation for his work in the Trobriand Islands. In the second, theoretical volume of his study called *Coral Gardens and their Magic*, he makes good use of the interlinear model of translation in order to recapitulate the history of how he himself has come to understand the culture of the islanders who are his subject there. It is a model involving not two languages but three, not just the Kiriwinian spoken locally and English, but Kiriwinian, English, and a third, intermediate language, which I shall call the language of translation. Here is Malinowski's own short account of the form in which he has chosen to publish his examples of native usage: 'We shall have in the first place to produce the texts, phrases, terminologies and formulae in native. Then we shall have to face the task of translating them. A word for word rendering is necessary to give a certain direct feeling for the language, which a free translation can in no way replace. But the literal translation is not sufficient because . . . such a translation simply never makes sense' (Malinowski 1935, Vol. II:10–11). Interlinear translation is here identified with a 'word-for-word' translation, the only appropriate setting for which, if it is to be projected at all, is in that strict collocation with the source which interlinearity alone permits. With the 'native' component of this model we need not I hope be concerned, beyond to say that what Malinowski gives of Trobriand usage has been transcribed into our own phonetic script, and a language without writing thus textualized in a form unknown to its speakers; as readers of it we are at the mercy of the transcriber since we have no way of knowing whether his forms and word divisions represent fairly those grasped by speakers of Kiriwinian or whether they have been decided upon for his own advantage. However, it is the purpose of the word-for-word rendering that is of interest, rather than whether 'word-for-word' is an accurate description of it (there can in truth be no such thing as a word-for-word translation of more than a few words at a time because no two natural languages are structurally close enough to allow it). Its purpose, Malinowski tells us, is 'to give a certain direct feeling for the [native] language'; but what sort of feeling can this be? It is the feeling quickly induced in readers whose native language is English that the grammatical and semantic categories employed by these islanders are not as our own. The 'certain direct feeling' for Kiriwinian is conveyed in English, of a strange, interlinear kind, but with a view to exhibiting the non-Englishness of local thought processes. Let me quote one of Malinowski's more straightforward examples of how he proceeds by way of his interlinear language from native utterance to 'free' translation (*ibid.*:14):

Waga	bi-la,	i-gisay-dasi,	boge	i-katumatay-da	wala
canoe	he might go	they see us	already	they kill us	just

were a canoe to sail, they would see us then they would kill us directly[2]

We can take it as read that this 'free' translation is entirely satisfactory; it makes a passable English sentence approved of by its author-translator, which is the only test we are in a position to apply to it. But what of the provisional, interlinear version of the native utterance, the preparatory work as it were out of which the final free version is to be constructed? It uses familiar English words but not in an order we can approve or quite make sense of; it promises a meaning but fails to deliver one. It calls for the expert's revision. The justification of this ill-formed string of English words is that it correlates as precisely as possible with the native string. The alienation effect of Malinowski's interlinear language starts to work straight away, when he uses the English nominal *Canoe* without either a definite or an indefinite article in front of it (and without the capital letter it has oddly and misleadingly been given in the native version; the same goes for the punctuation, of two commas, supplied in the source yet withdrawn from the English translation where it could alone belong). The canoe has subject position (or what English recognizes as such) in both the native and the interlinear sentence, but in the interlinear version a subject pronoun is introduced also, again infringing the grammatical norms of English; this is on the ground that verb forms in Kiriwinian must include a personal pronoun and that native noun forms incorporate a gender. Malinowski's auxiliary verb form *might* represents the translation of the prefixed b- which, as he explains, when added to the personal pronoun i, alters the character of the Kiriwinian verb in a variety of ways, making it 'very roughly' into a future form, or conveying 'the idea of potentiality', or else assimilating it to our own imperative. The English *might* has been chosen to represent this congeries of formal possibilities, whose diversity it takes Malinowski several lines to describe.

I shall not pursue the commentary on this particular interlinear version; like all other such versions it bears out his earlier promise that 'such a translation simply never makes sense'. But *must* an interlinear translation fail to make sense, or does it fail because the translator requires it to? In Malinowski's case one might well ask how far his literal versions of native word forms are determined by their (spoken) source and how far they represent the choice of a translator set on making his case at whatever cost. The technique of translation followed in *Coral Gardens and their Magic* is that to which many of us were exposed long since in school, in the handling of classical languages. In England it was known as the 'construe' (in American schools, I'm told, as the 'trot'), and it involved the same double act of translation, of first a 'word-for-word' version of some Latin or Greek sentence and then an improvement of this into an acceptably fluent and meaningful English sentence. This was only ever an oral exercise; the interlinear version was spoken, never written down. The stock teacher's question prompted by its obvious inadequacy as English was 'And what does that mean?'. The proper performance of the 'construe' thus entailed producing a literal translation which failed *conspicuously* to make sense; the clever pupil who rushed things and passed straight to fluency was penalized for having missed out a necessary stage of the translation process. The dispensable literal version was intended to demonstrate a formal grasp of the source sentence, in its grammatical as well as its semantic structure: to demonstrate that you knew how Latin or Greek worked form-ally; and the effect of being made to take this initiatory step was one of alienation followed by recovery as the quiddities of Latin were replaced by those of an accept-able English. It is a nice irony that Malinowski should follow this ancient pedagogic practice so closely in *Coral Gardens and their Magic* because, as someone professionally engaged in the encounter with alien but living languages, he has some severe things to say in that book about the 'typical philologist, with his firm belief that a language becomes really beautiful and instructive – ethically, logically and aesthetically valuable – when it is dead' (ibid.:viii).

Whether it is used in the schoolroom or in the ethnographer's accounts of his fieldwork, the word-for-word translation is a pedagogic contrivance, not a recognizable empirical stage in the process of translation. It is a model marked 'for display purposes only'. In its flagrant inadequacy or incompleteness it points beyond itself, to the 'free' or 'natural' translation to come, the one that we accept as a well-formed sentence of our language. Malinowski produces his own finished translations by a systematic rewriting of the interlinear ones, first by means of a 'grammatical commentary' on the native utterances in question, partly evidenced in the hyphenated form in which he prints these, the better to identify Kiriwinian word classes and morphology; and then by 'a contextual specification of meaning', in the course of which various kinds of vagueness and ambiguity in the interlinear rendering will be resolved and its inarticulate English words integrated syntactically. The procedure as a whole bears out Malinowski's empirical theory of meaning, according to which 'words are part of action and they are equivalent to actions, so that their meaning may be defined in terms of experience and situation' (ibid.:9). Thus, if we are to understand effectively what his Trobriand informants have earlier told him, we need the guidance of the ethnographer, whose own acquired knowledge of the indigenous culture will pad out the skeletal indications of the interlinear version. This is a traditional enough view of the translator's task, as being to ensure that his source is fully understood, if necessary by the glossing or analysis of certain obscure moments of it. The translator is by the nature of things an exegete, called upon to provide what the most weighty of the earlier theorists in England gave as his first Principle of Translation: 'a complete transcript of the ideas of the original work' (Tytler 1791/ 1907:9). Malinowski's three-parts model of translation in *Coral Gardens* takes on a mimetic, even a diegetic quality for thus summarizing his own experience in the field, where an original state of incomprehension faced with a native language little if at all known to him was over time replaced by knowledge based on the definitions and elaborations of key terms elicited by the questions he put to his informants. And so it is with us, as readers of Malinowski: the native utterances are beyond us and will largely remain so, since we have nothing to gain by learning them. Their inclusion shows, however, that this ethnographer is both more scrupulous and more methodical than the majority of his colleagues, whose normal practice was to cite, not whole sentences or sequences of sentences from native informants, but only certain key terms, chosen either because they were picturesque or because they were peculiarly 'untranslatable' and thus very well illustrative of the difficulties facing the ethnographer. With Malinowski these difficulties are dramatized in the form of his interlinear English, intended to reproduce native utterances that he himself characterizes as 'telegraphic'. As the typical example I have given shows, it lacks those connectives which we can be sure will be added, to make the sentence fully intelligible, once he goes on to give us the 'free' translation. Why in the interlinear version does he leave these out? Because, he writes, 'I want the reader to have as close a reproduction as possible of the bald clipped juxtapositions of the Kiriwinian language' (ibid.:27). That is, he wants his natives to sound not only strange but, relative to our own linguistic expectations, naive, when the asyndetic nature of what they say to him suggests a simple incapacity to recognize the logical relations between successive elements of the utterance. We can assume that the Kiriwinian language does not impress its native users as asyndetic, but that Malinowski wishes his own impression of that language as a stranger to be taken as a quality inherent in it. If we judge its scope and potentialities as being fairly conveyed in the interlinear translations, Kiri-winian is bound to appear a crude, even contemptible linguistic instrument; but then we might bring to mind a second laconic saying of Quine's, to the effect that 'wanton translation can make natives sound as queer as one pleases' (1960:58).

The interlinear translation as practised by Malinowski, or by generations of teachers of classical languages, is not permitted to reproduce a natural language in a fluent form; rather, it approximates to those intermediary languages such as pidgin which have developed in like contexts in order practically to bridge the gap between existing languages. But as with pidgin, the inference is that one of these languages, our own, is both lexically richer and syntactically more advanced than the other, to confer with whose users in a middle tongue thus demands an intellectual sacrifice on our part. Malinowski's middle tongue is intended to be neither one language nor the other, but English masquerading as Kiriwinian. The rules which he follows in con-structing it aim at the decontextualization of the native utterances. These he had first heard and recorded in a context which made them perfectly intelligible; that is, they were spoken to him on a given occasion by one or more local individuals as he pursued a particular line of enquiry. As printed on the page, however, utterances tend to revert to sentences, even when they occur in discursive sequences. The meaningful gestures and intonations of the informants have been lost, along with whatever other circumstances of the moment helped to determine their discourse or interchange with their visitor. The situation Malinowski finds himself in is that endured by any translator: he has a text in front of him which asks, if it is to be adequately translated, to be referred to a context. The ethnographer of course is fortunate beyond other translators, since the very thing he knows is that context, which, the bad interlinear moment once past, he can restore by the fullness of his commentary, expanding on the empirical evidence as cited until it becomes a synthesis of what he has learned over months or years in the field.

But how does decontextualization work, what must Malinowski get up to be-tween the lines in order to show us how badly we need him? His method is, wherever possible, to give one English term for one native term, and the same English term for the same native term; these English terms thus function not yet as translations but as what he calls 'mnemonic counters' or else 'aide-mémoires'. As such they bring to mind – to Malinowski's mind, not to ours, ignorant as we are of Kiriwinian – the native term while making that term seem mightily rigid in its English meaning; only once it is 'contextualized' is that rigidity dissolved and the Kiriwinian signifier shown to be a semantically very flexible item indeed. Malinowski's 'mnemonic counters' do the reputation of his natives much disservice at the interlinear level. Wholesale changes take place between the interlinear and the 'free' stages of the translation. In the example I have quoted, the interlinear, pidginlike phrase 'canoe he might go' (who does not hear echoes there of 'Mr Kurtz he dead'?) becomes in free translation 'were a canoe to sail', where the stopgap auxiliary *might* has given way to a refined conditional clause *were . . . to* – this is overdoing things, since Malinowski is translating sentences that were *spoken* to him and 'Were a canoe to . . .' belongs decisively to the written register of English. *Canoe* is now naturalized for us by the addition of an indefinite article; the generic verb *go* has been narrowed down to the contextual *sail*; and so on throughout Malinowski's examples. The transition from *go* to *sail* is espe-cially provocative; on what authority, one wants to know, did he decide that the native verb form *-la* should be generalized in the sense of *go* before its eventual specification as *sail*? Because this Kiriwinian verb has multiple uses, and thus potentially many contexts of use; *go* is therefore offered as its 'prime' meaning. But prime for whom?

The interlinear *go* is an imposition of the translator's, since the natives seem to lack the generic concept precisely mappable onto English as 'go', having instead a different categorization of the semantic field roughly determinable as that of *movement away from*. What Malinowski hopes to achieve by this method of imposed generalization is to get his readers to 'think in native', only with English terms. That is a contradictory ambition, as the duplicities of his interlinear translations show. But Malinowski errs only in asking too much of such a format, in mistaking it indeed for a distinct *method* of translation.

Interlinear translation is a peculiarly seductive format because it promises to actualize in front of us that hypothetical language between languages which commonsense models of the translation process have always presumed to exist. Common sense in the matter of translation is resolutely Platonist, Platonism being here the philosophical belief that meanings are entities independent of and thus transcendent of the sentences of the various natural languages in which we encounter them. Platonists have a solution to the problem of translation; natural languages may have few or no signifiers in common but they can still share their signifieds, so that identical meanings can be carried by different sentences in different languages. These transcendent entities are thus capable of materialization in many, perhaps in all natural languages, and the translator's task is to identify them in his source and transfer them from there to a second language. Thus common sense's most quotable advocate in English, Samuel Johnson, wrote of translators that 'he, therefore, will deserve the highest praise, who can give a representation at once faithful and pleasing, who can convey the same thoughts with the same graces, and who, when he translates, changes nothing but the language' (1759:120). 'Nothing but the language' sounds well enough, until one sets to asking what is there *except* the language. Or better, what is there once a translation has been made except for the two texts, the source and the version? Only the Platonist is willing to posit between these a third, abstract, or conceptual something, not itself a text presumably but distinguishable from both the texts we have, and usable as a reference by which to estimate their degree of synonymy.

But what if we disallow this convenient abstraction, or 'language of thought', which coincides with no one natural language yet informs them all? Contemporary philosophies of language, whether European or Anglo-American, are strongly against it. We have learned from the tough-minded nominalists, from Quine and Jacques Derrida, to be disbelieving of anything claimed as existing *between* languages, and disbelieving, by extension, of any theory which supposes that the process of translation involves a passage through a 'pure', sign-less, intermediate language. A rigorous empiricism allows us only two languages, a source language and a target language,[3] with no common denominator, a concept which profoundly alters the way in which we think about translation. The question of what translation is has been reformulated. Instead of naïvely supposing that translators are in the semantic haulage business, occupied in moving certifiably identical meanings from language to language, we can now only ask whether two sentences in two different languages 'mean the same', and that is to be decided at best approximately by evaluating their respective functions within their own language. The empiricist has no need of the substantive *meaning*, a more than dubious reification that easily leads our minds astray. In his canonical essay on 'Two Dogmas of Empiricism' Quine calls meanings into question as 'obscure intermediate entities, which may well be abandoned' (1963:22). Meanings are not referents, not physical things outside language, as translators know all too well, since what a translator trying to understand a text in another language is employed to provide is sequences of words of his own language, not a collection of objects referred to in the original. The only legitimate answer to the question of what a certain sentence means is another sentence of the same (or in the case of translation, a second) language. This process of semantic substitution or refinement is potentially endless, and the conception of translation may itself be redefined as being among what Quine calls 'the synonymy of literary forms'.

There are meaning-like entities it would be well to get rid of from any theory of translation at the textual level too: those commonly known as the 'sense' of a text. The 'sense' is a meaning writ large, a meaning somehow conceived of as pervading the entirety of the text under discussion. It is noticeable, however, that the 'sense' of a passage or, more mysteriously still, of a whole text is almost always what a translator is held by his critics to have failed to give us; it is an entity remarkable for its elusiveness, even though we must presume that whoever complains of the 'sense' of the source text having gone missing in the translation is able to produce evidence of its presence in the original. But then the 'sense' has ever stood opposed to that other entity, the 'literal meaning' of a text, and the translator who is taken to task for being too literal is also the one who has no hope of capturing the 'sense'. The notion of a 'sense' simply reintroduces the crucial notion of freedom as the prerogative of the translator, and in its higher, more ethereal form it becomes the 'spirit' of the text, that vitalizing entity forever opposed to the inertia of the 'letter'. As entities 'sense' and 'spirit' alike transcend the text and lift us again on to that utopian plane of 'pure' translatability, where the privileged translator can enter into immediate communication with his source without having to suffer the all too obviously mediate pains of literalism.

On that higher plane, amidst the green and easeful landscape of transcendental signifieds, the radical indeterminacy of translation argued for by Quine no longer holds; should a rabbit pop suddenly out of its scrape and a passing native exclaim 'Gavagai!', the inquisitive English-speaker will be able to establish beyond doubt that this item of the vernacular has an identical meaning to his own exclamation of 'Gosh, a rabbit!' and is not in fact some other wayward response to the same stimulus. Quine's indeterminacy thesis is after all so radical that it leaves us unable to determine even the stimulus, which is a labile 'event' itself occurring outside language and therefore open to different determinations in different languages. It is disconcerting for any translator to be brought to see that even 'events' in the world are language dependent, that there are, as Quine insists, no predetermined 'facts of the matter'. There is thus nothing 'out there' on which a source and its translation can be said to fix with an absolute synonymy of reference.

From a different philosophical direction, Derrida has done as much as Quine to prove the indeterminacy of translation, and to bring us to share in his own deep enjoyment of knowing that there can be no final arresting of the semantic flux. For him also there is no intelligible escape from natural language. The question of translation pervades his writings, as it must, since were translation possible in its 'pure' form, then his own philosophy of language and of meaning would collapse. The lesson of Derrida's anti-Platonism goes to the limit: it is that 'pure' translation, or the integral transfer of meanings from language to language, is not possible because it is not thinkable, since we have no way of establishing that it has taken place. In what language could the matter finally be determined? Misconceptions arise over translation because of the 'iterability' of linguistic signs, whose constant reappearance or repetition leads us to assume their 'ideality', as essences which transcend their various manifestations. This misconception was one with which Derrida took early and definitive issue in the thought of Husserl, whom he charged with determining Being itself as ideality, or repetition, and History as 'the transmission and reactivation of the origin' (Derrida 1967:58–59ff; my translation). His own philosophy of an absolutely strict, progressive temporalization, allowing no possibility of a 'pure', Proust-like identification of a stimulus in the present with the 'same' stimulus in the past, undermines Husserlian notions of the ideality of natural language forms and hence of their perfect iterability. As an empiricist resistant to any notion whatsoever of the intelligible transcendence of actual language events, Derrida thus cannot allow that 'pure' translation is feasible, suggesting that we stick instead to talk of 'transformation', which is a less ambitious idea: 'We shall not have and never in fact have had to do with any 'carrying' of pure signifieds which the signifying instrument – or 'vehicle' – leaves virgin and unscathed, from one language to another, or within one and the same language' (1972:31; my translation). For Derrida each actual manifestation of a sign or signs is a historical event in time and space and necessarily distinct from every other such manifestation; he will not allow any slack-minded lapse into what he witheringly calls 'the indigence of an indefinite iteration' (1978:102).

In the face of nominalism as uncharitable as this, what to say of the interlinear mode of translation, which purports to find forms of words that will plot a convincing route between one language and another across the semantic void that seems definitively to separate them? I shall say that in this ultraskeptical environment of thought the notion of interlinearity, and the notion of literalism which is linked with it, is more valuable than ever. Pyrrhonists such as Quine and Derrida do not seek to prevent translation from continuing, as an activity central to the diffusion of knowledge and culture; nor will the practising translator be deterred or depressed by learning of the theoretical impossibility of 'pure' translation. We have something called 'translation' even if we cannot be sure exactly what it is. What these philosophers have done is to fix the theorist of translation's mind on that obscure region where it should remain fixed, on between-ness, or the region sardonically referred to by Derrida as the 'entr'expression'. Interlinearity does so fix the mind. It sets us to puzzling over what occurs in the act of translation at such times as the translator feels himself to be between languages; or to questioning, more radically still, whether the words 'between languages' are themselves comprehensible.

Loaded experiments such as that conducted by Malinowski in *Coral Gardens and their Magic* do at least show that an interlinear language, in the form of an English that has gone native, cannot make sense. His may look an extreme case, of someone attempting to mediate between two wildly incompatible natural languages. Had he been doing his fieldwork in Provence or the Tyrol rather than in furthest Melanesia, Malinowski's task would have been simpler and his interlinear translations of his native informants' French or German no doubt a great deal closer to a well-formed English than are his versions of Kiriwinian. But the difference is one of degree, not of kind; there could never *not* be a space between two languages in which to insert interlinear translations and by doing so to characterize the failure of those languages to match up either formally or semantically.

The interlinear mode of translation has virtues, moreover, whatever one cares to believe as to the existence of an abstract or 'pure' language of thought. If, *contra* the nominalists, that hypothesis be allowed, then an interlinear language may attempt to indicate its hypothetical forms, as Malinowski tried to indicate them, by a process of decontextualization. Such an enterprise today might call on the support of Chomskyan grammarians, whose researches into syntax have led them to postulate structures, if not 'beyond' then 'below' the empirical level of actual language use, to invoke in extreme cases such new denizens of the linguistic deep as 'pre-sentential structures of a more abstract kind'. If these underlying structures are universal, or common to the species, they can be called in to underpin the common-sense belief that human thought processes follow certain rules by the fact of their being human, or biologically conditioned; which being so, at some suitably abstract level 'languages' might be claimed to be ideally intertranslatable. But that level turns out to be of a degree of abstraction or mathematization such that we might refuse to recognize it as a language at all; moreover, the problem of by what criteria to identify beyond argument one such structure with another seems to remain unsolved. Nevertheless, the assertion of a rationalist philosopher of language like Jerrold Katz that 'each human language community has the same stock of possible thoughts' (1978:219) will be of encouragement to those who persist in thinking that translation is determinable.

Katz's vertiginous hypothesis, of 'the same stock of possible thoughts', is very close to the sly and mind-numbing fantasy thought up by Borges in his story of 'The Library of Babel', whose title overtly declares it to be a contribution to the theory of translation. But Borges's library, unlike Katz's theory of language, has no room for abstractions; it is the dreadfully extended space in which all 'possible thoughts' have for once been materialized (as well as a very great many sequences of signifiers which are not thoughts at all). The Library is, however, for all its size, language dependent, containing as it does only the possible combinations (restricted by certain arbitrary rules of combination laid down by Borges) of the material signs of a particular writing system. Somewhere in the stacks of the Library of Babel are all the thoughts possible in whatever natural languages share that writing system; and, if you are an idealist, you may properly claim that certain volumes in the library, and certain bits of other volumes, constitute the 'pure' translations one of the other. The volume that is lacking, however, is one containing the extralinguistic proof that this 'purity' of translation is absolute.

But if 'pure' translation is not even conceivable, it remains desirable: desirable because inconceivable is what Derrida is saying. Whatever we achieve in translation falls short of an ideal of synonymy that is itself ineffable, the ineffable being the romantic, Derridian version of Quine's more scientific category of the indeterminate. But faced with this ultimate indeterminacy, or antifoundationalism, we can still engage in the work of translation shored up by the assumption that human beings of different cultures and environments are sufficiently alike psychologically for their languages to approximate to each other; let our common behaviour be, as Wittgenstein suggests, that 'system of reference by means of which we interpret an unknown language' (1953:82). In the real world we seldom if ever have to 'interpret an unknown language'; so-called 'radical' translation, from languages of which we know nothing at all (not even the fact that they are 'languages': suppose *gavagai* were to turn out to be the only sound Quine's native informant was able to make, to any stimulus at all?), is itself a hypothetical activity, a philosopher's device for severing the metaphysical links which we might otherwise believe to guarantee the ideal communicability of thoughts between natural languages, and for establishing each individual language as autonomous in respect of every other.

Languages may converge but not merge: it is in the act of translation that their apartness manifests itself. Or it is there that it should do so. And yet we hold that act of translation the most successful which contains no evidence at all of the apartness of languages, but only of a source text flawlessly naturalized, which is to say finally occluded. There is no hint of interlinearity in the translations that are the most prized and applauded, because interlinearity would be 'translationese' and who is ever heard speaking up for that? Someone should speak up for it; the case for 'translationese' is that it could represent, if intelligently used, an honourable refusal on the part of a translator seamlessly to indigenize his source; it could make visible the between-ness in which he is trapped. The translator who is caught between the lines expects to make his escape in the direction of his own language and away from the source; were an interlinear 'translationese' permitted to him it would mean that he could pay his respects to his source rather than to his eventual reader. 'Translationese' as we know it is involuntary and all that is read into it is the incompetence of the translator, together with the neglectfulness of his editor. A voluntary 'translationese', systematically followed, would be something else, a drawing of our attention to the irrevocably mediate status of the language of translation. An interlinear language does not have to be as patronizingly primitive as that employed by Malinowski; it need only allow certain 'purely' untranslatable characteristics of the syntax and lexicon of the source to show through in the translation. Interlinear English will always be English but not an altogether familiar English, its abnormalities being so designed as to acknowledge the derivative nature of what we are reading.[4]

Translators know very well how much their sources lose on their passage into another language; a greater tolerance of literalism in translation would bring some ease to their consciences and restore the lost balance between the claims to ultimate respect of the source and the brazen imperatives of the market. Much day-to-day translation may be hackwork, of sources themselves perishable whose integrity is thought scarcely worthy of defence. But the principles of translation derive not from this low kind of translation but from the highest kind, from the translation of masterworks whose claims to integrity are paramount and certainly come before any assuagement of the tastes of readers. If it is ever to be recognized as an ideal in translation, interlinearity can only start at the top, as its greatest advocate in the modern age recognized. For Walter Benjamin, translation, in its doomed striving to fuse one language with another, offers us in its flounderings the mystical 'prospect' of a pure language beyond languages; it displays the complementarity of languages, and does so all the more powerfully if the first language can be seen to be still present in the second, or else visible through it. How more compellingly to rest the case for interlinearity than on Benjamin's splendid architectural trope: 'For if the sentence is the wall before the language of the original, literalness is the arcade' (1970:79).

Notes

1   This is the standard practice, though publishers do depart from it and publish translations either anonymously or even without indicating that they are translations. Translations of the more academic sort may also carry footnotes supplied by the translator, and marked as being by him, where he feels the need to explain or justify some element of the text. Similarly, there are translations which declare themselves as such by giving the original form of certain key terms in parentheses after the translated forms, or by leaving key terms untranslated. These practices serve as at least intermittent reminders that what we are reading has an original 'behind' it.

2   The 'free' versions of the native utterances are given by Malinowski in the first descriptive volume of the work rather than in conjunction with the interlinear versions, so that comparison of the two is made rather laborious.

3   These are the terms customarily used by theorists of translation. The term target language is not only ugly but seems to place the translator in some extra- or else prelinguistic state where he must remain until such time as he has succeeded in finding the right words to match those in the source language. The notion of having a 'target' at which to aim in translating implies that the right form of words is already 'there' if only one can find it. Only where is 'there'?

4   An example of the hybrid 'language' this would call for is the one adopted by Ernest
     Hemingway in some of the dialogue of For Whom the Bell Tolls, where one or more of the
     speakers is Spanish and presumed to be speaking his native tongue. The following exchange,
     for example: ' "To me, now, the most important is that we be not disturbed here," Pablo said.
     "To me, now, my duty is to those who are with me and to myself." – "Thyself. Yes." Anselmo
     said. "Thyself now since a long time. Thyself and thy horses. Until thou hadst horse thou wert
     with us. Now thou art another capitalist more" ' (Ernest Hemingway, For Whom the Bell Tolls,
     Harmondsworth, 1955, pp. 18–19). The point is not whether Hemingway did what he was
     trying to do well but the fact that he should even have attempted it. 'Translated' dialogue of
     this kind is sure to irritate many readers, particularly those who know no Spanish and are
     therefore unable to see the rationale for such alien forms of English. It would be interesting
     to know whether the Spanish translator of For Whom the Bell Tolls took the author's cues and
     translated the 'Spanish' dialogue accordingly.

Chapter 4

Lawrence Venuti

TRANSLATION AS CULTURAL POLITICS: RÉGIMES OF DOMESTICATION IN ENGLISH

EDITOR'S INTRODUCTION

What I am advocating is not an indiscriminate valorization of every foreign culture or a metaphysical concept of foreignness as an essential value; indeed, the foreign text is privileged in a foreignizing translation only in so far as it enables a disruption of target-language cultural values, so that its value is always strategic, depending on the cultural formation into which it is translated.

WHEREAS STURROCK (THIS VOLUME) focuses on the source text, and on literalism and a specific textual format as a means of allowing the original to 'shine through', Venuti's much misunderstood position is quite different. His focus is on the target culture, and his aim is not to 'preserve' the source text as such but to disrupt dominant values and patterns in the target context. This position is outlined clearly in a more recent publication (Venuti 2000:469):

> ... an ethics that counters the domesticating effects of the inscription can only be formulated and practiced primarily in *domestic* terms, in domestic dialects, registers, discourses, and styles. And this means that the linguistic and cultural differences of the foreign text can only be signalled indirectly, by their displacement in the translation, through a domestic difference introduced into values and institutions at home. This ethical attitude is therefore simultaneous with a political agenda: the domestic terms of the inscription become the focus of rewriting in the translation, discursive strategies where the hierarchies that rank the values in the domestic culture are disarranged to set going processes of defamiliarization, canon reformation, ideological critique, and institutional change.

This view underpins Venuti's recurrent reference to the 'violence' of translation: translation is inherently violent because it necessarily involves reconstituting the foreign text in accordance with values, beliefs and representations that pre-exist it in the target language. The translator nevertheless exercises a choice concerning the degree and direction of the violence at work in his or her practice. Venuti draws on Schleiermacher's formulation of this choice as one between a domesticating method, which accommodates the foreign text to target-language cultural values, and a foreignizing method, which exercises pressure on domestic values in order to register the linguistic and cultural difference of the foreign text. Like Schleiermacher, Venuti favours the foreignizing method, but he points out that the ' "foreign" in foreignizing translation is not a transparent representation of an essence that resides in the foreign text and is valuable in itself, but a strategic construction whose value is contingent on the current target-language situation' – which means that he does not advocate *a priori* valorization of specific textual strategies (such as literalism, for instance).

Venuti advocates foreignizing translation in opposition to the Anglo-American tradition of domestication, which he describes in detail in this article and elsewhere. He regards this strategy as 'resistant' because, while avoiding the fluency that occludes the source language and culture, and despite enacting its own (inevitable) ethnocentric violence on the foreign text, it also challenges the norms and expectations of the target language and culture. To enact foreignization, Venuti advocates a strategy of symptomatic reading that involves the translator consulting a wide range of target-language cultural materials, both canonical and marginal. He expects the sheer heterogeneity of these materials to produce discontinuities in the translation that are symptomatic of – and alert the reader to – its ethnocentric violence. These discontinuities may be evident at the level of syntax, diction or discourse and allow the translation to be read as a translation.

Follow-up questions for discussion

- Eugene Nida's work and his advocacy of dynamic equivalence represent the extreme opposite of what is advocated by Venuti and Sturrock, and both scholars thus allocate much space to critiquing him. Sturrock, for instance, insists that 'As a way of redirecting the heathen into the paths of a Protestant godliness Nida and Taber's method may work miracles, but as a general recipe for translation its pragmatism is offensive; it is surprising, what is more, to find it coming from translators who have for their source the peculiarly authoritative word of God, which surely deserves better than to be so casually "fixed up" '. Compare the two critiques (Sturrock's and Venuti's) and consider how a supporter of Nida's work might respond to them.

- One of Venuti's objections to Nida's work is that his 'advocacy of domesticating translation is explicitly grounded on a transcendental concept of humanity as an essence that remains unchanged over time and space'. What arguments does Venuti present against humanism (in this article and elsewhere), and how do they relate to his understanding of subjectivity? What ethical implications do these arguments have for the practice of translation?

- Shamma (2009:90) argues that '[t]he major weakness of Venuti's argument . . . is that he confuses the *strategy* of translation (which is confined to the textual level) with its *effect*, which is realized only in its socio-political and intertextual dimension'. Note that this is not a question of disagreeing about what might count as foreignizing or domesticating in a given context, since Venuti himself does not confine 'foreignization' or 'domestication' to specific textual features. Shamma's point is that even the broad strategy of accommodating or challenging readers' expectations, of disrupting target language cultural values, does not in itself guarantee specific political effects in all contexts. Tymoczko (2007:211) elaborates a similar critique: 'Although at times foreignization may be an appropriate resistant technique in dominant cultures such as the United States, it is not at all suited to subaltern cultures that are already flooded with foreign materials and foreign linguistic impositions (often from the United States or other Eurocentric cultures) and that are trying to establish or shore up their own discourses and cultural forms'. Assess Shamma's and Tymoczko's argument and try to think of concrete examples from your own linguistic/cultural context to challenge or support it. You might also like to compare Shamma's and Tymoczko's position with Asad's discussion (in this volume) of the inequality of languages and the implications of this inequality for strategies and modes of translation.

Recommended further reading

Boyden, Michael (2006) 'Language Politics, Translation, and American Literary History', *Target* 18(1): 121–37.

Gentzler, Edwin (2002) 'Translation, Poststructuralism, and Power', in Maria Tymoczko and Edwin Gentzler (eds) *Translation and Power*, Amherst and Boston: University of Massachusetts Press, 195–218.

Lane-Mercier, Gillian (1997) 'Translating the Untranslatable: The Translator's Aesthetic, Ideological and Political Responsibility', *Target* 9(1): 43–68.

Shamma, Tarek (2009) *Translation and the Manipulation of Difference: Arabic Literature in Nineteenth-Century England*, Manchester: St. Jerome (Chapter 2: The Exotic Dimension of Foreignizing Strategies).

Tymoczko, Maria (2000) 'Translation and Political Engagement: Activism, Social Change and the Role of Translation in Geopolitical Shifts', *The Translator* 6(1): 23–47.

Venuti, Lawrence (2008) *The Translator's Invisibility: A History of Translation*, 2nd revd edn, London: Routledge.

A metalanguage is always terrorist.

Roland Barthes (trans. Richard Howard)

All violence is the illustration of a pathetic stereotype.

Barbara Kruger

I PROPOSE THESE TWO EPIGRAPHS as an extravagant but pointed metaphor for translation. The statement from Roland Barthes concludes his incisive 1961 review of Michel Foucault's *Histoire de la folie* (Barthes 1972). For Barthes, Foucault's history shows that madness is the discourse of reason about unreason, and this discourse, apart from the physical exclusions of exile, imprisonment and hospitalization which it makes possible, also excludes the discourse of unreason about unreason, hence reducing the object of which it professes knowledge. In Barthes's conclusion, a metalanguage, a second-order discourse that takes a prior signifying system as its object, is found to be reductive and exclusionary and thus likened to terrorism, violent action that is both intense and damaging, that intimidates and coerces, usually in the service of social interests and political agendas, often under the aegis of reason or truth. The epigram from the artist Barbara Kruger was part of a 1991 installation, in which the accusatory aphoristic statements that distinguish her photomontages were painted across the walls and floors of the Mary Boone Gallery in New York.[1] Here violence is likened to a metalanguage: it is action with the function of representation, a second-order discourse illustrating a prior stereotype, which can be seen as pathetic in its destructiveness, its reductive and exclusionary relation to a person or social group. Violence is the enactment of a cultural discourse that already constitutes a conceptual or representational violence. Reflection on translation in the context of Barthes's and Kruger's statements undoubtedly cheapens violent action, trivializing its serious physical and psychological costs, its brutal materiality. But such reflection will also illuminate the discursive conditions of violence by attending to the material effects of another metalanguage, the power of translation to (re)constitute and cheapen foreign texts, to trivialize and exclude foreign cultures, and thus potentially to figure in racial discrimination and ethnic violence, international political confrontations, terrorism, war.

The violence of translation resides in its very purpose and activity: the reconstitution of the foreign text in accordance with values, beliefs and representations that pre-exist it in the target language, always configured in hierarchies of dominance and marginality, always determining the production, circulation and reception of texts. Translation is the forcible replacement of the linguistic and cultural difference of the foreign text with a text that will be intelligible to the target-language reader. This difference can never be entirely removed, of course, but it necessarily suffers a reduction and exclusion of possibilities – and an exorbitant gain of other possibilities specific to the translating language. Whatever difference the translation conveys is now imprinted by the target-language culture, assimilated to its positions of intelligibility, its canons and taboos, its codes and ideologies. The aim of translation is to bring back a cultural other as the same, the recognizable, even the familiar; and this aim always risks a wholesale domestication of the foreign text, often in highly self-conscious projects, where translation serves an imperialist appropriation of foreign cultures for domestic agendas, cultural, economic, political.

Thus, the violent effects of translation are felt at home as well as abroad. On the one hand, translation wields enormous power in the construction of national identities for foreign cultures and hence can play a role in racial and ethnic conflicts and geopolitical confrontations. On the other hand, translation enlists the foreign text in the maintenance or revision of literary canons in the target-language culture, inscribing poetry and fiction, for example, with the various poetic and narrative discourses that compete for cultural dominance in the target language. Translation also enlists the foreign text in the maintenance or revision of dominant conceptual paradigms, research methodologies, and clinical practices in target-language disciplines and professions, whether physics or architecture, philosophy or psychiatry, sociology or law. It is these social affiliations and effects – written into the materiality of the translated text, into its discursive strategy and its range of allusiveness for the target-language reader, but also into the very choice to translate it and the ways it is published, reviewed, and taught – all these conditions permit translation to be called a cultural political practice, constructing or critiquing ideology-stamped identities for foreign cultures, affirming or transgressing discursive values and institutional limits in the target-language culture. The violence wreaked by translation is partly inevitable, inherent in the translation process, partly potential, emerging at any point in the production and reception of the translated text, varying with specific cultural and social formations at different historical moments.

The most urgent question facing the translator who possesses this knowledge is: What to do? Why and how do I translate? Although I have construed translation as the site of multiple determinations and effects – linguistic, cultural, ideological, political – I also want to indicate that the translator always exercises a choice concerning the degree and direction of the violence at work in his practice. This choice was given its most decisive formulation at the beginning of the nineteenth century by the theologian and philosopher Friedrich Schleiermacher. In an 1813 lecture on the different methods of translation, Scheiermacher argued that 'there are only two. Either the translator leaves the author in peace, as much as possible, and moves the reader towards him; or he leaves the reader in peace, as much as possible, and moves the author towards him' (in Lefevere 1977:149). Admitting (with qualifications like 'as much as possible') that translation can never be completely adequate to the foreign text, Schleiermacher allowed the translator to choose between a domesticating method, an ethnocentric reduction of the foreign text to target-language cultural values, bringing the author back home, and a foreignizing method, an ethnodeviant pressure on those values to register the linguistic and cultural difference of the foreign text, sending the reader abroad.

Schleiermacher made clear that his choice was foreignizing translation, and this has led the French translator and translation theorist Antoine Berman to treat Schleiermacher's argument as an ethics of translation, concerned with making the translated text a place where a cultural other is manifested – although, of course, an otherness that can never be manifested in its own terms, only in those of the target language, and hence always already encoded (Berman 1984).[2] The 'foreign' in foreignizing translation is not a transparent representation of an essence that resides in the foreign text and is valuable in itself, but a strategic construction whose value is contingent on the current target-language situation. Foreignizing translation signifies the difference of the foreign text, yet only by disrupting the cultural codes that prevail in the target language. In its efforts to do right abroad, this translation method must do wrong at home, deviating from native norms to stage an alien reading experience.

I want to suggest that in so far as foreignizing translation seeks to restrain the ethnocentric violence of translation, it is highly desirable today, a strategic intervention in the current state of world affairs, pitched against the hegemonic English-language nations and the unequal cultural exchanges in which they engage their global others. For the fact is that only 2–3 per cent of the books published in the US and UK each year are translations, whereas foreign titles, many from English, count for as much as 25 per cent (or more) of the books published annually in other countries.[3] And yet foreignizing translation has always been marginalized in Anglo-American culture. This method is specific to certain European countries at particular historical moments: formulated first in German culture during the classical and romantic periods, it has recently been revived in a French cultural scene characterized by postmodern developments in philosophy, literary criticism, psychoanalysis and social theory that have come to be known as 'poststructuralism'.[4] English-language translation, in contrast, has been dominated by domesticating theories and practices at least since the seventeenth century.

In 1656, Sir John Denham prefaced *The Destruction of Troy*, his version of the second book of the *Aeneid*, with the remark that 'if *Virgil* must needs speak English, it were fit he should speak not only as a man of this Nation, but as a man of this age' (in T. R. Steiner 1975:64–65). Denham saw himself as presenting a naturalized English Virgil. He felt that poetic discourse in particular called for domesticating translation because 'Poesie is of so subtle a spirit, that in pouring out of one Language into another, it will all evaporate; and if a new spirit be not added in the transfusion, there will remain nothing but a *Caput mortuum*' (ibid.:65). The 'new spirit' Denham 'added' to

Virgil belonged to Denham ('my Art', 'my self'), and he was acutely aware that it was specifically English, so that domestication was a translation method laden with nationalism, even if expressed with courtly self-effacement (ibid.):

> if this disguise I have put upon him (I wish I could give it a better name) fit not naturally and easily on so grave a person, yet it may become him better than that Fools-Coat wherein the French and Italian have of late presented him.

Domestication became the preferred method for English-language poetry translation by the end of the seventeenth century, when it received its authoritative formulation in John Dryden's *Dedication of the Aeneis* (1697). 'I have endeavoured to make Virgil speak such English', wrote Dryden, 'as he would himself have spoken, if he had been born in England, and in this present age' (in T. Steiner 1975:72–74). In Dryden's wake, from Alexander Pope's multi-volumed Homer (1715–26) to Alexander Tytler's systematic *Essay on the Principles of Translation* (1791), domestication dominated the theory and practice of English-language translation in every genre, prose as well as poetry. William Guthrie, for example, in the preface to his version of *The Orations of Marcus Tullius Cicero* (1741), argued that 'it is living *Manners* alone that can communicate the Spirit of an Original' and so urged the translator to make 'it his Business to be as conversant as he cou'd in that Study and Manner which comes the nearest to what we may suppose his Author, were he now to live, wou'd pursue, and in which he wou'd shine' (in T. R. Steiner 1975:96–99). Hence, Guthrie cast his Cicero as a member of Parliament, 'where', he says, 'by a constant Attendance, in which I was indulg'd for several Years, I endeavour'd to possess myself of the Language most proper for this translation'.

It is important not to view such instances of domestication as simply inaccurate translations. Canons of accuracy and fidelity are always locally defined, specific to different cultural formations at different historical moments. Both Denham and Dryden recognized that a ratio of loss and gain inevitably occurs in the translation process and situates the translation in an equivocal relationship to the foreign text, never quite faithful, always somewhat free, never establishing an identity, always a lack and a supplement. Yet they also viewed their domesticating method as the most effective way to control this equivocal relationship and produce versions adequate to the Latin text. As a result, they castigated methods that either rigorously adhered to source-language textual features or played fast and loose with them, that either did not sufficiently domesticate the foreign text or did so by omitting parts of it. Following Horace's dictum in *Ars Poetica*, Denham 'conceive[d] it a vulgar error in translating Poets, to affect being *Fides Interpres*', because poetic discourse required more latitude to capture its 'spirit' in the target language than a close adherence to each foreign word would allow. But he also professed to 'having made it my principal care to follow [Virgil]', noting that 'neither have I any where offered such violence to his sense, as to make it seem mine, and not his'. Dryden similarly 'thought it fit to steer betwixt the two extremes of paraphrase and literal translation', i.e. between the aim of reproducing primarily the meanings of the Latin text, usually at the cost of its phonological and syntactical features, and the aim of rendering it word for word, respecting syntax and line break. And he distinguished his method from Abraham Cowley's 'imitations' of Pindar, partial translations that revised and, in effect, abandoned the foreign text. The ethnocentric violence performed by domesticating translation rested on a double fidelity, to the source-language text as well as to the target-language culture, but this was clearly impossible and knowingly duplicitous, accompanied by the rationale that a gain in domestic intelligibility and cultural force outweighed the loss suffered by the foreign text and culture.

By the turn of the nineteenth century, a translation method of eliding the linguistic and cultural difference of the foreign text was firmly entrenched as a canon in English-language translation, usually linked to a valorization of transparent discourse. In 1820, a translator of Aristophanes, John Hookham Frere, unfavourably reviewed Thomas Mitchell's versions of *The Acharnians* and *The Knights*, their principal 'defect' being 'the adoption of a particular style; the style of our ancient comedy in the beginning of the 16th century' (Frere 1820). Frere faulted Mitchell's use of an archaic literary and dramatic discourse, English Renaissance comedy, because

> the language of translation ought, we think, as far as possible, to be a pure, impalpable and invisible element, the medium of thought and feeling, and nothing more; it ought never to attract attention to itself; hence all phrases that are remarkable in themselves, either as old or new; all importations from foreign languages and quotations, are as far as possible to be avoided . . . such phrases as [Mitchell] has sometimes admitted, 'solus cum solo', for instance, 'petits pates', &c. have the immediate effect of reminding the reader, that he is reading a translation, and . . . the illusion of originality, which the spirited or natural turn of a sentence immediately preceding might have excited, is instantly dissipated by it. (ibid.:481)

Frere advocated a fluent strategy, in which the language of the translation is made to read with a 'spirited or natural turn', so that the absence of any syntactical or lexical peculiarities produces the illusionistic effect of transparency, the appearance that the translation reflects the foreign writer's intention ('It is the office, we presume, of the Translator to represent the forms of language according to the intention with which they are employed'; ibid.:482) and therefore the appearance that the translation is not in fact a translation, but the original, still within the foreign writer's control, not worked over by the translator. Fluency produces an individualistic illusion, in which the text is assumed to originate fundamentally with the author, to be authorial self-expression, free of cultural and social determinations. Since fluency is here a translation strategy, it can be considered a discursive sleight of hand by which the translator domesticates the foreign text, causing its difference to vanish by making it intelligible in an English-language culture that values easy readability, transparent discourse, and the illusion of authorial presence.

And, once again, the domestication enacted by a fluent strategy does not necessarily result in an inaccurate translation. In 1823, the anonymous reviewer of William Stewart Rose's *Orlando Furioso* recommended this strategy in the pronouncement that

> the two characteristics of a good translation are, that it should be *faithful*, and that it should be *unconstrained*. Faithful, as well in rendering correctly the meaning of the original, as in exhibiting the general spirit which pervades it: unconstrained, so as not to betray by its phraseology, by the collocation of its words, or construction of its sentences that it is only a copy. (Anonymous 1823)

Fluency can be associated with fidelity because it means foregrounding the conceptual signified in the translation, checking the drift of language away from communication, minimizing any play of the signifier which calls attention to its materiality, to words as words, their opacity, their resistance to immediate intelligibility, empathic response, interpretive mastery. What the fluent strategy conceals with the effect of transparency, what it makes seem faithful, is in fact the translator's interpretation of the foreign text, the signified he has demarcated in the translation in accordance with target-language cultural values. The fluent translation is seen as 'rendering correctly the meaning of the original' because it constitutes an interpretation that conforms or can be easily assimilated to those values, not only the valorization of 'unconstrained' language, but also the understanding of the foreign text or literature that concurrently prevails in the target culture.

In Frere's case fluency entailed a linguistic homogenization that avoided 'associations exclusively belonging to modern manners' as well as archaism, that removed as many of the historically specific markers of the foreign text as possible by generalizing or simply omitting them. The translator will,

> if he is capable of executing his task upon a philosophic principle, endeavour to resolve the personal and local allusions into the genera, of which the local or personal variety employed by the original author, is merely the accidental type; and to reproduce them in one of those permanent forms which are connected with the universal and immutable habits of mankind. (ibid.:482)

Frere rationalized these admitted 'liberties' by appealing to a 'philosophic principle':

> The proper domain of the Translator is, we conceive, to be found in that vast mass of feeling, passion, interest, action and habit which is common to mankind in all countries and in all ages; and which, in all languages, is invested with its appropriate forms of expression, capable of representing it in all its infinite varieties, in all the permanent distinctions of age, profession and temperament. (ibid.:481)

In Frere's view, a fluent strategy enables the translation to be a transparent representation of the eternal human verities expressed by the foreign author.

The principle on which Frere's translation theory rests is liberal humanism, in which subjectivity is seen as at once self-determining and determined by human nature, individualistic yet generic, transcending cultural difference, social conflict, and historical change to represent 'every shade of the human character'. Frere's theory may appear to be democratic in its appeal to what is 'common to mankind', to a timeless and universal human essence, but it actually involved an insidious domestication that allowed him to imprint the foreign text with his conservative sexual morality and cultural elitism. He made plain his squeamishness about the physical coarseness of Aristophanic humour, its grotesque realism, and felt the need to explain it away as inconsistent with the author's intention: the 'lines of extreme grossness' were 'forced compromises', 'which have evidently been inserted, for the purpose of pacifying the vulgar part of the audience, during passages in which their anger, or impatience, or disappointment, was likely to break out' (ibid.:491). Hence, 'in discarding such passages', Frere asserted, 'the translator is merely doing that for his author, which he would willingly have done for himself' – were he not 'often under the necessity of addressing himself exclusively to the lower class' (ibid.). Frere's advocacy of a fluent strategy was premised on a *bourgeois* snobbery, in which the moral and political conservatism emerging in early nineteenth-century English culture resulted in a call for a bowdlerized Aristophanes that represented the 'permanent' class divisions of humanity, what Frere described as 'that true comic humour which he was directing to the more refined and intelligent part of his audience' (ibid.).[5] For Frere, 'the persons of taste and judgment to whom the author occasionally appeals, form, in modern times, the tribunal to which his translator must address himself' (ibid.).

Fluency is thus a discursive strategy ideally suited to domesticating translation, capable not only of executing the ethnocentric violence of domestication, but also of concealing this violence by producing the illusionistic effect of transparency. And it is this strategy that, with very few exceptions (the Victorian archaism of Francis Newman and William Morris, for example, or the modernist experiments of Ezra Pound and Louis and Celia Zukofsky), has continued to dominate the theory and practice of English-language translation to this day. Perhaps the clearest indication of this dominance is Eugene Nida's influential concept of 'dynamic' or 'functional equivalence' in translation, formulated first in 1964, but restated and developed in numerous books and articles over the past twenty-five years. 'A translation of dynamic equivalence aims at complete naturalness of expression', states Nida, 'and tries to relate the receptor to modes of behavior relevant within the context of his own culture' (1964:159). The phrase 'naturalness of expression' signals the importance of a fluent strategy to this theory of translation, and in Nida's work it is evident that fluency involves domestication. As he has recently put it, 'the translator must be a person who can draw aside the curtains of linguistic and cultural differences so that people may see clearly the relevance of the original message' (de Waard and Nida 1986:14). This is of course a relevance to the target-language culture, something with which foreign writers are usually not concerned when they write their texts, so that relevance can be established in the translation process only by replacing source-language features that are not recognizable with target-language ones that are. Thus, when Nida asserts that 'an easy and natural style in translating, despite the extreme difficulty of producing it . . . is nevertheless essential to producing in the ultimate receptors a response similar to that of the original receptors' (1964:163), he is in fact imposing the English-language valorization of transparent discourse on every foreign culture, masking a basic disjunction between the source- and target-language texts which puts into question the possibility of eliciting a 'similar' response.

Like earlier theorists in the Anglo-American tradition, however, Nida has argued that dynamic equivalence is consistent with a notion of accuracy. The dynamically equivalent translation does not indiscriminately use 'anything which might have special impact and appeal for receptors' (de Waard and Nida 1986:vii–viii); it rather 'means thoroughly understanding not only the meaning of the source text but also the manner in which the intended receptors of a text are likely to understand it in the receptor language' (ibid.:9). For Nida, accuracy in translation depends on generating an equivalent effect in the target-language culture: 'the receptors of a translation should comprehend the translated text to such an extent that they can understand how the original receptors must have understood the original text' (ibid.:36). The dynamically equivalent translation is 'interlingual communication' which overcomes the linguistic and cultural differences that impede it (ibid.:11). Yet the understanding of the foreign text and culture which this kind of translation makes possible answers fundamentally to target-language cultural values while veiling this domestication in the transparency evoked by a fluent strategy. Communication here is initiated and controlled by the target-language culture, and therefore it seems less an exchange of information than an imperialist appropriation of a foreign text. Nida's theory of translation as communication does not adequately take into account the ethnocentric violence that is inherent in every translation process – but especially in one governed by dynamic equivalence.

As with John Hookham Frere, Nida's advocacy of domesticating translation is explicitly grounded on a transcendental concept of humanity as an essence that remains unchanged over time and space. 'As linguists and anthropologists have discovered', Nida states, 'that which unites mankind is much greater than that which divides, and hence there is, even in cases of very disparate languages and cultures, a basis for communication' (1964:2). Yet the democratic potential of Nida's human- ism, as with Frere's, is contradicted by the more exclusionary values that inform his theory of translation, specifically Christian evangelism and cultural élitism. From the very beginning of his career, Nida's work has been motivated by the exigencies of Bible translation: not only have problems in the history of the Bible translation served as examples for his theoretical statements, but he has written studies in anthropology and linguistics designed primarily for Bible translators and missionaries. Nida's con- cept of dynamic equivalence in fact links the translator to the missionary. When, in *Customs and Cultures: Anthropology for Christian Missions* (1954/1975:250), Nida asserted that

> a close examination of successful missionary work inevitably reveals the correspondingly effective manner in which the missionaries were able to identify themselves with the people – 'to be all things to all men' – and to communicate their message in terms which have meaning for the lives of the people,

he was echoing what he had earlier asserted of the Bible translator in *God's Word in Man's Language* (1952:117): 'The task of the true translator is one of identification. As a Christian servant he must identify with Christ; as a translator he must identify himself with the Word; as a missionary he must identify himself with the people'. Both the missionary and the translator must find the dynamic equivalent in the target language in order to establish the relevance of the Bible in the target culture. But Nida permits only a particular kind of relevance to be established. While he disapproves of 'the tendency to promote by means of Bible translating the cause of a particular theo- logical viewpoint, whether deistic, rationalistic, immersionistic, millenaria, or charis- matic' (de Waard and Nida 1986:33), it is obvious that he himself has promoted a reception of the text centred in Christian dogma. And although he offers a nuanced account of how 'diversities in the backgrounds of receptors' can shape any Bible translation, he insists that 'translations prepared primarily for minority groups must generally involve highly restrictive forms of language, but they must not involve substandard grammar or vulgar wording' (ibid.:14). Nida's concept of dynamic equivalence in Bible translation goes hand in hand with an evangelical zeal that seeks to impose on English-language readers a specific dialect of English as well as a distinctly Christian understanding of the text.

To advocate foreignizing translation in opposition to the Anglo-American trad- ition of domestication is not to do away with cultural political agendas. Clearly, such an advocacy is itself an agenda. The point is rather to develop a theory and practice of translation that resists dominant target-language cultural values so as to signify the linguistic and cultural difference of the foreign text. Philip Lewis's concept of abusive fidelity can be taken as a first step in such a theorization: it acknowledges the equivo- cal relationship between the foreign text and the translation and eschews a fluent strategy in order to reproduce in the translation whatever features of the foreign text abuse or resist dominant cultural values in the source language (Lewis 1985). Abusive fidelity directs the translator's attention away from the conceptual signified to the play of signifiers on which it depends, to phonological, syntactical, and discursive structures, resulting in a 'translation that values experimentation, tampers with usage, seeks to match the polyvalencies or plurivocities or expressive stresses of the original by producing its own' (ibid.:41). Such a translation strategy can best be called resistancy, not merely because it avoids fluency, but because it challenges the target-language culture even as it enacts its own ethnocentric violence on the foreign text.

The notion of foreignization can alter the ways translations are read as well as produced because it assumes a concept of human subjectivity that is very different from the humanist assumptions underlying domestication. Neither the foreign author nor the translator is conceived as the transcendental origin of the text, freely expressing an idea about human nature or communicating it in transparent language to a reader from a different culture. Rather, subjectivity is constituted by cultural and social determinations that are diverse and even conflicting, that mediate any language use, and that vary with every cultural formation and every historical moment. Human action is intentional, but determinate, self-reflexively measured against social rules and resources, the heterogeneity of which allows for the possibility of change with every self-reflexive action.[6] Textual production may be initiated and guided by the producer, but it puts to work various linguistic and cultural materials which make the text discontinuous, despite its appearance of unity, and which result in meanings and effects that may exceed the producer's intention, creating an unconscious that is at once personal and social, psychological and ideological. Thus, the translator consults many different target-language cultural materials, ranging from dictionaries and grammars to texts, discursive strategies and translations to values, paradigms and ideologies, both canonical and marginal. Although intended to reproduce the source-language text, the translator's consultation of these materials inevitably reduces and supplements it, even when source-language cultural materials are also consulted, and their sheer heterogeneity leads to discontinuities in the translation that are symptomatic of its ethnocentric violence. Discontinuities at the level of syntax, diction, or discourse allow the translation to be read as a translation, revealing the strategy at work in it, foreignizing a domesticating translation by showing where it departs from target-language cultural values, domesticating a foreignizing translation by showing where it depends on them.

This method of symptomatic reading can be illustrated with the translations of Freud's texts for the *Standard Edition*, although the translations have acquired such unimpeachable authority that we needed Bruno Bettelheim's (1983) critique to become aware of the discontinuities. Bettelheim's point is that the translations make Freud's texts 'appear to readers of English as abstract, depersonalized, highly theoretical, erudite, and mechanized – in short "scientific" – statements about the strange and very complex workings of our mind' (ibid.:5). Bettelheim seems to assume that a close examination of Freud's German is necessary to detect the translators' scientist strategy, but the fact is that his point can be demonstrated with no more than a careful reading of the English text. Bettelheim argues, for example, that in The Psychopathology of Everyday Life (1960), the term 'parapraxis' reveals the scientism of the translation because it is used to render a rather simple German word, *Fehlleistungen*, which Bettelheim himself prefers to translate as 'faulty achievement' (ibid.:87). Yet the translator's strategy may also be glimpsed through certain peculiarities in the diction of the translated text:

> I now return to the forgetting of names. So far we have not exhaustively
> considered either the case-material or the motives behind it. As this is
> exactly the kind of parapraxis that I can from time to time observe
> abundantly in myself, I am at no loss for examples. The mild attacks of
> migraine from which I still suffer usually announce themselves hours in
> advance by my forgetting names, and at the height of these attacks, dur-
> ing which I am not forced to abandon my work, it frequently happens
> that all proper names go out of my head. (Freud 1960:21)

The diction of much of this passage is so simple and common ('forgetting'), even
colloquial ('go out of my head'), that 'parapraxis' represents a conspicuous difference, an inconsistency in word choice which exposes the translation process. The
inconsistency is underscored not only by Freud's heavy reliance on anecdotal, 'everyday' examples, some – as above – taken from his own experience, but also by a
footnote added to a later edition of the German text and included in the English
translation:

> This book is of an entirely popular character; it merely aims, by an
> accumulation of examples, at paving the way for the necessary assump-
> tion of *unconscious yet operative* mental processes, and it avoids all theoretical
> considerations on the nature of the unconscious. (ibid.:272n)

James Strachey himself unwittingly called attention to the inconsistent diction in his
preface to Alan Tyson's translation, where he felt it necessary to provide a rationale for
the use of 'parapraxis': 'In German "*Fehlleistung*", "faulty function". It is a curious fact
that before Freud wrote this book the general concept seems not to have existed in
psychology, and in English a new word had to be invented to cover it' (ibid.:viii n). It
can of course be objected (against Bettelheim) that the mixture of specialized scientific terms and commonly used diction is characteristic of Freud's German, and
therefore (against me) that the English translation in itself cannot be the basis for an
account of the translator's strategy. Yet although I am very much in agreement with
the first point, the second weakens when we realize that even a comparison between
the English versions of key Freudian terms easily demonstrates the inconsistency in
kinds of diction I have located in the translated passage: 'id' vs. 'unconscious';
'cathexis' vs. 'charge', or 'energy'; 'libidinal' vs. 'sexual'.

   Bettelheim helpfully suggests some of the determinations that shaped the scientistic translation strategy of the *Standard Edition*. One important consideration is the
intellectual current that had dominated Anglo-American psychology and philosophy
since the eighteenth century: 'In theory, many topics with which Freud dealt permit
both a hermeneutic-spiritual and a positivistic-pragmatic approach. When this is so,
the English translators nearly always opt for the latter, positivism being the most
important English philosophical tradition' (1983:44). But there are also the social
institutions in which this tradition was entrenched and against which psychoanalysis
had to struggle in order to gain acceptance after the Second World War. As Bettelheim
concisely puts it, 'psychological research and teaching in American universities are
either behaviorally, cognitively, or physiologically oriented and concentrate almost
exclusively on what can be measured or observed from the outside' (ibid.:19). For
psychoanalysis this meant that its assimilation in Anglo-American culture entailed a
redefinition, in which it 'was perceived in the United States as a practice that ought
to be the sole prerogative of physicians' (ibid.:33), 'a medical specialty' (ibid.:35),

and this redefinition was carried out in a variety of social practices, including not only legislation by state assemblies and certification by the psychoanalytic profession, but the scientistic translation of the *Standard Edition*:

> When Freud appears to be either more abstruse or more dogmatic in English translation than in the original German, to speak about abstract concepts rather than about the reader himself, and about man's mind rather than about his soul, the probable explanation isn't mischievousness or carelessness on the translators' part but a deliberate wish to perceive Freud strictly within the framework of medicine. (ibid.:32)

The domesticating method at work in the translations of the *Standard Edition* sought to assimilate Freud's texts to the dominance of positivism in Anglo-American culture so as to facilitate the institutionalization of psychoanalysis in the medical profession and in academic psychology.

Bettelheim's book is of course couched in the most judgemental of terms, and it is his negative judgement that must be avoided (or perhaps rethought) if we want to understand the manifold significance of the *Standard Edition* as a translation. Bettelheim views the work of Strachey and his collaborators as a distortion and a betrayal of Freud's 'essential humanism', a view that points to a valorization of the concept of the transcendental subject in both Bettelheim and Freud. Bettelheim's assessment of the psychoanalytic project is stated in his own humanistic versions for the *Standard Edition*'s 'ego', 'id', and 'superego': 'A reasonable dominance of our I over our id and above-I – this was Freud's goal for all of us' (ibid.:110). This notion of ego dominance thinks of the subject as the potentially self-consistent source of its knowledge and actions, not perpetually split by psychological ('id') and social ('superego') determinations over which it has no or limited control. The same assumption can often be seen in Freud's German text: not only in his emphasis on social adjustment, for instance, as with the concept of the 'reality principle', but also in his repeated use of his own experience for analysis; both represent the subject as healing the determinate split in its own consciousness. Yet in so far as Freud's various psychic models theorized the ever-present, contradictory determinations of consciousness, the effect of his work was to decentre the subject, to remove it from the transcendental realm of freedom and unity and conceive it as the determinate product of psychic and familial forces beyond its conscious control. These conflicting concepts of the subject underlie different aspects of Freud's project: the transcendental subject, on the one hand, leads to a definition of psychoanalysis as primarily therapeutic, what Bettelheim calls a 'demanding and potentially dangerous voyage of self-discovery . . . so that we may no longer be enslaved without knowing it to the dark forces that reside in us' (ibid.:4); the determinate subject, on the other hand, leads to a definition of psychoanalysis as primarily hermeneutic, a theoretical apparatus with sufficient scientific rigour to analyze the shifting but always active forces that constitute and divide human subjectivity. Freud's texts are thus marked by a fundamental discontinuity, one which is 'resolved' in Bettelheim's humanistic representation of psychoanalysis as compassionate therapy, but which is exacerbated by the scientistic strategy of the English translations and their representation of Freud as the coolly analyzing physician.[7] The inconsistent diction in the *Standard Edition*, by reflecting the positivistic redefinition of psychoanalysis in Anglo-American institutions, signifies another, alternative reading of Freud that heightens the contradictions of his project.

It can be argued, therefore, that the inconsistent diction in the English translations does not really deserve to be judged erroneous; on the contrary, it discloses interpretive choices determined by a wide range of social institutions and cultural movements, some (like the specific institutionalization of psychoanalysis) calculated by the translators, others (like the dominance of positivism and the discontinuities in Freud's texts) remaining dimly perceived or entirely unconscious during the translation process. The fact that the inconsistencies have gone unnoticed for so long is perhaps largely the result of two mutually determining factors: the privileged status accorded the *Standard Edition* among English-language readers and the entrenchment of a positivistic reading of Freud in the Anglo-American psychoanalytic establishment. Hence, a different critical approach with a different set of assumptions becomes necessary to perceive the inconsistent diction of the translations: Bettelheim's particular humanism, or my own attempt to ground a reading of translated texts on a foreignizing method of translation that assumes a concept of determinate subjectivity.

In many translations, however, the discontinuities are readily apparent, unintentionally disturbing the fluency of the language or deliberately establishing the linguistic heterogeneity that distinguishes a resistant strategy. Literary translations, in particular, often bear prefaces which announce the translator's strategy and alert the reader to the presence of noticeable stylistic peculiarities. But perhaps translations in other disciplines should also contain prefaces that not merely describe the problems posed by the foreign text and the translator's solutions, but rationalize the global strategy developed and implemented by the translator, including the specific kind of discourse chosen for the translation and the specific interpretations assigned to key concepts. Such prefaces will ultimately force translators and their readers to reflect on the ethnocentric violence of translation and possibly to write and read translated texts in ways that seek to recognize the linguistic and cultural difference of foreign texts. What I am advocating is not an indiscriminate valorization of every foreign culture or a metaphysical concept of foreignness as an essential value; indeed, the foreign text is privileged in a foreignizing translation only in so far as it enables a distruption of target-language cultural values, so that its value is always strategic, depending on the cultural formation into which it is translated. My goal is not an essentializing of the foreign, but resistance against ethnocentrism and racism, cultural narcissism and imperialism, in the interests of democratic geopolitical relations. Hence, my project is the elaboration of the theoretical, critical and textual means by which translation can be studied and practised as a focus of difference, instead of the homogeneity that widely characterizes it today. Once the violence of translation is recognized, the choices facing the writers and readers of translated texts become clear – however difficult they are to make.

Notes

1   Barbara Kruger, Mary Boone Gallery, 5–26 January 1991.
2   See also Berman (1985, esp. 87–91). Schleiermacher's theory, despite its stress on foreignizing translation, is complicated by the nationalist cultural programme he wants German translation to serve: see Venuti (1992b).
3   See the annual statistics for the American publishing industry presented by Chandler B. Grannis in *Publishers Weekly*, 19 September 1989, pp. 24–25, 9 March 1990, pp. 32–35, and 8 March 1991, pp. 36–39. For the British statistics, see *Whittaker's Almanack* for the years 1986 to 1991. The volume of translations published annually in a European country like Italy can be

gauged from Herbert R. Lottman, 'Milan: A world of change', *Publishers Weekly*, 21 June 1991, pp. s5–s11.

4   I discuss the impact of French poststructuralism on translation theory and practice in the introduction of my anthology (Venuti 1992a). The present article develops theoretical issues set forth in that introduction. Although I am theorizing translation from within Anglo-American culture, the foreign theoretical discourses I put to work considerably complicate my 'home' position, creating possibilities for cultural critique and resistance. In a previous article (Venuti 1986), I offer an assessment of current English-language translation that is indebted as much to Althusserian Marxism as to poststructuralism.

5   For the emergence of moral and political conservatism in early nineteenth-century England, see Quinlan (1941) and Stone (1977).

6   These remarks assume Anthony Giddens' concept of agency in *Central Problems in Social Theory: Action, Structure, and Contradiction in Social Analysis* (1979), especially chapter 2.

7   The same contradiction appears in Freud's own reflections on the therapeutic/hermeneutic dilemma of psychoanalysis in *Beyond the Pleasure Principle*, translated by James Strachey (Freud 1961:12):

> Twenty-five years of intense work have had as their result that the immediate aims of psychoanalytic technique are other today than they were at the outset. At first the analyzing physician could do no more than discover the unconscious material that was concealed from the patient, put it together, and, at the right moment, communicate it to him. Psychoanalysis was then first and foremost an art of interpreting. Since this did not solve the therapeutic problem, a further aim quickly came in view: to oblige the patient to confirm the analyst's construction from his own memory. In that endeavor the chief emphasis lay upon the patient's resistances: the art considered now in uncovering these as quickly as possible, in pointing them out to the patient and in inducing him by human influence – this was where suggestion operating as 'transference' played its part – to abandon his resistances.

It will be noted that although Freud intends to draw a sharp distinction in the development of psychoanalysis between an early, hermeneutic phase and a later, therapeutic phase, his exposition really blurs the distinction: both phases require a primary emphasis on interpretation, whether of 'unconscious material' or of 'the patient's resistances', which in so far as they require 'uncovering' are likewise 'unconscious'; in both 'the analyst's construction' can be said to be 'first and foremost'. What has changed is not so much 'the immediate aims of psychoanalytic technique' as its theoretical apparatus: the intervening years witnessed the development of a new *interpretive* concept – the 'transference'. It is also worth pointing out that this characterization of psychoanalysis as primarily therapeutic occurs in a late text that is one of Freud's most theoretical and speculative. Bettelheim's characterization of psychoanalysis, the basis for his rejection of the *Standard Edition*, smoothes out the discontinuities in Freud's texts and project by resorting to a schema of development (like Freud himself): 'The English translations cleave to an early stage of Freud's thought, in which he inclined toward science and medicine, and disregard the more mature Freud, whose orientation was humanistic, and who was concerned mostly with broadly conceived cultural and human problems and with matters of the soul' (Bettelheim 1983:32).

PART 3

Text, discourse and ideology

Chapter 5

Ian Mason

DISCOURSE, IDEOLOGY AND TRANSLATION

EDITOR'S INTRODUCTION

> . . . the discourse belongs to the user, who also belongs to it.

MASON'S UNDERSTANDING OF 'IDEOLOGY' as 'the set of beliefs and values which inform an individual's or institution's view of the world and assist their interpretation of events, facts and other aspects of experience' informs his definition of discourse as 'systematically organized sets of statements which give expression to the meanings and values of an institution'. He sets out to show how ideology influences translational choices in subtle (and largely subconscious) ways by investigating the traces of systematic ideological shifts in the language used in a text about Mexican history and its translation. The text and its translation appeared in a bilingual format in the *UNESCO Courier*. The analysis reveals that the source and target texts express two very different world views and ideologies. The source text concedes that the Spanish Conquistadors were the official chroniclers of Mexican history but states that there were also indigenous voices that remain under-represented; these voices have preserved the 'memory' of the peoples of Mexico. The discourse is one of a nation striving to forge its own destiny by actively searching for its past and recording it. In the target text, the role of memory is downplayed and 'the active search for the past and the task of recording it turn into a passive "view" of the past and a "desire" to interpret it'.

Although Mason's focus is very much on ideology and ideological skewing, he assumes that we are all constrained by the discourses that circulate in our environment and that there is thus 'no need to attribute the divergent discourse of the target text to any deliberate intention of the translator'. His recognition of the 'habitualization of discourse' (Fowler 1991:89) leads him to examine the linguistic patterning of the two texts in considerable detail in order to bring to the surface connections which are normally hidden from view precisely because they are 'habitualized'. He supports his claims with analyses at a variety of levels. Lexically, he points out many differences in the choice of vocabulary ('sabios' becomes 'diviners'; 'testimonios' becomes 'written records', and so on). He also analyzes the divergent structures of the two texts in some detail, particularly with reference to the flow of information or the linear arrangement of elements in the clause. The source text places 'effort', 'memory' and 'destiny' in theme position, providing a point of orientation at the beginning of sentences. The target text, by contrast, puts humans in theme position and places in rheme position (where new information is usually placed) verbs that do not portray these humans in a pro-active role: for example 'met with mixed fortunes', 'succeeded one another'. Cumulatively, the effect is one of projecting a view of destiny as passive observation rather than personal commitment.

In a postscript written specifically for this volume, Mason revisits the findings, methodology and theoretical assumptions of the initial study and surveys a number of recent developments that offer promising avenues for pursuing some of the issues raised in this study from alternative perspectives.

Follow-up questions for discussion

- How does Mason's position on the pervasiveness and power of discourse compare with Kahf's emphasis on placing the ultimate responsibility for distorted representations on the environment of reception rather than the individual translator?
- One aspect of discourse that Mason does not pursue in this study is its regulatory function, its ability to 'describe and delimit what it is possible to say and not possible to say' (Kress 1985/1988:7), as well as how and when to say it. You might like to compare his treatment of discourse with Jacquemet's (this volume), who stresses that 'discourse practices do not necessarily seek to depict the world: rather, they dictate the world by mobilizing tactics of social indexicality and strategies of social inequality advantageous to the dominant group(s) in charge of institutional decision-making'. How might the analysis of the *UNESCO Courier* text in Mason's study have engaged with this dimension of the function of discourse? How might the methods of analysis and the interpretation of findings be different if this regulatory function is taken into account?
- What definitions of ideology, other than that offered by Mason, are explicitly or implicitly used by other scholars of translation? What do these understandings of ideology have in common, and how do they differ from, feed into or overlap with notions such as 'culture', 'discourse', 'narrative', and 'power'?

Recommended further reading

Calzada Pérez, María (ed.) (2003) *Apropos of Ideology: Translation Studies on Ideology – Ideologies in Translation Studies,* Manchester: St. Jerome.

Cunico, Sonia and Jeremy Munday (eds) (2007) *Translation and Ideology: Encounters and Clashes.* Special Issue of *The Translator* 13(2).

Hatim, Basil and Ian Mason (1997) *The Translator as Communicator,* London & New York: Routledge.

von Flotow, Luise (ed.) (2000) *Translation and Ideology.* Special Issue of *TTR (Traduction, Terminologie, Rédaction)* 13(1).

I **N A FASCINATING WORK OF** translation criticism, Bruno Bettelheim (1983) describes how the official English translators of Freud distorted the language – and hence the meaning – of their source text, principally through systematic lexical selections that had the effect of rendering their target text more clinical, more scientific and less subjective than Freud's original. Whereas Freud had nominalized German personal pronouns (*das Ich, das Es, das Über-Ich*) to represent central concepts of his work, his translators preferred Latin forms (*Ego, Id, Super-Ego*), appropriate – they no doubt reasoned – to a scientific treatise in English. The Graeco-Latin influence did not stop there; *Besetzung* (occupation) became in translation *cathexis*, *Fehlleistung* (erroneous performance) became *parapraxis*, *die Seele* (soul) and the corresponding adjective *seelisch* became *mind* and *mental*; and many more examples could be given. The choices made by Freud's official translators were strongly motivated. In line with the best practice of context-sensitive translators, they kept the target readership constantly in mind and had a clear sense of the language appropriate to a particular area of social activity. They strove to render the target text more abstract, more learned and more scientific in order to ensure that it would appeal to the Anglo-American medical/scientific community and thus win acceptance for a set of ideas which, in the original, stemmed from a somewhat different European humanist tradition.

Thus, the translation gave rise to a perception of Freud – based on the Standard Edition of his works in English, through which he achieved worldwide renown – which is quite different from that of readers of the source text. In Joyce Crick's (1989) words, these translations made of Freud 'the anatomist of the mind rather than the doctor of souls'. Underlying the source text and the target text are two distinct ideologies, which Bettelheim identifies as humanism and behaviourism. For Peter Newmark (1991:59), Bettelheim 'goes beyond neutrality when he insists on the translator's respect for the original, on values beyond culturally and socially-bound translation norms, on a respect for the "literal truth" '. Such an objection is unfortunate in implying that there can be a single, objectively defined meaning of a text, independent of both producer and receiver. But behind this issue lurks another more familiar one: where do the translator's loyalties lie? With the letter of the source text or with the expectations of the readers of the target text?

As Siân Reynolds (1991) relates, the controversy continues to rage in the preparation of the complete edition of Freud in French. While Jean Laplanche, co-editor and president of the terminology committee for the translation, speaks of 'restoring Freud to Freud' by stripping away all of the accretions which have obscured the original text and by standardizing the vocabulary, others regret the terminological strait-jacket in which they feel the translation is being imprisoned. The end result, they fear, will be more the language of Laplanche than that of Freud. Moreover, the work may be posited on the outmoded notion of the attainability of a 'pure' translation carrying over a single definable body of meaning from source text to target text.

That such a monolithic view of meaning is erroneous is an underlying theme of this study, but one which has been ably argued elsewhere (e.g. Prince 1981) and will not be further elaborated here. Rather, our preoccupation in what follows will be with some of the questions raised by the issue of ideology in translation. How are ideologies to be objectively identified? Can they be pinned down in the use of discrete items of language? What should the translator's attitude be towards whatever is perceived to be the ideology of the source text? How far will the perceptions of the readers of the target text match those of the readers of the source text?

Tentative answers to questions like these can properly be attained only through systematic analysis of what goes on in the process of text production and reception.

As will be argued here, words are invested with meaning by virtue of their use within a context and their exchange between users. In the multiple processes involved in translation (source text production, source text reception, target text production, target text reception), the meaning potential of items within the language system (Halliday 1978) is exploited by a variety of users, each within their own context and for their own purposes. In the particular case we shall consider, alternative world-views and discursive histories create divergent discourses and texts in a situation in which equivalence is normally assumed.

Terminology

Before outlining a model for analysis and then applying it to a text sample, it will be necessary to define certain of our terms – namely, discourse, text, and ideology. The terms discourse and text are frequently used to refer to any undifferentiated stretch of language performance, spoken or written, as for example in the expressions 'text linguistics' or 'discourse analysis'. This usage is standard and unproblematic. But the terms will be used here in narrower senses which require definition. The term **text** in the sense of Hatim and Mason (1990) refers to a unit of structure which is deployed in the service of an overall rhetorical purpose – e.g. to expound or to argue. Kress (1985), following Foucault (1971), uses the term **discourse** to refer to systematically organized sets of statements which give expression to the meanings and values of an institution.

Language users have their own discursive history: their previous experience of discourses which, in turn, shapes their own perception and use of discoursal features. Discourse is thus both institutional and individual and gives expression to users' attitudes towards any particular state of affairs. It is in this sense that the term is used here. As such, it is of course closely bound up with **ideology** – not in the commonly used sense of a political doctrine but rather as the set of beliefs and values which inform an individual's or institution's view of the world and assist their interpretation of events, facts and other aspects of experience.

A model for analysis

In examining ideology in translation, we shall be concerned with the constraints governing the production and reception of texts and the rhetorical conventions of the cultural communities of source and target language. The constraints may be considered as belonging to three categories: genre, discourse and text. As semiotic categories, these are culture-specific in the sense that different cultural communities may have evolved their own intertextual conventions governing what constitutes a given genre, discourse or text. Basil Hatim (e.g. 1991), whose work underlies this analysis, has convincingly argued that there are cross-cultural differences in the use of persuasive strategies, giving rise, for example, to a preference in Modern Standard Arabic for **through-argumentation** and in English for **counter-argumentation**. Further, in an analysis of a translation into English of a speech given by the late Ayatollah Khomeini (Hatim and Mason 1991), we sought to show how systematic differences in Western and non-Western generic, discoursal and textual conventions create considerable difficulties for translators; and that whereas the strategy of relaying the unfamiliar signals of genre and discourse in unmediated form to the target text reader affords the latter the possibility of real insight into an unfamiliar text-world, the translator's options are more constrained in the case of signals of text structure. For example, a text-initial item such as English *Of course* or French *Certes* (certainly) is a clear signal of a concession within a counter-argumentative text structure. In such a case, the translator's decision will be determined not by some elementary lexical equivalence between source and target language but rather by the need to relay the appropriate structural signal to users of the target text.

Above all, it is our contention that these – genre, discourse and text – are the semiotic systems within which the expression of ideology is realized, and that the investigation of ideology in translation is best handled within such a framework.

Application: Ideology in translation

The data

The text sample reproduced in the Appendix appeared in the April 1990 edition of the *UNESCO Courier*, a monthly publication produced simultaneously in several different language versions. We may characterize the institution, UNESCO, and its official organ, the *Courier*, as being dedicated to the promotion of the cultures of the world, and to the dissemination of knowledge and understanding about them. Following Kress (1985), we have defined **genres** as conventionalized forms of texts appropriate to given types of social occasion. In this sense, the social occasion is the international dissemination of understanding, in the form of social history, of the peoples of Mexico. Unlike the case of Freud, discussed earlier, in which genre is modified in translation to meet different cultural conventions, source text (ST) and target text (TT) here belong to an identical generic specification: both have the same starting point, are aimed at similar international readers and have the same moderately didactic role. The channel of publication is the same: different language versions of the same periodical. Given this specification, we can expect that the primary rhetorical purposes of the article will be to expound (describe, narrate) but also to present a case and pass judgement (present argumentation and evaluation).

Lexical cohesion

The first and most obvious way in which ST and TT diverge from each other is at the level of individual lexical choice (see appendix). In a translation which is far from a slavish rendition of ST form, lexical shifts are to be expected. But the manipulation here involves in some cases a radical shift of values. *Prolongados esfuerzos* (Prolonged efforts; ST 1) become in translation *obstinate determination* (TT 1); *enfrentamientos* (confrontations; ST 26) becomes *war* (TT 25) and *encuentros* (encounters; ST 32) becomes *clash of cultures* (TT 30). Even more significantly, *sabios* (wise men; ST 10) become *diviners* (TT 9). Whereas the meaning potential of *sabios* covers both Western (i.e. purely rational) and non-Western forms of wisdom, the use of *diviners* tends to exclude the form of wisdom which is currently valued in the West. A different perspective is also apparent in making *testimonios* (testimonies; ST 39) into *written records* (TT 41), *el hombre indígena* (indigenous man; ST 33) into *pre-Columbian civilization* (TT 31) and *antiguos mexicanos* (ancient Mexicans; ST 44) into *Indians* (TT 45).

Yet something more systematic is at work in the realization of these two texts.

The Spanish terms *esfuerzos* (efforts) and *memoria* (memory) are announced as themes in the opening sentence of the source text and form cohesive networks throughout. In the case of *memoria*, there is multiple recurrence (ST 2, 7, 9, 30, 43). Beaugrande and Dressler (1981:55) note that recurrence is 'prominently used to assert and reaffirm one's viewpoint', and it is this discoursal value which is important here. *Memoria* is a term which takes on added meaning in societies where oral tradition is valued (although the Spanish term can also denote a written record or report, co-text here makes clear that 'memory' is the sense intended). It is clearly a keyword in the discourse; its recurrence is motivated by a rhetorical purpose which emerges in conjunction with other features we shall describe. *Esfuerzos* is echoed in co-referring items such as *búsqueda* (search), *luchar* (struggle), *quehacer* (task – with the added connotation of 'duty'), *creatividad* (creativity), to form what Halliday and Hasan call a chain of collocational cohesion – 'the cohesion that results from the co-occurrence of lexical items that are in some way or other typically associated with one another' (1976:278). We can now make an initial comparison of source text versus target text at the level of networks of lexical cohesion (Table 5.1). It is immediately apparent that neither the multiple recurrence of *memoria*, nor the notion of 'destiny', nor the collocational chain of 'effort' has been adequately maintained. Moreover, the first signs of a fundamentally different discourse emerge. When memory becomes *history* (TT 7) and *knowledge of the past* (TT 8), the direct links between past and present are severed. Memory as such is down-played, and the active search for the past and the task of recording it turn into a passive *view* of the past and a *desire* to interpret it. Creativity, meanwhile, has been reduced from whole 'ages' to occasional *bursts*, and the neutral *hubo* (there were; ST 25) has correspondingly been transformed into *were punctuated by* (TT 24).

Discourse indicators

At this point, we must address a procedural matter. Translation criticism as an activity has been censured for concentrating on the written text as a product divorced from the circumstances of its production and reception, and for ignoring the translation

Table 5.1 Recurrence and collocational cohesion

Source text	Target text
memoria (memory; ST 2)	memory (TT 2)
memoria (ST 7)	history (TT 7)
memoria (ST 9)	knowledge of the past (TT 8)
memoria (ST 30)	memory (TT 27)
memoria (ST 43)	—
destino (destiny; ST 4)	destiny (TT 5)
destinos (ST 10)	the future (TT 11)
destino (STT 22)	—
destinos (ST 22)	—
esfuerzos (efforts; ST 1)	obstinate determination (TT 1)
búsqueda (search; ST 4)	the way in which they view (TT 4)
luchar contra (struggle against; ST 8)	to save . . . from (TT 7)
quehacer (task; ST 11)	desire (TT 14)
épocas de gran creatividad (ages of great creativity; ST 25)	bursts of creativity (TT 24)

process. The cross-textual comparison of individual lexical items may seem open to such censure. But our interest in these items resides in their value as signs, and in the clues they provide to the construction of a text-world by text users. It is in this semiotic dimension that divergences become significant, rather than at the level of discrepancies between individual lexical items. A further example may serve to illustrate this point. *Mas de veinte siglos* (more than twenty centuries; ST 14) is relayed in translation as *two thousand years* (TT 12). Referentially, twenty centuries and two thousand years are equivalent; in traditional forms of analysis, the difference of expression would be put down to (presumably unmotivated) stylistic variation. Yet there is evidence in the ST of a discourse of emphatic appeal in the use of hyperbolic expressions, as shown in Table 5.2. Equivalence of referential meaning between items in the source text and target text is much less important here than relaying discoursal indices that contribute to an overall discourse of epic narration in which history, memory and destiny are seen as subject to human will and effort.

Theme/rheme arrangement

It was mentioned above that 'effort' and 'memory' constitute the themes of the initial sentence of the source text. (In Functional Sentence Perspective, the theme constitutes the topic of a sentence while rheme is the name given to whatever constitutes a comment on the topic.) A cursory glance at the developing text shows that these notions form a kind of hyper-theme that spans the themes of various sentences (see Table 5.3, in which the ST is represented in a literal English translation).

Thus, 'effort/memory/destiny' are the featured themes in parts of this discourse. In contrast, the target text at these points tends to put people(s) in theme position (see Table 5.4) and the dramatic *prever los destinos* (foresee the destinies; ST 10) becomes the prosaic *predictions of the future* (TT 10). But even within the thematic structure illustrated in Table 5.4 the choice of verb in the rheme does not portray humans in a

Table 5.2 Discourse of emphatic appeal

Source text	Target text
miles de vestigios (thousands of remains; ST 13)	countless remains (TT 11)
más de veinte siglos (more than twenty centuries; ST 14)	two thousand years (TT 12)
los muchos pueblos (the many peoples; ST 23)	peoples (TT 22)
gran creatividad (great creativity; ST 26)	creativity (TT 24)
el más grande de los traumas (the greatest of traumas; ST 44)	the traumatic fate (TT 44)

Table 5.3 Hyper-theme in source text

Theme	Rheme
(1) (Ancient . . . efforts to preserve the memory)	(constitute the first great chapter . . .)
(8) (That memory)	(was indispensable)
(11) (Such a task)	(lives on in thousands of remains)
(22) (The destiny – or destinies)	(experienced propitious times and fatal times)

Table 5.4 Hyper-theme in target text

Theme	Rheme
(1) Mexicans	have always exhibited
(6) they	have been engaged
(22) The people, or rather peoples	met with mixed fortunes

particularly pro-active role: they *exhibit* features and *meet* with their fate. Contrast too, for example, *interesarse por* (to take an active interest in; ST 7) with *have been engaged* (TT 6).

This theme/rheme arrangement is closely associated with the expression of discourse. Admittedly, word order and theme/rheme arrangement correspond to different textual norms in Spanish and in English, and one cannot be prescriptive about the translator's choices in this respect. Nevertheless, all of the textural devices of the source text noted so far combine in the expression of a discourse which relays an ideology: destiny as personal commitment rather than as passive observation. Our last category, text structure, provides further evidence of the discoursal shift in the translation.

Text structure

The dominant text-type focus of the source text is expository, although there is a substantial element of evaluation which gives rise, in the third paragraph, to an argumentative text structure. A concession is made, followed by a counter-argument. A formal – 'literal' – translation of the source text (ST 32–39; cf. TT 30–41) at this point might read as follows:

> About the greatest and most tragic encounters experienced by indigenous man [persons] would have to write such as the conquistador himself, Hernán Cortés in his *Letters of Account* and the soldier-chronicler, Bernal Díaz del Castillo in his *True History of New Spain*. But also the vanquished left their testimonies . . .

The effect of this source text structure is to downgrade the initial concession (the Spaniards were the official chroniclers of these events), relative to the counter-argument (**but** the indigenous people did write their own account); here, the second text element has a higher rhetorical status. In the target text, however, the counter-argument signalled by 'but' is missing:

> The vanquished peoples also left written records.

Moreover, the first element is upgraded by the addition of the term *pre-Columbian* (TT 31), making the arrival of a European the main historical milestone, and by a more detailed and at times laudatory rendering in *sent five remarkable letters [. . .] back to Spain between 1519 and 1526* (TT 33–35) and *who served under Cortés, fifty years after the event wrote* . . . (TT 37–38), which foregrounds the Spanish over the indigenous documentation – a clear rhetorical reversal in the achievement of a subtly different purpose.

The evidence for this claim might be judged insufficient: at first glance, there appears to be no overt concessive in the source text (equivalent to *Certainly . . ., Of course* . . . or *Although* . . .) and the item *pero* (but) might not, for all readers, carry the rhetorical weight I am attributing to it. Such a view, however, would overlook the modality of the verb form *habrían de escribir*, with its clear implied value of: 'it was natural that . . .' or: 'were bound to . . .'. Thus, the concessive is indeed present (though not expressed in the conventional adverbial manner of English) and the counter-argumentative structure is beyond doubt. Moreover, an identical structure occurs in a later portion of the text, not included in the excerpt reproduced in the Appendix. Here it is, rendered in my formal translation into English:

> To an extraordinary Franciscan monk, Bernardino de Sahagún . . . was owed the recovery of a great treasure of testimonies of the pre-Hispanic age. But there were also indigenous people who continued to write in their own language . . .

This section of the source text makes a strikingly similar point with its contrastive *but*, rhetorically subordinating the known Spanish accounts to the lesser known indigenous texts. In the translation, the adversative *but* has turned into a mere time-adverbial *meanwhile*, and the volume of writings suggested by *continued to write* gets lost in the simple *were writing*:

> An extraordinary man, the Spanish Franciscan Bernardino de Sahagún, . . . gathered invaluable, first-hand information on the pre-Columbian era. Meanwhile, indigenous chroniclers were writing in their own languages . . .

Overall, these divergent structures relay two different world-views or ideologies. Within a humanist discourse of people striving to forge their own destiny, and within an institutional framework (i.e. UNESCO) for the promotion of indigenous cultures, the rhetorical purpose of the source text structure is clear: in conceding that the Spanish Conquistadors were the official chroniclers of Mexican history, the text strongly counter-argues that there are indigenous voices, under-represented hitherto, which are equally worth listening to and which have preserved the precious legacy of 'memory' in their own written records. The text world constructed in the translation is radically different.

In sum, genre, discourse, and text are found to be mutually supporting entities within the producer's plan towards an overarching communicative goal. We can see how the sets of constraints imposed by genre, discourse and text are important variables in the translator's search for translational adequacy and how, as superordinate factors, they take precedence over incidental equivalences at the level of the referential meaning of individual lexical items.

A text-linguistic approach to descriptive translation studies

When I first discussed these two text samples with a group of Spanish linguists and English-language Hispanists, they were outraged at what they saw as a deliberate skewing by the translator of the intended meaning of the source text. Without access to the inner motivations and thought processes of the translator, we cannot state with any certainty what the intentions were. But I would suggest that there is no need to attribute the divergent discourse of the target text to any deliberate intention of the translator. Mediation, as 'the extent to which one feeds one's current beliefs and goals' into processing a text (Beaugrande and Dressler 1981:182), may largely be an unconscious process. And, as noted earlier, an individual's discursive history will shape his or her perception and use of discoursal features. As James Paul Gee (1990:174) notes, text users 'serve apprenticeships in social settings where people characteristically read, write, speak and listen in [certain] ways'; he continues: 'thus I am at one and the same time an active subject (agent) in the Discourse and passively subjected to its authority' (ibid.:176).

In this sense, the discourse belongs to the user, who also belongs to it. If such an account of discourse is well-founded, then it would suffice to explain our two divergent text samples. The reception and production of texts have been mediated through variant discursive histories. The results reveal two distinct ideologies, only one of which is entirely consistent with the conventional norms of the institutional setting of the texts.

Our analysis has been far from exhaustive. A comparison of the titles of the two texts would, for example, reveal further corroborative evidence of the divergent discourses we have described. But our aim here has been to show that there are implications both for descriptive translation studies and for translator training. Empirical studies must seek not to contrast disembodied entities or isolated phrases from the source text and target text but to trace generic, discoursal and textual developments which reveal ideologies and highlight the mediating role of the translator. If training programmes consider these important dimensions of text production and reception, the discussion of translators' techniques and strategies can be greatly enriched.

Postscript

In the years since this article was published, various scholars have commented from differing perspectives on the case study related in it. Venuti (1998b:2–3) drew on it as the opening example in his *Scandals of Translation*, thus associating the case with his project for an 'ethics of difference' (ibid.:82) in translation. Brotherston (2002:165–67) then took Venuti to task for claiming that the translation downgraded Mexican oral culture and thus implying that pre-Conquest Mexican history was essentially oral – in direct contradiction to what León Portilla was actually saying. Brotherston then proceeded to demonstrate the importance of written texts to the ancient Mexicans and the challenges to our conception of translation thrown down by the multi-layered meanings offered by the iconic script of some key texts. Munday (2001:100; 2007a:199) cites the case as an example of critical-linguistic approaches to the analysis of translation, opening up a discussion of the potential and limitations of such approaches. These studies open up substantial issues, which continue to occupy a central position in contemporary translation studies.

My own original aims were more modest. They were to show how the individual choices made by language users – and here, specifically, translators – on the surface of the text (**texture**) may provide evidence of underlying ideologies – in the sense of sets of the 'taken-for-granted assumptions, beliefs and value systems which are shared collectively by social groups' (Simpson 1993:5). In this way, such categories as cohesion (or transitivity, or modality) are lifted out of the realm of technical linguistics to become the tools for the construction of a text world, intertextually echoing other text worlds, discourses and genres. My source and target texts were chosen for the way in which they each reflected patterned behaviour, networks of expression projecting two contrasting discourses.

The analysis could, of course, have been more comprehensive. The contrasting perspectives of source and target text producers are, for example, reflected in patterns of personal reference. Whereas the ST presents processes in a relatively impersonal fashion, the TT adopts a resolutely third-person form of reference: *Mexicans* (1), *their society* (3), *they view* (4), *their identity* (5), etc., thus positioning the author as if he were an outside observer rather than a member of the subject group. Conspicuous too is the absence from the translation of ST anaphora and junction: *Así* (thus; ST 5), *Esa memoria* (This memory; ST 8), *Tal quehacer* (Such a task; ST 11), *Así, por ejemplo* (Thus, for example; ST 16), *Entre otros* (Among others; ST 39) provide a form of linkage which, while it might be associated with Spanish rather than English style, nevertheless signals a continuity and dynamism in the source text account. Clearly, evidence in support of the argument advanced in the article is not lacking.

In the intervening years, there have been a number of other studies in a similar vein, drawing attention to the role of textural devices in projecting ideology via discourses. For example, Schäffner (2003) analyses a policy document, jointly published by the leader of the Labour Party in the United Kingdom and of the Social Democratic Party of Germany in English- and German-language versions, a case of parallel text production. Adopting a critical discourse analysis approach, she relates textural decisions (lexical choice, metaphor) to contextual factors: the ideological positioning of both parties and the generally hostile reception of the text in Germany, thus providing an excellent example of politics at work in an intercultural environment (cf. also Meylaerts 2007). Bennett (2007) studies the ideological effects of the globalization of academic English, noting how micro-textual features (nominalizations, passives, etc.) impose alien norms on academic discourses in other cultures. Kang (2007) shows how translators' decisions in the genre of news reporting serve to reconstruct North Korea between US and (South) Korean versions of texts. Munday (2002) compares English translations of an article by Gabriel García Márquez, finding that choices made in the representation of processes (transitivity) and of interpersonal meaning (attitude) appear to be compatible with the ideological positions of the channels in which the translations are published (the Cuban *Granma International*, *The New York Times*, the *Guardian*). This leads to the question of whether such shifts in translation (including omission of some items) might be deliberate moves on the part of the translator or publisher.

In a separate study of different data, however, Munday (2007a) finds that ST institutional agendas are not necessarily inscribed in translation practice, citing cases where translators' decisions appear to run counter to the ideological outlook of the channel of publication. He concludes that translators tend to be 'guided by intuition and previous linguistic experience of the two languages alone' (*ibid.*:204). This statement matches the evidence presented in the present article, in the sense that the translator appears to present a detached outsider's view of Mexico and its history rather than a discourse representative of the UNESCO ideology of promotion of indigenous cultures. Munday (*ibid.*) also uses Michael Hoey's concept of **lexical priming** (the way in which a word 'becomes cumulatively loaded with the contexts and co-texts in which it is encountered' – Hoey 2005:5) to account for ways in which translators' language use depends at least in part on their previous socio-textual experience. This too is close to the conclusion drawn in the present article: that the reception and production of texts are mediated through variant discursive histories. The added significance lies in the fact that lexical priming can be empirically investigated through the techniques of corpus linguistics and therefore provides opportunities for more reliable supporting evidence in future work of this kind.

These studies and others not mentioned here considerably broaden our understanding of ways in which translators' decision making at the level of texture reflects higher-order concerns and influences. Among the many insightful notions that would be relevant to the analysis of the León Portilla translation are: institutional policies and recontextualisation (Kang 2007, Schäffner 2003), the translator as gatekeeper (Bennett 2007), and thus as a means of reinforcing or resisting power structures (Cunico and Munday 2007). Further, Hatim (2001:131–32), drawing on Bruce (1994), suggests **interdiscursive mixing** (competing discourses, the hijacking of one discourse in the service of another, discursive subversion, and so on) as an over-arching category that subsumes many kinds of textural moves involved in the projection of ideology, including those related here.

It will be noted that this discussion of discourse in relation to ideology constantly moves between the personal (translators' choices) and the public (ambient discourses). Baker (2006a) proposes narrative theory as an alternative account of these and similar phenomena in translation studies. In narrative theory a distinction is made between **ontological narratives** (narratives of the self) and **public narratives**, as 'stories elaborated by and circulating among social and institutional formations larger than the individual' (ibid.:33). Baker's account makes explicit the interaction between individual and collective perception and expression – an immensely useful insight for both translation and discourse studies, especially in situations where the individual voice and the public narrative conflict with each other.

These notions and others provide a much richer framework within which to conduct analyses of language and ideology in translation. In pursuing such studies, however, we shall have to confront some methodological problems, raised by Stubbs (1997) amongst others, about the practice of critical discourse analysis (CDA). One is that CDA studies typically do not aim at comprehensive coverage of the data, instead merely selecting elements in texts which support the argument being put forward. The present study might be accused of this failing since there are, of course, some counter-examples in the texts which go against the general trend. Occasionally, for instance, the translator does represent the discourse of effort and engagement: *a continuous battle* (TT 6–7), *the memory lives on . . .* (TT 27–28). So are we just cherry-picking evidence to suit our case? The logical way to counter this criticism would be to provide a full, quantitative analysis of shifts (and non-shifts) in the translation. The results that would emerge from such a study, however, would tell us very little about what is going on – and might even prove misleading. For numbers of shifts do not represent significance of shifts. In the first three lines alone of ST and TT, it is very difficult to quantify the precise number of shifts (there are many); and some which would have to be counted (e.g. *comunidad* becoming *society, conservar* becoming *safeguard*) are hardly significant. This problem was recognized long ago by van Leuven-Zwart (1990:88) in her pioneering study of translation shifts: the macro-structural impact of shifts depends not upon their quantity but upon their quality or significance. Qualitative assessment, including counter-examples as well as patterned behaviour, still seems to be the best way forward.

Another criticism of CDA is that one of its central claims – that discourses are both 'socially shaped and socially constitutive' (Fairclough 1995:131; cf. Gee 1990, above) – is often asserted but has not as yet been empirically substantiated. How could the relation between cause and effect posited in this double process be tested? Specifically, how can we tell that the sets of decisions that make up the translated text have any particular cumulative effect? I have described elsewhere (Mason 2009a) the beginnings of an attempt to investigate actual reader response to translated texts as a way of testing whether discoursal shifts have any effect on readers. It is, of course, a highly problematic undertaking – perhaps even a quixotic enterprise, as Hermans (1999:63–64) has suggested. Nevertheless, enquiry into the actual effects of translators' decision making on users of translations would add considerable support to the kinds of claims we wish to make about discourse and ideology in translation. If we wish to substantiate our beliefs about the role of translators in spreading or resisting the spread of narratives and discourses, it is to this area of enquiry that we should perhaps turn our attention.

APPENDIX

¿Tiene la historia un destino?

Miguel León-Portilla

1	Antiguos y prolongados esfuerzos por
2	conservar la memoria de sucesos que afectaron
3	a la comunidad integran el primer gran
4	capítulo de la búsqueda del ser y del destino
5	mexicanos. Así, ya en la época prehispánica
6	se afirma una forma característica de
7	interesarse por preservar la memoria de sí
8	mismo y luchar contra el olvido. Esa memoria
9	era indispensable a los viejos sacerdotes y
10	sabios para prever los destinos en relación con
11	sus cálculos calendáricos. Tal quehacer de
12	elaboración y registro de una historia divina y
13	humana perdura en miles de vestigios
14	arqueológicos que abarcan más de veinte siglos
15	antes de la llegada de los españoles en 1519.
16	Así, por ejemplo, las estelas de 'Los
17	Danzantes' en Monte Albán, Oaxaca, fechadas
18	entre 600 y 300 a.C., constituyen en el Nuevo
19	Mundo el más antiguo registro de aconteceres,
20	con sus años y días, nombres de lugares, de
21	reyes y señores.
22	El destino - o los destinos - de los
23	muchos pueblos que han vivido y viven en
24	tierras mexicanas tuvo tiempos propicios y
25	tiempos funestos. Hubo épocas de gran
26	creatividad y otras de crisis y enfrentamientos,
27	que llevaron a dramáticas desapariciones de
28	hombres y de formas de exisitir. Los mitos y
29	leyendas, la tradición oral y el gran conjunto
30	de inscripciones perpetuaron la memoria de
31	tales aconteceres.
32	Del más grande y trágico dc los cncuentros
33	que experimentó el hombre indígena habrían
34	de escribir personajes como el propio
35	conquistador Hernán Cortés en sus *Cartas de*
36	*Relación* y el soldado cronista Bernal Díaz del
37	Castillo en su *Historia verdadera de la Nueva*
38	*España*. Pero también los vencidos dejaron sus
39	testimonios. Entre otros, un viejo manuscrito
40	fechado en 1528, que se conserva ahora en la
41	Biblioteca Nacional de Par's, consigna en
42	lengua náhuatl (azteca) la memoria de lo que
43	fue para los antiguos mexicanos el más grande
44	de los traumas. (...)

Reprinted from: *El Correo de la UNESCO*, April 1990

History or Destiny?

Miguel León-Portilla

Mexicans have always exhibited an obstinate determination to safeguard the memory of the major events that have marked their society and this has coloured the way in which they view their identity and destiny. From pre-Columbian times they have been engaged in a continuous battle to save their history from oblivion. Knowledge of the past was the foundation on which their priests and diviners based their astronomic calculations and their predictions of the future. Countless archaeological remains from the two thousand years before the arrival of the Spaniards in 1519 bear witness to the Mexican desire to interpret and record the history of gods and man. The stelae known as danzantes ('dancers') at Monte Albán in the Oaxaca valley, on which are inscribed a record of the passing days and years, place-names and the names of kings and other notables, constitute the oldest known chronicle (600 to 300 BC) of the New World.

The people, or rather peoples, who succeeded one another on Mexican soil met with mixed fortunes. Bursts of creativity were punctuated by times of crisis and war which even led to the abrupt disappearance of entire populations and civilizations. The memory of these events lives on in the thousands of inscriptions and the legends of oral tradition.

The greatest and most tragic clash of cultures in pre-Columbian civilization was recorded by some of those who took part in the conquest of Mexico. Hernán Cortés himself sent five remarkable letters (*Cartas de relación*) back to Spain between 1519 and 1526; and the soldier-chronicler Bernal Díaz del Castillo (c. 1492-1580), who served under Cortés, fifty years after the event wrote his *Historia verdadera de la conquista de la Nueva España* ('True History of the Conquest of New Spain'). The vanquished peoples also left written records. A manuscript dated 1528, now in the Bibliothèque Nationale in Paris, recounts in Nahuatl, the language of the Aztecs, the traumatic fate of the Indians. (...)

The UNESCO Courier, April 1990

Chapter 6

Abé Mark Nornes

'PŌRU RŪTA'/PAUL ROTHA AND THE POLITICS OF TRANSLATION

EDITOR'S INTRODUCTION

>Documentary Film *straddled the space between the hidden and the public discourses, and the multiplicity of readings this position implies was built into all the translations.*

IN THIS CASE STUDY IN 'travelling theory' (Said 1991), Nornes supplements his analysis of the immediate text with an examination of the way in which Paul Rotha's work on documentary film was imported and received by Japanese theorists of cinema. Rotha's *Documentary Film* (1935) was well received in Europe and America, but it never attained the status it was to acquire in Japan following its translation by Atsugi Taka (first edition in 1938). Nornes explains this imbalance by reference to the events of the latter half of the 1930s, when Rotha's book first arrived in Japan, and especially Japan's invasion of China and the government's drumming up of nationalist feelings, with the subsequent ideological conversion of most progressive intellectuals into rabid nationalists. Of particular significance is a 1939 Film Law which mandated the forced screening of non-fiction films, thus raising the prestige of the genre and encouraging film specialists to theorize a documentary practice appropriate for the times.

Among other translational choices, the way in which the title of Rotha's book was translated is examined in detail in order to reveal the political ramifications of this translation act. Although most readers knew the term *dokyumentarii eiga* (documentary film), Atsugi chose to translate the title as *Bunka eiga-ron* (On culture film), and in doing so strongly connected Rotha's book with propagandist filmmaking. The term *bunka eiga* first appeared in Japanese texts around 1933, and was originally connected to the *kulturfilm* of Germany (primarily science films), but Japanese critics had begun to apply the term to a variety of non-fiction films by Japanese filmmakers. With the release of the 1939 Film Law, however, all documentary came under the rubric of *bunka eiga*. Nornes argues that the choice was an attempt on the part of the translator to quietly shift the terms of the Japanese documentary debate in a certain direction. The slipperiness of meaning ultimately meant that Rotha's book appealed equally to members of the entire political spectrum, and all participants in the debate claimed his thought to different ends. The article focuses on this struggle over meaning by examining a range of different choices in the various editions of the translation in order to explain how and why Rotha's book became a 'Bible' for both militarist and leftist documentary film makers and critics in Japan.

Follow-up questions for discussion

- The fourth and final 'movement' in Edward Said's model of how ideas and theories travel from one environment to another is one of transformation: a new theory is always 'transformed by its new uses, its new position in a new time and place' (1991:227). Based on the description provided by Nornes, consider the ways in which Rotha's theory was transformed in its new setting, and the mechanisms (textual, paratextual, institutional, etc.) by which this transformation, or range of transformations, was/were effected.
- In describing the routes by which Western theories of literature and narrative were introduced into China, Dan Shen and Xiaoyi Zhou (2006:146) argue that 'the validity and legitimacy of a particular theoretical approach to literature has as much, if not more, to do with the particular historical, political, and cultural constellation of a given nation as with any influence from outside'. What evidence, or counter-evidence, of this claim might be found in Nornes's study? To what extent does this claim overlap with the broader position outlined by Toury (1980, 1995), which stresses that translations are facts of the target system alone?
- Theoretical works, like literary texts, are often translated for an élite readership that is skilled in 'reading between the lines'. To evade censorship under authoritarian political régimes, translators encode hidden oppositional messages that they know can be deciphered by their educated readers. In doing so, they bolster their own as well as their readers' cultural capital and their claims to cultural leadership, and further create a common group defined by its intellectual skills and its oppositional mood (Baer 2006). To what extent can you see this pattern operating in the translations of Rotha discussed in this article, as well as in other case studies you might be familiar with?

Recommended further reading

Dan Shen and Xiaoyi Zhou (2006) 'Western Literary Theories in China: Reception, Influence and Resistance', *Comparative Critical Studies* 3(1–2): 139–55.

Said, Edward (1991) 'Traveling Theory', in *The World, the Text and the Critic*, New York: Vintage, 226–47.

Said, Edward (1994) 'Traveling Theory Reconsidered', in *Reflections on Exile and Other Essays*, Cambridge, Mass.: Harvard University Press, 436–52.

Sánchez, Dolores (2007) 'The Truth about Sexual Difference: Scientific Discourse and Cultural Transfer', in Sonia Cunico and Jeremy Munday (eds) *Translation and Ideology. Encounters and Clashes*. Special Issue of *The Translator* 13(2): 171–94.

Shohat, Ella (2006a) 'The "Postcolonial" in Translation: Reading Edward Said between English and Hebrew', in *Taboo Memories, Diasporic Voices*, Durham and London: Duke University Press, 359–84.

Susam-Sarajeva, Şebnem (2003) 'Multiple-entry Visa to Travelling Theory', *Target* 15(1): 1–36.

Zhang Longxi (1998) 'Western Theory and Chinese Reality', Chapter 5 of *Mighty Opposites: From Dichotomies to Difference in the Comparative Study of China*, Stanford, CA: Stanford University Press, 1998), 151–83.

OPEN ANY JAPANESE BOOK ON documentary and the 'theory' of Paul Rotha will be singled out as one of the most influential in the history of Japanese cinema. Although the writings of all the major Western film theorists, from Münsterberg to Eisenstein, were translated, none was as fiercely contested and discussed as Rotha's. No other theorist or critic had more impact on film practice or underwent as much 'processing'.

Rotha's influence in Japan may surprise the Western reader. His book *Documentary Film* (1935) was widely read throughout Europe and America, particularly within the educational film movement, but it was seen largely as promoting British documentary at the time, hardly as a theoretical 'Bible'.[1] His place in (our) history is basically as one of the central filmmakers of the British school, as an author and, occasionally, as John Grierson's antagonist. Thus, despite renewed interest in documentary in Euro-American film studies, one rarely if ever hears Rotha's name mentioned. Even book-length histories of the British documentary movement refer to *Documentary Film* only in passing. This would undoubtedly shock Japanese filmmakers and scholars, who refer to Rotha's name in the same breath with Eisenstein, Balázs, Pudovkin, Arnheim, Münsterberg, Moholy-Nagy and Vertov.

Imamura Taihei, in his 1952 overview of film theory, discusses Rotha in his final chapter – the author is even shown posing with *Documentary Film* in his portrait. Rotha's prestige has hardly weakened in the intervening years (Imamura 1952:184).[2] Thus, in 1960 Atsugi Taka offered a completely revised translation of Rotha's 1935 expanded volume. This in turn was reprinted in 1976 and in 1995.[3] Ironically, judging from his own papers, Rotha appears to have had no idea how influential he was in Japan, an indication of how disconnected Japan was from larger currents in film theory.[4]

This apparent imbalance may be partially explained by examining events of the latter half of the 1930s, when Rotha's book arrived in Japan. At the time, Japan was escalating its invasion of China, especially with the 1937 China Incident. On the home front, the government ensured the war reached into the daily lives of citizens everywhere by drawing on young men for cannon fodder and increasingly controlling behaviour. By mid-decade, police pressure, including mass arrests, imprisonment and occasional torture, had shut down the noisy Left. Most progressive intellectuals underwent ideological conversion to a rabid nationalism and an often racist nativism. Those who refused this course quietly retreated underground or chose their language carefully when in public. At the same time, the government placed elaborate restrictions on filmmaking, ranging from intricate censorship mechanisms to nationalizing entire sectors of the industry. This culminated in the 1939 Film Law, which mandated the forced screening of nonfiction films, or the so-called *bunka eiga* (culture film).

Along with the pressures of continental warfare, this legislation propelled documentary to a level of prestige comparable to the fiction film. Film journals were filled with articles by intellectuals as disparate as Hasegawa Nyozekan, Tosaka Jun, Kamei Katsuichirō and Nakai Masakazu, all attempting to theorize a documentary practice appropriate for the times. Given this atmosphere, the appearance of Rotha's *Documentary Film* – especially its 1938 translation – electrified the Japanese film world and was greeted with the respect accorded the most authoritative of theoretical systems. This intense interest eventually filtered into filmmaking itself, enabling Rotha to leave a very large theoretical mark.

Why Rotha? And, by extension, what did his writing mean in wartime Japan? A hint at the answer lies in the title of his volume – *Documentary Film*. The manner in which the title was translated alerts us immediately to the political ramifications of this translation act and suggests the complexity of these questions.

A variety of words were circulating in the Japanese film world to designate non-fiction filmmaking: *jissha eiga, kiroku eiga, nyūsu eiga, dokyumentarii eiga* and the like. The 1938 edition appeared with a title on the cover that may or may not be a mistranslation: *Bunka eiga-ron* (On culture film). First, the suffix *ron* (argument, discourse) appended to the title could be translated as *Documentary Film Theory*. This might have given Rotha's thought a heft we do not feel when reading the original English text. Second, an intertext for the *bunka eiga* is the *kulturfilm* of UFA in Germany. These were primarily science films; however, upon their successful Japanese release, some critics began using the term for a variety of nonfiction films by Japanese filmmakers.

The term *bunka eiga* begins to appear in Japanese texts as early as 1933, and all documentary came under the rubric of *bunka eiga* with the 1939 Film Law. Although most readers knew the term *dokyumentarii eiga* (documentary film), in choosing to use *bunka eiga* the translator strongly connected Rotha's book with propagandist film-making. Many of Rotha's contemporary critics pointed out the ambiguity of the film genre to which this title points. Few noted, however, that the title firmly inserted Rotha's thought into the discourse raging around the terms of the new Film Law, and Rotha's translation roughly coincided with the announcement of plans for these detailed government regulations over the film industry. Consequently, amid the fervent discussion about the new meaning and direction for nonfiction film, Rotha's cheerleading for the documentary found an enthusiastic audience. In one sense, this would appear to associate Rotha with a radically opposed politics; however, I would argue it could also be seen as an attempt on the part of the translator to quietly shift the terms of the Japanese documentary debate in a certain direction. Thus, the short answer to the question above is that Rotha's book meant many things indeed.

The long answer is that, because of this slipperiness, a curious situation arose in which Rotha's book appealed equally to members of the entire political spectrum, and all participants in this debate claimed Rotha's thought to different ends. This article will examine this struggle over meaning on many levels. To root out the most important issues, however, we must look to the media through which Rotha's thought came to be known: translation.

Consider this relatively obvious example: the 1938 edition mistranslates Rotha's 'Worker's Revolution' as the more innocuous '*Rōdōsha katsudō*', or 'Worker's Activities' (Rotha 1938:108). Only in the postwar revision did the proper translation appear: '*Rōdōsha kakumei*' (Rotha 1960:68). The reason is unambiguous; 'revolution' was a dangerous term in Japan in 1939, and a text containing it would never have passed censorship review. Authors, translators and publishers had been deflecting such trouble with authorities for nearly a decade by printing obvious synonyms and even substituting problematic words with XXs (called *fuseji*). Readers knew the protocol; when they came across *fuseji* or ambiguous words, they could read past them to the original meanings. The first edition of *Documentary Film* is sprinkled with many such examples, but analysis of such simple instances of intentional mistranslation only get us so far. First, as the example above suggests, there were entire communities of readers who were forced to conceal their true relationship to the book and, second, everyone knew the translator's command of English was dubious at best because it became one of the issues raised in the debates.[5]

We must dig far deeper into the issue of translation to appreciate the complexity of the highly politicized discourses circulating around Rotha's original text when it entered the Japanese linguistic world. Furthermore, shifting our analysis from simplistic notions of (one-way) 'influence' to the site of translation brings an array of larger issues into focus. For example, looking at the sheer volume of translation reveals much about the relationship between cultures (it follows that a lack of translation activity indicates a discourse stuck in an unhealthy short-circuit of desire).

When transferring texts from one language to another, the translator's approach to language and meaning is inseparable from larger historical and ideological currents in the target language. This new linguistic and cultural context often impinges on the translation while having little to do with the original text itself. In this situation, in which competing translations are circulated among overlapping readerships, a struggle over authority occurs – after all, can there be a more powerful position over cross-cultural discourse than that of the translator? We must look at the qualities of a given translation and ask who the translator is, what his or her relationship is to the original text, the author and the larger communities of readers. From this perspective, the difference between translation theory and documentary film theory is very slim indeed, since both fields involve representations weighed by a debt to an 'original', whether it be the source text or the world.

Documentary Film enters the Japanese linguistic world

Japan's pre-eminent prewar film theorist, Imamura Taihei, read Rotha's book and passed it on to Dōmei Tsūshin's Kuwano Shigeru. From there, the book surged into the film community (Okamoto Masao 1996:62–63). At one point, it came into the hands of Atsugi Taka, one of the first Japanese female filmmakers. Atsugi came to filmmaking as a leading member of the Nippon Puroretaria Eiga Dōmei (Proletarian Film League of Japan), or Prokino for short. After the breakup of Prokino in 1934 under police pressure, Atsugi began writing film criticism and translating foreign film theory. Along with other former Prokino members, she was also one of the dōjin producing the early film theory journal Eiga sōzō. This gave her concrete links to Yuibutsu Kenkyūkai (Materialism Study Society), or Yuiken, a group of leftist intellectuals organized by the philosopher Tosaka Jun.[6] Atsugi even wrote a review article in their Yuibutsuron kenkyū, probably the first mention of Paul Rotha's Documentary Film in print.

In the late 1930s, Atsugi began a long career in documentary screenwriting, working for Photochemical Laboratory (PCL), Toho, and Geijutsu Eigasha (GES). This afforded her the chance to bring Rotha's theory into practice. Above and beyond her own filmmaking activities, Atsugi's most influential project was a translation of Documentary Film, which she undertook at the request of her PCL supervisor; he was moving to JO Studios to become head of production and wanted to use the book as the text for study groups. Atsugi had been reading the English original and was glad to use the need for a translation as an excuse to finish the book. She published the first edition in the fall of 1938.

The translation had an enormous impact and went into second and third printings within a year. The book's influence spread in the late 1930s as critics debated

Rotha's terms and their implications for documentary filmmaking, often offering their own translations of the original in their quotations. Soon an alternative translation by Ueno Ichirō appeared in *Eiga kenkyū*, a film studies series put out by the magazine *Eiga hyōron*.[7] Study groups were devoted to Rotha's book in production companies and film studios. At Toho, where it was considered the documentary filmmaker's Bible, the Kyoto studio circulated its own handwritten, mimeographed translation within the company.[8] Before Atsugi's translation appeared, the original English-language book was even used for English practice at JO Studios (Makino Mamoru 1978).

About the same time, the original text came into the hands of Ōmura Einosuke and Ishimoto Tōkichi, whose reading of the book had a great impact on the formation of Geijutsu Eigasha. Thanks to Rotha's ideas, the company's early films, such as *Yukiguni* (Snow Country, 1939) and *Kikansha C57* (Train C57, 1940), strove to surpass the usual public relations film and bring documentary to a new, independent level (Tanikawa Yoshio 1990:194–95). Geijutsu Eigasha's own film journal, *Bunka eiga*, published enthusiastic debates about Rotha's book, as did most of the other serious Japanese film publications.

One of the major responses to the Rotha translation involved a knee-jerk reaction to his disdain for the 'story-film', which he said 'threaten[ed] to stifle all other methods of cinema' and 'tend[ed] to become an anesthetic instead of a stimulant' (Rotha 1935:70). The most vociferous of these critics displayed a nearly uncontrollable anger. In his book-length bibliographic survey of film literature, Okuda Shinkichi, for example, passes Rotha off with a flourish: 'I – and others – can only recognize [*Documentary Film*] as a little like drawing water for one's own field [i.e., self-serving]. Above all, Rotha's rejection of the feature film, and his view that documentary was the main path for cinema, is clearly ridiculous; even as a theory of art, it never exceeds shallow abstraction' (Okuda Shinkichi 1943:39; my translation).

The most scathing attack on Rotha came from Tsumura Hideo, who sarcastically wrote:

> Put a different way, Rotha's book is extremely heroic and vigorous. He praises documentary based on materialist socialism as the most valuable cinema of tomorrow. In contrast to that, it pulverizes the fiction film into dust, with writing like vicious gossip. The way it attacked fiction film was extremely rough with ideological tricks. I confess that this is one of the reasons which gave me the courage to criticize Paul Rotha. (1939:17; my translation)

This now-famous attack provoked a response from Takagiba Tsutomu, who ran Toho's Shinjuku News Film Theatre and was a frequent essayist on documentary film. Takagiba humorously rewrote Tsumura's article, substituting 'Tsumura' for 'Rotha' to turn the attack back on the Japanese critic (Takagiba Tsutomu 1940a). However well this strategy neutralized Tsumura's critique, it did not address the key issues: that Rotha's definition of 'fiction' in documentary was less than clear and that his book offered less a theory of documentary film than a specious promotion of government cultural policy. There is a grain of truth to the accusations against Rotha (his arrogance, his self-promotion of the English documentary, and his faith in government sponsorship), but the critical debate that actually affected Japanese filmmaking practice was over the problem of 'fiction' in documentary.

The most tempered discussion of this issue was offered by Kubota Tatsuo in *Bunka eiga no hōhōron* (The Methodology of the Culture Film, 1940). This was one of the more serious attempts to explore the phenomenon of the *bunka eiga*. Although he came out of a film production background (Shochiku's Kyoto studios), Kubota was very well read. He drew on the writing of Münsterberg, Arnheim, Balázs, Eisenstein, and other major film theorists. The book was ultimately a disappointment, however. Kubota's aesthetic agenda centred on expunging any influence of the *avant-garde* from documentary, positioning the *bunka eiga* with a hard and fast opposition between fiction film 'sensitivity' (*kansai*) and science film 'intellect' (*chisei*) (Kubota Tatsuo 1940a). Unfortunately, this dichotomy colours his discussion of Rotha as well. Kubota had originally intended to structure his entire book around *Documentary Film*, a measure of Rotha's prestige and influence over the very conception of nonfiction filmmaking. In the end, Kubota wisely saved his discussion of Rotha for the final chapter. After his careful discussion of the *avant-garde*, Kubota warns readers that although Rotha has his good points, his vague definition of 'dramatization', bolstered as it is by questionable examples such as Pabst's *Kameradschaft* (1931), could lead documentary to stray too completely into the world of fiction.

Kubota represents one brand of discussion that was occurring in the Japanese documentary community in which the relatively innocent-sounding debates about Rotha's conceptions of 'fictionality' and 'actuality' veiled struggles over the function of documentary in Japanese society. The written record on this discussion is decidedly one-sided. Rotha proposed a nationally sponsored documentary film committed to the enlightenment and unification of the citizenry, precisely the kind of cinema necessary for a country like Japan that was deeply embroiled in foreign warfare. Under the restrictive circumstances of 1930s Japan, however, many other important perspectives went unrecorded. In particular, one aspect of Rotha's appeal – his apparent sympathies for socialism – necessarily had to be concealed from the Japanese public sphere; restricted to private discussion, this discourse never appeared in the written record, posing a battery of problems for the historian. Traces remain, however, that provide access to these hidden spaces, and in the remaining pages I will explore their furthest reaches.

Battle of the translators

Like many other (underground) leftists in the documentary film world, Atsugi found Rotha's writing inspirational. Committed to social change, she saw cinema as a medium for critiquing everything from class discrimination to totalitarian political systems. Having spent the last decade immersed in Marxism and committing her life to demonstrating its relevance to filmmaking, criticism, and translation, Atsugi found a true compatriot in Paul Rotha. *Documentary Film* became the 'hidden sacred book' of filmmakers like Atsugi who opposed the direction their nation and film industry were taking. Only after the war was over, however, could they reveal their views publicly.

One can feel Atsugi's intense relationship with Rotha's book by scanning her personal copies, which she recently donated to the National Film Centre of Japan. Opening those pages provides both a thrill and a challenge to the historian. Her 1976 Miraisha version appears brand new and unopened. Her 1960 Misuzu copy contains only a few penciled-in notes and an inscription inside the cover: 'To Takeshi, the husband I love'.

Her first editions – Rotha's and her own translation – are far more intriguing. One can quickly detect a pattern in the highlighted sections. For example, in this time of stricture, she singled out the following sentence: 'There is little within reason and little within the limits of censorship that documentary cannot bring before an audience to state an argument' (Rotha 1935:156). Although there can be no doubt that she liked the sentence, she also filled other pages with obscure checks, question marks, circles and exclamation points. Strange symbols and many M.B.s lie mute in the margins. Bookmarks sit in curious passages. We will never know their significance, but three marks stand out for their powerful evocation of what this book meant at the height of the China War. Apparently, Atsugi took her own translation in hand and read it over the space of several weeks in 1939, because she left dates next to three paragraphs. At the time, the government was taking steps to convert all documentary into propaganda in support of the emperor's war, brilliant filmmakers were subverting these efforts with clever editing, and open resistance meant persecution. (Kamei Fumio's *Tatakau heitai* (Fighting soldiers, 1939) had just been suppressed, and the director would be in prison within a matter of months.) In this context, these three passages make Atsugi's cathexis with Rotha's text palpable. For this reason, they are worth quoting in full (Atsugi Taka's dates are included in square brackets):

> Relative freedom of expression for the views of the documentalist [sic] will obviously vary with the production forces he serves and the political system in power. In countries still maintaining a parliamentary system, discussion and projection of his beliefs within certain limits will be permitted only so long as they do not seriously oppose powerful vested interests, which most often happen to be the forces controlling production. Under an authoritarian system, freedom is permissible provided his opinions are in accord with those of the State for social and political advance, until presumably such a time shall arrive when the foundations of the State are strong enough to withstand criticism. Ultimately, of course, you will appreciate that you can neither make films on themes of your own choice, nor apply treatments to accepted themes, unless they are in sympathy with the aims of the dominant system. And in view of the mechanical and hence expensive materials of cinema, it will be foolish of the documentalist if his sympathies do not lie, or at least appear to lie, with those who can make production a possibility [June 28, 1939].[9]

The following is a critique of Flaherty's apolitical approach:

> In every location which he has chosen there have existed social problems that demanded expression. Exploitation of native labour, the practises of the white man against the native, the landlords of Aran, these have been the vital stories, but from them Flaherty has turned away . . . Idyllic documentary is documentary without significant purpose. It takes romanticism as its banner. It ignores social analysis. It takes ideas instead of facts. It marks a reactionary return to the worship of the heroic, to an admiration of the barbaric, to a setting up of 'The Leader' [July 6, 1939].[10]

Finally, here is a Pudovkin quote on the power of montage:

> I found the way to build up a dialogue in which the transition of the actor from one emotional state to another . . . had never taken place in actuality before the camera. I shot the actor at different times, glum and then

smiling, and only on my editing table did these two separate moods coordinate with the third – the man who made the joke [July 20, 1939].[11]

Atsugi's handwritten dates convert these translations from something in the public domain to something new and contradictory. They act as conduits, allowing those resistant discourses retained safely in hidden spaces to leak from between the lines. But this is only half the story, because the criticism and debate surrounding *Documentary Film* are an instance of oppositional discourses being coded into public view, camouflaged to deflect the threat of reprisals. To render this complicated discourse visible, we must return to the problem of translation. On the one hand, Atsugi wove her point of view into the very fabric of her translation, both in conscious and unconscious ways. On the other hand, intellectuals from far different perspectives engaged her in a veritable battle of the translators.

In the course of researching the subject of prewar Japanese documentary, I occasionally ran across copies of Atsugi's translation in used bookstores. Taking a volume in hand, one gains a material appreciation for the respect with which Rotha was viewed, from the high quality of the printing, binding and paper to the book's beautiful slipcase. Each time I found a copy of the Rotha translation, I pulled it off the shelf to see if it belonged to anyone I knew from my research. One of these dusty first editions contained quite a surprise: every single page had detailed annotations. Between every single line of the book – cover to cover – someone had diligently scrawled corrections to Atsugi's translation (see Figure 6.1). Inside the cover, this anonymous editor had written a message: 'This is a surprising book. She can't understand English. Japanese is pretty bad. Even Ms. Atsugi cannot argue with this. I don't understand how this person had the guts to translate it. This caused the chaos in this country's *bunka eiga* discourse. I'm sorry these corrections are a year late'. The original owner who requested this involved check of the translation was unclear; other than this message, there was only an illegible scrawl across the page. (Hereafter I will refer to this copy of *Documentary Film* as the *teiseiban*, meaning 'corrected version'.)[12]

The first edition of the Atsugi translation came out in September 1938, and whoever pored over Atsugi's work left us only with the message that the translation was so bad that its revision took the better part of a year. Actually, the existence of this *teiseiban* came quietly into public view in January 1940 – fourteen months after the original publication of the book – in a programme passed out at Takagiba Tsutomu's Shinjuku News Film Theatre. In addition to advertising the week's film slate, these pamphlets often contained in-depth essays printed in tiny type. The 18 January 1940 issue contained an article by Sekino Yoshio that asserted that the controversies over Rotha sprang primarily from the inexperience of the person who had translated him. Sekino wrote: 'Below, let us pick out two or three parts of interest from a corrected text pretty much black with corrections'.[13] He proceeded to compare passages from Atsugi's translation with corrections from the *teiseiban*. (With this in mind, the odd pencil slash inside the cover clearly reads 'Seki' in *hiragana* with a long tail.) In the following months, Sekino drew on the *teiseiban* for a series of lengthy articles in which he attempted to clear up the controversy surrounding Rotha's book (Sekino Yoshio 1940a, 1940b, 1940c, 1940d, 1940e, 1940f, 1940g).[14] These articles also became the basis for the book *Eiga kyōiku no riron* (Theory of Film Education; Sekino Yoshio 1942).

The main issues for Sekino involved the translation of terms such as 'story-film' and 'dramatization of actuality'. He attempted to contextualize Rotha's thoughts in terms of his development as a critic – the differences between *Film Till Now* and

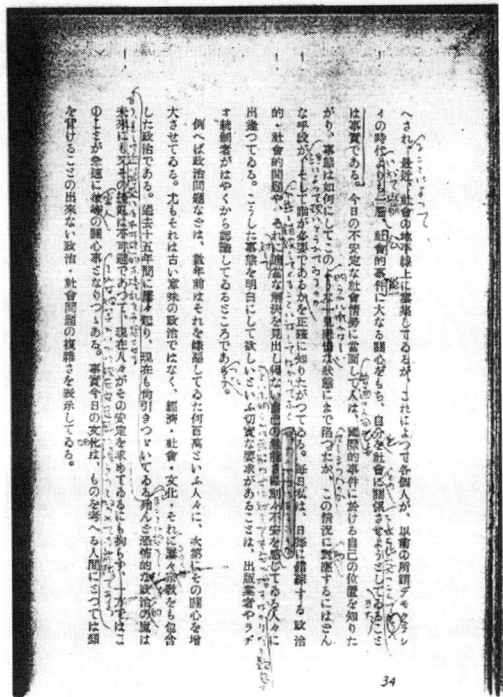

Figure 6.1 The *teiseiban*: cover to cover translation check.

Documentary Film – as well as the vast changes in English society. Sekino's success in reorienting the translation debate is difficult to judge, although it appears to have influenced his reputation as an authority on the topic. There is a good reason for this. In this series of high-profile articles, Sekino positioned himself less as a critic than as the translator. He gives a discreet nod to the help of the *teiseiban*, but the substance of his articles is unusual. Rather than provide his own interpretation of *Documentary Film*, Sekino all but retranslates the book. These articles were basically strings of extended quotes from the *teiseiban* with short passages of paraphrase inserted in between. Thanks to the corrections by Sekino's anonymous colleague, the new translations are quite good – for the most part, they are better than Ueno's or Toho's, and they are certainly better than Atsugi's. With its rows of exclamation point annotations, the *teiseiban* remains by far the best translation. Sekino ultimately does not offer an actual translation as such, however, since significant portions of the book are paraphrased or deleted. To be more specific, they are suppressed. Here is a typical, and relatively innocuous, example. Sekino's deletions are in italics:

> *Art, like religion or morals, cannot be considered apart from the materialist orderings of society.* Hence it is surely fatal for an artist to attempt to divorce himself from the community and retire into a private world where he can create merely for his own pleasure or for that of a limited minority. He is, *after all, as much a member of the common herd as a riveter or a glass-blower,* and of necessity must recognize his obligations to the community into which he is born. His peculiar powers of creation must be used to greater purpose than mere personal satisfaction (Rotha 1935:66; Sekino 1942:163).[15]

Sekino's reading, or more properly his selective translation, evacuates Rotha's Left-leaning politics and aligns *Documentary Film* with the dominant ideology of war-time Japan. Sekino effortlessly converts the passage above into an attack on individual-ism and a call for artists to serve the mission of the national polity. Elsewhere, extremely long series of extended quotations often skip a sentence or two in the middle when Rotha brings in the subject of class or Marxism. The segment of Rotha's audience to which Sekino belonged was enthralled with the Englishman's high moral tone and sense of 'mission'.

Sekino himself was far more than a film critic. After studying art at Tokyo University, he worked at the social education section in the Tokyo metropolitan government. In this capacity he promoted the use of film for education through publications, lectures, study groups like STS,[16] and regular *jidō eigahi* (children's film days).[17] In the latter stages of World War II, Sekino worked at Nichiei as the vice president in charge of *bunka eiga* production. Throughout the war, Sekino was a prominent theorist in the education film movement, meaning that he was not in the classroom trenches, where the real teaching was going on. With his articles on the Rotha controversy, Sekino moved beyond pedagogical issues and claimed a position of authority over the Rotha text and therefore over Japanese documentary film.

The Rotha we encounter through Sekino's articles speaks of responsible citizen-ship and the central role of cinema in educating the nation's populace. Sekino's Rotha heightens the stakes of these ideas by drawing the readers' attention to the worldwide sense of crisis – the theme that was so central to pre-Pearl Harbor Japan – but the British filmmaker's calls for peaceful settlement of conflict, disarmament and intelligent social critique are completely suppressed from Sekino's blow-by-blow 'translation = correction' of Rotha's book. With these themes purged from the text, one is left with a discourse on propaganda and the necessity for state support of documentary to the end of enlightening its citizenry. No wonder that Rotha's work was attractive to Sekino and to the new leadership emerging with the Film Law.

A further example of this political reinscription of Rotha is his emergence in Yamada Hideyoshi's *Eiga kokusaku no zenshin* (The Progress of National Film Policy), a 1940 book outlining the national film policies of all the major Western nations. The latter half of this book covers the situation in Japan and offers essays on the implica-tions of the new Film Law for various segments of the film industry. Its chapter on the deployment of film as an instrument of state propaganda cites Rotha as the international authority, posing the English filmmaker's innovations as the proper course for a nationalized film industry (Yamada Hideyoshi 1940:216).

Even more revealing than the ways in which Sekino intentionally mistranslated *Documentary Film*, in a manner analogous to Atsugi before him, are the differences between their actual texts. *Documentary Film* straddled the space between the hidden and the public discourses, and the multiplicity of readings this position implies was built into all the translations. The following example reveals how the differences between Atsugi and Sekino play out in their translations. This is one of Rotha's numerous digs at the powers that be, followed by its extant translations (emphasis mine; see Figure 6.1 above for the quote as it appears in the *teiseiban*):

Rotha: Every day I come across persons who manifest increasing anxiety not only at the growing complexity of political and social problems, but at the patent inability of *those in power* to find adequate solutions. (Rotha 1935:48)

Atsugi: Mainichi ni sakusō suru seijiteki, shakaiteki mondai ya, sore ni tekitō na kaiketsu o miidashi enai *jiko no munōsa* ni kokkoku fuan o kanjite iru hitobito ni deatte iru. (Rotha 1938:34)

Ueno: Mainichi watashi no au hitobito ga seiji mondai ya shakai mondai no shinkokuka suru fukuzatsusa ni tsuite fuan o kataru bakari de wa naku, *jibunra* ni tadashii kaiketsu o miidasu *nōryoku no nai koto* o gaitan suru no de aru. (Rotha 1939a:56)

Sekino: Taezu watashi wa, seijiteki, shakaiteki na jyaku mondai ga masumasu fukuzatsusa o mashite kuru koto ni taishite nominarazu, *torō no hitobito* ga sore e no tekitō na kaiketsu o miidashi enai to iu meihaku na muryokuburi ni taishite mo, fuan ga kuwaete iku bakari da to tansaku suru hitotachi ni ikiatte iru. (Sekino 1942:136)

Teiseiban: Mainichi watashi wa, seijiteki, shakaiteki mondai ga masumasu sakusō suru shite kuru koto ni tai shite bakari de naku, *kenryoku no chii ni aru mono* ga, sore ni taishite tekitō na kaiketsu o miidashi enai to iu akiraka ni munōryokusa ni taishite masu bakari da to tansaku suru hitobito ni deatte iru.

Rotha's original text sets up a relatively straightforward contrast between, on the one hand, common people who find themselves bewildered by the complexity of the world on the verge of war and, on the other hand, those in power who seem too incompetent to deal with the situation. Here Rotha's critical spirit comes out in force, but in 1939 such comments landed people in Japan in prison. All the translators seem to deal with this problem of potential censorship or reprisals in their own way; everything from choices of vocabulary to mistakes reveal the ideological undergirding of their respective translations. The *teiseiban* provides the best, most straightforward translation of the quotation's most problematic phrase, 'those in power': 'kenryoku no chii ni aru mono' (people in positions of [political] power). However, Sekino strays from the guidance of his *teiseiban* and substitutes this phrase with the rather vague 'torō no hitobito' (authorities, intellectuals), deflecting the criticism into ambiguous territory. Other decisions further weaken Rotha's criticism, as a rendering of this phrase back into English reveals: 'but at the clear powerlessness of authorities/intellectuals in finding appropriate solutions'.

Both Atsugi and Ueno completely erase 'those in power' from the sentence; the effect is to create a single group of common people who feel anxiety about the world's complexity and their inability to effectuate change. We might assume that the Japanese translators expunged Rotha's attack on the powerful to preempt punishment by their own authorities. Without more documentation, the case of Ueno is difficult to judge; however, Atsugi produced a postwar version of *Documentary Film* when threats of reprisal were not an issue. In this 1960 translation, she significantly revised the text with the help of two young scholars,[18] but although she completely rewrote this sentence, Atsugi retained the mistake. Even the 1995 'refurbished edition' (*shinsōban*) remains unchanged. In other words, Atsugi simply didn't understand the meaning in the first place.[19]

Atsugi's word choice is also significant. Ueno's exasperated, anonymous masses are literally the people Rotha has met on the street ('jibunra ni tadashii kaiketsu o miidasu nōryoku no nai koto o gaitan suru no de aru'), but the Marxist Atsugi does not shirk social responsibility and uses the much stronger 'jiko no munōsa', which places the burden of history on herself and the reader – it is the difference between 'their own inability' and 'our own incompetence'.

Atsugi's misprision circulates in a gray area between Rotha's original English text and its dim representation in Japanese; the latter reflects a conception of documentary cinema that combines Rotha's thinking with that of Atsugi's community of leftist filmmakers who restrict their politics to hidden spaces in the teeth of power.[20] Rotha himself said, 'I came nearest to becoming a Socialist in my Documentary Book'.[21] This was not lost on the filmmakers, who found themselves in a forest of pressure, especially since many had recently spent time in the so-called pig box (butabako, or slammer) for their filmmaking activities in Prokino. For some filmmakers, Rotha's book simply confirmed the direction in which they were already taking nonfiction film, and knowing that someone outside Japan thought the same way gave them a measure of confidence.[22] Many others, however, had a far deeper, hidden relationship with Documentary Film. Kuwano Shigeru worked at Dōmei Tsūshin's film unit before becoming the section head in charge of Nippon News at Nichiei. He was probably the second person in Japan to read Documentary Film, having received it from Imamura Taihei, himself a Marxist critic. In a 1973 book on documentary, he included a reminiscence about his wartime encounter with Rotha (Kuwano Shigeru 1973:201–202; my translation):[23]

> This book, for me, was a shock. He was choosing his words extremely carefully, but this is clearly what Paul Rotha was saying: The duty of documentary filmmaker was to somehow replace today's rotting capitalist society and construct a new socialist society, and indicate the clear, social scientific analysis of it [capitalist society] by the emergent classes – the proletariat and the farmers. There was no question that the so-called documentary, which started out as the news film, would become a strong weapon of the movement for social revolution. This has been evidenced by the Soviets. Even in Japan, which was under the violent oppression of a militarist government, each and every cut of the news film preserved a fragmentary 'truth'. Therefore, if we consciously shoot that at the location, and if we edit these scenes purposefully, the 'truth' of modern-day Japanese society – the anguish of the people, the necessity of collapse because of those contradictions – we could precisely indicate this to the people of the emergent classes of Japanese society . . . However, even though we can do this, what are we Japanese documentary film producers – no, what am I doing right now?!

As a filmmaker working in what were basically semi-government agencies (Dōmei Tsūshin and Nichiei), Kuwano was extremely limited by the form of the newsreel. He did try to include subversive moments in his films to direct spectatorial readings against the grain. For example, he recalls inserting a funeral pyre of some fallen soldiers with melodramatic narration, such as 'Even now, the soldiers' souls return to their hometowns, where wives and children quietly wait'. However, this was inevitably snipped by the censors, leaving Kuwano clinging to the hope that his documentary images of the fighting retained some grain of truth (Kuwano Shigeru 1973:201).

Filmmakers in the budding field of bunka eiga had far more latitude to code multiple readings into their films. This is the issue running quietly behind many of the debates over fiction in nonfiction film between 1939 and 1942. Filmmakers were working out the nature of this new brand of fictionality.

In the end, Rotha was exceedingly vague on this point, but Japanese filmmakers were looking for a prescription. Shirai Shigeru spoke of Rotha's influence on documentary production (1988:73), but had he not seen six or seven of the British school films at the Education Ministry – including *Drifters* (1929) and *Night Mail* (1936) – he would have had no idea what Rotha meant by 'dramatization of actuality'. Certainly the filmmakers who did not attend those screenings were handicapped in their reading of *Documentary Film* and the massive discourse it generated. Many articles discussed the definitions of Rotha's terminology and its translation (see Takagiba Tsutomu 1940b, 1940c, Atsugi Taka 1940a, Kubota Tatsuo 1940b) but the bulk of the writing was a continuation (and vulgarization) of earlier Yuiken debates concerning the epistemology of cinema – 'documentary as art' or 'documentary as science' (see, for example, Ueno Kōzō 1940a, 1940b). This argument itself, as Ueno Kōzō has suggested, was a structural continuation of earlier struggles over whether film was art; the aesthetic domain simply migrated from 'Cinema as Art' to 'Talkie as Art' to 'Documentary as Art' (Ueno Kōzō 1940a:33). However, in one of Atsugi's finest articles responding to her critics, we find her best definition of the core issue (1940b:82; my translation):

> In order for documentary film to have a meaningful existence as art, we must correctly recognize the essential meaning of this 'fiction'. This is what I want to state over and over again. To this same end . . . filmmakers' efforts must be more than the turning of the camera as it has been up to today. There needs to be more care for 'working' on works, more intensity, more like throwing one's entire soul into the hardships of a novelist.

> 'Poetry is more philosophical than history.' – Aristotle.

> Today we can find the meaning of this saying if, while native born to the turbulent breath of history, we seek in documentary film the possibility of finding poetry (fiction) in the very centre of that history (actuality).

In the midst of the spectacular war films of the day, a new kind of documentary emerged. Although some filmmakers were locating their filmmaking practice at the sites of greatest power (the Japanese military and the bureaucracy), other filmmakers were endeavouring to produce a new documentary film that (indirectly) pointed to the backwardness of the nation and to the sheer poverty and suffering in everyday life.[24] For their producers, these films were the finest examples of documentary being made. Ishimoto Tōkichi's *Yukiguni* set the pattern, recording the fight between Yamagata villagers and their fierce winters for nearly three years. *Yukiguni* was unusual for its long-term study, foreshadowing the Yamagata films by the most important postwar documentarist of the 1970s and 1980s, Ogawa Shinsuke. Indeed, Tanikawa Yoshio goes so far as to say that *Yukiguni* marked the start of Japanese documentary film (1990:195). Other films include Atsumi Teruo's *Sumiyaku hitobito* (People Burning Coal, 1940–41) and *Isha no inai mura* (Village Without a Doctor, 1939). The latter, Itō Sueo's first film, shows the terrible health conditions in a village in Japan and the government's obvious inability to provide adequate health care for all its people. Kyōgoku Takahide's *Ishi no mura* (Village of Stone, 1941) shows the severe manual labour at a rock quarry, and his *Hōmensen* (Field Diagnosis Boat, 1939) follows a medical group travelling the Sumida River to treat river workers.

Imaizumi Yoshitama turned his camera to the rough life of train workers in *Kikansha C57*. Ueno Kōzō's *Wagu no ama* (The *ama* of Wagu, 1941) contrasts the hardships of life for *ama*, or female shell divers (including steep pay inequities in comparison to men) with stunning underwater sequences that aestheticize the work itself. Mizuki and Atsugi's *Aru hobo no kiroku* (Record of a Nursery, 1942) shows the cooperative work of mothers and nursery school teachers in raising healthy, educated children. This impressive body of work arose from the competing claims over the significance of Paul Rotha's *Documentary Film*.

Although they were all inspired by Rotha, these filmmakers took varying positions *vis-à-vis* the use of reenactment and screenwriting in documentary. What they held in common was a striking exclusion of the war hysteria and its rhetoric and a focus on the difficult life of Japanese citizens, resulting in a socially conscious reportage that resisted the temptations of spectacular explosions and exotic locales. In this way, the filmmakers encoded into their very public media various degrees of discontent usually restricted to hidden spaces. The filmmakers perceived their efforts to be interconnected and dedicated to bringing documentary to an unprecedented level of excellence. Although they never gave themselves a collective name or identity, they did consider their combined efforts to be akin to a 'documentary movement' (see Kamei Fumio 1940, Kamei Fumio *et al.* 1940). Influenced by a British filmmaker and author, their films constitute the finest of the prewar Japanese documentary cinema and an instance of theory and practice finely tuned and in thorough interaction.

Notes

1   See Iris Barry's 'Review of *Documentary Film*' (1939), which discusses how people were nervous about Rotha's politics and his immodest pontification. See also the reviews by Frank Evans (1939), who discusses the social function of documentary (nothing on style), and Elizabeth Laine (1939), as well as unattributed reviews in *Times* (1939) and *Lady* (1939).

2   Imamura's book contains the best Japanese overview of Rotha. In contrast to the wartime debates, its reasoned overall critique reveals how narrowly the discussion was focused in 1940. This suggests how other issues were at stake besides the one explicitly on the table in 1938.

3   The 1960 edition involved a fairly extensive revision of the translation itself, although this translation has its own problems. The 1995 printing is billed as a 'refurbished edition' (*shinsōban*), but the only apparent difference is a new colour on the jacket.

4   Nothing in Rotha's personal files suggests he knew what the Japanese thought of his work. Quite the opposite, he clearly shared fears about the menace Japan posed to the West. In a letter to Eric Knight written at the height of Rotha's prestige in Japan, he wrote, 'I agree that the sooner America sees her immediate danger the better and that now more than ever is the time to come into this business . . . She actually [it sounds] is trying to appease the Japs which seems odd after all the examples of appeasement she's had before her. I agree with all your beliefs about the cementing of the English speaking peoples – at least that would be a beginning basis for reconstruction' (Letter, August 28, 1941, Paul Rotha Collection, UCLA, Box 26, 2001). After the war (in the 1960s, from the look of the paper and adjacent documents), in a statement written to someone in Japan, Rotha wrote, 'One day, perhaps, if I am still alive, I will come to visit to the land of Hokusai and Kurosawa and Ozu' – no mention of any Japanese documentarists, let alone his translation by Atsugi (Undated letter, Paul Rotha Collection, UCLA, box 82, folder 3, 2001).

5   In her postwar autobiography, her embarrassment over rushing the translation prematurely to print is clear (Atsugi Taka 1991:103–105).

6   Atsugi also married Yuiken philosopher Mori Kōichi.

7   Rotha (1939a) covers chapter 1 in Rotha's *Documentary Film*; Rotha (1939b) covers Rotha's chapter 2. Although there were many reports on the British documentary movement, Ueno

probably wrote the best; his study (Ueno Ichirō 1939) certainly contributed to his translation.

8   Paul Rotha, *Bunka eigaron* (On documentary film), *Chōsa shiryō* 4 (Kyoto: Toho Kyoto Satsueijo, n.d.), Makino Mamoru Collection, Columbia University. This mimeographed publication completes the Ueno translation, covering Rotha's chapter 4.

9   Atsugi Taka's personal copy of Rotha, *Bunka eigaron*, trans. Atsugi (1938), 150–52, Atsugi Taka Collection, National Film Centre of the National Museum of Modern Art, Tokyo. Original text is Rotha, *Documentary Film* (1952), 135–36.

10   Rotha, *Bunka eigaron*, trans. Atsugi (1938), 132. Original text is Rotha, *Documentary Film* (1952), 108.

11   Rotha, *Bunka eigaron*, trans. Atsugi (1938), 198. Original text is Rotha, *Documentary Film* (1935), 143.

12   I have deposited this book in the Makino Collection, Columbia University.

13   Sekino Yoshio, 'Tadashiki "documentary" riron no ninshiki no tame ni' (For the correct recognition of 'documentary' theory), *Bunka nyūsu Weekly*, 18 January 1940, 1, Makino Collection, Columbia University. The Makino Collection holds quite a few issues.

14   The other major series of articles by Sekino is Sekino Yoshio (1940h, 1940i, 1940j).

15   By way of contrast, Ueno's translation is complete and correct in 'Bunka eigaron josetsu' (see Rotha 1939a:79).

16   STS, or the Square Table Society, was an influential study group composed of a variety of intellectuals interested in film education. The group published its own *dōjinshi*: *Eiga zehi* and *Eiga dai-issen*. For a history, see Makino Mamoru's column in *Unitsūshin* between 26 September 1977 and 21 November 1977.

17   For an extensive discussion of Sekino's children's film days, see Gonda Yasunosuke (1931), especially 309–28. Gonda sandwiches this discussion between chapters on *kyōiku eiga* and dedicated children's theatres. In the 1930s, one of the main pedagogical struggles was over the manner in which cinema was used in education. In the course of much debate, educators narrowed the conditions of projection down to two possibilities: assembly screenings (*kōdō eishakai*) and classroom screenings (*kyōshitsu eishakai*). During assembly screenings, all the students in an entire school came into one big hall where the principal or some other official would provide the context for viewing the films through formal speeches and rituals such as singing the national anthem and paying respect to the emperor. Classroom screenings would take place in the classroom where students received the substance of their education. In this latter case, how the film was contextualized would be left entirely to the individual teacher. Although this will require further research, it appears that conservatives with nationalistic politics favoured assembly screenings because their 'total education' and 'group training' offered complete control over the films and conditions of reception. Teachers with more liberal attitudes opposed assembly screenings, however, because they replicated the structure of the nation or, more specifically, attempted to unify and control the thought of people. At the very least, classroom screenings narrowed film education to localized issues: 'This is how a volcano forms', and so on. This is yet another example of the battles taking place between totalization and difference as the public discourse became more oppressive. Those interested in pursuing this topic should start with the extended historiography of the film education magazines in Suzuki Kiyomatsu (1941).

18   One was Asanuma Keiji, Japan's best-known film semiotician.

19   Further evidence that Atsugi did not recognize the mistranslation may be found in the various copies she deposited at the Film Centre. None contains any corrections here, although she did underline the *adjacent* sentence in her 1960 edition.

20   This is not the only place where Atsugi's misprision reveals the nature of her (mis)reading of Rotha. Her translation (in all editions) provides many examples. Most critics refer only to how 'bad' it is. For example, in the afterword to his *Eiga riron nyūmon* (Introduction to Film Theory), Imamura Taihei (1952) points out how thankful we should be for the work of translators like Iijima Tadashi, Sasaki Norio and Atsugi Taka. He also warns readers to be cautious about trusting translation; ultimately; they must refer to the original, as Imamura has. He cites one example of misprision, and he singles out Atsugi: Rotha refers to some 'modern authorities' who call dialectical materialism 'out-of-date', but Atsugi translates this *saishin* as 'latest', 'brand-new'. Although Imamura picks a good example of mistranslation, he – like everyone else – does not ask what factors led to this particular

misreading. It does seem rather obvious. See Rotha (1935:182, 1938:270) and Imamura (1952:184).

21   Letter, Rotha to Eric Knight, 8 November 1938, Paul Rotha Collection, UCLA, Box 26, 2001.

22   This is how Kamei Fumio described his relationship to Rotha's book (Kamei Fumio et al. 1940). Various people had criticized *Tatakau heitai* (Fighting Soldiers), claiming that Kamei was Rotha's disciple. However, Akimoto Takeshi introduced the original book to Toho Studios when Kamei was in China shooting the film. Rotha was less a guidebook than an inspiration, especially the second half of the book on practical matters (this was the section translated and circulated within Toho).

23   On Kuwano, see Kuwano Shigeru (1941:70).

24   Atsugi discusses this phenomenon in her translator's afterword to the 1960 edition of *Documentary Film* (Atsugi Taka 1960:332).

Chapter 7

Mona Baker

REFRAMING CONFLICT
IN TRANSLATION

EDITOR'S INTRODUCTION

> *Rather than ignoring the choices that do not fit into the repeated pattern, recognizing the interplay between dominance and resistance allows us to elaborate a more complex picture of the positioning of translators and to embed them in concrete political reality.*

BAKER DRAWS ON NARRATIVE THEORY in an attempt to outline a theoretical approach to studying translation and interpreting that gives as much attention to the mainstream as it does to the marginal, to the workings of the system as well as the many acts of resistance against it, and that avoids the streamlining effect of dichotomies by acknowledging that the positioning of individual translators in relation to their texts, authors, societies and dominant ideologies is negotiated at every juncture, and can vary not only across texts but even within the same text. She starts by outlining some of the strengths of the narrative approach, compared with current popular approaches and against the backdrop of widespread political conflict at this moment in history. Among other advantages, narrative theory allows us to consider the immediate narrative elaborated in the text being translated or interpreted *and* the larger narratives in which the text is embedded, and this in turn allows us to see translational choices not merely as local linguistic challenges but as contributing directly to the narratives that shape our world. Every choice is considered – at least potentially – as a kind of index that activates a narrative, a story of what the world or some aspect of the world is like.

In addition to *narrative*, Baker makes use of the concept of *framing* to show how the 'same' narrative can be framed in very different ways by different narrators. She examines sites and strategies of framing, both around and within translations, using a wide range of examples, including some of the strategies employed by the web-based Middle East Media Research Institute, Arabic translations of Samuel Huntington's *The Clash of Civilizations*, English translations of statements by Osama Bin Laden in a collected volume published in Britain and the US, and English subtitles of a documentary film shot in Arabic in the Jenin camp in the Occupied West Bank. Baker concludes that the tension between dominance and resistance, which characterizes every aspect of our daily life, is often played out discursively, and that the interplay between the two can produce a range of choices that are difficult to streamline into specific types of strategy, since in the real world, and especially in situations of intense conflict, translators and interpreters vary their strategies in order to pursue concrete political goals rather than adhere to abstract principles or textual formats.

Follow-up questions for discussion

- One criticism of Baker's framework is that it makes the concept of narrative do a great deal of work, in other words, as Chesterman put it to her in an interview, 'the concept remains extremely vague and general; it is so wide that it explains everything – and therefore nothing' (Baker 2008:21). Baker's response is that 'narrative is not special in this sense; most key concepts in the humanities are similarly all-pervasive and similarly open to various definitions. The same could be said of 'culture' and 'context', for instance' (*ibid.*:21). Consider the pros and cons of working with such pervasive, fluid concepts, both in terms of research on and teaching of translation and interpreting.
- Israel (this volume) argues that 'translation projects undertaken by missionaries in the colonial context disturb neat polarities – such as those between colonizing and colonized, between complicit and resistance audiences and between "domesticating" and "foreignizing" translations – that continue to have currency in the present theoretical discourse on translation'. How does this argument compare with textual evidence of the negotiation of resistance and dominance in Baker's data, and to what extent can it be extended beyond textual interventions on the part of translators?
- In his critique of Foucault's theory of power, Said (1991:246–47) argues that 'there is always something beyond the reach of dominating systems, no matter how deeply they saturate society, and this is obviously what makes change possible, limits power in Foucault's sense, and hobbles the theory of that power'. To what extent is the tension between 'dominating systems' and that 'something' that remains beyond them and persists in resisting them negotiated and played out through various acts of translation and interpreting? How does narrative theory accommodate or explain this tension? What type of textual and non-textual evidence might we look for in order to make this negotiation visible?

Recommended further reading

Baer, Brian James (2006) 'Literary Translation and the Construction of a Soviet Intelligentsia', *The Massachusetts Review* 47(3): 537–60.

Baker, Mona (2008) 'Ethics of Renarration – Mona Baker is Interviewed by Andrew Chesterman', *Cultus* 1(1): 10–33.

Boéri, Julie (2008) 'A Narrative Account of the Babels vs. Naumann Controversy', *The Translator* 14(1): 21–50.

Gentzler, Edwin (1996) 'Translation, Counter-Culture and *The Fifties* in the USA', in Román Álvarez and M. Carmen-África Vidal (eds) *Translation, Power, Subversion*, Clevedon: Multilingual Matters, 116–37.

Gordon, Neve (2002) 'Zionism, Translation and the Politics of Erasure', *Political Studies* 50: 811–28.

THIS PAPER DRAWS ON CONCEPTS FROM narrative theory, sociology and the study of social movements to examine some of the ways in which translators and interpreters reframe aspects of political conflicts, and hence participate in the construction of social and political reality. The model of analysis I apply here is elaborated in greater detail in Baker (2006a) and elsewhere (Baker 2005, 2006b). It relies principally on the notion of narrative as understood in some strands of social and communication theory, rather than narratology or linguistics. Here, 'narrative' is used interchangeably with 'story': narratives are the stories we tell ourselves and others about the world(s) in which we live, and it is our belief in these stories that guides our actions in the real world. In this sense, narrative is not a genre, nor is it an optional mode of communication: narration, in the words of Walter Fisher, is 'not a mode of discourse laid on by a creator's deliberate choice but the shape of knowledge as we first apprehend it' (1987:193).

My choice of narrativity as a theoretical framework is motivated by a general dissatisfaction with existing theoretical notions that we tend to draw on in trying to explain the behaviour of translators and interpreters. In particular, much of the literature on translation tends to draw on the notion of norms, as elaborated in polysystem theory and the work of Gideon Toury. Norm theory encourages analysts to focus on repeated, abstract, systematic behaviour, and in so doing privileges strong patterns of socialization into that behaviour and tends to gloss over the numerous individual and group attempts at undermining dominant patterns and prevailing political and social dogma. Similarly, norm theory has nothing to say on the intricate patterns of interplay between repeated, stable patterns of behaviour and the continuous attempts at subverting that behaviour – the interplay between dominance and resistance, which is one aspect of translator behaviour I am particularly keen to highlight in my own work. Norm theory arguably also pays little attention to the political and social conditions that give rise to such patterns of dominance and resistance to them.

Another type of current theorizing that narrative theory allows us to move beyond is Lawrence Venuti's sweeping dichotomies of foreignizing and domesticating strategies (Venuti 1993, 1995), recast elsewhere as minoritizing and majoritizing strategies (Venuti 1998a). Apart from reducing the rich variety of positions that translators adopt in relation to their texts, authors and societies, these dichotomies also obscure the shifting positions of translators within the same text – they reduce the intricate means by which a translator negotiates his or her way around various aspects of a text into a more-or-less straightforward choice of foreignizing versus domesticating strategy. Even a brief glance at some of the texts I have been examining in my own research suggests that translators oscillate within the same text between choices that Venuti might regard as domesticating and ones he might regard as foreignizing. And, importantly, this oscillation serves a purpose in the real world – it is neither random nor irrational.

To balance the emphasis in norm theory on abstract, repeated behaviour and the streamlining effect of Venuti's dichotomies, what we need is a framework that recognizes the varied, shifting and ongoingly negotiable positioning of individual translators in relation to their texts, authors, societies and dominant ideologies. Hence my interest in narrative theory and my attempt to apply it to a wide range of written translations and oral interpreting events. Without claiming that narrative theory can single-handedly address all the weaknesses of current theorizing on translation, nor suggesting that current theorizing (norm theory and Venuti's dichotomies included) is not productive in addressing a wide range of issues relevant to the behaviour of translators and interpreters, I see the main, interrelated strengths of narrative theory as follows.

First, narrative theory does not privilege essentialist and reductive categories such as race, gender, ethnicity and religion; instead, it acknowledges the ongoingly negotiable nature of our positioning in relation to social and political reality. Narrativity, as Hall *et al.* argue, 'offers a way of conceptualising identity that is neither universal nor essentialist, but rather temporally and culturally specific' (2003:38). It thus allows us to move beyond the focus on supposedly inherent cultural differences and the type of identity politics that have informed much of the work on translation and interpreting so far, particularly work on cultural attributes and patterns of behaviour (for example, Katan 2004), on gender (Godard 1990, Simon 1996, von Flotow 1997) and on sexuality (Harvey 1998, 2003a, Keenaghan 1998). Without dismissing the importance and worth of this type of work, I would argue that it is now time to move beyond it. Identity politics, and frameworks that thematize difference in general, are the last model we need at this precise moment in history, when pernicious theories such as Samuel Huntington's 'clash of civilizations' (1993, 1996) are striving to highlight, and indeed invent, a whole panorama of differences – not to empower oppressed groups in the tradition of identity politics, but to justify the most criminal and dangerous of foreign policies. These politically motivated theories of difference allow the likes of Huntington to claim, for instance, that there is such a thing as a 'Muslim propensity toward violent conflict' (1996:258) and that '[t]he survival of the West depends on Americans reaffirming their Western identity and Westerners accepting their civilization as unique not universal and uniting to renew and preserve it against challenges from non-Western societies' (1996:20–21).

Pernicious theories and irresponsible foreign policies aside, it is also fair to point out that however attractive and potentially liberating in certain political contexts, identity politics has always suffered from some important limitations. The most serious of these is that it traditionally groups together people who share certain external attributes (women, blacks, homosexuals, Pakistanis) and disregards individual variation within the group. It also overdetermines the identities of individuals by giving precedence to one feature or attribute at the expense of others. What we need to be able to do instead is to locate individual translators and interpreters within the range of narratives they subscribe to and that inform their behaviour in the real world – including their discursive behaviour as translators and/or interpreters. This does not mean ignoring the obvious fact that our location in a particular cultural, racial or religious community at a given point in time is likely to influence our behaviour in specific ways. But narrative theory acknowledges that that influence is neither inevitable nor predictable. At this moment in time, for example, being Jewish could mean: (a) uncritical support for Israel and Zionism; (b) any number of variations on critical support for current Israeli policies; (c) refusing to self-identify as a Jew at all and taking no interest in the Middle East conflict whatsoever; (d) or, as is increasingly happening among large sections of the Jewish community, assuming a special responsibility to become heavily involved in activities designed to expose and undermine the Zionist enterprise. Even self-identifying as a Jew, then, does not tell us how a particular person might act in the real world, nor explain their behaviour, unless we know something about the kind of narratives to which they subscribe or can deduce them from the way they act and the discourse they produce.

Second, and following on from the above, narrative theory allows us to see social actors, including translators and interpreters, as real-life individuals rather than theoretical abstractions. Whitebrook argues that theory in general 'frequently fails to make the political agent concrete', and that 'character is treated as a matter of the variables an observer must assess when trying to understand or predict anyone's behaviour' (2001:15). Her critique certainly applies to theorizing about translation and interpreting, as does her proposal for adopting narrative theory as a way of breaking free from this abstraction:

> A turn to narratives allows for the de-personalized persons of theory, the bearers of a representative or typified identity, to be understood as separate persons – characters – with singular sets of characteristics, including but not confined to their political context and/or group identity. (Whitebrook 2001:15)

Third, narrative theory allows us to explain behaviour in dynamic rather than static terms – it recognizes the complexity of being embedded in crisscrossing, even competing narratives. Narrativity thus 'embeds the actor within relationships and stories that shift over time and space and . . . precludes categorical stability in action' (Somers and Gibson 1994:65). There is no scope here for streamlining behaviour or choices into macro categories such as foreignizing versus domesticating, acculturating versus exoticizing, nor of course faithful versus free – not even within the space of a single text. Equally, because the actor is always 'embedded' in relationships and stories, there is no question of assuming a privileged position from which we can claim 'objectivity' or 'neutrality' in relation to the narratives we are involved in translating, interpreting or indeed analyzing. Narrative theory encourages us to reflect on and question the narratives we come in contact with and that shape our behaviour, but there is no assumption here that we can suppress our subjectivity or stand outside those narratives, even as we reason about them.

Fourth, and most importantly in my view, narrative theory recognizes the power of social structures and the workings of the 'system' but does not preclude active resistance on a personal or group level. It pays equal attention to issues of dominance and resistance, to the ritual nature of interaction (in the tradition of Erving Goffman) as well as the means by which rituals are questioned and undermined. And finally, although hardly any of the work on narrativity in social and communication theory pays attention to issues of language, nor indeed translation, narrative theory does lend itself to being applied to both, and in a way that allows us to explain translational choices in relation to wider social and political contexts, but without losing sight of the individual text and event. This is one aspect of narrative theory that I have tried to elaborate in some detail in my own work and that I will attempt to demonstrate with an extended example at the end of this article.

Frames and framing

Narratives, as I explained above, are stories that we come to subscribe to – believe in or at least contemplate as potentially valid – and that therefore shape our behaviour towards other people and the events in which we are embedded. As used here, narratives are not chronologies, not undifferentiated lists of happenings: they are stories that are temporally and causally constituted in such a way as to allow us to make moral decisions and act in the real world.

Somers (1992, 1994, 1997) and Somers and Gibson (1994) suggest that narratives are constituted through four interdependent features. *Temporality* means that narratives are embedded in time and space and derive much of their meaning from the temporal moment and physical site of the narration. *Relationality* means that it is impossible for the human mind to make sense of isolated events or of a patchwork of events that are not constituted as a narrative. Every element in a narrative depends for its interpretation on its place within the network of elements that make up the narrative; it cannot be interpreted in isolation. The third core feature of narrativity is *selective appropriation*. Given that it is impossible to weave a coherent story by including every detail of experience, narratives are necessarily constructed according to evaluative criteria that enable and guide selective appropriation of a set of events or elements from the vast array of open-ended and overlapping events that constitute experience. The final and most important core feature of narrativity is *causal emplotment*. Causal emplotment 'gives significance to independent instances, and overrides their chronological or categorical order' (Somers 1997:82). It allows us to turn a set of propositions into an intelligble sequence about which we can form an opinion, and thus charges the events depicted with moral and ethical significance (Baker 2006a:65). It is our subscription to a particular pattern of causal emplotment in the Middle East narrative, for instance, that leads us to interpret another incident of suicide bombing in Israel as either a threat to Israeli security, providing evidence for the need for measures such as the Wall and targeted assassinations, or as an inevitable outcome of those very measures and hence providing 'evidence' that the solution lies in adopting other alternatives. These alternatives, in turn, will vary depending on more specific patterns of causal emplotment that distinguish one individual's narrative from those of others, even within the same broad group of, say, political activists. Not all activists in the Palestine Solidarity Movement, for instance, necessarily agree that the solution to the conflict lies in simply ending the Occupation along the 1967 borders. Some insist that it lies in reconfiguring Palestine/Israel as a single secular state for all its citizens, the 'One State Solution' as it has come to be known. Arguments for or against any solution are only coherent within the specific patterns of causal emplotment that distinguish one narrative from another.

For the above features of narrativity to become operative, and for a set of events to be constituted as a narrative with a specific pattern of causal emplotment, a considerable amount of discursive work has to be undertaken by those doing the narration. The notion of frame, and especially the more active concept of framing, can be productive in outlining some of the ways in which this discursive work is carried out. These notions are given several definitions in the literature, but broadly speaking they can be interpreted either passively, as 'understandings' that *emerge* out of the interaction, or actively, as deliberate, discursive moves designed to *anticipate* and guide others' interpretation of and attitudes towards a set of events. The first, generally passive definition of frames is characteristic of the work of Erving Goffman, who argues that 'an individual's framing of activity establishes meaningfulness *for him*' (1974:345; emphasis added). Similar definitions can be found in the work of other scholars who follow Goffman's lead. Tannen and Wallat (1993:60), for example, define frames as 'a sense of what activity is being engaged in, how speakers mean what they say'. The literature on social movements, by contrast, tends to treat framing as an active process of signification. For activists and those interested in studying their behaviour, the process of framing events for others is part and parcel of the phenomenon of activism; crucially, it involves setting up structures of *anticipation* that guide others' interpretation of events, usually as a direct challenge to dominant interpretations of the same events in a given society. This discursive work of framing events and issues for a particular set of addressees is important not only because it undermines dominant narratives of a given issue (the nuclear threat, Palestine, the so-called War on Terror), but also because it is a key strategy for forming networks and communities of activists, for enabling social movements to grow and attract adherents:

> While in daily life all social actors draw upon frames to engage in the production and maintenance of local meanings, frame analysts have recognized that the strategic process of frame construction and management is central to the mission of social movement organizations seeking to replace 'a dominant belief system that supports collective action for change' (Gamson et al. 1982:15). In this sense, framing processes provide a mechanism through which individuals can ideologically connect with movement goals and become potential participants in movement actions. (Cunningham and Browning 2004:348)

The notion of framing is closely connected to the question of how narrative theory allows us to consider the immediate narrative elaborated in the text being translated or interpreted and the larger narratives in which the text is embedded, and how this in turn allows us to see translational choices not merely as local linguistic challenges but as contributing directly to the narratives that shape our social world. Here, we consider every choice – at least potentially – as a kind of index that activates a narrative, a story of what the world or some aspect of the world is like. Some choices, particularly those relating to how we label an event, place or group, as well as the way we position individuals and communities in social and political space through the use of pronouns and adverbs of place, among other things, allow us to frame the narrative for others, in the social movement, activist sense of framing.[1]

Translators and interpreters working between Chinese and English, for instance, are aware that the 1997 events in Hong Kong can be referred to either as *The Handover of Sovereignty*, the standard reference in English, or (literally) as *The Return to the Motherland*, the standard reference in Chinese.[2] Also, they are generally aware that these choices do not exist in free variation but have serious implications in the real world. Similarly, in translating a text about the events of 1956 in the Middle East, one has to choose between two competing designations, neither of which poses a local linguistic challenge as such.[3] The first choice, prevalent in western discourse and embedded in a narrative that has currency in the West, is to refer to these events as *The Suez Canal Crisis*. The choice of *The Suez Canal Crisis* immediately activates the narrative of the invading powers: for Britain, France and Israel, it was useful and expedient to narrate these events as a political crisis. The designation that has currency in the Arabic-speaking world, on the other hand, and practically no currency in the West, is *The Tripartite Aggression*. This default choice in Arabic activates quite a different narrative framework, one that is embedded in the consciousness and alignments of those on the receiving end of that attack. Translators do not necessarily replace *The Suez Canal Crisis* with *The Tripartite Aggression* in rendering an English text into Arabic. They might reproduce the designation in a close translation, perhaps because they subscribe to a narrative of translation as a neutral and 'professional' practice. But even then, their choice will have implications for promoting and legitimating one or the other narrative. And there are other choices: translators may leave the designation itself as it is but comment on it or even challenge it in the introduction or footnotes to the text. While the choice of *The Handover of Sovereignty* or *The Suez Canal Crisis* might frame the narrative in a particular way, this very frame can in turn be challenged, and the entire narrative *reframed*, at a variety of points or sites in and around the text.

The point, then, is not to treat any specific translational choice as random, with no implications in the real world. Nor does narrative theory encourage us to treat a given choice (such as *The Suez Canal Crisis*) as a realization of some broad, abstract norm linked to other abstract choices such as choosing to stay close to the syntactic structures of the source text because there is an overriding norm of adequacy rather than acceptability[4] in the target culture at a particular moment in time. The narrative theory framework encourages us to avoid these broad abstractions and to think of individual choices as embedded in and contributing to the elaboration of concrete political reality.

Sites and strategies of framing

Processes of (re)framing can draw on practically any linguistic or non-linguistic resource to set up an interpretive context for the reader or hearer. This may include exploiting paralinguistic devices such as intonation and typography, visual resources such as colour, image and layout, and of course linguistic devices such as tense shifts, deixis, code switching, and the use of euphemisms. Language users, including translators and interpreters, can also exploit features of narrativity (temporality, relationality, selective appropriation and causal emplotment) to frame or reframe a text or utterance for a set of addressees. Translators of written text can do so in the body of the translation or, alternatively, around the translation. This distinction can be very important in some contexts because of the key role that the notions of accuracy and faithfulness tend to assume in the context of professional – and particularly politically sensitive – translation.

For instance, neoconservative organizations such as MEMRI,[5] which specializes in circulating translations of carefully selected Arabic source texts to elaborate a narrative of Arab societies as extremist, anti-semitic and a threat to western democracies, are very careful about the accuracy of their translations, since their credibility can easily be undermined if their opponents were to identify and publicize a list of errors in these translations, whether the errors in question are presented as deliberate or not. Most of the framing in which MEMRI and its close affiliate, Watching America,[6] engage is effected outside the text/translation proper. For a start, the narrative feature of selective appropriation allows MEMRI and Watching America to frame the Arab World as extremist and dangerous by simply choosing to translate the worst possible examples of Arabic discourse, which they also circulate to the media and Congress free of charge. Interestingly, MEMRI now has a special category of what they consistently call 'reformist' writers: a few voices from the Arab World and Iran that are translated and quoted on the site now and again; these 'reformists' argue for freedom of thought, women's rights, and so forth. The occasional 'cosmetic' selection of a non-extremist source serves to give a veneer of balance to MEMRI's coverage, at the same time as reinforcing the overall portrayal of the Arab World and Iran as a hotbed of extremism that suppresses the very few sane voices in the region – voices that are now magnanimously being given space on an American site.

Secondly, while keeping the actual translation very close to the original, MEMRI and Watching America can change the title of a text to frame the narrative as extremist, threatening or simply 'discursively alien'. For example, a recent English translation of an article from the Palestinian newspaper *Alhayat Aljadeeda* is posted on the

Watching America website under the title 'Oh, America . . . Oh, Empire of Contradictions'.[7] Closely backtranslated, the original Arabic title is far less flowery and 'exotic': it reads 'Signs on the Road: America and Democracy!!!'.[8]

Third, Watching America inserts images, complete with suitable captions, in the English text that frame the translated narrative as part of the broad, meta-narrative of the War on Terror. Figures 7.1 and 7.2, for instance, together with the accompanying captions, appear in the translation of the article from *Alhayat Aljadeeda*.

Figure 7.1 Palestinian Authority Prime Minister Ismail Haniyeh Prays Before a Speech, Most Likely for Funds . . . Most Likely to Come from Iran.

Figure 7.2 A militant from the Al-Aqsa Martyr's Brigade on the West Bank, During an Event to Remember One of the Many Acts of Violence that Have Taken Place There.

Fourth, and perhaps most importantly, each English translation of an article from an Arab newspaper is accompanied by a suitably annotated link to a video clip, provided by MEMRI, which acts as a further framing device, encouraging the reader to interpret even the most reasonable of Arabic discourse as one that hides an extremist subtext. The article from *Alhayat Aljadeeda* is accompanied by a video link with suitable annotations, as shown in Figure 7.3.

Interestingly, translations from other languages do not receive this treatment: translations from Chinese, Spanish, French, Dutch and a host of other languages are offered on the Watching America site *without* links to MEMRI videos that serve to demonize the community in question. The only other language that receives this special treatment (or is subjected to this framing strategy), as may be expected, is Persian.

Apart from images, captions, and the manipulation of titles, paratexts are an important site of framing in book translations: they include cover images and blurb, introductions, prefaces and footnotes. Cover images and blurbs are not generally provided by the translator,[9] but prefaces, introductions and footnotes normally are. Two Arabic translations of Samuel Huntington's *The Clash of Civilizations* were released within a very short period of time, the first in 1998 in Egypt (translated by Tal'at Al-Shayib) and

VIDEO FROM PALESTINE: PRAISE FOR SUICIDE BOMBING AT HAMAS FUNDRAISER

Iqra TV, Palestine: Excerpts from a fundraising speech delivered by Yemenite Cleric Abd Al-Majid Al-Zindani, Mar. 23, 00:08:18, Via MEMRI

'After efforts, policies, and plans failed, and when people almost despaired, the whole world was surprised by a certain decision of Hamas. What was the decision? An intifada. An Intifada? Where? In Palestine. In Palestine!'

Figure 7.3 Yemenite Cleric Abd Al-Majid Al-Zindani. Annotated video clip accompanying Alhayat Aljadeeda article, courtsey of MEMRI.

the second in 1999 in Libya (translated by Malik Obeid Abu Shuhayaa and Mahmoud Mohamed Khalaf). Both translations feature extensive introductions. The Libyan translation carries two. The first, by both translators, consists of four pages and offers a summary of the content of the book, tells us that it has been extremely controversial, and goes on to state the following (Huntington 1999:11; my translation):

> Given what we have noted of the chaotic structure and incoherence of the text and the flaws in the methodology adopted by the author, and in an effort to identify the underlying agenda of the clash-of-civilizations thesis, it was necessary to deconstruct the mechanisms and assumptions of the clash-of-civilizations discourse. Dr. Malik Obeid Abu Shuhayaa [one of the two translators] has therefore prepared a study of the political and intellectual assumptions of the clash-of-civilizations discourse and the mechanisms it relies on in outlining its conceptual apparatus, persuading others, and acquiring supporters. This study is entitled 'An Initial Contribution towards Awareness of the Other: The Assumptions and Mechanisms of the Clash of Civilizations'.

The study itself, written by one of the translators, as indicated in the above quote, constitutes the second introduction. It runs into an impressive 49 pages and directly challenges Huntington and his theory. The Egyptian translation released in 1998 has a 19-page introduction, not by the translator but by an Arab intellectual (Salah Qunswah), similarly undermining the thesis of the book and challenging its main tenets (Huntington 1998). All three introductions (two in the Libyan and one in the

Egyptian translation) precede the Arabic versions of Huntington's own preface to his book and pre-empt the reader's response to the arguments presented in the source text. They frame the translated texts that follow them in very negative terms, encouraging the reader to interpret Huntington's thesis from a specific angle even before they start reading it.

Footnotes are often also provided by translators and can serve a similar framing function. *Messages to the World: The Statements of Osama Bin Laden* (Lawrence and Howarth 2005), for instance, offers heavily annotated translations of Bin Laden's speeches, making extensive use of footnotes to reframe his personal narrative – and through this the narratives of Islamic fundamentalism, the so-called clash of civilizations, and the 'War on Terror' – as a direct outcome of western foreign policies rather than the product of a mentality that, in the War-on-Terror discourse, is normally depicted as sheer, inexplicable evil. In his review of the volume in the *London Review of Books*, Charles Glass notes that Bin Laden 'does not appear to be deranged, as his detractors insist he is. His message is plain: leave the Muslim world alone, and it will leave you alone. Kill Muslims, and they will kill you' (Glass 2006:14). How is this impression achieved?

The book is edited by Bruce Lawrence but the individual speeches and statements are translated by James Howarth. The main introduction by the editor (Lawrence and Howarth 2005:xi–xxiii) and the Translator's Note (ibid.:ix–x) make it clear that the editor explicitly takes responsibility for the mini introductions provided at the beginning of individual translations of Bin Laden's statements, and the translator for footnotes accompanying each translation. Together, the introductions and the footnotes frame Bin Laden as rational, as well as witty, educated and lucid. For instance, the mini introduction by the editor to a letter from Bin Laden posted on the internet on 6 October 2002, and appearing in the collection under the title 'To the Americans' (ibid.:160–72), tells us the following:

> This portrait of the US follows a call to the American people to convert to Islam. Fantastical as the prospect of such a conversion must be – as the letter itself implies ('I doubt you will do so') – the appeal has a practical function within the umma. Its purpose is to answer Muslim critics of 9/11 who argued that al-Qaeda did not offer Americans an opportunity to convert to Islam before attacking them, thereby violating God's ruling: 'We never punish until we have sent a message.' The exhaustive detail of the letter is bin Laden's proof to Muslims that he has explored every avenue to resolve this war by peaceful means, and given proper warning of the destruction that will be visited upon Americans if they refuse to listen to his advice. (ibid.:160)

A footnote by the translator to another statement made by Bin Laden in an interview with an Australian journal and appearing earlier in the same collection ('The Saudi Regime'; ibid.:31–43) makes the same point, striving again to depict Bin Laden as rational and as possessing considerable political acumen (ibid.:32):

> [22] Throughout the volume, the 'invitation to Islam' denotes the Arabic term *dawa*. Dawa is particularly significant in the context of bin Laden's later statements to America and its allies after 9/11, in which he offers them a chance to convert before further assaults, thereby 'clearing the decks in Islamic terms: he has warned and invited before attacking.' (Michael Scheuer, *Imperial Hubris: Why the West is Losing the War on Terror* [Potomac, 2005], p. 153).

In addition to portraying Bin Laden as rational (rather than deranged), the introductions and footnotes also give us an impression of him as 'human', smart, witty. The translator in particular makes a point of explaining witty wordplays in Bin Laden's discourse that undermine his normal portrayal as 'our enemy' – we do not normally credit our enemies with verbal dexterity or a sense of humour. Here are two examples. The first (ibid.:194) comes from what the editor, in his mini introduction, describes as 'the first and only statement of bin Laden that is framed as a sermon'. It is part of a 53-minute audiotape published on various websites and in the al-Hayat newspaper.

Main Text
They sought to be with God, and deprived themselves of sleep while injustice was being done. They poured out the water of life, not the water of shame.[24]

Footnote
[24] This is a play on words in Arabic; 'ma' al-hayat' ('water of life') and 'ma' al-mahya' ('water of shame') use variations on the same root.

The second example comes at the end of an audio-taped statement aired on al-Jazeera on 4 January 2004 ('Resist the New Rome'; ibid.:236):

Main Text
If Bush's call for peace was honest, why hasn't he spoken about the one who slit open the bellies of pregnant women in Sabra and Shatila or the planner of the surrender process,[3] the 'man of peace' [Ariel Sharon]; why did he not just come out and say 'we hate freedom and we kill for the sake of it'?

Footnote
[3] Bin Laden is making a pun here. 'peace process' is 'amaliyat al-salam', but here he talks about 'amaliyat al-istislam,' the surrender process. The word for surrender is a cognate of the word for peace.

Footnotes such as the above, together with arguments and descriptions outlined both in the general introduction to the volume as well as mini introductions to individual translations, cumulatively serve to portray Bin Laden as rational and competent, although the editor makes it clear that this does not mean he approves of Bin Laden's methods of expressing his grievances. The point he makes, and which the individual choices made by the translator indirectly support, is that a very different narrative, with a different pattern of causal emplotment, can account for the current ills of the world. Rather than explaining the so-called War on Terror as a necessary response to the horrors inflicted on an innocent West by deranged extremists from the Islamic World, this new narrative of Bin Laden suggests that the West is not innocent, and that its so-called War on Terror and similar atrocities are responsible for the horrific but 'rational' extremism we are now witnessing. This narrative resists the effort to divest violence of all historicity by portraying figures like Bin Laden simply as deranged extremists.

Framing within the translation: an extended example

An Arabic documentary entitled Jenin Jenin was directed by Mohamed Bakri and released in 2002 following the Israeli attack on the Jenin camp in the Occupied West Bank. The documentary is shot in the Jenin camp in Arabic but is clearly aimed at an international audience: it was subtitled into English, Hebrew, French, Spanish and Italian (Mohamed Bakri, personal communication). The version with English subtitles seems to be aimed predominantly at an American audience, as we will see shortly. The following examples from the documentary demonstrate two attempts at (re)framing that respond to larger narratives circulating beyond the immediate text and cannot be explained by resorting to norm theory or Venuti's foreignizing versus domesticating dichotomy. Both examples are discussed from different angles in Baker (2006a:99–100, 64–66).

The Vietnam frame

The first instance of (re)framing activates a narrative framework that seems to have been judged as more effective in the target context. At one point in the documentary, an old Palestinian man expresses his shock at what happened in Jenin and the world's apparent indifference and reluctance to intervene to protect Palestinians. He ends his contribution by saying, literally in Arabic, 'What can I say, by God, by God, our house/home is no longer a house/home'. The subtitle for this frame is 'What can I say? Not even Vietnam was as bad as this' (see Figure 7.4).

The decision to replace the original reference to the destruction of Palestinian homes with a reference to Vietnam would traditionally be interpreted in translation studies as an attempt to 'acculturate' the source text, to render it more intelligible to the target audience (in this case envisaged as predominantly American). But this is not a very productive or satisfying explanation. Had this been the primary motivation here, it would have made much more sense to refer to a more recent and hence more salient event, such as 9/11. After all, Vietnam arguably has less resonance among a young American audience than 9/11, and appealing to the memory of the latter is thus more likely to secure the emotional involvement and sympathy of a wider

أنا عارف والله العظيم، والله العظيم، بيتنا ما صار بيت

Figure 7.4 Screen shot from Jenin Jenin.

section of American viewers. To appreciate the motivation for this translational choice and its implications, it is necessary to refer to the wider narratives in circulation at that time, in Palestine and internationally.

First, the immediate narrative of what actually happened in the Jenin camp and elsewhere in Occupied Palestine in April 2002 was and continues to be heavily contested – from why the Israeli Defence [sic] Forces invaded the camps, to how many houses they demolished and how many people they killed, and so on. One of the discursive loci of contestation at the time concerned the widespread description of the Jenin event in the English-speaking media as an 'incursion'. Activists in the Solidarity movement insisted that 'incursion' was far too sanitized a description for the full-blown and sustained assault that left the camp in ruins and many people dead. The reference to Vietnam in the above subtitle reframes the event as a war of aggression, rather than a minor raid as the term 'incursion' tends to suggest. Vietnam was certainly no incursion: it is widely perceived as a vicious and bloody war, among large sectors of the American public as well as internationally.

Second, one narrative that continues to have considerable currency among Palestinians as well as the growing international solidarity movement in support of Palestinian rights is that America is as responsible for Israeli atrocities as Israel itself – that Israel could not possibly get away with its oppression of Palestinians were it not for the extensive support it receives from the United States. The choice of Vietnam here activates that public narrative. Far from being either foreignizing or domesticating, the choice to evoke the narrative of Vietnam encodes both accommodation to dominance and resistance to it. It accommodates to dominance by opting for a reference (Vietnam) that has resonance for the dominant American audience, rather than one that can equally signal unjust and bloody acts of aggression but would have no resonance for that dominant public: Kashmir, for instance, or even Darfur. It encodes resistance by simultaneously framing America as aggressor and signalling that the American audience is complicit in the injustices perpetrated by their government – and can choose to challenge them, just as they did in the case of Vietnam.

The secular frame

Another interesting attempt at reframing the wider Palestinian narrative by recasting aspects of the speech of several Palestinians interviewed in this documentary concerns the treatment of the recurrent word *shaheed*. The standard equivalent for this word in English is *martyr*, but this is problematic for two reasons. First, *shaheed* does not semantically map onto *martyr* in full. In Arabic, *shaheed* is generally used to refer to anyone who is killed violently, especially in war, whether they choose to be involved in that war or not, and irrespective of their religion. It therefore does not have the overtones of militancy and extremism that the term *martyr* has come to acquire in English, in connection with the Arab and Islamic world.[10] Second, *martyr* readily evokes associations of Islamic fundamentalism in this type of context, and using it repeatedly would play into the hands of those who would portray the Middle East conflict as a religious war, fuelled by young deranged Muslims in search of virgins in paradise.[11] The subtitles consistently opt for different equivalents when the word *shaheed* is used by Palestinians interviewed on the documentary, as in the following examples (see Baker 2006a:64–66 for further examples):

Example 1

"لسه بندوّر شهدا من تحت الأرض".

Backtranslation
We are still pulling **martyrs** from underneath the ground.

English subtitle
We are still pulling **victims** out of the rubble.

Example 2

"متخلّفين عقليًّا استشهدوا عندنا، معاقين استشهدوا عندنا، أطفال استشهدوا عندنا، نساء استشهدوا عندنا".

Backtranslation
We have mentally retarded people who have been **martyred**; we have disabled people who have been **martyred**; we have children who have been **martyred**, we have women who have been **martyred**.

English subtitle
They **killed** some mentally disabled people, children and women in the camp.

The choice of equivalents such as *victims* and *killed* in the above examples (and *corpses* and *dead* in other instances, discussed in Baker 2006a) rather than *martyr* helps to frame the larger Palestinian and Arab narrative in more secular terms.

There are two exceptions in the entire documentary. The first occurs towards the end in a scene involving a young Palestinian girl of about seven or eight years old who had been expressing defiance and determination to survive throughout the documentary. She draws an extended analogy between the Jenin camp and a 'tall, tall towering tree', which 'consists of leaves', with every leaf 'inscribed with the name of a *shaheed*, a *muqawim* [resistance fighter]' (my translation). The subtitles retain the metaphor and the reference to 'martyrs' in this instance, arguably because the innocent-looking, if defiant, young girl does not exactly fit the image of a deranged extremist in pursuit of paradise:

> The camp is like a tall, eminent tree. The tree has leaves, and each leaf of the tree bears the name of a **martyr**.[12]

The second instance in which the term *martyr* is used occurs in the final credits, and is therefore not a 'subtitle'. The documentary starts with the following dedication (reproduced here as is, without correction):

> Dedicated to
> The Executive Producer of 'Jenin'
> IYAD SAMOUDI
> who was murdered at alyamoun
> at the end of the filming by
> Israelian soliders on 23/06/2003
> Mohamed Bakri

The final credits include the following text:

> Executive Producer
> The **martyr**
> lyad Samoudi

These apparently conflicting choices in the treatment of *shaheed/shohadaa* reflect the interplay between dominance and resistance that is part and parcel of everyday life. They cannot, and should not, be treated as unmotivated, random choices on the part of translators and those who work with them, nor should they be swept under the carpet because they do not fit into existing theoretical frameworks and conceptual dichotomies.

Concluding remarks

To sum up, narrative theory allows us to make sense of these apparently conflicting strategies, such as those relating to the choice of equivalents for *shaheed* at different points in the *Jenin Jenin* documentary, as well as ones (like the choice of *Vietnam* above) that are simultaneously foreignizing and domesticating. By contrast to static, power-insensitive concepts like 'norms', narrative theory recognizes that dominance and resistance not only shape our behaviour and discursive choices, but that they are also always in a relationship of tension. This tension is often played out discursively, and the interplay between the two can produce a range of choices that are difficult to streamline. Rather than ignoring the choices that do not fit into the repeated pattern, recognizing this interplay between dominance and resistance allows us to elaborate a more complex picture of the positioning of translators and to embed them in concrete political reality.

Notes

1   Framing, in this sense, is not restricted to activism, however – although even this of course depends on how one defines activism. Some of the examples I discuss later come from sources I would personally regard as too pernicious to be labelled 'activist'. They include advocacy groups like the Middle East Media Research Institute (MEMRI) that set out to demonize Arab and Islamic communities and actively pit the West against the rest.

2   Similar choices in the Chinese context include *The Tiananmen Massacre* versus *The Tiananmen Incident* or *The Tiananmen Protests*. The source for these examples is Dr Kevin Lin, lead interpreter for the Foreign Office in Britain.

3   In 1956, Egypt was attacked by Britain, France and Israel following Egypt's decision to nationalize the Suez Canal, which connects the Mediterranean Sea with the Red Sea and Gulf of Suez.

4   In Toury's (1980, 1995) framework, the initial norm that governs any translation involves a choice between adequacy and acceptability. A translation will either subscribe to the norms of the source text, language or culture (and will hence be adequate) or to the norms of the target language and culture (and will hence be acceptable). Adherence to source norms determines a translation's adequacy with respect to the source text; adherence to norms originating in the target culture determines its acceptability within that culture.

5   See www.memri.org. For a detailed discussion of MEMRI and its translation activities, see Baker (2006a:73–76, 108–109).

6   See www.watchingamerica.org.

7   http://www.watchingamerica.com/alhayataljadeeda000003.shtml.

8   http://www.alhayat-j.com/details.php?opt=1&id=22102&cid=394.

9   For interesting analyses of covers and blurbs of published translations, see Watts (2000), Harvey (2003b), Asimakoulas (2005).

10   *Martyr* of course has very different associations in other contexts, for instance in the discourse of Christianity.

11   MEMRI, among other neo-conservative organizations, tends to blur the distinction between 'Arab' and 'Muslim' in an attempt to promote this specific narrative: that the conflict in Palestine/Israel is ultimately a religious conflict between Jews and Muslims, rather than a political conflict over territory and resources.

12   Note that the subtitles nevertheless tone the image down by omitting 'resistance fighter'.

PART 4

The voice of authority: institutional settings and alliances

Chapter 8

Marco Jacquemet

THE REGISTRATION INTERVIEW: RESTRICTING REFUGEES' NARRATIVE PERFORMANCE

EDITOR'S INTRODUCTION

The [asylum] interview . . . was based on a well-oiled routine. The UN caseworker would ask short questions, through the interpreter, to determine an applicant's name, date of exit from Kosovo, prior contacts with relief organizations, and number and whereabouts of close relatives. Together, officer and interpreter would also check the authenticity of identity documents . . . Then the UN officer would turn the entire proceeding over to the interpreter, who took the initiative in evaluating the applicant's claim of being Kosovar.

THE THEME OF NARRATIVE REMERGES in this article by Jacquemet, who examines the role played by interpreters in registration interviews run by the United Nations High Commission on Refugees in Tirana, Albania, following the end of hostilities in 2000, and at a point when many Albanians were trying to pass for Kosovars in search of a relatively easier life in Kosovo. The UNHCR mission became focused on investigating the asylum seekers' claims of being Kosovar refugees, and the priority for both caseworkers and interpreters became identifying bogus claims by Albanian citizens. Jacquemet describes the registration process as 'one of the technologies of power set up by humanitarian relief agencies for managing mass displacements of people'. His data analysis demonstrates clearly that managing asylum seekers is largely achieved by denying them the opportunity to tell their stories, and that 'in most cases the task of stopping storytelling fell heavily to the interpreters who, because of their interactional role, represented the first line of defence against unobstructed narratives'. The fact that refugees were not allowed to tell their stories caused considerable frustration and anguish, since for them the asylum interview was understood to involve retelling the story of their ordeal in detail, which would afford them 'a therapeutic moment in the search for closure of a usually traumatic experience'. The UNCHR's insistence on denying refugees this moment, with the active help of the interpreters, was seen by refugees as a lack of interest in their predicament, and hence a lack of 'humanity' on the part of the organization.

Beyond participating in enforcing the institutional agenda of preventing refugees from telling their stories, interpreters in the interviews recorded by Jacquemet are shown to play the role of institutional gatekeepers in other ways, actively managing the interaction even before the interview itself has started:

> From the moment the asylum-seekers approached them to set up interviews, the interpreters turned into communicative detectives – they tuned their ears to accents, checked clothes and communicative behaviour, and observed women's gazes and postures. As a consequence, before the interview proper had even started, the interpreters in many cases had already made up their minds, often based on the conviction that they had detected the 'wrong' accent . . . or other non-Kosovar clues. This bias was then carried over into the interview proper, with potentially life-changing consequences.

Jacquemet looks in detail at the interactional strategies and verbal tactics used between UNHCR agents (caseworkers and interpreters) and asylum seekers. He explores UNHCR's tactics for stopping stories by examining micro-sequences of institutional encounters during the registration process. He demonstrates, for example, that the standard way of preventing refugees from launching into a narrative was to enforce a strict question and answer format. The case worker would pose very precise and detailed questions designed to determine the asylum-seeker's link with Kosovo, and the ever-vigilant interpreter would stop any attempt at storytelling immediately in its tracks and ensure that the answer did not exceed the terms of the question.

Follow-up questions for discussion

- Jacquemet stresses the power of the institution in determining meanings even beyond the immediate encounter when he argues that 'stories not only recreate and comment on prior events, but in the process allow a particular recollection of these events to become a text, transposable to a variety of different contexts. In institutional settings, this means that stories can be lifted from their interactional context to enter the public record, thereby acquiring legal force'. How does this compare with Asad's discussion (this volume) of the authority that anthropology as an institution exercises over its subjects and the role of what he calls 'textualization' in this process?

- Jacquemet's description of the various tasks performed by interpreters in his data, in their role as institutional aides and gatekeepers, complicates the issue of interpreter positioning – and assumed neutrality – considerably. The picture he paints is not restricted to the context of asylum registration interviews, nor even to wartime interpreting specifically – cf. Palmer and Fontan (2007) and Davidson (this volume). What are the ethical implications of this positioning and how might a professional code of practice articulate some of these implications in order to encourage more reflexivity in the profession? You might find it helpful to read Stahuljak (this volume) to see how some interpreters negotiate the balance between institutional/client and other types of loyalty in difficult settings.

- Jacquemet offers us some information about the interpreters in his data (that they were Kosovar refugees themselves, that they were fluent in the Gheg variety of Albanian spoken in Kosovo, that they were all male and mostly from an urban, college-educated milieu, and that they were recognized as 'community elders' although in some cases they were still in their twenties). Compare this type of broad, group description, typical of interpreting studies, with the detailed information we often get on individual translators in studies of literary translation – for example, what Nornes (this volume) tells us about the trajectories of translators like Atsugi. Do you think this downplaying of the trajectories of individual interpreters is necessary or even inevitable in interpreting studies, or can you envisage a different approach to interpreting data that gives more visibility to the interpreter as a unique individual?

Recommended further reading

Barsky, Robert F. (1996) 'The Interpreter as Intercultural Agent in Convention Refugee Hearings', *The Translator* 1(2): 45–64.

Mason, Ian (2004) 'Conduits, Mediators, Spokespersons: Investigating Translator/Interpreter Behavior', in Christina Schäffner (ed.) *Translation Research and Interpreting Research*, Clevedon: Multilingual Matters, 89–97.

Palmer, Jerry and Victoria Fontan (2007) ' "Our Ears and Our Eyes". Journalists and Fixers in Iraq', *Journalism* 8(1): 5–24.

Pöllabauer, Sonja (2004) 'Interpreting in Asylum Hearings: Issues of Role, Responsibility and Power', *Interpreting* 6(2): 143–80.

'Refugees should stay home'.

Italian Senator Umberto Bossi, leader of the Lega Nord, an anti-immigrant political party.

Tirana, Albania

WINTER 2000. THE SOUTHWESTERN Balkans were in a suspended state of calm, as if someone had pushed the pause button in a war video game. The legions of NATO officials and journalists who watched the war from the relative safety of Tirana had, for the most part, cleared out. To the north, NATO air power had succeeded in chasing Serbian forces out of Kosovo. This region of the Yugoslavian Federation, in which NATO had engaged its military power to protect the Albanian majority from Serbian 'ethnic cleansing', had become a somewhat autonomous zone under international protection. Though the border between Kosovo and Serbia remained sealed, communications and transport between Albania, Kosovo, Macedonia and Montenegro had improved dramatically since the war's conclusion in July 1999.

Meanwhile, the swell of people passing through the United Nations High Commission for Refugees (UNHCR) Registration Office in Tirana to apply for refugee cards had subsided. Still, the appointment schedule was filled to capacity. Each morning five or six families patiently waited their turns. One by one, each family was invited into a small inner office to be interviewed by UNHCR staff who would determine the legitimacy of the applicants' asylum claims.

In the warmth of this office the asylum-seekers sat down next to an interpreter, across the table from a UNHCR officer. During the interview they heard the hum of computers in the background, as well as the noise of power generators in the backyard – the international community's audible affirmation of power and auton-omy from a local government unable to deliver electricity. Outside the UNHCR office, Tirana was a mess. Because of the need for heating during the freezing Balkan winter, the energy supply was spread thin. Electricity was available just two to three hours a day. Since the former Communist régime chose electricity to be Albania's sole form of energy, this meant that one could do practically nothing outside those hours. People could not heat their homes, cook, run water to wash dishes or clothes (because pressure was maintained by electric pumps), take warm showers, watch television, or use other electronic appliances.

As a result it seemed that everybody in Albania wanted out. For a brief period during the Kosovo War, the invasion of Albania by NATO military personnel, inter-national news organizations and aid agencies had allowed Albanians a taste at home of the western life they had previously only glimpsed on the TV screens or heard about from returning migrants. Anybody who could speak a foreign language was hired for $100 a day by foreign news media. Spare rooms could be rented to foreign-ers for $50 a day. Drivers were in constant demand. Money was finally flowing in a country where the average pension was $60 per month. However, by fall 1999 all of this was gone, leaving behind only a handful of agencies in need of Albanian workers. Even shadowy entrepreneurs trafficking in dope, humans and weapons had moved their operations to Kosovo – by then the ultimate lawless zone.

Before the war, Albanians who could not leave by legal means were left with only one option: to take the gommoni, rubber speedboats that could bring them to Italy in two hours, but were also liable to lose their passengers overboard in the choppy Adriatic waves. Even once would-be migrants made it to Italy, they were often inter-cepted by the Italian police, interned in prison-like camps, and sent back at the earliest opportunity. But with the Kosovo War, Albanians found a new avenue: they could try to pass for Kosovar refugees. By the winter of 2000 a growing number of Albanians, locked out of rich countries by immigration restrictions, increasingly resorted to scoring an asylum card as the only legal means of achieving the right to migrate.

This was perhaps the most ironic development of the Kosovo crisis, and the most telling evidence of the quality of life in Albania. Among the asylum applicants in the UNHCR Registration Office on any given day there may have been a number of Albanian citizens desperately seeking to be recognized as Kosovar refugees. While most people designated as 'refugees' have had this label imposed upon them, Albani-ans sought it out and, when they attained it, saw it as a godsend. Besides a weekly allowance of food and cash for lodging, refugee status brought the right to medical treatment (in the most urgent cases, even air evacuation to a European Community hospital) and, most importantly, the chance to be resettled abroad in western Europe, the United States, or Canada.

As a result, the UNHCR mission in Albania had evolved from providing legal documentation to refugees and mediating between refugees and humanitarian organ-izations, to investigating the asylum-seekers' claims to be Kosovar refugees. The priority of the Registration Office (for both staff and interpreters) became identifying bogus claims for this status filed by Albanian citizens. Every interview conducted by the office's staff and interpreters included careful screening of the identity of the asylum-seekers – a process that depended heavily on the interpreters' fluency in multiple Albanian dialects as well as in English.

In their interactions with asylum-seekers, caseworkers and interpreters made a point of never asking the would-be refugees to tell any stories of their ordeal. During the interview, they abandoned their curiosity for narratives in an effort to determine the asylum-seeker's objective link to Kosovo. In short, stories were denied a role in the determination of the refugees' status. Refugees perceived this denial both as a lack of trust on the part of the caseworkers and as a sign that their suffering did not count in this bureaucratic encounter. This in turn caused serious problems in refugees' perception of the asylum process and, more importantly, in their ability to utilize their encounter with relief workers as a therapeutic moment in the search for closure of a usually traumatic experience. As a result, these interviews were experienced as confrontations rather than as exchanges based on trust, and some refugees found themselves resorting to angry posturings to vent their frustration with the bureaucratic handling of their case.

In documenting such a denial of narratives, this article first addresses the link between stories and credibility, then looks at the UNHCR's treatment of refugees' attempts to launch a narrative performance. Finally, it discusses how the denial of narratives was interpreted by refugees as a symptom of the relief organization's lack of 'humanity', resulting in an antagonistic stance that hindered any chance for an open and frank exchange, which led to serious consequences for the entire asylum process.

Narrative performances and credibility

The link between refugees' stories and their referential value is fraught with ambiguity and paradox. As Knudsen remarked in his contribution to *Mistrusting Refugees*, after the first interaction with the asylum process, refugees learn that a carefully crafted interview is a ticket for an easy certification process while a mismanaged one can cause delays, even application denials: 'Any incongruity has serious consequences if judged to be a deliberate deception intended to advance one's position in the departure queue. Inconsistencies must, therefore, be minimized, not only in the personal data reported but also in the life history presented' (1995:22).

Refugees must manipulate their experience – inevitably messy, complicated and confusing – to provide a straight, simple narrative reality perceived to fit the requirements of the asylum process. The resulting narrative performances are scattered along a continuum between understatement and overstatement. Quite often, refugees tend to understate their experience. Val Daniel, in his research on Tamil refugees, pointed out the 'unshareability and incommunicability of pain and terror' (1996:139): the telling of an act of torture or execution is believed to be too monstrous for words, the experience to be unlike any other, making it impossible to relate. Asked to explain their ordeal, refugees rely on stock narratives that couch that pain in acceptable scenarios that can be shared with people who have not experienced their unutterable suffering.

At the same time, we find many cases where these narratives are overstated. For instance, the British writer Caroline Moorehead, one of the country's most eloquent defenders of asylum rights, was reported in the *New Yorker* to be saddened by the fact that each refugee, knowing the odds against asylum – knowing that asylum itself involves a kind of triage – has to describe a past that is more horrific than the one his compatriot, and often his friend, has just recited to the person who will assess their cases (Kramer 2003).

Either understated or overstated, refugees' stories run the risk of losing a measure of their truth, of their integrity, and thus of their credibility. This is partly due to the fact that these stories are not shared casually with friends, but are told to strangers in institutional settings invested with the infinitesimal techniques, tactics and devices through which authority, legitimacy and dominance operate.

How should the international agencies in charge of refugees respond to this conundrum? Should they simply trust the refugees? Should a therapeutical concern for the healing power of narratives overwrite a bureaucratic concern for precise information and accurate facts? Or should they altogether cease listening to the refugees' stories?

In 2000 the UNHCR office in Tirana opted for the latter. Its decision not to rely on narratives reflected a common-sensical suspicion on the part of UN officers of the power of stories. To explain this suspicion we can point to three phenomena which constitute the inner workings of narrative performances: *persuasion, entextualization*, and *participation framework*. In other words, the motives at the basis of UN officers' refusal to collect stories stemmed from a resistance (more or less below the level of awareness) to the structural and rhetorical capabilities of narratives.

First, stories persuade by appealing to a human need for syntagmatic coherence. Stories string individual and separate facts into a compelling isotopic plot, able to increase the credibility not only of the entire narrative but also of single facts (Greimas 1982). Defence attorneys, for instance, are known to encourage their clients to provide testimony in a narrative form, precisely to enhance their credibility (O'Barr 1982, Jacquemet 1996, Hirsch 1998, Conley and O'Barr 1998, Taslitz 1999). By refraining from assessing refugee narratives, the UNHCR sought to establish 'objective' criteria for the assessment of each individual 'fact', evaluating each case by running through a checklist of facts instead of listening to the narrative development of a personal history.

Second, as Briggs argues in his study of conflict talk: 'the art of connecting words to form narratives provides humans in a wide range of societies with powerful tools for creating and mediating conflict and in doing so, constituting social reality' (1988:272). Stories constitute social reality through the process of *entextualization*, that is: 'the process of rendering discourse extractable, of making a stretch of linguistic production into a unit – a text – that can be lifted out of its interactional setting' (Bauman and Briggs 1990:70). Through distinctive features of narration (framing devices, reported speech, metalinguistic statements) stories not only recreate and comment on prior events, but in the process allow a particular recollection of these events to become a text, transposable to a variety of different contexts. In institutional settings, this means that stories can be lifted from their interactional context to enter the public record, thereby acquiring legal force.

Finally, narrative performances such as storytelling allow participants to reframe and transform social relations. As Goodwin (1990) pointed out, stories operate on the *participation framework* of the people involved in the performance. In many cases, stories can dramatically alter the relationships among participants, making it possible for people to align themselves with particular narrators and be recruited into the storytelling performance to declare their position *vis-à-vis* the characters and events in the story. Storytelling thus has the capacity to transform power alliances among participants, to force them to take sides: stories are in fact addressed to everybody in reach, and these people become an active audience charged with the task of evaluating the story and declaring their disposition towards the matter under examination.

These three factors (persuasion based on isotopy, entextualization, and participation framework) would considerably reduce the power of an interviewer to control and unilaterally manage a verbal interaction. This is, in my opinion, the reason for the UNHCR's policy against allowing refugees to engage in open, unobstructed narratives. But how was this discouragement of stories achieved in the on-going flow of an institutional interview?

In the next section, I will look in detail at the interactional strategies and verbal tactics used between UNHCR agents and asylum-seekers in the aftermath of the Kosovo War. After introducing the socio-political context of these interactions, I will explore UNHCR's tactics for stopping stories by examining micro-sequences of institutional encounters during the asylum registration process.

The registration procedure

The registration process is one of the technologies of power set up by humanitarian relief agencies for managing mass displacements of people. Together with the refugee camp (see Malkki 1995), the registration process establishes an ordered, replicable, and consistent operation that depends on smooth interactional routines to achieve its goal of surveillance, discipline and control. In this way, the registration process may be considered a discourse practice. As we know from Foucault (see for instance his inaugural lecture at the Collège de France, 1972a/1981), discourse practices do not necessarily seek to depict the world: rather, they dictate the world by mobilizing tactics of social indexicality and strategies of social inequality advantageous to the dominant group(s) in charge of institutional decision-making.

The caseworkers

The UNHCR international staff in Tirana in 2000 came from all over the world – Spain, Uganda, Peru, Japan. Most of them were young, and were on their first or second UN mission, in many cases under temporary contracts renewable every six months. The majority had been hastily recruited for Kosovo emergency and had been quickly deployed to the field after minimal training (in most cases provided by individual nations and not by the UN). Their duty during the registration process was to find a clear and substantial connection between the asylum-seeker and his or her purported Kosovar origin. They routinely spoke in English (the official language of this global organization) for internal communication, to direct their local staff (all fluent in English and usually another international language), and to communicate with the interpreters. Their lack of cultural and linguistic awareness was at times quite pronounced. Behaving like postcolonial players, they seemed unable to grasp and understand the complexities of local interactions, and as a result relied heavily on their staff, and especially on the interpreters, for almost all their dealings with the refugees. This placed a heavy burden of responsibility on the local staff and again especially on the interpreters, who were left squarely in charge of the registration process.

The interpreters

The UNHCR interpreters, Kosovar refugees themselves, played a pivotal, though often unrecognized, role in managing the interaction between asylum applicants and the international community represented by the UNHCR. They were the most transidiomatic of speakers among Kosovar refugees. They were fluent in the Gheg variety of Albanian spoken in Kosovo, able to detect its differences from the Gheg spoken across the mountains in Northern Albania, conversant in Albania's standard language, and effective in an English-language environment. All were male and most came from an urban, college-educated milieu. They were recognized as 'community elders' by both refugees and the UNHCR, although in some cases they were still in their twenties.

At the peak of the registration drive during the Kosovo War, the UNHCR employed twelve interpreters, who were scattered all over Albania: near the check-points at the Kosovo border, in the refugee camps and in the temporary offices opened by the UNHCR in the main Albanian towns. At that time registration inter-views were hastily conducted while the interviewees were waiting in line for food or shelter. The interviews lasted five minutes at the most – a short time indeed to determine whether someone really came from Kosovo, if he or she belonged to a Kosovar family, if he or she was a Kosovo Liberation Army member.

Once the emergency ended, all interviews were moved to the UNHCR head-quarters in Tirana. Only the best of the interpreters were retained, and were given more time and responsibility for addressing asylum requests. Interpreters were also in charge of scheduling interviews and helping asylum-seekers fill out the many forms required prior to the interview.

These pre-interview screenings were somewhat problematic, since they inevit-ably biased the interpreters' assessment of the asylum-seekers. Instead of relying on hard evidence, in most cases interpreters' first impressions were heavily influenced by such communicative factors as accent, looks or politeness. From the moment the asylum-seekers approached them to set up interviews, the interpreters turned into communicative detectives – they tuned their ears to accents, checked clothes and communicative behaviour, and observed women's gazes and postures. As a con-sequence, before the interview proper had even started, the interpreters in many cases had already made up their minds, often based on the conviction that they had detected the 'wrong' accent (i.e. a North Albanian accent when speaking Gheg) or other non-Kosovar clues. This bias was then carried over into the interview proper, with potentially life-changing consequences.

The interview

The interview itself was based on a well-oiled routine. The UN caseworker would ask short questions, through the interpreter, to determine an applicant's name, date of exit from Kosovo, prior contacts with relief organizations, and number and whereabouts of close relatives. Together, officer and interpreter would also check the authenticity of identity documents (if they had not been lost or destroyed at the border by Serb police). Then the UN officer would turn the entire proceeding over to the interpreter, who took the initiative in evaluating the applicant's claim of being Kosovar.

This relay was usually achieved by the caseworker (C) asking the interpreter (I) to ask the would-be refugee (R) a question about Kosovo's toponymy (see Table 8.1).

The interpreter/questioner would initially limit himself to probing the applicant's knowledge of his or her alleged area of origin. Most people, such as the man above, would answer this query with a long list of toponyms. If an interpreter did not know the applicant's home town, he would compare the applicant's description with the

Table 8.1
03/08/00 [1]

R = young man		
C ↔ I		
01	C	so can you ask him some questions about this part of kosovo?
I ↔ R		
02	I	pa thuma tash ndonjë fshat të rrethinës së malishevës aty? (now, can you name any village of the malisheva area?)
03	R	po (. .) është – belanica/ thuj mbas qysh i thone belza – baja – (yes . . there is – belanica/and after it I say belza – baja)
04		prejucaki – seniti- është:: (. .) si e ke emrin – është klecka një – (preucaki – seniti- then:: . . what's its name . . . klecka, this is a –)
05		një lagje komplet në prizren – sa thashë unë – pese t'i thashe – (a – large neighbourhood in prizren – how many I mentioned – five?)
06		(. .) pastaj vjen durgazi – vjen bllaca – vjen kemecia – asht – (. . . then there's durgazi – then bllaca – then kamenica – that's it)
C ↔ I		
07	C	yes he knows well that region.

sketches of villages and towns drawn by other refugees at the request of the UNHCR. Or he would ask about the nearest large town, the villages that one passes en route to that town, or the name of the most important mosque or bridge in the area. Here again, he would often consult maps drawn up exclusively to verify the answer's accuracy.

If, in the pre-interview screening, the interpreter's first impression of dealing with a compatriot had been positively reinforced by the applicant's responses, the interview was conducted in a relaxed mood. Sometimes the interpreter would preface questions about Kosovo with disclaimers about the need to follow 'procedure'; at other times he might even suggest the right answers. A smooth interview would, in this case, last only a few minutes.

On the other hand, if an interpreter suspected the accent, behaviour, or look of the asylum-seeker, then the interview quickly turned into a rigorous interrogation. Family members were separated and interviewed in succession. Knowledge of local geography and Kosovar practices were probed over and over again. Some people, unable to answer, blamed their ignorance on the isolation of their lives. Women, in particular, would claim never to have left their houses after their wedding days (a claim eagerly corroborated by their husbands, who proudly confessed that they were 'religious fanatics').

If people were unsure about toponyms, the interpreter would test knowledge of local farming and cooking terminology, or Yugoslavian bureaucratic practices. After the interpreter was satisfied, he would give the officer a synopsis, in English, of his questioning and the applicant's responses; sometimes he would give his assessment alone of the case (as in line 7 above).

The majority of the asylum-seekers were somewhat puzzled at having to describe their town or region to prove that they came from there, and sometimes did not comprehend the connection between this line of questioning and their asylum application.

Table 8.2
03/09/00

R = young woman		
C ↔ I		
01	C	can you ask her some questions?
I ↔ R		
02	I	Yes – mirë si ashtu thotë – na thuni ca lagje të gjakovës –
		(yes – well, how – so she says – name us some neighbourhoods in giakova)
03		diçka për gjakovën
		(some things about gjakova)
→ 04	R	do të dij ça kam bërë atje?
		(does she want to know what I did there?)
→ 05	I	JO. lagjet lagjet e gjakovës
		(NO – neighbourhoods, neighbourhoods of gjakova)
06	R	rrugët?
		(streets?)
07	I	Rrugët – mëhallat – mund t'na i thush?
		(streets – city quarters – can you tell us?)
08	R	Po
		(yes)

Most asylum-seekers, such as the university student interviewed above, thrown off by the topographic inquiries, instinctively sought to provide autobiographical narratives (line 4, where she asks whether they wanted to know some narrative details of her life in Gjakova). However, as we already mentioned, the UNHCR was not interested in narratives, and the interpreter was quick and forceful in rejecting the asylum-seeker's offer of personal stories (line 5). This active discouragement of narratives stood in striking contrast with asylum-seekers' expectations about the registration interview: that the entire process of becoming a refugee would entail the reconstruction of their past lives and the deliberate, exquisitely detailed telling of the story of their ordeal. In this case, the university student could only reply to the interpreter's questions with a meek 'yes' (line 8) before producing a list of Giakova's streets.

Yet the power of syntagmatic coherence was often too great to resist and some applicants, even in recalling toponyms, managed to give detailed narrative descriptions of the area, walking the interpreter through the village streets: at the left is the mosque, the market is down on the right, home is just on the other side of the stream.

Preventing stories

Both caseworkers and interpreters put considerable effort into trying to prevent asylum-seekers from relating unobstructed narratives. The case-workers' main concern was to restrict the interview through punctual and detailed questions with the goal of determining the asylum-seeker's link with Kosovo. This concern was readily apparent in one of the first encounters I observed, in which a young woman arrived at the office with an identity card (supposedly, but unverifiably hers – identity cards produced during the war did not have pictures) cut in two. She asked to have a new one issued to her. The caseworker, suspecting identity fraud, decided to interrogate the woman regarding the card. After asserting that it had been cut during a car accident, she tried to launch into a narrative that would provide some credibility to her claim of being a refugee (see Table 8.3).

By bringing the young woman back to the issue of the card (line 18), the caseworker seeks to avoid the open-ended development of the narrative. At the same time, this move might be read as demonstrating callous disregard for the highly traumatic story being told by the woman. Note also the interpreter's freedom in relaying the events, where the statement 'my uncle and father stepped on a mine' (line 10) is rendered as a wounded father (line 13) and a dead uncle (line 17).

While in the case above control of the interaction was mostly achieved by the caseworker, in most cases the task of stopping storytelling fell heavily to the interpreters who, because of their interactional role, represented the first line of defence against unobstructed narratives. The simplest way to prevent storytelling was achieved by implementing a strict question and answer format (see Table 8.4).

Most of the time asylum-seekers tried to expand the question and answer format into a more conversational structure, which in most cases meant trying to launch a narrative explanation of their case. However, the ever-vigilant interpreters were quick to stop any attempt at storytelling in its tracks. As soon as an answer departed from the expected script and especially if it seemed to lead into a story, the interpreter promptly redirected the asylum-seeker to the solid ground of well-known toponyms (see Table 8.5).

In the case above, as soon as the asylum-seeker moves to launch a narrative (see the two-story preface cues in line 6: 'because' and 'I went' mark the motive and deictical pronominalization for the story), the interpreter quickly overlaps (=), interrupts the other, and directs him to stick to the question. Metalinguistic awareness,

Table 8.3
02/07/00

R = young woman		
(. .)		
I ↔ R		
08	R	jo jo jo – kur kina ardhë në shqipëri – na kanë – kanë sjellë në (no no no – when we came to Albania we were pushed to Albania)
09		shqipëri serbët – na kanë – qit nëpër rrugë – nëpër mal kish pasë dhe (by the Serbs – they – drove us away – into the mountains –)
10		një minë – asht ra mixha jem baba – (a mine was there – my uncle and father stepped on it)
C ↔ I		
11	I	she explain something during the war how they came here –
12		Albania
13		(. .) and she said on the mine my father cut the leg –
14	C	Yeah
15	I	and my uncle lost his life
16	C	and?
17	I	he were – he was died.
→ 18	C	and what's the relation with this card?

Table 8.4
02/07/00

R = adult male		
C ↔ R		
01	C	but did you obtain a – uh passport in kosovo?
I ↔ R		
02	I	po ju a keni marrë pasaportë në kosovë a keni marrë pasapor= (did you obtain a passport in Kosovo a passport did you)
03	R	=janë djegë (they are burned)
C ↔ R		
04	C	before the war
I ↔ R		
05	I	PARA lufte/ para lufte para lufte a keni pasë ju pasaportë? (BEFORE the war, before the war did you have a passport?)
06	R	po po (yes yes)
07	I	po po apo jo? (yes, yes or no?)
08	R	po pasaportë – (yes passport)
09	I	keni pasë? (did you have one?)
10	R	kemi pasë e janë met andej ato hupë (we had them but we left them behind, they are lost)
I ↔ C		
11	I	he repeat the same thing,
12		we lost the passport, we lost the documentation

ever present in any good interpreter's bag of tricks, is here so heightened that the interpreter recognizes story cues as soon as they emerge. He is thus able to pre-empt the actual launching of the story, thereby avoiding the more difficult task of stopping a narrator in the middle of his performance.

As Goodwin (1990) reminded us, stories have the power to engage participants in a speech event and impede early unilateral exit from the event. Particularly in the case of a one-on-one interaction, obligations imposed by the interactional order (such as those described in Goffman 1974) make it quite difficult for the listener to interrupt the storytelling without serious face loss for everybody involved. It is much easier to halt a story before its full emergence by resorting to metalinguistic directives (such as the 'come on! name me the villages' in lines 7–8) that successfully restore control of the exchange to the interpreter.

Another tactic used to halt refugees' attempts to launch narratives was offered by the particular sequential organization of turn-taking set up by the need to interpret. Other researchers (Berk-Seligson 1990, Davidson 2000) have already pointed out the gate-keeping role played by interpreters. Rather than serving as a neutral conduit between caseworker and asylum-seeker, the interpreter is an active participant in the exchange, maintaining parallel and related conversations with the other two

Table 8.5
01/28/00

R = man in his forties		
C ↔ I		
01	C	can you ask him some question about the region?
02	I	Yes
I ↔ R		
03		tash a mundet me thanë diçka për uh uh – rrethin e deçanit –
		(now can you say something about uh uh – deçan county –)
04		katundet rreth decanit a mund i thuni?
		(the villages around deçan can you name them for me?)
05	R	iznici-raxhaja-ralia-deri deri (. .)
		(iznici-raxhaja-ralia-deri deri . .) [pause]
06		në plavë e në guci e i kam shtëtit unë e =jam ken=
		(up to plava and gusi I have been there because I went to –)
→ 07	I	= hajde =
		(come on!)
08		thumi katundet e rrethit të deçanit
		(name me the villages in deçan county)

Table 8.6
01/28/00

R = old man		
I ↔ R		
01	R	jo unë po t'thome se unë jam shëtit e jam kon atje – për –
		(no I am saying I have been around and I was there – for –)
02		më ka rasti që të ngrihem q'aty –
		(I had the chance to go up there –)
03	I	jo uh – të rrethit të deçanit katundet
		(no uh – [tell me about] deçan county, the villages)
04	R	t'i thashë – këvralla – elebi – s'jam marrë me atë punë unë veç –
		(I told you: këvralla – elebi – I didn't just walk around but –)
05		(xx) në postë jam – arrë me –
→		(once in the post office I dealt with –)
I ↔ C		
06	I	=he doesn't know.

participants, keeping each informed of the other's general drift. In the material under study here, this role is boosted by the interpreter's power to silence one of the other speakers (that is, the asylum-seeker) by simply ceasing to translate and selecting the caseworker as next speaker (see Table 8.6).

In the case above, as soon as the asylum-seeker begins a story (line 5), the interpreter quickly overlaps and interrupts him by switching to English and directly addressing the caseworker, producing a realignment in the participation framework. Moreover, the interpreter does not limit himself to addressing the caseworker, but uses this opportunity to assess the communicative performance of the asylum- seeker (line 6). This behaviour on the part of the interpreter points to his role as 'interpreter-judge' – a label devised by Davidson (2000) in his study of interpreters in medical encounters: instead of serving as an advocate for interpreted asylum-seekers, the interpreter acts as an informational gatekeeper, assuring a smooth interactional routine while maintaining a role of prominence in the exchange. His interpreting competence allows him not only to control the flow of the interaction but also to pass judgement on the asylum-seeker being interviewed.

The next case, a stringent interrogation of a young woman claiming to have been attacked by Serbian soldiers, clearly shows the interpreter's personal involvement in determining the asylum-seeker's credibility. Here again, as soon as the asylum-seeker attempts to initiate a story involving Serbian policemen, the interpreter stops her by asking a fact-seeking question regarding their uniforms (see Table 8.7).

Table 8.7
02/07/00

R = young woman		
I ↔ R		
01	I	çfarë uniforme kanë pasë? (What was their uniform?)
02	R	kur na – (when we –)
03	I	çfarë ngjyre kanë pasë? (What colour?)
04	R	Ngjyrë – unë kur jam ardhë vetëm për shqipni kam pa ma së shumti serb – (color – while coming to Albania I saw mostly Serbians –)
05		ata ishin me ngjyrën – qashù ngjyrë ushtarake – (they had the colour – a military colour, like this)
06	I	çfarë? (which?)
07	R	sikur ajo ngjyra [points to green sweater] (like that colour)
08	I	kjo? [points to green sweater] (this one?)
09	R	e si ajo – (yes like that –)
I ↔ C		
10	I	this kind of colour [points to green sweater]
11		the uniform – uniform
12	C	uh uh – serbian force/
13	I	serbian police
14	C	uh uh
R ↔ I ↔ C		
15	R	edhe me maska në kry – (and with masks on their heads)
16	I	and with some masks=
17	R	=ne na kanë vjedh- kur kemi ardhè këndej na kanë vjedhé= (they robbed us – when we came here they robbed us=)
18	I	=but is not true

After having forced the young woman to identify the colour of Serbian police uniforms (lines 1–9), the interpreter dismisses the case as a false claim (Serbian police uniforms, he knows, are black). He quickly loses interest in this case and ends up declining to translate the asylum-seeker's last turn (line 17), offering instead his assessment of the mendacity of the interviewee (line 18).

Against the procedure

Most of the asylum-seekers in Tirana resented the UNHCR procedure, finding it a demeaning and final trauma in their already traumatic adjustment to life as a refugee. They were particularly shocked by the implicit lack of trust underlying the registration interview. Moreover, the apparent callousness with which they were asked to recall toponyms of an area severely damaged by war made a deep impression on them. The refugees' perceptions of the lack of trust and callousness of the UN officers gave rise to the most common complaint about the interview process: its utter disregard for refugees as human beings.

This perceived lack of interest for refugees as human beings features prominently in the next case examined here, the clamorous and at times quite emotional outburst of a man in his forties, well-known in the UNHCR offices for his self-appointed role as protector of refugee rights. This 'procurator' (P), a 'certified' Kosovar refugee himself, had taken up the cause of an elderly couple denied refugee status because they failed to provide any factual information linking them to Kosovo. After having learned from the couple about the denial, he burst with them into the UN office demanding an explanation for the dismissal of their case (see Table 8.8).

The UNHCR caseworker's response to the procurator's outburst is typical of bureaucrats trying to shield their work from criticism: she appeals to a higher form of authority, in this case the 'procedure' (which the interpreter promptly translates, line 1) of establishing a link to Kosovo through detailed questions (line 9). By citing an abstract, impersonal principle, the caseworker is trying to dilute responsibility for

Table 8.8
31/01/00

I ↔ P		
01	I	ashtu- sipas procedurës – (so – according to the procedure)
02	P	po sipas procedurës – PERSE – PERSE? – (according to procedure – WHY – WHY –)
03		DUHET ME DITE PERSE ARESYEN UNE (I HAVE TO KNOW THE REASON)
04		procedurën PO e LEXOJ – PO PSE? – (I READ THE procedure – BUT WHY?)
I ↔ C		
05	C	Ok – if he (xxx)
06	I	he say why –
07		I follow the procedure and at the end
08		they are not resulted to be kosovars – then why? – why?
09	C	because we cannot find their link with kosovo

I ↔ C ↔ P

10	I	sepse nuk mund të gjejmë lidhjen e tyre që kanë me kosovën/ (because we can't find the link they have with kosovo/)
11	P	po more – po more – po kjo është e palogjikshme – (yes sir – yes sir – this is illogical)
12	I	it's – it's illogic – they are kosovars
13	P	po – po – kein logic hier – wie verstahen/ (ok ok, there's no logic here, understand?)
14		keine logik (no logic)
15		(..)
16		po – keine logik – (right, no logic)
17		po kjo s'ka një logjikë mre burrë – (but this is illogical man)
18		qysh bohet – po këto nuk janë buburreca mor – (how can that be – they are not fleas –)
19		janë dy njerëz të thjesht – t'vjetër – (they are simple people, simple, old)
20	C	if they are (xxx)
21	P	bitte?
22	C	i think – we have already told you
23	I	ne iu thamë – (we told them)
24	C	what we can tell you?
25	I	çka mund t'ju themi? (what can we tell you?)
26	P	mor në rregull – atëhere thuj që ne jemi të pakënaqur – (well all right – then tell her we are not satisfied –)
27		që kundërvenia juaj nuk ka logjikë (that her way of confronting [refugees] is illogical)
28	I	we are not satisfactory
29	C	Yes
30		(..)
31	C	but I have to work up here –
32	P	Përgjegjësinë – KUSH E MERR PËRGJEGJËSINË – (responsibility – WHO HAS THE RESPONSIBILITY?)
33	I	ajo thotë kam punë të tjera thotë – (she says I have other work to do she says)
34	C	so please go to OFR
35	P	në rregull – thuj – thuj – ne nuk e meritojmë këtë mënyrë – (all right – tell her – tell her – we don't deserve this attitude)
36	I	we are not deserving to be treated like this
37	P	und I say you goodbye

[P storms out of the office]

her own decision (on the concept of responsibility in verbal exchanges, see Hill and Irvine 1992).

This strategy is countered by the procurator's claim that the procedure is illogical (line 11, reinforced in his next turn by code-switching to very rudimentary German, 'keine logik') and does not allow for a humane treatment of the asylum-seeker (lines 18–19: 'they are not fleas/they are simple, old people'). The appeal to necessary procedural steps is interpreted as evidence that the caseworker has an 'attitude problem' (line 35), and that she turns a request for help into an 'illogical way of confronting [refugees]' (line 27). Any attempt at establishing rapport between caseworkers and asylum-seekers is clearly compromised.

The perceived disregard for the humanity of refugees is again displayed in the final case examined here, an interview with a Kosovar lawyer (one of the few educated individuals whom I observed undergoing the procedure). After having described (correctly) the toponymy of the area around Prishtina (Kosovo's main city), the lawyer objects vigorously to the UNHCR line of questioning (see Table 8.9).

Table 8.9
03/05/00

I ↔ R		
01	R	kështu që ndihem shumë i ofendum (well, I feel very offended)
02	I	për çka? (what for?)
03	R	për pyetjet rreth prishtinës për fshatrat e ma tjerat – (for the questions about Prishtina and villages and so on)
04		kam marrë me qindra njerëz/ (I sheltered many people in my house)
I ↔ C		
05	I	and I – I feel that uh – my feelings is – is that
06		I am like offenced – offenced –
07	C	uh uh
08	I	from this – kind of questions
09	C	uh uh
10	I	you know – because you are not believing to my words
I ↔ C ↔ R		
11	R	Uh – më fal – jam ofendum – (excuse me but I'm offended)
12	I	yes he says I'm offenced
13	R	jam i vetmi avokat këtu që kam qenë (xxx) (I am the only lawyer here that has been xxx)
14	I	because I am a lawyer –
15	R	në kosovë – i vetmi avokat jam që jam i akuzum/ (in kosovo – the only lawyer who's been accused)
16	I	and he:: was charged in kosovo
16	R	baza e akuzes është= se i kam = (the charge is I had)
17	C	=uh sorry sir=

18		I'm sorry sir but we have a procedure
19		we believe you but we follow procedure
20		(. .)
21	R	ska problem
		(well . . . no problem)

This exchange features not only the caseworker's ready invocation of 'procedure' to avoid personal responsibility for her questions, but also the interpreter's awareness of the UNHCR office's underlying mistrust of asylum-seekers.

When the lawyer/refugee vents his displeasure with the interview and tries to recount his experience with political dissent before the war (line 4), the interpreter quickly identifies for the caseworker the basic issue behind the lawyer's displeasure: the lack of trust (line 10). While other refugees made this point explicitly, the issue of trust does not come to the foreground in the lawyer/refugee's complaint. He seems mainly interested in telling his story, rather than complaining about the lack of trust. Nevertheless, his second attempt to begin a narrative is cut short by the intervention of the caseworker, again with an appeal to the need 'to follow procedure' (line 19).

By appealing again to procedure, the caseworker tries to minimize responsibility for her own questions, and their underlying implication of mistrust. The issue, as implied by the caseworker, is not suspicion of the present interviewee, but a more formal principle of equal treatment for everybody which, as in any institutional setting, is guaranteed through universally applied procedural means.

It is interesting to note that both the caseworker's and the interpreter's responses prevent the refugee from telling his story of political dissent that started well before the war. Twice silenced, by the end this interviewee can only give up on his narrative, and after a pregnant pause (line 20), acknowledge the authority of the UNHCR office over the interview process.

Conclusion

> Refugees should not be seen solely as a burden. Without underestimating the humanitarian and security issues related to the presence of large refugee populations, it must be recognized that refugees are not merely the beneficiaries of humanitarian aid. They can make positive contributions. Rather than marginalizing refugees, our challenge is to find ways of empowering them, so that they can contribute to our societies. We must ensure respect for the individual dignity and worth of each and every refugee. (Ruud Lubbers, United Nations High Commissioner for Refugees, in a speech to the UNHCR headquarters in Geneva, December 12, 2001)

Why should we care that asylum-seekers in Albania were systematically denied the chance to tell their stories in the UNHCR registration procedure? After all, most people applying for refugee status have endured experiences far more traumatic than the interviews examined above.

The UNHCR in Tirana made it a practice to discourage the refugees from sharing narratives. But if it wanted to do so, it should have clearly spelled out its reasons to the interviewee, to allow them to make sense of the proceedings.

Storytelling is precisely one of the practices refugees have for making sense of their experience, by exploring traumatic events in front of an audience and hearing comforting responses. Refugees use storytelling to locate themselves in a specific space and time, countering on the symbolic plane the material dislocation they have had to endure. By denying asylum-seekers the opportunity to tell their stories, the UNHCR office may have succeeded in saving time on interviews and avoiding the persuasive force of narratives, but this policy carried hidden costs for both itself and the refugees: the agency lost credibility as an advocate for displaced people and the refugees lost the opportunity to use the interview as the first step in their road to recovery.

Through its 'procedure', the UNHCR may have caught some bogus applicants, but in so doing it may have seriously jeopardized its relationship with 'true' refugees. By abruptly launching a barrage of questions without proper framing, that is, without giving the interviewees any explanation about why they were being asked to recite Kosovar toponyms or why they were not allowed to engage in storytelling, the UNHCR turned a neutral conduit (the interview) into an absurdist (and at times antagonistic) exchange. With their future on the line, the refugees were subjected to judiciary techniques that made very little sense to them, except that they knew that a wrong answer could lead to a denial of their application.

The abrupt switch to factual questions very soon into the interview did more than just signal to all asylum-seekers that they were 'suspects' in the eyes of the UNHCR and that their stories were irrelevant: it disempowered them, turning them into automatons asked to recite toponymic lists. Moreover, deprived of a clear explanation of the proceedings, the refugees left the UNHCR office baffled and frustrated. In other words, by being reduced to automatons and kept in the dark about the UNHCR's rationale for handling these encounters, they were denied their agency.

If the UNHCR is sincerely concerned with 'finding ways of empowering' the refugees and ensuring 'respect for their dignity' (in the words of its High Commissioner quoted above), its officers need to do a better job of explaining their methods and procedures to people seeking their help. In Tirana such an explanation was never properly offered, and as a result the UNHCR came to be perceived by refugees as an institutional, insensitive body of bureaucrats, disinterested in their agency and their suffering.

Note

1   The transcripts identify the date of the interview, the gender and age of the refugee, and the primary axis of conversation (caseworker-interpreter: C ↔ I, interpreter-refugee, I ↔ R, or multi-party C ↔ I ↔ R). The interpreters' English turns are left in their original form. I use the following transcription conventions:

=	latching turns	=/=	overlapping turns	CAPS	loudness
(text?)	difficult to hear	(xxx)	impossible to hear		

Chapter 9

Brad Davidson

THE INTERPRETER AS INSTITUTIONAL GATEKEEPER: THE SOCIAL-LINGUISTIC ROLE OF INTERPRETERS IN SPANISH-ENGLISH MEDICAL DISCOURSE

EDITOR'S INTRODUCTION

> Interpreters frequently engaged in furthering the physician's perceived agenda for the discourse. This happened, not only because of time pressures, but because hospital based interpreters are, in the end, members of the hospital community where they work and interact daily; they are institutional insiders, and ally themselves as such.

DAVIDSON'S STUDY AND DETAILED analyses provide further examples of the way in which interpreters tend to align themselves with institutions and to strengthen institutional voice, often at the expense of the voices of other participants, in this case the patients. The institutional setting in this case, US public and private hospitals, is less conflictual than that examined by Jacquemet, but Davidson nevertheless identifies the same consistent attempt by interpreters to keep patients 'on track', in the interest of fulfilling institutional agendas.

Time pressures and other factors create an institutional culture in which patients are made aware, from the minute they enter the medical facility and until they leave it, that their time is less valuable than that of the physician and other medical staff. 'Patients who used interpreters had this message delivered in even stronger terms', according to Davidson. Far from acting as 'advocates' for vulnerable patients, many of them recent immigrants from the Third World, interpreters perform the role of informational gatekeepers whose main priority is to keep the interview 'on track' and the physician on schedule. To this end, they often interpret selectively, and often offer their own answers to patients' questions without the physician necessarily being aware of it (thus acting as covert co-diagnosticians). Davidson explains this by arguing that direct questions have been found to pose a threat to the physician's authority within the medical interview, and hence that 'the interpreters' habit of *answering* questions might be viewed as a move to insulate the physician, and thus the institution of the clinic, from patient challenges to its authority'.

While accepting that interpreters can never act as conduits or mere echoes, as is some-times expected of them, Davidson insists that they can nevertheless interpret evenly, and that they do not have to work as an extra gatekeeping layer in medical settings. Interpreters' wholesale alignment with the institution 'is both unethical and a truly poor form of interpre-tive practice', and the gap between the 'official' conceptualization of their role as conduits and their actual, covert functioning as co-diagnosticians creates a vacuum of responsibility that has a negative impact on the provision of medical care. The slippage between what they are officially expected or asked to do and what they actually do allows the practice to continue unmonitored and unevaluated.

Follow-up questions for discussion

- Davidson notes that there is 'considerable slippage . . . between how the tasks that hospital personnel set for interpreters are believed to work in practice, and the actual functions and linguistic actions that interpreters perform'. This point has been made by other scholars of interpreting, most notably Wadensjö (1998) and Diriker (2004), in relation to a variety of settings (conference, court, medical, business, etc.). How and why does this slippage arise, in your view? Is it a question of unreasonable expectations on the part of other participants, of inadequate performance on the part of interpreters, a combination of both, or are there other factors that complicate interpreter-mediated encounters and that require more reflexivity on the part of both interpreters and those who rely on their services?

- Bolden (2000:395) suggests that most physicians, at least in western countries, adopt what she refers to as the 'voice of medicine', which 'is characterized by its focus on decontextualized descriptions of reality in terms of its objective features', and that medical interpreters orient themselves to this institutional voice. This results in a con-flict between two voices: the 'voice of medicine' and the 'voice of the lifeworld', the latter referring to 'patients' narrative, contextualized, subjective accounts, especially those presenting the causally contingent nature of the symptoms' experienced by the patient (ibid.:413). How does this observation relate to both Davidson's and Jacquemet's analyses in terms of the role played by interpreters in preventing narrative performance, and why should various institutions (not only medical ones) wish to suppress the 'voice of the lifeworld' as Bolden calls it?

- As opposed to the kind of institutional alliance exemplified in this study, some scholars and practitioners have called on interpreters to adopt the perspective of the patients – or less empowered participants in general – and to function as their advocate and ally. McKee (2004:124), however, critiques this recommendation in the context of interpret-ing for the Deaf community in New Zealand, arguing that such advocacy is 'potentially paternalistic and counterproductive to developing greater autonomy in the long run'. Consider the practical and ethical merits and shortcomings of each position.

Recommended further reading

Angelelli, Claudia (2004) *Re-visiting the Role of the Interpreter: A Study of Conference, Court and Medical Interpreters in Canada, Mexico and the United States*, Amsterdam & Philadelphia: John Benjamins.

Beaton, Morven (2007) 'Interpreted Ideologies in Institutional Discourse: The Case of the European Parliament', *The Translator* 13(2): 271–96.

Bolden, Galina B. (2000) 'Toward Understanding Practices of Medical Interpreting: Interpreters' Involvement in History Taking', *Discourse Studies* 2(4): 387–419.

Merlini, Raffaela and Roberta Favaron (2005) 'Examining the "Voice of Interpreting" in Speech Pathology', *Interpreting* 7(2): 263–302.

Wadensjö, Cecilia (1998) *Interpreting as Interaction*, London & New York: Longman.

'Interpreters are the most powerful people in a medical conversation.'

Head of Interpreting Services at a major private U.S. hospital, May 1999.

IN THIS ARTICLE, I EXAMINE THE linguistic and social roles played by hospital-based interpreters in medical discourse. The need for interpreters has become a fact of contemporary medical practice; one study of 83 US public and private hospitals found that 11 percent of all patients required the services of an interpreter (Ginsberg et al. 1995). Since Shuy (1976), a growing number of researchers has become interested in close linguistic analyses of medical discourse, but very little has been said to date about the linguistic and social role of the interpreter in cross-linguistic medical discourses. Yet these encounters are common, and it is the interpreter, the only conversational participant with the ability to follow both sides of the cross-linguistic discourse, who is uniquely positioned within these discourses to control the flow of information necessary for the achievement of the participants' medical and social goals.

In addition, in an era of massive population movements, the increase in number and frequency of cross-linguistic medical encounters can also be viewed as an increase in an institutional form of cross-cultural encounter (Blackhall et al. 1995, Erzinger 1991, Marcos and Trujillo 1984, Martinez et al. 1985, Phillips et al. 1996, Thamkins 1995), with the interpreter acting as the point of negotiation and exchange between the social contexts inhabited by the physician and the patient (Davidson 1998, 1999, Kaufert and Koolage 1984). In this article, then, I explore the contextually and historically situated nature and role of the interpreter within these socio-medical interactions.

That there *is* a social component to hospital interpreting is itself a reasonably uncontroversial, but largely unstudied, hypothesis. Hospital administrators and physicians alike insist that it is both possible for, and the duty of, medical interpreters to interpret without adding or subtracting meaningfully from the content and intentions, and thus the effects, of utterances (to the degree to which she does do so, she is considered incompetent). The problem lies in that most, if not all, serious analyses of interpretation acknowledge that perfection in interpretation is unattainable. At the very least, differences in linguistic form lead, inevitably, to differences in meaning and reception, however small, and semantically 'identical' utterances in different languages vary greatly in their social and contextual evaluation by speakers (Bendix 1988, Cartellieri 1983). In addition, the time constraints placed on interpreters force them, in the cases I observed, to do more than simply change the nuances of utterances: they edit, and in some cases delete wholesale, conversational offerings on a regular basis. There is considerable slippage, then, between how the tasks that hospital personnel set for interpreters are believed to work in practice, and the actual functions and linguistic actions that interpreters perform.

The question remains as to what are the patterned ways in which the interpreter influences the discourses she interprets through these small, and in some cases not-so-small, changes in linguistic form; what is the 'interpretive habit' of the socially positioned agents known as 'interpreters' in a typical medical encounter, and how do they conceive of their role in achieving conversational goals? Interpreters interpret *for a reason*, because there is some communicative or social goal that needs to be met; they do not simply wander upon two speakers shouting at each other in different languages and offer their services. From this point of view, the measure of the interpreter's success may not be an abstract count of how 'accurate' they are, but rather the degree to which she allows, through her actions, the speakers first to negotiate and then to achieve their goals for the speech event in question.

The mediated negotiation of conversational goals, however, is no trivial matter; such goals are determined, for each conversational participant, by historical contexts that frequently preclude any analysis of social equality between the primary speakers. Many researchers have already noted that even same-language medical discourse can be viewed as a form of interaction between unequals, in which patients, as clients of the institution of the hospital clinic, find it difficult to establish a voice outside of the expected parameters of medical practice (Mishler 1984, Waitzkin 1991, West 1984, Wodak 1996). In the data examined in this article, the addition of a conversational mediator (the interpreter) increases tremendously the patient's difficulty in making herself, or her agenda for the discourse, heard. The fact that the patients for whom these interpreters are speaking are recent immigrants, mostly from the Third World, highlights the fact that what interpreters are mediating in hospital discourse is not only the diagnosis and care of patients, but also a form of cross-cultural encounter between immigrants and agents of the institutions of the First World; it is these agents who both provide services to these immigrants while simultaneously educating them as to their role within the modern nation-state (cf. Gupta and Ferguson 1997).

Background

Historically, most analyses of interpretation have been based on an oral model of *translation*, which has meant that most analyses of interpretation have focused on *monologues*. Students of discourse have rarely focused their attention squarely on interpretation itself, instead producing in passing a tacit model of discourse interpretation as a sequence of discrete linguistic conversions of isolated utterances. Interpreters are seen as conduits, not conversational participants. For example, Hymes (1972), in his famous SPEAKING mnemonic, lists the interpreter's role as that of 'spokesman' or 'sender', but not as a 'source' or 'addresser'; similarly Goffman (1981) calls the interpreter an 'animator', or one who makes noises, but not an 'author' or 'principal', one to whom the meaning of utterances can be attributed (see also Clark 1992, 1996).

But in interpreting a monologue one does not need to worry about turn-sequence, the rights of hearers to become speakers, or even the level at which the primary speaker is being understood by the audience; monologues involve one-way transmission, and the audience is largely unable to respond or to act in setting the agenda for what will be discussed. However, the act of oral interpretation of *discourse* is very different (cf. Roy 1999); it must take into account all of these factors, but it is often reduced, in passing analyses, as the interpreter's obligation to be a perfect echo of the primary interlocutors.

The interpreter as conversational participant

Recently, however, students of language and discourse have turned their attention to the nature and, to some degree, consequences of the interpreter's role as an historical agent. This has led to a number of works that examine the role of the interpreter or translator as linguistic and social intermediary (Bassnet and Trivedi 1999, von Flotow 1997, Hatim 1997, Hatim and Mason 1989, Rafael 1993, Roy 1999, Snell-Hornby 1988, Venuti 1998b, Wadensjö 1998). All of these works share the common analysis that interpreters or translators, far from 'merely' converting and conveying the words of others, are centrally employed in the work of mediating the achievement of conversational or interactional goals, and that to a large degree responsibility for the achievement of these goals lies squarely with the interpreter herself. Interpreters do not merely convey messages; they shape and, in some very real sense, create those messages in the name of those for whom they speak. The context of the interpreted speech event itself has also received considerable attention, and the influences of the social and historical facts surrounding an interpreted speech event are seen to influence greatly the interpreter's choices and the resulting outcomes of the interaction (cf. Rafael 1993).

Institutions and the mediation of post-colonial discourses

One significant factor influencing the manner and effects of interpretation is the location of interpreted speech events within a historical-political timeline. With the exception of business or diplomatic interactions, the majority of interpreted discourses in the US take place within the context of state-sponsored or -run institutions (the hospitals, schools, and judicial/legal system), between agents of those First World institutions and the Third World immigrants who require or are subjugated to the services provided. Institutional discourse is defined, in large part, by the fact that institutionally defined goals and the institutionally reinforced habits for achieving them provide clear signposts for how communication should, and does, proceed, at least to those speakers familiar with the institution in question (Bourdieu 1977, Cicourel 1983, van Dijk 1993, Gupta and Ferguson 1997, Schegloff 1992, Wodak 1996, inter alia).

These institutional interactions thus stretch the notion of 'neutrality' in interpretation to the limit, as interpreters 'are *always* placed in this contested arena between being providers of a service and being agents of authority and control' (Candlin, in the introduction to Wadensjö 1998:xvii; emphasis in the original). Wadensjö writes:

> As do all professionalized intermediaries, interpreters work at providing a particular *service*. Simultaneously, they – of necessity – exercise a certain *control*. Obviously there is a potential conflict between the service and the control aspects, which sometimes surfaces in dilemmas reported in the literature on institutional communication. It largely remains to be investigated how this conflict is handled in institutional interpreter-mediated talk, where the gatekeeping is, in effect, doubled. (1998:68–69, emphasis in the original)

Institutional interpretation has, then, a potentially disruptive social component that cannot be ignored.

There have been several excellent studies of interpreted courtroom discourse, all of which have pointed to the legal habit of selecting, privileging and codifying certain utterances as 'facts' (Scheppele 1989) as being the dominant factor in determining how interpreters are allowed, and not allowed, to interpret (Berk-Seligson 1990, Edwards 1995, Hewitt 1995, Mikkelson 1998). In this article, I examine the 'interpretive habits' of hospital interpreters through a close analysis of their actions within the structured speech event known to physicians as the medical interview; these habits are influenced directly by both the medical habit of differential diagnosis and the institutional reality of chronic time shortages in contemporary clinical practice.

Medical discourse and medical interpretation

There have been numerous, detailed studies of physician-patient discourse, focusing primarily on the difficulties patients and physicians have in communicating effectively with each other (Ainsworth Vaughn 1994, Cicourel 1983, Frankel 1990, Hein and Wodak 1987, Mishler 1984, Robins and Wolf 1988, Sarangi and Stembrouk 1996, Waitzkin 1983, 1991, West 1984, West and Frankel 1991, Wodak 1996, inter alia). Most of these analyses centre on one type of medical discourse, the named speech event 'medical interview'; this is a structured, practised interaction between the physician and the patient, taught in medical schools, designed to quickly elicit the patient's complaint(s) so that they may be diagnosed and treated. Medical interviews are thus a type of verbal and physical investigation, a matching of unorganized experiences against familiar patterns and processes of human vulnerability to disease. The overt, elaborated goals of the medical interview are: (1) from the data provided, determine what, if anything, is wrong with the patient; (2) elaborate a plan of treatment for that ailment; and (3) convince the patient of the validity of the diagnosis so that treatment will be followed. However, the elicitation of medical 'facts', or from another point of view the creation of medical facts through medical practice, is heavily influenced by a social evaluation of the meaning and importance of whatever facts are thus uncovered or created (Foucault 1963, Waitzkin 1991); the practice of medicine, like the practice of interpreting, has a social dimension that cannot be ignored.

Diagnosis is, then, an interpretive process in which the patient's physical and verbal data is passed, by physicians, through a grid of medical meanings (biological and social) and re-analyzed, so that 'irrelevant' input from the patient may be excluded and the story of the disease constructed (Foucault 1963, Kleinman 1988, Mishler 1984). Indeed, this is the unmarked use of the word 'interpreting' in medical contexts; when I first told the physicians at the General Medical Clinic I would be conducting a study of interpreting, they universally assumed that I meant a study of the ways in which physical and verbal input are re-read as signs and symptoms of disease processes.

In fact, very little has been said about the concrete forms or effects of interpretation of medical discourse. There are exceptions to this trend (Bendix 1988, Erzinger 1991, Marcos and Trujillo 1984, Martinez et al. 1985, Weaver 1982), but the majority of literature written about medical interpretation has come from two camps: physicians who use interpreters (Baker et al. 1996, 1998, David and Rhee 1998, Ebden et al. 1988, Putsch 1985, Vasquez and Javier 1991, Woloshin et al. 1995), and interpreters themselves (Haffner 1992, Juhel 1982, Kaufert and Koolage 1984). The physicians generally lament the difficulties of diagnosing patients, establishing a clinical relationship, or providing adequate care to patients when using an interpreter; the interpreters tend to focus on their role as 'linguistic ambassadors' for the patient, a stance in favour of overt 'advocacy' interpretation. Neither group, however, rests their arguments on analyses that explore exactly *how*, in discourse, interpreters advocate or obfuscate the conversational process.

It is not surprising that physicians have taken a recent interest in interpretation: it would be hard to imagine a physician in practice or training today who has not had to use an interpreter at least once to converse with a patient. At Riverview General Hospital, the large, public county hospital in Northern California where I conducted my research, the recent increase in interpretation is readily apparent in Table 9.1. While Riverview may be unusual in the degree to which multilingualism pervades everyday life, it is typical in the way that the number of patients who need interpreters has increased in the last two decades. It is also typical in that Spanish is both the most prevalent non-English language, and in that it will remain so for the foreseeable future (cf. Berk-Seligson 1990). For this reason, in addition to the fact of my own bilingual abilities in English and Spanish, Spanish language visits were chosen as the subject of study.

Methods and data

In the Spring and Summer of 1996, I conducted fieldwork at Riverview General Hospital's General Medicine Clinic (GMC), the outpatient unit of the internal medicine division of the hospital. The patients there were undergoing treatment for a variety of long-term illnesses, ranging from chronic back pain to stroke rehabilitation to diabetes to congestive heart failure; their physicians were also the primary care physicians within the hospital hierarchy, meaning that patient referrals to other specialist physicians and clinics were orchestrated by these internists.

Data collection centered on the ways in which hospital-based interpreters were utilized within the clinic, how their presence during medical interviews helped to shape the course and content of those interviews, and how they mediated the potential clash of goals between the achievement of the overt institutional goals of diagnosis and treatment that are set by standard medical practice, and the not-necessarily identical goals held by the patients. I approached the study as a political, social, and linguistic enterprise, with an eye towards answering the following questions:

- What is the role of the interpreter within the goal-oriented, learned form of interaction known as the 'medical interview'?
- What is the 'interpretive habit', and how does one engage in the practice of interpreting?
- If interpreters are *not* neutral, do they challenge the authority of the 'physician-judge' (cf. Foucault 1979), and act as patient 'ambassadors' or 'advocates' (as

Table 9.1 Riverview General Hospital patient demographics, by year

Year	# of patients seen	# of patients requesting interpreter	% of total patient population
1981	67,000	14,000	21
1993	133,000	53,000	40

Spanish-language visits in 1993: 34,000 (25% of all visits)

Haffner 1992, Juhel 1982, and Kaufert and Koolage 1984 suggest); or do they reinforce the institutional authority of the physician and the health-care establishment, and should we create a model for the 'interpreter-judge'? (cf. Foucault 1979)

In order to answer these questions, I observed both the interpreted medical interview itself, and the institutional context that supported and gave meaning to this speech event. Every physician and interpreter asked, and almost every patient, agreed to participate in the study, most of them enthusiastically. It was typical for patients, especially patients waiting for an interpreter to arrive, to tell me that they thought it was an excellent idea for someone to study how physicians talked to patients, largely because they thought it wasn't very well at all.

The interpreters who form the focus of this article were professional in the sense that they were paid employees of the hospital; none, however, had any formal degree in interpretation or translation, and in this they appeared to be quite typical of all of the hospital interpreters I have observed or spoken with in Northern California. The specifics of training are different from hospital to hospital in the San Francisco Bay Area, but in general they constitute nothing more than a period of time following an interpreter on her daily rounds, an assurance that the interpreter in question is actually bilingual in the relevant languages, and paperwork documenting that the interpreter is informed (somewhat) about issues of patient confidentiality. In this sense Riverview General was 'normal' – interpreters were neither trained extensively nor supported institutionally, and they performed their work in an *ad hoc* vacuum of accountability; the hospital monitored if they were present at a certain number of physician–patient encounters, but expressed virtually no interest in determining what they actually *did* in these encounters.

The data reported on here come from observations of over one hundred patient visits, 50 of which were both observed and audiotaped. For those interactions that were taped, all participants were requested to fill out a questionnaire, and most were interviewed, at the end of the visit. The audiotaped encounters included visits with both hospital-based staff and family members acting as interpreters, and also mono-lingual interviews conducted all in English or all in Spanish with no interpreter. There was a total of 10 Spanish-English, professionally interpreted medical interviews taped. These 10 visits were matched with 10 English-English visits, as closely as possible, for similarity of patient, physician and interpreter age, race, religion and ethnicity, and for nature of the interaction (first time visit, routine check-up) and the patients' illnesses (diabetes, high blood pressure, etc.). The data presented here, then, represent an exhaustive accounting of the data collected on hospital-based interpreters specific-ally. The analyses of linguistic data below are drawn from the set of 20 fully tran-scribed medical interviews, and from the ethnographic and survey data collected on the clinic as a whole.

The interpreter in medical interviews

During the study at Riverview, one factor stood out as being overwhelmingly con-textually salient: the scarcity of time in modern medical institutions. The amount of time patients spent waiting for their physician, the even longer amounts of time spent waiting for interpreters, and the brevity of the physician–patient–interpreter encounter, added to the time constraints on modern medical practice in general, seemed to be overriding factors in how interpreted medical interactions took place. In myriad ways, all patients were shown that, from the minute they entered the clinic until the minute they left, their time was not as valuable as that of the physician, or of any other member of the clinic (cf. Elliot 1999). Patients who used interpreters had this message delivered in even stronger terms. Often they were left alone in window-less examining rooms, sometimes for up to an hour, while they waited for the interpreter to arrive. In such cases the physicians would not wait, but rather would move on to the next patient.

The interpreter as co-interviewer

One common scenario for interpreted medical interviews at Riverview was, then, that the interpreter would arrive while the physician was busy elsewhere, and she would begin some form of interaction with the patient before the physician arrived. This had two effects. The first was that, from the physician's point of view, the process of elaborating a Chief Complaint (a named entity in medical practice, usually written in chart notes as the abbreviated 'CC') from the patient was (apparently) simplified; the interpreter might greet the physician at the door of the examining room with an announcement of whatever the patient had specified as his or her problem, as in Excerpt 1, where 69 lines of transcript have occurred before the physician enters the room. The second effect was, however, that the interpreter thus set the focus of the initiation of the interview, and would occasionally go so far as to conduct the initial portions of the interview herself (see Excerpt 1).

It is impossible, in this stretch of text, to construe what the interpreter is doing as 'merely' conveying information. She is essentially running the interview, not inter-preting sequences of utterances. She asks the questions, and begins the physical exam; her only interaction with the doctor is a request to help her find a stool for the patient to elevate his foot, and at line 99 the beginning of a recapitulation to the physician of what was said in his absence. In taking charge of the interview, she is preventing a potential initial greeting phase between the physician and patient, and nowhere does she ask the patient, nor allow the physician to ask the patient, what exactly has brought him to the clinic today. Note that in line 70, the patient expresses an interest in hearing what his physician has to say about his problem, but it is the interpreter with whom he converses.

The interpreter has not, however, misunderstood the patient's earlier expressions of concern over his foot, which is, as becomes clear throughout the interview, his true Chief Complaint; nor does the physician seem concerned that the interpreter is conducting the preliminary physical exam. The only problem, then, is that the inter-preter has sacrificed completely the notion that the physician and the patient are participating, at this moment, in a conversation with each other.

The patient and the physician appear to understand that the interpreter is not interpreting, in the strict sense, but rather maintaining parallel and related conversa-tions that inform them, approximately, of the other's general verbal offerings. They frequently make it clear when they want the interpreter to actually interpret by telling her explicitly to do so. Excerpt 1 is taken up, below, a little further along in the interview.

The interpreter is still not following a model of strict sequential interpretation: the only straightforward sequence of utterance–interpretation happens in lines 210–212. Even a request for interpretation may not be granted. In lines 201 and 210,

Excerpt 1 (from Visit 30):[i]

(Dr enters the room)

70	Pt	Anda, a ver que dice el doctor.
		Well, let's see what the doctor says.
71	Dr	Hi:!
72		how are you doing?
73	Int	Doctor, I was looking for something to put over there because he
74		wants to show you his:
75	(1.5 seconds)	
76		foot but I didn't find something.
77	Dr	Oh.
78		Let's see:=
79	Int	=One of those (xx)s, or.
80	Dr	Maybe he: re, no:
81	Int	Maybe in the (xx). ((banging noises – searching for a stool))
82	(2 seconds)	
83	Dr	Wouldn't surprise me.
84	(6 seconds)	
85	Int	At least we are not (xx).
86		Levante(te?) un poquito la pierna. (louder than previous English)
		Lift your foot a little bit.
87	Pt	Sí, sí, señora.
		Yes, yes, ma'am.
88		Ahora bien.
		Okay now.
89		[x]
90	Int	[¿Cuál] es el malo?
		[Which] is the bad one?
91	Pt	¿Mande?
		Excuse me?
92	Int	¿Cuál es el [enfermo?]
		Which is [the 'sick' (bad) one?]
93	Pt	[Éste.]
		[This one.]
94	Int	A ver,
		Let's see,
95		quitense el caletín y el [XXX] por favor.
		take off your sock and [XXX] please.
96		[(loud banging noise)]
97	Pt	Oh, no.
98	(2 seconds)	
99	Int	He says that, ah,
100		You explained to him the last time then ah, . . .

[i] []	overlapping turns	
=	simultaneous beginning of one speaker's turn/end of another's turn (latching)	
:	Lengthening	CAPS Loud
Italics	translation of Spanish	(text?) difficult to hear
(noise)	description of non-verbal noise	
(xx)	impossible to hear; each x is one syllable, if syllables can be discerned	
((text))	description of physical actions, or meta-commentary on discourse	

Excerpt 1 (from Visit 30), continued:

195	Int	He says he feels:
196		good except his foot,
197	(.5 seconds)	
198		ah: =
199	Dr	=can I see his other foot?
200	Int	A ver,
		Let's see,
201	Pt	Dígale que,
		Tell him that,
202	Int	Y, y it stops when, when,
203		it's worse, when he walks.
204	(3 seconds)	
205	Pt	Y yo, ya sí me siento bien.
		And I, now I feel good.
206	(2 seconds – Dr takes off Pt's sock and looks at other foot).	
207		Ah, (que esos?) no los pongo, si no los (pide?).
		Ah, (that these?) I won't wear these, if he doesn't (ask?).
208	Int	Oh my god, it's totally (xx) – (very softly, aside to Dr).
209	(1.5 seconds)	
210	Pt	Dígale que eso no me duele, eso es solo como una reventadita.
		Tell him that this doesn't hurt me, it's like a little eruption.
211	Int	He says that one is nothing, and it's like a little,
212		(xx?)
213	(3 seconds)	
214		¿Pero se acuerda que así le empezó el otro?
		But do you remember that the other one started this way?
215	Pt	Sí, así como está ése.
		Yes, just like this one is.
216		Que bien que Ud. se acuerde.
		How good that you remember.
217	Int	I mentioned that remember then the other one start the same way.
218	Dr	I know. ((e.g. that the other foot started the same way))
219	Int	And he said, yeah, that's good that you remembered that.

the patient expressly asks the interpreter to interpret his words by prefacing his statements with *dígale*, 'tell him', but the patient's subsequent offering after line 201, presumably the 'I feel good now' in line 205, is not interpreted. It is not only the patient who has his offerings left untranslated, however; line 199 from the physician is not put into words, either, although his request to 'see [the patient's] other foot' is fulfilled. Notice also that the interpreter, who knows the patient from past inter-actions, comments upon the state of the patient's foot as being the same way that the other foot started to have problems (line 214), a comment which elicits a response from the patient directed at her ('Ud.', line 216) and not the physician; only when this interaction, initiated by the interpreter herself, is completed does she recount what she has said to the physician.

The patient's problem is not minor: he is in danger of having his toes amputated as a result of complications from unmanaged diabetes. The physician knows this, the interpreter knows this; the one conversational participant who does not seem to grasp the severity of the problem is the patient himself, who at the end of the interview remains unconvinced by the physician's warnings that if his diet does not change he will lose, not only his toes, but eventually his feet as well. The patient manages to get a referral to the wound management clinic to have his feet cleaned, which was his initial goal; but if one of the institutional goals of a medical interview is to not only elaborate a diagnosis and plan of treatment, but also to convince the patient of the validity of the diagnosis and plan, this interview has failed in that the patient leaves completely unconvinced that his problems are as severe as the physician and interpreter tell him they are. It is not possible to say with certainty that this is the result of the interpreter's actions; what is clear, however, is that the patient's voice is significantly modified by having to speak through an interpreter, and that the interpreter is frequently speaking, not as an echo, but in her own voice.

Quantifiable patterns of interference in interpreted medical interviews

One could ask at this point, as did many of the physicians who took part in this study (acting perhaps as devil's advocates), what is the harm in the interpreter assisting the physician in conducting the medical interview, especially if time is short and it speeds the interview process along? The first response would be that nowhere is it stated that speed is the *primary* goal of a medical interview; these are institutional constraints, but they are universally decried as having a detrimental effect on the physician–patient experience. Time is scarce in hospitals today, however, and interpreters are conscious of their role as facilitator and editor; during one interaction (visit 11), after several minutes of conversation with the patient in the absence of the physician, the interpreter looked at me and said, 'you chose one that's hard to keep on track'. The patient had been providing a detailed history of the difficulty he had had at various clinics affiliated with Riverview General. The interpreter's statement made it clear that she felt this was extraneous information, and that it was her job to keep the patient on track, as measured against what *she* believed to be relevant information for a medical interview. It was not clear that the patient's narrative was, however, irrelevant; the 'Social History' relating to an illness is part of the routine medical interview, coded in patient charts under the heading 'SH'.

The consistent attempt to keep patients 'on track' led to a number of quantifiable phenomena in the discourse. Tables 9.2 and 9.3 show how patient-generated direct questions were dealt with in the two sets of interviews. For both sets of interviews, almost all of the direct questions asked were answered. However, for the patients using an interpreter over half (18/33) of all of the questions which were directed at the physician were answered by the interpreter, without the physician ever hearing the question. The significance of this pattern of short-circuiting question-and-answer sequences between patients and physicians is not only that patients are receiving answers from their interpreter and not their physician; it is also that physicians have no idea that their interpreted patients are asking questions at all, which increases the likelihood that these Hispanic patients will be seen as 'passive' (cf. Baker *et al.* 1998, Erzinger 1991) and also prevents the physician from following up on difficult questions or questions that display a deep misunderstanding, on the part of the patient, as to what the diagnosis or plan of treatment are.

Another possible analysis for this treatment of direct questions is that these questions pose a threat to the physician's authority within the medical interview (Ainsworth-Vaughn 1994). In medical interviews it is the physician, and not the patient, who typically asks the questions (Mishler 1984). We have already seen in Excerpt 1 that interpreters are themselves capable of producing spontaneous requests to patients, thus taking on the physician's right to ask questions; the interpreters' habit of *answering* questions might be viewed as a move to insulate the physician, and thus the institution of the clinic, from patient challenges to its authority. We will return to this issue below.

In a related vein, patients' physical complaints themselves, the *raison d'être* of the medical interview, are often lost in the conversational shuffle. Tables 9.2 and 9.3 show the number and content of identifiable patient complaints from two matched interviews, interviews 6 and 7. They have been chosen for detailed comparison because of the large number of similarities they share: both interviews took nearly the same time, and dealt with 'typical' patient complaints at the GMC – chronic discomforts that did not appear life-threatening and which were difficult to diagnose and subsequently treat. Both interviews took place on the same day, with the same physician, and the patients were roughly the same age. Both the English-speaking patient in visit 7 and the Spanish-speaking patient in visit 6 produced new complaints, in addition to a number of vaguely-defined and difficult to treat conditions that had been addressed in previous visits. The two visits were also representative in that, given roughly similar clinical scenarios, in comparison to the same-language visit the interpreted visit was marked, as were nearly all of the observed interpreted visits, by severe communicative difficulties. These were of a type and to a degree that far surpassed the 'normal' communicative difficulties encountered by same-language patients and reported in research on physician–patient discourse.

The complaints offered by the English-speaking patient were all addressed directly, in one form or another, and nearly all of them were diagnosed and treated; for the Spanish-speaking patient, however, most of his complaints were left undiagnosed and untreated, most significantly the one complaint that he is most concerned with (see Excerpt 2, in the next section below). This was due to one of three processes: to the physician not hearing the complaint because the interpreter didn't pass it along; to the physician hearing the complaint but not addressing it, leaving the interpreter

Table 9.2 Treatment of patient-generated direct questions in 10 same-language visits

	# of questions from patient	Answered by physician	Not answered by physician
Total	55	53	2

Table 9.3 Treatment of patient-generated direct questions in 10 interpreted visits

	# of questions from pt	Passed on to Dr	Not passed on to Dr	Answered by Dr	Answered by interp	Not answered
Total	33	15	18	12	17	4

Table 9.4 Complaints addressed and diagnosed in visits 6 and 7

	Diagnosis supplied	Treatment suggested
Complaints: visit 6, Spanish		
Vision (new)	No	No
Foot pain	No	No
Arm/hand pains	Yes	No
General pains	Yes	Yes
Mood	No	Yes
Complaints: visit 7, English		
Wrist pain (new)	No	Yes
Cough (allergy)	Yes	Yes
High blood pressure	Yes	Yes
Frequent urination (new)	Yes (possible diagnosis)	Yes
Prostate node (new)	Yes	Yes (urologic referral)

with nothing to say to the patient; or to the physician hearing and addressing the complaint, but the interpreter not passing the physician's commentary on to the patient. The majority of the patient's complaints, in visit 6, were left without a concrete or even partial diagnosis or plan of treatment. Notice also that the final diagnosis for most of the Spanish-speaking patient's complaints are general pains, which the physician sees as related to his 'mood'; his illnesses are considered psychosomatic, to a large degree, which is common for patients who speak Spanish (Erzinger 1991, Marcos and Trujillo 1984). The English-speaking patient, a recovering intravenous drug abuser, was no less depressed, but his complaints of physical discomfort were taken seriously enough by the physician to have them addressed individually and concretely. One of the most negative effects of interpretation at Riverview, in fact, is the tendency for physicians to see patients who can't speak for themselves, as a result of the conversational difficulties, as 'cranks' or patients who complain of phantom problems (Davidson 1998). What is left to examine is the role played by the interpreter in interview 6, to determine what part she played in thwarting the elaborated goals of diagnosis and care delivery.

The loss of patient complaints

In Excerpt 2 we see portions of the interview in visit 6, which took place between a Spanish-speaking male patient in his mid-40s, an English-speaking, male, Anglo physician in his mid-30s, and a Spanish-dominant, professional female interpreter in her mid-40s (a different interpreter from that in Excerpt 1). This is not the first visit between the patient and the physician, who have known each other for three years; the interpreter, too, knew the patient, as this was the 'third or fourth' time she had interpreted for him. The excerpt begins after the patient and the physician had already had a chance to interact, briefly, an interaction that I observed; the patient had enough English to say his 'eyes hurt', but he could say no more than this, at which point the physician decided to call the interpreter (why, after a 3-year clinical relationship, the physician decided to call the interpreter *after* trying to converse with the patient, remains unclear). The patient had been left waiting in the examining room for over 45 minutes, as the physician moved on to his next patient rather than wait for the interpreter to show up.

The excerpt begins, then, with the physician and the interpreter (and myself) arriving in the exam room to see the patient, who has at this point been waiting alone in a windowless room. Notice that the interpreter is licensed, in the physician's first turn, not simply to interpret, but rather to explore 'what did [the patient] mean by this?' (line 23) when he said his 'eyes hurt'. From the very beginning of the interaction, she becomes responsible, then, for not only conveying information, but for first collecting it, in immediately usable fashion, in the name of the physician. The interpreter's subsequent actions should be judged in the light of this request from her institutional superior, the physician for whom she is interpreting, to actively clarify the patient's verbal output.

Notice also that, from the beginning, we hear the physician, patient and interpreter struggling to construct a coherent account of the patient's Chief (or at least initial) Complaint about his eyes, but that they fail to establish anything more than that the patient's eyes have a problem relating to 'burning', 'tearing', and cloudiness or a possible complete loss of vision. The interaction was perhaps even more muddled than the transcript shows; when the interpreter struggles to convey exactly what the patient has said, it is because what he is saying is not entirely clear, a fact which is not commented upon by either the physician or the interpreter. The problem of definition, central to medical diagnosis, is never resolved.

Excerpt 2 (from visit 6):

15	Dr	Mr. X was telling me – no, come sit *here*.
16		We have all these chairs, no there's two chairs.
17		Grab a seat.
18		Ok,
19	Int	mm-hm.
20	Dr	So: he was telling me tha:
21		he was having problems no: w, he said, with his vision.
22		He said sometimes he can't see at all.
23		What did he mean by this?
24	Int	Mm-hmm.
25		Dice el doctor que está teniendo problemas con la vista
		The doctor says that you are having problems with your vision
26		que unas veces
		that some times
27		no puede V E R?
		you can't S E E?
28	Pt	Ah, sí, sí, xx en la: la vista, se me,
		Ah, yes, yes, xx in the:, the vision,
29		empieza a salir agua
		water starts to come out
30		aunque estoy en xxx
		even though I am in xxx
31		y-y: como que tengo chile allí
		and-and like I have chili there
32	Int	Eyes get teary,
33		and, burning, feels like,

34		hot chili.
35	Dr	Hot chili. But it's not that his eyes go black
36		it's that his eyes ar: e.
37	Int	Pero no es que la vista se le
		But it is not that your vision
38		se le ponga totalmente oscura, negra.
		goes completely 'obscure' (opaque), black.
39	Pt	Bueno: =
		Well: =
40	Int	=Es simplemente que le arden los ojos.
		=It's simply that your eyes burn.
41	Pt	A veces se me pone, se me va la vista.
		Sometimes it gets, sometimes my vision goes.
42		Cuando pasa esto se me va la vista.
		When this happens my vision goes.
43	Int	Se le va la vista=
		Your vision goes=
44	Pt	=Sí
		=Yes
45	Int	ah:. ¿que muy oscuro?
		ah:, what very dark?
46	Pt	Muy oscuro.
		Very dark.

One aspect of this transcript fragment seems immediately apparent, which is that this opening phase of the interview, which phase typically concerns the elicitation and elaboration of the patient's complaint, neither clarifies nor furthers the physician's understanding of what, exactly, is wrong with the patient's eyes. To this point in the transcript, very little has been established beyond the fact that the patient's eyes hurt him, they may go dark, and they burn. The doctor has entered, in his attempt to clarify the patient's complaint, what the colonial missionary Father Murillo, cited in Rafael, referred to as ' "a labyrinth without a clue" . . . beset with digressions and non-sequiturs' (Rafael 1993:133); while Rafael is referring to the difficulty in hearing cross-linguistic confessions from native Tagalogs in the colonial Philippines, the phrase could easily apply to the physician's attempts at clarification and definition of the patient's problem with his eyes.

The confusion that is evident in the transcript was equally evident in the actual interview; the physician was visibly upset that he could not get a clear picture from the patient of what was wrong, and the patient was also visibly upset that he was asked the 'same' question over and over. Clark (1992, 1996) describes the 'achievement' of a contribution to a discourse as the moment when both parties understand what has been said, and believe that the other also understands; at this point in the excerpt, nothing substantial that would aid in diagnosis has been achieved in the medical interview.

It should be noted here also that the interpreter's changes to the dialogue are not entirely related to problems inherent in the act of linguistic conversion itself. Her insertion in line 40, for example, of the evaluative adverb *simplemente*, 'simply', to modify the question about the patient's eyes burning, is a judgement that is hers and hers alone. The physician, by his negative question, implies this relative scale of severity (burning eyes are less serious than loss of vision), but it is the interpreter who puts this implication into concrete form. In addition, her follow-up question to the patient at the end of the fragment, in line 45, represents a small but significant departure from the notion that the interpreter conveys all and only what was said; she is asking the patient to clarify, to her, what he is saying, before she attempts to pass this information along to the physician. In the end, lines 47–83 do not serve to pin down the complaint, and the physician finally moves on. In lines 84–85, below, he turns from the problem of definition of symptoms to the question of duration of these (still vaguely defined) symptoms, asking, 'Ok, so, how often does this happen?'.

To this point in the encounter the patient can infer from the interpreter's offerings that both he and the physician understand that he is concerned about his eyes, and that the physician now shares this concern. But when the patient reports that his eyes burn and get teary, the question that is addressed to him in reply to this report is the negative, 'but it is not the case that you lose your vision' (lines 37–38). What may be inferred, by the patient, from this question is that the physician has taken the patient's reported symptoms, not as a positive affirmation of illness, but rather as a negative affirmation of a more serious illness. The patient then states that he *does* lose vision when his eyes tear and water, although he then modifies that, after being led by the interpreter (line 45) to agree that, instead of losing sight, his vision goes 'very dark'.

I do not wish, here, to overstate the analyses of what the conversational participants are attempting to achieve with their turns-at-talk; it is not possible to say, with absolute certainty, the goals of the different conversational offerings that each participant proffers. Epistemic and emotional states are not available for definite analyses, and it is impossible to fully catalogue the intended effect of utterances. It is possible to claim, with some very high degree of certainty, that the interview in Excerpt 2 has very quickly become bogged down in an attempt, on the part of the physician, to determine what exactly the nature of the Chief Complaint is, centring, not on a differential diagnosis, but on the establishment of an agreed upon set of symptoms that the patient is reporting. With this in mind, it is noteworthy that the physician chooses to move on in the interview at all, from defining the complaint to finding out about the temporal markers of diagnosis, that is, frequency, intensity, and duration of the (as yet undefined) symptoms (lines 84–85, below).

The next transcript fragment from visit 6 shows how the question of the patient's eyes is resolved within the interview. Here the interpreter's role as co-diagnostician comes to the fore: the physician asks for a further clarification of time-of-onset of the complaint, to which the patient answers in an indirect, but entirely relevant, fashion. The interpreter, however, ignores the patient's offerings in lines 105–111, and instead re-tracks him to give a strictly temporal answer to the physician's initial question.

Lines 101–116 are critical to this analysis. After a string of successful closed questions (lines 85–100), the physician asks for how long the patient has been suffering these (uncertain) symptoms (lines 101–103), and the interpreter relays this question (line 104). But the answer, from the patient, is not a direct one: instead he replies that he has been trying to tell the physician for quite some time that his eyes are bothering him, but that he is unsure if the physician has heard (and by implication understood) him or not (lines 105–111).

The reply is indirect, but relevant. The patient is not simply replying to the question, but is rather addressing himself to the inferable basis of the question; this is that a commonly-held and agreed upon medical fact has not been established, despite

Excerpt 2, continued:

84	Dr	Ok, so,
85		And how often does this happen?
86	Int	Uh, ¿cuánto le sucede esto?
		Uh, how often does this happen to you?
87	Pt	Pues, uh:,
		Well, uh:,
88		unas dos veces yo creo al mes,
		about two times I think a month,
89		me sucede.
		it happens to me.
90	Int	two times
91		[a month.]
92	Pt	[más o menos]
		[more or less]
93	Int	[more or less.]
94	Dr	[Twice a month.] For how long?
95	Int	¿Por cuánto tiempo le [(xxx)]?
		For how long does it [(xxx)] (to you)?
96	Pt	[me dura como:]
		[it lasts (me) like:]
97		(1 second)
98		a veces me dura casi media hora.
		Sometimes it lasts almost a half hour.
99	Int	Sometimes he takes, ah, i-it lasts
100		uh-h, half an HOUR when it happens
101	Dr	Ok, right
102		So::
103		And how long has it been going on for?
104	Int	¿Y por cuánto tiempo le ha venido sucederle esto?
		And for how long has this been happening to you?
105	Pt	Pues, yo traté de decirle al doctor de
		Well, I tried to tell the doctor
106		de hace más,
		more than,
107		cuatro cinco visitas para atrás
		four five visits ago
108	Int	mm-[hm]
109	Pt	[que] ya me estaba sucediendo.
		[that] it was already happening to me.
110		Pero:,
		But,
111		Que no sé si él me entendía o no.
		I don't know if he understood me or not.
112	Int	Pero, ¿hace,
		But, since,

Excerpt 2, continued:

113		ha-hace cuándo que le comenzó a,
		Si-since when did this start,
114		a suceder esto?
		to happen to you?
115	Pt	Mas o menos como un año, yo creo.
		More or less about a year, I think.
116	Int	About a year.
117	Dr	Ok. (9 second pause)
118		And it goes away by itself?
119	Int	Ah:
120		y, it.
121		Así como le viene esta molestia,
		And as this discomfort comes to you,
122		se le quita sola.
		it goes away by itself?
123	Pt	Me quita, sí.
		It goes away (from me), yes.
124	Int	Yes, it goes away by itself.

the patient's repeated attempts to establish it over time. The patient does not believe that the physician has assimilated his complaint into the medical record, and the patient has every reason to suspect this is the case given the nature of the physician's question in line 103. The patient does not know if a crucial piece of information has been accepted by the physician, and suspects, correctly, that it has not, because he has never had a reply, in this or prior visits, that would make it possible for him to infer that this is the case. The interpreter's subsequent action, which is an attempt to re-focus the dialogue on the immediate semantic basis of the physician's original question (lines 109–114), is met with a reply of 'one year' (line 115).

The interpreter's verbal actions in lines 104–116 are critical. Having been asked to initially determine 'what the patient meant' by his complaint about his eyes, the interpreter has moved on to determining the relevance of an utterance to the process of diagnosis at hand: the physician has asked a question, presumably in anticipation of a strict temporal reply, and the patient answers with a more complicated, albeit entirely relevant, answer about the nature of the question itself. The interpreter here evaluates the patient's response and dismisses it as irrelevant ('but . . .', line 112) to the initial closed question, denying its entry into the discourse. The interpreter is acting as pre-filter for patients' utterances, screening them for relevance to the physician's questions: as noted earlier, however, converting data by passing it through a grid of medical meanings is the central component of the process of diagnosis itself. In addition, it is entirely possible that the interpreter here is not merely screening the patient's answer for relevance, but that she is deleting it wholesale, to protect the physician and the institution of the hospital from the critique that the patient's complaint has been repeatedly ignored.

This manoeuvre effectively obliterates the chance that in this visit, as in prior visits, the patient will be able to establish the medical fact that, not only do his eyes bother him, but that he has been attempting to report this problem for quite some time. With respect to patient complaints in general, the physicians who took part in this study often spoke about the importance of determining, not only the exact complaint, but why the complaint has become significant or urgent enough to be brought up by the patient *now*. The fact that the report has been made repeatedly, over time, is important, because it supplies the physician with the information that this complaint is neither trivial nor recent. The physician, however, does not question the interpreter with regards to what the patient has said in lines 106–111; he hears a coherent reply to a closed question, and moves on.

Far from being a valid CC, the report of burning eyes now becomes a somewhat trivial complaint, for how bad could it be if a year has passed and only now the patient is bringing the symptom to the physician's attention? The physician's subsequent question, in line 118, adds credence to the analysis that, because the physician receives a strictly temporal reply via the interpreter, he no longer takes the patient's complaint seriously: the question, 'it goes away by itself?', may be read, in a medical context, as the question, 'is this ailment self-limiting (e.g. self-correcting), and do I need to seriously address it?'. Self-limiting ailments, such as colds (which go away in a few days regardless of the medical care delivered or withheld) are generally considered non-issues by medical practitioners, because there is nothing that can be done, medically, to fix them. When the reply comes back that yes, the symptom cures itself (line 124), the physician quickly works, over the next 50 lines of transcript, to move the interview past the report. When the physician hears, finally, that perhaps the patient's need of glasses may in the future give permanent relief, he resets the interview with an open question, still in search of a valid CC upon which to focus.

Notice that the question in lines 182–186 can be read as serving several functions: the first, of course, is to reset the interview, so that a 'valid' Chief Complaint may be identified and addressed. Another, however, is that the physician here is himself trying to keep the patient on track, by asking him to pre-evaluate, on his own, what is most medically important. One final message which might be read into this question is that the physician may be serving notice to the patient that he has wasted a certain amount of time with his complaint about his eyes, and that there is now time for only one more of his complaints to be addressed before the physician will close out the interview. The problem is that the patient's problem with his eyes is, in fact, a valid Chief Complaint. The interpreter's pre-evaluation and *de facto* editing of the patient's contributions to the interview result, in this case, not in keeping that patient 'on track', but rather in un-tracking the achievement of the institutional goals (diagnosis and treatment) of the interview itself.

Excerpt 2, continued:

179	Dr	Oh, good.
180	(8 seconds).	
181		And:,
182		Is there any, other,
183		main thing that is bothering him today?
184		I know there's a lot of problems,
185		but if there was only one
186		other thing he was gonna tell me about today, what would be choose?

Conclusions and discussion

In this article I have outlined the role of interpreters in one form of medical discourse, the internal medicine 'medical interview'. The linguistic data, both quantitative and qualitative, points strongly away from a conclusion that interpreters are acting as 'advocates' or 'ambassadors' for interpreted patients, but are rather acting, at least in part, as informational gatekeepers who keep the interview 'on track' and the physician on schedule. While the interpreters do in fact convey much of what is said, they also interpret selectively, and appear to do so in a patterned (non-random) fashion. There is no evidence in the data presented here (nor in the larger data set) of interpreters putting forth the patient's agenda vigorously, as is claimed by Haffner (1992) and others. This is not the inevitable role that interpreters must take in hospital discourses, however, and the reasons they act in this way at Riverview is largely a result of their position within the hospital hierarchy.

The practice of medical interpreting is not highly valued within the hospital clinic; when I began my study, I was told by a sympathetic physician that he had also been interested in studying interpreters, but had been told by a hospital administrator not to do 'any studies that tell me I need to hire more interpreters; we can't afford the ones we have now'. There were only seven full-time Spanish–English interpreters at Riverview General Hospital, not nearly enough to take care of the 33,000 patients who needed Spanish interpretation, even given the large number of bilingual physicians and family-member interpreters utilized in individual clinics. The training given to these interpreters was scant; the requirements for becoming an interpreter at Riverview were a good grasp of both English and Spanish, and the ability to translate 50 medical terms on a test with complete accuracy. There was no training in discourse processes, and the training for how medical interactions worked was on-the-job. Physicians, for their part, received absolutely no training in how to use interpreters, beyond being told how to call them to come interpret.

The clinic staff were also consistently wrong in their predictions of who would need an interpreter, and more often than not would be forced to call an interpreter for an unscheduled interpretation, rather than scheduling in advance. Consequently, the interpreters were always running behind, postponing scheduled interpretations and answering pages through the day that added to a large list of patients who needed their services. In addition, during my study over 100 nurses were fired at the hospital, at the same time that the physicians themselves were being asked to see more and more patients in a shorter and shorter time period.

These time pressures all gave rise to competing mandates for the interpreters. Institutionally, they are officially required to act as an 'instrument', saying all and only what has been said; in practice, however, they are encouraged to keep the interview short, and to keep patients 'on track'. In competition, it was almost always the latter requirement that won out, and interpreters frequently engaged in furthering the physician's perceived agenda for the discourse. This happened, not only because of time pressures, but because hospital based interpreters are, in the end, members of the hospital community where they work and interact daily; they are institutional insiders, and ally themselves as such.

The larger ramifications of the interpreter's role in medical discourses are also significant. Of the power of institutional encounters to define citizens' relations with the state itself, Foucault writes (1979:304):

We are in the society of the teacher–judge, the doctor–judge, the educator–judge, the 'social–worker'-judge; it is on them that the universal reign of the normative is based . . .

All that is needed to make this quote perfectly relevant to the analysis at hand is to add the words 'the society of the interpreter-judge', for it is interpreters with whom and through whom recent immigrants interact with institutions of the state.

Interpreters are not, and cannot be, 'neutral' machines of linguistic conversion, both because they are faced with the reality that linguistic systems are not 'the same' in how they convey information contextually, and also because they are themselves social agents and participants (albeit special ones) in the discourse. It is possible for them to interpret evenly, however, and it is not the case that professional, hospital based interpreters need to work as an extra gatekeeping layer through which patients must pass in order to receive medical care. One could argue, as I would, that the interpreters' wholesale alignment with the institution of Riverview General Hospital (which is, not coincidentally, their employer) is both unethical and a truly poor form of interpretive practice.

As stated earlier, however, it is the context of communication that is fundamental in defining how the interpreter will carry out her role, and how she should be judged in that role; given that the physicians' command was, first and foremost, to keep the interview short, interpreters at Riverview may in fact be doing a good job at a bad task. The real issue is that they are doing a job that is different, in daily practice, from the job they are typically assumed to be doing. This means that they are not trained, nor licensed within the institution (i.e. they cannot write referrals or prescriptions, and may not make notes in the patient's permanent record), to do the things they are in fact doing (collection and analysis of data; establishing a 'therapeutic rapport' with the patient); nor are they given any form of institutional support for the true nature of the work that they do. The construction of the interpreter as a simple instrument of semantic conveyance is only possible when those who hire and use interpreters imagine that it is possible for interpretation to be the task of merely echoing content faithfully. It is this conceptualization of the interpreter's work that renders her daily practice of acting as co-diagnostician invisible, which in turn engenders a vacuum of responsibility, both within the discourse and with respect to the delivery of health care to non-English speaking patients in general. This slippage, between what interpreters are asked, officially, to do, and what they are really doing in daily practice, allows the practice to continue unmonitored and unevaluated; the invisible nature of the interpreter's role as co-diagnostician is the effect, rather than the interpreter's incompetence being the cause, of the broad dissatisfaction physicians and patients at Riverview express towards medical interpreting in general.

Chapter 10

Hephzibah Israel

TRANSLATING THE BIBLE IN NINETEENTH-CENTURY INDIA: PROTESTANT MISSIONARY TRANSLATION AND THE STANDARD TAMIL VERSION

EDITOR'S INTRODUCTION

The immense power and institutional authority the Bible Society gained, partly by a process of self-authentication, meant that key components of the processes of translation were under its direct or indirect control.

ISRAEL FOCUSES ON INSTITUTIONALIZED religion and examines issues relating to Bible translation that engaged the attention of missionary translators connected to the Bible Society in the Madras Presidency and Ceylon, in particular the production of a standard Tamil version of the Bible in nineteenth-century India. She places in context the Bible Society's push for standardization and uniformity of Bibles, arguing that the insistence on standard translations underpinned an effort to create an abstract, standard Christian subject who would transcend differences among cultural communities in India, including differences in religious beliefs.

What is particularly interesting about Israel's analysis is that it does not assume a process of unidirectional influence, emanating from missionary institutions and imposed onto passive Indian subjects. Instead, she engages with the dynamic of negotiation between the goals of the Protestant missionary project of conversion and the demands of their Protestant converts, as well as the role played by translators in this process. In the complex cultural and linguistic landscape of India, the translators had to find ways of keeping the Bible both distinct *and* familiar, to ensure that it would be recognized as scripture and at the same time not be confused with the scriptures of the existing religious groups in the region. In doing so, and given that language is a major marker of identity, the translators had to build a suitable Protestant vocabulary in each language, one in which the new converts could express their religious identity in language that signalled a clear break from their previous religious affiliations. They set out to achieve two types of uniformity: uniformity of vocabulary and style within a single language version (making it possible for this version to qualify as a 'standard' translation), and uniformity of Christian terminology across the 'standard' translations for the various language groups in India. The entire process was carefully controlled and monitored by the Bible Society: from providing printing infrastructure and finance for each translation project, to selecting the languages into which the Bible would be translated, who undertook the translation, what principles they were instructed to adopt, and so on.

Focusing on the specific case of the Protestant Tamil community, Israel argues that some sections of the community collaborated with the missionary project, not out of fear or conviction, not as passive or consenting audiences, but because it served their own, local interests to do so at that point and because they saw an opportunity to fight the hegemonic colonial institutions within their own structures. Thus, despite the power of the institutions behind this missionary project, 'the history of Protestant Tamil translations', she concludes, 'when viewed from the bottom up, from the standpoint of the various sections of Protestant Tamils, indicates that the Protestant Tamils have assimilated the translated Bible and its message on their own terms'.

Follow-up questions for discussion

- One of the ways in which the Bible Society implemented its agenda of uniformity and standardization was to print the Bible without any commentary or exegetical notes whatsoever: the Bible and nothing but the Bible. This 'effectively cut short doctrinal disputes over the text of the Scriptures' and presented the Bible as the unmediated Word of God. Compare this with the practice of providing extensive commentary and exegesis in other contexts of Bible translation, as well as translations of the Qur'an or Buddhist scriptures, for instance. How might both scenarios (commentary or no commentary) serve similar or different ends in different contexts?

- Israel explains that the English King James Bible, itself a translation, came to function as the original text for most nineteenth-century translators in India, and each of the various language versions based on it came to be known as the 'authorized version' in that language. Any dispute over ambiguous meaning was settled in favour of the King James version, with the relevant passages translated according to the interpretation found in the English text rather than the Greek or Hebrew originals. Niranjana (1990:775) describes a similar practice in the same region during the same period, where the missionaries also translated Indian religious texts into European languages then used these European translations as *the* authoritative texts, on the basis of which they then 'berated Hindus for not being true practitioners of Indian religion'. Consider the extent to which these two examples might reflect a common reconfiguring of the relationship between original and translation in colonial contexts.

- Israel's description of the skill with which Protestant Tamils assimilated Protestant Christianity on their own terms reminds us that dominance is never absolute, and that resistance comes in many forms. Consider some of the ways in which translation participates in both projects, i.e. supporting dominance and encoding resistance.

Recommended further reading

Dodson, Michael S. (2005) 'Translating Science, Translating Empire: The Power of Language in Colonial North India', *Society for Comparative Study of Society and History*, 809–835.

Lai, John T. P. (2007) 'Institutional Patronage: The Religious Tract Society and the Transla-
    tion of Christian Tracts in Nineteenth-Century China', *The Translator* 13(1): 39–61.
Rafael, Vicente (1988) *Contracting Colonialism: Translation and Christian Conversion Under
    Early Spanish Rule*, Ithaca: Cornell University Press.

FROM ITS BEGINNINGS IN THE EARLY eighteenth century, the
evangelical project of Protestant missions focused on the translation of the Bible
into different languages. This was also the case in the history of Protestant mission
in India. The two primary objectives of the Protestant missionaries in nineteenth-
century India were, firstly, to assimilate the Bible through translation into the language
cultures of India; and, secondly, as a result of this, to create a Protestant identity for
their converts. Missionary translators discussed several strategies of translation in
order to achieve these objectives. A particular concern of the nineteenth-century discourse on Bible translation, and one that was peculiar to the intellectual and political
context of nineteenth-century India, was the desire to arrive at standard translations
of the Bible in as many of the Indian languages as possible. Such translations would
serve to create a uniform Protestant culture in India.

Besides examining the arguments offered in favour of standardization and
exploring how the process of standardization worked in practice, the present essay
investigates how far this objective was achieved in the case of the Tamil Bible. I will
argue that although the nineteenth-century Tamil version was accepted as the standard translation by the Protestant Tamil community, the reasons for this did not concur
with the intention of the Protestant missionaries in South India. For Protestant missionaries, a single, standardized version of the Tamil Bible signified both a unified
Protestant Tamil community separated – horizontally, as it were – from the other
religious communities in Tamil society and a vertical link to the universal church.
Protestant Tamils, however, supported the establishment of one standard version
because it helped them to establish a 'history' for the community (enabling them to
speak of a Protestant Tamil tradition) and to set up horizontal ties with the other
Tamil communities of faith (by gaining recognition from the other religious communities). I contend that translation projects undertaken by missionaries in the colonial context disturb neat polarities – such as those between colonizing and colonized,
between complicit and resistance audiences and between 'domesticating' and 'foreignizing' translations – that continue to have currency in the present theoretical
discourse on translation.

The understanding that the spread of Christian 'truth and Scriptures' in India, as
elsewhere outside Europe, depended on the excellence of the vernacular versions
(Gulliford 1898:456) encouraged theoretical debate on language, translation and
religious terminology to take place in nineteenth-century India. While only a few
missionaries were involved in the actual process of translating the Bible into Indian
languages in the nineteenth century, others who were working in the field were
drawn into the debate and contributed in building up a collective notion of how
Bible translation should proceed in India. This, on occasion, included comments
and observations from some members of the Indian clergy. The result was not a
homogenous and finished set of rules or procedures to be followed by Bible translators. Rather, there were frequent contradictions, disagreements, contrary experiences and criticisms. These points of concurrence and conflict point to the matrix of

assumptions and controversies, linguistic and otherwise, that influenced the path of Bible translation in the nineteenth century and after. Similarly, the contradictory pressures within the receiving Indian cultures also influenced the project of Bible translation. Thus, the translated Bible was the product of both the Protestant missionary project of conversion and the demands of their Protestant converts.

The Bible was introduced in India within the rhetorical discourse of 'true' and 'false' scriptures in the early eighteenth century. This had a bearing on the translation of the Bible into Indian languages, as the truth claims of and for the Bible had to stand the test of translation into several exotic and alien languages. By the nineteenth century, missionary literature and religious tracts were published in each language the Bible was translated into, proposing to give rational proof that the Bible was the true 'Veda'; that it must logically replace the Hindu Scriptures; and that in spite of its appearance of being multiple or split across languages, it was ultimately one. For the missionary translators, the act of translating the Bible functioned as a medium for defending Christianity and missions both from the attacks of Western rationalists and sceptics and from the superstitious, false beliefs of the East. That the Bible could be translated into any language without loss of meaning served as proof of its divine nature; while the irrationality and darkness of the local beliefs could be dispersed by the translated Bible. The translation and dissemination of the Bible across the globe was for many, as claimed by an enthusiastic missionary, 'the noblest service on earth'.

For Protestant missionaries, translating the Bible was translating Christianity in order to establish it in alien and at times hostile environments. The important role that the Bible was expected to play in replacing all other scriptures put added pressure on the translators to arrive at 'correct' methods of translation that would keep the Bible distinct and yet familiar; that is, although recognizable as scripture it would not be confused with the scriptures of the existing religious cultures in India. This meant that translation 'difficulties' or translation 'problems' encountered during earlier attempts at Bible translation in Europe were further multiplied in the Indian context. It also meant a struggle with languages whose religious vocabularies were closely connected to other religious practices, supposedly rendering them 'inappropriate' or 'inadequate' for expressing Christian concepts and practices. Since language is one of the markers of identity, one of the primary tasks of the missionary translators was also to build a suitable Protestant vocabulary in each language, so that the new Indian Protestants would be able to express their religious practices and identity in a vocabulary that was distinct from their previous religious affiliations.

The question of how religious or technical terms ought to be translated from one language into another was a source of much controversy. In order to translate ideas, terms had to be translated and most religious terms available to translators in India were ones that already conveyed the ideas of other religions. The general opinion among the missionaries was that 'Christian thoughts cannot buy ready-made clothes at Hindu stores' (Anon. 1899:138). There was disagreement over whether technical terms of the Bible should be translated at all, or merely transferred intact or transliterated. If translated, whether it should be into existing terminology or into terms coined especially for the Bible. It was recognized that some of the best religious terms were those employed by the Hindus with peculiar Hindu meaning. But for this very reason such terms were considered 'unsafe' for use in the Bible (Wenger 1876:8). Those who recommended the use of Hindu terms warned that it was also imperative to know the exact meaning and value of terms and the current coin of Hindu thought (Anon. 1889:6). They suggested that Hindu terminology could be adopted if it could be 're-baptised into our holy faith', because 'it is not words that give value to ideas but ideas that give value to words' (Jones 1895:50).

The choice of one over the other depended on the translator's opinion of whether the Bible should be made familiar to its readers or not. Translation into an existing term meant that the Bible would be more familiar to the Indian reader, but with the risk of being confused with the previous meaning of the recycled term. However, others felt that Bible translators who wanted to express Christian truth and be faithful to the original could not avoid strangeness. This was recommended even if it meant that the Hindu would be repelled by the strangeness of the translation. The editor of *The Harvest Field*, a Protestant missionary journal published by the Wesleyan Methodist Society in South India, gives two reasons in support of this view. Firstly, the Bible according to him was not just a literary production but contained a religion; and secondly, the reader who was repelled by any uncouth phrases was unworthy to realize the new ideas conveyed by them. In comparison, he gave the example of the *Bhagavad Gita* translated into English and pointed out that the translation could not avoid sounding foreign because of the presence of technical Sanskrit terms, but this was better, he argued, than Vedantic ideas disguised in English masks (Anon. 1899:138).

Further, there was discussion on whether the Indian languages had an adequate vocabulary and linguistic standard to make them capable of receiving the Bible. Hindi, according to one missionary,

> offers special difficulty as a medium for the expression of Biblical truth. Hindi is the speech of a people to whom pantheism in some form is as natural as Calvinism is supposed to be to a Scotsman. We have no word in Hindi for 'person', none for 'matter', as distinct from 'spirit'. The word for 'omnipresence' suggests rather universal pervasion than what we mean by presence. There is often difficulty in finding exact words even for moral ideas. [. . .] Neither is there any word which connotes the same thought as our word 'ought', so that, naturally, Hindi has no word for 'conscience'.[1]

William Greenfield (1830:62), while defending the Serampore Maratta Version, pointed out the shortcomings of the Marathi language to support Bible translation:

> . . . there is not in this language a subjunctive or potential mood, or a passive voice, and scarcely a word denoting the operations of the mind. In translating, therefore, from the copious language of the Greeks, or the ruder language of the Hebrews, innumerable words and phrases must occur which have no corresponding term in Marat'ha, but without which the peculiar tenets and doctrines of the Christian religion cannot be explained.

Unfortunately, lack of a biblical lexicon was cited as proof of the lack of conceptual and moral values, which therefore needed to be written into these languages and cultures (Sugirtharajah 2001:65). Other languages, such as Bengali, were praised for being 'extremely rich and Copious', but even so Bible translation would improve them further: according to Carey, Bengali was a language that was not understood by the common people who had a limited dialect, however, 'publishing the Bible must make it [Bengali] more known to the Common People'.[2] Though some other languages besides these were declared sufficiently developed to be able to express biblical ideas, there was always the need to stretch, bend and 'perfect' these languages 'as a medium for the expression of Christian truth'.[3]

Several of the theoretical questions on Bible translation debated in nineteenth-century India had already been under discussion for many centuries in Europe, but they acquired new dimensions in the Indian context. Some of the binary opposites between which the debates swung, or that were invoked as part of the debates, were faithful versus free, transference versus translation, literal versus idiomatic, obscure versus clear, sense-for-sense versus word-for-word, the original and its translation, standard versus multiple versions. Further, 'misrepresentation', 'mistranslation' and 'uniformity' were terms employed in the discourse on translation to fix the parameters of assimilating Protestant Christianity through biblical translation. However, these defining terms of Bible translation were discussed in the context of introducing Protestant Christianity and the Bible in opposition to the religious systems that were already present in Indian society. This important function envisaged for the Bible put added pressure on the translators to arrive at the 'correct' methods of translation that would keep the Bible distinct from the existing scriptures available to Indians. The quest, in other words, was for a text that would be recognizable as scripture. In what follows, I focus on the overarching missionary concern to produce standard versions of the translated Bible, their interest in achieving uniformity at several levels, and the implications of this concern for Protestant converts in India. I examine in particular the case of the Protestant Tamil Bible and the implications of translation strategies for the Protestant Tamil community.

One of the primary aims in missionary circles was to achieve uniformity in and through Bible translation. 'Uniformity' and 'standardization' were two linked concerns that underlay the nineteenth-century translation debate. Uniformity of two kinds was aimed for: uniformity of vocabulary and style within a single language version that would qualify it as a 'standard' translation; and uniformity of Christian terminology across several or all language groups in India. A standard version implied a translation that used a set of Protestant terminology accepted as standard, a standard level of the language, and a standard translation for all social classes and all Protestant denominations. Most revision committees gave 'uniformity of rendering' as one of the important principles that guided them but spent more time on disputing the rendering of such terms that were considered essential for establishing a standard terminology. The result that Protestant missionary translators hoped for was the creation of a homogenous Protestant readership with a distinct and standard Protestant identity.

An institutional agenda for creating standard versions

The primary agency responsible for creating interest in uniformity and standardization was the British and Foreign Bible Society (BFBS). The society, originally founded in 1805 in England to fill a shortage of Bibles in Wales and other parts of Britain, rapidly expanded in the following decades by establishing 'Foreign Auxiliaries' all over the world. Within a short period of time, the society claimed that it was the largest distributor of 'authorized' versions of the Bible in languages and dialects in which the Bible had never been printed before. Amidst controversy, and on occasion severe criticism in England of the Society's aims and methodology, contemporary reports and histories published by the British and Foreign Bible Society represent it as a success and as vital to missions.[4]

The beginning of the nineteenth century showed a shift in the practice of Bible translation in India. Before the 1800s, Bible translation was carried on within particular mission societies, and criticism from other societies was not viewed as constructive but as a threat to the doctrines of the society in question. However, there was a perceptible change from the early nineteenth century after the entry of two societies of primary importance to the history of Bible translation in India. The first of those was the Baptist Society, which was established in Serampore, in Bengal in 1793. The second was the British and Foreign Bible Society (BFBS), which opened its first Indian auxiliaries in Calcutta (1811) and Madras (1820). Both societies were actively involved in the translation of the Bible into as many Indian languages as was possible at the time: the former was the first society to start translating into the languages of northern and eastern India, and the latter the first to coordinate and organize Bible translation and revisions all over India. The BFBS attempted to institutionalize the task of Bible translation in the major Indian languages. Whereas earlier, Bible translators had worked in comparative isolation with occasional help or comments from colleagues, Bible translations in the nineteenth century were mostly group efforts at translation by committees appointed by the BFBS. By the mid-nineteenth century, the BFBS had established a network that linked translators and their readers, translations and responses to them, and production and finance more formally than in earlier centuries when these were left to individual interest and enterprise. The BFBS very quickly became a nodal point that coordinated with all other Protestant mission societies, whereby they drew upon the financial and human resources of these societies and offered in return the translated Bible to be distributed in their mission fields. Although there were some humble claims to being a 'handmaiden' to other missionary societies, the Bible Society more frequently projected itself as the pillar supporting the rest of the missionary enterprise. It did not 'send' missionaries to the field but recruited missionaries from their stations to participate in the process of translation. Equally important, the BFBS also initiated debate on Bible translations that later developed into formal rules and guidelines for Bible translators, revisers and editors.

The immense power and institutional authority the Bible Society gained, partly by a process of self-authentication, meant that key components of the processes of translation were under its direct or indirect control. From material concerns (those of providing printing infrastructure and finance for a translation project) to the ideological (into which languages the Bible would be translated and when, who would translate, the principles of translation to be followed, and what was an acceptable translation), the Bible Society has dominated almost the entire field of Bible translation for the last two hundred years. The Society appointed translation committees, often financed the entire translation project in a certain language, provided resources such as libraries equipped with source texts and language dictionaries, prescribed certain guiding principles and rules to follow. It also controlled the time within which a translation project was to be completed, coordinated opinion, requests and response from different Protestant denominations, printed the translation, distributed the version widely through an elaborate system of 'agents' and 'colporteurs', and sold it at a very low price.

The Bible Society enjoyed much success because of certain decisions it took regarding Bible translation. In order to survive as an institution within the context of constant Protestant infighting, it made uniform and standard versions a part of its manifesto. A 'standard' translation, if such a version could be agreed upon, would make both the translation and its publishers acceptable to all Protestant denominations. Printing the Bible unaccompanied by exegetical notes or interpretative commentary was a strategy to achieve this. It effectively cut short doctrinal disputes over the text of the Scriptures. It enabled the presentation of the Bible as the unmediated Word of God in keeping with the Protestant emphasis on the self-sufficiency of Scripture for human comprehension. Henry Martyn, in a sermon he preached in Calcutta in 1811 to 'promote the objects of the British and Foreign Bible Society', assured his audience that, according to him, one of the most important principles was the Society's decision to print only the text of the Bible. 'You may be assured', he declared, 'that they will not depart from this rule, because the very existence of the Society depends upon their adherence to it. The certainty that nothing will be given but the Bible, and that without note or comment, is the only principle, upon which Christians of all denominations will unite in it, or could do so legitimately' (1811:15). Such a Bible was also more acceptable to most Protestant denominations in the mission field, as the mass-produced 'standard' text suited the needs of all Protestant sects without highlighting the confusing doctrinal controversies to new converts.

Another decision of the Bible Society which had far-reaching effects on the translated Bible in India was the recommendation of the 'original' source text to be used for translation. While the Hebrew and Aramaic books of the Old Testament and the Greek New Testament were acknowledged as the original to be used for translation, missionaries until the nineteenth century had taken the help of other language translations such as Luther's German version or the Dutch translation. Of the many translations that were available, the Bible Society determined to use the English King James Version as a standard of reference. From the nineteenth century, the English King James Version gradually began to replace the importance and position even of the 'originals'. This meant that conflict over passages or terms with ambiguous meaning were translated in accordance with the interpretation of the English translation rather than the Greek and Hebrew originals. It seems, for all practical purposes, that the English translation functioned as the 'original' for most nineteenth-century translators in India. As a result, virtually every language in India has a nineteenth-century version (based on the English King James Version) that is popularly known as 'the authorized version'. This, in turn, came to be known as the 'original' in each language and thus a text that could not be changed through revisions or retranslations. Though the clergy today acknowledge that each such translation is outdated and needs revision, the laity has resisted published attempts at modern translations. Connected with the missionary translators of the past and bolstered by its textual proximity to the English Version, these 'standard' nineteenth-century translations of the Bible Society continue to exist in the popular imagination as the original Word of God. Hence, the 'original', within the discourse of institutionalized religion, can never be displaced entirely: it is usually replaced by a translation, which is given the same status as the original. More importantly, marketed as uniquely coherent, self-referential Bibles, sanitized of undesirable local cultural elements, these translations were acceptable as 'standard', their languages invested with authority and sanctity by the laity.

The Bible Society usually attempted to gain the support of all the missionary societies working in an area to establish consensus and acceptance that the finished translation was a 'standard' version, that is, the result of standard procedures of translation and capable of establishing a standard of Christian terminology in the particular language. The Bible Society's project of providing standard versions using standard terminology worked in conjunction with other secular and political projects of the British Empire. The introduction of print media and the establishment of standardized higher education in the nineteenth century, for instance, created a class of literate Indians who were equipped both to function in the processes of imperial government and to participate in Protestant culture if they so desired. It seems that the Bible Society established an 'empire' based on the Bible to equal the Empire. The Bible Society's resourcefulness in coordinating translation committees, mobilizing financial aid, providing paper and printing facilities in order to disseminate Bibles around the globe, coincided with other channels for the mediation of imperial culture and authority to peoples who were actual or potential imperial subjects. As a sign of the success of this project, translated Bibles were displayed in the Bible Society stall at the Great Exhibition of 1851 as one of the many exotic artefacts of Empire. Further, translation and empire were clearly connected in the language used to represent the successful spread of translated Bibles: often this was the language of empire, of conquering (through the Word) and of establishing a kingdom (of God).

Uniformity and unity: the case for standard versions

From the mid-nineteenth century onwards, a 'standard' version in each language was seen as essential for achieving denominational unity among Protestants belonging to each language area of India. By then, each language had more than one translation of the Bible. True of most Indian language translations, this was particularly noticeable in the history of Tamil Bible revision: one of the important justifications given for starting each revision of existing translations – and there have been at least six such revisions since the nineteenth century – was the need for a single Tamil Bible for all Tamil denominations.

The simultaneous use of several Tamil translations had often been referred to as an 'evil' that must be overcome by the establishment of the standard Bible. The Madras Committee reportedly thought that no considerations should weigh against a hopeful progress of labours 'that propose to furnish a population of 11 millions with a standard version of the Holy Scriptures and so to remove what is at present a serious evil, the use of various versions in the congregations of Tamil Christians' (Letter, Rev E.E. Jenkins, Madras 1860). One of the Tamil Translation Committee members, E. Sargent, supported work on the new standard Tamil version because 'it would be a wrong to our Native Church here to increase the evil which we intended to remove, by adding to the many other Versions now in use, instead of offering a complete version which would take the place of all others'. One Bible for all churches would imply unity between all missionary societies and a united church in each language area. The Revision Committee of the Tamil Bible (1869) justified revising the existing Tamil versions by claiming to unite all the Protestant denominations of the Tamil church:

> . . . considering the evils arising from the existence and use amongst Tamil Christians of a variety of versions of the Tamil New Testament, it was felt by all who were interested in the circulation and study of the Holy Scriptures, in the success of Missionary labours in the Tamil country, and in the spiritual welfare of the Tamil people, that it was in the highest degree desirable to make another effort, on a well-considered and comprehensive plan, to secure to the Tamil people the advantage of a version of the New Testament which should be worthy of being accepted by all, and which should tend, if possible, to bind together all religious communities in the Tamil country, however they might differ in other particularities, by the bond of a common record and standard of faith, expressed in a common speech. (Anon.1869:2–3)

More importantly, a single, standard translation proved the existence of one God and one voice speaking to all readers of the holy text, and one religion. This Tamil translation was published in 1871 as the *Union Version* and eventually did 'take the place of all others'. It is significant that the nineteenth-century Tamil version was referred to as the 'Union' Version in Tamil Protestant circles. Two years after its publication, Ashton Dibb wrote:

> It has often been cast in the teeth of Protestant Missions that the Protestant Church presents to the native mind such a variety of sects, so many divisions, so many sub-divisions, and so much mutual opposition, that it cannot discover which among us has the true religion. To all this it is the common and obvious answer that the Bible is the point of union. (1873:123)

Clearly, the standard version of the Tamil Bible was meant to unite all Protestant Tamils under one banner: one God, one Bible, one church, which would create one Protestant identity. The *Union Version* is still considered the standard Tamil version by a majority of Protestant Tamils. However, the fact that the Tamil Bible continued to be extensively revised[5] after the publication of the *Union Version* indicates that the desired unity was not simply the result of a standard Tamil version. Instead, other extra-linguistic factors, such as Tamil social and cultural practices, worked either in conjunction or in competition with the Protestant missionary translation project.

Uniformity and unity: the case for a standard Protestant terminology

Fixing linguistic standards for all Indian language translations was another strategy towards standard versions. This ranged from adopting common principles of revision to a common terminology for the fundamental terms lying at the foundation of Protestant teaching (Wilhelm Dilger, in Gulliford 1898:454–55). The suggestion was to use Sanskrit as a base to formulate a standard terminology for all other languages. An 'Editorial' in *The Harvest Field* of December 1898 pointed out that it was necessary to look at the question of Bible revision from a wider standpoint than the individual version. Even if all the Indian languages could not be brought under one standard, it suggested that, since Indian language groups shared many characteristics in common, it would be 'possible to determine some of the terminology and also of the idiom of several languages at the same time'. The four Dravidian languages (Telugu, Tamil, Kannada and Malayalam) were an example of such a group where common terminology could be developed from Sanskrit roots. However, around the mid-nineteenth century, Robert Caldwell (1814–91) had proposed the theory that Tamil (along with the other three south Indian languages) had a separate lineage from those Indian languages that derived from Sanskrit. It is apparent that there were two parallel but opposing moves within the missionary handling of Indian languages, which threatened the uniformity they strove for. On the one hand, Protestant missionaries were arguing for a standard Protestant terminology in all Indian languages based on the Sanskrit language. On the other, missionary scholars of south Indian languages were pointing out that the linguistic roots of Tamil were not of Sanskrit origin.

Nevertheless, there were several attempts from the nineteenth century onwards to compile a list of biblical terminology in the major Indian languages to ensure that a standard Protestant vocabulary developed across the languages. John Murdoch's

Renderings of Scriptural Terms in the Principal Languages of India (1876) listed important terms from Hebrew, Greek and English and their equivalents in ten Indian languages. In the Preface, however, Murdoch acknowledged that this attempt at standardization might not be a complete success: 'Complete uniformity of rendering is impossible, for in most cases the original terms and those in the vernacular are not exactly synonymous. Still, there might be greater uniformity than at present' (1876:n.p.). This effort continued till the end of the nineteenth century. The Madras Missionary Conference of December 1902 reported:

> Many will be interested in the recommendation made that a list of biblical terms should be drawn up which have no equivalent in the Indian languages, and which convey no meaning to the ordinary Indian reader, such as Pharisee, Passover, Sabbath, &c.; and that this list in English, with brief explanations also in English, should be submitted to the Bible Society for sanction in order that a vernacular translation of these terms may be added to the various Indian versions. (Weitbrecht 1903:493)

In 1957, J.M.S. Hooper compiled a 'comparative word list' for Greek New Testament terms in sixteen Indian languages. The aim was 'to select words which have undergone a change in meaning through being used to represent Christian ideas, or which present special problems of translation against the background of Hindu or Muslim thought' (Hooper 1957:vii). Believed to be of interest and value to all who were concerned with accurate translation, the Introduction stated that, '[f]ew more important services can be rendered to the Indian Church than thus to help it to an accurate understanding and careful use of its biblical terminology' (ibid.).

However, a few nineteenth-century missionaries questioned whether a standard terminology was possible. Wilhelm Dilger, Chairman of the Malayalam Bible Revision Committee stated:

> I am not sanguine as to the possibility of adopting a common terminology for all Dravidian languages. There may be a number of terms that can be used in most or all of these languages, because most of the technical terms have to be drawn from Sanskrit. But it is a well-known fact that Sanskrit words acquire different shades of meaning as they come to be used in different Dravidian languages. (in Gulliford 1898:451)

Goudie, a Protestant missionary in south India, suggested another method by which standardization could be achieved between languages: 'I think it highly desirable that the vernacular versions of the Bible given to the Indian Church should be derived from a common text' (ibid.:450). H.U. Weitbrecht, writing on translating the New Testament into Urdu, gave two reasons why this was important. Firstly, it would remove a potential stumbling block for Christian Indians, many of whom could read more than one language and therefore could compare one version against another. Secondly, it would prevent attacks from non-Christians, like their Islamic opponents who were 'constantly on the watch for evidence to prove the corruption of our Scriptures' (Weitbrecht 1900:26).

A further type of standardization under discussion in the nineteenth century was that of romanizing Indian languages so that missionaries sent to any part of India would be able at least to read the Bible in the language before gaining fluency in it. This idea was discussed quite seriously and some books of the Bible were printed using the Roman script for different Indian languages. However, the project never took off because its proponents were defeated by the variants in vowels that each language possessed, which made standardization of script almost impossible. There was also talk of 'uprooting' all existing Indian languages to replace them with English – to facilitate both governance and conversion. Although such attempts to control indigenous languages were successful in other cultures, in the Spanish colonies in South America and some British colonies in Africa for instance, most Indian languages by virtue of having a strong written literary tradition proved resistant to standardization through the imposition of the English language and the Roman script.

Protestant missionaries encouraged the idea that uniformity could forge connections not only within India but also with a wider Protestant community outside the country. The reaction of Nehemiah Goreh, an Indian clergyman, suggests that some Protestant Indians were beginning to desire this sense of being connected to Protestants in other countries. When the appropriate title for Christ was discussed during revisions of the Urdu and Hindi Bibles in the third quarter of the nineteenth century, Goreh claimed he preferred using *Yesu Krist* to *yeshu*, as it was 'adopted by the whole Christian body throughout the whole world, and why should we Indians, or rather the natives of the North-west Province only, differ from all Christians in this respect?' (T.S.W. 1875:502).

The aim of creating a set of terms that could be instantly recognized as Protestant across all the major Indian languages was never a complete success. In Tamil, for instance, the religious idiom of the language became a site for conflict because it revealed parity rather than an absence of concepts and vocabulary between the contending religions. Protestant Tamil translations had to exploit this correspondence instead of inventing a whole new vocabulary. This put immense pressure on the Tamil language to signal differences in religious doctrines and practices in such a way that Protestant Tamils could articulate a difference in belief while drawing on the same set of religious terms that the rival faiths had access to. Although the main religious 'other' for Protestant missionaries were the Hindu communities, Protestant missionaries (and later Protestant Tamils) were as eager to differentiate themselves from the Catholic use of Tamil terms. Thus, the discussion of various terms from Tamil religious discourse revealed the central paradox in Protestant missionary use of Tamil to assimilate Protestant Christianity: communicating difference in religious beliefs and practices while using existing terminology from other religious discourses.

Further, although Protestant missionary translations had a huge impact on the different languages of India, there were other factors that governed the development of each language. Language movement within Tamil in the twentieth century, for instance, was governed by political and social developments that attempted to reorganize the relationship between the Tamil language and its community of speakers around issues of race, caste and religion. This change was politicized through the 'Pure Tamil Movement', which from the 1930s sought to 'cleanse' Tamil of Sanskrit influence. This meant that the sanskritized Tamil terminology of the *Union Version* no longer offered the politically correct terminology for the twentieth century. Groups within the Protestant Tamil community have attempted to create an alternative standard of Protestant terminology. Paradoxically, however, dominant sections within the Protestant Tamil community have resisted all attempts to revise the terminology of the *Union Version* to suit the new political climate. They cite Protestant Tamil tradition as a strong factor for the preservation of the archaic nineteenth-century terminology.

Uniformity and unity: the case for a standard audience

Religious conversion was not the only effect that the translated Bible was expected to produce. It was also supposed to begin a larger civilizing process that was later perfected by the missionary. A missionary working in Tanjore, South India, wrote to the Society: 'the moral conduct, upright dealing and decent dress, of the native Protestants of Tanjore, demonstrate the powerful influence and peculiar excellence of the Christian religion. It ought, however, to be observed, that the Bible, when the reading of it becomes general has nearly the same effect on the poor of every place' (Buchanan 1811:58). The Calcutta Auxiliary Bible Society, in its history of Bible translation in India, quoted a missionary in South India to justify the Bible Society's role in circulating the Bible:

> If ever a sincere Christian could doubt of the good effects of the gospel upon a heathen land, I would propose to him, as a means to solve his doubts, to come and reside for some time in the Tinnevelly district; and to enquire into the mental state and conduct, both of those who have not received the Word of God and are comparatively ignorant of it, and of those who have received it: having no doubt whatsoever, that the result of the enquiry of such a man would clear up all his doubts. (Anon. 1854:6)

Thus, the translated Bible, while translating souls from a 'heathen' to a 'godly' state, also translated their depraved minds, morals and bodily states to a superior level of existence.

Moreover, regardless of the historical and cultural specificity of each individual's past, the convert was encouraged to fit into the universalized category of a 'Protestant'. Thus, the emphasis on standard translations and terminology can be seen as part of an interest in creating a homogenous Protestant readership. As Sue Zemka (1991:104) has argued: 'The Bible Society based and justified its existence on the belief that the exposure to Holy Scriptures created an abstract Christian subject with similar attributes of behaviour and belief regardless of cultural conditions, material environment, or preexisting religious beliefs'. The aim was to remove local cultural practices, deemed as 'heathen', and replace them with Protestant ethics and values. The Protestant register of the languages used in the translated Bibles was meant to provide the convert with a distinct vocabulary to express this move towards the Protestant faith.

Again, the contradictory responses from two sections of the nineteenth-century Protestant Tamil community point to the extralinguistic factors, socio-political and cultural, in South India that affected the formation of Protestant Tamil identity. Where one group of Protestant Tamils resisted the Protestant mission's attempt to direct Protestant identity in a particular direction through institutional efforts at translating the Bible, another section of Protestant Tamils colluded with the missionary agenda. In both instances, the caste identity of each group played an important part in Protestant Tamil response.

In the early decades of the nineteenth century, Evangelical Lutherans of Madras and Tanjore wrote several letters and petitions protesting against revisions of existing translations. Large sections of the Evangelical Lutherans, who belonged to the high caste Vellala group, showed their self-consciousness as a religious community in their engagement with the question of Bible translation. They combined the issue of Bible translation with other differences that the congregations had with the missionaries: the observance of caste distinctions, the observation of Protestant and Tamil feast days, the use of Tamil musical instruments, and the writing of Protestant poetry according to Tamil poetic and religious traditions. All of these were referred to as 'cruelties' imposed by the missionaries on the Protestant Tamil congregations. They protested against the proposed revision of the (eighteenth-century) Tamil Bible on the grounds that the highly Sanskritized version used a 'pure' Tamil that best represented the Protestant Tamils as a community and themselves as belonging to a caste that enjoyed a high social standing in Tamil society. This use of language to represent religious community has a long tradition in South India. In the long history of religious rivalry in Tamil society, religious language and poetry had functioned as a powerful instrument with which to express religious identity. Assailing the literary quality of Tamil had figured largely in earlier conflicts between Tamil Saiva, Buddhist and Jaina sects (Monius 2001). Inability to speak or sing good Tamil had been used to 'expose' the perceived foreignness of Buddhist and Jaina poets in medieval Tamil society, an issue that was brought up again at the entry of Protestant Christianity into Tamil society in the eighteenth century.[6] The rivalry between these religious systems had been expressed in claims about the use of 'pure' 'literary' or 'correct' Tamil where the ability to use pure Tamil was viewed as an indication of knowing the true God. In this context, they were conscious that a peculiar form of Tamil had developed amongst Protestants, which was derogatorily termed 'missionary' or 'Protestant' Tamil, from which they wanted to dissociate themselves. Protestant Tamil congregations dominated by the Vellala caste at the beginning of the nineteenth century were keen to maintain a particular version of the Tamil Bible as representing appropriate language use, and thus their own religious identity.

However, in the second half of the nineteenth century other caste groups in the Protestant Tamil community colluded with the missionary project because it was in their interest to do so. Upwardly mobile low-caste groups, such as the Nadars, who had converted in large numbers to the Protestant faith in the second half of the nineteenth century, found that the missionary programme enabled them to ascend the social ladder through literacy, education and government jobs. In contrast to the Protestants belonging to the higher caste Vellalas who were reluctant to give up cultural practices that signalled their high status in Tamil society, these low-caste groups assimilated Protestant missionary interpretations of language and cultural practices. The missionary project to translate Protestant Christianity and the Bible into Tamil 'high' culture while simultaneously providing a distinct religious and social identity offered lower-caste groups the opportunity to create an alternative social identity under the banner of a Protestant identity. These groups enthusiastically accepted the new translation of the mid-nineteenth century and went on to locate their Protestant identity in the highly Sanskritized 'Protestant Tamil' of the *Union Version*. The widespread rejection of all attempts to either revise this translation or retranslate the Bible into modern Tamil in the twentieth century indicates the internalization of a religious discourse to the extent that the particular Tamil used in the 'standard' version was venerated as Protestant, and more significantly, as God's language. For them, the *Union Version* has acquired besides the religious, a symbolic power, and functions in the present to mark boundaries of identity and otherness. The technical terminology of the *Union Version*, which helped to shape the sacred areas of Protestant Tamil lives, had gradually come to be understood as the correct way to speak about the church and its doctrines. 'Protestant Tamil' had become the only appropriate language for Protestant worship and expression of devotion.

Interestingly, these latter sections of Protestant Tamils, who have gained a dominant status within the community in the twentieth century, have continued to resist the retranslation of the Bible into tanittamil ('pure' or de-sanskritized Tamil). They are unwilling to exchange one set of special linguistic symbols (Protestant Tamil terms) for another ('pure' Tamil terms). Rather than viewing the heavily Sanskrit-oriented Protestant Tamil as a handicap, majority opinion sees it as marking their identity. This specific religious language 'began to serve as a socio-religious marker that helped to reaffirm the identity of denominational Tamil Christian communities through their own dialect or 'branch language' (kalaimoli), which clearly distinguished them from other religious groups' (Bergunder 2002:215).

Paradoxically, a majority of Protestant Tamils in the present participate in the political, economic and larger social discourses of Tamil mainstream culture in the desanskritized tanittamil. However, they function in parallel in the archaic and peculiar Tamil of the nineteenth-century Union Version within the church and the family. Most Protestant Tamils lead a double life in terms of language use: they use the politically correct 'pure' Tamil in the public domain; however, in the private spheres of the family and worship, they slip into the Protestant Tamil of the Union Version with ease. For most, there is no apparent conflict in this practice but it is convenient in serving to mark their Protestant heritage.

Conclusion: whose standard version?

In the specific case of the Protestant Tamil community, it can be argued that some sections of the community colluded with this missionary project because it was in their interest to do so. Upwardly mobile low-caste groups, such as the Nadars, accepted, comparatively easily, the introduction of the Union Version as a 'standard version'. Whereas Protestants belonging to higher caste groups, such as the Vellala caste, were reluctant to give up cultural practices that signalled their high status in Tamil society and resisted the Protestant mission to 'civilize' them according to Western cultural codes. It is possible to say then that social and political imperatives within Tamil society at times worked in conjunction with the Protestant project to translate and civilize: thus, sections of the Protestant Tamil community have functioned as a 'standard' audience for the translated Bible at different points in the history of Protestant Christianity in South India.

Why did the project of creating a standard Protestant Tamil audience through the translation of the Union Version succeed in the second half of the nineteenth century? First, one of the reasons for the comparatively easy establishment of the term in Protestant usage could be the spread of literacy, especially amongst Protestant Tamil converts in the second half of the nineteenth century. Unlike the previous century where literacy and the reading of the Bible was confined to the few literate Tamil catechists and high-caste groups, Protestant congregations in the nineteenth century were moving towards becoming a reading audience. Where, in the eighteenth century, the laity depended largely on the authority of the clergy and a memory created out of aural effect, with the increase in literacy there was a shift towards the primacy of the Bible as the authoritative basis of truth. The movement of the Bible from the church to the home meant that this translation became the first version that was known intimately and at an individual and personal level by Protestant Tamils. An important component of this personal devotion was the memorizing of passages from the Bible. Memory, now created from the reading of a written text, helped to entrench Protestant Tamil terminology on a mass level, a previously unknown phenomenon in Protestant Tamil society.

Second, the relatively short history of the Protestant Tamil community (as compared to the other religious traditions in Tamil society) resulted in a need to establish a 'past' for the community. Located in a culture of long and well-established religious traditions, one of the projects of Protestant Tamils has been to establish an unbroken thread of tradition and continuity from the early eighteenth century. The Tamil Bible could function as one such link with the past if there was only one standard version. Further, it confirmed their status as a religious community if they were seen not to have internal squabbles over their central sacred text: they often showed awareness of the derisive gaze of rival religious groups (especially Hindu and Catholic Tamil communities), none of whom had the similar problem of possessing multiple translations that were meant to indicate one sacred text. While Protestant missionaries also laboured to arrive at one translation that could be established as a standard version to represent the Protestant Tamil community, their motive was different. For Protestant missionaries, one version of the Tamil Bible signified a unified Protestant Tamil community separated on a horizontal plane from the other religious communities in Tamil society but united vertically to the universal church. Protestant Tamils, however, supported the establishment of one version because it provided them a vertical link with their past (so that it was possible to speak of a Protestant Tamil tradition) as well as set up horizontal ties with the other Tamil communities of faith.

A third reason, as mentioned earlier, was the factor of caste hierarchy. The Protestant Tamil community comprises heterogeneous sections, some complicit with and others resisting hegemonic moves from the missionary establishment. The translated Bible both produced compliant converts and initiated radical forms of resistance against Christian missions, affected by identities formed around other social factors such as caste groupings. Elite caste groups (such as the Vellala), in the early nineteenth century, resisted what they saw as missionary interference in their high social position. In the nineteenth century, low-caste groups that wanted to improve their material and social status colluded with the translation project of the Protestant missionaries in South India. By the early twentieth century, they became the economically dominant caste group within the Protestant Tamil community and have put up a determined resistance to any changes in language or translation. Conflict over language use signals the lack of a shared religious experience, and hence of a shared religious identity. Although there were attempts by Protestant Tamils to posit religious identity as an essentialized reality, separable from caste, they found that faith, even as a subjective experience, could not be disengaged from caste and community. Thus, the project of creating a 'standard audience' of Protestant Tamils, split between the public and private realms of experience, has continued to remain an unstable one, escaping fixed definitions.

To conclude, although the Protestant Tamil community's acceptance of the *Union Version* as the standard translation seems to point to the success of a hegemonic translation project in colonial South India, the success depended both on Protestant missionary strategies and on the internal pressures of Tamil society. Protestant Tamils have participated as much in the South-Indian context of inter-religious antagonism expressed through disagreements over language use as responded to the Protestant missionary agenda for setting up differences between Protestant Christianity and other belief systems. The skill shown by Protestant Tamils in assimilating Protestant Christianity on their own terms is a counter-assimilative move to that of Protestant missionaries. If the history of Protestant translations in Tamil society is viewed from the top down, from missionary records and the official missionary position, then the assimilation of Protestant Christianity into Tamil culture appears to participate in other hegemonic strategies of colonial power that sought to impose a rigid defini-tion of how religious communities ought to relate with one another. However, the Protestant translators' belief in the cultural transparency of the Bible and its mobility across cultures was at odds with their translation experience. The translators' inability to gain complete control over language was apparent even as they claimed that the Bible could be revealed in any language. On the other side of the unstable and unfixed text of the Bible, Protestant Tamils have been contesting their right to control lan-guage by rejecting, assimilating, appropriating or reinterpreting Protestant Tamil vocabulary. The history of Protestant Tamil translations, when viewed from the bot-tom up, from the standpoint of the various sections of Protestant Tamils, indicates that the Protestant Tamils have assimilated the translated Bible and its message on their own terms. Thus, in the colonial context, the hegemonic agenda of a translation project may be fulfilled not because of passive or consenting audiences, but because the audience saw the radical possibilities offered by the project to fight hegemonic institutions within their own social structures.

Notes

1   From 'Indian Notes' (1897:910), *The Church Missionary Intelligencer: A Monthly Journal of Missionary Information*. 'Indian Notes' was a running feature in *The Church Missionary Intelligencer* (1849–1906), continued as *The Church Missionary Review* vols 58–78 (1907–1927).
2   Carey, Letter to the Society for Spreading the Gospel among the Heathen, 13 August, 1795.
3   Preface to *kiristhava Siddantham: An Introduction to Christian Doctrine* (1939: iii), A. Arul Thangaiya (trans.), Madras: SPCK.
4   Histories written by George Browne (1859) and William Canton (1904–10), C.S. Dudley's *Analysis of the System of the Bible Society* (1821), the *Bible Society Annual Reports*, to name just a few.
5   *Revised Version* (1956), Common Language New Testament (1975), and the *Tiruvivilium* (1995).
6   According to Monius, the Tamil language emerged as a basic means of articulating religious, cultural and political orientation, as a highly valued indicator of cultural and religious identity, and arguably remained so into the modern era (2001:84).

PART 5

Individual voice and positionality

Chapter 11

Theo Hermans

THE TRANSLATOR'S VOICE IN TRANSLATED NARRATIVE

EDITOR'S INTRODUCTION

> *What is needed . . . is a model of translated narrative which accounts for the way in which the Translator's voice insinuates itself into the discourse and adjusts to the displacement which translation brings about. The model, that is, needs to incorporate the Translator as constantly co-producing the discourse, shadowing, mimicking and, as it were, counterfeiting the Narrator's words, but occasionally — caught in the text's disparities and interstices, and paratextually — emerging into the open as a separate discursive presence.*

TRANSLATORS AND INTERPRETERS do not necessarily or merely function as institutional gatekeepers, echoing and strengthening the 'voice of authority'. They also have a voice in their own right, which is not always seamlessly subsumed within the voices of primary interlocutors. In the case of translated fiction, the focus of Hermans' article, we become more aware of the translator's discursive presence when the translated text 'call[s] on the explicit intervention of a Translator's Voice through the use of brackets or of notes, and they then remind the reader of this other presence continually stalking a purportedly univocal discourse'.

The issues raised and succinctly summarized in this article are elaborated in considerably more detail in Hermans' later work, especially *The Conference of the Tongues* (Hermans 2007). The main question posed is whose voice comes to us when we read translated discourse in general and translated fiction in particular. 'Does the translator, the manual labour done', Hermans asks, 'disappear without textual trace, speaking entirely "under erasure"?'. The answer, both here and in his later work, is a categorical 'no'. Existing narratological models tend to overlook the discursive presence of the translator, perhaps because the translator's voice often remains entirely hidden behind that of the Narrator and may be impossible to detect in some translated texts. But it is always there, and we become particularly aware of it in situations which give rise to contradictions or fissures that have to be resolved through the translator's intervention. Three types of situation involve 'performative self-contradictions' that pressure the translator to 'come out of the shadows and directly intervene in a text which the reader had been led to believe spoke with only one voice'. The first is where the text's orientation towards an Implied Reader is directly at issue, as when it contains topical references and allusions that call on the translator to intervene by providing background information to ensure that communication can proceed smoothly. The second is when the text is characterized by self-reflexiveness and self-referentiality, as when it exploits puns or polysemy, or when it addresses the translator directly (as in some of Derrida's works). The third involves cases of 'contextual overdetermination', features or statements which create a credibility gap that readers can only resolve by reminding themselves of the fact that they are reading a translation. One example is reading Descartes in an English translation proclaiming that he is writing in French not Latin. Here, the reader recognizes that '[t]here is, clearly, another voice at play, duplicating and mimicking the first one, but with a timbre of its own'. Hermans illustrates all three cases and the different ways in which translators deal with them with reference to several translations of a single book, the Dutch novel *Max Havelaar* by Multatuli, first published in 1860.

Beyond illustrating the mechanics of how and why the translator's voice can break through the widespread illusion of transparency and univocality, Hermans explores the ideological motivations for assimilating the translator's voice into that of the narrator in existing narratological models. The standard oppositions within which we locate translation (creative vs. reproductive, original vs. derivative, etc.) are cultural and ideological constructs that serve to maintain established hierarchies and safeguard the notion of univocal speech, to project an orderly universe populated by single voices issuing from distinct and identifiable sources. Translation is recognized as an activity that continually risks producing a proliferation of voices and meanings, and must therefore be controlled through the ideology of transparency and the suppression of the translator's discursive presence.

Follow-up questions for discussion

- Hermans describes as 'untenable' existing models of narrative that assume that the translator is located outside the discursive situation as a 'mere' reporting voice, a voice that simply repeats verbatim what is said by others. Elsewhere, Hermans (2007:69–76) discusses the issue of reported speech at length and suggests that the complexity of the reporting act and the difficulty of distinguishing clearly between various types of direct and indirect speech create 'a degree of ambivalence as to exactly whose voice and viewpoint receive articulation in a translation', and that we might then think of translation as 'a form of direct speech affected, or infected, by indirect speech' (*ibid.*:75). Consider the ideological and ethical implications of this suggestion, including, for example, the extent to which a translator or interpreter may be held responsible for what they 'report' or 'quote'.

- Sakai (1997:9–10) argues that the translator 'regulates communicative transactions, but her mediation must be erased in the representation of translation according to which the message issued by the writer in one language is transferred into an equivalent message in another language, which is then received by the readers'. Consider the impact of this erasure on the translator or interpreter herself, especially in situations of conflict or ethical dilemma (cf. Stahuljak, this volume). Might this erasure also have implications for the status of translators in society?

- Despite the emphasis on translated fiction, Hermans does devote some attention to interpreting, an activity rarely addressed by theorists of literary translation. His point of departure is that the illusion of transparency is just as dominant in written translation as it is in interpreting, despite the fact that the latter 'involves the simultaneous physical presence of two individuals and two voices in the same space', and that 'there are good grounds for arguing that very much the same factors, and the same illusion of transparency and coincidence, are at work' in both genres. Consider some of the factors that might be operative in both contexts and those that might separate them and hence require a different type of model to account for when and how the interpreter's voice becomes 'audible' – not as a 'carrier without a substance of its own' or a 'transparent vehicle', but as a distinct discursive presence.

Recommended further reading

Baker, Mona (2000) 'Towards a Methodology for Investigating the Style of a Literary Translator', *Target* 12(2): 241–66.

Hermans, Theo (2007) *The Conference of the Tongues*, Manchester: St. Jerome.

Munday, Jeremy (2008) 'Discursive Presence, Voice, and Style in Translation', Chapter 1 of *Style and Ideology in Translation*, London & New York: Routledge, 11–41.

Sakai, Naoki (1997) 'The Subject of Translation/the Subject in Transit', from the Introduction to *Translation and Subjectivity: On 'Japan' and Cultural Nationalism*, Minneapolis & London: University of Minnesota Press, 11–17.

1

WHEN BORIS YELTSIN SPEAKS THROUGH an Interpreter, do we really want to hear the Interpreter's voice? We listen, surely, because we want to know what Yeltsin has to say. To the extent that we are conscious of hearing the Interpreter's voice, it is as no more than a minor distraction. We regard – or better: we are prepared, we have been conditioned to regard – the Interpreter's voice as a carrier without a substance of its own, a virtually transparent vehicle. Anything that takes away from this transparency is unwelcome 'noise' in the information-theoretical sense of the term.

At the same time we know perfectly well that, unless we understand Russian, the Interpreter's voice is all we have. It is all we have access to, all we can make sense of on this side of the language barrier. Even when on radio or television, for example, we can still hear Yeltsin's Russian in the background, we do not understand those words and so we shut them out, realizing they are being broadcast alongside the interpretation only to authenticate the Interpreter's re-enunciation. We are not unduly bothered about not having direct access to Yeltsin's language because we know we can trust the Interpreter's professionalism. We trust that the Interpreter's words are an accurate and truthful copy or reproduction of Yeltsin's words. This trust, underpinned as it is by a number of professional and institutional guarantees, allows us to accept, or to project, the Interpreter's discourse as matching Yeltsin's, as constituting the equivalent of it, as coinciding with it, as being, to all intents and purposes, identical with it.

Of course, as soon as we stop to reflect on the various asymmetrical inter-lingual and intercultural processes taking place in the operation, we realize we are entertaining an illusion. The translation never coincides with its source, it is not identical or equivalent in any formal or straightforward sense, and it remains to be seen how the notion of the one discourse 'matching' the other is to be filled in. But the illusion is there, and necessarily there. It is part and parcel of what we, in our culture, have come to understand by 'translation'. It fits, that is, our ideology of trans-lation, which is backed up by a vast amount of translation theory and history and by all manner of institutionalized agreements governing relations between primary and secondary texts, up to and including such things as intellectual ownership, copyright laws, authorized translations, legally certified copies, professional codes of conduct, etc. Translation, in this context, is delegated speech, and the delegate has no executive powers.

The illusion, then, the necessary illusion, is one of transparency and coincidence as exponents of equivalence. As the Interpreter's voice falls in with, coincides with and in so doing – paradoxically – disappears behind Yeltsin's voice, the physical experience of hearing two distinct voices speaking more or less simultaneously is suppressed, or sublimated, and in practice we consider the two voices to be wholly consonant. Even as we listen to the one voice we are able to follow, we negate its presence because we recognize its substantial and institutionally endorsed conformity to the primary enunciation, which, we accept, has integrity, authority, and therefore primacy. We conclude that 'Yeltsin has said so and so'. Because it has no substance of its own, the re-enunciation in the other language assumes the quality of direct quotation.[1]

2

Although interpreting, as a rule, involves the simultaneous physical presence of two individuals and two voices in the same space, there are good grounds for arguing that very much the same factors, and the same illusion of transparency and coincidence, are at work in written translation, and in translated fiction. Perhaps the illusion is even stronger here.

Consider for a moment a certified translation of a degree certificate. The stamp issued by a third party declaring the translation to be a 'true copy' of the original reminds the user that this is a translation: the stamp marks the distance between original and translation (usually also identifying the sworn translator by name), but at the same time as formalizing their differential status it asserts that the copy is 'as good as' the original. Next, consider a translation, say, of a safety regulation in a large international concern, which first issues the new regulation in the head office and then has it translated into a number of languages for use in its subsidiary plants. In each country this version subsequently becomes one regulation among several, and the translators' interventions, including their proper names, are completely erased. Whether the translators are the firm's own employees or the job was contracted out to a translation agency, all concerned have every reason to take it for granted that the translation constitutes a truthful copy of the original. Translators, after all, like inter-preters, speak in someone else's name and thus they are expected to subscribe to what Brian Harris has called the 'true interpreter' norm, or the 'honest spokesperson' norm, which 'requires that people who speak on behalf of others . . . re-express the original speakers' ideas and the manner of expressing them as accurately as possible and without significant omissions, and not mix them up with their own ideas and expressions' (Harris 1990:118). The translator is expected to observe total discretion.

Although nowadays many works of translated fiction routinely carry the translator's name and in this respect resemble the 'certified copy', in the way they are read they are mostly closer to the second case just mentioned. While reading translated fiction, readers are normally meant to forget that what they are reading is a translation. The translator withdraws wholly behind the narrating voice. So whose voice comes to us when we read a translated novel? Common usage is indicative. We tend to say that we are reading Dostoyevsky, for example, even when we are reading not Russian but English or French or Spanish words. This blotting out, this 'erasure' of the translator's intervention is paradoxical. In contrast to simultaneous or especially consecutive interpreting, with two speakers sharing a given physical space, when we read translated fiction we have only the translated text in front of us. The primary voice, the authoritative originary voice, is in fact absent. And yet we casually state it is the only one that presents itself to us. And in practice we do so largely, perhaps wholly, on the strength of the hierarchy implied by the order (and, more often than not, the size) of the names on the title page:

NOVEL by Writer X
Translated by Translator Y

The question arises: is the illusion of 'I am reading Dostoyevsky' all there is to it? Does the translator, the manual labour done, disappear without textual trace, speaking entirely 'under erasure'? Can translators usurp the original voice and in the same move evacuate their own enunciatory space? Exactly whose voice comes to us when we read translated discourse?

The question can be examined from a variety of angles, including an ideological one. In what follows it is treated first and foremost as a narratological issue, asking about the voice that produces the discourse that we read, and therefore asking about the discursive centre from which the text issues. Let us remind ourselves of the standard representation of narrative communication[2] (see Figure 11.1).

This scheme represents the normal situation, without reference to translation. What we read is a discourse produced by a Narrator. In translated fiction, who exactly articulates the translated discourse? Is it the same Narrator as in the source text? Does

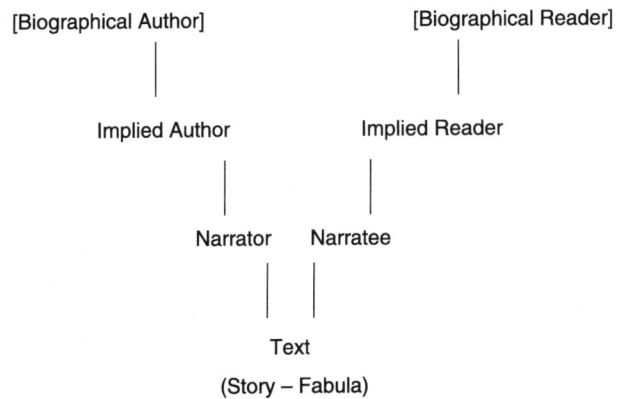

Figure 11.1

this then mean that the translator, as Biographical Translator, is like the Biographical Author: another name on the title page, indicating an entity located firmly outside the narrative discourse?

As it is, narratology does not distinguish between original and translated fiction. The main narratological models currently available (Booth, Stanzel, Genette, Rimmon-Kenan, Bal, Chatman, Prince) are designed to apply to narrative texts in general, irrespective of whether they are original or translated. In what follows I will argue that these models overlook a presence in the narrative text that cannot be fully suppressed.[3] Translated narrative discourse, it will be claimed, always implies more than one voice in the text, more than one discursive presence. It may be that in many narratives this 'other' voice never clearly manifests itself, but it should neverthe-less be postulated, on the strength of those cases where it is manifestly present and discernible. And it is only, I submit, the ideology of translation, the illusion of transparency and coincidence, the illusion of the one voice, that blinds us to the presence of this other voice.

3

The claim, then, is that translated narrative discourse always contains a 'second' voice, to which I will refer as the Translator's voice, as an index of the Translator's discursive presence. The voice may be more or less overtly present. It may remain entirely hidden behind that of the Narrator, rendering it impossible to detect in the translated text. It is most directly and forcefully present when it breaks through the surface of the text speaking for itself, in its own name, for example in a paratextual Translator's Note employing an autoreferential first person identifying the speaking subject.[4] And then there are shades and degrees in between.

As far as I can make out, the 'other' voice in translated narrative texts is likely to manifest itself primarily in three kinds of cases. They all involve what may be termed 'performative self-contradiction' in that the Translator's self-denial runs into obvious, textually traceable contradictions. In each case there is a certain pressure on the Translator to come out of the shadows and directly intervene in a text which the reader had been led to believe spoke with only one voice. They are

(1) cases where the text's orientation towards an Implied Reader and hence its ability to function as a medium of communication is directly at issue;
(2) cases of self-reflexiveness and self-referentiality involving the medium of communication itself;
(3) certain cases of what, for want of a better term, I will refer to as 'contextual overdetermination'.

In each case the degree of visibility of the Translator's presence depends on the translation strategy that has been adopted, and on the consistency with which it has been carried through. Since each of the three cases listed, and certainly cases (1) and (2), involve a kind of communicative short-circuiting, a fissure within the discourse which draws attention to the linguistic and pragmatic dislocation that comes with translation, the resulting incongruity in the translated text needs to be accounted for in one way or another. Some translation strategies will effectively paper over the cracks and leave the reader unaware of the other voice. My interest here is in those instances where the translated text itself shows visible traces of a discursive presence other than the ostensible Narrator. Before illustrating the case with reference to a particular translation, a further word about the first two cases mentioned above; the third will be elucidated later, with reference to a concrete example.

As for (1): Unlike interpreting, where speaker and interpreter more or less simultaneously address a physically present if linguistically mixed audience, written translations normally address an audience which is not only linguistically but also temporally and/or geographically removed from that addressed by the source text. To the extent that a Reader is implied by and implicated in the overall 'intent' (Chatman) and orchestration of narrative fiction, translated narrative fiction addresses an Implied Reader different from that of the source text, since the discourse operates in a new pragmatic context. All texts are culturally embedded and require a frame of reference which is shared between sender and receiver to be able to function as vehicles for communication. The various forms of displacement that result from translation (Folkart 1991:347ff. speaks of a 'décalage traductionnel') threaten this shared frame of reference. It is therefore not surprising to find that it is precisely with respect to the cultural embedding of texts, e.g. in the form of historical or topical references and allusions, that the Translator's Voice often directly and openly intrudes into the discourse to provide information deemed necessary to safeguard adequate communication with the new audience. As a rule, translations, and certainly modern translations of canonical literary fiction, stop short of reorienting the discourse so radically that the orientation to the original Implied Reader disappears altogether. The translated text can therefore be said to address a dual audience, and thus to have a 'secondary' Implied Reader superimposed on the original one. This can lead to hybrid situations in which the discourse offers manifestly redundant or inadequate information, or appears attuned to one type of Reader here and another there, showing the Translator's presence in and through the discordances.

As for (2): 'self-reflexiveness' and 'self-referentiality' are used here as rather broad terms covering various instances which have been discussed as exemplifying untranslatability by, among others, Jacques Derrida. Obvious cases are texts which affirm their being written in a particular language, or which exploit the economy of their idiom through polysemy, wordplay and similar devices. We are dealing, then, with instances in which language collapses upon itself, as it were, or, as Derrida would have it, 're-marks' itself. It is of course possible that the translated text solves the problems so discreetly that no trace of a 'second voice' is left behind. But sometimes translations run into contradictions and incongruities which challenge the reader's willing suspension of disbelief; or the translated text may call on the explicit intervention of a Translator's Voice through the use of brackets or of notes, and they then remind the reader of this other presence continually stalking a purportedly univocal discourse.

Examples of linguistic self-referentiality are not hard to find, and they are not restricted to narrative texts. In translations of many of Derrida's essays meta-linguistic notes or comments are added by translators in their attempts to cope with the French puns. Nowhere is this more in evidence than in 'Survive: Journal de bord', where the lower band of the page, the 'journal de bord', openly challenges the translator to render the French puns ('pas de méthode', 'point de méthode', the series 'écrit, récit, série', etc.); again and again the English translation has recourse to square brackets in an effort to keep up, overtly displaying the translated nature of the text by showing the translator's hand (see, for example, Derrida 1991:256ff.).

Derrida's discussion, elsewhere,[5] of a rather different instance of language affirming itself concerns the final chapter of Descartes' *Discours de la Méthode*, where in the French original the author declares that his book is written in French and not in Latin. The Latin translation omits this embarrassing sentence, to avoid the self-contradiction of a statement in Latin declaring it is not in Latin but in French. Derrida regards this as a case of institutional and statutory untranslatability, which is a perfectly valid observation. For the reader of the Latin version, however, the omission is not detectable and therefore does not reveal the translator's presence in the translated text as such. In translations into languages other than Latin, where the sentence is translated, the self-contradiction may be less glaring, but it is still obvious enough. When the English version has: 'And if I write in French . . . rather than in Latin . . . it is because . . .' (Descartes 1968:91), the anomaly of reading an English text which declares, in English, that it is actually in French creates a credibility gap which readers can overcome only by reminding themselves that this is, of course, a translation. But in so doing those readers also realize that the voice producing the statement cannot possibly belong to Descartes, or to Descartes alone. There is, clearly, another voice at play, duplicating and mimicking the first one, but with a timbre of its own. Derrida himself exploits the paradox in his 1984 address 'Ulysse gramophone', which opens with the sentence: 'Oui, oui, vous m'entendez bien, ce sont des mots français', and leads to an inevitable if self-conscious self-contradiction in the English translation: 'Oui, oui, you are receiving me, these are French words' (Derrida 1992:256).

4

In the following pages I will illustrate these points in more detail, with reference to several translations of a single book, the Dutch novel *Max Havelaar* by Multatuli, first published in 1860. With its complex narrative structure, *Max Havelaar* provides instances not only of cultural embedding and linguistic self-referentiality, but also of 'contextual overdetermination', all of them, to varying degrees, bringing the Translator's voice to the textual surface. I will refer to two English translations, by W. Siebenhaar (1927) and Roy Edwards (1967, re-issued as a Penguin Classic 1987); and to the French and the Spanish translations by Mme Roland Garros (1968) and Francisco Carrasquer (1975), respectively. There are other translations, including older renderings into English and French as well as versions into German and other languages, but the four considered here will do for the purposes of the present exposition. The Dutch text referred to is the standard scholarly 'historical-critical' edition (1992), which is based on the novel's fifth and last edition (1881) to appear during the author's lifetime.[6]

The Biographical Author of *Max Havelaar* is Eduard Douwes Dekker (1820–1887), who wrote under the pseudonym Multatuli. The novel was dedicated to Everdine Huberte van Wijnbergen.[7] In its barest essence the book tells the story of Max Havelaar, a Dutch civil servant in the colonial administration in the Dutch East Indies in the 1850s. Witnessing the exploitation of the local population by the native élite, he protests in vain to his immediate superior. When he ignores the administrative hierarchy and brings a charge against the local ruler he is relieved of his post and resigns in disgust.

The novel's unusual richness, however, springs at least in part from its narrative structure and its use of different narrators. The opening chapters employ the homodiegetic narrator Batavus Droogstoppel, an Amsterdam coffee broker and the epitome of Dutch *petit-bourgeois* values and hypocrisy. One day Droogstoppel runs into a former schoolmate, the destitute Sjaalman, who leaves him a bundle of documents which Droogstoppel reckons he can use for a book on the coffee trade. However, he delegates the writing to a young German trainee in his firm, the romantic Stern who, assisted by Droogstoppel's son Frits and probably helped by Sjaalman himself, writes an altogether different book, which is being composed as we read. Stern thus becomes the narrator of the dramatic story of Max Havelaar and his wife Tine in the East Indies. As the novel continues, Droogstoppel occasionally breaks into Stern's discourse to voice his disapproval of the way Stern is handling his material. In the Havelaar episodes, meanwhile, the Stern-Narrator dishes up other stories as well as documents purporting to authenticate Havelaar's conflict with his superiors. The novel's concluding pages contain the main surprise, as another first-person Narrator identifying himself as Multatuli suddenly takes over from Stern, dismisses Droogstoppel, and addresses the Dutch King with an impassioned plea to stop the oppression of the natives in the East Indies.

The different narrative levels in *Max Havelaar* may be represented schematically as follows:

DROOGSTOPPEL (in Amsterdam)
= I-Narrator$_1$
'you' addressee = the Dutch reader
→Droogstoppel delegates narration to
    STERN (in Amsterdam)
    = I-Narrator$_2$
    'you' addressee = the Dutch reader
    → story of **Max Havelaar**, wife Tine etc.
    (in Dutch East Indies)
Final pages: 'I, MULTATULI' takes over as Narrator from Stern and Droogstoppel
= I-Narrator$_3$
'you' addressee = the Dutch King

As it happens, there is in *Max Havelaar* an instance similar to the Descartes case mentioned above. In the Dutch text Max Havelaar quotes a poem in French which he says he wrote himself and which is also reproduced in French (MH:127). As Havelaar is Dutch, the poem serves as a signal to the reader, suggesting Havelaar's literary talent and linguistic abilities, favourably contrasting him with the dreary Droogstoppel figure. The French translation, unable to translate the French poem into itself, merely quotes it (Garros:186). But it adds a Translator's Note: 'En français dans le texte (N.d.T.)'.[8] The reason for rupturing the discourse and intervening by means of a paratextual note is clear enough: the surplus value signalled in the original by the use of a different language risks being lost on the French reader. The note itself, however, with or without its curious ambiguity ('dans le texte' is obviously redundant if it means the French text, so it must refer to the Dutch original), reminds its readers that this is a translated text – and at the same time alerts them to the presence of an altogether different voice, breaking through the narrative voice ostensibly established by the discourse. In contrast, a poetic dialogue in German also reported by the Narrator as having been penned by Havelaar (MH:157–160) is left, unannotated, in German in the French translation (Garros:225–228), revealing not a glimpse of the Translator's presence – except in the dissonance between a Note identifying the language of a French poem in a French text and remaining silent on how to read a poem in a foreign language.

5

Before going on to consider examples of different ways in which, and degrees to which, the Translator's presence makes itself felt in translations of *Max Havelaar*, it may be useful to point out that they all concern instances where the presence of an enunciating subject other than the Narrator becomes discernible *in the translated text itself*. This means we are *not* looking at cases where only the comparison with the source text will show the intervention of a (biographical) translator, however revealing these manipulations, additions or omissions may be from an ideological or other such point of view. In the Havelaar narrative, for example, the Narrator at one point describes the layout of Havelaar's house in the Indies. In the Dutch, and in the French translation, this is done by means of numbers: imagine a rectangle divided into twenty-one compartments, three across, seven down, etc. (MH:136; Garros:198). In both the Spanish and the English versions diagrams are added as visual illustrations, without paratextual comment (Carrasquer:190; Edwards:224). Since the Spanish and English texts themselves provide no discernible trace of a linguistic subject other than the Narrator as the source of the diagrams, and consequently the intervention by (presumably) the biographical translator can be detected only through a comparison with the source text, such instances are not relevant to the argument being pursued here.

Hence, although the cases highlighted below mostly issue from source text cruxes, they do not focus on the retrospective comparison between translation and original. Rather, as different translations opt for different solutions, some bring the Translator's discursive presence clearly into view while others do not, or to a lesser extent. In each case the assumption is that, given the dominant conception of transparent translation in modern fiction, the reader's awareness of reading a translation lies dormant, leaving intact the notion that (with the exception of embedded narrative and character speech) there is only one Narrator speaking at any one time. As long as there are no markers in the text suggesting another voice, all is well. The following instances, however, concern places where another presence insinuates or parachutes itself into the text, breaking the univocal frame and jolting the reader into an awareness of the text's plurivocal nature.

5.1

A couple of examples will suffice to illustrate the rather obvious case of cultural references which, as a result of the displacement brought about by translation, threaten to be left in a vacuum and prompt the Translator to rupture the narrative frame by means of paratextual Notes.

In Chapter 9 of *Max Havelaar*, in a passage marking a sudden transition from Stern as Narrator (of the Havelaar story) to Droogstoppel as Narrator (of his own story), reference is made to Abraham Blankaart, a fictional character from the Dutch novel *Sara Burgerhart* (1782) by Betje Wolff and Aagje Deken. The name is first dropped in the Stern narrative, and taken up by Droogstoppel. That its recognition requires a Dutch cultural frame of reference is evident from Droogstoppel's comment that his own son Frits has obviously been lending young Stern a hand, for, as he says, 'this Abraham Blankaart is much too Dutch for a German' (MH:95). Ironically, in a note added by Multatuli himself to the fourth edition (1875) and retained in subsequent editions (Multatuli 1992, II:xxxvii), he wondered how many of his own generation still recognized the literary allusion (MH:263), suggesting that even within a specific cultural continuum shared frames of reference are time-bound phenomena.

Both English translations and the Spanish version at this point break into the text to insert a Translator's Note explaining the reference (Siebenhaar:122–123; Edwards:134–135; Carrasquer:155–156).[9] The French translation retains the name, without an explanatory note; a second occurrence of the name, in the next paragraph, has been omitted (Garros:142–143). This seems consistent, and at first sight does not allow the reader a view of the Translator's discursive presence. But before this passage other instances have occurred where Translator's Notes, identified as such, explained linguistic or cultural issues arising from the source text (Garros:36, 38, 58, 60, 87, 108, . . .). It is precisely the inconsistency in the provision of paratextual information designed to safeguard the shared frame of reference which creates a disparity at the discursive level: the helpful voice which came to the French reader's rescue on other occasions remains inexplicably silent here. The deliberate silence of the voice, withholding information which is expected, signals the presence of a discursive subject different from either of the two homodiegetic Narrators whose words we read. As we are reading a translation, this 'differential voice' can only be the Translator's.[10]

A similar inference can be made, incidentally, with respect to the proper names in several of the translations. *Max Havelaar* is set in a particular place and time: the Netherlands and the Dutch East Indies in the 1850s. The proper names of the Dutch characters are recognizably Dutch. Some, like Havelaar, Bastiaans, Busselinck, Verbrugge, are proper names in the conventional sense; others are more Dickensian, motivated names, holding out an invitation to the reader to activate their latent semantic load. Roy Edwards' English translation copies most of the names intact, including, for example, the suggestive 'Droogstoppel' (paratextually annotated as meaning 'Drystubble', 'Dryasdust', which is the way the name was rendered in the two previous English translations). With a name like 'Slimering' (Dutch: 'Slymering'), luck is on the Translator's side, as minimal adaptation preserves the satirical intent without revealing the Translator's presence. But the pompous preacher Wawelaar appears in the text as 'Parson Blatherer', creating a sudden incongruity within the pattern of proper names which stretches the reader's willingness to suspend disbelief: an obviously Dutch character, in a Dutch setting, with so transparent and apposite an English name, yet without explanation? Given the otherwise consistent discourse of the Narrators delivering the story, the source of the disparity must surely be attributed to another discursive presence.

5.2

The name of the character Sjaalman in *Max Havelaar* is a special case. This is not a proper name at all, as Droogstoppel, the Narrator at this point, declines to tell us the person's real name (which the reader will infer later). It is first introduced as a descriptive term (the man with the shawl, or scarf), then contracted into 'de Sjaalman' (the Shawl-man), and Droogstoppel subsequently decides to continue to call the man 'Sjaalman' as if that were his name. The first occurrence of the designation is accompanied by Droogstoppel's metalinguistic comment to the effect that his son Frits prefers the English word 'shawl' to Droogstoppel's good old Dutch 'sjaal'. It is the first in a series of linguistic quibbles through which Droogstoppel characterizes himself as a pedant:

In-plaats van een behoorlyken winterjas, hing hem een soort van sjaal
over den schouder – Frits zegt: 'shawl', maar dit doe ik niet – alsof hy zoo
van de reis kwam. (MH:10)

The translations render the passage as follows:

Instead of a suitable winter coat, he had a kind of shawl hanging over his
shoulder – Frits says 'Châle': he is learning French, but I keep to our good
old language – as if he had just come from a journey. (Siebenhaar:12–13)

Instead of a decent winter coat he had a sort of scarf dangling over his
shoulder – we call it a *sjaal* in Dutch, so Frits has to call it a 'shawl', which
isn't even right, just to show off his English – as if he – the scarf-man,
I mean – was just back from being on the road. (Edwards:27)

Aunque en lugar de llevar gabán, como habría sido lo propio, colgaba de
sus hombros una especie de bufanda or largo chal – Frits dice pañuelo
de cuello, pero yo no paso por ahí – como si acabara de llegar de algún
viaje. (Carrasquer:22)

Au lieu d'un pardessus convenable, une sorte de châle couvrait ses
épaules, comme s'il rentrait de voyage. (Garros:36)

Neither Garros (on this page) nor Carrasquer upset the reading process, and hence
the fictional universe, as neither text leaves the language the reader is engaged in.
Garros omits Frits' use of a foreign term, and Carrasquer employs an intralingual
variant. As Sjaalman's descriptive designation turns into a proper name, the Spanish
version continues with 'Chalman'. At that stage the French translation runs into a
linguistic problem: since 'homme au châle' will not double up as a proper name in
French, the transition from designation to name cannot take place within the terms
first set out for it. The problem is solved by cutting into the text's linguistic homogeneity: the next occurrence has: 'Un jour, le Sjaalman que j'avais devant moi était
avec nous' and the novel term 'Sjaalman', more than halfway between designation
(*le* Sjaalman) and proper name (Sjaalman capitalized), is elucidated in a Translator's
Note: 'Littéralement: homme au châle (N.d.T.)' (Garros:38). But the linguistic trans-
gression, the Note and the fact that the reference is to the source language of a
translation, break the narrative frame. The agent responsible for this discursive act
cannot be the Narrator.

Siebenhaar solves the 'sjaal/shawl' problem by substituting 'shawl/châle',
English/French for Dutch/English, culturally not dissimilar as a pair, and so the
reader's awareness that in fact Droogstoppel is Dutch and speaks Dutch remains
largely dormant (not wholly, as the reader knows that Droogstoppel's 'our good old
languae' is Dutch, not English). Edwards' triad 'scarf/sjaal/shawl' does remind the
reader of Droogstoppel's native language – and more than that, since Dutch is not
only the language of Droogstoppel as character and (homodiegetic) narrator, but
also, inescapably, the source language of the translation as a whole. The occurrence,
in the translated text, of a metalinguistic statement bearing coincidentally on both the
fictional world (Droogstoppel as a fictional character) and its framing context (a novel
translated from the Dutch) highlights a paradox. As readers, we accept the convention, which also operates, for example, in historical fiction or in narratives set in

foreign lands, that we read words in one language while we know that the fictional characters, to the extent that they resemble lifelike individuals existing in identifiable locations, must have spoken a different language. In this crux in the English *Max Havelaar* the metalinguistic reference draws attention to that convention itself. This is no doubt partly because it involves the source language of the whole work, as the Translator's paratextual Notes remind us time and again. A further reason is that the 'sjaal/shawl' issue is only one of a series of similar instances of linguistic point-scoring between Droogstoppel and his son, some of which are presented within the terms of the English language while others draw on Dutch. These disparities within the discourse itself prevent the conventional suspension of disbelief and bring into focus the linguistic as well as pragmatic displacement consequent upon the act of translation.

The following passage provides additional illustration. This is Droogstoppel again, taking on Frits on a point of language:

> . . . en dat ook de suikerraffinadeurs – Frits zegt: *raffineurs*, maar ik schryf *nadeurs*. Dit doen de Rosemeyers ook, en die *doen* in suiker. Ik weet wel dat men zegt: *geraffineerde* schelm, en niet: *geraffinadeerde* schelm . . . (MH:29)

> . . . and that also the sugar-*raffinadeurs* – Frits says refiners, but I write *raffinadeurs*; this the Rosemeyers do also, and they *are* sugar people; I know, one speaks of a *refined* scoundrel, and not a *raffinadeur* scoundrel . . . (Siebenhaar:36)

> . . . and that the sugar refiners, *raffinadeurs* as we say in Dutch – Frits says *raffineurs* but I say *raffinadeurs*; the Rosemeyers do too, and they're *in* sugar. I know one talks about a *geraffineerd* scoundrel, and not a *geraffinadeerd* scoundrel . . . (Edwards:54)

> . . . y que también los refinadores (Frits dice 'refineros', pero yo hago como los demás, incluídos los Rosemeyer, y eso que trabajan en el ramo del azúcar; ya sé que se dice un carterista 'refino' y no refinado, . . . (Carrasquer:53).

> . . . et que les raffineurs de sucre et les marchands d'indigo dussent y joindre les leurs. (Garros:61)

The Spanish translation again solves the linguistic problem within its own linguistic terms and the French version has suppressed it altogether; neither allows a glimpse of the Translator's discursive presence. Both English versions go beyond their own language. The Siebenhaar translation has Droogstoppel using a non-existent English word (the *OED* does not list 'raffinadeur') coupled with Frits' 'refiners'. Apart from the psychological inconsistency in Droogstoppel as a character/narrator who normally insists on solid Dutch values and is here found using a term which the English reader might conceivably (if erroneously) take to be French, there is little to suggest another voice speaking alongside the Narrator's.

In the Edwards' version Droogstoppel specifically refers to Dutch as his own language, bringing in three terms: 'refiners', 'raffinadeurs' and 'raffineurs'. Curiously, Droogstoppel's discourse here short-circuits itself, as he writes, in English, 'sugar refiners', only to declare in the same breath, 'but I say *raffinadeurs*', a Dutch word. The issue of whether scoundrels are '*geraffineerd*' or '*geraffinadeerd*' will not only be lost on the English reader (both forms contain Dutch morphemes), but will draw further attention to Dutch as the real language of Droogstoppel's fictional world – and as the language of a book which, when the fictional narrative is shattered in the final pages, closes with a direct address by a Dutchman (see below) to the Dutch King. This pulls very closely together the different levels of language which are involved: the language of the fictional characters and narrators, the language of Multatuli's address to the King, and the source language of the translation. What is striking, however, is not so much the paradoxical nature of this situation – convention keeps that under control – but the linguistic anomaly in Droogstoppel's own usage. That anomaly points to a different discursive *locus*, not reducible to Droogstoppel's speech act.

5.3

Max Havelaar is a complex novel not only because of its different narrative levels, but also because it plays, ingeniously and decisively, on the distinction between fiction and non-fiction. A crucial aspect of this is the way in which the narrative levels are linked. Some of these links are immediately obvious, others are established piecemeal, through association, inference, and a number of subtle shifts and hints.[11] In this way it gradually becomes clear to the reader that Max Havelaar, who only appears as a character in Stern's narrative, is in fact the same person as the Sjaalman who later (but, as we read, in the opening chapters) runs into Droogstoppel in Amsterdam and leaves him the documents from which Stern constructs the Havelaar story. Stern also copies the correspondence detailing Havelaar's conflict with his superiors. However, when in the book's final pages Multatuli himself takes over, he radically changes the perspective, emphasizing the factual truth underlying the fictionalized Havelaar story (including the factual truth of the correspondence) and declaring the novel form to have been a mere ploy, since the book is really a tract written in self-justification. Together with a number of other indications (detailed in Sötemann 1972:67–69, 276–280) this leads to the inescapable conclusion that Havelaar, Sjaalman and Multatuli are all the same individual, thus linking the most deeply embedded narrative level, the Havelaar story, with the framing discourse and the name on the cover and title page.

   In the narrative, Havelaar's wife is never called anything but Tine, although she has a handkerchief with the letter E in the corner, her grandfather is a 'Baron van W.', and we learn her initials: E.H.V.W. In the Droogstoppel narrative, Sjaalman's wife is never mentioned by name, but there are certain parallels with Tine. The book's dedication to 'E.H.v.W.' (manuscript and first three editions) and, from the fourth edition onwards, to 'Everdine Huberte Baronnesse van Wynbergen' (MH:1), leaves little doubt that the person in question is the wife of – well, of a pseudonym? 'Multatuli' is evidently a pen-name (Latin: 'multa tuli'), which the bearer himself translates in the text: 'I, Multatuli, who have borne much' ('ik, Multatuli, "die veel gedragen heb" ', MH: 235) just as it is said several times of Havelaar that he had suffered much. No, Tine/Everdine is evidently the wife of Eduard Douwes Dekker, inventor of Multatuli.[12] The chain of identification thus stretches beyond the pseudonym to the Biographical Author, exploding the fictional frame and revealing the book as autobiography, since Dekker = Multatuli = Sjaalman = Havelaar, and the Author = Narrator = Character (Genette 1991:83).

   It is also possible, of course, to read the claim to factual truth in the novel as being made within the limits of the fictional world presented by the narrative. The buck then stops with Multatuli rather than with Eduard Douwes Dekker. In that case the dedication is presumably also part of the fictional universe, and Everdine/E.H.v.W. is then indeed the wife of Multatuli. But this does not affect the identification of Havelaar's wife with Multatuli's dedicatee.

Now, at the novel's deepest narrative level, the story of Max Havelaar, we are at one point presented with a conversation between Havelaar, his wife Tine and some Dutch friends; they discuss the fact that Mrs Slotering, a native woman who is the widow of Havelaar's predecessor and lives in the same compound as the Havelaars, prefers to keep to herself. Tine remarks she can very well understand Mrs Slotering's keenness to run her own household (we learn the real reason later), and asks her husband:

> 'Weet je nog hoe je myn naam vertaald hebt?'

to which Havelaar replies:

> 'E.H.V.W.: eigen haard veel waard'. (MH:121)

In the translations the exchange is rendered as follows:

> 'Do you remember how you once translated my initials?'
> 'E.H.V.W. *Eigen haard veel waard.*'
> Translator's Note: Own hearth great worth (One's own hearth is worth a good deal) (Siebenhaar:159)

> 'Do you remember how you once translated my initials: E.H. v. W.?'
> 'Yes. *Eigen haard veel waard.*'
> Translator's Note: 'Literally "one's own hearth is worth much". Cf. "There's no place like home" ' (Edwards:170)

> '¿Te acuerdas de cómo interpretaste mis iniciales como si fueran siglas de una máxima: E.H.V.W.?'
> '— Ya lo creo: 'Eigen Haard, Veel Waard.'
> Translator's Note: 'Literalmente: "El propio es el hogar que mucho vale", pero aquí se refiere a que vale mucho lo que uno hace y la casa propia gana si la administra y cuida la misma dueña. Las iniciales corresponden a: Everdina Huberta van Wijnbergen'. (Carrasquer:199)

> [Omitted] (Garros:179)

The extent to which the initials are 'contextually overdetermined' will be clear by now. Both the immediate pragmatic context of the conversation and the complex chain of identification linking the fictional character Tine with the book's dedicatee bear directly on the passage. This severely reduces the Biographical Translator's room for manoeuvre, as the task consists of combining the initials (ultimately, those of a historical person, and therefore not open to manipulation) with an appropriate four-word proverb in which each word begins with a certain letter. Even the Spanish translation, which on other occasions coped with metalinguistic statements within the terms of Spanish, is at a loss here. The French version omits the exchange, sacrificing one of the strongest links in the identification chain, which in turn directly affects the book's status as representing fact or fiction (irrespective of whether the claim to factual truth is seen as being made within the fictional world only).

In so doing, however, the translated French text as it stands shows no trace of the Translator's discursive presence in this particular instance. In the Siebenhaar, Edwards and Carrasquer versions a sudden abyss opens up, even if we disregard the Translator's Note. As in some of the other examples listed above, the translated discourse operates under the convention that although Havelaar and company are Dutch-speakers, we read their words, and the presentation of their actions, in English or Spanish. This convention routinely spans the credibility gap by putting in place a suspension bridge, the willing suspension of disbelief. This convention collapses here. Since the Havelaar circle in this scene, as in most other scenes in the book, is monolingual, the sudden shift from English or Spanish to Dutch and back again creates a severe discursive anomaly, a crevice. Oddly enough, the Narrator appears not to register the anomaly: the voice leaps out of and back into its language of narration as if it were speaking independently of its linguistic medium. It is the other voice, the one which co-produces the text, the Translator's, which picks up on the disparity and provides an explanation in the form of a paratextual Note.

The Note in each case also translates the untranslatable. In the source text, Tine's question regarding Havelaar's having once 'translated' ('vertaald') her initials into a proverb rather than a proper name, prompts an intralingual response: the initials transposed into a proverb. In the English and Spanish versions, we get what we expect of translation, an interlingual shift. But instead of transforming the unfamiliar into the familiar, the shift (from English/Spanish to Dutch in the text) only produces an incomprehensible string ('eigen haard veel waard'), the opposite of translation. Since the discourse itself does not remark on this incongruity, the assumption must be that this is Dutch, Havelaar's 'real' language, which we knew was there but were meant to gloss over – but also, coincidentally, the 'original' language of the book as a whole. The Translator's Note confirms this by translating the Dutch proverb (though not the initials, for that transposition, barring a linguistic fluke, can only take place in Dutch) and showing the intractability of the problem. In invoking, explicitly or not, the book's dedication and thus going beyond the immediate Havelaar scene, the Note brings the translated nature of the entire discourse into the picture, self-referentially and self-reflexively. The combination, then, of the non-translation of the initials, the reversion to Dutch and the deferred translation of the Dutch proverb defines the discursive position of the Translator's voice.

6

The discussion in the preceding paragraphs was designed to show the presence of the Translator's voice, as a discursive presence, in translations of *Max Havelaar*. If the points made have any validity, it is worth considering some broader and more general claims. Indeed, while we may have been concerned with the detail of one particular novel, and a particularly complex one at that, the issue would appear to be of some wider theoretical import.

6.1

What the discussion of *Max Havelaar* in translation will have shown is that the Translator's voice is always present as co-producer of the discourse. The Translator's voice may remain hidden behind the voice(s) of the Narrator(s) for long stretches. In some narratives it may never become clearly discernible at all, and in those cases we have to fall back on positing an Implied Translator as the source of the translated text's invention and intent. However, the inference from the *Havelaar* case must be that it is not only reasonable but necessary to postulate the presence of the Translator's discursive presence in translated fiction, because it is possible to cite specific cases which clearly bring that 'other' voice to the surface, for example in instances where its intervention is seen to cater for the needs of the Target Text reader (as a consequence of the cultural and pragmatic embedding of texts and the displacement resulting from translation), or in cases where the discourse short-circuits itself through linguistic self-referentiality or contextual over-determination.

Hence even in those instances where the Translator's discursive presence is not directly traceable, it is a presence that must be posited, just as we must also posit a Target-Culture Implied Reader superimposed on the Source-Culture Implied Reader. It also follows that, if a theoretical model of narrative communication is to be comprehensive, it must create room for instances like those highlighted here.

This makes untenable the model of translated narrative which simply assumes that every enunciation has a source (every text implies the presence of a voice producing it) and that the translator's presence does not interfere with that discursive situation, being located outside it as the reporting voice which repeats, verbatim, the words spoken by the first voice. That model, simplified, looks like this:

(text)
[I say: (text)]
{I translate: [I say: (text)]}

What is needed, rather, is a model of translated narrative which accounts for the way in which the Translator's voice insinuates itself into the discourse and adjusts to the displacement which translation brings about. The model, that is, needs to incorporate the Translator as constantly co-producing the discourse, shadowing, mimicking and, as it were, counterfeiting the Narrator's words, but occasionally – caught in the text's disparities and interstices, and paratextually – emerging into the open as a separate discursive presence. In Schiavi (1996), the theoretical case for an Implied Translator is argued and an alternative model proposed. In practice, many translated narratives indeed do not allow us to go further than the terms of that model, because what has been called here the Translator's voice or the Translator's discursive presence in the text is wholly assimilated into the Narrator's voice. It is only in specific cases that the 'other' voice becomes dissociated from the one it mimics.

6.2

The further question arises: Why do current approaches to narrative have this blind spot when it comes to the Translator's voice? Why do *we*, as readers, prefer to ignore this 'other' discursive presence?

The reason, it seems to me, lies in the cultural and therefore also the ideological construct which is translation. This takes us straight back to the dominant concept of translation in our culture: translation as transparency and duplicate, as not only consonant but coincident and hence to all intents and purposes identical with its source text; the view of translation as reproduction, in which the translation is meant to reproduce the original, the whole original and nothing but the original; the image of a translation being 'as good as' its original, except in regard of status. A translation is a 'good' or a 'proper' or a 'real' translation, we tend to say, if there are no loose ends, no foreign bodies; it should not contain anything that might affect the integrity of the original. Translators are good translators if and when they have become transparent, invisible, when they have spirited themselves away. Only a Translator who speaks 'under erasure' can be trusted not to violate the original. The loyal absence of the one guarantees the primacy and aura of the other.

This hierarchy governing the relation between original and translation is nothing new. Historically it has been construed in a number of ways, mostly around oppositions such as those between creative versus derivative work, primary versus secondary, art versus craft, authority versus obedience, freedom versus constraint, speaking in one's own name versus speaking for someone else. In each pair it is translation which is circumscribed, hemmed in, controlled, subordinated. And in case we think these are after all natural and necessary hierarchies, it may be useful to remind ourselves of the fact that in our culture the male/female distinction, too, has been constructed in terms of very similar oppositions of creative versus reproductive, original versus derivative, active versus passive, dominant versus subservient.

Deep down, of course, we know − as soon as we stop to think about it − that the oppositions in which we have placed translation are cultural and ideological constructs. But they still structure our way of thinking about these issues, because they are ingrained in our culture and in our mental habits and projections. To abandon them, and to abandon the control mechanisms which they keep in place, would be to upset established hierarchies, to deny the primacy and inviolability of the original, to stress the intertextual transformative streak in all writing, to assert the plurivocality of discourse. And to let in plural voices means destabilizing and decentring the speaking subject, and creates the prospect of a runaway inflation of voices and meanings.[13]

Translation therefore needs to be controlled, to be kept under the lid, because it is recognized as an activity that continually risks producing this kind of proliferation and dissemination. Translation is controlled through the ideology of transparency, identity, reproduction, the translator's absence from the translated text. This allows us to suppress the loose ends, the hybridity of translation: we pretend they do not exist − or at least that they ought not to exist, so as not to endanger the notion of univocal speech, the single voice issuing from an identifiable source. And so we say that we read Dostoyevsky, that we hear Yeltsin: we do not *want* to hear the Translator's voice. However, as this essay has tried to demonstrate, that discursive presence is there − not only in exceptional circumstances in unusually complex books, but always. For in the final analysis it is impossible not to ask how far the plurivocal nature of translation extends. A translation as a rule addresses an audience different from that addressed by the original. If this adjustment calls for the recognition of a Target-Culture Implied Reader, for positing an Implied Translator and for the possibility of discerning the Translator's discursive presence in certain cases and under certain circumstances, then there is nothing to prevent extending this principle from translated narrative to translated texts in general. Translation is irreducible: it always leaves loose ends, is always hybrid, plural and different.

Notes

1   The notion of translation as re-enunciation, and its relation to quotation and reported speech, is taken from Barbara Folkart (1991).

2   Different theorists use different terms for the various elements in the diagram. The triad 'text', 'story' and 'fabula' is from Mieke Bal (1985). I follow Rimmon-Kenan (1983), Chatman (1978, 1990) and others in assuming an Implied Author and an Implied Reader, despite Genette's reservations (1983).

3   This makes the present essay complementary to Giuliana Schiavi's 'There is Always a Teller in a Tale' (1996), which argues the case for positing an Implied Translator in the translated text. My focus is on those instances where another discursive presence, another voice, becomes discernible in the text itself. Both essays posit an Implied Reader specific to the translated text.

4   In the case of a paratextual note there is a difference between a Translator's Note and other possible Notes. In the context of narrative fiction, Notes would normally be attributed to a Narrator, and signal the intervention of a different Narrator or a switch to a different narrative mode (as in, say, John Fowles' *The French Lieutenant's Woman*). In principle, Translator's Notes could be presented in exactly the same way and be indistinguishable from other Notes (i.e. be detectable only through comparison with the original). However, in our translational culture the translator's professional ethos and other institutional rules and conventions forbid this option: Translator's Notes are normally identified as such. This gives them a different status, which raises a theoretical problem. The main point, however, is the observation that Translator's Notes break through the narrative discourse in a way different from other Notes; the voice which produces the Translator's Notes is clearly a different voice, with an identity of its own.

5   In *Ulysse gramophone* (1987) and in *Du droit à la philosophie* (1990); see Segers (1994).

6   I will henceforth refer to the Dutch text (volume 1 of the 1992 edition) as MH. The translations will be referred to by the name of the translator (Siebenhaar, Edwards, Carrasquer, Garros) immediately followed by the page number.

7   In the fifth edition (1881) the dedication is 'To the revered memory of Everdine Huberte, Baroness van Wijnbergen, loyal wife, heroic, loving mother, noble woman' (Dutch: MH:1). The manuscript (printed edition: Multatuli 1949) bears only the dedicatee's initials: 'To E.H. v. W.' (Dutch: Multatuli 1949:1). The importance of the dedication will become clear later.

8   'N.d.T.' stands for 'Note du Traducteur', i.e. Translator's Note. Interestingly, the abbreviation makes it clear that the producer of the Note is the translator as a textual presence, a voice, not to be confused with the Biographical Translator. How else to explain the use of the masculine (generic?) 'Traducteur' when it was Mme Roland Garros who translated the book?

9   In view of what was said in Note 4 above, this obviously raises the question of how Multatuli's Notes (from the 1875 edition on) relate to Translator's Notes. Both are paratextual, and as such interrupt the narrative flow. Since 'Multatuli' is both a Narrator in the text and the name on the cover and title page of the book (which, as we shall see, plays on the distinction between fiction and non-fiction), and since the introduction to the Notes (MH:239–246) clearly indicates that he is their provider, the linguistic subject of these Notes is beyond doubt. They appear as a kind of editorial intervention, associated with the name on the cover and title page rather than with the 'I, Multatuli' who enters as a Narrator in the book's final pages. This is partly because Multatuli-as-Narrator does not appear until the very end, and partly because many of the comments go well beyond the novel's narrative world, e.g. in commenting on the editor of the first edition of 1860.

10   The term 'differential voice' is Barbara Folkart's, who in the section in question develops an argument similar to mine: '. . . le ré-énonciateur ne se manifestera dans l'énoncé qu'il produit que sous forme de déviances, tant pragmatiques et référentielles que sémiologiques'. She goes on to speak of 'un ensemble hétéroclite de déviances (dont la saisie requiert une analyse plus ou moins poussée, du moins une confrontation avec le texte de départ . . .)' (Folkart 1991:394–95). As I hope to have shown, the Translator's 'differential voice' can be seized in the translated text itself, without confronting it with the source text.

11   The following discussion, like all such discussions, is indebted to Sötemann (1972), the classic and detailed study of the structure of *Max Havelaar*. Since Sötemann's study refers to the printed edition of the manuscript (Multatuli 1949), it does not address issues like those raised in Note 9 regarding the 'editorial' status of the Notes in the 1875 and subsequent editions.

12   Everdine van Wijnhergen died on 13 September 1874, hence the extended dedication in

the fourth edition, which came out in October 1875 (Multatuli 1992, II:538). Although in the manuscript and the first three editions of *Max Havelaar* the initials E.H. v. W. do not explicitly identify the dedicatee as the author's wife, the conclusion seems inescapable, as indeed Sötemann (1972:23, 275ff.) has shown.

13   This is an idea which Karin Littau developed in several seminars and conference papers, with reference to Foucault, Barthes and Derrida. See Littau (1993).

Chapter 12

Maria Tymoczko

IDEOLOGY AND THE POSITION OF THE TRANSLATOR: IN WHAT SENSE IS A TRANSLATOR 'IN BETWEEN'?

EDITOR'S INTRODUCTION

> The problem with translators for dominant centres of power is not that translators are between cultures and cultural loyalties, but that they become all too involved in divergent ideologies, programmes of change, or agendas of subversion that elude dominant control.

IN A SEMINAL ARTICLE THAT IS WIDELY quoted in the literature, Tymoczko sets out to interrogate the trope of 'in betweenness' and to explore the reasons for its current popularity. She argues that ideological aspects of a translation are inextricable from the 'place of enunciation' of the translator, and that this place is not simply geographical but also temporal *and* ideological. The ideology of a translation is not located in the translated text alone, but also in the voice and positioning of the translator, and our understanding of this positioning has been influenced by the tendency to speak of translation itself as an *in between* space. The idea of *betweenness* has led some to try and figure an *elsewhere* that a translator may speak from, an elsewhere that is separate from both source and target cultures and that 'is often seemingly not simply a metaphorical way of speaking about ideological positioning, but ... *ipso facto* affords a translator a valorized ideological stance'.

Tymoczko dismantles the trope of in-betweenness by first offering a number of explanations for the popularity of this metaphor, which include the actual physical position that the interpreter occupies in community interpreting and the etymology of *translatio* and its widespread use in Western translation theory. One of the explanations she offers is the influence that poststructuralism has exercised on translation scholars: the concept of *between per se* is central to poststructuralist thought. The romantic sensibility that underpins the metaphor of in-betweenness is rejected as both misleading and élitist: 'If the place of enunciation of the translator is a space outside both the source and the receptor culture, the translator becomes a figure like romantic poets, alienated from allegiances to any culture, isolated by genius'. The suggestion that translators somehow occupy a space between is not supported by historical studies, which demonstrate that translators do affiliate, and do pursue specific agendas. Moreover, scholars who use the trope of betweenness uncritically, who talk about hybrid spaces being located between the certainties of national cultures, assume that national cultures are monolithic and homogenous and fail to recognize the hybridity and dynamism of all cultures.

From an ideological point of view, Tymoczko insists that one of the most serious weaknesses of the discourse of *in betweenness* is that it fails to understand the nature of engagement, to acknowledge that 'translation as a successful means of engagement and social change – like most political actions – requires affiliation and collective action'. She concludes that '[t]he ideology of translation is indeed a result of the translator's position, but that position is not a space between'.

Follow-up questions for discussion

- Drawing on Georg Simmel's analysis of money, where he suggests that the fact that money can be used for a variety of ends 'place[s] it somehow between all qualities and thereby deprive[s] it of any specific psychological coloration', Cronin (2000b:139) argues the following: 'though they are important agents of circulation and openness and renewal in society, translators (who occupy in-between spaces, and are therefore not "one-sided", and who, in addition, tend to work in many different areas, particularly in smaller markets) do not have the distinctive "coloration" of those who are less nomadic and multifarious in their activities'. While Cronin's comment is offered in the context of accounting for the invisibility of translators and distrust for their 'hybrid' position, it is nevertheless formulated as a general statement. To what extent, and in what respects, does this generalization conflict with Tymoczko's analysis of the positionality of the translator?

- Bachmann-Medick (2009: 34) argues that '[t]he notion of culture needs to be pushed towards more openness and dynamism, for the "third space" is by no means simply a place or condition *between* different cultures, but is also a strategy of proliferating non-homogeneous layers *within* a particular culture'. Adopting this understanding of third space means that '[o]ur habituated notion of culture as a location of solid belonging and coherence would then cede to a notion of culture as translation, transition and development'. To what extent do these ideas differ from or overlap with Tymoczko's position, as outlined here?

- Here and elsewhere (Tymoczko 2006, 2007), Tymoczko pays more attention than most to the metaphors used to talk about translation and argues that '[b]ecause metaphors have ideological power and also structure our thought and our lives, it is important to investigate their implications and to ascertain that they have intellectual integrity'. Apart from *in-betweenness*, what other metaphors have been used to describe translation, and what are the ideological implications of these metaphors? You might like to consult, in particular, Chamberlain (1992), Stahuljak (2004) and Cheung (2005).

Recommended further reading

Bachmann-Medick, Doris (2009) '1 + 1 = 3? Intercultural Relations as a Third Space', trans. Kate Sturge, in Mona Baker (ed.) *Critical Concepts: Translation Studies*, Vol. II, London & New York: Routledge.

Batchelor, Kathryn (2008) 'Third Spaces, Mimicry and Attention to Ambivalence: Applying Bhabhian Discourse to Translation Theory', *The Translator* 14(1): 51–70.

Mason, Ian (2009b) 'Role, Positioning and Discourse in Face to Face Interpreting', in Raquel de

Pedro Ricoy, Isabelle A. Perez and Christine W. L. Wilson (eds) *Interpreting and Trans-lating in Public Service Settings: Policy, Practice, Pedagogy*, Manchester: St. Jerome, 52–73.

Metzger, Melanie (1999) *Sign Language Interpreting: Deconstructing the Myth of Neutrality*, Washington, DC: Gallaudet University Press.

Pym, Anthony (1998) 'Intercultures', Chapter 11 of *Method in Translation History*, Manchester: St. Jerome, 177–92.

Stahuljak, Zrinka (2004) 'An Epistemology of Tension: Translation and Multiculturalism', *The Translator* 10(1): 33–57.

SOME OF THE MOST SEARCHING AND revealing discussions of trans-lation in the last decade have focused on questions of ideology; indeed, there has been a productive, ongoing academic dialogue about various facets of the issue, extending for years now, with contributions from people from all parts of the globe. Raised principally by those who have an investment in social engagement, questions about the translator as an ethical agent of social change have gone to the heart of both the practice of translation and the theory of translation (see Hermans 1999, Pym 1998, Tymoczko 2000). Part of the ongoing conversation, this essay is an attempt to clarify issues pertaining to the position of the translator by teasing out some philosophical implications of contemporary discourses about translation. Although successful cultural programmes do not necessarily depend on clear and logical philosophical premises, in my experience a firm cognitive and theoretical foundation makes it more probable that a cultural project will draw together groups of people and inspire them to work in concert.

For at least a quarter century now, it has been generally agreed that translation is a text about a text or, to put it another way, a form of metastatement (see, for example, Holmes 1994:23–33, Lefevere 1985, 1992a). If we put this seemingly innocuous observation in an ideological context, then we must recognize that the ideology of translation is quite complex. A translation's ideology is determined only partially by the content of the source text – the subject and the representation of the subject – even though this content may itself be overtly political and enormously complicated as a speech act, with locutionary, illocutionary and perlocutionary aspects of the source text all contributing to the effect in the source context. The ideological value of the source text is in turn complemented by the fact that translation is a metastate-ment, a statement about the source text that constitutes an interpretation of the source text. This is true even when that metastatement is seemingly only a form of reported speech (cf. Jakobson 1959:233) or quotation uttered in a new context, for in quoting a source text, a translator in turn creates a text that is a representation with its own proper locutionary, illocutionary, and perlocutionary forces which are determined by relevant factors in the receptor context. Thus, even in a simplified model, the ideology of a translation will be an amalgam of the content of the source text and the various speech acts instantiated in the source text relevant to the source context, layered together with the representation of the content, its relevance to the receptor audience, and the various speech acts of the translation itself addressing the target context, as well as resonances and discrepancies between these two 'utterances'.[1]

A concrete example of this layering is found in the well known rewriting and staging of Sophocles's *Antigone* by Jean Anouilh, produced in Paris in 1944 during the Nazi occupation of France. Clearly Sophocles's text had its own ideological significance in its original context. Produced for the Great Dionysia festival held annually in Athens, as a statement about the dangers of tyranny and the importance of heroic resistance to tyrants, *Antigone* implicitly *celebrated* Athenian democracy and attempted *to instill independence and moral responsibility* in its audience, as well as *pride in and allegiance to* the city-state of Athens itself, among other things.[2] When Anouilh transposed Sophocles's play into French and staged it for his own time, however, those early ideological meanings were overwritten with contemporary meanings: he was implicitly commenting on the Nazi occupation of France, *inciting his contemporaries and encouraging resistance* against the Nazis, *calling for them to act out* against Nazi usurpation. Here I've tried to emphasize the words associated with the illocutionary and perlocutionary dimensions of Sophocles's work and Anouilh's refraction, as well as to indicate briefly some of the relevant contextual dimensions that must be considered in determining the ideology of Anouilh's play.

Ideological effects will differ in every case of translation – even in translations of the same text – because of the translator's particular choices on all these various levels – on the levels of representation of the subject matter, as well as representation of the relevant locutionary, illocutionary and perlocutionary effects of the source text, and on the relevant locutionary, illocutionary, and perlocutionary acts in his or her own name as translator. That is, the ideology of a translation resides not simply in the text translated, but in the voicing and stance of the translator, and in its relevance to the receiving audience. These latter features are affected by the place of enunciation of the translator: indeed they are part of what we mean by the 'place' of enunciation, for that 'place' is an ideological positioning as well as a geographical or temporal one. These aspects of a translation are motivated and determined by the translator's cultural and ideological affiliations as much as or even more than by the temporal and spatial location that the translator speaks from.

Although more extensive and more precise vocabulary pertaining to the ideology of translation has been developed in the last few decades, these issues of enunciation have been implicitly recognized for years in writing about translation, even if not stated explicitly in the terms that I have used above. Thus, for example, the affiliation and place of the translator were a concern in translation theory as early as 1813 when Friedrich Schleiermacher stated that 'just as a man must decide to belong to one country, just so [a translator] must adhere to one language', affiliating himself thus with one particular culture, assumed by Schleiermacher to be the translator's native land (in Lefevere 1977:84; cf. discussion in Pym 1998:181 ff.). The issues behind Schleiermacher's concerns have continued to be central in translation scholarship and theory. More than 150 years later, for example, in attempting to delineate a descriptive approach to translation, Gideon Toury took up questions pertaining to the position of translation and translators, stating categorically that translated texts are 'facts' of one language and one textual tradition only, namely the target culture's (1980:82–83), and that translators are 'persons-in-the-culture' of the target system (1995:40).[3] Although one might contest Toury's argument on these points, disagreement should not obscure the importance of his addressing issues of positionality for the evolution of translation studies.

A very nice – albeit brief and circumspect – pragmatic survey of the variety of places the translator can write from is found in an early essay by Norman Simms (1983). Simms shows how the politics of translation intersects with the translator's position. This is true, he indicates, no matter whether the translator is a member of a postcolonial culture using translation into an imperial language as a means of cultural advocacy, or whether the translator holds one of the many possible subject positions within which translation is produced for members of the target culture itself in a specific ideological complex. Descriptive studies and theoretical arguments by many writers, including Simms, illustrate that the translator can be positioned within the receptor culture (the most common case), within the source culture (as, for example, in the case of authorized translations of Mao's writings into English that were undertaken in the People's Republic of China during the period 1949–79), or elsewhere (as in a third culture, the case when German philologists translated Irish literature into English and published them in German series, or when US Bible translators translate the New Testament into South American native languages).

Despite the fact that the affiliation and orientation of the translator have been a continual topic in writing about translation for more than a century, the issues remain an active concern in the field, particularly as they impact on questions of the ideology of translation. These questions about the place of enunciation of the translator – both the ideological positioning and the geographical and temporal positioning – are related to the recent development within translation studies of a tendency to speak of translation itself as a place or space somehow disjoined from (or mappable over) the actual physical and cultural space that the translator occupies, and somehow distinct from the ideological position of the translator as well. Particularly employed by progressive and engaged writers on translation theory and practice, translation has been characterized as a place or a space in *between* other spaces. The locution *between* has become one of the most popular means of figuring an *elsewhere* that a translator may speak from – an elsewhere that is somehow different from either the source culture or the receptor culture that the translator mediates between – as well as the culture the translator lives in – an elsewhere that is often seemingly not simply a metaphorical way of speaking about ideological positioning, but that *ipso facto* affords a translator a valorized ideological stance. An exploration of this discourse – including aspects of its origin, logic, rationale, usefulness, and import – takes us to the heart of the ideology of translation.[4]

Let us begin by considering specific recent instances of the figuration of translation as *a place between*. Sherry Simon offers convenient examples in her excellent and provocative book entitled *Gender in Translation* (1996). She speaks (ibid.:162), for example, of 'the blurred edge where original and copy, first and second languages, come to meet. The space "between" becomes a powerful and difficult place for the writer to occupy'. She compares the domain of translation to the domain of a person with multiple cultural affiliations: 'the space which Bhabha works in is the liminary terrain of the translational, that hybrid space which stands between the certainties of national cultures but does not participate in them' (ibid.:153). In her usage Simon follows Gayatri Spivak, whose essay 'The Politics of Translation' (1992) has become one of the most influential explorations of the ideology of translation. Spivak alludes to translation as an activity 'where meaning hops into the spacy emptiness between two named historical languages' (ibid.:178), clearly using spatial figurations. Similarly, in 'Translation and the Postcolonial Experience', Samia Mehrez asserts, 'these texts written by postcolonial bilingual subjects create a language "in between" and therefore come to occupy a space "in between" ' (1992:121). Although examples could be multiplied,[5] these instances suffice to indicate the type of usage that has proliferated. Why are scholars and theorists inclined to use the metaphor of translation as a space – a space 'in between' – in talking about the ideology of translation and in delineating a valorized position for the translator to occupy?[6]

Before addressing this question directly, we must make a brief detour to consider what sorts of answers might be considered adequate. We should note that a question like 'why do scholars use the spatial metaphor of between?' admits different responses, depending on the different types of causality to be considered. There are many types of causality. As a starting point on the types of answers provided for the question 'why?', we can consider the sorts of causes that might be given for natural phenomena, say the phenomenon of a sneeze. In this case we could note, first, the proximate cause; in the case of a sneeze, the proximate cause is the contraction of the muscles involved in producing a sneeze. Second might be the ultimate cause or the functional cause; the ultimate cause of a sneeze is to expel material from the breathing passages. Third could be the ontogenetic cause, the developmental reason for a phenomenon; in the case of a sneeze, the ontogenetic cause is that the organism is exposed to irritants which must be ejected from the organism. Fourth might be the phylogenetic cause. In biological phenomena, the phylogenetic cause is the causality associated with the characteristics of the organism's nearest relatives; thus, in the case of a human sneeze, the phylogenetic cause is that primates sneeze, hence human beings sneeze. There would be other ways to respond to such a physiological question as well, but these answers suffice for the present context.[7]

As is apparent, within the domain of this simple biological example, there are many different ways to answer the question 'why?'. Moreover, other natural sciences would recognize forms of causality proper to their own domains, with adequate explanation differing from one domain to another (Salmon 1998:323). In addition to the types of causes admitted by the natural sciences, also to be considered are the types of causalities accepted by other disciplines, including the social sciences and the humanities. There are anthropological answers to the question 'why?', philosophical answers, and so forth. These various ways of approaching causality – and the question 'why?' – are not mutually exclusive, nor do the answers invalidate one another (ibid.:74). Thus, in trying to answer the question before us in the domain of translation studies, we should expect a number of different ways to respond that are at once disparate and yet do not necessarily undermine or contradict each other. We must also implicitly delineate a theory of causality for translation studies itself.

To turn to the main question before us, therefore, one way to answer the question 'why has speaking of translation as a *space between* become popular in translation studies?' is, of course, to seek answers within these established frames of causality. We might, for example, turn to phylogeny and seek a phylogenetic cause. That is, because primates are imitators, humans are imitators: as the English proverb puts it, 'monkey see, monkey do'. Thus, with respect to an academic discourse of the sort we are considering, we see our colleagues using a particular figure of speech, a trope, or a discourse, and as imitators we tend to take up such things ourselves without much reflection. Perhaps the phylogenetic cause in this instance has to do with the specific behaviour of our nearest relatives and ancestors in an intellectual or critical sense. From an individual's point of view, the reasoning behind the use of these expressions goes something like this: *between* is a trendy term; if critic X can use the phrase, so can I; indeed perhaps, so should I, insofar as I see myself in her lineage – or phylum – of thinkers. Clearly in the case of intellectual pursuits, a phylogenetic cause for behaviour, while perhaps good for accruing patronage, is not the best intellectual reason to adopt a mode of thinking or speaking: we might want to be careful in such circumstances of the impulse to imitate without critical reflection. Moreover, from a phylogenetic perspective, particularly the phylogenetic perspective of creatures who can elect their intellectual lineages and choose their critical and theoretical forebears, we must ask ourselves whether there are other lineages, other contemporary thinkers, whom we as translators and translation theorists might wish to claim as close 'relatives' or 'ancestors', who must be considered as we approach these questions regarding translation as being a *space between*. Obviously, a phylogenetic reason for spatializing translation is not the strongest rationale for the use of these tropes.

A second reason for the easy acceptance of the discourse of translation as a space between may reside in the actual physical location which the translator assumes in the archetypal translation encounter, namely the position of the translator-as-interpreter. In many situations of interpretation, from community interpretation to certain affairs of state, the interpreter literally stands between two speakers, performing the necessary vocalizations of interpretation, turning physically back and forth as the work proceeds, occupying a physical space between the principals. This physical positioning we might identify as the proximate cause for considering translation as a space between and for conceptualizing the translator as speaking from in *between*.[8] Although this proximate cause deserves our consideration in assessing the idea of translation as a space between, we should be wary of an uncritical generalization of one physical aspect of the interpreter's role to other domains of the activity, particularly the symbolic domain of language transfer. Moreover, it is questionable how far the physical location of the interpreter can serve as a literal or metaphorical guide to the ideological positioning of a translator of written texts.

Perhaps a stronger reason for conceptualizing translation in spatial terms has to do with the meaning and history of the words used for translation in certain Western languages. Such a reason may be looked on as the ontogenetic – or developmental – reason for translation being figured in terms of space in Western translation theory. The source of the English word *translation* is the Latin word *translatio*, which means 'carrying across'. Used originally in the very concrete sense of moving things through space, including both objects like the relics of saints and cultural phenomena like learning and power, its meaning was extended relatively late in time, during the fourteenth century, and applied to the activity of interlingual translation in English (OED s.v.). This usage was pioneered by Bible translators in what seems to be a metaphoric extension of more central semantic meanings of the word, which included the movement from earth to heaven, as well as the transference of things from one spot to another on earth.

This lexical shift is interesting in the context of earlier usages in the Western tradition. In Old French in the twelfth century, for example, to *translate* in the sense of textual mediation between languages was to put '*en romanz*'; this was standard usage all over the francophone world, which at the time included the British Isles, and such textual mediation could be rather literal, as indicated in certain saints' lives, but more typically involved fairly free adaptation permitting radical shifts of all sorts in vernacular materials (Tymoczko 1986).[9] When the term *translation* comes into use in English in the fourteenth century, it seems to be associated with a new esthetic of translation, one more text based, more oriented to the source text, more literal, and less associated with the informal standards of medieval vernacular literature, *ad hoc* oral interpretation, and other sorts of refractions: in short, with translation strategies that are seen as more appropriate for the growing movement to translate the Bible into the vernacular languages. In this regard, the earliest citation of the word in the OED is suggestive: in 1340 in his prologue of his translation of the Psalms, Hampole writes, 'in the translacioun i folow the lettere als mykyll as i may'.

Implicit, then, in the English word *translation*, and as well in the words used for *translation* in the Romance languages deriving from the Latin root *trans-ducere*, 'to lead across' (e.g. French *traduction*, Spanish *traducción*), is the idea of a *between*, a *space*, that such an act of mediation will cross or bridge. In this historical sense of the word *translation*, there are similarities with the Greek concept of *metaphorein*, which gives the English term *metaphor* and which also involves the etymological sense of carrying across, namely a carrying across of an idea or relationship from one field of reference to another. Both terms – *translation* and *metaphor* – involve extensions of a known concept (specifically the physical act of carrying across) to new ideas, respectively the transposition of texts from one language to another and the transposition of an idea or relationship from one conceptual field to another.

When we explore the rationale for these words denoting interlingual translation as involving a *between* in a concrete sense, we can hypothesize that these modes of speaking derive from an implicit recognition that ideas and knowledge, modes of understanding and learning, are all ultimately local, bound to a specific place, a specific cultural framework, and a specific linguistic mode of construing the world. Indeed, stated this way, such a view seems singularly modern, congruent as it is with contemporary views that meaning is language specific; these arguments have been developed within translation studies by scholars such as J. C. Catford (1965). Such a framework is also stressed by contemporaries writing about the phenomena of globalization. Anthony King, for example, argues that the 'autonomy of cultural competence exists at the local level' (1997:17; cf. Hannerz 1997:124) and 'meaning only exists within a language game, a discourse, practices, etc., negotiated locally and discontinuously' (King 1997:159).

In earlier times, however, before the modern age, the local nature of knowledge and ideas to be translated was less abstract and philosophical. Indeed, translation of such local knowledge might involve a very concrete crossing of space, for it often presupposed physically transporting yourself (*translating* yourself or *carrying yourself across*) to a new place so as to learn about the ideas current in that place, as a precondition of transposing those ideas from one language to another, from one local cultural system to another. As an alternative to translating yourself across space, of course, you could choose to translate some source of knowledge across space to yourself; such a source of knowledge might take a variety of forms – it might be a scroll, a codex, or even a learned person (such as a wise man, captive, slave, or other native of the source culture), who could then serve as a source and interpreter of that distant local knowledge. Some mixture of the two alternatives was also possible: you might undertake a journey to secure a relic and bring it through space to your own land, so as to have leisure in your own space to make the transposition from one language to another. This idea of translation is graphically illustrated in the ancient Chinese legend about the journey to secure Buddhist scriptures from India so they could be translated into Chinese; this tale is at the heart of the legend of Monkey, one of the most popular and productive literary complexes of Chinese culture, but it intersects with actual historical practice as well. In fact the Chinese versions of Buddhist scriptures were textually translated in the Great Wild Goose Pagoda, still standing in Xi'an at the eastern terminus of the ancient Silk Road, after copies of the Buddhist scriptures had been physically translated along that road to China. The legend of Monkey memorializes for us the material conditions of a time when translation East or West involved travel and transport across and through space.

This conceptualization of translation, then, derives from a time when the movement of religious relics through space was not in fact so very different from the transportation of the precious physical and material bases of new knowledge to be transposed into a receiving language. Such a source of learning – whether a scroll, a codex, or a person – was itself a relic of another culture, another time or space. Because in former times the translator himself might have to undertake or to under-write a dangerous journey across space in order to secure a precious document or source for translation, to undertake translation was to undertake adventure: the trans-lator was a culture hero, one who would brave danger for the sake of knowledge. (The appropriation of this concept of translator as culture hero in itself might be an attractive feature of the current discourse in translation studies of *between*, especially when used by translators themselves.)

A reason for the appeal of the discourse of translation as a space between, there-fore, is our continued awareness of the residual sense of these older meanings associated with words in Western languages pertaining to translation, such as *transla-tion* in English or *traduction* in French, as well as our historical sense of the difficulty in ancient times of transposing and expanding cultural knowledge everywhere in the world. In this regard, skilled speakers of English still know what the translation of a saint is, and most people are still aware that *trans-* in *translation* means 'across', a meaning we retain cognitively in part because of our knowledge of other words with the same formant, words such as *transcontinental* or even the automobile name *TransAm*. Although it is suggestive to consider these old meanings and associations of the Western words for translation, we must nevertheless be careful of simply and uncritically accepting such old ideas. Not only do old concepts sometimes cease to be relevant as time passes, but they do not always offer theoretically useful perspec-tives.[10] We should also be especially careful about claiming as universal a theoretical assertion that is based on the particularities and histories of a few Western European languages. It is not at all certain that such a claim would hold for other languages where the words for translation have different meanings and historical associations (for example, Arabic *tarjama*, originally meaning 'biography').

A more compelling attraction of the notion of translation as a space between – a reason that might be seen as a functional or final cause – is the importance of the concept of *between per se* in poststructuralist thought. In challenging the binary conceptualizations of structuralism which dominated critical thought in the mid twentieth century in Europe, poststructuralists emphasized alternatives to the op-positional structures and polar opposites of the structuralists. The concept of *between* epitomizes those alternatives – it suggests that not only the poles but also all the positions in between the poles are open for occupation. Moreover, poststructuralists were not alone in mounting such critiques and in searching for alternatives to binar-ies; they were part of widespread and generalized developments in intellectual history that explored similar issues in many domains. Perhaps the most notable intellectual development in this regard is an alternative to classical logic that goes by the name of 'fuzzy logic'; proponents of fuzzy logic advocate alternate ways of viewing basic logical principles, rejecting a fundamental principle of classical logic which says that a proposition cannot be both *a* and *not-a*, a principle called the law of the excluded middle. Fuzzy logic, by contrast, allows that a proposition can be both *a* and *not-a*. The standard example usually offered of the difference between fuzzy logic and classical logic is the glass half full of water. Is such a glass full or not full? For fuzzy logic such an entity poses no problem, whereas it does for classical logic. Along with poststructuralism and fuzzy logic, developments that reject absolute contrasts can be seen as part of the intellectual shift associated with the breakdown of positivism in the West.

Although the views of poststructuralists have been enormously useful in under-mining structuralist binaries, there are limitations in the concept of *between* as a solution to the problems of structuralism, for not all alternatives to a polarity or a binary figuration lie on a line between the two contrasted elements. For example, not all the alternatives to Claude Lévi-Strauss's famous contrast between *le cru et le cuit* ('the raw and the cooked'), can be placed on a single linear scale.[11] Thus, not all polarities have a single continuum that we could call *in between*. Moreover, it should be remembered that there are some things that do indeed operate on binary principles – for example, digital computers – and some properties that do follow classical logic.[12]

Whatever its logical limitations, as a metaphor *between* has other values for poststructuralists. Poststructuralist thought has been notable in opposing the idea of an absolute origin, the idea that values, cultural concepts, or systems of knowledge are grounded on a bedrock of certainty, that they rest on essentialist cultural foundations upon which all else can be built with security. Instead critics in this tradition view ideas, knowledge, thought, language and culture as all being in process, between the uncertainties of the constructions of the past and the uncertainties of the constructions of the future. Rather than being founded upon fundamental or essential realities, such human constructions as language and culture rest upon a chain of signifiers and in turn generate a succeeding chain of signifiers. This conceptual framework has made the term *between* useful, signifying the uncertainty that is inevitably associated with cultural constructions.

There is a third value of *between* as well, related to a more personal and political domain of motivation, that has made this metaphor appealing to poststructuralists. The emergence of poststructuralism is associated with the generation of 1968, and the politics of that generation have coalesced with its critical stances. Motivated by a desire to escape collusion with unsatisfactory political systems and rejecting the compromised, polarized politics of the Cold War, some poststructuralists sought an alternative positioning for their ideological stance, repudiating affiliation with either side in the Cold War. In the period before the dissolution of the Eastern bloc, this desire to escape from and to avoid being trapped by the polarized dominant political alternatives came to be symbolized in certain circumstances by the concept of a *space between*. This is part of the reason for the attraction of the discourse in translation studies as well.

There have been many compelling reasons, thus, for criticism to fasten on the expression *between* and for the term to suggest positive ideological connotations. The concept has been absorbed into translation studies not only because of its use by poststructuralist theorists of translation but also because of its congruence with other aspects that make spatial metaphors congenial and that make gaps in time and space relevant to the activity and process of translation: the physical dimension of interpretation, the history of translation in the West, and the history of words for translation in certain Western languages. Although there are no doubt many other causes for the popularity of the discourse of translation as a *space between*, this brief survey suffices to establish its attraction to scholars. Let us turn then to an evaluation and critique of the discourse to assess its implications for the ideology of translation.

An imperative question is whether this concept of translation as a space between is applicable to all facets of translation, particularly the linguistic dimension of translation. In this regard, we must ask whether poststructuralism is the only intellectual lineage to consider in applying the concept of a space between to translation and in using the notion in the discipline of translation studies. Here I think we must acknowledge that if language is seen in part as a formal system, a code (as it generally has been in modern linguistics), then a spatial concept of translation – the concept of the translator as bridging a gap, a *between*, which the translator can be located within – has a very limited utility in translation theory. That is, when translation is conceptualized in terms of transfer between languages as *systems*, this spatial metaphor of translation breaks down.

In very schematic terms, here is why. In theories of systems, one is seen as acting or operating within a system. In the event that one transcends the limits of a given system, one does not escape systems altogether or fall between systems, but instead one enters another system, generally a larger system that encompasses or includes the system transcended. This is not simply a view of contemporary systems theorists (cf. Luhmann 1995). It can be traced back to the work of Kurt Gödel, whose insights and formulations on mathematics have influenced all of twentieth-century intellectual history. In the incompleteness theorem Gödel demonstrates that questions can always be posed within any formal system (say, arithmetic) which cannot be answered in terms of the formal system itself, and that answers to such questions are formulated not outside of systems altogether but within the framework of another more encompassing formal system.

Such views are not restricted to the domains of mathematics and logic as Gödel has articulated them, or to the domain of systems theory *per se*. This is also the direction that anthropology and ethnography have taken: these disciplines have come to acknowledge that an ethnographer or anthropologist can never stand in a neutral or free space between cultures, but of necessity operates within some cultural framework, notably the constraints of his or her own primary cultural system. Increasingly in the social sciences such cultural frameworks within which research is conducted are expected to be acknowledged and specified in the work in some fashion (see, for example, Clifford and Marcus 1986). Indeed, it is only by recognizing the position that the investigator holds within a system that one can understand the ideological contingencies and presuppositions of the investigation itself.

Clearly these arguments have relevance for both translators and writers about translation. In extending such arguments and applying such models to translation, we must recognize, for example, that insofar as translators mediate between cultures, the concerns of anthropology and ethnography are relevant to translation; insofar as languages are formal systems, the findings of logic and systems theory should apply to linguistic activities like translation. Thus, one can argue that in the act of translation, when a translator interrogates a source text on the basis of a target language, the translator transcends the source language as a formal system, without simply switching to the target language as a formal system. Conversely, when the target language is interrogated using the source text as the basis of the examination, the translator transcends the target language as formal system without simply reverting to the system of the source language. The transcendence of both linguistic codes in fact puts the translator into a formal system that encompasses both languages, rather than being restricted to either. How large such an encompassing system will be has to do with the closeness of the two languages and two cultures in question, the breadth of the linguistic purview of the materials translated, and so forth. Whatever the extent of these parameters, however, the translator doesn't altogether leave the system of language *per se*, nor does the translator strictly speaking leave the domain of either or both languages. That is, one must conceptualize the translator not as operating *between* languages, but as operating either in one language or another, or more properly in a system inclusive of both SL and TL, a system that encompasses both.[13] With respect to a theory of formal systems, there can be no in *between*, no free space that exists outside systems altogether, separate from a more encompassing system: any inquiry or statement or position will fall within the framework of such a larger system. Thus, we can think of systems as a series of Chinese boxes, so to speak, with given systems always nested inside more inclusive ones.

To insist upon a *between* existing with respect to languages is to abandon what the modern age has agreed upon with respect to systems. Such a view of a *between* as occurring in translating from one language to another or from one culture to another *as systems* is, therefore, incompatible with a view of languages as formal systems that actually *construct* meaning rather than as structures that merely reflect external, language-free meaning. This is the heart of the argument I am making here, and the point must be emphasized and underscored. Spatial metaphors of translation may be useful and even perhaps natural in some contexts having to do with translation, as the ontogenetic and proximate causes considered above indicate; moreover, the concept of *between* may be useful in certain considerations of language as a (single) system, as poststructuralist arguments about the binaries of structuralism indicate. From the perspective of translation as movement from one system of language and culture to another, however, the philosophical implications and limitations of the concept of *between* which have been discussed here must be clearly understood. They return us to retrograde Platonic notions of meaning that were ascendant in the nineteenth century, in which meanings and ideas were thought to exist apart from and above any linguistic formulations.[14]

In her 1987 work entitled *Borderlands*, focusing on identity questions of the Spanish-speaking community that lives in the Southwest of the United States, near the Mexican/US border, Gloria Anzaldúa writes (1987:20):

> Alienated from her mother culture, alien in the dominant culture, the woman of color does not feel safe within the inner life of her Self. Petrified, she can't respond, her face caught between *los intersticios*, the spaces between the different worlds she inhabits.

As in the quotes we began with from Simon, Spivak and Mehrez, Anzaldúa here conceives of a *space between* cultures, from which one can (or cannot) speak – or, *mutatis mutandis*, translate. Although Anzaldúa is not writing primarily about translation, her writing demonstrates the tendency to use a spatial figuration of between for cultural interface, and her work has in fact been used by writers in translation studies as a means of elucidating the positioning of the translator. Anzaldúa returns us to the central topic of this essay. In view of what has been said about both the causes for its popularity and the critiques that can be levelled against it as a concept, what are the implications for the *ideology* of translation in the use of the discourse of translation as a space between?

Certainly a first implication is that this discourse grows out of Western views of translation – notably the history of the words in the Romance languages and in English for the concept of translation. Thus, *prima facie* this is not a discourse that is easily transferable to other cultural systems – including cultures with other European languages. The view of translation as a space between is a model, moreover, that grows out of a particular Western capitalist paradigm of the translator as an isolated individual worker who independently acts as mediator of languages. It does not fit other paradigms of translation, including the practices used in the People's Republic of China, for example, or practices in China throughout time for that matter, where teams of translators have traditionally worked together, with each member of the team operating primarily within a single linguistic and cultural framework. In the latter paradigm of translation practice, the first stage of translation is performed by a person with primary knowledge of and even loyalties to the source language and culture, followed by a polishing stage undertaken by someone with clear loyalties to the receptor language and culture (for example, a native in the receiving language often with minimal or no knowledge of the source language), with the whole process under the eye of an ideological supervisor.[15] Such teams and their members are *ipso facto* together and severally rooted in a specific cultural context and even an institutional framework. One could even argue that the primary translation situation throughout history everywhere and still today in most developing countries – namely oral interpretation – can hardly be modelled as occurring in a space between, where space is understood in terms of culture rather than the physical location of the interpreter. Thus, it is problematic to ground an ideological theory of translation in the historical linguistics and practices of a specific group of Western languages and cultures: *between* is a questionable premise for those seeking ethical geopolitical change, for it is a model based on a framework primarily grounded in a rather limited range of Western experiences.

Equally problematic are the traces of romantic sensibility lurking behind this discourse. Rather than promoting a view of a translator as embedded in and committed to specified cultural and social frameworks and agenda, however broad, the discourse of translation as a space between embodies a rather romantic and even élitist notion of the translator as poet. If the place of enunciation of the translator is a space outside both the source and the receptor culture, the translator becomes a figure like romantic poets, alienated from allegiances to any culture, isolated by genius. This view of the translator is obviously congenial and perhaps even welcome to models of translation that efface the difference between translating and (original) writing, between translator and writer. It also coalesces with the model of the translator as a *déclassé* and alienated intellectual cut loose from specific, limiting cultural moorings and national affiliations, suggesting in turn comparison with the political meanings of *between* to poststructuralists who rejected the political polarizations of the Cold War.[16] Again, however, we may question whether such ideas about the translator are in fact typical of translators and translation practices worldwide, and whether they are likely to result in the use of translation for progressive ideological purposes.

Moreover, the concept of the translator as occupying a space between is hardly one that fits with historical research in translation studies, nor does it fit with materialist analyses of translation. Over and over again descriptive studies of translation have demonstrated the connection of all facets of translation – from text choice to translation strategy to publication – with ideology, and they have established how translations are grounded in the politics of particular places and times. Rather than being outside cultural systems, descriptive and historical research on translation indicates that translation is *parti pris* and that translators are engaged, actively involved, and affiliated with cultural movements (see, for example, Lefevere 1992a:ch.5, Tymoczko 2000). Historical research rarely supports the view that translators are characterized by romantic alienation and freedom from culture, whatever their place of enunciation.

In part the (intentional) alienation implicit in the model of translation as a space between reflects dissatisfaction with dominant discourses in dominant cultures, a feeling one can sympathize with. However, to suggest that the only alternative to dissatisfaction with dominant discourses is departure from a culture is, ironically, to affirm implicitly or explicitly the view that culture is a homogeneous construct. Here Sherry Simon's definition of 'the translational' as 'that hybrid space which stands between the *certainties* of national cultures but does not participate in them' (1996:153, my emphasis) stands as an example of the dubious implications of translation as a space between: we must note that Simon's trope depends on national cultures being monolithic, homogenous, and characterized by 'certainties'. These implications of a cultural *between* contrast markedly with contemporary ideas about culture that stress the heterogeneity of culture and that assert that any culture is composed of varied and diverse – even contradictory and inconsistent – competing viewpoints, discourses, and textures (see Hall 1997), which, paradoxically, Simon herself elsewhere espouses and enjoins in translation studies (Simon 1996:137). Recent scholarship in many fields has delineated the coexistence and maintenance of minority and divergent views within cultures. Clearly, from a logical point of view, the introduction of or adherence to ideas and values from another culture does not *per se* eliminate a translator – or anyone else, for that matter – from being part of her own culture. The suggestion that such influence – or even commitment to 'foreign' ideas – moves a person to a position outside her culture (without even granting the subject a position in the other culture, as the use of *between* suggests) is a very peculiar notion that contravenes work about heterogeneity and hybridity that has emerged in recent explorations of the conditions of the diasporic modern world and that can be projected backward in time as well. One can, of course, choose to reject such views and assert that the only discourses of a culture that count are dominant discourses, but to do so would put one very much out of the mainline of current explorations of culture as a varied and heterogeneous construct. Such a position would clearly not be a step forward for translation theory. It is important therefore to look at the logical implications of vocabulary before it is adopted, interrogating in this regard the ideological discourse of translation as a space between.

Finally, from the point of view of the ideology of translation, the discourse of translation as a space between is problematic because it is misleading about the nature of engagement *per se*. Whether translation is initiated for political purposes from a source culture, from a receptor culture, or from some other third culture, translation as a successful means of engagement and social change – like most political actions – requires affiliation and collective action. The discourse of a space between obscures the necessity of such collective work – even if it is the minimalist collective action of attending to the practical needs of getting a translation published and distributed. Effective calls for translators to act as ethical agents of social change must intersect with models of engagement and collective action. This the discourse of translation as a space between abandons.

As Anthony Pym has chronicled (1992:chapter 7), the loyalty of translators is a leitmotif in translation history. Questions about the loyalty of a translator arise not because the translator inhabits a space between, with affiliations to that space between, but because the translator is in fact all too committed to a cultural framework, whether that framework is the source culture, the receptor culture, a third culture, or an international cultural framework that includes both source and receptor societies. Loyal to dissident ideologies internal to a culture, or to affiliations and agendas external to a culture, the translator can easily become the traitor from within or the agent from without. The problem with translators for dominant centres of power is not that translators are between cultures and cultural loyalties, but that they become all too involved in divergent ideologies, programmes of change, or agendas of subversion that elude dominant control. The ideology of translation is indeed a result of the translator's position, but that position is not a space between.

Notes

1   On speech act theory see Austin (1975), Searle (1969) and Sperber and Wilson (1995). The ideological aspects of reported speech have been discussed by Vološinov (1971:149.ff.) and Parmentier (1993). A comprehensive study of translation as reported speech is found in Folkart (1991); see also Gutt (2000), Hermans (2000:269) and Mossop (1998).

2   *Antigone* is the first of the Theban plays written by Sophocles, performed in Athens probably in 442 or 441 B.C. At the time the democratic system was firmly entrenched in Athens and the prevailing ideology emphasized free speech, free association, and open access to power, limited by loyalty to the laws of the *polis*. These ideals were being actively negotiated with the Delian League and Samos, in particular, having been established in Samos initially by a campaign of 40 ships from Athens. At the period of Sophocles's play, however, the oligarchs of Samos were seemingly fomenting secession from pro-Athenian rule. In 441–40, after the staging of the play, Athens responded with a second expedition to Samos, this time a hosting of 60 ships under the leadership of Pericles and Sophocles himself, designed to remove the rebels and restore democratic, pro-Athenian rule to the island. Thus the play was staged against a highly politicized historical background and its discourses were probably ideological in very specific ways, in addition to the general ones emphasized here. See Sophocles (1999:1–4, 1973:3–4).

3   These notions have been hotly debated. See, for example, Pym (1998:179 ff.) and Hermans (1999:40 ff), as well as sources cited. The impact of translation on many contemporary writers – from Borges to Kundera – whose status 'at home' was immediately enhanced by the translation of their works into English or French is a trivial refutation of Toury's view, despite the importance of his insights about descriptive approaches to translation in general.

4   This is a topic that more people than myself have set their minds to. I am particularly indebted to Annie Brisset with whom I've had conversations on this topic and who has herself published on this topic (1997). Although we come to similar conclusions, we approach the issues from somewhat different directions. The importance of understanding the implications of discourses and metaphors about translation for both the history of translation and the theory of translation has been increasingly recognized. Groundbreaking studies with implications for the ideology of translation are found in Hermans (1985b) and (Chamberlain 1992). On the general significance of metaphors for the structuration of thought, see Lakoff and Johnson (1980). Because metaphors have ideological power and also structure our thought and our lives, it is important to investigate their implications and to ascertain that they have intellectual integrity.

5   For example, the trope is integral to the argument in Iser (1995). Brisset (1997) offers an excellent critique of Iser's position, arguing that his view is ultimately utopian rather than programmatic for translation *per se*.

6   Translation studies is not alone in using spatial metaphors. They have become popular in other domains of contemporary culture and are perhaps most remarkable in language pertaining to computer activities, as exemplified by such terms as *cyberspace, chat rooms, Web sites*, and so forth. Koppell (2000) suggests that spatial vocabulary has been adopted in the domain of computers to give it status, notably to avoid comparisons with television, to avoid downgrading it to the status of a mere medium, and to avoid the suggestion that Web denizens are passive recipients of electronic signals. Metaphors of space make the Internet seem more intriguing and exciting, helping to sell computers and related products. Moreover, spatial metaphors are part of what has allowed the government to consign decisions about the Internet to profit-seeking companies and commercial interests, skewing its development to favour the corporation rather than the individual or society as a whole.

7   Also troubled by issues of causality, Pym rests a similar discussion on the types of causalities distinguished by Aristotle: the material cause, the final cause, the formal cause, and the efficient cause (1998:144–59). I am adopting a somewhat broader framework than Pym does, incorporating current thinking about causality in the contemporary sciences. For a general discussion of causality and explanation, see Salmon (1998); I am also indebted to Julianna Tymoczko for aspects of the argument, as well as to Irven DeVore.

8   This is perhaps one factor inspiring the title *Between* for Christine Brooke-Rose's novel about a simultaneous interpreter, who literally mediates in the sound channel between the speaker's voice and the audience's ear. In written studies about translation, it is also related to

the graphological representation of the translator (and the translator's mediation) as positioned between the source language and text on the one hand, and the target language and text on the other, realized variously in diagrams, such as the following: ST + SL $\rightarrow$ Translator $\rightarrow$ TT + TL.

9   Vernacular translation procedures in the Middle Ages show certain congruences with the processes of translation in oral tradition (Tymoczko 1990).

10   For example, Descartes's view that animals (but not humans) are machines is one that few would be inclined to accept in a post-Darwinian period, in light of the vast evidence built up by the life sciences in the last century, illustrating the essential continuities between human beings and other animals.

11   The structuralists' dichotomy of the raw and the cooked no longer convinces in part because experience in our own kitchens shows other options. The raw, the cooked, and the rotten. The raw, the cooked, and the burnt. The raw, the marinated, and the cooked. The raw, the fermented, the salted, the pickled, the dried, and the cooked. Or, when things are *à point*, the perfectly raw-and-cooked. While I take sides with the poststructuralists here, at the same time, it's also clear that these alternatives do not fall on a single scale between the raw and the cooked. Is the dried more or less cooked than the salted, for example? And how does each of those relate to the rotten? Impossible to say, because there is no single criterion that would govern such assignments. See my treatment of these issues as they relate to translation in Tymoczko (1999:chapter 4).

12   Logicians often offer as an example the property 'pregnant': a person is either pregnant or not pregnant – you can't be half-pregnant, or a little pregnant, or on the continuum between pregnant and not-pregnant.

13   This is what lies behind Pym's concept of an interculture (1998:chapter 11). His diagram of the translator's position (ibid.:177) indicates that the translator inhabits the junction or union of two linguistic and cultural systems, represented as the space shared by two overlapping circles, but one could perhaps more accurately diagram the situation as two small circles enclosed within a larger one, a schema more compatible with some conceptions of bilingualism explored in translation studies (see, for example, Oksaar 1978). Actually both representations are very schematized and ultimately inadequate representations of the complexity of human cultures and languages which are open systems rather than closed ones, as the circles in such diagrams would suggest.

14   The implications for an assessment of Spivak, for example, are thus clear: although she is at the cutting edge of bringing French poststructuralist theory into an English-language context, her views of translation as a movement between formal systems are paradoxically fairly regressive philosophically and at the same time somewhat naive, ironically implying a Platonic view of language.

15   In the early days of translation in China, there were often even more stages, with oral recitation or reading of the source text by a speaker of the source language conjoined with ad hoc oral translation of the text passage by passage by a bilingual. The material was then transcribed into written language by a third team member, and polished and finalized by yet a fourth, the latter two of whom might not know the source language at all.

16   Not to mention the drop-out mentality of the generation of '68 in the United States.

Chapter 13

Moira Inghilleri

NATIONAL SOVEREIGNTY VERSUS UNIVERSAL RIGHTS: INTERPRETING JUSTICE IN A GLOBAL CONTEXT

EDITOR'S INTRODUCTION

. . . in the arc of activity across the asylum system, interpreters are pivotal players in the emergence of a global society, not in some over-idealized linguistic or cultural conduit role but as participants in discourse. They enable the system to function by ensuring both the flow of communication and of applicants.

INGHILLERI EXAMINES THE POSITIONING of interpreters within régimes that rely on dichotomies such as insider/outsider, national/universal, and open/closed borders, focusing specifically on exclusionary policies aimed at asylum seekers. The asylum system partakes of both national and international discourses and agendas. It situates the nation state within a global society, responding to issues of international order and responsibility, but is ultimately designed to construct asylum seekers as outsiders (to the nation state) and constrain their transnational right to belong. Following a discussion of the rise of the nation state, the concept of universal hospitality, and the impact and management of migration in a globalized world, Inghilleri focuses on the extent to which the communicative rights granted to or claimed by interpreters and translators in this context reflect the politics of belonging that informs current immigration policies and practice. She supports her analysis with data drawn from interviews she conducted with adjudicators, solicitors, interpreters and interpreter coordinators working in the UK asylum system.

Participants in the political asylum adjudication system, described here as 'the roughest of rough games', have no clear understanding of the role that is or should be played by the interpreter. The interpreters involved in the asylum process have their own social and political backgrounds and histories, which are often closely linked to those for whom they interpret, as acknowledged by one of the interpreter coordinators interviewed in this study: 'It can be very difficult for interpreters to be interpreting in situations which might be very similar to the ones they themselves have come through'. The interpreters themselves know they cannot suppress their own subjectivities, that their own experiences have a bearing on their assessment of what is going on; one interviewee explains: 'I know what the pain of torture feels like. When you are hung in chains, for example, you sweat, lots of people never mention this, I think they are lying'. Nevertheless, given the high stakes involved, and that 'asylum cases are won or lost based on the competing "ontological" narratives of applicants and "public" narratives of the receiving countries', all participants are invested in the illusion that a comprehensive and totally objective rendering of their case, whether for or against persecution, is possible and necessary. As such, their view of what might work for or against this aim will vary. Even 'the *objective* norms of interpreting themselves', Inghilleri explains, can be perceived as either a hindrance to this aim or as enabling its fulfillment. Similarly, the interpreter's own background, in terms of political or national allegiances, may or may not become an issue. Interpreters themselves seem unsure about the boundaries of their role. Inghilleri's data demonstrates the complexity of their positioning and their own, shifting perception of it. Ultimately, she concludes, the status and role of interpreters in this context remain largely vulnerable to exercises of power outside of their control.

Follow-up questions for discussion

- Two solicitors interviewed by Inghilleri express their concern over the cooptation of interpreters into the asylum system thus: 'The Home Office interpreters quite often get sucked into the Home Office system, so they are a part of the Home Office machinery, they've got a vested interest in weeding out the ones to be refused, and they're part of that culture'. How does this compare with the findings of Jacquemet and Davidson (both in this volume)? What are the ethical implications of such cooptation, and how might trainers sensitize would-be translators and interpreters to these implications?

- The insistence on neutrality and impartiality is generally motivated by a desire to deny or suppress interpreter subjectivity in order to ensure 'unmediated', comprehensive transfer of the 'message'. And yet, Inghilleri suggests that 'the maintenance of impartiality, an interpreting norm perceived as a reflection/guarantor of objectivity, is firmly grounded in the subjectivity of the interpreter'. What does she mean by this, and what definition of subjectivity might be deduced from this discussion? Does it mean the same as 'personal' or 'ontological' narrative, for instance (Baker 2006a, this volume), or ideology (perhaps as defined by Mason, this volume)?

- Drawing on Beaugrande and Dressler (1981:182), Mason (this volume) defines mediation as 'the extent to which one feeds one's current beliefs and goals' into processing a text. How does this understanding of mediation conflict with or feed into conceptions of impartiality in contexts such as those described by Inghilleri? What other definitions of mediation (a widely used but rarely defined term) might be deduced from the literature on interpreting?

Recommended further reading

Barsky, Robert (2007) 'Activist Translation in an Era of Fictional Law', *TTR* 18(2): 17–48.

Inghilleri, Moira (2008b) 'Asylum', in Mona Baker and Gabriela Saldanha (eds) *Routledge Encyclopedia of Translation Studies*, 2nd edn, London & New York, 10–13.

Maryns, Katrijn (2006) *The Asylum Speaker*, Manchester: St. Jerome.

Tipton, Rebecca (2008) 'Reflexivity and the Social Construction of Identity in Interpreter-
Mediated Asylum Interviews', *The Translator* 14(1): 1–19.

G LOBAL RELATIONS CREATE AND ATTEMPT to sustain hybrid
economic, social and political networks that inevitably involve some form of ongoing linguistic or cultural 'translation' to ensure their function. There is a wealth of
literature on the subject of globalization from a range of disciplinary perspectives (e.g.
political philosophy, international relations and migration studies), each of which
directly or indirectly considers the effects of global mobility on local, national and
transnational constructions of identity and belonging. Interestingly, however, there is
little or no recognition in this literature of the role of translators or interpreters in global
processes of communication. Indeed, within familiar discourses of global relations,
concepts like hybridity, transnationalism or deterritoriality are treated largely as
un-self-conscious conditions or consequences of globalization. While there is much
attention to questions regarding the effects of these conditions on, for example, the
role of the nation-state and the re-construction of national or postnational identities,
there is less mention of the communicative processes involved in such transformations.

Within translation studies, global processes of communication are at the centre
of analysis of cultural and linguistic textual representations. Studies within the 'cul-
turalist' paradigm, foregrounding concepts such as hybridity and *métissage* derived
from postcolonial, postmodern and/or multicultural discourses, have revealed how
historical and existing inequalities at the national, regional and global level contribute
to the suppression and emancipation of cultural and linguistic realities. Although
these studies have tended to take the literary text as their starting point – and to
view nations and national identities in fairly static terms (Robinson 1997a) – there
is increasing interest within this paradigm in the specific conditions of globalization under which translated texts are produced, circulated and read (Gentzler and
Tymoczko 2002, Cronin 2003) and in the translator's agency with respect to contact
and changes to the global order (Buzelin 2005). A recognition of the global nature
of translation activity has also been central to polysystems and descriptive translation
studies (Even-Zohar 1978, Toury 1995). Systems approaches, while maintaining a
stronger focus on the binary nature of the source-target linguistic/cultural interface,
crucially locate processes and products of translation beyond the translator and the
text and within complex configurations of macro-social and historical contexts.

Interpreting research on micro-contexts of utterances and the ways in which
power and identity and 'communication rights' are played out between officials,
interpreters and their clients, has also revealed some of the complexities of the
'contact zone' of interpreted interactions (Mason 1999, Hale 2004, Bot 2005). The
types of contexts that have been analyzed in interpreting research (e.g. legal, educational, health and social services) are crucial public spaces for the attainment of
social and legal rights. They constitute the actual microcosms of the 'transnational'
spaces that are conceptualized in the abstract in philosophical and political discourses
of globalization and imagined and deconstructed in hybrid postcolonial literary
texts. Where refugees, immigrants or guest workers – among the key agents of
globalization – are involved, intercultural, interlingual communication becomes a
central part of the process in which global relations of power are played out.

The asylum interpreting process involves an array of contexts in which interpreters are involved. This carries from the initial port of entry interview through the development of narratives taking place within the solicitors' offices, through the Home Office interviews, and ultimately, and different again, in the appeals courts. No one of these moments can be isolated as the critical one. Outcomes are the product of activity across this process and therefore any analysis that focuses on one of these domains alone will be likely to be deficient. The process is therefore an arc of activity across which we must look.

What happens at the surface level of interaction is more often than not a micro-drama through which a larger social and political reality is acted out in a refracted form. Accounts of courtroom or immigration hearing interactions have recourse only to speculations concerning motivations or interpretations of intended meaning, providing little sure foundation other than interpretive plausibility, much as literary criticism does. While in interpreting research this has done much to reveal the complexity of the interpreter's role, under these conditions it is very easy to miss fundamental social and political realities. Through understanding and awareness of the whole arc of activity, the chances of distorting perspectives are diminished.

This paper explores the interface in interpreted encounters in the political asylum process between the notion of a 'fixed' national identity/subject and that of a more globally defined, multicultural, de-territorialized one. The right to asylum is simul-taneously a national issue and an international issue. It is thus a crucial context in which some of the key issues surrounding globalization are enacted (e.g. national sovereignty, the construction of individual/collective identities and rights, and the question of territorial and symbolic borders). The paper will focus on the contribu-tion of the wider historical and political context in constructing asylum seekers as outsiders and limiting the extent of their transnational 'right to belong'. It will then consider the extent to which the 'communicative rights' granted to or claimed by interpreters and translators within interpreted interactions reflect the 'politics of belonging' that informs current immigration policies and practice.

Formation of the nation-state

The organization of the world into distinct and autonomous states has been the central organizing principle in the West since the mid-seventeenth century, when territorial boundaries supplanted religious ones (Donnelly 2003). Since its forma-tion, the modern state has principally functioned in juridical terms – as an 'entity in which the people are bound together, even defined, by their common participation in and subordination to (democratic public) law' (Donnelly 2003:64).

Significantly, the modern state was defined in relation to and as a response to questions of international order and responsibility. Thus, the relationship between the notion of a global society and the sovereignty of nation-states – and its moral and political consequences – is not a new one.

It is generally accepted that this relationship takes on political, but more import-antly, symbolic importance in Europe from the time of the Peace of Westphalia in 1648 (Jackson 2005:82):

> After Westphalia the language of international justification gradually shifted, away from Christian unity and toward international diversity based on a secular society of sovereign states that acknowledged common practices and principles of international law.

The origins of the modern state are thus rooted in a vision of political society that is at once internationalist, based on 'natural law' – which holds that all humans are equal members of the community of humankind – and nationalist, based on 'positive law' – which holds that individuals have the right to form political associations in the form of independent states (Jackson 2005:127–28). Under positive law, relations with other sovereign states are viewed as voluntary and contingent, and a private matter for individual states alone (Held 2002:4).

Since the inception of the notion of state sovereignty, efforts have been made to recognize and/or reconcile the inherent tension between moral universality and national political autonomy with respect to human rights. In the realm of political philosophy, Hobbes, for example, writing in 1651, viewed the international world as a 'state of nature' with no normative bonds or ties between states (Jackson 2005:110). Hobbes likened this to a perpetual 'state of war' in which 'all men are equal in body, ambitions, and reason and there is no common power to restrain them' (Doyle 1997:114). Nations were compelled to protect themselves from this anarchic state of affairs by operating according to their own self-interests, protecting their liberal principles and practices from the illiberal laws of nature (Cole 2000:165–66). Kant would later attempt to reconcile this view through an appeal to a cosmopolitan world society united in solidarity over fundamental human rights. Kant was more optimistic about the possibility of an internationally based 'state of peace' based on a pacific union of liberal democratic states, which would gradually be extended as non-liberal states disappeared (Doyle 1997:257). In *Perpetual Peace*, Kant argued for a set of common values and principles, shared by individuals as well as states, based on a universal law of right rooted in human reason, in 'nature' itself (Kant 1957:31–32). Kant's idea of a cosmopolitan law involved agreement on 'conditions of universal hospitality', defined as follows (*ibid.*:20–21):

> Hospitality is the right of a stranger not to be treated as an enemy when he arrives in the land of another. One may refuse to receive him when this can be done without causing his destruction; but, so long as he peacefully occupies his place, one may not treat him with hostility. It is not the right to be a permanent visitor one may demand. A special beneficent agreement would be needed in order to give an outsider a right to become a fellow inhabitant for a certain length of time. It is only a right of temporary sojourn, a right to associate, which all men have. They have it by virtue of their common possession of the surface of the earth, where, as a globe, they cannot infinitely disperse and hence must finally tolerate the presence of each other.

In establishing the idea – at the time of its formation – that the modern democratic state draws its very legitimacy from conformity to universal human rights rooted in human reason, moral and political responsibilities became inextricably linked.

Globalization, the nation–state and the management of migration

The relationship between a sovereign state's moral-legal requirement to offer temporary sojourn to 'strangers' and the right of the state to control the type and extent of their stay continues to inform twenty-first-century refugee and asylum policies. Despite the development of international human rights agencies, conventions and the positive collective humanitarian actions of states in times of global crisis, the will of the sovereign state continues to serve as the ultimate arbiter over who is judged a worthy stranger.

The relationship between state sovereignty and cosmopolitan law has come under increased scrutiny in the context of more recent transformations of the global economy. While there is little debate over the fact of the global interconnectedness of modern nation-states, there is disagreement over whether 'globalization' is a positive phenomenon leading to the erosion of the independent political authority claimed in the name of sovereignty (see Held et al. 1999). Whatever one's position in contemporary debates over this issue, the issue of migration has emerged as central to questions of mobility and membership in the present global order. Migration practices and policies have become an explicit focus of interest for politicians, social scientists and philosophers alike. Migration-related questions concerning, for example, the nature of citizenship, the right of nation-states to act in their own self-interest, and the obligations of the 'international community' toward migrants, forced or otherwise, are in evidence in political and academic debates at both an intra-national level and an inter-national level. Such questions address the very essence of what it means to 'belong' in a global society. Although migration is acknowledged to be an inevitable consequence of the establishment of global economic networks, it is frequently portrayed by governments and perceived by members of the public as a potential threat to the internal economic or cultural order and stability of a sovereign nation (Statham 2003), often creating divisions between members of the same society. As Jordan and Düvell (2003:62) note:

> [Immigration] mobilizes resentment of those made insecure by their vulnerability to a global competition; it taps into rivalries between excluded groups; it links the fate of immobile and impoverished ethnic minority communities with the threat of mobile and resourceful new-comers, seen as further subverting the protection of citizenship. It allows the politics of nationalism and 'race' to be rekindled and exposes the fragility of liberal democratic institutions.

Although the national media frequently portray social and economic conflicts as primarily an outcome of tensions between citizens/insiders and migrants/outsiders, divisions among different types of migrant groups can be equally corrosive to an individual's or a group's sense of belonging. Such divisions may originate in or become perpetuated by the immigration policies and practices of receiving countries. Whatever the historical precedents, the motivations for current migration to and between countries have tended to be falsely portrayed, particularly in the developed world, in either economic or political terms. The persistence of this either/or interpretation of the causes of migration is evident in the pejorative categorization of the 'bogus' asylum seeker in cases where an asylum claim is believed to be based on 'economic' rather than political reasons. This charge is highly problematic given that, at the present time, the United Kingdom and the European Union are positively encouraging the managed recruitment of highly-skilled and unskilled workers from outside the Union (Jordan and Düvell 2003:68). Several points can be made in this regard. First, most asylum seekers are themselves 'highly-skilled and unskilled workers' who are willing and able to contribute to the economic and social life of the receiving country. Secondly, it is increasingly difficult to make a distinction between 'refugee' and 'economic migrants' (Crisp 2003:81) as most individuals and groups seeking asylum migrate as a result of a combination of factors deriving from the consequences of civil war, ethnic conflicts, and other forms of social and political violence. Thirdly, in the past, during times of economic boom, policies toward all immigrants, including asylum seekers, have been more accommodating (Joly 1996). In the current climate, despite the fact that applicants for entry may share similar social and economic characteristics, receiving countries operate discriminatory policies in order to control overall numbers (Jordan and Düvell 2003:69):

> . . . the crisis arises not from world migration movements but from the lack of a political rationale for integrating them; for reconciling them with other humanitarian demands for protection, or ethical principles of distribution, and for the internal rules of membership of liberal democratic states. Furthermore the diversity and complexity of migration processes in an integrated world economy challenges policy makers to frame consistent rules and apply them fairly to a whole range of different kinds of migrants.

The migration 'crisis', attributed to the rising numbers of people seeking asylum worldwide since the 1980s, has justified stricter controls at the borders of receiving countries. But while there has been a significant overall increase in migration since that time, the overwhelming majority of displaced persons still either remain in their countries of origin or seek refuge in neighbouring countries. Despite this reality, globalization has played a role in the increased migration to Western Europe and North America. Since the end of the Cold War, many of the world's principal refugee populations have come from countries that have not had a significant role in global economic expansion and are therefore of little geopolitical significance to the West. As a consequence, the West has tended to turn its back on any long-term economic commitment in the form of refugee assistance programmes, for example. Neighbouring states in the developing world have been increasingly reluctant and unwilling to accept sole moral or financial responsibility for the political conflicts in their regions (Crisp 2003:78). In addition, unlike the situation during the Cold War, many asylum claimants currently come from countries with whom Western Europe and North America share or seek to develop close political and/or economic ties or are considered of strategic importance in the 'global war on terror'. Receiving countries have thus attempted to strike the right balance with their immigration policies – attempting to operate effectively, economically, politically and morally, as global partners while at the same time protecting their own national interests and those of their citizens.

Migration and the politics of belonging

Contemporary debates originating from western liberal democracies over migration, citizenship and belonging have predominated in countries with well-established histories of migration. In the United States and Canada, the debate tends to centre around the issue of assimilation, comparing the styles and patterns of cultural and economic assimilation of European and East Asian immigration from the late nineteenth century and early twentieth century to post-1960s immigration originating largely from the developing world (Portes 1997, Alba and Nee 2003, Reitz 2003). In western Europe, debates are focused on the continued impact of colonialism on contemporary migration patterns and practices and on the current and future status of guest workers and their families imported to countries such as Germany, Switzerland, The Netherlands and France during the period of industrialization following the Second World War (Joppke 1998, Geddes and Favell 1999). Underlying these debates is an interest in the extent to which immigrant groups, past and present, contribute to a sense of a 'national collectivity' and an increased recognition of the role played by their maintenance of 'transnational' ties and allegiances. For some, this implies a diminished importance for traditional forms of nationhood and citizenship (Soysal 1994, Jacobson 1996). Others, however, emphasize the renewed relevance of the liberal democratic state as a crucial public site for constructive dialogue between national and transnational affiliations (Schuck 1998, Benhabib 2004).

The issue of asylum occupies a distinct position within these debates as refugees and asylum seekers are normally perceived primarily in terms of their potential to be returned or contained. In this way, questions of long-term citizenship rights or assimilatory potential are secondary, although significant factors in determinations of admission. With the implementation in recent decades of far stricter interpretations of the 1951 Geneva Convention's criteria for what constitutes a refugee, most asylum seekers fail to obtain formal refugee status. Instead, because of individual states' adherence to the principle of non-refoulment,[1] those claimants who are not deported outright, returned after a negative determination or held indefinitely in the category of asylum seeker are permitted to remain with some form of temporary status until such time as conditions in their country are considered safe. However, without the formal status of 'Convention refugee' – which in most countries has usually led to the rights and benefits of permanent residence – both the quality of rights and conditions of settlement often remain vague or undetermined. Indeed, some non-governmental organizations have argued that governments have deliberately categorized refugees in this way in order to avoid the commitments involved in the Convention status (Joly 1996:11; see also Joly 2002). By conferring temporary refugee status without any legal commitment to extend this to permanent residence or opting to hold applicants in reception/detention centres for the duration of the application process, nation-states visibly mark asylum seekers as outsiders whatever the eventual outcome of their claim. In doing so, states demonstrate an increasing ambivalence to the idea of universal hospitality and global inter-connectedness.

In addition to the political and economic influences involved in the management of migration, a strong justification for increasing border control has also been the protection of national cultures and identities. The political philosopher Michael Walzer (1983:39), for example, has argued that:

> The distinctiveness of cultures and groups depends on closure and without it, cannot be conceived as a stable feature of human life. If this distinctiveness is a value, as most people (though some of them are global pluralists and others are local loyalists) seem to believe, then closure must be permitted somewhere. At some level of political organisation, something like the sovereign state must take shape and claim the authority to make its own admissions policy, to control and sometimes restrain the flow of immigrants.

Such a view suggests a relationship between the control of migration and the maintenance of cultural cohesion in the context of a sovereign state. Implied here are two distinct sites of 'closure' – one that exists between diverse members of the same nation, and another that distinguishes members of a nation from would-be or non-members. Walzer has argued that, despite their differences, members of a national culture mutually construct a political culture and identity. In a liberal democracy, this gives them the right to exercise their self-determination, including the right to limit or restrict membership to others. Such restrictions are applied both to internal members (e.g. permanent residents, guest workers, third-country nationals) and to external non-members.

In the case of refugees and asylum seekers, the question of 'closure' is closely linked to territorial boundaries. A nation-state exercises its legal right to refuse entry through deportation, stricter border controls, and reception/detention centres that contain and effectively cordon off asylum seekers from the rest of the public. Provision of foreign economic and development aid itself has a twofold purpose, to fulfil a humanitarian duty of assistance and to discourage migration to donor countries.

Political asylum, universal human rights and the 'trans-national'

Given the continuation of the significance of the nation-state with respect to the international politics of human rights, it is worth considering the impact and relevance of claims about the increased role of universal human rights and 'transnational belonging' to refugee populations across the globe.

Some suggest that patterns of migration associated with globalization have done much to erode images of permanent resettlement and assimilation with regard to the movements of peoples (Carens 2000, Papastergiadis 2000). Papastergiadis has argued that the 'conditions of hospitality' for migrants should reflect this changing nature and should take into account the historical reality of flexible borders and the increasingly 'complex networks of responsibility that link a person to the past and to the future' (2000:57). Similarly, Soysal claims that transnational norms and the discourse of human rights have begun to erode the boundaries of nation-states, suggesting the advent of a postnational model of membership and citizenship with respect to migrants (1994:142):

> In the postnational model, universal personhood replaces nationhood – and universal human rights replace national rights. The rights and claims of individuals are legitimated in ideologies grounded in a transnational community, through international codes, conventions and laws on human rights, independent of their citizenship in a nation-state. Hence, the individual transcends the citizen. This is the most elemental way that the postnational model differs from the national one. Universal personhood as the basis of membership comes across most clearly in the case of political refugees, whose status in the host country rests exclusively on an appeal to human rights.

Soysal's claim that the idea of the nation persists mostly as an 'intense metaphor' (ibid.:162) is not predicated on the erosion of the nation-state qua state; rather, she argues that the persistence of legal and illegal migration into Europe, for example, indicates a weakening in the state's ability to successfully curtail entry. She locates this weakening in 'ideologies grounded in a transnational community' and supported by human rights legislation such as the 1948 Universal Declaration of Human Rights and the 1950 European Human Rights Convention.

While these authors make insightful points regarding contemporary migration in the context of globalization, much of their argument relates more pertinently to migrant groups or national minorities who are already inside the boundaries of the nation-state and who have or ought to have rights to move back and forth legally between territories. As discussed above, however, the movement of refugees and asylum seekers remains more restricted and arguably more dangerous. While it is true that states have begun to attend more to internationally recognized human rights (Forsythe 2000, Donnelly 2003), it is also true that in terms of foreign policy agendas human rights issues are not 'even close to the top' (Donnelly 2003:172). Moreover, despite their increasingly influential role in monitoring, education, relief operations and developing human rights norms, global human rights régimes such as the United Nations High Commission for Refugees, the UN Human Rights Committee and the UN Commission on Human Rights have limited international decision-making powers (ibid.I:138). Recently Louis Gentile, a UN High Commission for Refugees Protection Officer, has argued that the notion of significant progress in protecting human rights is a myth (2002:40–41):

> The human rights problem today is not about establishing principles but about practice, and it is in analysing the human rights situation on the ground, in judging progress in the practical application and respect for human rights principles, that this myth begins to disintegrate.

Thus, while expansive conceptions of human rights and transnational norms may be in evidence, the continuation of national policies of exclusion has not significantly altered the rights of refugee and asylum seekers. On the contrary, in the current climate, these rights have become increasingly suspended, with humanitarian considerations or concerns for 'universal personhood' the lowest priority for receiving countries.

The political philosopher Seyla Benhabib has attempted to fuse the idea of 'transnational belonging' with that of a territorially based democratic political culture – of nationhood with personhood. She argues for a constructive inclusive dialogue between the established and the excluded inhabitants of a nation-state that does not depend on prior shared understandings based in ethnocultural commonalities or on permanent territorial allegiances. She suggests that although the precise interpretation of human rights must be considered in light of the 'concrete historical traditions and practices of a given society', claims to the validity of such interpretation must be 'context-transcending' (Benhabib 2004:123); that is, the exercise of political agency must be considered valid not due to a shared national identity and culture, but to a belief in and commitment to moral cosmopolitanism.

Benhabib envisions a type of transnational dialogue, accomplished through what she terms 'democratic iterations', borrowing the notion of iteration from Derrida for whom it suggests the indeterminacy of meaning from one context to another; that is, that in the repetition of a linguistic utterance, the 'performative force' of the utterance breaks from prior established contexts of socially established meanings. Benhabib takes up this idea, arguing that diverse linguistic, cultural or religious practices, for example, can and must be taken up in a political context of debate that does not require as a precondition the type of closure (and the fixed, shared meaning this notion implies) referred to above (ibid.:179):

> By democratic iterations I mean complex processes of public argument, deliberation and exchange through which universalist rights claims and

principles are contested and contextualised, invoked and revoked, posited and positioned, throughout legal and political institutions, as well as in the associations of civil society. These can take place in the 'strong' public bodies of legislatures, the judiciary, and the executive, as well as in the informal and 'weak' publics of civil society associations and the media.

Benhabib's concern is to establish the minimal discursive norms and the fair and equal procedures necessary for reaching compromise and agreement between conversational partners in multicultural societies. Importantly, she wishes to do so without collapsing the distinction between moral and cultural discourses. That is, she wishes to acknowledge the possibility of a context-independent universalist moral language that can coexist with the complexities of and potential overlaps in the moral, ethical and evaluative discursive frameworks within which different cultural/national groups conduct their lives (Benhabib 2002:40–42).

The notion of a democratic iteration offers the possibility of the emergence and re-emergence of meaning – and thus social knowledge – that is not weighed down and over determined by prior contexts or positions. It suggests that the capacity of the force of an utterance to assume new contexts – which Derrida suggests emanates in language itself – creates the necessary and sufficient conditions for the emancipatory potential of partners in cross-cultural contexts of communication to create new meanings that will themselves remain unfixed to any one context. Benhabib is interested in the potential of the decontextualized, dis-closed utterance to challenge existing forms of legitimacy. At the same time, however, she acknowledges that whether an individual or group is judged worthy of equal treatment and respect as conversational partners – their right to recognition – will ultimately determine the type and extent of their participation in public deliberations (2002:56).

Bourdieu takes up this last point in his critique of the idea that social transformation can emerge out of linguistically constituted moral or cultural validity claims. Bourdieu insists that the efficacy of speech derives not from language but from the institutional conditions of its production and reception (1991:111):

> It is clear that all the efforts to find, in the specifically linguistic logic of different forms of argumentation, rhetoric and style, the source of their symbolic efficacy are destined to fail as long as they do not establish the relationship between the properties of discourses, the properties of the person who pronounces them and the properties of the institution which authorises him to pronounce them.

Central to Bourdieu's claim regarding the intractable authority that language derives from social relations of power is the belief that this authority is maintained through the collaboration of those it governs through the functioning of the habitus – the social mechanism capable of producing this complicity based on misrecognition. For Bourdieu, language cannot perform a break with context – and the power of language cannot be invoked linguistically, authority comes to language from the outside (ibid.:109); hence the impossibility of the emergence of 'discursive gaps' that might challenge socially pre-established grounds of legitimate meanings. For Bourdieu, where an individual or group's language has no prior authorization, it cannot participate equally in the type of transnational 'democratic iterations' and the production of new forms of legitimacy envisioned above. For Bourdieu, this would require substantially more than a break with context, it would necessitate a break with the social conventions and modalities of practice that are inscribed in language and embodied or enacted through the habitus.

The interpreted encounter: transnational iteration or authorized discourse?

Acts of interpreting and translation are instantiations of language attempting to function in a context in which it has no prior authorization. In the case of most public service contexts, including the political asylum context, interpreters and translators actively participate in negotiating the prior social conventions of usage that serve to constrain but also engage their clients as conversational partners. As active agents in the 'transnational' spaces to which Benhabib and others refer, they contribute both consciously and unconsciously to the interplay or tension between the force of 'democratic iterations' and that of 'authorized language' as they help or are hindered in the negotiation of linguistic and cultural meanings between the established and excluded inhabitants of a nation-state.

In the political asylum system these negotiations take place in a climate in which the continuation of national policies of exclusion significantly restricts the right of refugees and asylum seekers to be heard. As discussed above, nationhood, not universal personhood, remains the reference point for claimants' rights of entry, significantly limiting the conditions for the emergence of a discourse of 'transnational belonging' or moral cosmopolitanism. In interpreted asylum events, the force of linguistic utterances – for both claimants and the state – remains located firmly in the context of national cultures and identities. Yet at the same time, translation and interpreting play a central role in the development of expansive conceptions of human rights and transnational norms, which in turn effect the extent of an applicant's right to participate in a constructive inclusive dialogue within the asylum system. It is thus a crucial context in which to develop a more stable and shared understanding of the interpreter's role. The 'communication rights' granted to or withheld from interpreters as well as those claimed and enacted by interpreters themselves are central to this development.

Despite established codes of practice and an increased awareness of the interpreter's role, there is still much uncertainty and inconsistency among all participants in the political asylum adjudication system – adjudicators, solicitors, interpreters, Home Office representatives and claimants alike – regarding the exact nature of this role in interpreted encounters. Different approaches to training also contribute to these uncertainties. The conflicting perceptions and expectations of and by interpreters are an outcome of a further set of uncertainties over the 'objective' nature of asylum adjudication on the one hand, and communicative practices on the other. The asylum process is the roughest of rough games. Beneath some of the interactional surface each participant in an official hearing can be in bad faith. Discussions within the solicitor's office between an asylum seeker, a legal representative and an interpreter involve the joint production of a narrative that will achieve the objective of winning the right to remain in the United Kingdom. The underlying motive of the Home Office's counter-narrative against a claimant's credibility is to return the applicant to his or her country of origin or an alternative 'safe' country. The particular discursive moves of any or all of the participants in evidence in interpreted interactions are directly informed by both the local communicative and global political processes described above.

The interpreters involved in this process do not come from nowhere. They too are socially and politically situated. They are therefore operating at the grinding edge of macro-political realities. Given that asylum cases are won or lost based on the competing 'ontological' narratives of applicants and 'public' narratives of the receiving countries (Baker 2006a:4; see also Barsky 1996, Blommaert 2001, Jacquemet 2005, Maryns 2006), both sides have a stake in believing in and seeking to ensure that their case for or against persecution is relayed as comprehensively and 'objectively' as possible.

In some instances, it is the *objective* norms of interpreting themselves that are believed to work for or against this aim, as the following examples suggest. In Example 1, in response to my question, the adjudicator describes as 'unfortunate' but nevertheless 'appropriate' the rule that interpreter and expert roles must be clearly distinguished from one another despite her own instincts against this distinction in the particular hearing described.

Example 1

M: If there were any queries about a political fact or a cultural fact or a social fact, a practice of some kind that takes place or doesn't take place, would you be comfortable with an interpreter making any clarification along these lines?

A: Terribly tempting, and I had the other day a Nepalese with a Gurkha, with a wise looking, to me a retired Colonel from the Gurkha Regiment I would have thought, who was doing some work as an interpreter and I was simply dying to ask him because I felt that from this man we could have got some balanced view that we would not have had from the so-called expert reports, but no it's not appropriate. No, it's not their job. If they're clued up about their country then they ought to be putting themselves forward as experts, so unfortunately, no.

In Example 2, however, this same adjudicator acknowledges as 'silly' the bureaucratic consequences of another rule that interpreters (if willing and able) cannot do sight translations of short documents because they are written and not oral forms of communication.

Example 2

But sometimes, it's just silly, because you're faced with the prospect of adjourning something otherwise, because a letter had just come in, and it's nobody's fault, it seems that it's just come in and there's twenty words to be interpreted, well if nobody minds and the interpreter will read it out for me, that's fine.

At other times, it is the interpreter's *subjectivity*, based on political or national allegiances, that is felt to have an effect on a case. In Example 3, an interpreter coordinator working in a major UK detention centre describes to me the difficulty of being aware of interpreters' actual or possible manipulation of claimants' stories. In the case he describes, the interpreter, a native of the Czech Republic, is interpreting for a Roma Gypsy. In Example 4, this same difficulty emerges for another interpreter coordinator over the issue of recruitment.

Example 3

IC: I've known of a situation where the client has turned round to the legal rep and has tried to say I don't want this person tomorrow because, you know, I don't trust him and we were told by the Home Office interpreter that our interpreter had said 'Look, you know, that's not true, what you're claiming it's not like that in the Czech Republic', and, you know, there are problems, that's why we tend to use tried and tested people.

M: Yes, the client would feel the interpreter was misrepresenting him.

IC: Yes, it's like telling a story and missing out details. They leave out dates, they could leave out names and places. And it has happened, it goes on, and you pick it up the next day when you're in there and you've got a different interpreter sitting next to you and you feel that your client is saying something different to what the client said yesterday, and at the end of it you say to your client 'you told me this yesterday' and then he says 'no I said this', and you've got to make that judgement whether it's your client or whether it was the interpreter and most times the adviser will be able to make an assessment. And then you say 'look fine you told me this yesterday, but I need to make representation, which one do you want me to go with'? Because then if you go against what they've said in the Home Office interview you've got to justify it really well because it raises that credibility thing again.

Example 4

I can remember I was recruiting Turkish interpreters around Christmas time and there was one who was really good and I thought, oh yes, maybe we could take her on. I was having trouble finding the right person actually, Turkish, and getting a bit exasperated. And then one of the caseworkers here sort of filled me in and said, don't take her on, her husband's in the PKK [a Kurdish independence party] and they're really extreme. So it's like aaah. So if they're very well known in the community for one reason or another then, you know, again you've got to have the clients' trust of uppermost concern.

In Example 5 and Example 6, two solicitors express their concern about different forms of cooptation of interpreters into the asylum system itself.

Example 5

The Home Office interpreters quite often get sucked into the Home Office system, so they are a part of the Home Office machinery, they've got a vested interest in weeding out the ones to be refused, and they're part of that culture because they're all behind locked doors and they all come in at the same time and so I think that's an additional pressure in terms of the Home Office interpreting which you don't get in court.

Example 6

By [names a London Underground Station] you'll see a sign that says [names an interpreter, X]. [X] brings them to law firms. They will turn up at such and such a time outside such and such a tube station and the interpreter will pick up clients and take them to firm X. What on earth goes on in his office I shudder to think. Are cases being concocted? There's stuff that goes on.

Interpreters are also divided, sometimes within themselves, over the issue of boundary maintenance in interpreted interactions. In Example 7, an interpreter coordinator and trainer refers to this difficulty for interpreters in general.

Example 7
It can be very difficult for interpreters to be interpreting in situations which might be very similar to the ones they themselves have come through. And I know how difficult interpreters find it sometimes well (a) to remain impartial, which they have to be able to do obviously, but (b) not to get emotionally sort of caught up with it, even if they manage to remain impartial in the actual interview. But actually how it leaves them feeling, it's a big issue.

Example 8 illustrates this difficulty. The interpreter, himself a torture victim, discusses interpreting for applicants whom he feels, based on his own experiences of torture, tell lies about theirs in order to conform to the official established criteria for establishing persecution and thus strengthen their chances to be granted asylum.

Example 8
I have witnessed liars get granted asylum and genuine refugees be refused. I have been tortured so I know what torture is. When I hear people say they have been tortured for 5 to 10 minutes with electric shock I know they are lying as it only takes 1 or 2 minutes to make an impact. I know what the pain of torture feels like. When you are hung in chains, for example, you sweat, lots of people never mention this, I think they are lying . . .

For this interpreter, however, there is no question of challenging these accounts; in his view, both the 'liars' and the 'genuine refugees' are equally victims. As he says about the 'liars', 'you gotta do what you gotta do'. It is an interesting example of how personal experience, national and political allegiances and impartiality come to intersect in particular ways in interpreted events.

In this instance, the maintenance of impartiality, an interpreting norm perceived as a reflection/guarantor of objectivity, is firmly grounded in the subjectivity of the interpreter and his view of the asylum system as an institution in which facts can be manipulated on both sides in order to win.

Despite the evidence in the above examples of a range of 'communicative rights' claimed by or withheld from interpreters, given the present constitution of the interpreting profession as a 'zone of uncertainty' (Inghilleri 2005), the status of interpreters' knowledge remains largely vulnerable to exercises of power outside of their control, more authorized discourse, less democratic iteration. Nevertheless, as these examples make clear, in the arc of activity across the asylum system, interpreters are pivotal players in the emergence of a global society, not in some over-idealized linguistic or cultural conduit role but as participants in discourse. They enable the system to function by ensuring both the flow of communication and of applicants. In this role, they may codify, clarify or challenge the cultural and linguistic boundaries used to symbolize national and political agendas. They are excluded and empowered, traitors and truth tellers, nationalists and internationalists, embodying the paradoxes of transnational discourses of belonging, out of which both conflict and consensus emerge.

Note

1   The principle of non-refoulment is one provision of the 1951 Convention that remains strictly implemented by signatory states. Under this provision, governments are prohibited from returning a refugee 'in any manner whatsoever to the frontiers of territories where his life or freedom would be threatened on account of his race, religion, nationality, membership of a particular social group or political opinion' (Joly 1996:8).

PART 6

Minority issues: cultural identity and survival

Chapter 14

Michael Cronin

THE CRACKED LOOKING GLASS OF SERVANTS: TRANSLATION AND MINORITY LANGUAGES IN A GLOBAL AGE

EDITOR'S INTRODUCTION

The issue of translation and minority languages is not a peripheral concern for beleaguered fans of exotic peoples gabbling in incomprehensible tongues but the single, most important issue in translation studies today. The hegemony of English in the fastest-growing area of technological development means that all other languages become, in this context, 'minority languages'.

CRONIN REGRETS THE FAILURE OF translation scholars to address the issue of minority on several levels, including their failure to include theoretical contributions from minority languages in anthologies of translation studies, and the lack of willingness to acknowledge that those working with minority languages will have distinct points of view and experiences. Advocacy of non-fluent, exoticizing strategies, for example, may make sense for translators working in a major language, but for a minority language, non-fluent strategies can pose a threat to their very survival. From the perspective of minority languages, Cronin distinguishes between *translation-as-assimilation*, where speakers of a minority language allow themselves to be assimilated through self-translation into a dominant language, and *translation-as-diversification*, where they resist assimilation by retaining and developing their language through translation.

One important argument elaborated by Cronin is that for minority languages to survive they must resist being ghettoized, which means that they must have a presence, mostly through translation, in all areas of life, in all disciplines, and must not confine themselves to the realm of the aesthetic. Here, the role of scientific, technical and commercial translation in identity formation for minorities must be recognized and explored. Minority languages must pay as much attention to their technical, commercial and scientific translators as they do to their literary translators, and must develop 'languages that can service all areas of life and not simply the bruised ego of historical loss'. Minority languages must also learn from tradition-ally dominant languages (like French and German), that have come under pressure from English, how to respond to assimilationist translation pressures. Cronin notes that the new information economy of signs and spaces is generating pressures on translation to become a uniform, transparent medium of fluid exchange (cf. Raley, this volume). Here, English increasingly functions as a universal means of exchange, and time becomes an oppressive factor that forces translators to produce assignments within increasingly short response-periods. Moreover, the exponential growth in information that is a characteristic of the new global economy results in increased pressure to produce new terminology, a pressure that is particularly acute for minority languages. Often, new terms from a major language will be left untranslated in the minority language, thus gradually eroding the native resources. 'Even where they are translated', Cronin explains, 'terms and expressions articulate a world-view, a particular interpretation of events, that cumulatively erase the space of difference between languages'. Cronin ends by discussing a range of desiderata to support minority languages in translator training and research, and by means of minoritizing major languages through heteroglossia.

Follow-up questions for discussion

- In calling for increased attention to scientific and technical translation, Cronin states that '[f]or speakers of minority languages . . . the aestheticization of language can be profoundly disabling'. Consider how a poststructuralist might respond to this claim, in the context of minority languages specifically. Consider also how theoretical writing on translation might respond to this call.

- House (2006:356) claims that two processes that are normally part of the translation act, namely re-contextualization and cultural filtering, 'are . . . today in danger of being undermined by the dominance of global English and the concomitant omnipresence of Anglophone communicative conventions'. Bennett (2007:154) goes further, and calls this process 'epistemicide'; she justifies her choice of term by arguing that 'the way that a particular culture formulates its knowledge is intricately bound up with the very identity of its people, their way of making sense of the world and the value system that holds that worldview in place'. 'Epistemicide', she suggests, 'as the systematic destruction of rival forms of knowledge, is at its worst nothing less than symbolic genocide'. What role does or can translators play in this process, both in the context of 'minority' languages in the traditional sense and, following Cronin, in the context of translating into any language other than English today.

- One issue that Cronin does not engage with in this article is the position of the translator within the minority language group, as insider or outsider. McKee (2004:114) points out that '[w]hereas interpreters who work between minority and majority language groups are usually cultural members of the minority community, sign language interpreters are by necessity not Deaf, and are thus identified by Deaf people as outsiders and members of the dominant culture'. Is she correct in assuming that interpreters of spoken language are normally cultural members of the minority community? What are the implications of each position, as insider or outsider, and are these implications restricted to interpreting or might they also arise in the case of translation? Consider, for example, who might be involved in translating between Africaans or English and, say, Zulu or Xhosa in South Africa.

Recommended further reading

Apter, Emily (2001) 'Balkan Babel: Translation Zones, Military Zones', *Public Culture* 13(1): 65–80.

Bennett, Karen (2007) 'Epistemicide!: The Tale of a Predatory Discourse', *The Translator* 13(2): 151–69.

Branchadell, Albert and Lovell Margaret West (eds) (2005) *Less Translated Languages*, Amsterdam & Philadelphia, John Benjamins.

Cronin, Michael (2008) 'Minority', in Mona Baker and Gabriela Saldanha (eds) *Routledge Encyclopedia of Translation Studies*, 2nd edn London & New York: Routledge, 169–72.

McKee, Rachel (2004) 'Interpreting as a Tool for Empowerment of the New Zealand Deaf Community', in Sabine Fenton (ed.) *For Better or For Worse: Translation as a Tool for Change in the South Pacific*, Manchester: St. Jerome, 89–132.

Venuti, Lawrence (ed.) (1998) *Translation and Minority*, Special Issue of *The Translator* 4(2).

BUCK MULLIGAN AND STEPHEN DEDALUS are on the top of the Martello tower in Sandycove, Dublin. Buck Mulligan has finished shaving and he extends the mirror in Stephen's direction:

> – Look at yourself, he said, you dreadful bard.
> Stephen bent forward and peered at the mirror held out to him, cleft by a crooked crack, hair on end. As he and others see me. Who chose this face for me? This dogsbody to rid of vermin. It asks me too.
> – I pinched it out of the skivvy's room, Buck Mulligan said. It does her all right. The aunt always keeps plainlooking servants for Malachi. Lead him not into temptation. And her name is Ursula.
> Laughing again, he brought the mirror away from Stephen's peering eyes.
> – The rage of Caliban at not seeing his face in the mirror, he said. If Wilde were only alive to see you.
> Drawing back and pointing. Stephen said with bitterness:
> – It is a symbol of Irish art. The cracked lookingglass of a servant.
> (Joyce 1971:13)

Let us place the opening section from James Joyce's *Ulysses* alongside Charles Dickens' description of the making of plate glass in an article he wrote with W. H. Wills for *Household Words* in 1851. Dickens and Wills describe the slow ascension of a cauldron of red-hot glass:

> The dreadful pot is lifted by the crane. It is poised immediately over the table; a workman tilts it; and out pours a cataract of molten opal which spreads itself, deliberately, like infernal sweet stuff, over the iron table; which is spilled and slopped about, in a crowd of men, and touches nobody. 'And has touched nobody since last year, when one poor fellow got the large shoes he wore filled with white-hot glass.' (Cited in Armstrong 1996:127)

Here we have two images of glass, one of the looking glass, the glass as reflection, and the other of the plate glass, a shop-window, the transparent medium. Plate glass is one of the great technological innovations of the nineteenth century and Isobel Armstrong notes in 'Transparency: Towards a Poetics of Glass in the Nineteenth Century' that 'whereas "human labour" is "legibly expressed" for ever on other artefacts, glass, exasperatingly, erases this connection, its own invisibility making the conditions of its production invisible' (ibid.:128–29). The analogy with translation is telling, and this article will pursue a connection with the poetics of glass – the dual themes of *transparency* and *reflection* – to draw attention to the valuable if fragile connections between translation studies and minority languages in the modern world.

Invisible minorities

Count Dracula, the Transylvanian marginal and accomplished linguist, also looks into a shaving mirror, that of Jonathan Harker in *Dracula*, but he does not see himself (Stoker 1993:25). He remains disturbingly invisible. Speakers of minority languages looking into the disciplinary mirror of translation studies can also experience the troubling absence of the undead.

In the otherwise excellent *Routledge Encyclopedia of Translation Studies* (Baker 1998), there is no single, separate entry for translation and minority languages. There are informative and insightful historical entries on languages that have at various stages occupied a minor position in world culture, but the absence of a specific theoretical focus on the translation problematic for minority languages is significant. In Douglas Robinson's substantial and important *Western Translation Theory: from Herodotus to Nietzsche* (Robinson 1997b) there are 124 texts by 90 authors. However, the source texts for the anthology are overwhelmingly confined to five languages, namely Latin, ancient Greek, English, French and German. Two texts were originally written in Italian, one in Finnish, one in Spanish and one in Portuguese. There are no theoretical texts from Dutch, Danish, Norwegian, Irish, Catalan, Breton or Welsh, to name but a few of the translation languages of the Western world. Not one of Europe's lesser-used languages merits an entry in the anthology. The silence is all the more surprising in that minority-language cultures are translation cultures *par excellence*. Until recently, 70% of the books produced in the world originated in four languages: English, French, Russian and German. If we take children's literature for example, 3% of the output in Britain and the United States are translations. This compares with 70% in Finland, 50% in Italy and 33% in the Netherlands (O'Sullivan 1998:5).

If translation has traditionally suffered from lack of visibility then there is a sense in which translators working in minority languages are doubly invisible at a theoretical level. First, there is the general failure to include theoretical contributions from minority languages in translation theory anthologies. The anthologies that have appeared in English under the editorship of Rainer Schulte, John Biguenet and Andrew Chesterman are further evidence of exclusion (Schulte and Biguenet 1992, Chesterman 1989). Second, there is not always a willingness to acknowledge that translation perspectives from the point of view of minority languages will not always be those of major languages. Advocacy of non-fluent, refractory, exoticizing strategies, for example, can be seen as a bold act of cultural revolt and epistemological generosity in a major language, but for a minority language, fluent strategies may represent the progressive key to their very survival. Maolmhaodhóg Ó Ruairc, in his preface to *Dúchas na Gaeilge*, a study of Irish-English translation difficulties, describes the principal difficulty facing the translator of Irish:

> Má táimid neadaithe i ndomhan an Bhéarla. ní mór bheith san airdeall nach trí mheán an Bhéarla, faoi bhréagriocht na Gaeilge, a chuirtear friotal ar smaointe ár gcroí. Da mb'amhlaidh a bheadh, ba thúisce a bháfaí an tsainiúlacht Éireannach ná dá gcríonfadh an Ghaeilge féin. Ní fios an bhfuil sé ró-dhéanach cheana. (Ó Ruairc 1996:xiii)
>
> (If we find ourselves in an English-speaking world, we must guard against expressing our innermost feelings through English under a false Irish veneer. Should this happen, Irish distinctivness would disappear even more quickly than the language itself. Maybe, it's already too late.)
>
> (my translation)

Minority languages that are under pressure from powerful major languages can succumb at lexical and syntactic levels so that over time they become mirror-images of the dominant language. Through imitation, they lack the specificity that invites imitation. As a result of continuous translation, they can no longer be translated. There is nothing left to translate. The defence of the particular, the promotion of the naturalizing strategy can be derided as the last refuge of the essentialist, but it can be seen equally as the *sine qua non* of genuine hybridity. Indeed, it could be claimed that in this context, strong identities produce interesting differences. Rather than universalizing one particular strategy in translation practice, it would arguably be more useful to oppose *translation as reflection* to *translation as reflexion*. The first term I define as the unconscious imbibing of a dominant language that produces the numerous calques that inform languages from Japanese to German to Irish. The second term refers to second-degree reflection or meta-reflection, which should properly be the business of translation scholars and practitioners, namely the critical consideration of what a language absorbs and what allows it to expand and what causes it to retract, to lose the synchronic and diachronic range of its expressive resources. The work by Maurice Pergnier (Pergnier 1989) on anglicisms is one example of how such an approach might work; but more generally, like Dedalus on Sandymount strand in Dublin, translation scholars in minority languages must explore the limits of the transparent, the 'limits of the diaphane' (Joyce 1971:42).

There is a certain urgency about exploring the effects of translation on minority languages because of the parlous state of many languages in the modern world. According to the UNESCO *Atlas of the World's Languages in Danger of Disappearing*, up to a half of the 6500 languages spoken on the planet are endangered or on the brink of extinction. Some linguists claim that a language dies somewhere in the world every two weeks. In 1788, there were around 250 aboriginal languages in Australia, now there are 20. The arrival of Portuguese in Brazil led to the disappearance of 75% of the languages spoken in the country, and of the 180 indigenous languages still remaining, few are spoken by more than 10,000 speakers (Wurm 1996). The role of translation in this process of linguistic impoverishment is profoundly ambiguous. Translation is both predator and deliverer, enemy and friend. What happens to a people when they lose their language is not that they lose language. *Homo linguae* is not silenced, he or she speaks another. The speaker is in effect translated into another language. Irish history between the seventeenth and twentieth century is largely the story of that translation process. In the late sixteenth century, 90% of the Irish population were Irish-speaking, now less than 10% are fluent in the language and there are no Irish-speaking monoglots left. Translation is never a benign process *per se* and it is misleading to present it as such. From the perspective of minority languages, we must distinguish therefore between translation-as-assimilation and translation-as-diversification. Language speakers can either be assimilated through self-translation to a dominant language or they can retain and develop their language through the good offices of translation and thus resist incorporation. In a report on efforts to save a North American indigenous language, Tlingit, spoken on the Prince of Wales Island in the Gulf of Alaska, the journalist from *Time* magazine tells us that the Tlingit speakers try to record as much of the language as possible 'by translating just about anything they can get their hands on into Tlingit, from Christmas carols like *Jingle Bells* to nursery rhymes such as *Hickory Dickory Dock*' (Geary 1997:38). It is striking in this instance that translation (into English) – which has reduced Tlingit to its marginalized, peripheral position – should also be seen as one of the primary means for its survival.

Minority languages and science and technology

Speaking to the Press Club in Dublin in 1896, a graduate of Trinity College Dublin, W. J. Rolleston, declared that Irish was not a suitable instrument for thought or for a cultured people. The language had disappeared for all practical purposes and the Irish had willingly let it go. He then issued a challenge:

> He said he would take a piece of prose from a scientific journal and give it to someone in An Conradh for translation. He would then give the translation to another Irish speaker for translation back into English. The English translation could then be compared with the original in the journal. (O Fearaíl 1975:5)

Douglas Hyde, a future president of Ireland, translated the text into Irish and Eoin MacNéill translated it into English. Rolleston compared the English translation with the original and later declared publicly that he was satisfied that Irish was capable of being used in the modern world. The anecdote has the flavour of Jules Verne, the translation wager in the cigar lounge. However, it does highlight the significance of the relationship between translation, minority languages and science and technology. For Rolleston, accession to modernity was scientific. It was the ability to express the concepts of science that would define a language as a fit instrument for the modern age. He was not articulating an idle prejudice but the deeply-held belief of many minority-language activists. Writing in 1926, the Breton author and thinker Roparz Hemon declared:

> Ma ne striver ket da zaskoriñ d'ar brezhoneg e wir lec'h evel yezh ar ouiziegezh, al lennegezh, ar gelennadurezh hag ar Stad, evel yezh hor sevenadurezh en ur ger, ma n'anzaver ket splann n'eo ket ar brezhoneg ur gevrenn eus hor buhez vroadel, hogen ur benveg evit an holl, an istorour, an arzour, ar sonour, an espernour, kenkoulz hag ar c'houer, ar micherour, ar c'hlasker-bara, ne dalvez ket ar boan stourm evitañ. Lezomp eñ diouzthu da vervel. (cited in Gwegen 1975:76)
> (There is no point in fighting for the Breton language if we do not try to restore it to its true position as a language of knowledge, literature,

teaching, the State, and culture and we may as well let it die now if we do not state clearly that Breton is not a separate compartment of our life but can be used by everyone, by the historian, artist, musician, economist as much as by the farmer, worker and beggar.) (my tanslation)

Many works of translation theory and history celebrate the messianic role of translation in its work of aesthetic rescue, from Luther's Bible to Florio's Montaigne to Pope's Homer. For speakers of minority languages, however, the aestheticization of language can be profoundly disabling. Edmund Spenser's Irenius in *A View of the Present State of Ireland* (1596) admits that Irish-language poetry in translation is 'sprinkled with some pretty flowers of their own natural devise' (Spenser 1970:75), but if language becomes mere decoration or ornament then we are back to the specular exoticism of Orientalism and Celticism. The desired presence of the minority language in all areas of life, in all disciplines, the refusal of the aesthetic ghetto, demands a much greater reflection than has hitherto been undertaken on the role of scientific, technical and commercial translation in identity formation for minorities.

In this context, let us take one area of contemporary life, the Internet. Al Gore told the following story on a return from one of his foreign trips:

> Last month, when I was in Central Asia, the President of Kyrgyzstan told me his eight-year-old son came to him and said, 'Father, I have to learn English.' 'But why?' President Akayev asked. 'Because, father, the computer speaks English.' (cited in Lockard 1996:4)

The President's son was right. Current estimates are that 80% of email and data content are in English, a language that is not spoken as either a first or second language by three quarters of the people on the planet (Geary 1997:43). Writing on the omnipresence of what he calls 'Cyber-English', Joe Lockard (1996:5) claims:

> Non-English speakers have remained the permanent clueless newbies of the Internet, a global class of linguistic peasantry who cannot speak technological Latin. The overt language/classism that shapes the US English advocacy of mandatory English has long been an unstated de facto policy throughout most of the Internet.

He argues that in terms of language hierarchy, a new language class emerges whose online syntax and vocabulary embodies metropolitan norms, distinguishing them from those whose cyber-English remains more limited, 'in terms of transglobal class architecture, language/class is coming to represent the delineation between textual nation languages and *supra*-national cyber languages, a class division where advantage steadily accrues to those with a widely-employed cyber language' (*ibid*.:2).

These distinctions at one level are not new. Aramaic, Persian, Greek, Latin, French, to name but a few, are languages which have had imperial functions and where social prestige was affirmed through mastery of specific language norms (Kiernan 1991:191–209). The significance of the current situation lies in the spatial extent of cyber-English and the consequences of temporal compression (now tremendously quickened by the global cultural economy) for translation.

If the telecommunications revolution has involved the globalization of English, then the very terms of our discussion here are altered. The issue of translation and minority languages is not a peripheral concern for beleaguered fans of exotic peoples

gabbling in incomprehensible tongues but the single, most important issue in translation studies today. The hegemony of English in the fastest-growing area of technological development means that all other languages become, in this context, *minority
languages*. As I have argued elsewhere, the notion of a minority language is not a static
but a dynamic concept (Cronin 1995:85–103). Minorities are always relational, one
is a minority in relation to someone or something else. All languages, therefore,
are potentially minority languages and in the case of the Internet, most languages
have been *minoritized*. There are of course web sites and browsers in many languages.
Software localization is big business and multilingual web development is an expanding area. However, if present trends continue, particularly in software development,
then all languages on the Net other than English will be – in translation terms –
minority languages. The consequences for translators are many and relate principally
to the lessons of minority language experience and the extended teleological chain
of translation in the modern world.

The lessons of minority languages and teleological chains

Major languages have much to learn from minority languages. As vocabulary, syntax
and cultural memory come under pressure from English, dominant languages are
simply experiencing what minority languages have been experiencing for many centuries, and it would be instructive for the former to study the responses of the latter
to assimilationist translation pressures. This, in turn, places an onus on translation
scholars in minority languages to become more visible in translation studies debates.

A salient feature of globalization is time-space compression, the ability of
goods, people, currencies, bits of information to circulate at ever greater speeds. The
dematerialization of money has been a hugely important factor in the advent of the
post-Fordist economy and the consequent acceleration of exchange (Harvey 1989).
The late nineteenth-century sociologist Georg Simmel argued in his eassy 'On the
Psychology of Money' (1889) that any uniform and generalized means of exchange
was a means of lengthening the teleological chain and money was one such form
of exchange. What he understood by a teleological chain was that the difference
between what he called 'primitive' and 'cultivated' conditions could be measured by
the number of links that lie between immediate action and its ultimate end. A characteristic of modernity that is frequently cited is its growing abstraction, the increasing
number of links between actions and ends (Berman 1983:87–129). However, something must link the links, and Simmel sees money as a prime example of the intermediate link. Money, as means of exchange, is a way of converting personal volition
into goods and services, whereas in a direct barter system you are dependent on
person B wanting your goods *a* at the same time as you are attracted to their goods *b*.

> Therefore it is of the greatest value for the attainment of our goals that
> an intermediate link be inserted into the teleological chain, one into
> which I can convert *b* at any time and which can, in turn, be converted
> into *a* – roughly in the same way that any particular force, for instance,
> falling water, heated gas, or windmill sails, can be converted into any
> particular type of energy once it is introduced into the dynamo. (Simmel
> 1997:234)

Once equivalence is established and one has the equality of all things through an accepted means of exchange, there results a certain smoothness, a grinding down of sharp corners, that eases and accelerates the circulation of things. The French translation thinker Charles Batteux, for his part, links money, trade and translation in his *Principes de littérature* (1747–78). Here he recommends the use of what we would now call 'transposition' in translation practice and declares:

> Let him [the translator] take the scales, weigh the expressions on either side, poise them every way, he will be allowed alterations, provided he preserve to the thought the same substance and the same life. He will act only like a traveller, who, for his conveniency, exchanges sometimes one piece of gold for several of silver, sometimes several pieces of silver for one of gold. (Batteux, in Robinson 1997b:198–99)

Batteux's analogy has a singular purchase on translation reality at the end of our millennium. The new information economy of signs and spaces with the rapid movement of symbols and bytes is generating pressures on translation to become a uniform and generalized means of exchange, a transparent medium of fluid exchange. The translator becomes like the demon in James Clerk Maxwell's *Theory of Heat* (1872), a perfectly neutral space of transmission. Eurospeak becomes in more ways than one the speech of the Euro. The drive towards zero resistance, full equivalence, transparent immediacy that is implied in this reading of translation as intermediate link generates real translation pressures.

The first point to note is that English is adopted increasingly as the kind of universal means of exchange envisioned in Simmel's theory of money. The advertisement for *Visa* credit card in Guarulhos airport, São Paolo, Brazil that proclaims 'It's fluent in every language' is articulating a deep truth. Credit cards are emblematic of the new paper economy where money circulates at greater velocity, and the language of the advertisement is not Portuguese but English. If the credit card is the universal means of financial exchange then English is the universal means of linguistic exchange. The *Visa* vision of polyglossia is frictionless monoglossia.

A second feature of the current situation is the tyranny of real-time where translators increasingly have short response-periods for translation assignments. Time pressure has always existed but modems, translation memories, CAT tools greatly increase temporal expectations in a world of short-batch production and time-to-market constraints. Software localization provides many examples of growing time constraints. Localizing *Windows* '95 and *Office* '95 meant the release of the products in twenty languages within 165 days of the US original version. The office documentation entailed the translation of 134,000 words and the Help functions involved the translation of over 1,200,000 words (Poor 1996:1). The localization ideal of 'sim-ship', where all language versions are released at the same time and if possible at the same time as the original language version, means there is less and less time to do a translation. Any resistance offered by the text or translator slows down the process. If accelerated velocity is the chief characteristic of the post-industrial economy, then the pressure is on the translator to approximate more and more to the ideal of *instantaneous transparency*. Here, time (speed of execution) annihilates space (the place of the translator).

A third characteristic of global modernity is the exponential growth in information that is characteristic of the new post-Fordist economy. The growth in the quantity and delivery of information in all areas, from informatics to the media, has brought in its wake enormous terminological demands. As this information circulates more and more rapidly, there is increasing pressure on all languages other than the language of generation (usually English) to find equivalents, though the pressure is particularly acute in the case of minority languages due to lack of resources. Writing on the terminological pressures on Irish-language broadcasters in Ireland, Máirín Nic Eoin notes:

> Is é an deacracht is mó . . . ná nach bhfuil an soláthar in ann freastal ar an éileamh atá ann faoi láthair. Nuair a chaithfidh an craoltóir an scéal a chur amach go gasta, agus gan go leor ama aige nó aici go minic le foinsí údarásacha ar nós an Choiste Téarmaíochta a cheadú, ní hiontas ar bith go mbeidh garbhaistriúcháin in úsáid ar uairibh in áit leaganacha cruinne cearta a mbeadh machnamh éigin ar a gcúl. (Nic Eoin and Mac Mathúna 1997:7)
> (The biggest difficulty at present is that supply cannot meet demand. When a broadcaster has to get a story out quickly, without having much time to consult authoritative sources such as the Terminology Committee, it is no wonder that rough translations are sometimes used instead of accurate terminology that is well thought out.) (my translation; the *Coiste Téarmaíochta*/Terminology Committee is the State body responsible for the establishment of Irish-language terminology in Ireland.)

The temptation is to opt almost invariably for the reflective rather than the reflexive mode of translation in these circumstances. In addition, languages always carry a coefficient of power and the terminology of a major language can carry a socio-economic prestige, resulting in more and more terms appearing untranslated in the minority language (*ibid.*:4). Even where they are translated, terms and expressions articulate a world-view, a particular interpretation of events, that cumulatively erase the space of difference between languages (*ibid.*:19).

Lastly, new technology allows a much greater lengthening of the teleological chain of translation, as is evident from the management of localization projects. Tom Grogan, the Managing Director of International Translation and Publishing in Ireland, for example, has characterized a typical localization project as evaluated and managed from Ireland, translated in Japan, France and Italy, engineered in India, reviewed in the United States and finally assembled in and shipped from Ireland (Grogan 1997:52). There is a danger in the future of translation being seen as a low rather than high value-added activity as translation is outsourced to low-cost production centres, with a consequent deterioration in working conditions for translators working in these centres.

The translation ideal that permeates globalization-as-homogenization has often found lyrical expression in the literature of science fiction. In *The Hitch-Hiker's Guide to the Galaxy* (1979), Arthur Dent finds himself aboard a Vogon spaceship after planet Earth has been destroyed to make way for a hyperspace bypass. Ford Prefect, an extra-terrestrial friend, slaps a Babel fish into Arthur Dent's ear so that he can understand the unchivalrous welcome of the Vogons. Arthur Dent looks up 'Babel Fish' in *The Hitch-Hiker's Guide to the Galaxy* where he reads that the 'Babel fish is small, yellow and leech-like, and probably the oddest thing in the universe' (Adams 1979:49). After a pseudo-scientific description of its operation, Dent learns that 'if you stick a Babel fish in your ear you can instantly understand anything said to you in any form of language' (*ibid.*:50). However, transparency has not resulted in felicity. The entry for the Babel fish concludes unhappily (*ibid.*): the poor Babel fish, by effectively removing all barriers to communication between different races and cultures, has caused more and bloodier wars than anything else in the history of creation.

Our translation schools might be seen at one level as aquaria for the Babel fish of the future, but science fiction has to be distinguished from technological reality. Minority languages arguably need to be as concerned about their technical, commercial and scientific translators as they are about their literary translators, for cultural as well as pragmatic reasons. Literatures in minority languages need languages that can service all areas of life and not simply the bruised ego of historical loss. They need to move out of the ghetto of self-aggrandizing antiquarianism and see translation in all its dimensions as cultural, because culture is about a whole set of human activities not one subset that is privileged by the gaze of the commanding other. A significant element of translation activity in eighteenth-century and nineteenth-century Ireland was the translation/recovery of prestigious literary and historical texts (Cronin 1996:91–166). To translate these texts was to counter the charges of ignorance and barbarity levelled against the Irish by earlier English propagandists and prove the antique excellence of Irish language and culture. The difficulty for a minority language in this situation is that it gets fixated on a symbolic combat whose terms have been defined by a more powerful Other, so that minority-language translators confine themselves to the translation of high-culture texts and neglect all the other realms of human experience that constitute a culture.

Pathologies of universalism and difference

Glass, as Armstrong points out, is a transitive material and looking is always triangulated, there is always the viewing subject, the viewed object and what you view it through or with (Armstrong 1996:145). Translation is also triangulation, the broken middle that, as Gillian Rose points out, prevents a violent and dogmatic synthesis of binary opposites (Rose 1992). The French historian François Furet in Le passé d'une illusion analyzes the particular appeal of totalitarian ideologies in our century and describes Nazism as a pathology of difference and communism as a pathology of the universal (Furet 1995). Staying with translation as triangulation, it is possible to argue that translation lies between the pathology of universalism and the pathology of difference.

The pathology of universalism is implicit in language triumphalism, the sense of manifest destiny that informs the comments by Dinesh D'Souza in his The End of Racism, where he argues: 'We risk an American Babel, a breakdown of communication, if everyone does not speak a shared language. For reasons of practicality, this language must be English, which is rapidly becoming the global medium of intercultural communication' (D'Souza 1995:122). Here, pragmatism is the foot soldier of ideology and Babel a synonym for Armageddon. The nirvana of intercultural communication masks the violence of language loss. For the universalist, translation is an obstacle to – not an agent of – intercultural communication.

The pathology of difference, on the other hand, is parodied by the bilingual Irish novelist Flann O'Brien in The Poor Mouth, where the President of Grand Feis (festival) in Corkadoragha addresses the crowd:

> Gaels! he said, it delights my Gaelic heart to be here today speaking Gaelic with you at this Gaelic feis in the centre of the Gaeltacht. May I state that I am a Gael. I'm Gaelic from the crown of my head to the soles of my feet

> – Gaelic front and back, above and below. Likewise, you are truly Gaelic. We are all Gaelic Gaels of Gaelic lineage. He who is Gaelic, will be Gaelic evermore. I myself have spoken not a word except Gaelic since the day I was born – just like you – and every sentence I have ever uttered has been on the subject of Gaelic. (O'Brien 1973:54)

Here language is fetishized and all contact with the other is a form of contamination. The language is idealized and the speakers are ennobled. Joep Leerssen in *Mere Irish and Fíor-Ghael* (1996:288) describes the response of Irish-language poets to derogatory representations of their language and craft by Tudor propagandists. For these poets, the speech of the English

> (both in its contents and its linguistic medium) stamps them as uncouth, blubbering, simpering, stupid blockheads and bullies – this is in complete contrast to the mellifluous and harmonious *Gaeilge ghlic* and the clever speakers of that well-wrought language.

Here, Babel is betrayal, translation a form of capitulation. Minority languages that are constantly under social, economic and cultural pressure must, of course, often champion difference, if only to offer cogent reasons for their own survival. However, the rhetoric of difference can ultimately breed a conformism as stifling as the gospel of universalism.

Common conditions

Difference does not have to result in the pathology of closure. A celebration of difference can lead to an embrace of other differences, the universalism lying not in the eradication of the other but in sharing a common condition of being a minor other. It is interesting, in this context, to study the fortunes of inward translation in Ireland, a country which speaks a major world language and one of Europe's lesser-used languages. In the recent *Irish Guide to Children's Books*, almost half the Irish language titles were translations. Though the source language of the majority of the titles was English, over a third came from other languages such as German, Italian, Swedish, Welsh and Russian. On the other hand, the number of children's titles translated into English and published by Irish publishers has been negligible. Christine Nöstlinger's *Elf in the Head*, published by Poolbeg in 1992, and three novels by the Belgian author Ron Langenus, published by the Wolfhound Press, are notable exceptions. Irish Anglophone publishers, like their British and US counterparts, are eager to sell and reluctant to buy translation rights (O'Sullivan 1998:5).

The Ireland Literature Exchange, an organization established in 1994 to promote the translation of literature in Ireland, has been extremely successful in promoting the translation of Irish literature into other languages, yet it has so far failed to subsidize the translation of even one foreign title into English (*Bord na Leabhar Gaeilge*, another State body, is responsible for funding translations into Irish). Translation does not exist in a vacuum, of course. It is part of an interpretive community, a community that will have a greater or lesser degree of openness to foreign literatures and cultures. Dedalus, not Stephen, but a diarist for *The Sunday Times*, recently commented on the shortlist for the IMPAC literary prize. This prize is in financial terms the largest literary prize in the world and is awarded annually in Dublin. He notes that one of the authors on the list is Guy Vanderhaeghe and adds, 'crazy name, crazy guy'. He points out with leaden irony that last year's winner was a Spaniard, 'No doubt you will all have read, possibly in one sitting, last year's winner, *A Heart so White* by Javier Marias' and concludes, 'We shall only award the prize to impenetrable books, published abroad, that few can read' (Dedalus 1998). This kind of critical prejudice makes the publication and reception of translations in a major language like English even more fraught than it already is and is further demonstration that major is likely to mean minor in translation terms.

What about the other Dedalus and his shaving mirror? The cracked looking glass of the servant might be the description of any minor language speaker who sees himself or herself reflected in the language of the major other. This is the case of the Breton described by Gwegen (1975:73) who is persuaded to give up his old language clothes for the trendy fashions of the capital:

> Un beau jour, poussés par la curiosité, nous nous sommes regardés dans une glace, et nous avons poussé un cri! L'habit 'made in Paris' nous allait comme un sac! Les grands couturiers de la capitale avaient oublié de prendre nos mesures.
> (One fine day, piqued by curiosity, we looked at ourselves in a mirror and cried out saying that the outfit 'made in Paris' didn't suit us at all. The great fashion designers of the capital had forgotten to take our measurements.) (my translation)

The mirror here is presented as the oracle of a language and political truth. If we stay with this image of the looking glass, what kind of future can we see for minority languages in translation studies?

Training

Market demands, history and cultural proximity often lead to economies of scale that mitigate not only against translation into and out of minority languages but also between these languages. Much more needs to be done to encourage translation exchanges between lesser-used languages on the planet and translator-training institutions need to explore ways in which this can be done. These exchanges have training implications. Translation, by definition, requires translators and the tendency in minority languages can be for more unusual language combinations to be handled by more or less gifted, well-meaning amateurs. Training of translators in a minority language can usually only be justified economically if a major language is involved, but translator-training institutions have to argue beyond the rationale of the accountant for more inclusive training programmes that have minor-minor language combinations.

Research

As noted at the beginning of this article, minority languages are still largely invisible in translation studies. This problem needs to be addressed both at the level of historical research into the past experience of minority languages and at the level of theory itself. There are many problems to which theory might direct its attention. For example, when an Irish-language poet wants to translate an Estonian writer, he or she will almost invariably have recourse to a crib in a language they both understand, usually English. How does the use then of filter languages impact on translation practice in minority languages? Does the intermediate link in this instance vitiate source-specificity? Can the practice be called translation or is it something else? In a different but related context, writers in a minority language have frequent recourse to auto-translation into a major language. They do this to facilitate their presence as writers/translators in other languages. Does this practice create a different translation dynamic from translation between two major languages? Does the frequent practice of auto-translation create not a *literature-in-translation* but a *literature-for-translation*? There are many, many more questions that might be explored in the context of minority languages that would make translation theory more inclusive than it is at present.

Heteroglossia

Caliban may have wondered at his own reflection and cursed Prospero for teaching him his language, but knowing the language of the master made his revolt more widely articulate. Irish critics like Declan Kiberd see the Irish mass translation of the nineteenth century as the ultimate subversion, taking the language of colonial ruler and using it to drive him out (Kiberd 1995). This process of colonial and post-colonial appropriation of major languages has been much studied in its impact on literary expression. The movement can be theorized alternatively as the **minoritization** of major languages through heteroglossia (Deleuze and Guattari 1975). This minoritization can of course become the basis of a movement in translation that affirms identity through minoritized translation. The Irish Literary Renaissance at the turn of the century was largely driven by a belief in the virtues of such minoritization (Cronin 1996:131–43). Lady Gregory, one of the pioneers of the Renaissance, translated four plays by Molière into Hiberno-English between 1906 and 1926, as part of a project to make Hiberno-English a fit instrument for the translation of world literature (Gregory 1910, 1928). Lady Gregory's translation work was conceived of primarily as an act of cultural self-confidence. Tudor England, Classical France and Romantic Germany had considered the translation of Greek and Roman classics to be part of the process of nation-building. Translating Molière into Hiberno-English would affirm national specificity and the literary potential of a language that would no longer be the comic signature tune of the Stage Irishman. As a major language like English spreads more and more widely, the phenomenon of heteroglossia is likely to figure even more prominently in discussions on translation and minority languages, and the heteroglossic translation practice of Gregory will become more and more common.

Retreat from language

There is a final point of a more general nature, and this has to do with the consequences for translation of the minoritization of language itself. Here, the problem is the very translation of modernity. George Steiner in a 1961 essay, 'The Retreat from the Word', argued famously that in the seventeenth century significant areas of truth, reality and action receded from the sphere of verbal statement. He claimed that

> With the formulation of analytical geometry and the theory of algebraic functions, with the development by Newton and Leibniz of calculus,

mathematics ceases to be a dependent notation, an instrument of the empirical. It becomes a fantastically rich, complex and dynamic language. *And the history of that language is one of progressive untranslatability.* (Steiner 1979:33; emphasis in original)

The history of the mathematicization of scientific knowledge is also, however, one of radical and accelerated translatability. Gillian Beer argues that the use of mathematics has 'speeded up communication between scientists to a startling degree, as if the Tower of Babel had been built in a day once the workers found a common discourse' (Beer 1996:321–22). This mathematicization of enquiry has certainly resulted in that withdrawal from the word that Steiner sees at work as much in the human and social as in the physical sciences, but it has also, in my view, determined the current hegemony of English as a source language in translation and as a target language in language teaching. The pre-Babelian promise of mathematics is mirrored in the *reineSprache* of English as if, in a sense, the minoritization of all language becomes the majoritization of one. The condition of mathematical transparency that allows topologists of different nationalities to gather together in a community of understanding around the blackboard or VDU is the globalizing impulse behind English as the world language. However, this minoritization of language results in English becoming – in translation terms – a minority language in that it is not a language of translation but a language for translation (Venuti 1995). This retreat from the word directly affects minority languages not just through the privileging of one language but because increasingly they become, in the techno-scientific area, languages of reception rather than generation, locked into dependency like Joyce's hapless bard. On the other hand, the increasing importance of knowledge-intensive, design-intensive production in the world of disorganized capitalism (viz. the importance of the expressive, symbolic function in popular music, advertising and tourism) could heighten rather than minimize the importance of cultural and linguistic diversity as a source of economic and cultural renewal in a global age (Urry and Lash 1994).

Night has fallen on the 16 June 1904 and Leopold Bloom and Stephen Dedalus make their way into the backyard of 7 Eccles Street. There they gaze up at the 'heaventree of stars hung with humid nightblue fruit' (Joyce 1971:619). Bloom's thoughts turn to astronomy:

> Meditations of evolution increasingly vaster: of the moon invisible in incipient lunation, approaching perigree: of the infinite lattiginous scintillating uncondensed milky way, discernible by daylight by an observer placed at the lower end of a cylindrical vertical shaft 5000 ft deep sunk from the surface towards the centre of the earth.

Another earlier observer of the heavens, the British astronomer John Herschel, had seen the earth's atmosphere as a transparent film, that like glass bent the light so that the objects Stephen and Bloom gaze at are never quite where they appear to be nor are they, the viewing subjects, quite where they think they are. Isobel Armstrong (1996:144–45) points to another important conclusion of Herschel's work:

> Almost as important as this displacement of the viewing subject was the fact of the earth's motion. This means that anything like the idea of

the earth as a fixed point has to be given up. It is important he says in his work on the telescope, in 1861, to relinquish the notion of the earth as a foundation. Our motion in relation to that of another object has to be calibrated. With this we move to a world of continuous relational adjustments.

The notion of fixed points in translation studies is also deeply problematic. The power nexus between languages is constantly shifting so that our translation relationships have to be endlessly calibrated. Moving away from foundational notions of translation, it will be in a conception of translation as a 'world of continuous relational adjustments' that minority languages will finally have a major role to play in the discipline of translation studies.

Chapter 15

Alexandra Jaffe

LOCATING POWER: CORSICAN
TRANSLATORS AND THEIR CRITICS

EDITOR'S INTRODUCTION

> . . . *most translations are done in order to make a document accessible to people who cannot read it*
> *in the original. A translation that openly violates this pragmatic, communicative function acquires*
> *a certain metalinguistic force: it ensures that the translation will be 'read' as a political statement.*
> *Given the fact that not all Corsicans speak or read Corsican but all Corsicans speak and read*
> *French, translations from French to Corsican actually narrow rather than broaden the reading*
> *audience and thus constitute one of these open violations.*

J AFFE ANALYZES AN INTERESTING debate that was ignited in Corsican cultural and literary circles, spilled into the public domain and received considerable media
coverage following the translation of a French novel into Corsican in 1989. The debate, which
drew contributions from linguists and writers actively involved in promoting Corsican language
and culture, concerned the way in which translations in Corsica could be politicized and
made to symbolize power relations on a wider historical and societal level. Political resistance
to French domination in Corsica has been fought, as elsewhere, on the level of language and
culture. The Corsican language forms the centrepiece of an activist claim to political autonomy,
and as such has value in and of itself, as a pure, autonomous code rather than a communicative
practice.

Jaffe offers a detailed analysis of the role of diglossia in maintaining a hierarchical,
oppositional relationship between Corsican and French. Diglossia here means that Corsican is
excluded from the powerful public sphere and relegated to informal and family domains, while
French dominates education and public life. For activists and translators seeking to promote
and empower Corsican, this situation needs to be reversed, and the balance of power between
Corsican and French tipped in order to influence attitudes and practices. Hence the importance of *writing* in Corsican. 'Because the power of French was reflected in its command of
public domains', Jaffe explains, 'writing in Corsican also played the critical symbolic role of
displacing the sole dominion of French in literary, public and official contexts'. Disagreement
over the status of translation arose because while it contributed to creating a corpus of written

documents in Corsican, it did not contribute to establishing an independent Corsican literary tradition. The debate analyzed here brings various perspectives to bear on assessing what translating from the dominant to the minority language did to the existing imbalance of linguistic power. Those who assessed translation negatively interpreted its symbolic value from within the diglossic model and wanted to police the boundaries of the Corsican literary corpus. For them, any use of French as the source language constituted an implicit acknowledgment of its superiority. The translators took a different view: they argued that 'translation into the minority language encoded a *reformulated* social order in which habitual relations of power were reversed and the "minority" language was established as the set of conventions to which the majority language had to submit'. Moreover, translation gave them an opportunity to activate elements of oral style that had been largely unexploited because of the restricted size of the corpus of Corsican literature. Characters could be given identities and made to speak dialects from distinct micro-regions. The translators also rejected the exclusionary logic of minority self defence, the logic of rejecting everything that comes from the dominant culture. Here, translating 'was a way of demonstrating a new confidence in Corsican language and identity by acting *as if* it were a language of power'.

Follow-up questions for discussion

- Jaffe's focus in this article is on translating *into* the minority language, as a means of empowering it and extending the domains within which it can function. What role might translating *out of* the minority language play, and is it a feasible enterprise in the case of a language like Corsican, with very limited circulation and a restricted body of written material? How does translation into/out of Corsican compare with translation into/out of Scots, or Irish, or Breton, as discussed in the literature?

- In a study largely focused on Gikuyu, Peterson (2004:9) states: 'Niranjana, Venuti and other radical translators obscure . . . colonized people's own acts of translation and composition. In Niranjana's and Venuti's model, translation is a liberating act of scholarly genius. But in central Kenya as elsewhere in the colonized world, translation was always more than a scholarly project. Translating was a popular activity, a continual, continuing strategy of political argumentation'. How does this statement relate to Cronin's critique of the suppression of minority language experience in theoretical work on translation? What practical steps can we take to ensure that more minority voices come to inform the theorizing and teaching of translation and interpreting?

- Very few studies have analyzed public debates or even reviews of translation. Diriker (2003/2005) exceptionally offers an analysis of how simultaneous interpreting and interpreters were presented in the Turkish press between 1998 and 2003. Unlike Diriker's study, however, the translators in Jaffe's article are not merely the objects of debate but actively contribute to it as full participants. This is not a particularly unusual phenomenon, despite the lack of studies in the field (see, for instance, contributions by translators to various newspaper columns and literary magazines). Using databases such as St. Jerome's *Translation Studies Online* and Benjamins' *Bibliography of Translation Studies*, try to locate any studies that analyze public debates or press coverage of translation and/or interpreting, whether or not translators contribute to them. What themes do these studies focus on? How might they be extended and what value might they have in terms of refining theoretical models and/or training translators?

Recommended further reading

Corbett, John (1998) *Written in the Language of the Scottish Nation: A History of Literary Translation into Scots*, Clevedon: Multilingual Matters.

Cronin, Michael (1995) 'Altered States: Translation and Minority Languages', *TTR* 8(1): 85–103.

Diriker, Ebru (2003/2005) 'Presenting Simultaneous Interpreting: Discourse of the Turkish Media, 1988–2003', originally published in *The Interpreter's Newsletter*, revised version published in *Communicate*, the webzine of AIIC. (Available online: http://www.aiic.net/ViewPage.cfm/page1742.htm).

Findlay, Bill (2004) *Frae Ither Tongues: Essays on Modern Translations into Scots*, Clevedon: Multilingual Matters.

IN 1989, A TRANSLATION OF A FRENCH NOVEL, *Knock*, into Corsican by the Corsican writer and translator Jean-Joseph Franchi ignited a small but intense debate in Corsican cultural and literary circles. The debate was on the nature of translations from French into Corsican, or rather, about the various ways in which such translations could be politicized and made to symbolize power relations on a wider historical and societal level. This debate spilled over into the public domain, and received considerable media coverage. Translators and their critics shared fundamental assumptions about language, identity and power but disagreed about the function/outcomes of translation in the project of resistance to French language domination. This disagreement rested in part on their contrasting focuses on language-as-system versus language as practice/experience. Yet the analysis I will provide in this paper also shows that in some respects, translators challenged the insistence on a monolingual-monocultural norm and its essentialist view of relationship between linguistic, political and cultural identity. Translators also resisted the hobbling of personal artistic freedom imposed by the politics of language in contexts of minority language revitalization. Personal freedom became a metaphor for collective liberation, and suggested a model of resistance that located power in the prerogative to set and choose criteria of value.

In this paper, I use this debate over the politics of representation on Corsica to explore how enactments of linguistic and social identity are shaped by ambient ideological structures, and how 'dominant' ideologies of language and identity can be resisted or transformed. Analysis of this debate over the value of translations illustrates John B. Thompson's general point that the minority experience and acceptance of dominance is not uniform; that we should not assume that the social reproduction of relations of inequality involves or requires perfect consensus (1984:Chapter 2). In the translation debate in Corsica we can see the ample space for dissent and contestation created by local interpretations of dominant ideas about the connection between language, identity and power.

Corsica is one of the many places in Western Europe where there has been language shift away from a 'regional', predominantly oral language (Corsican) towards the official, written language of the state (French).[1] In the early seventies, the Corsican ethnonationalist movement was the catalyst for efforts at language revitalization. The philosophies and strategies of the past thirty years of Corsican language activism have been shaped by a number of ideological and political forces. These include macro-level language politics: the influence of dominant European ideas about the link between language, cultural identity and nationhood/autonomy. They also include how these broad themes have been translated into specific French language policies. Corsican language activists have also been influenced by academic explanations about the causal connections between French language policies and popular language attitudes and linguistic practices.

A central element of what I am labelling as 'dominant language ideology' is the conflation of language, culture and national identity. This is the foundation of Western European 'cultural nationalism', in which having a unique language is proof of a unique culture, which in turn legitimates claims to political sovereignty (Hobsbawm 1990, Anderson 1983, Balibar 1991, Grillo 1989). The influence of this dominant language ideology is evident in numerous postcolonial contexts and in many places in the developing world. It is also one of the most widespread scientific ideologies of language: as Blommaert (1996) points out, many linguists and socio-linguists involved in language planning in multilingual contexts subscribe to an 'organic' model of language and culture, and to the assumption that linguistic/cultural homogeneity is 'normal'.

In Western Europe, France has one of the longest histories of using the dominant language as a symbol of political/social incorporation and exercising State control through what Cameron (1995) calls 'verbal hygiene'. Not surprisingly, therefore, political resistance to French domination in Corsica has been played out on linguistic and cultural terrain. Corsican nationalists made the Corsican language a centerpiece of their claims on peoplehood and political autonomy. As Handler (1988), Gal (1989) and others have pointed out, when language plays this key role in the legitimation of political boundaries, it is not language as communicative practice that is invoked, but rather language as a bounded, pure, autonomous code. In other words, in the European politics of language, there is a monolingual norm and an essentialist philosophical bias (cf. Lüdi 1992, Blommaert and Verschueren 1992).

All of the actors involved in the translation debate were self-labelled culturels ('culturals'): teachers, linguists and writers who had been actively involved in the promotion of Corsican language and culture for years. In these circles, the sociolinguistic concept of diglossia had been widely circulated, and constituted the baseline for both their understanding of the processes involved in language shift and their strategies for the revitalization of Corsican. Diglossia described the hierarchical, oppositional relationship between Corsican and French. It indexed language practices (specifically, the exclusion of Corsican from the powerful public sphere) as well as language attitudes. These were intimately connected, for the dominance of French in education and public life and the restriction of the use of Corsican to informal and family domains led many Corsicans to view the languages as intrinsically intimate/solidary (Corsican) or distant/powerful (French). When Corsican intellectuals wrote and talked about a 'diglossic mentality' they were referring to the way that this compartmentalization of values effectively reproduced and legitimated Corsican's low status. Diglossia was seen as the outcome of both the practical and the symbolic domination of French, which not only had enormous pragmatic value but was also the centre of French ideologies of moral and civic virtue (Lüdi 1992, Weinstein 1990). Reversing language shift thus involved tipping the balance of power between Corsican and French in order to simultaneously influence attitudes and practices.

How does one tip that balance of power? One major trend in Corsican language activism was to claim/build for the minority language the attributes and domains of power from which it had been excluded. This is why *writing* assumed such an important role in the process. Writing in Corsican was central to a number of strategies. First of all, the writing of grammars, orthographies and dictionaries played a key role in the construction of Corsican linguistic identity and legitimacy. These texts 'proved' that Corsican met conventional and dominant criteria of 'languageness': that it had internal unity and structure, and was clearly differentiated from other linguistic codes. Secondly, because the power of French was reflected in its command of public domains, writing in Corsican also played the critical symbolic role of displacing the sole dominion of French in literary, public and official contexts. All Corsican texts could be seen as game pieces in a war for symbolic territory. In the context of French language ideology, the production of written literary texts had particular value as a legitimation of Corsican's claim to be a real language. As late as 1991, during a debate over a proposed law on Corsican language education, a non-Corsican senator who was critical of the measure said: 'Mais où sont vos Rimbaud?' (Where are your Rimbauds?) in a reference to the lack of a literary tradition in Corsican that was clearly made to disparage Corsican's language status. It is here that we begin to see the crux of the disagreement over the status of translation. Translation contributed to the corpus of written documents in Corsican, but it did not contribute to the goal of establishing an independent Corsican literary tradition.

The political nature of translation

There is an underlying political dimension to all translations, for each act of translation posits a relationship of power (whether equal or unequal) between languages and cultures. In contexts which are by definition hierarchical, the political significance of translation is heightened. Well before the postmodern critique of ethnographic practice, Crick (1976a) underscored the issue of power in his definition of anthropology as 'translation-for'. By this he meant that translation is never neutral: it is an ideologically-grounded interpretation which is intimately linked to issues of power and legitimacy of the translator/anthropologist and his or her discipline (1976a:166). Gupta (1990) also points out the ways in which the process of cultural translation serves to ratify the authenticity of the anthropological construction of 'self' and 'other'. Writing about translation in another context in which power relations are imbalanced (colonialism), Rafael points to 'the fact that translation lends itself to either affirmation or evasion of the social order' (1988:211). Translation is by definition a commentary on power relations, a point also made by Klor de Alva (1989:143).[2]

Thus translation is metalinguistic and metacultural activity which makes explicit contrasts and conflicts between modes of discourse and models of linguistic value and power which are able to remain buried or implicit in much of everyday life and in some other forms of writing. The interpretation of the 'meta' message of translations in contexts of ethnic and/or linguistic militancy takes place against two backdrops: (1) knowledge of the role and meaning of translation in conventional contexts and (2) knowledge of cultural and linguistic hierarchies.

As for (1), most translations are done in order to make a document accessible to people who cannot read it in the original. A translation that openly violates this pragmatic, communicative function acquires a certain metalinguistic force: it ensures that the translation will be 'read' as a political statement. Given the fact that not all Corsicans speak or read Corsican but all Corsicans speak and read French, translations from French to Corsican actually narrow rather than broaden the reading audience and thus constitute one of these open violations. In the preface to his bilingual French-Corsican book *Cavalleria Paisana*, Rochiccioli (1982:9) writes: 'To write in French and hope to be read is a form of optimism. To write in Corsican and cling to the same hope is to dream in vain'. In the case of the translation of *Knock*, the metalinguistic dimension is not just part of the message; it is the message.

As for (2), there is a precedent for the successful political use of symbolic translations by other Western European ethnic minorities. Typically, ethnic militants have made an issue of translation of official and legal documents into the minority language as a way of asserting their right to cultural and linguistic difference and the government's responsibility to legitimize their language and culture. These translations of the key forms and legal texts of government bureaucracies are counter-symbols which draw on the dense and powerful associations of power, rationality and value of the dominant state. The Welsh nationalist movement, for example, has successfully imposed a parallel Welsh-language structure of forms and documents (Khleif 1980). This is also true of the Basques (Urla 1987), the Catalans (Woolard 1989), and the Québecois (Handler 1988).

However, this particular brand of militant translation has been very little used in Corsica, probably because nationalist or autonomist parties have never had political control. There was a brief (and I suspect, not entirely serious) production of Corsican identification cards, but no other official forms have been translated. In sum, attempts to create official documents in Corsican have been sporadic and have usually met with apathy or disapproval from the political class.

Thus the symbolic literary translation that sparked the debate was not building on a base of existing militant practice. No one had any experience of the social effects of such translations. Translators and their critics brought a variety of theoretical perspectives to their assessment of what translating from the dominant to the minority language did to the existing imbalance of linguistic power. The critics of translation looked at translation from a macropolitical perspective: they interpreted its symbolic value from within the diglossic model. The translators argued from the 'bottom up'; they used the micropolitics of their own experiences as a metaphor for sociolinguistic relations of power in translation.

The critics

In a magazine article devoted to translation, Santarelli wrote:[3]

> [for many people, translation is] a dangerous symptom of a serious psychological complex that keeps Corsican literature in a state of infantile dependence on its French 'big sister' . . . a destructive force which prevents it from finding its unique voice . . . with Corsican creation in crisis, translation is an evasion of the facts: the language is moribund. It is premature to waste time and energy on translating foreign works while Corsican literature is only in its first stammerings . . . (1989:21)

An angry reader wrote in to amplify on this theme, stating that the 'soul of the nation' was best served by documents created in its own language, and called translation 'imported foreign philosophy, the reproduction of outside identity'. 'If Corsican culture is sterile', he concluded, 'then better not to deceive ourselves with transla-

tions, and to wait with patience for future literary harvests of genuine identity'
(Anonymous 1989).

It is obvious that these criticisms have nothing to do with the author's creativity,
the artistic validity or the cultural fidelity of the text of the translation. They stem
from the knowledge of a political context in which

> translation has been largely a one-way street: the small nations hasten to
> translate all that is worthwhile of the great nations' literature into their
> own language but not vice versa . . . Small nations cannot afford to be
> parochial and ignorant, while the great, it seems, can. And do. (Boldizsar
> 1979:xi)

The interpretation of translation primarily as a symbol of defeat in a cultural power
struggle was expressed in less extreme terms by the literary editor of the Corsican
page in the island's weekly magazine. He argued that in the current sociological
context, only page-by-page bilingual editions of translations had pedagogical value
and that only translations of works that had not been translated into French had
philosophical merit. Translation in any other form was simply a 'trap' into which
minority languages in 'diglossic' situations were often lured. Like the other critics, he
assumed that the primary motive for translation was to prove the value, or raise the
stature of the language in the idiom of power. 'Scrivi tu è scrivi toiu, O Ghjuanghjasè'
(Write of yourself and of your own, O Jean-Joseph) he wrote, advising Franchi not
to waste his considerable creative talents on more translations (Fusina 1989b:61).

It was true that Franchi had translated Montesquieu and other French classics,
and could be suspected of being motivated by the hope that some of the status and
legitimacy of the original text would rub off on the minority language. But he had
made no particular claims for the greatness of Knock; one of his primary motivations
for choosing it, he wrote, was that it was widely read in schools (Franchi 1989b). In
Franchi's view, translating a familiar text was pedagogically useful. But the ordinari-
ness of the original text was a much more subtle and specific issue than the ones the
critics were engaging. They were using Franchi's work as emblem of all translation
from the French, and they interpreted his motives against the backdrop of the history
of Corsican language planning. That is, as language activists themselves, the critics had
often heard arguments such as: 'Corsican has no grammar – it has no literature – it is
incapable of expressing abstract ideas' from both Corsicans and French as a way of
rationalizing French language dominance. They also knew that there was already a long
(and I would argue inevitable) tradition in Corsican language activism of countering
such arguments by attempting to show that Corsican met French criteria of linguistic
value. They recognized that this form of resistance to French left the French-Corsican
hierarchy undisturbed, since France and French were still the sources of authority.

While all the translators vociferously denied that they were using the French texts
as entrance exams for Corsican legitimacy, some of their comments suggested otherwise. For example, D. Geronimi was challenged during a literary gathering to explain
why he had translated Waiting for Godot. One of his responses was that the translation
served to 'put the language to the test'. In his written rebuttal to criticism of his
translation of Knock, Franchi phrased the value of translation in these terms:

> You say that Corsican is concrete? Certainly, and this is its opportunity to
> bring to European consciousness this mass of images and sensations which
> until this day have remained literally virgin. (1989b:59, emphasis added)

Here, 'literally' can be translated as 'literarily'; for the virginity of Corsican has to do with the written, not the oral tradition. Franchi's statement is based on the cultural norm that attributes superior status and value to written genres, and suggests that the value of the Corsican language is virtual until it is put into writing, which allows it to be measured and assessed in some wider social context. I do not want to make too much of these comments, because they are only part of a complex set of linguistic and social motivations that I will expand on below. But I do believe that they reflect an underlying tension of experience. That is, all Corsican writers, in their natural desire to legitimate their activity, have only French literary precedents to turn to. As Niranjana puts it, people in postcolonial contexts live lives that are already always 'in translation' (1994:38). One could argue that for any educated Corsican, French literature was an inevitable point of reference for all acts of reading and writing (including in Corsican); that even when they wrote original works and did not translate, the implicit comparison between the hegemonic French literary tradition and Corsican literary production was unavoidable. We can see this in the remarks made by Jacques Thiers in a newspaper interview regarding the publication of his book *A Funtana d'Altea*, in Corsican. He refused the label of 'novel', because

> being able to write a novel in Corsican is seen as one of the ultimate proofs of the dignity of our language. But do we really need to have novels to believe that Corsican is a distinct language? This is why I prefer to say that my book is a story. Corsican writers do not write in order to show that Corsican is a language. (Cerani 1991)

The critics of translation viewed any use of French as the source language as an implicit acknowledgment of the superiority of French. They wanted to exercise power by policing the boundaries of the Corsican literary corpus. Given the power imbalance between French and Corsican, it was important to withhold from French any ownership of the 'source' text. Translators challenged this reading of the authority of the source text, offering a reverse reading of the relations of authority between source and target language. Rafael provides the groundwork for this sort of reading in his discussion of the relationship of translation to social process. Translation, he writes, 'arises from the need to relate one's interest to that of others and so to encode it appropriately . . . it thus coincides with the need to submit to the conventions of a given social order' (1988:210). The translators took the position that translation into the minority language encoded a *reformulated* social order in which habitual relations of power were reversed and the 'minority' language was established as the set of conventions to which the majority language had to submit. They claimed that this symbolic empowerment of Corsican was heightened in translations for which there was no practical need, since historically, the 'need' for translations in either direction had been defined and imposed on the minority by dominant linguistic and social groups. That is, they were arguing that in their translations, the power balance was on their side since French was being used for Corsican purposes.

Translation as practice: the translatable and the untranslatable

The translators' reformulation of the power structure was based in part on their experience of the constant tension, in the act of translation, between what can and what cannot be translated; between the power of the translator to breach chasms of linguistic equivalence and the power of language to resist this forced journey from one culture and frame of reference to another. This tension is central to much of the abundant literature on translation, in which the proof of the translators' skill lies in their ability to recognize its limits: to identify what cannot be completely successfully communicated across languages and cultures. In a volume entitled *Small Countries, Great Literatures*, the editor remarks in the introduction that '*Latva, lasnak* is untranslatable. *Seen, seeing* appears incomplete in English, while the Hungarian has disarming force' (Boldiszar 1979:ix).

Writers on translation always return to the topic of the untranslatable. Rabassa (1984:24) comments on the untranslatability of local experience of words. He gives the example of the problem the name of a tree posed in a translation he made from Spanish to English. The tree, which has no English counterpart, was identified by its Mayan name in the Spanish text. None of the available choices of translation seemed satisfactory. The local flavour and exoticism connoted by the linguistic contrast of the Mayan name in the Spanish text could not be faithfully reproduced by using either the Mayan or the Spanish name for the tree in the English text. The experiential equivalent (a tree called by an exotic, indigenous name in English) would be geographically inauthentic. In a similar vein, Tedlock (1989:167) writes about the untranslatability of names in his one act play dramatizing the translation of *Popol Vuh*. The characters debate whether or not a proper name in a Mayan text that means 'crocodile' in Nahua should be left in Mayan or written 'crocodile' in English. And Eva Hoffman (1989:272) reflects on her sister's adult decision to use her Polish name in her English life jars her ear:

> Its syllables don't fall as easily on an English speaker's tongue. In order to transpose a single word without distortion, one would have to transport the entire language around it.

It is the knowledge of the 'entire language' and culture that translators are reminded of by failures in translation. In one respect, their mastery of two codes and movement between them emphasizes linguistic and cultural boundaries. This is the 'going across' in the experience of translation. When translators talk about the untranslatable, they often reinforce the notion that each language has its own 'genius', an essence that 'naturally' sets it apart from all other languages and reflects something of the 'soul' of its culture or people. Three comments by Franchi illustrate this point. In a magazine article in which he discussed translation, Franchi used, and then reflected on his use of a Corsican idiom. He wrote: 'Quant'au reste, inutile de "*piattassi daretu un ditu*" . . . tiens! Comment dit-on cela en Français?' (As for the rest, it's useless to '*hide behind a finger*' . . . tell me, how do you say that in French?) (1989b:58). In a fieldwork interview, Franchi also told me an anecdote which emphasized the role of translation in maintaining the integrity and boundaries of both languages in question. He recounted that he had 'faithfully' translated Yves Morel's song *Tu ne me quittes pas* into Corsican for a Corsican singer. The singer, he said, had then 'ruined' the translation by 'Corsicanizing' the original music and singing so that the words, so clearly articulated in the original version, were unintelligible. Here, Franchi emphasized the translator's obligation to render the *essence* of the original – the relation of words to music, the tone, the style – in a manner that was also faithful to the structures and style of the target language. In another part of the interview, he took up the topic of language boundaries once again, asserting that the very nature of Corsican guaranteed a distance between source text and translation. He explained that because Corsican is less standardized and more archaic than other latinate languages, a Corsican version of a text would never be 'a simple copy of the original' that he claimed one would find, for example, in a translation from French to Spanish.

But the 'untranslatable' is also a momentary failure, for translators often do arrive at felicitous translations. These successes are made possible by translators' knowledge of the social, contextual and experiential grounds of meaning in the two languages and cultures that they broker. The process of translating heightens and hones the translator's experience of cultural and linguistic mastery. Translation requires what the Corsican poet Biancarelli described to me as 'un œuil intermédiaire' (an intermediate eye). For him, translating was a rich source of self-knowledge and creative stimulus; it was a metalinguistic experience, an orchestration of the tension between two sets of metaphors. Translators also talked about the exercise of the imagination that translation provoked in the search for a phrase, a tone or a style that they might never have considered in the absence of the requirement to shuttle between two worlds of discourse.

There is another sense in which translation was particularly empowering for Corsican writers. They were able to experience what Roland Barthes calls the *jouissance* (pure pleasure) of the text which comes from playing with or violating norms of style, grammar, register and so on in Corsican. I emphasize this because this *jouissance* can usually only be experienced in languages with a written tradition. A writer who creates an original text in Corsican cannot violate a norm because there are hardly any (except for the hegemonic French norms); today, even Corsican spelling norms are contested. Translation gave these authors a chance to activate the sociolinguistic elements of oral style that, because of the small corpus of Corsican literature, were largely unexploited. In the translation of *Knock*, the characters were given identities and Corsican dialects from distinct microregions. As a stylistic strategy, the author was playing off the reader's understanding of the social connotations of accent and dialect and regional identity in *both* French and Corsican. This was one of the reasons why it was important for the text to be familiar: it allowed a wide public to appreciate his stylistic strategies. Reviews in the paper printed bits of the dialogue, asking 'what do you think of character x speaking as if he came from Sartène?'. The point is that the meaning of the author's use of Corsican dialects was sharpened and focused by its relationship with the French work; a similar strategy in an original Corsican work might not have had the same resonances.

Furthermore, as another translator, Jean-Marie Arrighi, pointed out to me, translation provided a unique opportunity to experience that *jouissance* without risk for Corsican. This was because translation provided the writer with an outside language of norms which could be violated, thus sparing the fragile oral code from a form of play it might not withstand. That is, there were norms in Corsican, but they were uncodified norms of usage; in Arrighi's words, 'one does not feel free to break with those norms which it is still a question of trying to save'.

In the arguments so far for and against translation, we can see that translation does not just reflect static relations of social power; it is a forum in which linguistic and social authority is discursively constituted. And, as Balibar writes (joining to some extent the translators' position), 'it is in translations that the weaker partner appropriates the language of the stronger' (1987:19). This point is illustrated in Rafael's (1988:xi) elegant analysis of the meaning of translation for Tagalogs and Christian missionaries. Seen from a Tagalog perspective, translation of Spanish texts and discourse was a way of domesticating the forces of Spain and Christianity, it was 'a process of demarcation and appropriation' which subverted the notion of linguistic consensus.[4] Similarly, Crowley (1996:118) notes that for Irish Protestants, the translation of the Bible into Irish was a way of taking popular control of the word of God; it was a form of liberation from English social control.

We can readily draw the analogy with the Corsican case, where translators saw themselves as appropriating linguistic space and the critics of translations took the latter perspective, substituting the authority of French for God's will. In the Corsican case, we can also note the tension (in the translators' discourse) between adherence to an essentialist model of language which emphasizes the naturalness of linguistic and cultural boundaries and the expression of a sense of personal pleasure and identity in which Corsican and French are not separated but integrated.

Another important theme in Corsican translators' defence of their craft was that producing or reading translations involved an intense and simultaneous experience of both the universal and the particular in a way that emphasized cultural interactions rather than cultural boundaries. Several translators emphasized that the positive experience of the particular was generated by a *dialogue* with another culture in the act of translation. For example, in the literary forum mentioned above, Geronimi declared: 'I translated *Waiting for Godot* because I am not Becket. I wanted to write it as if Becket were Corsican, as if he had never known another language than Corsican'. Franchi justified his translations in similar terms: 'so that the [Corsican] language has the chance to know, to experience the works in question' (1989b:59). Santu Casta, who translated *The Little Prince*, said in an interview in *Kyrn*, 'All cultures are inter-twined. It always does good to go and see and try to understand the ways others see life, the world' (1990:35). Often, translators selected their source texts because of their relevance to Corsican society. Biancarelli, for example, chose to translate *Waiting for Godot* for its theme of the absurd, for the confrontation between tradition and modernity and the conflict and confusion of identity that he felt characterized Corsican society. A similar theme (as well as the book's familiarity) had motivated Franchi's choice of *Knock*. On another occasion, Biancarelli had translated Gabriel de Lorca in order to explore cultural rather than thematic resonances.

Very explicitly, the translators rejected the exclusionary logic of minority self defence – the wholesale rejection of all that is 'foreign', especially if it comes from the dominant culture. They insisted on the 'link with the outside' (Geronimi), 'the impossibility of living in autarchy', and the necessity of 'rubbing up against other writers and cultures' (Biancarelli). In the introduction of his translation of some short pieces by Woody Allen and John Steinbeck (from the French) for the radio, Petru Mari (1986:1) wrote to an imaginary skeptical audience:

> Yes, of course our literature is able to produce the same pearls as any other
> . . . what do you say? That we don't need anyone? Yes, but if we want to
> do without them, they will certainly do without us . . . what do you think
> of that?

All of the translators insisted that this relationship with the other was not a dependent one.

Walking the line between alienation and empowerment

Crowley (1996:51) writes that

> The monoglossic language, at once familiar and foreign, necessary but felt
> to be alien . . . presents the colonial subject with a problem: how to engage
> in that language without, in using the oppressor's language, reinforcing
> one's own dispossession.

This dilemma is a fundamental one which is not perfectly resolved for those who
defend the practice of translation. One response to this dilemma is to emphasize non-
equivalence in the form of the text. James Joyce, Crowley adds, did so by using the
dominant language in such a novel way as to make it new and make it his. What we
find in the Corsican context is a move by several Corsican authors to avoid labelling
what they did as 'translation'. Petru Mari (cited above), Jacques Fusina (who had
translated an opera and several song lyrics), and Santu Casta (who had translated *The
Little Prince*) all insisted that they only 'adapted' or 'interpreted'. While it was not
necessarily the case that 'adaptations' were more different from the original texts than
'translations', using the term 'adaptation' stressed the significance and the authenticity of the final text in Corsican terms, rather than its fidelity to the original. Mari
made it clear that for him, the question was less what translators could do for the
original than what the original could do for them. The foreign voices in the text
might be 'imported' (as one of the attacks on translations had claimed), but they
were firmly in the representational control of their importers. Mari commented that
he had not invested a great deal of time in the mechanics of translation: 'I did it
quickly', he told me, 'with an ear for how these pieces would work on the radio for a
Corsican audience'.

The preface to Grimaldi's (1989) bilingual collection of stories (*U stringagliulu di
sigolu*) is a strong expression of non-equivalent adaptation philosophy. Although this
is not a completely parallel example (the author wrote the original in Corsican and
had someone else do a French version), the description of that version is illustrative
here:

> [it] is neither a direct translation, nor even an adaptation . . . the French
> text is born out of the Corsican one, without being dependent on it; there
> is no hierarchy in this musical piece, where the two versions are like point
> and counterpoint. (Fusina 1989a:5)

Here, we can note that the rhetorical force of the emphasis on equality and independence in 'adaptations' depends on the contrast with 'translations', and thus reinforces
the association of translation with linguistic hierarchy.

Some of the authors mentioned so far – Franchi, Fusina, Biancarelli, Geronimi –
had superlative command both of written French and written Corsican. They belonged
to the very top echelon of the Corsican bilingual intelligentsia. Their exceptional
linguistic facility was a vital ingredient in the experiences of personal linguistic
empowerment which served as the basis for their judgements about the sociolinguistic meaning of translations.

The experience and the meaning of translation were rather more ambiguous for
those who could not alternate between the two written codes with the same agility.
Perhaps the most reflective and self-conscious of these was Jean-Marie Arrighi. He
had translated some official reports of the Regional Assembly's Cultural Council, of
which he was a member. He did this because he was committed to the principle
of using translations as a way of legitimizing Corsican in the political domain. His
experience of translating, however, was ambiguous. To be sure, the process highlighted

the difference between the two languages. But it also underscored his very different levels of mastery and experience of Corsican versus French. As he tried to translate, he realized that his abstract thoughts were in French; he could only voice them in Corsican with great and painful effort. Translation made him struggle with his French intellectual heritage; although he rejected its powerful, authoritative and authoritarian linguistic ideology, his entire academic identity and practical consciousness was a function of his experience in this system. For Arrighi, creating an abstract, intellectual document in Corsican was a difficult exercise in which he inevitably reworked French models of expository prose in his head. If Arrighi used his experience of translation as a metaphor for its political significance (as the previous translators did), it was the dominance of French and the weakness of Corsican in public, literary domains that prevailed.

Another question raised for Arrighi by his experience of translation had to do with the nature of the linguistic and cultural divide between Corsican and French. From a political perspective, using Corsican in official domains (and thus, creating new registers in the minority language) was a step forward in a process of linguistic development and legitimation. But from another more emotional and experiential vantage point, this 'new' Corsican had no cultural resonances. As he translated, Arrighi sometimes had the impression that he was forcing Corsican into a mould which had no intrinsic value in the Corsican universe. Was a bureaucratic Corsican a 'deformation' of Corsican? Was it recognizable as Corsican to the average reader? In these questions we can see a reflection of the workings of the diglossic model: the compartmentalization of domains of practice and experience is translated into judgements about linguistic essence. That is, the things that Corsican and French are habitually used to do are read in the popular imagination as part of their inherent capacities.

Arrighi translated the documents because of his conviction that occupying public space with Corsican was important. But his own experience told him that he could not completely control or predict the effect of these symbolic translations on popular attitudes. On the one hand, it was possible that texts such as the ones he produced could be the catalyst for new understandings and acceptance of different registers of Corsican. That is, they might chip away at the logic of diglossia, with its polarized and essentialized identities. On the other hand, the texts might be dismissed out of hand as irrelevant and/or 'not Corsican'. At the time that Arrighi wrote, it was very difficult to gauge the results of any piece of writing in Corsican, since the reading and writing public was so very small.

One of Arrighi's responses to the dilemma posed by the imbalance in his mastery of written Corsican and French was to write the Corsican version first. He did this to insure a radical difference between the two texts; in particular, to prevent himself from producing a text with Corsican words and French linguistic and conceptual structures. Writing the Corsican text first forced him to ask himself, 'how would one think this in Corsican?' and finding an authentic Corsican voice to express those thoughts. This voice was partly his, partly his ancestors'; Arrighi himself had not thought these abstractions in Corsican before. Ultimately, he said that his experience of writing these documents was linguistically integrative. He noted that expressing the abstract in a language he had only known as concrete was a way of rediscovering the inherent metaphorical nature of all signs for abstractions, rediscovering the 'pensée sauvage' in the language of reason and owning them both, in their simultaneous sameness and difference.

But Arrighi did acknowledge that for the inexpert translator, it was indeed the source document and language that dominated. This, I believe, is the nature of most bilingual Corsicans' experiences of translation in their everyday lives. When older speakers of Corsican heard people make errors in French or in Corsican, they often attributed them to failures in translation. These failures of translation were interpreted within the framework of their experience of French language domination and the stigma attached to speaking Corsican. Thus 'not being able to find the right words' in Corsican was a form of linguistic alienation that also symbolically highlighted the power of French to erode minority language competence. But the converse, 'not being able to find the right words' in French, was seldom seen as proof of the uniqueness and authority of Corsican; it was experienced as a failure to command French that was personally embarrassing and disempowering.[5]

The potential for translation to highlight linguistic alienation is illustrated quite dramatically in a class of 'surrogate' translations. One author and illustrator of children's books, Francette Orsoni, does not write in Corsican, but said that she 'felt in it'; her stories emanated from childhood images of the village and the world of the fantastic, both of which she associated with Corsican. She created a rudimentary text in Corsican, gave it to a 'specialist' friend and collaborated with him over the Corsican turns of phrase, which came 'naturally' to him. Even though they did not 'come naturally' to her, she represented them as her latent Corsican voice: she knew when the Corsican text was 'right'.

Another writer (Mattei 1971) had a book of poems he wrote in French translated by a friend in much the same fashion and for the same reason, although his edition was bilingual, with Corsican and French versions printed on facing pages. Mattei, however, made no claims for his own Corsican competence. In a poem thanking his translator, he wrote:

Je remercie Nicole	I thank Nicole
Qui sait avec adresse	Who has the skill
Et avec délicatesse	And delicacy
Utiliser ses connaissances	To use her knowledge
N'importe qui	Not anyone
Ne peut traduire de la poésie	Can translate poetry
Je dis que la langue maternelle	I say, the mother tongue
Est à celle adoptée	Is to the one I use
Qu'une flamme moderne	Like a modern light
Est au feu de cheminée	Is to the fireplace's fire
Elle est froide et fade	It is cold and pale
Et sort de moi toujours	And always comes out of me
toujours forcée	Forced
De toutes ses articulations	In all its articulations
Cette langue sans chaleur	This language without warmth
Me fait peu envie	Hardly attracts me
Comme un fruit hybride	Like a hybrid fruit
Issu des pires conjonctures	Born of the worst circumstances
On m'a toujours reproché	I have always been reproached
Le français de mon écriture	For writing in French

Both Orsoni's and Mattei's works are a curious blend of alienation and intense connection with the language and its cultural resonances. The alienation is particularly striking in Mattei's poem, where he characterizes the language that he commands in writing (French) as 'forced', 'cold' and culturally inauthenticating. There is also Mattei's use of the metaphor of the 'hybrid fruit' to describe his own mixed identity. Far from exploiting the association of horticultural hybrids as a positive source of genetic resilience, Mattei represents hybridization as a disastrous genetic aberration. This metaphor shows the strength of the monocultural-monolingual norm, with its images of linguistic and cultural purity: hybridization equals bastardization. These two authors' very desires for surrogate translation invoke an ideology in which the value of the final product is called into doubt: is not the 'translated' text a hybrid one?

Surrogate translators were also sometimes used in the nationalist press, and the end results were no less ambiguous than the texts described above. An editor of an autonomist newspaper told me that he felt a political obligation to print serious articles in Corsican. But he and most of the members of his staff did not feel they were competent to write such Corsican texts. The editor tended to draw on a pool of specialists, sending them a French text to turn into a Corsican piece. These same people were called upon to produce Corsican pamphlets and programme announce-ments for political events. The meaning of these translations can be interpreted in a number of different ways. On one hand, the fact of translation was very thinly disguised. The common knowledge that there was a handful of language specialists producing in Corsican emphasized the marginality of writing in Corsican even amongst people who were politically committed to Corsican language and culture. In this sense, these translations drew attention to the lack of fit between political will and linguistic practice, as well as to the power imbalances between French and Corsican that were the causes of the belated development of Corsican literacy. On the other hand, the translation created Corsican linguistic space whose meaning was not entirely bound to the context of its production.

Representation and representativity: politics versus creative licence

As we have seen, translators' discussions of the meanings of translation often revolved around their personal experience of translating. In many cases, translation was experienced as a rich arena of creative practice, a source of self-discovery and height-ened metaphorical awareness. The nature of the criticisms of translation show, however, that cultural production in Corsica is often cast and always interpreted as political. Writing in Corsican entails social responsibility to represent and promote Corsican culture and language; personal, creative, artistic fidelity takes a distant sec-ond place.[6] For a Corsican writer, all creative choices in the process of writing – the use of French versus Corsican, genre, register, topic, spelling – are also political and ideological positions about the nature of Corsicanness.

The political facet of minority expressive culture often coincides with Corsican writers' and artists' personal and political agendas; an overwhelming percentage of Corsican expression is both politically-oriented and focused on Corsicanness. To take a popular example, there is the following commentary from a record jacket of the group A Filetta, whose very name (the fern) is 'a symbol of tenacity and rootedness':

> the themes taken up are meant to be representative of the joys, the sor-rows, the suffering and also the hopes of our people. In them, we denounce repression, the abandonment of the terrain, the loss of our language . . .

The moment writers or singers strayed from this path, however, they risked being seen as traitors by other cultural militants. On a personal level, this pressure was fatiguing and frustrating, and ran counter to individual expectations of artistic liberty and the pleasures of self-expression. This was brought home to me one day in a conversation with Fusina, one of the key figures from the 'seventies generation' of linguistic militants. As we parted, he said that frankly, he was 'just tired'; tired of having to represent something, tired of being a symbol. He just wanted to write, for himself. We can find echoes of this sentiment in comments made by Geronimi (the translator of Becket) and Thiers (the author of numerous works in Corsican and French). Challenged to explain why he had translated from French in the literary meeting alluded to above, Geronomi enumerated all the social justifications for translation. Repeated questioning from the audience then drew a slightly defensive response: 'I did it for me, for my pleasure', he said, looking around the room in a way that dared anyone to challenge his right to textual *jouissance* and self-representation. Similarly, in the newspaper interview cited above, Thiers' response to the journalist's query about why he wrote a book in Corsican was:

> Pleasure! pleasure! When we speak about Corsican . . . we speak about its ruined state, its protection, and of sacrifice. Certainly, there is little to rejoice in, but should we refuse our enjoyment and never speak about the satisfaction and liberation we get from expressing ourselves in Corsican? (Cerani 1991)

In addition to being an assertion of individual rights, the translators' claim that they translated for their own pleasure had a political and ideological foundation. In fact, I would argue that it was through staking a claim to artistic freedom that Corsican translators proposed their most radical reworking of concepts of linguistic power.

Specifically, the translators appeared to be aware that the social ideology of art reflects relations of power; that the relentless insistence on cultural representativity and fidelity to the exclusion of any other form of expression was in itself evidence of a 'colonized' mentality. Translating was a way of demonstrating a new confidence in Corsican language and identity by acting *as* if it were a language of power. Powerful languages are threatened neither by other languages nor by individual activity. Waiting, as the one critic recommended, for Corsica to produce a body of literature that could stand up to French was a denial of the value of both Corsican linguistic history – an oral tradition – and of present-day literary activity, with the normal range of talent and genres it represented.

It is in this sense that the personal experience of power in translation from French into Corsican had a unique political weight. It has to be remembered that most of these writers had not come by their mastery of two languages painlessly. For those who learned French for the first time in school, the first translations they experienced were violations of categories of identity and knowledge embedded in their knowledge of their mother tongue. The shock caused by these translation experiences is well documented, as it occurs in most immigrant contexts. Thus, as Eva Hoffman writes (1989:106), these were translations in which

> the signifier [is] severed from the signified . . . 'river' in Polish was a vital sound, energized with the essence of riverhood, of my rivers, of my being immersed in rivers. 'River' in English is cold – a word without an aura.

Even personal names, the most intimate link of language and self, are strangely altered in this first translation of cultures in school. Richard Rodriguez (1982:11) remembers his first day in an American school, his first extended contact with English:

> The nun said in a friendly but oddly impersonal voice, Boys and Girls, this is Richard Rodriguez. (I heard her sound out: *Rich-heard Road-ree-guess*). It was the first time I had heard anyone name me in English . . .

And Eva Hoffman (1989:105) recounts the day she and her sister are given English versions of their Polish names:

> My sister and I hang our heads wordlessly under this careless baptism . . . the twist of our name takes them a tiny distance from us – but it's a gap into which the infinite hobgoblin of abstraction enters. Our Polish names didn't refer to us, they were us as surely as our eyes and hands. These new appellations . . . are not us. They are . . . disembodied signs pointing to objects that just happen to be my sister and myself.

This symbolic violation, for Hoffman, for Rodriguez and, I suspect, for Corsican writers, heralded their entry into a world they had to obsessively translate – a world of words that they had to possess, precisely *because* they had been cut off from the resonances of those words as children. It was a quest, as Rodriguez says, for a sense of identity and individuality in the public language, a desire to belong in order to escape undifferentiated otherness. For Hoffman, liberation from the need, and then the desire to translate, signalled the end of her personal sense of alienation. For Rodriguez, this liberation took the form of being able to use the public language to address an anonymous reader, to write about intimate subjects – in short, to dissolve his diglossic experience of Spanish and English. In a sense, Corsican writers can be seen as taking up translation from French as a way of asserting this sort of liberation. Rather than working within dominant structures of value by reversing the habitual identities of source and target language, they took hold of the power to define the meanings of linguistic acts, and declared their translation into Corsican a demonstration of their freedom from the *requirement* to translate (possess) French and a manifestation of their desire to possess Corsican. That is, they defined power as the prerogative not to censor those acts that could be interpreted as powerless.

Conclusion: the perils of asserting virtual power in written genres

What is the difference between asserting this sort of power through literacy and literature and asserting it in oral practice? By way of answering this question, let me contrast Petru Mari's translation of Steinbeck's and Woody Allen's plays for radio with some of the other kinds of documents we have considered.

First of all, Mari's published text was a by-product of a translation that had been intended for purely oral consumption. Mari told me that he had only published the translation at the urging of one of his academic friends. In the original broadcast, the textual and foreign origins were clearly subordinated to the entertainment value of the spoken piece. Moreover, since the original texts were in English, they were not accessible to most Corsicans in the original. They were not, therefore as purely symbolic – and hence, as political – as Franchi's translation of Knock. They required no prior knowledge of the originals; their meaning and value was not dependent on a bilingual consciousness or a literary background. They were accessible, therefore, to a majority of radio listeners. The political was also de-emphasized by the programming patterns at the radio station. Broadcasts alternated between French and Corsican throughout the day, in all varieties of programming. This meant that the choice of language in any one broadcast did not carry particular ideological weight. Because of this language policy, listeners could enjoy the programming throughout the day without having to have perfect competence in Corsican. And the fact was, there were many Corsicans who could enjoy a radio programme in Corsican who were not capable of or interested in reading a Corsican text. The radio, in other words, played to the sociolinguistic reality of the island.

In contrast, the literary translations were premised on the existence of a fairly sophisticated, or at least, a strongly motivated audience. The sophisticated reader, like the translator, would experience the translated text as the expression of universal themes as well as a celebration of Corsican linguistic and cultural particularities. Since the meaning of the translated text would be located in both French and Corsican worlds, as well as in the dynamic space of movement between them, the sophisticated reader would be able to savour, alternately, a divided and an integrated cultural and linguistic heritage. The experience of reading would constitute a new experience of linguistic hierarchy, for the relations between French and Corsican would either be levelled or reversed.

The problem was that there were so very few of these sophisticated readers to write for. The translations in question were thus written for a virtual audience. This meant that these translations were simultaneously writing *as if* Corsican were a language of power (that had nothing to lose from translation) and *as if* Corsican were a language of widespread, everyday literacy in Corsican society.

The latter fiction, it seems to me, is what made the social and symbolic status of translation on Corsica so volatile, so precarious. Part of this has to do with the way that the emphasis on the written rather than the oral risks what Bourdieu and Boltanski (1975) call 'the fetishism of language'. As Bonn (1985:193) puts it, one of the fundamental paradoxes of writing in a minority language is that:

> a project which makes out to be looking for a place in which to express being as identity ends up looking for this place in the quest itself: in writing. . . . a 'place' which is impossible to seize and hold . . . identity becomes confused with the desire for identity . . . is the existence of discourse of place whose function is to refer to itself possible?

We can easily recognize the way that French-Corsican translations magnify the self-referential quality of minority literature. Bonn suggests that such a discourse can never truly be about *place* – shared, embodied, situated experiences of identity. Writing about cultural 'places' can be complex, ambiguous, unresolved; the boundaries and borders can be fuzzy and loose. Expert translators found such a place in the dynamic of translation, but for most Corsicans, the location of translation was a detached and abstract domain.

Here it bears reiterating that it was the experience and the intellectual consciousness of diglossia that made literacy and literature so important in Corsican militant circles. Diglossia was a result of symbolic and practical dominance; writing was therefore inevitably interpreted from within this framework.

In the translation debate, we can see some of the consequences of this implicit framework of experience and interpretation. First, there is the powerful hold of 'essential' linguistic and cultural identities; as we have seen, concepts of linguistic 'essence' and boundaries permeate the arguments of both translators and their critics. Embedded in this linguistic and cultural essentialism is a logic of oppositional identity. At least at some level, translators like Franchi were attempting to transcend this logic. But they did so on terrain that was almost exclusively defined in terms of that logic: writing was defined as a place for displacing French control.

Here, the self-referential quality of purely symbolic translations was a handicap, since it drew attention to power relations of literary production and consumption. As we have seen in the examples of (mild to extreme) linguistic and cultural alienation, translation from the dominant language automatically invokes the experience of linguistic hierarchy. Arrighi's example also illustrates that when writing is detached from vital social practices and exists purely as a symbol, it is the macropolitics of diglossic relations that often prevails. Because of the depth and intensity of Corsicans' shared experiences of powerlessness, subtle representational strategies of expert translators are swept aside by simple, oppositional meanings. In recognition of this, we find Arrighi turning to translation tactics (doing the Corsican version first) that ensure radical difference.

The translation debate underscores an old idea: how critical it is for ideological and political control to be instantiated in everyday practices. As Corsican activists certainly know, French language dominance has been embedded in multiple ways in Corsican social life. This has been difficult for Corsican language activists to replicate for Corsican, for unlike the French state, they have had no access to economic, institutional or political coercion to further the cause of the minority language. Translators tried to locate power in the prerogative to deny and transcend linguistic hierarchy, but did not have a strong enough base of consumers to instill this new vision of power in lived experience. The mere presence of French in the ghost of the original overshadowed the political implications of the translators' craft, and as a result, the non-apologetic, non-dependent aspects of literary translation were only perceived by a very few. In the absence of a healthy spoken language and a sophisticated reading public which is literate in two languages, translation in Corsica was left with contested, virtual value – a pale 'as if' in the face of a problematic reality.

Notes

1   See for example Khleif (1980) on Welsh, Woolard (1989) and DiGiacomo (1999) on Catalan, Boyer (1991) and Garavini (1988) on Occitan, McDonald (1989) on Breton, Urla (1988) on Basque.

2   Klor de Alva also observes that the politics of translation 'are more likely to be configured by the unspoken and usually unperceived assumptions making up the reigning ideas and exegetical rules that guide the translator' (1989:143).

3   Here and elsewhere in the paper, translations from French and Corsican are my own.

4   Although, from the point of view of Spanish missionaries, translation was an act of linguistic appropriation and an exercise of power for different reasons. They saw translation as the illustration of the 'natural' relationship of the world and God's will: 'the promise of a fully transparent language ruling over linguistic diversity' (Rafael 1988:7).

5   Gobard views the inability to translate as one of the foundations of diglossia and linguistic alienation. He writes: 'To know two languages apart from one another, without being able to translate one into the other, is precisely the diglossic situation that risks to end

in the different specialization of each of the languages' (1976:179). See also Bourdieu (1982:64).

6   This is revealed in the nature of three out of six questions asked of Santu Casta, the translator of *The Little Prince*, in a magazine interview: (1) *Traduttore, traditore?* ('translator, traitor?'), (2) Why translate from a language everyone understands to one that only few do?, (3) How does the text you chose relate to Corsican culture? (Anonymous 1990).

PART 7

Translation in world systems

Chapter 16

Pascale Casanova

CONSECRATION[1] AND ACCUMULATION OF LITERARY CAPITAL: TRANSLATION AS UNEQUAL EXCHANGE[2]

Translated by Siobhan Brownlie

EDITOR'S INTRODUCTION

> . . . far from being the horizontal exchange and peaceful transfer often described, translation must be understood, on the contrary, as an 'unequal exchange' that takes place in a strongly hierarchized universe. Translation can therefore be described as one of the specific forms that the relationship of domination assumes in the international literary field. It is an important factor in the struggles for legitimacy which occur in this universe, and one of the principal means of consecration of authors and texts.

THE TWO PAPERS IN THIS SECTION, by Casanova and Heilbron, attempt to place translation within the universe of international exchanges and to study it as a factor in the struggle for legitimacy in the literary and political fields. They are specifically concerned with the role translation plays in consecrating authors and texts, and hence in the distribution and transfer of cultural capital.

Casanova's model (see also Casanova 1999/2004, 2005) draws heavily on Bourdieu's concept of *capital* as accumulated prestige (whether economic, social or cultural). She assumes that literary capital is relatively independent of linguistic capital; literature, she maintains, operates in 'another world, whose divisions and frontiers are relatively independent of political and linguistic borders' (Casanova 2005:72). Casanova nevertheless stresses the theme of inequality and power struggle, and rather than talk about centre and periphery (as Heilbron does, this volume), she prefers to distinguish between dominating and dominated languages in the literary sphere. Dominating languages have considerable literary capital, partly because of the number of texts considered universal which are written in these languages. Dominated languages have little literary capital and fall into four distinct sub-groups. The first covers languages that lack an established writing system, and which therefore cannot benefit from translation in the world literary market. The second includes languages with a short history of use, for example those recently created or recreated following political independence. These languages rely heavily on translation to establish a literary corpus (cf. Jaffa, this volume) and to enter the world literary market. The third group consists of established languages that are used in 'small' countries and have relatively few speakers (for example, Dutch). And the fourth consists of languages with large numbers of speakers and great literary traditions that are not valued in the international literary markets (Arabic, Chinese).

Casanova identifies four scenarios and argues that the significance of translation in any of these scenarios depends on the respective position of the source and target languages, the author, and the translator: (a) translation into a dominated language of a text written in a dominating language; (b) a text in a dominated language is translated into a dominating language; (c) translation into a dominating language of a text written in a dominating language; (d) translation into a dominated language of a text written in a dominated language (a rare occurrence). She is particularly interested in the first two scenarios, which she analyzes under the two headings: 'Translation as accumulation of capital' and 'Translation as consecration'. Translation as accumulation of capital occurs when writers from a dominated literary field attempt to enter the world literary market by 'nationalizing' (i.e. translating) the great literary masterpieces which are considered to have universal value, for example, Shakespeare or Racine. This allows them to import capital and prestige, and Casanova thus describes the process of translating the major texts of a dominating language into a dominated language as a 'diversion of capital'. Translation as consecration involves 'introducing the periphery to the center in order to consecrate it' (Casanova 1999:133) and is dependent on the capital of the translator and other agents involved in the process. The translation of dominated authors is 'an act of consecration that gives them access to literary visibility and existence' (*ibid.*:135) – that grants them a certificate of literary standing. In initiating the opposite process, i.e. in making the centre – and what has been consecrated in the centre – known in the periphery by translating and importing its major works, translators/authors and/ or other agents play 'an essential role in the process of unifying literary space' (*ibid.*:134). They also perpetuate the dominance of the centre through this process.

Follow-up questions for discussion

- Casanova's idea of a 'world republic of letters' that is relatively independent of the political sphere challenges postcolonial studies that proceed from the opposite direction: 'Postcolonialism posits a direct link between literature and history, one that is exclusively political ... [and hence] runs the risk of reducing the literary to the political, ... often passing in silence over the actual aesthetic, formal or stylistic characteristics that actually "make" literature' (Casanova 2005:71). How would you assess her analysis of this link (in postcolonialism and in her own work)? Can the two positions be reconciled?

- Beecroft (2008:54) argues against models such as Casanova's, which assume 'national literatures' as the unit of analysis. Such models, Beecroft maintains, are 'now clearly inadequate, both because a number of languages and their literatures transcend national borders, and because the de-centring of the nation-state brought about by contemporary global capitalism alters literary circulation'. To what extent do you agree with Beecroft's critique, and how might Casanova respond to it?

- One of the themes Casanova touches on in passing is the interdependence of translators and other agents of mediation: 'translators are not discoverers or consecrators operating alone; they are part of a complex chain of mediators which includes bilingual readers, travellers, specialists, publishers, critics, literary agents, etc.'. Consider the implications of this interdependence, both in the literary and non-literary fields. Does a similar interdependence characterize the work of interpreters, at least in some contexts?

Recommended further reading

Beecroft, Alexander (2008) 'World Literature Without a Hyphen: Towards a Typology of Literary Systems', *New Left Review* 54 (Nov–Dec): 87–100.

Casanova, Pascale (1999/2004) *La République mondiale des lettres*, Paris: Éditions du Seuil; trans. M. B. Debevoise as *The World Republic of Letters*, Cambridge, MA: Harvard University Press.

Casanova, Pascale (2005) 'Literature as a World', *New Left Review* 31 (Jan–Feb): 71–90.

Moretti, Franco (2000) 'Conjectures on World Literature', *New Left Review* 1 (Jan–Feb): 54–68.

Moretti, Franco (2003) 'More Conjectures', *New Left Review* 20 (Mar–Apr): 73–81.

> . . . [the translator] deals with the elements of both languages as if they were mathematical symbols that can be reduced to the same value by increasing or decreasing them.
>
> On the Different Methods of Translating, Friedrich Schleiermacher

MY CONCERN IN THIS PAPER IS WITH THE SPECIFIC problems posed by literary translation (see Holmes *et al.* 1978, Meschonnic 1973, 1999, Ladmiral 1979). Literary translation is normally defined as the movement of a text from one language into another in an equal linguistic exchange. This operation is supposed to be neutral and symmetrical; it is conceived as a linear and 'horizontal' transfer. Comparative literary studies in its most traditional form presupposes closed national fields which are synchronous, of equal power and with no real relation apart from the visible interaction of the exchange of translations. In exactly the same way, literary translation, (pre)conceived as a 'simple' operation of transfer, presupposes the existence of national languages which are equal and juxtaposed. This monadic representation of national languages, which can be deduced in part from the incorporation of intra-national divisions, leads to a vision of translation as a simple matter of conveying texts from one national literary field to another. This is why studies of translation usually concentrate on one kind of relation, the transfer of a text in one language into a text in another. Distortions of the source text resulting from translation are examined, or else the gap between the source text and the target culture is analyzed. What is studied is two more or less superposable realities, two texts or two contexts which do not have a real relationship with each other.

If we depart from the national point of view, inverting the normal vision and placing the practice of translation in the universe of international literary exchanges, that is, in the world literary field, we can formulate the hypothesis that translation as normally defined is a preconstructed object, a sort of screen-notion which prevents appreciation of the real stakes of the international circulation of literary texts. Instead of envisaging translation within linguistic and national boundaries alone and as the singular transformation of a single text, I propose here to analyze it from the vantage point of the international 'observatory', to use Fernand Braudel's term (1979:9). The transnational point of view re-establishes relations, hierarchies and power struggles between national fields, and thus inverts the presupposition of equivalent national and linguistic entities and the representation of the literary world as the juxtaposition of self-sufficient universes which are closed and irreducible one to the other, with separate and autarkic languages of equal power. The literary and linguistic inequalities and hierarchies which organize the world literary field reveal another economy of linguistic exchange: far from being the horizontal exchange and peaceful transfer often described, translation must be understood, on the contrary, as an 'unequal exchange' that takes place in a strongly hierarchized universe. Translation can therefore be described as one of the specific forms that the relationship of domination assumes in the international literary field. It is an important factor in the struggles for legitimacy which occur in this universe, and one of the principal means of consecration of authors and texts. Adopting this point of view could also make it possible to go beyond conceiving a translation as a singular relation between a text and its transcription, by reinscribing each translated text in the world network of relations of literary domination, of which translation is one of the forms.

Structure of the world literary field

Before undertaking an analysis of translation in this light, it is necessary to outline, if only briefly, the structure of the international literary field, which enables us to understand the dual national and linguistic hierarchy in which all the operations of translation are inscribed.

Since the Herderian national revolution, the world literary field, formed by the combination of almost all the national literary fields, has been structured in a durable manner, according to both the volume and age of literary capital and according to the correlative degree of relative autonomy of each national literary field. The international literary field is organized according to the opposition between, on the one hand, at the autonomous pole, the literary fields which are the most endowed with capital, and on the other hand, the most deprived national fields or emergent fields which are usually dependent on national political authorities. There is a structural homology between each national field and the international literary field: the national fields are also structured according to the opposition between an autonomous cosmopolitan pole and a heteronomous national and political pole. The opposition is seen in the rivalry between 'international' and 'national' writers. The position of each national field in the world structure depends on its proximity to one of the two poles, that is, on its volume of capital. The world literary universe can therefore be represented as an entity formed of the entire group of national literary fields, which are themselves bipolarized and situated differentially (and hierarchically) in the world structure according to the relative weight which the international pole and the national (and nationalistic) pole hold in each field.

The unequal distribution of literary capital in the literary universe is matched by an unequal distribution of linguistic-literary capital. Political science has demonstrated the political and social inequality of languages: Abram de Swaan (1993, 2001), for example, has described a linguistic-political capital attached to languages. The unequal distribution of this capital explains why languages are more or less used in a particular market (scholarly, professional, familial, national, international, etc.). According to Swaan, it is possible to understand linguistic hierarchies by proposing what he calls 'floral figurations'.

For my part, I have tried to show that it is not only this strictly linguistic capital that is attached to each language, but there is also a literary capital, or linguistic-literary capital, which is relatively independent of linguistic capital (Casanova 1999). This capital depends on prestige, on the literary beliefs attached to a language, and on the literary value which is attributed to it. These factors in turn depend on the age of a language, the prestige of its poetry, the refinement of literary forms developed in it, traditions, the literary 'effects' associated, for example, with translations, and their volume, etc. This is what is evoked when we speak of 'the language of Shakespeare', 'the language of Racine', or 'the language of Cervantes'.

In order to measure the actual volume of this capital, I propose to use criteria from political sociology in the study of the literary universe, but I shall replace the binary 'centre/periphery' – which has only spatial or hierarchical implications – by the 'dominating/dominated' opposition, which implies a structure of domination and power struggles. Central languages will not be contrasted with peripheral languages; rather, dominating languages will be contrasted with dominated languages, which is far from being a simple semantic change, since it transforms the perspective of the analysis and the type of theoretical tools employed.

Abram de Swaan sees what he calls the 'emerging world linguistic system' as a system structured by multilingualism: the centrality of a language in the system can be measured by the number of multilingual speakers who speak the language in question. In other words, even in the political-economic universe the number of speakers of a language is not sufficient to establish its centrality. In a system described as a 'floral figuration', that is, a structure where the dominated languages are linked to the centre by polyglots, the more multilingual people speak a language, the more this language dominates the universe (de Swann 1993). In the same way, in the international literary field, if this same configuration is adopted, the volume of linguistic-literary capital of a language can be measured, not by the number of writers or readers of the language, but by the number of literary polyglots who use it, and by the number of literary translators who are instrumental in the circulation of texts from or towards the literary language.[3]

The unequal distribution of this capital organizes the linguistic-literary field according to the opposition[4] between dominated literary languages and dominating literary languages. Dominated languages have been recently nationalized (that is, have become national languages relatively recently), are relatively deprived of literary capital, have little international recognition, a small number of national or international translators,[5] or are little known and have remained invisible for a long time in the great literary centres. Dominating languages are endowed with a relatively large volume of literary capital due to their specific prestige, their age, and the number of texts which are considered universal and which are written in these languages.

Dominated languages do not constitute a homogenous group. They can be divided into four distinct sub-groups. First there are oral languages, or languages whose writing system has only recently been established. These are by definition deprived of literary capital because they lack a writing system;[6] they are unknown in the international field and cannot benefit from translation. Included here are certain African languages (Yarouba, Gikuyu, Amharic, etc.) and some Creoles.[7] Then there are languages which have been created or 'recreated' recently, and which have become national languages following political independence (Catalan, Korean, Gaelic,

Hebrew, Neo-Norwegian). There are few speakers of these languages, few texts are written in them, they are used by few polyglots, and have no or few traditions of exchanges with other countries. They can gradually acquire an international presence by promoting translation. The languages of ancient cultures and traditions used in 'small' countries, such as Dutch, Danish, Greek, and Persian, constitute the third category of dominated languages. They have quite an important history and prestige, but few speakers; they are used by few polyglots, and are little recognized outside national borders, that is, they are accorded little value in the world literary market. Some languages of broad diffusion, finally – such as Arabic, Chinese and Hindi – are also dominated in the literary sphere, because although they have great literary traditions and a large number of speakers, they are little known or recognized in the international literary market. This structural inequality, which means that translation must be defined as a power struggle, also prevents assigning translation a single significance. Its significance depends on the respective position of the three poles which found it: language, or more specifically the source language and the target language; the author of the source text; and the translator. In order to understand the real stakes (which are often denied) of the translation of a text, it is necessary to describe first the position which the source language and the target language occupy in the universe of literary languages. Then the translated author must be located in the world literary field in two ways: firstly, according to the place the author occupies in his or her national literary field, and secondly, according to the place this field occupies in the international literary field. Last to be analyzed are the position of the translator and of various consecrating agents who participate in the process of consecrating the work. According to the respective positions at the three levels and their objective 'distance' in the literary field, it will be shown that the stakes of translation vary and that this single word encompasses in fact a series of 'function-operations' which are quite distinct from each other. There is, for example, 'translation-accumulation' when, through a collective strategy, the dominated national literary fields attempt to import literary capital; or 'translation-consecration' when the dominating consecrators import a text from a dominated literary field.

The position of languages and authors

In order to describe the various possible positions of languages in the linguistic-literary domain, the following can be distinguished: the translation into a dominated language of a text written in a dominating language; the same operation in the opposite direction – a text in a dominated language translated into a dominating language; the translation into a dominating language of a text written in a dominating language; and lastly the translation into a dominated language of a text written in a dominated language (a rare occurrence). It is the first two scenarios which interest us here. Because of the incommensurability of their stakes and therefore of their significance in the world literary market, they cannot be treated together and must be analyzed in distinct ways.

Translation as accumulation of capital

If writers from dominated national literary fields wish to enter the world literary competition, they must work on importing capital, on gaining heritage and nobility by 'nationalizing' the great universal texts which are recognized as universal capital in the literary universe. 'Nationalizing' is achieved by translating those texts into the national language. The translation of texts from a dominating literary language into a dominated literary language can be analyzed as a 'diversion' of capital.

The 'programme of translation' (Berman 1984:29) of the German Romantics can be described from this perspective. Germany was late in constituting its national identity compared with other European nations, and German was very much a dominated language with respect to literature. So from the end of the eighteenth century and during the first half of the nineteenth century, in parallel to the 'invention' of a popular national literature, the Germans instituted a collective strategy of annexation and appropriation of the literary and philosophical resources of Greek and Roman Antiquity by means of translation into German. This 'nationalization' of a foreign and very noble culture enabled the Germans to catch up, so to speak, and to gain a tradition that they lacked through an initial accumulation of capital.[8]

This also represented an opportunity to rival the most prestigious literary nations of the time (in particular France), which had the greatest national classics recognized internationally. Germany's ambition was made known quite openly as one of the biggest collective tasks for the common good. Friedrich Schleiermacher, one of the great translators of Plato into German (from 1799), wrote the following in 1813, acknowledging the collective and national nature of the undertaking: 'An inner necessity, in which a peculiar mission of our nation is expressed clearly enough, has driven us in *large numbers to translation*; we cannot go back, and must go on'. Later he speaks of 'the true historical goal of *translation on a large scale*, as it is now indigenous to us' (Schleiermacher 1999:91; my emphasis).[9]

At the same time there was an attempt to transform the German language, or more precisely, the language was 'made literary' (*littérarisé*) through importing literary capital into the language itself. This 'Greekization' of German was an operation of literary ennoblement which can also be described as a strategy for increasing the volume of capital.

> In his Introduction to *Agamemnon* by Aeschylus (1816) Humboldt (2000) makes explicit this annexionist conception of translation: 'Think how the German language, to cite only one example, has profited since it began imitating Greek meter. And think how our nation has progressed, not just the well-educated among us but the masses as well – even women and children – since the Greeks have been available to our nation's readers in an authentic and undistorted form. It is impossible to overstate the importance of the service Klopstock rendered to the German nation with his first successful treatment of ancient meter or the even greater service of Voss,[10] who may be said to have introduced classical antiquity into the German language' (Humboldt 2000:37–39).[11] Importing what is considered to be the very model of culture into the German language and literature would allow German to rival the greatest literary languages. Goethe states as a fact what was at the time a self-fulfilling prophecy: 'Germans have contributed for a long time to mutual mediation and recognition. Those who understand German are in the market where all the nations present their merchandise' (cited in Strich 1946:47). Schleiermacher adds: 'our nation seems to be destined, because of its respect for things foreign, and because of its disposition toward mediation, to carry all the treasures of foreign art and scholarship, together

with its own, in its language, to unite them into a great historical whole, as it were, which would be kept safe in the center and heart of Europe; so that now, with the help of our language, everyone can enjoy, as purely and perfectly as it is possible for the foreigner, that which the most varied ages have brought forth' (Schleiermacher 1999:91).[12]

The gain in literary capital was reinforced by the work of linguists and philologists who contributed their specialist knowledge to the struggle against the domination of the French language. Comparative studies of the grammar of Indo-European languages in fact raised the Germanic languages to the same rank of seniority and nobility as Greek and Latin by placing the Germanic languages in a central position in the Indo-European family of languages and by decreeing the superiority of Indo-European languages over others. At the same time, such linguistic study provided the German language with an extraordinary heritage and therefore with a new 'literariness' which raised it to the level of Latin in the system of legitimacy defined by linguistic-literary seniority. According to this logic, it is easy to understand the development of theories of translation central to Romanticism: as if to reinforce the collective effort at gaining literary capital for the German nation, it was necessary to declare the French translations of Greek and Latin texts to be obsolete, and therefore to theorize what the 'true translation' should be like. The German theory of translation and the practice which it entailed were founded on a precise and firm opposition to the French tradition in this sphere. In France at that time translation practice had not the slightest care for faithfulness to the source text: the dominating position of French literature and of the French language motivated translators to appropriate and adapt foreign texts to the French literary aesthetic and categories of thought. 'Who would claim that anything has ever been translated into French from either the classical or the Germanic languages?' (ibid.), says Schleiermacher. 'It's as if they [the French]', adds Schlegel, 'required that every foreigner in France should behave and dress according to French habits and preferences, which means that they actually never knew any foreigners' (1964:17). 'For feelings, thoughts, and even objects, the French proceed in the same way as for foreign words which are adapted to the French language: for each foreign fruit, the French demand a replacement which has grown on their own soil' (Goethe 1819:255–56).

In order to set themselves in opposition to the French tradition, Germans theorized the principle of 'faithfulness'. 'If, however, translation is to give the language and spirit of a nation that which it does not possess . . ., then the first requirement is always fidelity', stated Humboldt (2000:39).[13] In opposition to the 'Frenchifying' of texts, in other words, their reduction to aesthetic categories which claimed to be universal, the Germans advocated 'faithfulness', that is, objective truth, the reliable and verifiable reference to the original text. The Germans guaranteed conformity of the target text to the source text, and hoped thus to make German the only benchmark language; after eighteenth-century French, German would become the new 'Latin of the modern world'. During the era when the immense project of German translation was under way, the German language laid claim to the title of new universal language.

It is thus that the idea of a real and objective accumulation of literary capital and linguistic-literary capital developed among German intellectuals. Goethe wrote the following: 'Independently of our own production, we have already achieved a high degree of culture thanks to the *full appropriation* of what is foreign to us' (quoted in Berman 1984:26; my emphasis).[14] In *Der Begriff der Kunstkritik in der deutschen Romantik*, Walter Benjamin himself wrote *a posteriori* as if it were an obvious truth: 'The durable accomplishment of Romanticism was the annexation of Romantic artistic forms to German literature. The Romantics' effort was consciously directed at the *appropriation*, development, and purification of those forms' (Benjamin 1974:76; my emphasis).

As well as the simple accumulation of capital during periods of foundation of the national and political unit, there is also the operation of 'temporal acceleration' in numerous dominated fields which, having entered the competition earlier, are bi-polarized. In these fields which are generally European (that is, dominated among dominating entities), translations have been the privileged instruments of struggle of the most autonomous writers. Translations have enabled the importing of central norms which decree and attest to modernity. Generally the translators are writers and polyglots[15] who can be situated among international writers following the major dichotomy which structures national fields. These writers wished to break away from the norms that governed their literary fields, and sought to introduce works of modernity as defined in the literary centres. There are numerous examples. The poet Daigaku Horiguchi imported Verlaine, Apollinaire, Jammes, Cocteau and Morand into Japan during the 1920s, and thus contributed to overturning the aesthetic norms of the emerging Japanese literary space.[16] The Hungarian writer, Dezsö Kostolanyi[17] (1885–1936) translated Shakespeare, Byron, Wilde, Baudelaire and Verlaine. Borges proposed Spanish versions of Crane, Cummings, Faulkner and Warren. Danilo Kis[18] translated into Serbo-Croatian the Hungarian poets Petöfi, Ady, Radnotti and Atilla Jozsef, the Russians Mandelstam, Essenine and Marina Tsvetaïeva, and the French Corneille, Baudelaire, Lautréamont, Verlaine, Prévert and Queneau.

These mediators played a role which in a way is the opposite of the international mediators of the great capitals: they did not introduce the periphery into the centre in order to consecrate it; rather they imported modernity decreed at the literary Greenwich meridian and made it known in their national field. This is why they played an essential role in the process of unification of the world literary field: it is possible to imagine a literary world map which is designed in accordance with the dates of the translation of the great heretical texts, that is, the founding texts of modernity. This literary geography would show the objective aesthetic distance from the different literary fields to the legislating centre.

> The case of the Chinese literary field is telling in this regard: in a universe closed to almost any literary imports since 1949, the playwright Gao Xingjian (2000 Nobel prize for literature) published in 1981 a text entitled 'First essay on the art of the modern novel'[19] in which he presented the technical and stylistic innovations of 'modern' literary authors and movements as diverse as Beckett, Surrealism, Aragon, Eluard, Prévert, Robbe-Grillet, Dadaism and Perec. All these writers, who are considered in the unified regions of the world literary field as 'classics of modernity', were presented for the first time in China. Gao had become a translator of French and had had the opportunity to read numerous literary works in secret. Before Gao no other Chinese writer had ever had access to these texts, nor had any idea of the series of stylistic, formal, rhetorical, and aesthetic innovations which revolutionized literature since the end of the nineteenth century, a time when the Chinese literary field was 'put on hold'.[20] Gao's book was of considerable importance in China, and through the polemic it gave rise to, it marked an important event in the Chinese literary universe. The redistribution of positions which it caused contributed to pushing the Chinese field into the world literary field in

spite of its heavy dependence on the political authorities (Dutrait 2001, Curien 2001).

The Chinese case illustrates very precisely the measurable consequences of the time gap (it is also a matter of literary time) existing between national literary fields which have entered the international competition at different dates.[21] When the time gap between spaces is significant, translation is the only means of making up literary time. In other words, it is an instrument of 'temporal acceleration': translation allows the whole of a national field which is temporally very distant from the literary centres to enter into the world literary competition, by revealing the state of (aesthetic) struggles at the literary meridian. Translation is therefore a very efficient weapon in the world competition: it allows an entire literary field to change its position in the international field, and to displace the whole of that universe through its autonomous pole.

The reader may have noticed that we have included under the label 'translation' a text which is not a linguistic transformation properly speaking. But Gao's text, which introduces and analyzes foreign works, is a kind of 'introduction' which plays the same role that a translation can play, because of its significant aesthetic and temporal transformation of a national literary field. Later on, indeed, I propose to enlarge the notion of translation to include numerous 'functions' which are not normally subsumed under the term 'translation'.

Translation as consecration

Earlier I described the structural homology between each national field and the international field. But this is not a simple analogy. By relying on and referring to the autonomous pole of the world field, each national field succeeds in emerging, and then in becoming autonomous. The structural homology is the product of the form of the world field, but also of the process of its unification: each national field appears and is unified according to the model and thanks to the specific consecrating agencies which allow international writers to legitimize their position internationally. Thus, not only is each field constituted according to the model and thanks to the autonomous consecrating agencies, but the world field itself tends to become autonomous through the constitution of autonomous poles in each national field. In other words, the writers who claim a (more) autonomous position are those who know the law of the world literary field, and who use it to struggle within their national field and to subvert dominant norms. The autonomous world pole is therefore essential for the constitution of the whole field, for its 'becoming literary' ('littérarisation'), and for its progressive denationalization: the autonomous pole is a bulwark not only because of the theoretical and aesthetic models that it provides for writers everywhere in the world, but also in terms of its editorial and critical structures which support the enterprise of universal literature. There is no 'miracle' of autonomy: each work from a space less endowed with literary resources, which has the ambition of being called literature, only exists in its relationship with the networks and consecrating power of the most autonomous places. The most consecrated creators, the great heroes of literature, only emerge in alliance with the specific power of autonomous international literary capital.

The struggles for unification of the international field are waged mainly in the form of rivalries in the national fields. Within a national field, national writers – those who identify with the national definition of literature – are opposed to international writers – those who have recourse to the autonomous model of literature. The translation of works from a dominated language into a central language is one of the ways in which the world field becomes autonomous: translation allows autonomous poles in the dominated national fields to appear and be reinforced. In dominated fields, struggling for access to translation is the same as struggling for the constitution of an autonomous pole, that is, for recognition at the autonomous world pole of works which conform to criteria defined at the literary Greenwich meridian.

It is the same international protagonists in each national field who employ all the resources of literary import-export in order to create or reinforce their positions. In the situation described earlier, they are importers, translators themselves; they import legitimate international works from the autonomous pole in order to divert literary resources and thus contribute to the process of autonomization of their national field. They can also at the same time be exporters and struggle for their own texts to be translated, that is, legitimized and consecrated in the literary centres.

Linguistic-literary inequality implies that the literary value of a text – its value on the market of literary goods – depends, at least in part, on the language in which it is written. This inequality has such powerful effects that it can objectively prevent (or at least make difficult) the recognition or the consecration of writers of dominated languages. The Danish novelist Henrik Stangerup speaks of his mother tongue as a 'miniature language'; the nineteenth-century Danish poet Oehlenschläger is for him the symbol of this linguistic marginality: 'This Napoleon of poets, as titanic in his productivity as Hugo or Balzac, [was] worthy, if only he had written in an international language, of conspiring at their sides against the stupidity which knows no national barriers' (Stangerup 1987:219). In the same way, Brazilian critics point out that two of the greatest Portuguese-language naturalist novelists, the Portuguese Eça de Queiros and the Brazilian Machado de Assis, have remained practically unknown in the international literary universe: 'Their perhaps excessive national glory is matched by a discouraging international obscurity', notes Antonio Candido (1995:236).

The linguistic-literary hierarchy is so implacable that the metaphor of the 'cage' comes up often among dominated writers. Gomez Carillo had become a famous author, and according to Max Daireaux, had 'conquered the maximum celebrity that a Latin American author could have [in the 1920s]' (1930:32). Yet Carillo said in 1930: 'For a writer whose spirit is universal to even a small degree, the Spanish language is a prison. We can write tons of books, even find readers, but it's exactly as if we'd written nothing: our voices don't pass through the rungs of our cage!' (ibid.). Similarly, more than thirty years later, the translation of the Pole Witold Gombrowicz into French allowed him, as he said, to 'demolish [his] Argentinian cage' (1968:55–56).

This is why in the world literary universe translation is both one of the main weapons in the struggle for literary legitimacy and the great authority of specific acts of consecration. For a dominated writer, struggling for access to translation is in fact a matter of struggling for his or her existence as a legitimate member of the world republic of letters, for access to the literary centres (to the critical and consecrating authorities), and for the right to be read by those who decree that what they read is worth reading. Salman Rushdie, a British writer of Pakistani origin, for whom the problem of translation ought not to exist, says nevertheless that immigrant writers are like 'translated men' (Rushdie 1991:17). This is a way of expressing the fact that translation is constitutive of literary dependence, that it belongs to the very gesture of dominated writing. In other words, in the dominated regions of the literary field, translation is the only specific means of being perceived, becoming visible, of existing. Far from being simply a 'naturalization' (in the sense of change of nationality), translation is much more: it provides a certificate of 'literariness', in Roman Jakobson's sense – 'that which makes a given work a work of literature'.[22] If a work is translated into one of the great literary languages, it becomes literary immediately; it is legitimate. Translation then functions as a kind of right to international existence. It allows a writer not only to be recognized as a literary figure outside his or her national borders, but even more importantly it brings into existence an international position, an autonomous position inside the national universe.[23] At the same time the group of translated texts marks out the borders of the most autonomous territories in the world literary field: the texts themselves designate what is literary (i.e. what is universal) and what is not.

It is well known that the English translation (in 1859) of the Persian poet Omar Khayyam (1050–1123) made an English 'classic' of this poet's work. The self-translation before the First World War of the Indian poet Rabindranath Tagore from Bengali into English earned him the Nobel prize. The French translation of the Iranian writer Sadegh Hedayat's work, La Chouette aveugle, in 1953 gave this writer an existence in both Paris and Tehran. The self-translation of Milan Kundera from Czech into French in the 1970s made him one of the most internationally consecrated writers in recent years. The translation of Gao Xingjian's plays into Swedish earned him the Nobel prize in 2000, and so on.

As mentioned above, the significance of translation does not depend only on the position of the source and target languages, but it also depends on the position of the translated authors, both in their national field and according to the place that this field occupies in the world field. This accounts for the fact that translation is a means of consecration for all dominated authors: authors writing in dominated languages (discussed above); writers in dominating languages who come from dominated national literary fields (the position of the national field in the international field); as well as writers occupying dominated positions within dominating literary fields (the position within the national field).

Thus there are a number of cases of consecration of writers from dominated literary fields being the immediate and direct result of the translation of their works into one of the great literary languages. The international consecration of the Irishman James Joyce resulted from the translation into French of Ulysses, supervised by Valery Larbaud and published in Paris by Adrienne Monnier in 1929 – this translation allowed Joyce to escape the censorship and moral attacks that he had come under in the main English-speaking centres and to become one of the great writers of modernity. The first German translations of Ibsen's plays from Norwegian allowed him to escape from what he felt was a Scandinavian prison;[24] the Yiddish poet Morris Rosenfeld, who immigrated to New York, became well known beyond Jewish political circles in 1898 as a result of the English translation of his book Lider bukh (Songs of the Ghetto) (Howe 1999:428).

Defining the translation of dominated authors as a specific form of consecration resolves a series of problems arising from the belief in the symmetry of translational transactions. If translation can be described as an operation through which a text from a deprived literary area succeeds in imposing itself as literary with regard to the legitimate authorities, then the whole series of strategies which aim to facilitate traversing the literary border can be included in the category of 'translation': self-translation, transcription, writing directly in the dominating language, lexical transformations of the dominating language, double symmetrical translation, etc. Interlinguistic translation would only be one of the possible 'translations', that is, one of the linguistic-literary strategies developed by the dominated in their struggle for legitimacy.

These diverse modes of access to literary recognition, which present a continuum of solutions for escaping literary destitution and invisibility, cannot be dissociated from each other. There is no real boundary between them, and a writer may adopt any of them at different stages of his or her consecration. It is possible therefore to locate all degrees and types of text transformation in the itinerary of numerous writers at the various stages of their consecration.

These strategies can also be understood from the point of view of dependence and independence: the translator is in competition with the author and on occasion can even cancel out the author, and certain strategies thus provide solutions by means of which authors can avoid the arbitrariness, prejudices, ethnocentrism, ignorance and supposed skill of mediators and translators, in order to maintain control over the transformations of their texts when and as much as they wish.

For each case which I shall now briefly mention,[25] it is necessary to distinguish between the position of each writer and the position of his or her national or mother tongue. Two types of dominated writer can be differentiated. The first writes in a dominated language which is part of a group of languages among which there are dominating languages (this applies to European languages as described above): this writer is dominated in the literary domain. The second type of writer is dominated politically and a product of the process of decolonization. This writer maintains a relationship with the dominating language which is inseparably political and literary: there is dual domination, both political and literary.

From the point of view of the writer, self-translation is one of the most efficient ways of independently ensuring the traversal of the literary border and totally avoiding dependence on the translator.

> The Swedish playwright August Strindberg decided in the 1890s to work on his international recognition. He undertook to retranslate, that is, to rewrite some of his texts in French, because he was displeased with the services of his translator and with the reception of his plays in Paris. Nabokov, who had begun his career as a Russian novelist in Berlin in the 1920s, before 'becoming' an American novelist, translated his Russian works into English after reading what he considered a very bad English translation of his novel *Camera obscura*. Upon discovering this text in 1935 he wrote the following remarks which are quite revealing about the conflictual relationship between authors and translators: '[this translation] was loose, shapeless, sloppy, full of blunders and gaps, lacking vigor and spring, and plumped down in such dull, flat English that I could not read it to the end; all of which is rather hard on an author who aims in his work at absolute precision, takes the utmost trouble to obtain it, and then finds the translator calmly undoing every blessed phrase' (Nabokov, cited in Boyd 1990:419).[26]
>
> The Pole Witold Gombrowicz, exiled in Argentina, translated his novel *Ferdydurke* into Spanish in the 1950s as a first attempt to get out of his Argentinian-Polish 'cage'. We know that Joyce refused to depend totally on Valery Larbaud; he was closely involved in the revised translation of *Ulysses*. The title page of the 1929 French edition of the book specifies the roles of the various participants and establishes a subtle hierarchy among

them, giving the author an important role: 'Complete French translation by Auguste Morel, assisted by Stuart Gilbert, revised in its entirety by Valery Larbaud and the author'.

The strategy of self-translation is provisional or ongoing, as the case may be. It presupposes that the author is bilingual – this is another indication of literary dependence which characterizes, among others, writers from formerly colonized countries. Rachid Boudjedra, an Algerian novelist, translated his novels from the 1970s onwards from Arabic into French and also the other way round, which enabled him to occupy a dual position as Algerian author in France writing in French and as national author in Algeria writing in Arabic.[27] Similarly, Mazizi Kunene, the Zulu poet from South Africa, produced works which were situated in the to and fro between two languages: he wrote epics in Zulu which traced the history of his people, and then translated and published his texts in Great Britain.[28]

When self-translation seems too artificial or when it seems to double the work of writing, it may be more efficient for the writer to write his or her texts directly in the language of translation. Adopting the dominating literary language – which is always a painful decision – is often provisional, and motivated by the desire to speed up the process of consecration.

> Strindberg became a French writer for a few years: he abandoned translating his works and wrote directly in French between 1887 and 1899, producing *Plaidoyer d'un fou* and the famous *Inferno* which were published in Paris.[29] He then translated these works into Swedish. Nabokov departed for the United States during the Second World War and became an American novelist. E.M. Cioran adopted French as his writing language, because after being exiled in Paris he realized that writing his texts in Rumanian would have excluded him from any publishing opportunities. Beckett in a sense always practised the two strategies, since through the elaboration of his bilingual works he undertook both self-translation and writing in a foreign language throughout his life. He thus avoided the intrusion of a translator and the choice of a national literary language, that is, political and national naturalization. Among Indian novelists, authors who gain the greatest visibility and international recognition are those who choose English rather than national and/or regional languages as their literary medium.
>
> Politically and linguistically dominated writers whose mother or national tongue is very deprived of literary prestige – such as Somalian Nurudin Farah and Zulu Njabulo Ndebele – have no other choice but to convert, from the literary point of view, to the language of colonization.

The 'importing' of a language into another, the last of our solutions to the problem of linguistic-literary dependence, is another compromise adopted by numerous authors who produce 'digraphical' works (to use Alain Ricard's term – Ricard 1995:esp. 151–72). These texts are written both in the dominated language and the dominating language, in the mother tongue and the language of colonization. These authors have perfected a style which allows them to avoid the filter and distortions of translation, without betraying their linguistic and/or national origin.

Here are some cases. Jean-Joseph Rabearivelo (1903–1937), a

Madagascan, managed to inject Malagasy syntax and vocabulary into French, specifically in a text entitled *Traduit de la nuit* (Translated from the Night). The Ivory Coast writer Ahmadou Kourouma claimed to achieve, at least in his first novels, a 'malinkization' of French.

The same process of linguistic importing and mixing applies to 'mental gallicism', which was created and theorized by the Nicaraguan poet Rubén Dario at the end of the nineteenth century in order to challenge the conservatism and conformity of Spanish poetry. 'Mental gallicism' is a kind of 'Frenchifying' of Castilian poetic language; it was one of the sources for the process of renewal of Spanish poetry which constituted 'modernism'.

Joyce's undertaking in *Finnegans Wake* can be understood according to the same logic. Seeking to escape from English, which was for him both the language of writing and the language of colonial domination, he wrote a text which is truly untranslatable, a novel whose existence in the literary sphere depends neither on translation nor on translators.

Another very similar strategy is to subvert, distort and attack the language from the inside, making it an instrument of criticism. One of the many authors who have done this is the Nigerian Ken Saro-Wiwa in his 1985 novel written in 'rotten English', *Sozaboy*.

The position of consecrators

The translator is the last participant we shall situate in the world literary field in order to complete this attempt at presenting a model. Once the translation has been done, the position of the translated text (or author), and notably its degree of legitimacy, will depend on the translator's position. Because translation is one of the forms of transfer of literary capital, the value of translation and its degree of legitimacy depend on the capital of the translator-consecrator himself or herself, and on the linguistic-literary capital of the target language (to which must be added the capital of the publisher, the prestige of the series or of the journal in which the text is published, etc.). In other words, it is possible to deduce the degree of legitimacy of the translated book from the position of the mediator in his or her national field, from the position of the target language, and secondarily from the position of the publisher of the translated book. The greater the prestige of the mediator, the more 'noble' the translation, and the greater its consecrating power.[30]

A genuine understanding of the role of translators requires situating them within a context, a continuum of functions and agents: translators are not discoverers or consecrators operating alone; they are part of a complex chain of mediators which includes bilingual readers, travellers, specialists, publishers, critics, literary agents, etc.

At one extreme of this continuum are the 'ordinary mediators'. These are almost invisible protagonists of the literary universe, who are largely forgotten by literary history and have no power of consecration themselves. They are translators and/or specialists of the target literary field, which they provide with information about literary innovations in the countries they visit or know. In a way they are points of reference which can be used in reconstituting the sum of the networks and circuits through which literature transits and transmutes. In studying the trajectory of such mediators it would be possible to produce a cross-section depiction of the literary field at a particular point in time. Henri Hoppenot was one of these essential and invisible mediators in Paris between the wars. He was, for example, one of Larbaud's informants on Latin America. The 'ordinary mediator' owes his existence to the act of mediation itself.

At the other extreme there are the 'consecrated consecrators' or the consecrators whose power of consecration depends on the degree of their own consecration. These consecrators, who could also be called 'charismatic consecrators', consecrate on their own behalf, as compared with 'institutional consecrators' who are in a way the third pole of this domain. Institutional consecrators are those who belong to the academic or scholarly establishment, for example academic translators.

In the case of a consecrator who is himself or herself highly consecrated and who translates a text, the translation is itself an effective instrument of consecration which does not have to be reinforced by commentaries, analyses, reviews or prizes. Examples include André Gide translating *Typhoon* by Joseph Conrad in 1918 and *Song Offerings* by Rabindranath Tagore in 1913. By producing the translation the translator designates a text which is worth reading, understanding and commenting on. In the case of charismatic consecrators – writers, intellectuals, and translators – who can consecrate personally, we could speak of a kind of inter-consecration or exchange of capital.

> The translation of *Ulysses* by Joyce, supervised by Larbaud, was in itself an immense consecration. Larbaud discovered *Ulysses* through the first episodes of the book published in *The Little Review*, and his reaction was enthusiastic. The name and prestige of Valery Larbaud as discoverer-consecrator-translator were so great that his mere proposal (in 1921) to supervise a translation of *Ulysses* led to Sylvia Beach's decision to transform her bookshop *Shakespeare and Company* into a publishing house with the sole purpose of publishing *Ulysses* in its original version, and also to Adrienne Monnier's decision to publish the French translation. Although Joyce was renowned in English-speaking literary milieux, in particular among the American expatriates in Paris, he found it impossible to get his novel published at the beginning of the 1920s. His texts were considered scandalous and had been published by small publishers who were plagued by British and American censorship. The issues of *The Little Review* in which *Ulysses* appeared in episodes were regularly seized and burnt on the grounds of obscenity, until the secretary of the New York Society for the Prevention of Vice managed to get publication of the review banned (see Joyce 1995). The mere designation of a text by a great consecrator as 'a must for translation' is sufficient to consecrate it as a great literary text. The same story can be told of William Archer and G.B. Shaw, who consecrated Ibsen in London – the first through his translations[31] and the second through his critical essay (see Casanova 2007).

It may also happen that when the translator is highly consecrated, the consecration of an author is so efficient that it leads to the wider recognition of an entire literary field, and therefore to the shift in position of a national field in the world structure. At the time of his discovery of Joyce's *Ulysses* and even before the translation of this work, Valery Larbaud wrote: 'His works do for Ireland what Ibsen's did in his time for Norway, Strindberg's did for Sweden, and Nietzsche's did for Germany in the nineteenth century . . . In short, it can be said that with the works of James Joyce, and in particular the novel about to be published in Paris,[32] Ireland is making a sensational entrance into European high literature' (Larbaud 1936:233–34).

In the opposite situation, when the translator is little endowed with or lacks specific capital, that is, when he or she has little consecrating power, the exchange of capital is entrusted to other better endowed mediators (preface-writer, analyst, prestigious critic, etc.). Since the translation in this case only represents the initial accumulation of necessary capital, other actors in the literary field must take over from the translator. The nature and role of those actors depend on the position of the translator, the initial degree of legitimacy conferred by the translation itself, and its place of publication.

An example of the contribution of a series of actors to the process of consecration is the case of the French translation of Gombrowicz's work. The first step was the translation of his work into French by Constantin Jelenski; then came the renown that followed the publication of his novel Ferdydurke by the publisher Maurice Nadeau; the final touch to his consecration was the commentaries and analyses by the writer Dominique de Roux, who was editor of Cahier Gombrowicz, published by the Editions de L'Herne in 1971. It is interesting to note that once a writer has been canonized and his works have become classics, the process is reversed, and it is then the writer who consecrates the translator. This was the case for Maurice-Edgar Coindreau, the French translator of Faulkner.

For consecrator-creators translation is not the only means of consecration. The preface or critical essay is a form of consecration which is both more valued and more efficient. Paradigmatic examples include the preface by Gidé to the novel by the Egyptian Taha Hussein, Le Livre des jours (Paris, Gallimard, 1947); Sartre's preface to l'Anthologie de la poésie nègre by Léopold Sédar Senghor (Paris, PUF, 1969); The Quintessence of Ibsenism written and published by G.B. Shaw in 1891; more recently, William Boyd's preface to Sozaboy by the Nigerian novelist Ken-Saro-Wiwa (London, Longman, 1985) and the preface by Marguerite Yourcenar to the work of the Japanese novelist Yukio Mishima (Paris, Gallimard, 1981). It is because they are themselves consecrated authors that these great consecrators 're-create' works, and often become privileged commentators on the works that they translate and/or consecrate.

Translation may well be an essential operation in struggles for literary legitimacy and one of the principal means of consecration for authors and texts. It nevertheless remains an ambiguous activity. Translator-mediators are special experts whose task is to select texts and thus determine the boundary between literature and non-literature, between what is 'a must for translation' and what is not, between the international and the national, the universal and the particular, modernity and archaism, etc. They grant a value to the texts, and are therefore somewhat like foreign exchange brokers who determine and fix the value of imported texts: to use Valery Larbaud's expression, 'the spiritual gold of the world' passes through their hands.

But the domination which they exercise requires that they 'discover' writers who are not native but who conform to their literary categories. This is why translation is also a form of annexation, and therefore a kind of universalization through the denial of difference: works are diverted for the benefit of the central resources. In this way, as Paul Valéry says, 'universal capital increases' (1960:1091). Mediators from the centre reduce foreign literary works to their own categories of perception, which are set up as universal norms. In this process the historical, cultural, political, and especially the literary context is forgotten; though it is precisely this context which would enable the works to be understood in their specific richness. This is the price to be paid to the great literary nations in order to obtain a permit of universal circulation. Thus the history of literary celebrations is also a long series of misunderstandings and misappreciation that result from the ethnocentrism of the great literary intermediaries (notably the Parisians and the Londoners) and the process of annexation which is perpetuated in the very act of literary recognition.

Notes

1   I have used the term 'consecration' and its derivatives in this paper, following Susan Emanuel, translator of Bourdieu's *Les Règles de l'art*. [Tr.]
2   This article reports on work in progress. My aim is to emphasize a particular function of translation, taking into account the difference between linguistic capital and literary capital, and the specificity of the transfer of literary capital.
3   See Ganne and Minon (1992), who distinguish between 'intraduction' (intranslation), the importing of foreign literary texts into the national language, and 'extraduction' (extranslation), the exporting of national literary texts.
4   There is in fact a continuum, such that the whole series of possibilities and positions can be observed in their continuity.
5   To take an example, in France the number of translators of English on the one hand, and of Korean or Catalan on the other, is a fairly accurate indication of the amount of literary capital of these languages.
6   Or the writing system is in the process of becoming standardized.
7   Although some of these creoles are beginning to acquire a literary status and codified writing system due to the activities of writers.
8   The same process can be observed in the African translations of Shakespeare, in particular the Swahili translations promoted by Julius Nyerere, ex-president of the Republic of Tanzania (*Julius Caesar* in 1963 and *The Merchant of Venice* in 1969). See Nkashama (1992: 339–50).
9   Quoted here from the English translation by Waltraud Bartscht (Schleiermacher 1992:53–54). [Tr.]
10   Johann Heinrich Voss undertook translations of Homer into German (*The Odyssey* in 1781 and *The Iliad* in 1793) which became true 'classics' of the German language.
11   Quoted here from the English translation by Sharon Sloan (Humboldt 1992:57). [Tr.]
12   Quoted here from the English translation by Waltraud Bartscht (Schleiermacher 1992:53–54). [Tr.]
13   Quoted here from the English translation by Sharon Sloan (Humboldt 1992:57). [Tr.]
14   Quoted here from the English translation of Berman's book, by S. Heyvaert (Berman 1992: 11). [Tr.]
15   For instance, in the German field at the end of the eighteenth century, A.W. Schlegel had a perfect mastery of the major modern European languages, as well as Greek, Latin, Medieval French, Old German, Occitan and Sanskrit. He translated Shakespeare, Dante, Petrarch, Boccacio, Calderon, Ariosto and numerous lesser known Italian, Spanish, and Portuguese poets.
16   See Tachibana (2000). The translation of *Ouvert la nuit* by Paul Morand, undertaken by Daigaku Horiguchi, was published in 1924. Then his great collection of French poetry, *Figures au clair de lune*, which contains 340 poems by 66 poets, was published in 1925. Poets represented include Valéry, Mallarmé, Verlaine, Gourmont, Régnier, Laforgue, Apollinaire, Claudel, Fort, Moréas, Louÿs, Max Jacob, Cocteau, Reverdy, Soupault, Picabia, Eluard, etc.
17   Dezsö Kostolanyi is the author of a very ironic short novel, entitled *Le traducteur cleptomane* (The translator-kleptomaniac), Paris, Viviane Hamy, 1994.
18   Jewish Yugoslav writer (1935–1989) born on the Yugoslav-Hungarian border, considered today as one of the greatest writers of that country.
19   *Xiandai xiaoshuo jiqiao chutan*, Canton, Huacheng chubanshe, 1981.
20   Certain works had, however, been translated and circulated secretly since the writer Beidao called literary translation in China, which had long been marginalized, a 'silent revolution' (Beidao 1993).

21   See Bourdieu (1992:226): 'in the space of the artistic field as in the social space, distances between styles or lifestyles are never better measured than in terms of time'; quoted here from the English translation by Susan Emanuel, (Bourdieu 1996:159). [Tr.]

22   See Jakobson (1921:11): 'The object of the science of literature is not literature, but "literariness" – (*literaturnost*), that is, what makes a given work a literary work' (Jakobson, quoted in Eichenbaum 2001:1066. [Tr.]). See also Eichenbaum (1965).

23   Which also reinforces the autonomous pole of the world field.

24   The first German translations of Henrik Ibsen's plays were published in 1872.

25   I shall only discuss a few of the most representative positions and solutions along the continuum of very sophisticated strategies.

26   Vladimir Nabokov, letter to Hutchinson & Co., 22 May 1935.

27   Self-translation is not the same when undertaken by a writer who writes in a dominated language among dominating languages, and by a writer from a colonial empire: the type of domination is different, although the strategy is the same.

28   *Zulu Poems*, London, 1970; *The Ancestors and the Sacred Mountains*, London, 1982.

29   *Inferno* was published by Mercure de France in 1898.

30   By contrast, in the case of the translation of a commercially successful book – an international best-seller, for example – the position of the translator, the field of origin of the author, the relationship between the two languages and the place of publication of the translation are sufficient to determine the position of the text at the heteronomous pole of the literary field.

31   The complete works of Henrik Ibsen were published in translation by William Archer, in London, 1890–91.

32   He is referring here to the forthcoming publication in Paris of *Ulysses* in English, published by Sylvia Beach.

Chapter 17

Johan Heilbron

TOWARDS A SOCIOLOGY OF TRANSLATION: BOOK TRANSLATIONS AS A CULTURAL WORLD SYSTEM

EDITOR'S INTRODUCTION

> The more central the cultural production of a country is, the more it serves as an example to other countries, and the less it is itself concerned with the cultural production from other countries. Instead of assuming that translations 'normally' occupy a marginal position (Even-Zohar 1990:50), it is far more accurate to say that their role varies significantly, and that the variation depends on the degree of centrality in the international translation system.

L IKE CASANOVA, HEILBRON FOCUSES on modes of circulation that allow intellectual works to develop a presence on the world stage, and the role of translation in this process. Also like Casanova, he argues that cultural exchanges have a dynamic of their own, and that transnational cultural exchange is a largely autonomous field, with its own economic, political and symbolic configuration.

The basic units of the world-system of translation are language groups rather than nation-states, and the aim here is therefore to analyze the structure of translation flows between these language groups. Existing sources of data for conducting this analysis, for example book statistics available in each country and databases such as the *Index translationum*, are all flawed; the answer may be to cautiously combine international and national translation statistics as well as the findings of case studies where these are available. The starting assumption is that a language is more central in the world-system of translation when it has a large share in the total number of translated books worldwide, bearing in mind that the system itself is dynamic and that this position therefore changes over time. Centrality is key in structuring translation flows, with more translations flowing from the core to the periphery than the other way around. Moreover, communication between language groups situated at the periphery will also tend to pass through the centre. Thus, 'the more central a language is in the translation system, the more it has the capacity to function as an intermediary or vehicular language'. Another consequence of this structure concerns variety: the more central a language is, the more types of books are translated from it. Finally, fewer translations are undertaken into languages situated at or near the centre of the international translation system, which explains why translations constitute a very small percentage of the total book production in English.

Follow-up questions for discussion

- Heilbron draws a broad, somewhat flat picture of translation flows that relies purely on the overall centrality of a language in the international translation system, without regard to specific historical or political contexts. How might his model account, or be refined/extended to account, for the observation by Hale (2008:218), namely that it is possible to identify zones of influence within the broad pattern of translation flows? How would the model explain the fact that in Northern European countries such as Denmark and the Netherlands 'German is the second most translated language after English, while in southern Europe French is everywhere the second most translated language' (*ibid.*), and bearing in mind that similar patterns could at one time be identified in relation to Russian in some parts of the world?
- Speaking of literary forms, Moretti (2003:75) claims that 'movement from one periphery to another (without passing through the centre) is almost unheard of'. He does not refer here to peripheral cultures existing within the same region (for example various language groups in India) but to those that belong to different regions, such as Norway and Portugal. To what extent does this claim overlap with Heilbron's analysis of translation flows? And to what extent does this analysis reflect the realities of translation?
- Consider some of the implications of the international world system of book translations, as described by Heilbron, for phenomena such as retranslation, self translation, pseudotranslation, as well as forms and practices of interpreting, including relay interpreting in international settings, and audiovisual translation (the use of a pivot language, the circulation of Japanese anime, or animated films, etc.). To what extent might Heilbron's model be adapted to account for patterns and sub-patterns of flow in these and similar contexts?

Recommended further reading

Hale, Terry (2008) 'Publishing Strategies', in Mona Baker and Gabriela Saldanha (eds) *Routledge Encyclopedia of Translation Studies*, 2nd edn, London & New York: Routledge, 217–22.

Heilbron, Johan and Gisèle Sapiro (2007) 'Outline for a Sociology of Translation: Current Issues and Future Prospects', in Michaela Wolf and Alexandra Fukari (eds) *Constructing a Sociology of Translation*, Amsterdam & Philadelphia: John Benjamins, 93–107.

Hermans, Theo (1999) *Translation in Systems*, Manchester: St. Jerome.

Sapiro, Gisèle (2008) 'Translation and the Field of Publishing', *Translation Studies* 1(2): 154–66.

L ANGUAGES HAVE THEIR OWN RULES AND regulations, they are marked by peculiarities of different kinds and vary greatly in their number of speakers. But whether linguistic communities are large or small, whether their languages have peculiar or more common features, they are all connected to each other by multilingual speakers, thus constituting an emerging world language system (de Swaan 1993). Polyglots assure the communication between the speakers of various languages, either by communicating directly in a foreign language or by translating from one language into the other. Whenever people are deprived of direct access to a language, translations offer the possibility of indirect access.

Although a growing number of people learn a foreign language and English has become the *lingua franca* of international exchange, much of the communication between language groups still depends on translation and translators. Processes of translation, here meant in the literal sense of the word, represent an intriguing object of study for the social sciences, although there is strikingly little social scientific literature available. In sociolinguistics translations are commonly ignored (Coulmas 1997), in economics there is little more than an occasional paper (Mélitz 1998), and other relevant fields, like the new book history, do not have much more to offer.[1]

Translations have traditionally, at least since Cicero, been commented upon by translators themselves. In the late eighteenth century, German scholars broadened the scope of reflection, and they have been joined, more recently, by linguists. The practitioners themselves, while reflecting on their craft, have argued mainly about the stages of the translation process and about the respective merits of literal versus free translation.[2] German philosophers and literary scholars at the end of the eighteenth century started to discuss questions of translatability more broadly as a matter of cultural difference, often related to national identity. Schleiermacher's essay 'Über die verschiedenen Methoden des Übersetzens' (published in 1913) became the seminal text for the hermeneutic view of translation (Berman 1984). Linguistic theories of translation, which have developed especially since the Second World War, have also been concerned with translatability but their approach has been related to the issue of the linguistic equivalence of languages.

One of the leading scholars in the recently established field of translation studies, Gideon Toury, has argued that the traditional discourses on translation were all oriented towards the source-text or the source-language (Toury 1980).[3] By concentrating on the relationship with an original, the underlying concern was an invariably normative one: what is the 'proper' translation of a given text? If translators tend to betray the original, *traduttore, traditore* as the Italian saying has it, which deviations from the original may be considered legitimate and which are not? Translation theory was thus more concerned with 'potential' than with actual translations. This problematic, which served as the basis for translators' training, was not a sound starting point for an empirically based understanding of the actual process of translation.

Against the predominantly 'normative' approach, scholars like Itamar Even-Zohar and Toury have called for a 'descriptive' perspective, based on the analysis of actual translations. Following the lead of the Russian formalists, these polysystem theorists have argued that translations need to be understood in relation to the system in which they function, in relation to a particular set of translation norms, for example, or, where literary texts are concerned, in relation to the literary system of the target-culture (Even-Zohar 1990, Toury 1995). 'Translations', in the words of Toury, 'are facts of target-cultures; on occasion facts of a special status, sometimes even constituting identifiable (sub)systems of their own, but of the target-culture in any event' (1995:29). For the sociological approach of translations which I will explore here, the conceptual shift from source-text to target-context offers a fruitful but insufficient point of departure.

Transnational cultural exchange

Considered from a sociological perspective, translations are a function of the social relations between language groups and their transformations over time. They are therefore by no means self-evident, a fact which the terminology itself recalls. In classical Greek, for example, there is no proper word for translation, only *hermeneuein*, but that also means to interpret, to explain. The Latin *translatio* is closer to the current meaning, but is a more general term as well, referring to the various forms of transfer, including the transfer of power, as in *translatio imperii*. The more specific and modern sense of the word 'translation' emerged only in the Renaissance, when Italian humanists started to distinguish between *translatio* and *traductio*. The latter term, and the corresponding verbs in Italian and French, *traducere* and *traduire*, referred specifically to the translation of texts from one language into another, and especially into the vernacular.

Translations into the vernacular had existed well before the Renaissance, but the printing press gave the vernaculars, and translations in the vernacular, an entirely new social significance. With the formation of national states, standard languages were codified and much of the translation activity in early modern Europe was bound to the evolving relations of cooperation and conflict between nation states.

The actual practice of translation obviously exists in a great variety of forms and contexts: interpreting in political and diplomatic settings; subtitling and dubbing in the media; high-culture literary translation; as well as a range of more standardized, technical and professional translations in law, technology and commerce. If meaning is determined by use, as the pragmatist adage says, translation practice must be analyzed specifically within the field or the subfield in which it actually functions.

In this article I am concerned with one major form of translation: the translation of books. Book translations represent an identifiable and broad category: they are published and distributed in a similar manner; they are registered, counted and classified as a particular category of cultural goods; and they are destined for a wide variety of audiences. Sociologically such translations can be studied from various angles. By analyzing translations, questions can be raised about the way in which cultural goods circulate outside their context of production (Bourdieu 1990), one can try to unravel the relationship between different countries and cultures (Schoneveld 1983), study the role of intermediary centres (Dirkx 1995), decipher the complexities of cross-cultural (mis)understanding (Oz-Salzberger 1995), consider translators as a professional group (Heinich 1984), or analyze the evolution of the system of transnational communication itself, for example by studying the social organization of the market for translation rights, the role of literary agents or the functioning of international book fairs (Sorá 1998).

This article focuses on what is perhaps the most general issue in the sociology of translation: the translation of books considered as an international system. The objective is to present a structural analysis of the international flows of translated books, and to demonstrate why such an analysis is indispensable for understanding the actual translation process. Two more specific questions are central in this respect. How can one account for the uneven flows of book translations between various language groups? And how can one explain the varying role of translations within different language groups? In proposing an answer to both questions, the various activities involved are considered to be interdependent and are therefore best understood as constituting an international or even a world-system. The analysis of this world-system, and the position which various language groups occupy within it, is a precondition for understanding the role of translations in specific local or national contexts. The significance of translations within language groups, for example, is shown to depend primarily on the position of the language within the international system.

This emerging world-system of translation, however, does not quite correspond to the predominant view in world-systems theory. Transnational cultural exchange is not simply the reflection of the structural contradictions in the world economy, as leading proponents of world-systems theory have maintained (for example, Wallerstein 1991). Cultural exchanges have a dynamic of their own which is based on a certain autonomy vis-à-vis the constraints of the world market. Instead of conceiving the cultural realm as merely derivative of global economic structures, it is more fruitful to view transnational cultural exchange as a relatively autonomous sphere, as an international arena with economic, political and symbolic dimensions. This specific constellation, itself part of broader structures, is best conceived as a transnational cultural field, in Pierre Bourdieu's sense, or as an emerging cultural world-system in Abram de Swaan's term (de Swaan 1995). Such a view avoids both the economism of certain varieties of world-systems theory and the culturalism which tends to prevail in cultural studies.[4]

Within this general orientation, I argue that the dynamics of the international translation system is based on a core-periphery structure and outline some of the main consequences of such a model for the understanding of translation practices. In the final part of the article the limits of the general model proposed will be discussed, together with suggestions on how it may be developed and further refined.

The international system of translation

As the basic units of the world-system of translation are language groups, the object of analysis is the structure of the translation flows between these language groups. Language groups do not always coincide with nation states: some of the more central languages – English, German, French, Spanish – have a supranational character. The flow of book translations between these language groups can be analyzed by using book statistics, which regularly include figures for translations. In relying on these figures, however, a great deal of caution is required. Contrary to the normal primary use of official statistics, the statistical material itself has to be critically examined before it can be used.

International translation statistics have been produced since the 1930s. The Institute for Intellectual Collaboration, which formed a part of the League of Nations, started during the interwar years with annual publications about translated books, the *Index translationum* (1932–40). The activity was part of the initiatives after the First World War to promote international collaboration and mutual understanding between nations. After the Second World War, Unesco resumed publication of the translation statistics; they have been published in the Unesco series of *Statistical Yearbooks* ever since. A closer look at these statistics reveals that they are not very reliable. The most obvious problem is one of definition. What is considered to be a 'book' or a 'title' varies from country to country. Certain publications qualify as a 'title' or a 'book' in one country, whereas they are considered to belong to the 'grey' literature in other countries and are therefore eliminated from official book statistics. Such is the case for doctoral dissertations, school books, governmental, parliamentary and administrative documents, and annual reports from enterprises. When it is reported that 21 percent of the published books in Spain in 1982 were translations, this percentage does not have the same meaning in other countries. Rigorous comparisons between translation ratios are therefore impossible on the basis of the Unesco figures.

When analyzing the Unesco statistics for one country alone, precisely in order to avoid such definition problems, it turns out, furthermore, that they exhibit great fluctuations over the years. According to the Unesco figures, 14 percent of the published books in the Netherlands were translations in 1979, a percentage which has risen to 34 percent five years later. Such a fluctuation is highly improbable and it does not correspond with the data provided by the Dutch agency, the *Stichting Speurwerk*, which produces the national book statistics for the Netherlands. Their figures indicate that the percentage of translations in national book production is more regular, varying between 22 percent and 25 percent between 1979 and 1984 (Heilbron 1995). The Unesco data are therefore not very reliable: it remains unclear to what extent they are actually comparable, and even for single countries they exhibit very improbable fluctuations. Unfortunately, these figures are the only international data which are readily available. I will therefore use some of them, but merely in an indicative manner to highlight structural patterns. I will refrain from giving any tables and breakdowns in categories and sub-categories of books, because in the form in which they are usually published they suggest a degree of accuracy which is misleading if not unfounded.

If one cautiously combines the international translation statistics with some of the more reliable national data and with what is known from several case studies, a coherent model can be constructed of the structural dynamics of the international translation system. I will outline somewhat schematically its main properties and illustrate their significance for understanding translation practices.

A hierarchical structure

The international translation system is, first and foremost, a hierarchical structure, with central, semi-peripheral and peripheral languages. Using a simple definition of centrality, one can say that a language is more central in the world-system of translation when it has a large share in the total number of translated books worldwide. The international figures available unambiguously indicate that English is by far the most central language in the international translation system. More than 40 percent of all the translated books worldwide around 1980 were translated from English (Curwen 1986:21, Venuti 1995:14). Over the years, from 1960 to about 1987, this percentage seems to have gone up, despite the fact that the percentage of English books in the total number of books worldwide has decreased (Mélitz 1998:36–37). On the European continent the position of English is even more predominant, with about 50–70 percent of published translations being undertaken from English.[5]

Following the ranking downwards, three languages also have a central role, although their share is significantly smaller than that of English: French, German and Russian. Each of these languages had a proportion somewhere between 10 percent and 12 percent of the international market for translations around 1980. It follows from these figures that three-quarters of the total number of translated books worldwide were translated from four languages only. The international translation system is thus marked by a very uneven distribution and is firmly dominated by English.

After these central languages, with English in a kind a hyper-central role, approximately six languages have a semi-peripheral role, to use Immanuel Wallerstein's terminology, each with a proportion of 1–3 percent of the total number of translated books. In 1978, for example, these languages were: Spanish, Italian, Danish, Swedish, Polish and Czech.[6] These semi-peripheral languages, however, cannot be separated very clearly from the peripheral ones. Contrary to the distinctions between hyper-central, central and semi-peripheral, which are relatively clear cut, the differences between semi-peripheral and peripheral languages are far more gradual. One might say provisionally and for analytical purposes that all languages with a share of less than one percent of the world market occupy a peripheral position in the international translation system. Among these peripheral languages, then, are Chinese, Japanese, Arabic and Portuguese, each representing a very large number of speakers, yet occupying a peripheral position in the translation system. The size of language groups is clearly not decisive for their degree of centrality in the translation system.

A dynamic constellation

But the structure of the international translation system is obviously not a static but a dynamic constellation. The position of language groups changes over time, central languages may lose something of their share, more peripheral languages can improve their positions in the international ranking. The translation system is a historical system, marked by a specific genesis and minor and major transformations over time. The major changes are long-term processes. When considering the relations between English, French and German, for example, one observes that both the hegemony of English and the relative decline of French have a long history. French was the most central modern language in early modern Europe, more important than English or German. The first major change in the constellation occurred at the end of the eighteenth century. For geo-political and geo-cultural reasons, French lost some of its centrality, as is indicated in the translation statistics for the Netherlands. The proportion of books translated from French declined fairly rapidly during the last decades of the eighteenth and the beginning of the nineteenth century (Korpel 1992). German especially profited from the French decline; English also gained but the growing share of translations from English was a relatively slow process for quite some time. The breakthrough of English probably occurred only after the Second World War, when the hegemony of the US gave English a decisive advantage over its main rivals.[7]

Changes in the international position of languages do not generally occur abruptly. They require a cultural reorientation which takes at least a change of generation, and often more than that. Changes in the position of languages and language groups occur suddenly only if the position of a language depends closely on the political power of a régime. The central position of Russian, for example, which is clear from the Unesco statistics for the 1980s, will undoubtedly have declined rapidly since 1989. Its predominant role in the system of international translations was based on the domination of the Soviet Union over Eastern Europe, implying obligatory and quasi-obligatory translations in nearly all fields, not merely those which were bound to the Marxist–Leninist orthodoxy. Since the fall of the Soviet empire, the use of

Russian has declined sharply in Eastern Europe, just as, undoubtedly, translations from Russian have.

The consequences of centrality

Distinguishing languages by their degree of centrality not only implies that translations flow more from the core to the periphery than the other way around, but also that the communication between peripheral groups often passes through a centre. What is translated from one peripheral language into the other depends on what is translated from these peripheral languages into the central languages. In other words, the more central a language is in the translation system, the more it has the capacity to function as an intermediary or vehicular language, that is as a means of communication between language groups which are themselves peripheral or semi-peripheral.

The role of French in early modern Europe is a case in point. Given the central position of French in European culture, not only French books but also translations into French attracted special attention from authors, translators and publishers. French translations were often retranslated into other languages. Although known as the *belles infidèles*, unfaithful adaptations to indigenous norms of elegance and clarity, French translations were nevertheless commonly retranslated into other languages. The most widely translated Spanish authors, Cervantes and Gracián, were translated into German from their French translations. English philosophers were translated into Italian on the basis of their French rather than their English editions, and English literature appeared in German most often while being translated from the French (Blassneck 1934, Von Stackelberg 1984, Graeber, 1991). The retranslation of French translations, which was common practice during the seventeenth and eighteenth centuries, fell into disrepute at the end of the old régime, when nationalism became a political and cultural force. German and English literature gained wider recognition and translations into French lost their exemplary role.

The retranslation of translations, indirect or second-hand translation, has become much less common. To a certain extent, however, the phenomenon persists. Even when the translations themselves are far more often made directly from the original language, the decision to publish a translation from a peripheral language still depends on the existence of a translation in a central language. Literary translations from Spanish into Dutch after the Second World War, for example, were nearly always preceded by their translation into one of the central languages. This was particularly the case for the most prominent authors (Borges, Cortázar, García Márquez, Vargas Llosa), who were all translated into French or English before being published in Dutch (Steenmeijer 1989). Although these books were translated from Spanish, many signs indicated that the English or French translation had actually served as the example. The choice of the title, the text on the cover, the quoted praise from reviews, all revealed the exemplary role of the English or French translation.

There were only a few cases in which Dutch publishers published a translation before their English or French counterparts. But they paradoxically confirm the dominant role of central languages. Not only were these translated authors 'minor' writers, who were discovered by Dutch specialists, but their translations into Dutch were not well received, either by the critics or by the public. They illustrate, *a contrario*, that peripheral and semi-peripheral language groups tend to follow the example of the international centres, including books, etc., that are imported into the centres.

Much of the international communication about books works in this manner and is dependent on the role of the leading centres of the international system. Once a book is translated into a central language by an authoritative publisher, it immediately catches the attention of publishers in other parts of the globe. The simple fact that an American or English publisher will publish an author from a semi-peripheral language is used extensively by the original publisher, because it is the best recommendation for publishers elsewhere to acquire the translation rights. The international recognition of Dutch literature is a good example of the leading role of literary centres in the translation business.

Translations from Dutch and Flemish have been made for centuries. Although a few literary figures in the sixteenth and seventeenth centuries seem to have had a certain international renown, none of them entered the canon of world literature (Schenkeveld 1991). In the eighteenth and nineteenth centuries very few books were translated from Dutch, and it was only from the end of the nineteenth century onwards, following the European recognition of Russian and Scandinavian literature, that the number of books translated from Dutch started to rise. It increased more or less regularly, with a total number of approximately 500 or 600 titles per year since the 1960s.[8]

Despite the relatively steady growth in the number of translations during the twentieth century, Dutch literature has remained largely unknown. Until recently not a single Dutch writer was internationally acknowledged as a major literary figure. Financial support and sustained translation efforts proved insufficient, and the lack of literary recognition outside the Netherlands seemed an inescapable fate (van Noesel and Janssen 1985, Vanderauwera 1985, Paul 1990). The lack of success was attributed to the doubtful quality of the translations, to the fact that they were published by small and often marginal publishing houses, and to the virtual absence of good translators, who would not only produce proper translations, but who could also inform publishers, write reviews and train future translators.

The change started during the 1980s when a few Dutch authors were published by well-established literary publishers; some of the translators won literary prizes.[9] The emerging interest was not restricted to a single country; the breakthrough occurred in Germany, and from there spread to other literary centres as well as to more peripheral language groups. Compared with other centres in the international translation system, German publishers were best prepared for Dutch authors, since Germany was the only country with a central position which had a tradition of translating Dutch literature and incorporating it into a national cultural strategy. Since the end of the Napoleonic wars, Germanists had come to consider the Low Countries as a cultural province of Germanic culture, and as a minor but not irrelevant ally against French civilization (Kloos 1992). Dutch and Flemish were perceived as a kind of *Platt-Deutsch* and popular novels especially were translated into German to meet the rising demand.

Apart from popular writers, some of the more established literary figures were also translated, but their role remained a very minor one. It was only in the 1980s that leading German publishers started to publish translations of major Dutch writers: Suhrkamp published Cees Nooteboom, Klett-Cotta Hugo Claus and Hanser Harry Mulisch. Their books were favourably received by literary critics and some sold quite well. More translations followed and German critics acclaimed Cees Nooteboom, in particular, as an outstanding European writer. When in 1993 the Netherlands was the focus of the international book fair at Frankfurt, the conditions were favourable for the German recognition to snowball. Since then the number of translated Dutch authors has substantially increased, as has the number of languages in which their work is translated.

The Dutch case illustrates the essential role of prominent cultural centres in the international diffusion of literatures from the semi-periphery. International cultural centres are not only interested in the diffusion of their own goods, they also have a vested interest in transit trade and the benefits this offers. Symbolic and economic transit profits are an essential component of the working of the international cultural system.

The example of Dutch literature also shows that dependency on the international centres works the other way around. Once a peripheral literature has had some degree of international recognition, the recognition abroad will contribute to and may indeed interfere with indigenous reputations. In the Netherlands it was common to speak of the 'big three' of postwar Dutch literature: Willem Frederik Hermans, Gerard Reve and Harry Mulisch. Some would add a fourth, Hugo Claus. For decades their reputation was not seriously threatened by anyone, not even by Hella Haasse and Nooteboom. But since Haasse and Nooteboom enjoy a growing international fame, whereas Hermans and Reve do not, the indigenous canon is undermined. Especially in small countries, the process of canonization is increasingly affected by the international market place.

Centrality and variety

The more central a language is in the international translation system, the more types of books are translated from this language. Book statistics in the Netherlands distinguish 33 categories of books, ranging from 'religion' and 'law' to 'prose' and 'history'. Only the translations from the most central language, English, are represented in all 33 categories. Translations from German are found in 28 categories, translations from French in 22 categories, from Italian in 10 categories, etc. Centrality, in other words, implies variety. Since the small number of books translated from peripheral languages is generally concentrated in very few categories, the opposite also holds true: book translations from peripheral languages lack the variety that increases with the degree of centrality.

The limits of monopolization

Since the international translation system is so firmly dominated by one hyper-central language, one might presume that translations from other languages will decrease, leading to a virtual monopoly for translations from English. Jacques Mélitz has explicitly suggested such a possibility in his economic model of the world book market: 'If the market in one particular language is sufficiently larger than any other, the total lack of technical barriers to diffusion can lead to the exclusive translation of imaginative works from that particular language into the rest' (Mélitz 1998).

The available statistics for the Netherlands do not confirm Mélitz's hypothesis. In fact they suggest a different pattern, which needs to be checked for other countries. As far as the Netherlands is concerned, the enormous growth of translations from English has not diminished the translations from other languages; it has essentially diminished the role of indigenous books. In order to perceive this effect the usual mode of calculating proportions has to be revised. The proportion of translations from a certain language is commonly calculated only as a percentage of the total number of translations. It is in many ways more accurate, however, to calculate the percentage of translations from a certain language as a proportion of the total number of books published. In that way book production in the indigenous language becomes part of the competition. And it is possible, indeed, that translations from English have not replaced translations from other foreign languages but mainly indigenous books. That, at least, has been the case for the Netherlands, where translations from English increased from 2 percent to 17 percent of total book production during the years 1946–90. In the same period translations from German increased from 1.4 percent to 4.3 percent, translations from French from 0.6 percent to 2.2 percent, and translations from 'other languages' from 1.2 percent to 2.7 percent (Heilbron 1995). Thus although English has profited far more from the growth of translations than any other foreign language, these other languages have also increased their share in national book production.

The levels of cultural importation

The structure of the world-system of translation also determines the level of importation. The more central a language is in the international translation system, the smaller the proportion of translations into this language. The most central languages tend to have the lowest proportion of translations in their own book production. In the UK and the US less than 5 percent of all published books are translations, a figure that has hardly changed since 1945. In France and Germany, the proportion of translations is consistently higher, fluctuating between 10 percent and 12 percent of national book production during the postwar period. In Italy and Spain the relative weight of translation is more important, at approximately 12–20 percent. In countries with more peripheral languages like Sweden and the Netherlands, 25 percent of all published books consist of translations, and in Greece the proportion amounts to more than 40 percent.

These figures, although incomplete and at best indicative, clearly suggest an inverse relationship between the centrality of a language in the international translation system and the proportion of translations in national book production. The more central the cultural production of a country is, the more it serves as an example to other countries, and the less it is itself concerned with the cultural production from other countries. Instead of assuming that translations 'normally' occupy a marginal position (Even-Zohar 1990:50), it is far more accurate to say that their role varies significantly, and that the variation depends on the degree of centrality in the international translation system. The core of an international cultural system has the highest status; it is carefully observed, followed and emulated, and at the same time it is much less oriented towards products and producers from outside the centres.

The same can be observed in international exchange among the sciences. As indicated by citation patterns, scientific research in the US is the most central and most prestigious part of the scientific world-system. But scientific production in the US is also characterized by the lowest percentage of foreign references, foreign co-authors and publications abroad. The percentages of foreign references in scientific articles and foreign publications in US citations are both about 25 percent. In Japan and the European countries the figure lies somewhere between 40 percent and 71 percent; for the developing countries it varies between 70 percent and 92 percent (Schott 1991). Instead of an equilibrium between import and export, the reality of transnational exchange is a process of uneven exchange. For every book that is translated from Dutch, for example, there are six books translated into Dutch. Imbalances of this kind characterize the very structure of transnational exchange.

In order to understand the structure of the international flows there is no need to invoke the peculiarities of national cultural traditions. Comparing the proportion of 10–12 percent translations in France, for example, with the significantly higher percentage for Sweden, one might deplore the relative closure of French culture. Some even consider this to be a specific feature of French culture. Wasn't Chauvin a Frenchman? Comparing the French with the UK's much lower percentage of translations, one might be equally tempted to invoke the opposite argument, namely that it testifies to the very richness of the French cultural tradition. The traditionally high esteem for culture then appears as being reflected in a high level of translations.

Neither one of these arguments is necessary for explaining the level of cultural importation. The proportion of translations in France corresponds to the international position of French in the world-system of translation, and is perfectly comparable with the role of German and the proportion of translations in Germany. As argued above, it is not so much the national tradition, but rather the international position of national cultures, which determines the level of cultural importation.

Towards a sociology of translation

The sociology of translation may well become a new branch of the sociology of culture and a promising domain for the study of the cultural world-system. As a research field it can draw on social science research on culture, international exchange and globalization, as well as on a variety of publications in the field of translation studies. Some of the most interesting work in translation studies has been inspired by polysystem theory. Polysystem theorists have rightly shifted the analytical focus from an exclusive concern with the source text to the more broadly conceived target culture. But to understand the role of translations in a target culture, it is by no means sufficient to analyze them as being part of the literary system of the target culture. It is essential, as I have tried to show, to consider target cultures as a part of an international system, of a global constellation of language groups and of national or supranational cultures.

To develop and refine the approach outlined, two directions seem appropriate. On the one hand, numerous questions may be raised about the international cultural system, its genesis and its actual functioning. The analysis of the international translation system can benefit from comparisons with other transnational systems and from the continuing debate about globalization. On the other hand, there are questions to be raised about the significance of such an international system for the understanding of specific translation practices. There is obviously no simple and immediate transition from analyzing a world-system to analyzing a national publishing industry or particular translation strategies. The world-system is concerned with the most general set of conditions, and for a more complete survey, it is necessary to link these conditions to the social dynamics of the publishing business and its different segments.

In certain categories of books, for example, translations are virtually absent, in others they have a major role. In what is regularly the largest category of books, schoolbooks, translations have practically no role whatsoever. The market for schoolbooks is in a way protected, not so much by economic barriers, but by national regulations and control agencies. Other market segments are more open: in the categories of prose and children's books translations have a major and sometimes predominant role and there are typically no official instances and far fewer regulatory institutions. The social organization of the market is thus a crucial dimension for assessing the role of translations, and the sociology of markets is very relevant (Swedberg 1994). A more complete sociological analysis may therefore seek to connect the dynamics of the international translation system with the actual working of the book market and its various segments.

Notes

1   In the remarkable project directed by Roger Chartier and Henri-Jean Martin (1982–86) on the French book trade, which contains more than 3000 pages, there is not a single chapter on translations or translators. Literary history also tends to ignore translations since it is commonly conceived as national history. The only literary domains in which translations are a regular part of the research agenda are reception studies and comparative literature. In both fields, however, the scope of the work is generally restricted to canonical literary works.

2   For historical texts on translation, see the anthologies of Lefevere (1992b) and Robinson (1997b). Historical overviews are presented in Ballard (1992), Delisle and Woodsworth (1995), Kelly (1979), Rener (1989), Steiner (1975) and Van Hoof (1991).

3   Translation studies is a recent, interdisciplinary field which emerged in the 1970s and 1980s in a few small countries (Belgium, Israel, the Netherlands). It was based on attempts to unite different elements from previous approaches into a single framework. The pioneering statement was given by James S. Holmes, an American translator living in Amsterdam, at the International Congress of Applied Linguistics in 1972. The full text of his paper, 'The Name and Nature of Translation Studies' (1972), existed only as a mimeographed pre-publication for 15 years. When it was eventually included in the posthumous collection of Holmes' papers (Holmes 1988:67–80), translation studies were in the process of gaining some institutional recognition. For overviews of the field and its history see Gentzler (1993) and Baker (1998).

4   In the literature on cultural globalization, the work of Ulf Hannerz is particularly illuminating (Hannerz 1992, 1996). For an interesting comparison see the analysis of the international system of modern sports (Van Bottenburg 1994).

5   Besides the figures reproduced in Curwen (1986), Barret-Ducrocq (1992), Venuti (1995) and Mélitz (1998), I have consulted the Unesco *Statistical Yearbooks* for 1965–85.

6   This list, based on the Unesco figures for 1978, is somewhat different from the grouping of Venuti (1995), who has taken the Scandinavian languages, as well as Greek and Latin, together.

7   Book translations from English have an ever growing share in the number of books published in the Netherlands. In 1946, 39 percent of all translated books were translations from English; in 1990 the proportion was up to 65 percent (Heilbron 1995).

8   These approximate figures are based on the bibliography of translations from Dutch which is produced by the Royal Libraries of The Hague and Brussels. The absolute numbers are less significant than the trend they indicate (see Heilbron 1995).

9   Important translation prizes were awarded to Philippe Noble for his French translation of E. Du Perron's *Le pays d'origine* (1980) and to Adrienne Dixon for her translation of *Rituals* (1983) by Cees Nooteboom.

PART 8

The making of literary traditions

Chapter 18

Samah Selim

PHAROAH'S REVENGE: TRANSLATION, LITERARY HISTORY AND COLONIAL AMBIVALENCE

EDITOR'S INTRODUCTION

> The act of translation in the colonial context inevitably performs an ambivalent and simultaneous gesture of appropriation, collusion and critique on a variety of levels — from the purely formal to the broadly historical — and therefore far from being a straightforward or naïve act of linguistic transfer, translation typically rewrites the web of discourses, codes and conventions of the literary text in keeping with the conflictual and 'intensely social nature' of its cultural histories.

SELIM USES TRANSLATION AS A CRITICAL category with which to question normative European models of literary history. Literary history, she argues, is a powerful instrument enlisted by the nation state in its attempt to claim legitimacy and authenticity, and as such partakes of and contributes to the various political and discursive practices that have shaped the relationship between Europe and its others in modernity. Thus, for example, Arabic literature was for a long time 'characterized primarily in terms of historical collapse and critical dystopia', such that literary modernity was understood as a renaissance in which Arabs attempted, with limited success, to appropriate and copy European modes and forms; centuries of literary production in the Arab World, from thirteenth-century Baghdad to nineteenth-century Beirut, were simply rendered invisible in this process, in both Western *and* Arab literary histories. Also obscured, or denigrated, in this perspective was a thriving marketplace of popular fiction in Egypt in the early twentieth century. Selim demonstrates that translation was 'the major trope' employed to effect this erasure. Literary histories dismiss pre-*bildungsroman* fiction as a deeply flawed history of translation, one in which valued concepts of equivalence and purity were disregarded. One consequence is that a rich corpus of popular fiction came to be 'contained within the stabilizing and minor category of "translation"'.

Selim outlines an alternative model of the practice of writing (and reading) outside of the dominant nineteenth-century Romantic tradition by foregrounding translation as a key process in the creation and diffusion of texts, genres and literary schools. She does so by examining an

Arabic translation published in Cairo in 1906 of *Pharos the Egyptian*, a bestselling Edwardian novel about ancient Egypt, situating the novel in both its British and local contexts in order to show how the conservative discourse of degeneration in Edwardian Britain both overlapped and collided with nationalist, reformist discourses in turn-of-the-century Egypt. Rather than focus on colonial difference and rigid dichotomies, she explores the community of social interests across the imperial divide, and in so doing offers us a glimpse into the ambivalent representations that lie at the heart of literary histories and that continue to structure the way we think about cultural identities.

Follow-up questions for discussion

● In her critique of Moretti's work, Kristal (2002:73–74) argues 'in favour of a view of world literature in which the novel is not necessarily the privileged genre for understanding literary developments of social importance in the periphery; in which the West does not have a monopoly over the creation of forms that count; in which themes and forms can move in several directions—from the centre to the periphery, from the periphery to the centre, from one periphery to another, while some original forms of consequence may not move much at all; and in which strategies of transfer in any direction may involve rejections, swerves, as well as transformations of various kinds, even from one genre to another'. Consider this statement critically in light of Selim's critique of modernity as well as Heilbron's model of translation flows (this volume).

● Beecroft (2008:88) argues that models of world literature such as those elaborated by Casanova and Moretti (see Moretti 2000, 2003) have 'the unintended effect of re-inscribing a hegemonic cultural centre, even as their avowed desire is to globalize literary studies'. How might studies such as Selim's contribute to questioning and destablizing this 'hegemonic cultural centre'?

● Rastegar's work on the interaction between Persian and Arabic literature through translation during the nineteenth century overlaps with but departs from Selim's study in significant respects. In particular, he sets out to demonstrate that in the case of Persia, 'modernity in the literary or other cultural fields emerged through multiple intercultural interactions and diverse processes of circulation' (2007:374); in other words, modernity does not have to flow from the West to the East but can also evolve out of East-East interaction. Consider how studies of literary and other forms of translation might develop and extend this insight, not only in the context of the Arab World or Persia, but in relation to the West's many others.

Recommended further reading

Friedman, Susan Stanford (2006) 'Periodizing Modernism: Postcolonial Modernities and the Space/Time Borders of Modernist Studies', *Modernism/Modernity* 13(3): 425–43.

Kristal, Efraín (2002) 'Considering Coldly – A Response to Franco Moretti', *New Left Review* 15 (May-June): 61–74.

Lefevere, André (1992) *Translation, Rewriting and the Manipulation of Literary Fame*, London & New York: Routledge.

Rastegar, Kamran (2007) 'Literary Modernity between Arabic and Persian Prose: Jurji Zaydan's *Riwayat* in Persian Translation', *Comparative Critical Studies* 4(3): 359–78.

Selim, Samah (2004b) 'The *Nahda,* Popular Fiction and the Politics of Translation', *MIT Electronic Journal of Middle East Studies* 4: 70–89.

IT IS BY NOW GENERALLY ACCEPTED that the writing of literary history is – like history *tout court* – teleologically driven and politically useful, serving as it most often does to prop up the cultural claims of a particular language, ethnic group or national hegemony; as Hutcheon argues, 'literary histories not only create continuities, but in the process, confer legitimacy' (2002:7). It might even be argued that literary history is one of the most powerful vehicles by which the nation state projects its legitimacy and authenticity within and beyond its own borders, and as such, it has played – and continues to play – a central role in the foundation and reproduction of the socio-political structures of modernity, including those of imperialism. Literary history is therefore not innocent of the broader political and discursive practices that have shaped the relationship between Europe and its others in modernity.[1] Walter Mignolo has called this relationship 'the colonial difference': 'the outside that is declared as such from the inside' (2002:156). For Mignolo, the colonial difference is both a process and a place: the process of Western discursive self-formation, and the place of its other; of minority, difference and negation; the place where History becomes history and Literature becomes literature (*ibid.*:158).

For scholars working in Arabic literature, some kind of cognizance of the colonial difference has become unavoidable, particularly because of the way in which it structures the field as a whole. The discipline of English Literature, for example, constructs its subject as an integrated and uninterrupted tradition with its own internal historical and formal logic, from *Beowulf* to Virginia Wolf. On the other hand, until quite recently, Arabic literature was characterized primarily in terms of historical collapse and critical dystopia. The Anglo-European philological tradition read classical and early medieval Arabic literature in terms of a larger narrative of rise and fall, or creeping decadence. Literary modernity was then constructed as a renaissance that appropriated and copied – usually imperfectly – European modes and forms. The six-odd centuries in between decline and renaissance – from thirteenth-century Baghdad to nineteenth-century Beirut – were thereby rendered largely invisible.

The 1980s inaugurated a poststructuralist onslaught against the discipline itself: literary history was declared 'almost moribund' (Hutcheon 2002:4) because of its seemingly inescapable teleological bent and its inevitable penchant for constructing and naturalizing various 'fictions of power'. Feminist and postcolonial literary histories were tarred with the same brush, reproducing as they did the same fiction of origins and the same genealogical mechanisms as their patriarchal and imperial counterparts. While Linda Hutcheon has made a convincing argument that the way we reflect about the past has direct bearing on how we act in the present, and that therefore, what she calls the 'interventionist strategies' of minority scholars remain an important political tool for historians of literature (*ibid.*:6–8), my intention in what follows is not to recuperate a marginalized tradition or to reconstruct a new canon for the Arabic novel. Rather, this paper will attempt to sketch out an alternate model of the practice of writing (and reading) outside of the dominant but historically contingent nineteenth-century Romantic tradition by foregrounding translation as a key process in the creation and diffusion of texts, genres and literary schools – in other words, as a central axis of comparative literary history. As I hope to show, this is one way to climb out of the neo-Hegelian teleologies of cultural praxis that continue to shape the way we understand the movements of modernity.

While the first part of the paper will outline some of the key questions involved in this 'translational turn' in literary history, the second part will focus on a specific Arabic translation published in Cairo in 1906 of *Pharos the Egyptian*, a bestselling Edwardian novel about ancient Egypt. I will situate the novel in both its British and local contexts in order to show how the conservative discourse of degeneration in Edwardian Britain both overlapped and collided with nationalist, reformist discourses in turn-of-the-century Egypt.[2] In a way then, the paper suggests a critique of 'the colonial difference' in literary history, as well as a cartography of the ambivalent historical and textual territories of literary rewritings from a post-Romantic point of view.

Translation and literary history

Building on the earlier work of Gideon Toury and Even-Zohar in polysystems theory, Susan Bassnett and André Lefevere argued for a cultural turn in translation studies in the 1990s. Their claim was that translation, like all writing, is never transparent: 'There is always a context in which the translation takes place, always a history from which a text emerges and into which a text is transposed' (Lefevere and Bassnett 1990:11). Translation is always then doubly contextualized, since the text has a place in two cultures and two literary systems. The elusive search for some kind of normative equivalence between free-floating source texts and target texts which had characterized much of modern translation theory in the West had produced a loaded rhetoric of possession and value to describe the translated text – 'fidelity' versus 'treachery', 'bastardization', 'usurpation' and so forth.[3]

More recently, scholars have begun to interrogate the binary categories of 'translation' and 'original' institutionalized in the nineteenth century along with the very discipline of national literature via German Romanticism. The simultaneity of these two processes is important. Nation-building, essentialist concepts of national culture and the reification of solitary, unique genius – of originals versus copies – were all part of the way in which the hierarchies of colonial modernity were constructed and projected both inside and outside Europe. Lefevere (1990:24) explains that '[l]iterary histories, as they have been written until recently, have had little time for translations, since for the literary historian, translation has had to do with 'language' only, not with literature – another pernicious outgrowth of the 'monolinguization' of literary history by Romantic historiographers intent on creating 'national' literatures preferably as uncontaminated as possible by foreign influences'.

Before the eighteenth century (and I may venture to add, in all the major literary traditions), originality was not in and of itself considered an aesthetic value in relation to literary production. Instead, imitation, free adaptation and commentary were variously privileged in the circulation of poetic forms. Romanticism changed all this however. The 'spirit' of a nation was understood by Herder and Schlegel to be reflected in its language and, in turn, in the original literary text, understood as an organic and self-contained form. Nonetheless, German Romanticism used translation as a strategic tool for dismantling the dominance of French models and mediations in its eighteenth-century literary culture and directly accumulating world literature in the German language. At the same time, the institutionalization of north European national literatures and genres was being assimilated to colonial epistemologies and projected outwards to the rest of the world as a series of universal categories. This is how European literary history and literary culture as a whole (mainly, those of France, England and Germany) became the 'original' while the literary history and culture of the exterior of Europe was reduced to the status of copy.

Since translation is the key trope through which this narrative of power operates, translation studies is a useful site from which to launch critical studies of culture and the cultural discourses that have structured colonial modernity. Translation has been the most basic, if largely invisible, mechanism in the production and circulation of new genres, devices and motifs across modern literary cultures. Translations of classical Greek and Latin texts produced major transformations in European vernaculars and poetics from the sixteenth century onwards, for example. The classical Arabic *maqamah* was transformed by the Spanish Picaresque and led to the emergence of seventeenth- and eighteenth-century novelistic forms in France and England through translation. Anglo-American imagism was directly shaped by Ezra Pound's translations of East Asian poetic forms like the Japanese Haiku. The same can be argued for the movement of South American magical realism into European postmodernisms.[4]

The examples multiply once we take into account the entire nexus of texts that make up a literary polysystem, and not just its high cultural forms. Popular literature has historically circulated through a variety of non-normative techniques of translation, including anonymous rewritings, forgeries and pseudotranslations. The eighteenth-century French *conte* was transformed by Antoine Galland's adaptation of the *Thousand and One Nights* (1704–1717), and English gothic was initiated by Horace Walpole's pseudotranslation, *The Castle of Otranto* (1764). The nineteenth and early twentieth centuries witnessed the spread, through an onslaught of semi-anonymous adaptations and pseudotranslations, of the detective fiction genre, from England to the rest of Europe, Latin America, the Middle and Far East, transforming narrative techniques and literary motifs along the way (Varende 2000). These are just a few examples of the absolute centrality of translation in literary history in and beyond Europe. But the colonial difference functions partly by repressing these movements and by constructing translation instead as a metaphor for its civilizing mission.

In his later work, André Lefevere arrives at the conclusion that translation is itself a form of rewriting and that therefore all texts are essentially rewritings or refractions of other texts. Most people, he argues, never even come into direct contact with the originals of the literary canon, but rather come to know them through the generic 'translations' that alone guarantee their survival: abridgements, anthologies, commentaries and film adaptations for example (Lefevere and Bassnett 1990:10). The colonial difference collapses under the force of this perspective. Arguments about original and copy, fidelity and betrayal become irrelevant for the translation historian. What matters are the dialogical chains of relationships constructed between source text and target text and their respective social, historical and literary contexts.

Southern intellectuals – particularly South American ones – were already grappling with these issues from the beginning of the twentieth century at least. In Brazil, the *Antropophagia* movement was a direct response to the problem of translation as a colonial régime of power. Haroldo de Campos, Fernando Ortiz and Octavio Paz' various poetics of 'transcreation' and 'transculturation' emerged from this earlier moment in the 1920s. In his theory of 'mistranslation', Jorge Luis Borges makes visible the invisible operations historically initiated by translation in all literary cultures. He insists that since origins are always unstable, originality is not an aesthetic value in and of itself. Instead, he emphasizes 'the importance of the displacements that occur when one goes from an original to a translation, and how these displacements create the potential for new and unexpected meanings' (Waisman 2005:65). I am particularly interested here in his notion of the text as a 'movable event'; a kind of rough draft that circulates, both diachronically and synchronically, and constantly mutates along the way, depending on a variety of contingent rewritings and rereadings. Equally important is Lawrence Venuti's insight into the political nature of translation – what he calls its 'scandalous' status. On the one hand, translation régimes uphold hegemonic cultural and institutional structures; on the other, individual translations can be made to disrupt and challenge these selfsame structures (Venuti 1998b:1). Needless to say, this is a pragmatic position for intellectuals thinking and writing from the so-called margins, from 'the colonial difference'. I want to turn now to one such marginal/central moment in the Arabic context; the modern Nahdah, which was historically also a significant translation moment and which produced, among other things, a series of new literary genres, including the novelistic.

Translation, genre and the literary Nahdah in Egypt

The origins of the Arabic novel are usually located in the Nahdah, understood as that historical moment in the early nineteenth century when Arab intellectuals began to acquire the cultural and scientific knowledge of the West, thereby initiating a modern 'renaissance' that rescues the region from centuries of decadence and stagnation. The story of the Nahdah is closely entwined with the history of the Arabic novel. This history is supposed to begin with the translation, adaptation and imitation of the European novel towards the end of the nineteenth century. In orientalist discourse, the extent to which Arab writers were able to reproduce this idealized European genre became a kind of yardstick with which to measure the progress and value of the Nahdah as a whole. In this respect, European commentators were generally pessimistic. For example, Alexander Hamilton Gibb used modern literature as a way of identifying what he saw as the faultlines in the larger Nahdawi project. Writing on what he called 'neo-Arabic literature' in 1929, Gibb set up the rigid dialectic characteristic of orientalism, irreconcilably pitting 'Western scientific methods' against an 'orthodox Muslim world view' in order to explain the sterility of Arab literary modernity (Gibb 1982).

Translation occupies a curious position in writing in and about this period, because of the way in which it was understood to function as a vehicle of modernity. On the one hand, translation was supposed to help backward Arab societies acquire all kinds of European knowledge. On the other, it was viewed with great suspicion, as a form of destabilizing penetration of supposedly stable national cultures. This ambivalence is most visible in discourses about culture, and especially about literature and translation. To Nahdawi intellectuals, the novel in particular was a very controversial genre, at first, for the same reasons that it had been controversial in Europe – as a morally corrupting and socially dangerous literary form. Later, nationalist intellectuals sublimated these social concerns into an attack that was based on the idea of its 'foreignness' – another cultural instrument of colonialism. It was only much later, somewhere in the late 1920s, that the genre came to be accepted in Arabic after it had been domesticated through the practice of various 'national literature' schools. Realism and the bildungsroman came to be the preferred literary forms of the new bourgeois intelligentsia, while Romance – and therefore the entire corpus of fiction produced in Arabic from the middle of the nineteenth century to the beginnings of the twentieth – was rejected as a decadent and foreign, anti-national literary mode. This is a critical tradition that runs all the way through from social theorist Ahmad Lutfi al-Sayyid at the beginning of the twentieth century to literary scholar Abd al-Muhsin Taha Badr at its end. The thriving fin de siècle marketplace of popular fiction has been largely invisible in Arabic literary history. When it does appear, it is as a sign of the social and cultural decadence that the project of renaissance struggles against.

'Translation' was the major trope through which this erasure was accomplished. In practically all literary histories of the period, pre-bildungsroman fiction is dismissed as a deeply flawed history of translation – a disreputable stage in the modernization of Arabic literature. Good translation was a jealously guarded literary zone that reproduced European Romantic concepts of equivalence in order to guarantee the purity of its foundations. Bad translation cared nothing for origins and genealogies. It raided, plagiarized and fabricated its sources and invented an entirely new literary syntax that drew on heterogeneous – and indeed, it was supposed, mutually exclusive – narrative languages and frames of reference. A process of displacement thus occurs whereby a rich corpus of fiction is contained within the stabilizing and minor category of 'translation'. The two terms – 'translation' and 'popular fiction' – come to stand for each other, the implication of course being that the popular is itself foreign to national culture.

Pharos the Egyptian appeared in English in 1899, and was translated into Arabic by Muhammad Lutfi Jum'ah in the popular serial Musamarat al-Sha'b (The People's Entertainments) seven years later, in 1906 (Boothby 1899; Jum'ah 1906a, 1906b). Khalil Sadiq, the publisher of The People's Entertainments, billed it as 'the most widely circulating illustrated social fiction weekly in Egypt'. The serial was printed at The People's Press, which was also owned by Sadiq and which published separate book editions of full-length novels, as well as other kinds of material, from manuals of modern French jurisprudence to popular anthologies of classical literature. The serial, which ran from 1904 to 1911, was offered through subscription but also had numerous distribution points in Cairo, as well as in the provinces and as far away as Syria and South America.[5]

Sadiq was keen on casting his literary enterprise as a service to the nation, and he regularly editorialized about the noble and didactic function of novels. On the other hand, Sadiq was also an astute businessman and equally invested in promoting the idea of a thriving marketplace in which literature would circulate as a commodity much like any other. Sadiq resolved the evident tension between these two poles – and tried to forestall his highbrow critics – by constructing a liberal literary discourse based on the ambiguous idea of profit, simultaneously moral, social and economic. He opened the pages of the Entertainments to the most divergent types of texts – translations, adaptations and original works ranging from the complex and stylistically sophisticated to the most slapdash and linguistically handicapped – and all for the price of a penny an issue. The serial started out as a bi-weekly publication featuring one complete novel of around eighty pages per issue. Due to readers' demands however, by its third year it had become a weekly, publishing multi-issue novels of up to 1000 pages each.

The Entertainments was definitely popular in its range of provocative and easily accessible fiction. But it also recruited a group of authors and translators – Muslims, Christians and Jews; native Egyptians and Syrian émigrés – whose professional activities as lawyers, journalists, police officers and civil servants endowed their work with a deeply embedded social knowledge and sometimes also a genuine sense of social commitment. Some young contributors to the serial went on to make names for themselves as bona fide men of letters: Muhammad Lutfi Jum'a, Muhammad Kurd Ali, Muhammad al-Siba'i and Salih Jawdat, for example. Ahmad Shawqi, 'prince of poets', and fiction writers Mahmud Khayrat and Niqula Haddad published original novels in the *Entertainments*. But even the less well-known contributors were prolific and professional writers in the most basic sense of the term. Ahmad Hafedh 'Awad and Niqula Rizqallah were two of these. Both were newspaper editors, the former at *Al-Mu'ayyid* and the latter at *Al-Ahram*. 'Awad published ten novels in the *Entertainments*, including two original works, entitled *Al-Yatim* (The Orphan) and *Al-Hal wal-mal* (Life and Property); Rizqallah published fifteen multi-volume adaptations (of works by Victor Hugo and Alexandre Dumas, among others) and unattributed or falsely attributed adaptations like *Al-Sa'ilah al-hasna'* (The Pretty Beggar) and *Lusus baris* (Thieves of Paris).[6]

Muhammad Lutfi Jum'ah was a lawyer, writer, translator and political activist who was frequently in and out of trouble with both the local and colonial authorities in Egypt.[7] He was an ardent disciple of Muhammad Abduh (a highly influential liberal reformer of the time, whose lectures Jum'ah attended while a student in Tanta and with whom he corresponded until the latter's death in 1905) and was closely associated with the Egyptian political leader Mustafa Kamil and his National Party from 1906 onwards. Born into a modest family in Alexandria in 1886, his education was marked by the syncretic trajectory typical of the period: from the local *Kuttab*,[8] to a private Coptic primary school in Tanta, then to the Khedival School in Cairo and on to the Syrian Protestant College of Beirut, where he spent a year before returning to Cairo to work as a journalist and translator. From 1905 to 1906, he worked as an editor at the newspaper *Al-Dhahir* then joined the editorial staff of *Al-Liwa'* – the organ of Mustafa Kamil's National Party. Like many intellectuals of his generation, Jum'ah pursued postgraduate studies in France. He received his Ph.D. in Law from the University of Lyon in 1911. During these years (1908–1911), he campaigned extensively for Egyptian independence in conferences and parliamentary commissions in Geneva, Brussels and London, and founded two European-based newspapers to that effect: the first, *Sawt al-sha'b* (The Voice of the People), was an Arabic language paper published out of Geneva. The second, *Misr* (Egypt), in English, was published variously in Geneva, Florence, Lyon and London, and continued publication after Jum'ah's return to Egypt in 1912 under the editorial direction of Wilfred Scawen Blunt and Edward Brown (see al-Tamawi 1993, Jum'ah 1991).

Jum'ah's repertoire was vast and remarkably varied. He authored numerous plays, short stories, novellas, essays, scholarly monographs and translations in and of the social sciences, political philosophy and Pharaonic and Islamic history.[9] He is perhaps best remembered today as the author of *Layali al-Ruh al-Ha'ir* (Evenings of a Bewildered Soul, 1912) – a romantic, *maqamah*-like narrative that is often compared by critics to the famous Egyptian poet Hafidh Ibrahim's *Layali Satih* (Satih's Evenings, 1909). Curiously – or perhaps appropriately – his two-part translation of *Pharos the Egyptian* is rarely mentioned in any of the relevant bibliographical sources. In 1906 the function and status of the novel was still a matter of social and moral debate in the Arabic context – this, in spite of the fact that Jum'ah's generation of writers and intellectuals was highly eclectic and open-minded in terms of its disciplinary and generic concerns and interests. The turn of the twentieth century was decidedly a period where the boundaries between genres and disciplines – as between notions of 'high' and 'low' culture – had yet to be established.[10] This is what made it possible for a non-canonical and now largely forgotten periodical like Salim Sarkis' short-lived *Majallat Sarkis* (Sarkis' Magazine, 1905) to publish translations of popular fiction by Sarkis himself as well as by a popular translator of the period like Tanius Abduh alongside poems by the neoclassicist Ahmad Shawqi and the young Romantic Khalil Mutran as well as a regular cultural column by essayist and fiction writer Muhammad al-Muwaylihi. According to Ahmad Tahir Hasanayn, the review gave rise to a literary salon whose members included Salim Sarkis, Khalil Mutran, Tanius Abduh, Muham-mad Kurd Ali, and the journalist and religious reformer Muhammad Rashid Rida (Hasanayn 1983:122–25). On the other hand, *Al-Diya'* (1898–1906), the journal of the prominent neo-classicist poet and lexicographer Ibrahim al-Yaziji, featured adaptations of British detective and crime fiction (twenty-three stories by Arthur Conan Doyle alone) as well as original fiction by Labibah Hashim, among others (*ibid.*:107–108).

Jum'ah's own interests and output reflect this voracious and wide-ranging movement between genres, styles and cultural commitments: from classical Greek to Islamic philosophy, from ancient Egyptian history to Shari'a studies and Quranic exegesis, from vernacular popular fiction to poetic Realism. We might then con-jecture that Jum'ah's translation of *Pharos the Egyptian* has simply gone the way of the hundreds of other titles of popular fiction produced by prominent and less promin-ent writers and intellectuals of the period. Unfortunately so, for it uncovers a window onto a key historical moment in the conflicts and collusions initiated by the colonial encounter, and as such represents an important historical and literary document.

Edwardian anxieties and colonial concerns: 'imperial gothic' and ancient Egypt

Pharos the Egyptian, by bestselling but now largely forgotten Australian author Guy Newell Boothby, belongs to a late Victorian genre variously called by critics Edward-ian Gothic, Trance Gothic, Supernatural Romance or, most commonly, Imperial Gothic. Patrick Brantlinger (1988) has defined the genre of Imperial Gothic as an expression of the deep social anxieties of the late Victorian and Edwardian periods.[11] A fantastic combination of imperialism, scientific materialism and occultism was projected in various ways onto the far reaches of the British Empire, where 'strange gods and unspeakable rites supposedly still had their millions of devotees' (Brantlin-ger *ibid.*:228). Brantlinger identifies the genre's three principal themes as 'individual regression or going native; an invasion of civilization by the forces of barbarism and demonism; and the diminution of opportunities for adventure and heroism in the modern world' (*ibid.*:230). Boothby's *Pharos the Egyptian* belongs to the second thematic category, that of 'invasion fantasy', like other more or less well-known novels of the period, from Bram Stoker's *Dracula* (1897) to H.G. Wells' *War of the Worlds* (1897).

Briefly put, in the invasion fantasy strain of Imperial Gothic, a hostile and implacable alien force threatens to attack, colonize and destroy the very foundations of civilization, primarily understood as being British. In Erskine Childer's *The Riddle of the Sands* (1903) this alien force is Bismarck's Germany; in Stoker's *Dracula* it is the demonic empire of the living dead to be engendered in England by the Count himself, the last of a bloodthirsty and atavistic conquering race. In *Pharos the Egyptian*, it is an immortal ancient Egyptian priest who spreads a deadly plague across Europe. In Rider Haggard's *She* (1887) and Stoker's *The Jewel of Seven Stars* (1903) it is a vengeful or power-hungry Ancient Egyptian queen, bent on destroying democracy and ruling first Britain, then the world.[12]

Invasion fantasy fictions sublimated a group of interconnected ideologies and pseudo-scientific practices that characterized the period. Social Darwinism, criminology, theories of degeneration and the would-be science of eugenics were all articulated around the anxieties provoked by domestic social conflict, rapid urbanization, economic stagnation and the perceived waning of empire. The 'advanced state of rottenness' that George Bernard Shaw identified in Britain in 1889 expressed obsessive ruling-class worries about 'fitness', 'national efficiency' and racial and cultural decadence that characterized the end of the century, and that came to a head in the aftermath of the Boer War (Brantlinger 1988:230; see also Porter 1982, Pick 1996:176–221). 'Outcast London' became the central trope around which these biological theories of decline were articulated, since it was primarily in the industrial metropolis that the concerns and objects of the period were located: 'from cretinism to alcoholism and syphilis, from peasantry to urban working class, *bourgeoisie* to aristocracy, madness to theft, individual to crowd, anarchism to feminism, population decline to population increase' (Pick 1996:15). Scientific theories of degeneration projected anxieties of national decline onto the restive, overworked and underfed masses of urban Britain. The trope of the exponentially self-reproducing mob, the figure of the sickly slum-dweller, sinister immigrant and raving feminist or anarchist all inspired various responses of discovery and control, most notably the new sciences of criminology and eugenics – themselves diffused through translations of scientific research across nineteenth-century Germany, France, Italy and Britain. The disenchanted new-liberal perception of democracy, mass society and urban life that shaped this moment destabilized the British establishment's sense of imperial mission and the very 'viability of the ideology of a cohesive and unified ruling race' (ibid.:184). Invasion fictions played on these anxieties, but also largely served to exorcise them, and to end with the comforting re-assertion of dominant domestic and political values: vampire and mummy destroyed, democracy saved and the monstrous woman brought back into the fold of virtuous femininity.

Pharos the Egyptian, along with Haggard's *She* and Stoker's *The Jewel of Seven Stars*, can be situated in another, even more specific context – that of the Egyptological Romance, or Mummy Fiction, that was all the rage in late Victorian Britain and that eventually gave birth to Boris Karloff's famous cinematic mummy (Daly 1999:84–117, Lupton 2003). Arthur Conan Doyle, Bram Stoker and Rider Haggard are some of the best known authors in this subgenre. However, far from representing one of the 'dark places of the earth', Egypt, in the Victorian imagination, came to be constructed as a central yet deeply ambivalent temporal and physical space. On the one hand, biblical archeology and the emerging field of Egyptology appropriated Ancient Egypt to European historical narratives; as a genealogical point of origin or scriptural authentication, as an imperial model, or as a cryptic site of civilizational difference. These appropriations were domesticated and popularized in Victorian England in the forms taken by mid-century Egyptomania. In an era of political and social turmoil, 'Egypt was seen as providing a spectacular point of stability, its antiquity equating with certainty, its monuments and monumentality contrasting with dissolution' (Rice and MacDonald 2003:7). On the other hand, to the British traveller and administrator of the colonial period, modern Egypt provided a living laboratory for the scientific racism being developed by nineteenth-century evolutionary ethnology (Champion 2003). John Barrell has documented the genocidal fantasies inscribed in Victorian tourist literature on the standard Nile tour; fantasies in which anxieties about racial typing fused with zoological metaphors to produce the modern inhabitants of Egypt as less than human and hence entirely dispensable

(Barrell 1991). The following fairly typical quote is from the 1857 travel narrative *Boat Life in Egypt and Nubia*, by the American lawyer William Prime, who was fond of likening modern Egyptians to dogs and pigs: 'Two hundred people were lying around me, and I asked who and what they were, and what part they formed in the grand sum of human valuation? Literally nothing. They are not worth counting among the races of men. They are the curse of one of the fairest lands on this earth's surface' (cited in Barrell 1991:115).

Ancient Egypt however retained its status as a place of mystery and monumentality. Occultism and the nostalgia for a lost martial or archeological heroism combined in the work of Edwardian writers to produce Egypt as an irrational and sexy imperial alternative to the humdrum mass society of *bourgeois* democracy. Rider Haggard's *She* begins with a locked chest mystery that contains the documentary evidence of a secret and startling genealogy. In the familiar comfort of rooms at Cambridge, the narrator's impeccably English friend confesses to him that 'my sixty-fifth or sixty-sixth lineal ancestor was an Egyptian priest of Isis, though he was himself of Grecian extraction, and was called Kallikrates. His father was one of the Greek mercenaries raised by Hak-Kor, a Mendesian Pharaoh of the twenty-ninth dynasty, and his grandfather, I believe, was that very Kallikrates mentioned by Herodotus' (Haggard 1887:10). This Egyptian ancestor's quest for revenge, bequeathed through the generations, takes the family from Egypt to Athens to Rome to Charlemagne's Brittany, and finally to England, where, by the nineteenth century, they have become boring middle-class British citizens: 'Sometimes they were soldiers, sometimes merchants, but on the whole they have preserved a dead level of respectability, and a still deader level of mediocrity' (ibid.:11).

Colonial Egyptology was one of the practices that made these kinds of fantastic appropriations possible. From the early years of organized looting of artifacts, to the somewhat more regulated archeological excavations of the late nineteenth century, European museums – and particularly the Louvre and the British Museum – were able to amass, classify and display the most significant collections of Ancient Egyptian art in the world (Reid 2002, Fagan 2004). The sciences that grew up around these collections detached Egyptian antiquity from the rest of Egyptian history and claimed it as the sole preserve of western scholarship. Until the second decade of the twentieth century, Egyptians were actively prevented from training as Egyptologists by the European experts and administrators resident in Cairo. Only bitter inter-European rivalries and, later, policies set by the new nationalist-controlled parliament allowed them to slowly gain a toehold in the field.

Nonetheless, nationalist intellectuals – like Jum'ah himself – were keenly interested in Egyptian antiquity from the late nineteenth century onwards.[13] To the colonial intelligentsia, ancient Egypt came to be associated with nation building and national prestige, as it was of course in Europe. The same holds true for the modern Egyptian state both pre- and post-colonial. From the reign of Muhammad Ali (1769–1849) onwards, the state astutely used archeological regulation as a negotiating tool with European governments, as well as a mechanism for bringing the unruly and isolated South of the country – rich in sites and artifacts – under firmer central control (Colla 2000:177, 278–85). Writers and intellectuals – including Ahmad Kamal, the first professional Egyptian Egyptologist – understood that the ability to acquire and interpret the languages and symbols of this distant historical past was one key to political self-determination. Archeological nationalism was not therefore just some naïve, or hysterical colonial mythology, but rather a shrewd sizing-up of the relationship between historical practice and political power in the context of the imperial modern nation-state system. Clearly, this was one of the main reasons why Jum'ah chose to translate Boothby's novel, offering as it does a forceful vision of the glory of imperial Egypt, and no less, by the pen of a British subject. While Jum'ah however deliberately appropriates the text to a nationalist agenda, his interest in the strain of degeneration discourse that runs throughout the novel is fascinating and offers much food for thought about the community of nineteenth-century liberal social discourses across the colonial difference.

Elliot Cola's use of the term 'ambivalence' in this context offers a subtle and productive way of describing the kinds of colonial negotiations that play themselves out in a text like *Pharos the Egyptian* and its Arabic translation. Cola prefers the notion of ambivalence to that of 'hybridity' because of the ontological dimension of the latter term, and because 'ambivalence' captures the intensely social – and hence conflictual – nature of the history of colonialism and nationalism in Egypt; 'a history of struggles and competitions . . . governed by relations of domination between a range of actors motivated by divergent, and even self-conflicted interests and desires' (Colla 2000:169–70). He illustrates this point through an analysis of the ancient Egyptian artifact as simultaneously an aesthetic object and an exchangeable commodity circulating between England, France and Egypt.

Translation, I propose, represents an equally significant site of historical ambivalence in the sense offered by Cola, because it offers a window into those vertical relations of colonial domination, but also, no less importantly, into certain horizontal acts of recognition across seemingly fixed cultural identities. The act of translation in the colonial context inevitably performs an ambivalent and simultaneous gesture of appropriation, collusion and critique on a variety of levels – from the purely formal to the broadly historical – and therefore far from being a straightforward or naïve act of linguistic transfer, translation typically rewrites the web of discourses, codes and conventions of the literary text in keeping with the conflictual and 'intensely social nature' of its cultural histories.

The translator strikes back: *Pharos the Egyptian* and the degenerate city

Pharos the Egyptian opens with a classic device of the gothic genre. A brief exchange of letters between two old Oxford friends introduces a strange manuscript addressed to them by a third long-lost friend from their university days. Cyril Forrester, a young and successful English artist, casts his narrative in the form of a terrible, shameful secret. Forrester is the son of a famous Egyptologist. One day, while taking an evening stroll on the banks of the Thames, he meets a mysterious and repulsive stranger – an extremely old and fabulously wealthy foreigner, endowed with strange powers. The stranger begins to haunt Forrester, appearing, with his young and beautiful ward at all the same social events at which he is a guest. He finally arrives at Forrester's doorstep in the middle of the night, and demands the young artist's prize possession: a perfectly preserved Egyptian mummy inherited from his father. The mummy, Pharos claims, is that of a powerful royal magician, and moreover his direct ancestor. When Forrester refuses to hand it over, Pharos hypnotizes him and steals the mummy anyway. Forrester tracks Pharos down to Sicily, where Pharos seduces him with his magnetic charm and his hashish cigarettes, persuading him to accompany himself and his beautiful and mysterious young ward to Egypt, where he intends to rebury the mummy in its proper resting place and hence right the wrong done to him and his family by Forrester's Egyptologist father. This task accomplished, Pharos tricks

Forrester into the heart of the Great Pyramid of Giza, where he has him injected with a deadly strain of the Plague. As planned, Forrester survives a bout with near-death in the desert and, totally unawares, slowly returns to England, spreading the plague across Europe in his wake and finally bringing it to London itself, causing millions of deaths, untold suffering and the complete breakdown of social infrastructure.

At the end of the novel, Pharos the Egyptian reveals himself to be the great magician Phtahmes, cursed to immortality by the Gods of Ancient Egypt for having betrayed the Biblical Pharaoh Menephtah. Phtames had deliberately deceived his master about the infinitely superior powers of Moses, which in turn had caused the plagues visited on the land of Egypt, including the death of all its first-born sons. The European plague is Pharos' attempt to redeem himself in the eyes of the gods and to find eternal rest. However, the narrative ends with these same gods refusing Pharos' act of propitiation. Instead, they condemn his spirit to eternal destruction for 'using the power vouchsafed thee . . . for thine own purposes and to enrich thyself in the goods of the earth' – a reference to the origins of Pharos' fabulous wealth in illicit antiquities trading (Boothby 1899:229). The novel ends with Forrester and Pharos' ward escaping a decimated Britain together at sea and to a life of exile and wandering.

The novel faithfully reproduces all the essential ingredients of the Gothic genre – landscapes, interiors, plot construction and characterization, including the central trope of the doppelganger. Bootheby works this device of the Gothic uncanny however into a heightened and historically inflected register. Like Dracula, Pharos' wealth, urbanity and exquisite taste mask the ruthless and cruel malevolence that is a necessary ingredient of Gothic villains. Unlike Dracula however, his malevolence is attenuated by the remarkable relationship of complicity that is constructed through-out between Pharos and Forrester, his tortured instrument. Pharos' 'extraordinary individuality' (ibid.:29) compels the act of filiation on Forrester's part which will prove to be Europe's doom:

> His presence had been repulsive to me ever since I had first set eyes on him. I hated the man as I had hitherto deemed it impossible I could hate any one. Yet, despite all this, by some power – how real I cannot expect anyone to believe – he was compelling me to shield him and behave towards him as if he had been my brother, or at least my dearest friend. I can feel the shame of that moment even now, the agonizing knowledge of the deep gulf that separated me from the man I was yesterday, or even an hour before. (ibid.:43)

This Gothic ambivalence takes on added meaning in the context of mummy fiction, where heroes tend to identify on some level with übermench Egyptian characters, usually feminized and hence also sexualized – the lustful, power-hungry mummy-queen intent on destroying democracy and reinstituting good old-fashioned Egyptian style autocracy: 'a Diana in jackboots who preaches materialism in philosophy and fascism in politics' (Norman Etherington, cited in Brantlinger 1988:234). In Pharos the Egyptian, the mysterious complicity between Pharos and Forrester is partly referred to mesmerism – a popular turn-of-the-century fad and phobia. But it is primarily rooted in a set of discourses and values shared between villain and victim.

Pharos' historical grievance is described at great length throughout the novel. The following is an exemplary passage:

> 'Thy father, was it wretched man,' he cried, shaking his skeleton fist at

me, while his body trembled like a leaf under the whirlwind of his passion, 'who stole this body from its resting-place? Thy father, was it, who broke the seals the gods had placed upon the tombs of those who were their servants?' . . . Then turning to the mummy, he continued, as if to himself, 'Oh mighty Egypt! Has thou fallen so far from thy high estate that even the bodies of thy kings and priests may no longer rest within their tombs, but are ravished from thee to be gaped at in alien lands? But by Osiris, a time of punishment is coming. It is decreed and none shall stay the sword! (Boothby 1899:33–34)

This complaint, with which Forrester strongly sympathizes, is rooted in that particular Edwardian neurosis that mixed all kinds of occultisms with racialized fantasies of power projected onto imperial Egypt. From the conservationist polemics of Amelia Edwards to the mystical venerations of Rider Haggard, a certain disgust with mass tourism and popular spectacle, or the rational middle-class sensibility of the museum exhibit produced the reaction against what Haggard attacked as, 'the trade in the dead' (Brantlinger 1988:238–53; see also Gregory 2004).[14] In Jum'ah's translation, this narrative of restitution and sacred trust dominates the Arabic text as an explicit parable of colonial revenge through numerous Arabic additions to Pharos' various monologues. Moreover, Jum'ah carefully excises most of the passages that construct Forrester's elaborate and tormented interiority, thereby stripping him of his character and hence his status of Gothic victim (and incidentally making the novel a lot shorter and less repetitive). More importantly, he deletes the biblical sub-plot that identifies Pharos as the mendacious rival of Moses, removing in the process the entire narrative motor that fixes Egypt within imperial Christian historical time and that establishes Pharos' immortal villainy. This strategy entailed considerable editorial work on Jum'ah's part, since numerous brief references to the pharaonic subplot as well as long passages describing flashbacks or dream sequences are scattered throughout the English text. The lengthy chapters at the end of the novel that depict the human pathos of a London shattered by death and disease are also deleted in the translation. On the one hand, this translational strategy transforms the human subjects of modern Europe into those same dispensable or invisible multitudes of Victorian colonial fantasy. On the other, it marks a kind of deliberate hesitation or silence in the face of English novel's awesome genocidal imaginary. Jum'ah strips the novel of its ambivalent moral economy: Pharos the villain becomes Pharos the Avenger, and Forrester becomes simply his puppet-like accomplice – a victim emptied of his victimhood. Jum'ah elaborates a minor remark in Pharos' confession at the end of the novel into a grandiloquent and typical statement of purpose: 'And so I was sent, by the gods' command, to take vengeance on the corrupt, iniquitous nations, on the Europe that this Plague will annihilate as a just reward for its tyranny and ignorance' (Jum'ah 1906b:138; my translation). In the Arabic text, Pharos is destroyed by a well-placed knife in the heart, rather than by the gods' outraged decree (ibid.:139).[15]

But the trope of historical revenge is only one of Jum'ah's translational concerns. The real climax of both Boothby's novel and of Jum'ah's translation is the tour of 'Outcast London' on which Pharos takes Forrester after their return to England and before the Egyptian plague begins to decimate its population. Pharos' declaration that he will show Forrester 'London as I see it in my character of Pharos the Egyptian' is rife with over-determined meaning as it circulates between the English and the Arabic text, for it plays on and finally erases the last vestiges of fixed moral identities on which the genre presumes (Boothby 1899:201; Jum'ah 1906b:117). The degenerate city becomes the shared object of both Pharos and Forrester's gaze, and hence, through the translation process, of the Arabic reader as well.

The full force of Edwardian degeneration discourse is displayed in this series of social tableaus that Pharos unveils to his accomplice in one long night and over ten pages of text. The City, with all its massed human detritus, is offered up as the spectacle of a diseased organism; a modern Sodom and Gomorra calling for divine retribution. Together, Pharos and Forrester descend the ladder of English society – from scenes of 'that luxury and extravagance which is fast drawing this great city to its doom' to the filthy thieves' dens of London's darkest alleys (Boothby 1899:202). This unfolding vision of titled blacklegs, lascivious *bourgeois*, incompetent parliamentarians, scantily-clad females, constitutional drunks, thieves and murderers leaves Forrester sick at heart for 'the sorrow and the sin of London', as well as 'the callous indifference to it displayed by Pharos' (ibid.:210). Jum'ah adds passages of his own invention to this sequence in order to elaborate on these 'sorrows and sins' – passages that emphasize a set of moral concerns of particular interest to the Egyptian middle classes of the period: sexual debauchery and alcoholism (Jum'ah 1906b:120–24). His answer to this issue of Pharos' 'callous indifference' is, as I have mentioned earlier, to delete the London tour's fantastic conclusion from his translation – the last two chapters, which describe the devastating aftermath of the London plague and which successfully invoke the cathartic horror employed by the invasion fantasy genre as a whole. However, the spectacle of the diseased urban microcosm nonetheless remains as an urgent question in the social imaginary of both the English novel and its Arabic translation.

In his *Faces of Degeneration*, Daniel Pick makes the case that the conception of degeneration as it emerged in Europe between 1848 and 1918 was largely the product of a broad crisis in liberal social optimism in the face of real and threatened revolution: 'the socio-biological theory of degeneration emerged in and beyond the 1880s most powerfully as a counter-theory to mass-democracy and socialism' (1996:218). It can certainly be argued that Egypt experienced a comparable moment around the turn of the century; a moment however in which optimism and crisis existed side by side in a precarious social and discursive tension. As in Europe, translation was one of the means through which this tension was managed and coded for consumption by national middle classes.

The issue of national decadence was very much on the minds of Egyptian intellectuals at the turn of the century. The major reform movement initiated by the *Nahdah* in Egypt was at least partly shaped through the translation of conservative Darwinian and Utilitarian nineteenth-century European social thought, namely theorists like Gustave Le Bon, Hippolyte Taine, Herbert Spencer and John Stuart Mill (Mitchell 1988). From the 1890s till the 1920s, liberal reformist intellectuals like Ahmad Fathi Zaghlul and Muhammad 'Umar produced an Arabic discourse of Egyptian cultural decadence that partly drew on concepts of racial history and evolutionary psychology to describe and analyze the social pathology of the modern Egyptian character. The slothful, vice-ridden and unruly urban and rural masses, as well as, to a lesser extent, the dissolute and acculturated aristocracy were targeted by liberal intellectuals as the source of Egypt's backwardness and dependency. Though these discourses were never fully articulated in terms of the kinds of biological determinisms produced by nineteenth-century European scientism, they nonetheless represented a powerful disciplinary tool in the hands of emergent national élites.[16] In Egypt, the capital city was also identified as a microcosm of this national decadence. While Outcast London certainly works as a metaphor of *imperial* depravity in Jum'ah's translation, it can also be read as an opaque and open-ended translation of Outcast Cairo.

Alcoholism and drug addiction, vagabondage, insanity, sexual debauchery and the various forms of urban criminality which they produced were also all linked in this strand of Egyptian reformist discourse to anxieties of social malfunction and national breakdown. On the other hand, the unchecked importation of European social and sexual mores was perceived as a disease that afflicted the upper echelons of urban society. Though these social concerns and the discourses they produced are primarily associated with the 'school' of liberal reformers focused around Ahmad Lutfi al-Sayyid and the Ummah Party, they were nonetheless strongly echoed in the writings of die-hard nationalists from Abdallah al-Nadim to Mustafa Kamil himself.[17] At the same time, the country at large was being consumed by social unrest. From the ʿUrabi uprising of 1881 and the bitter occupation and restorations of the following years, to the massive urban migrations and broad labour unrest of the period and the dramatic stock market crash of 1907, Cairo was a city just waiting to explode – which is exactly what happened a decade later in 1919. Muhammad Farid's remark about a Port Said strike in 1894 – 'This European disease has spread to Egypt' – was, as Lockman points out, emblematic of the general nationalist attitude towards labour activism as a sign of larger social 'disorder' and 'sickness' imported from abroad (cited in Lockman 1994:171). It comes as no surprise then that socialism was a topic of intense debate during this period, and that for the most part, both liberal and nationalist intellectuals like Jumʿah polemicized extensively against what they saw as a foreign threat to an emergent social order.[18] Jumʿah's translations, Al-Sahir al-khalid/ Al-Intiqam al-haʾil, are thus texts that 'translate' the whole gamut of jarring social and political pressures characteristic of the period itself – colonialism and the cultural utopias and dystopias it brings into being; social mobility and social conflict in an era of dramatic economic transformation.

Jumʿah's translation has had no place in canonical versions of Nahdawi literary history precisely because it lies outside the major narrative of the emergence of the nation as a unified ontological subject. Nonetheless, the questions of national decadence that it raises are surely linked to a whole range of social and textual representations that eventually crystallized into the concept and practice of 'National Literature' and of realism as a whole in Egypt. The trope of the diseased city as a metaphor of a dislocated colonial modernity is a defining one in modern Egyptian literature, as is its dialectical opposite – the primordial and authentic countryside, ancient repository of Egypt's national identity. Pharos the Egyptian and its Arabic translation afford us a glimpse into the ambivalent representations that lie at the very heart of literary histories, beyond essentialist binaries – like 'tradition' and 'modernity' – that continue to structure the way we think about cultural identities. Colonial difference here collapses into the nuances of historical correspondence and the community of social interests across the imperial divide. Studying the historical network of translations allows us to map these correspondences and complicities in a move beyond complacent articulations of difference and minority.

Notes

1   By Europe's 'others', I also mean those subaltern groups within its own imagined geographical borders: women, the poor, ethnic and religious minorities.

2   As both Daniel Pick and Patrick Brantlinger have shown, degeneration discourse in Europe

– and particularly in Britain – was also characterized by internal socio-political dissonances and contradictions. Many British socialists of the period used the language of degeneration in their writings, and prominent Fabianists were interested in the possibilities of eugenics, for example. However, it is not my intention in this paper to delve into the complex social and intellectual history of degeneration politics in England, but rather to focus more broadly on its circulation as a set of potential social languages in *fin de siècle* Egypt.

3   Modern Arabic literary scholarship has adopted this critical structure wholesale, *tashwih* (mutilation) being the favourite metaphor for translation practices that are not based on strict equivalence.

4   However, not all of these historical examples have the same normative function. While the Greek and Latin translations of the poets of the *Pléiade* served to reinforce the construction of Europe's classical origins, the Arab sources of the Spanish school of Toledo's extensive translations seem to have played no role in the formation of European self-identities. See Lefevere (1990:14–28) for an overview of European practices of translation from antiquity to the twentieth century.

5   Sociological studies of the specifically *literary* production of the period are unfortunately nonexistent. Therefore it is almost next to impossible to retrieve publication and distribution figures and to reconstruct readerships, except on the basis of the evidence found in the periodical itself. These figures are given by Khalil Sadiq in his editorial columns. Might it be possible then to guess at the social composition of its readers by casting an eye on the regular advertisements published in its pages? Lawyers, pharmacists, doctors, confectioners and haberdashers all advertised in the *Entertainments*. Can we then assume that – much like the authors and translators themselves – its readership was largely male, largely middle-class and largely professional?

6   Of the eighty novels published in the *Entertainments*, twelve are original compositions, thirteen are translations of known French and English authors, twenty-seven present themselves as translations that cite the name or part of a name, or simply the initials of a (so far) untraceable European author, and the rest – twenty-eight novels – merely state on the frontispiece that they have been adapted 'from the French' or 'from the English'.

7   Jum'ah's nationalist sympathies apparently led to his failure in the final exam at the Khedival School, and he left in 1903 without having matriculated. After his return from his brief sojourn in Beirut, he received a degree from a Teacher's Training College in Darb al-Jamamiz and went on to teach translation at the Helwan Primary School from 1904 to 1905, but was forced to resign from his post after a dispute with the Headmaster regarding some Quranic verses that he had translated into English. In 1906, Jum'ah was fired from his editorial post at *Al-Dhahir* after having given a speech at the Jubilee of the Khedive Abbas Helmi in which he attacked the *Entente Cordiale* and the Khedive's collusion in this betrayal of Egypt. In 1908, he was expelled from the Khedival College of Law due to yet another speech he gave at the College on the occasion of Mustafa Kamil's death.

8   The *kuttab* was a traditional Islamic elementary school, originally attached to a mosque.

9   Among his translations are two novellas by Arthur Conan Doyle, Plato's *Symposium*, Machievelli's *Prince* and an abridged translation of James Joyce's *Ulysses*. His monographs include *Hukm Nabuliun* (Napoleon's Rule, 1912), *Muhadarat fil-Tarikh wal-Iqtisad* (Lectures on History and Economics, 1912), *Rasa'il fi 'ilm al-ijtima'* (Essays on the Social Sciences, 1912), *Tarikh Falasifah al-islam* (History of Islamic Philosophy, 1927), *Hayat al-sharq* (The Life of the East, 1932), and his vast oeuvre, *Thawrat al-Islam wa batal al-anbiya' Abu al-Qasim Muhammad Ibn Abdallah* (The Revolution of Islam and the Hero of Prophets Abu al-Qasim Muhammad Ibn Abdallah, 1939/1958). His literary works include *Fi buyut al-nas* (In People's Houses, 1904), *Fi wadi al-humum* (In the Valley of Sorrow, 1905), *Aidah* (1932/1934), and *Mukhtara* (1941/1942) – the latter a historical novel set in Mamluk times – in addition to numerous unpublished works. See al-Tamawi (1993).

10   Nicholas Daly (1999) has argued that a similar situation existed in Edwardian Britain, where the dividing line between what Q.D. Leavis has called 'middlebrow fiction' and the literature of high modernism was still fluid and largely indistinct, both in critical terms and in terms of the vibrant social and professional networks of contemporary writers.

11   Edwardian England played host to a whole range of mystical and supernatural fads and practices, from the Rosicrucian revival and The Hermetic Order of the Golden Dawn to cabalism and mesmerism. Many prominent writers and politicians of the period were

associated with these movements – W.B. Yeats, Bram Stoker, Aleister Crowley, Arthur Conan Doyle and Arthur Balfour, for example. See Laqueur (2006).

12   The genre became so ubiquitous by the end of the century that P.J. Wodehouse produced a parody in 1909, The Swoop . . . A Tale of the Great Invasion, 'in which Britain is overwhelmed by simultaneous onslaughts of Germans, Russians, Chinese, Young Turks, The Swiss Navy, Moroccan brigands, cannibals in war canoes, the Prince of Monaco, and the Mad Mullah, until it is saved by a patriotic Boy Scout named Clarence Chugwater' (Brantlinger 1988:235). It is worth noting that our present period has witnessed a revival of this genre in cinematic science fiction. Independence Day inaugurated the Bush Junior era's war on terrorism, and a variety of film remakes of classics like The Planet of the Apes and The War of the Worlds have proved to be huge box office successes.

13   Jum'ah attended lectures on Hieroglyphics while studying in Lyon. He translated the Instruction of Ptah-hotep from the English version of the British Egyptologist Battiscombe Gunn (1918) and published his translation in a volume entitled Al-Hikmah al-mashriqiyyah (Eastern Wisdom) in which he dealt with Pharaonic history. See al-Tamawi (1993:23).

14   In his essay of the same name, Haggard (1981:147) was especially offended that the mummies of Egypt's ancient kings and queens should be displayed in Egyptian museums, and he demanded that some 'great Christian Power' rescue these 'poor fallen folk' (namely, modern Egyptians) from the spectacle of such desecration. Brantlinger (1988:228) notes that 'imperialism itself, as an ideology or political faith, functioned as a partial substitute for declining or fallen Christianity and for declining faith in Britain's future'.

15   In Boothby's novel, Pharos literally crumbles and shrinks into a shrivelled monkey-like creature then disintegrates into an ectoplasmic mess after a vision in which the gods' eternal curse is pronounced through the medium of his telepathic ward. Jum'ah's removal of the Biblical subplot in Al-Intiqam al-ha'il obviates the logical necessity of this retributive ending. Instead, it is Pharos' ward who, in a fit of despair and rage, stabs him to death.

16   It is interesting to note in this context that Farah Antun – along with his brother in-law Niqula Haddad, one of the first Arab intellectuals to advocate socialism, flirted with eugenics during his Fabian phase (see Reid 1975). See Donald M. Reid, The Odyssey of Farah Antun: A Syrian Christian's Quest for Secularism, Minneapolis: Bibliotheca Islamica, 1975.

17   See Selim (2004a) for a discussion of Abdallah al-Nadim's cultural politics. See also Lockman (1994:183–85). Lockman notes that the attitude and strategies of the National Party towards the 'reformable' poor – and particularly urban workers – began to change around 1908 when the Party began to enlarge its social base.

18   Ahmad Husayn al-Tamawi (1993:47) claims that Jum'ah's lifelong concern for the plight of the poor in Egypt as well as the influence of writers like Turgenev, Tolstoy, Meredith and Daudet demonstrate his ongoing interest in socialism. Al-Tamawi goes on to note that this interest had its natural limits and that Jum'ah strongly attacked communism in various publications.

Chapter 19

A. E. B. Coldiron

TRANSLATION'S CHALLENGE TO CRITICAL CATEGORIES: VERSES FROM FRENCH IN THE EARLY ENGLISH RENAISSANCE

EDITOR'S INTRODUCTION

Once one reads past the high canon's editorially sanitized selections, the early decades of print seem frankly and excitingly strange, variable, even chaotic, and so inextricably bound up with translation as to make single or simple accounts unlikely. Translations so un-Wyattesque, so absolutely un-Surreyan, challenge not only the predominating account of English Renaissance poetry's Petrarchan origins, but also a venerable model of literary history, the translatio studii.

L IKE SELIM, COLDIRON IS INTERESTED in questioning national historiographies of literature, specifically literary canons, and does so by using translation as a site of critical enquiry. Also like Selim, she focuses on less élite readerships. A study of translation reveals that in the period between 1501 and 1558, almost half the printed English verse was translated and, significantly, about six times more lines were translated from French than from Italian. This complicates a number of long-held critical assumptions, especially the presumed Italian roots of English Renaissance poetry. The core of the article engages with the special theoretical and historical challenges that these translations present to some of the central narratives of English Renaissance poetry.

Though now uncanonical and largely invisible, the body of translations analyzed by Coldiron are shown to have appeared at a crucial moment (the introduction of print), when new technologies expanded readerships and altered whole systems of literary production, distribution and reception. The facts of translation make visible a fairly clear line around the culture of print: it was dominated by French-derived, versus Italian-derived, poetry. The translated French verses, moreover, were not Petrarchan in origin (they did not imitate Petrarch, nor were they post- or anti-Petrarchan in character). They fell under four main thematic groupings: verses about women and gender relations, religious verse, moral verse containing a critique of court or of power, and 'low-georgic' or practical verses. Each grouping is examined separately and shown to invite further questions about the literary canon and to connect to larger issues in the field. For example, instances of translator intervention in rendering

French verses in the first grouping challenge us to see early modern French and English discourses on gender as distinct, when our tendency may be to lump them together. All four thematic subsets, taken together, are shown to have implications for a history of English poetics. The translations analyzed invite us to develop more inclusive, more comprehensive explanations of textual transmission and transformation and new models of literary change.

Follow-up questions for discussion

- 'The challenge of translation', for Coldiron, 'is to read not in comfortable, relatively static epistemes but to read across national, "movement", and period categories and to think instead in terms of polysystems. This means treating translations (and all texts) as dynamic rather than static: to watch them as moving creations against moving cultural backgrounds'. To what extent does polysystem theory, including its application and extension by Toury (1995), respond to this challenge, and to what extent might it be refined or combined with other approaches to answer the types of question raised by Coldiron more adequately?

- Coldiron describes a situation where translations from French dominated in the new medium – i.e., print – whereas translations from Italian were more likely to appear in manuscript form. This enables her to speak of 'a "language decorum" of media, a presumed suitability between medium and language content'. Consider the range of media in which translations currently circulate, in general and in your own language combination(s): for example, Internet, various types of audiovisual media, video phones and web cams (for sign language interpreting), etc. Can you observe a similar decorum between language, genre and type of media?

- Arguing against linear and teleological models that explain literary change in terms of influence, especially those which assume that 'texts are passed from one (higher, older) culture to another (lesser, younger), usually through the good offices of appropriately servile translators', Coldiron proposes meme theory as a potential alternative framework for 'thinking of translation and literary history'. To what extent does the treatment of meme theory in translation studies to date respond to the challenge posed by Coldiron? You might like to consult, in particular, Chesterman (1997), Vermeer (1997), and Pöchhacker (2004:51–61).

Recommended further reading

Coutts, Angela (2002) 'The Gendering of Japanese Literature: The Influence of English-Language Translation on Concepts of Canon in the West', *Japan Forum* 14(1): 103–125.

Even-Zohar, Itamar (1990) *Polysystem Studies*, Tel Aviv: The Porter Institute for Poetics and Semiotics, and Durham: Duke University Press. Special issue of *Poetics Today*, 11(1).

Sajdi, Dana (2009) 'Print and Its Discontents: A Case for Pre-Print Journalism and Other Sundry Print Matters', in Samah Selim (ed.) *Nation and Translation in the Middle East*, Special Issue of *The Translator* 15(1): 105–38.

Smith, Michael (1974) 'English Translations and Imitations of Italian Madrigal Verse', *Journal of European Studies* 4(2): 164–77.

Toury, Gideon (1995) *Descriptive Translation Studies and Beyond,* Amsterdam: John
    Benjamins.

LITERARY TRANSLATIONS POSE SERIOUS challenges to our
canons and to critical narratives about those canons.[1] Critical categories are
built upon linguistic, temporal and national boundaries: we largely teach and study
national, monolingual literatures and literary periods, and many of us still identify
ourselves as, for instance, French medievalists or specialists in the Spanish Golden
Age. While cultural and comparative approaches to literature, like approaches by
theme or by theory, do cross these boundaries, period, nation and authorship still
provide the chief conceptual and institutional frameworks for literary study. From
their birth, however, translations transcend and disrupt those frameworks, adding a
name to the 'author' line and extending the reach of a work beyond its first language,
era and nation. In their particulars, they may also complicate critical discussion of
such features as genre, imagery, allusion, rhetorical figures, even forms and metres.[2]
Because any feature of a literary work operates both synchronically and diachronically
– that is, both in a literary system and in a literary history – virtually any such feature
is subject to the system-crossing, history-leaping play of translation. In their very
existence, then, translations counter the framing terms of our standard critical practice and can serve as important sites of critical inquiry.

   This essay finds one such site in the late-fifteenth- and early-sixteenth-century
verse translations from French to English. The period between 1476 and 1557
(which is to say, between England's first printing house and first poetic miscellany)
saw experiments in poetics and technology that connect with nearly every wider
ideological and aesthetic change that we have called 'Renaissance' or 'early modern'.[3]
Some of the defining features of the literature we have periodized as 'Renaissance'
are an intensive intertextuality, a concern for *imitatio* and *aemulatio,* and an extensive,
multifaceted and generative use of translation. It is not news, then, that almost half
the English verse printed from 1501–1558 was translated (Ringler 1988:6). The
news? Of this translated plurality, about six times more lines were translated from
French than from Italian. In other words, English readers had more French-born than
Italian-born verse available to them in print, by a margin of roughly six to one. This
single fact about the translation of early printed verse complicates a number of
long-held critical assumptions (most obviously, about the Italian roots of English
Renaissance poetry). What follows is a discussion of the special theoretical and historical challenges these translations present to some of our central critical narratives
about English Renaissance poetry.

Textual production, translation and criticism

This is a large body of verse, more than 100,000 lines, until now not even identified
as a corpus; little of it exists in modern editions. Now relatively undercanonized,
these translations appeared in a time of rapid, radical technological change and were
profoundly implicated in the processes of print. The early English printers who
shaped and presented this verse to a widening readership – William Caxton, Wynkyn
de Worde, Robert Copland, Richard Pynson, Robert Wyer, and others – were all

engaged in printing translations from French. Most of the printers were themselves translators of verse, several of them bilingual, born or having lived in France or Burgundy.[4] Not only the verse but the techniques of presentation and the production technologies came to England from the continent. Given such strong practical connections to France, it makes sense that the early printers' verse output was significantly French-derived. Yet most scholarship on the English poetry of this period tells the story of Italian influence, especially Petrarchan influence, and tells it as the main critical line on the history of Renaissance poetics. Furthermore, this period, preceding a 'golden' latter-sixteenth century, is too often dismissed as the 'drab age', represented in canons and curricula only by the usual suspects, the Skelton-Wyatt-Surrey triumvirate. This disjunction between the large quantity and small canonicity of this verse parallels the disjunction between the strong Frenchness of the verse and the strong Italianist emphasis in criticism: both reveal a mismatch between the facts of translation and the critics' approaches. In other words, the facts of translation expose significant gaps in our constructions of literary history.

Some editors have actually widened such gaps with well-intentioned textual interventions. Because editors of early-sixteenth-century manuscripts generally modernize spelling and render difficult hands in clean modern typefaces, material originally in manuscript may now be paradoxically easier to read than the (mostly unedited) early printed texts. Now available on microfilm or as digitized images from EEBO (Early English Books Online), most early printed texts are in, for instance, blackletter, textura or Caxton typefaces, with orthography closer to Middle than modern English. (Figure 19.1 is a typical example of sixteenth-century English blackletter or gothic typeface.)[5] What early printed material is edited often regularizes or suppresses the very technical aspects that were undergoing importation and change, like typeface styles or page layout. Modern editions, trying to improve legibility and access, tend to omit woodcuts, colophons and printers' devices, thus rendering

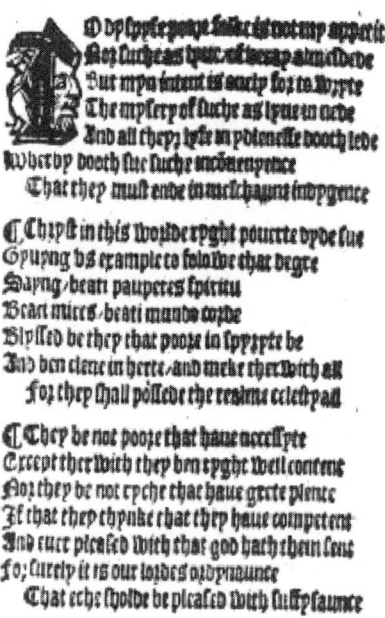

Figure 19.1 *The Hye Way to the Spyttell Hous* (London: Copland, c. 1536), STC 5732, page 1.[6]

invisible the early readers' and writers' complex negotiations with the new medium. During these decades, English writers' relation to the means of production was being re-shaped, and English readers' horizons of expectation (Jauss 1982) for the printed book were first set, so visual and physical aspects of the book are not idle concerns. In general, new media draw on aesthetic techniques of older media; in early film, for instance, the fade-to-black mimics the fall of a theatre curtain, and is thus comprehensible to audiences as a closural signal. Likewise, production values in early print mimic those of manuscript culture in certain ways: typefaces imitate script, woodcuts stand in for (and sometimes copy) illuminations, title pages and colophons extend the conventions of *incipit* and *explicit*, and the larger printed initials we now know as drop caps simulate rubricated initials. Readers and writers alike were learning, with the help of continental printers' methods and texts, how to handle the particular capacities of the new medium. Though now uncanonical and largely invisible, the translations treated here appear at a crucial moment, when new technologies expanded readerships and altered whole systems of literary production, distribution, and reception.

The challenge of translation thus points first at our accounts of media, readerships and language literacy. Some very strong critical threads have tied early modern English poetry to Petrarchan origins. Petrarch's poetry was copied in manuscript, as were the poems of his main English translators, Wyatt and Surrey. Those translations occur in a particular medium that implies relatively restricted social contexts: the world of poetic manuscripts, largely the courtier's world, was not the world of all England, and was not even the world of all literate England. Because Petrarch's poetry was not even printed in English until after 1547 (Lord Morley's *Trionfi*), most criticism overlooks these first, crucial decades of print and the less-élite readerships developing then. (I say 'less-élite' rather than 'non-élite' because there were always noble and royal readers of print, and because anyone who could read or buy books enjoyed comforts not available to everyone.) The so-called 'two readerships' of early modern England, manuscript and print, have usually been thought of in terms of social class, but they probably do not divide neatly along élite versus less-élite lines. Readerships surely overlapped and shared common texts, attitudes and experiences; Harold Love, H. R. Woodhuysen and Arthur Marotti, among others, have shown that scribal publication and transmission made manuscripts more widely available than was previously thought, and Steven May, for instance, has well countered the old 'stigma of print' idea (May 1981).[7] Yet the facts of translation make visible a fairly clear line around the culture of print: it was dominated by French-derived, versus Italian-derived, poetry. Are we safe to say that readers of printed verse were increasingly not bilingual readers? The new and growing print readership would presumably appreciate the content and qualities of French verse but may have required translations – or so the printers seem to have guessed.

The fact of translation from French is usually announced in these works' titles and paratexts, as if Frenchness were a good selling point or carried some special authority. Typical examples are the anonymous [H]*istory of Kyng Boccus, and Sydracke . . . translatyd by Hugo of Caumpeden, out of frenche*; *The dreme of the pylgremage of the soule translated out of Frenshe in to Englysshe with somwhat of addicion*; *Here foloweth a lytell treatyse of the Beaute of women newly translated out of Frenshe*; and the *Certayne treatyse most wyttely deuysed . . . entitled Lamant mal traicte de samye. And nowe out of French in to Englysshe*. The printers retain other kinds of French visibility, too, such as woodcuts or initial styles. Figure 19.1 shows an English translation that uses a reduced French-style anthropomorphic initial T; Figure 19.2 shows a typical French large-initial L.[8] Many works preserve French names, place names, or oaths, and a few preserve French refrains. Although there is little hard

Figure 19.2 Alain Chartier, *Les Demandes d'amours* (s.l.: s.n., s.d. [c. 1500]), title page. Reproduced with the permission of the Bibliothèque nationale de France, from Gallica, No. No-0264.

evidence of the two readerships' differing language-literacies, the printers' consistent advertisement of translation from French indicates their judgement that the new readers had French tastes but English literacy. This is not to say that the two media, script and print, divide neatly on language lines either, for there was plenty of French and French-originated verse in English manuscripts (see Ringler 1988, Beal 1990–1997). Still, the printers clearly chose French as their chief vernacular source, and translators like the influential Anthony Woodville and the prolific Andrew Chertsey clearly chose the new medium for their poetic appropriations from France. Any relation between content-providers and medium is a fluid one, of course. But this strong mutual preference, and the deliberate, visible Frenchness of the early imprints may mean that print – the latest thing – was somehow seen as more appropriate for French works, while Italian-born works were somehow naturalized more easily in manuscript than in print. Perhaps French works and Frenchness in general were more widely commodified because they were thought to be more salable, more popular. Practicalities like the skills and connections of particular translators or the availability of texts to particular printers surely favoured the conjunction of Frenchness and printed verse. In light of this corpus, we may be able to speak of a 'language decorum' of media, a presumed suitability between medium and language content. In any case, the surprising facts of translation complicate the questions of how audiences are distributed around media and how content and media conjoin.

Before the Italianist scholars reading this essay fling down the volume in disgust, a few qualifications are needed. Clearly, the size of the corpus, its production values, and its quantity relative to Italian-derived verse challenge our canons and our usual accounts of literary history of this period. But the Italianist or Petrarchist line of scholarship has been enormously productive and successful and has charted, for example, the development of English sonnets, the silencing and revoicing of women in early modern lyrics, the relation of poetry to Tudor court politics, the importance of patrons, and more. Furthermore, studies of Wyatt's and Surrey's translations of Petrarch into English helped establish our disciplinary habit of looking back in time and to the continent for literary sources, analogues and methods (looking, in other words, in the same directions the English poets themselves had looked). To the idea of Renaissance as a revival of the classics, a long line of scholars after Jacob Burckhardt's 1860 *Die Kultur der Renaissance in Italien: Ein Versuch* has drawn attention to an extra layer of vernacularity – the English re-birthing of the Italian fourteenth century's re-birthing of the classical past, in which Petrarch was a chief midwife, his own work richly varied and vast, both maieutic and generative itself. Scholars preferring 'early modern' have also seen Petrarch as an originator of subjectivity and modern consciousness (though that view is not unquestioned). It would be hard to overestimate the enduring importance of Italianist early modern studies, and this essay is no 'Oedipal ritual of Burckhardt-bashing' (Starn 1998:122). Nothing here should be taken to minimize either the contributions of Petrarch to the European Renaissance or the contributions of scholars of English Petrarchism, whose work has been foundational to our discipline. But the significant Frenchness of the verse translated for early English print is a direct invitation to learn things quite new, quite distinct from all that has been brought forth during the Petrarchists' long, fruitful hegemony.

One might first try to explain these translations as French-filtered Petrarchan verse making its inexorable move into English via a language that more English printers happened to know. This explanation would make sense if the translations were Petrarchan in origin, if they imitated Petrarch or were post-Petrarchan or anti-Petrarchan in character. If that were the case, we could treat this large corpus with the usual methods of the influence study. These translations, however, demand other methods, for they are almost entirely not Petrarchan, are not French vehicles in which Petrarchan material comes early to England. There are no sonnets, first of all, in these 100,000+ French-born lines, no *canzoni*, and no love-lyric sequences. Not that those features exhaust the possibilities in Petrarch, but curiously enough, there are also no flamboyant antitheses, no grand patriotic laments like the 'Italia mia', no idealized Laura figure (though there is Chartier's *Belle Dame Sans Merci*), no self-laureation, no post-Augustinian introspection. What exactly characterizes all this French-born verse in English print? The translated verses fall fairly well under four main thematic groupings: verses about women and gender relations, religious verse, moral verse containing a critique of court or of power more generally, and what I am calling 'low-georgic' or practical verses. These four groupings are arbitrary conveniences, and the themes interesect and overlap, but this rough thematic division clarifies the nature of the translations in their historical contexts. Each grouping also invites further questions and connects to larger issues in the field.

The corpus

First, many of the translations are about women and gender relations. The relatively small English appropriation of the truly vast body of early modern French writing about women, sex and love is selective but varied. Ranging widely in genre and style, these verses include romances, treatises, debate poems, a farce, epigrams, and several long poems on marriage. What idealizing of women can be found here comes from a chivalric rather than strictly Petrarchan tradition.[9] French chivalric-romance and related shorter forms (e.g. the *complainte amoureuse*, the *demande d'amour*, the *débat*) appear alongside misogynist and misogamous poems.[10] The *Castell of Love*, Marie de France's *Lanval*, and the *Life of Ipomydon*, for instance, like the amorous inscriptions in *Lamant mal traicte de samye*, the love-poem in *Blanchardyn and Eglantine*, the Chaucerian *Complaynts of*

Mars and Venus and the *Complaynt of the herte thorough perced with the lokynge of the eye* typify the romance and romance-related translations here. Although French romance ideals fill many lines of translated verse, they are not imported without question. Christine de Pizan's 'Letter of Cupid', like the anonymous translation of Octavien de Saint Gelais' version of Dido's lament, put in print a darker spin on romance themes. The *Belle Dame Sans Merci* has a negative answer to every lover's plea. The *Castell of Labour*, with six editions in English between 1503 and 1525, inverts many romance conventions, its essentially economic critique set in a couple's bedroom at night. In fact, several longer poems in a satiric, misogamous and misogynist vein descend variously from the traditions of the *Miroir de Mariage*, the *Lamentations* of Mathéolus, and the French anti-clerical farce, *The Complaynte of them that be to soone maryed*, *The Complaynte of them that ben to late maryed*, the long satiric tales of the *Fyftene Joyes of Maryage*, and *A Mery Play betwene Iohan Iohan the husbande, Tyb hys wyf, and syr Ihann the preest* (John Heywood's translation of a misogamous farce), certainly balance in vivid, earthy, anti-idealizing tone the rather larger number of romance lines.

Sometimes the translator adds the misogyny. When Robert Copland, for instance, versifies the prose *Chemin de L'Hôpital*, he adds a section at the end asking why there are no women among the many classes of foolish, wretched, destitute folk in the estates-satiric 'Hospital'.

> Copland
> Yet one thyng I wonder that ye do not tell
> Come there no women this way to swell [?]
> Porter
> Of all the sortes that be spoken of afore
> I warraunt women enow in store
> That we are wery of them euery day
> They come so thycke that they stop the way
> The systerhod of drabbes, sluttes, and callets[11]
> Do here assorte / with theyr bagges and wallets
> And be partener of the confrary
> Of the mayteners of yll husbandry
> Copland
> A lewd sorte is of them a surety . . .

In this case the translator has taken a French text that does not mention women at all and has created what we might too charitably call gender-inclusive stanzas, specifying misogyny within the French work's general misanthropy.[12]

A more complex tension between romance ideals and misogyny shows up in the anonymous *Lytell treatyse of the Beaute of women*. The remarkable title woodcut, with its devil-jester, lute and cautionary inscription ('peccati forma femina est . . .'), illustrates this tension and suggests the moral dangers of beauty (see Figure 19.3).[13] This cut is a functional part of the translation, since the French versions do not have such cuts (the edition of 1497, for instance, presents a sedate 'teaching' scene of young aristocratic women reading). Women are great and gracious, says the translator, and their praises need to be sung (and translated). But 'The woman sholde haue the forehed hygh & fayre' like a romance heroine to be acceptable, for otherwise she is quite ugly and probably also evil. Women's physical and moral qualities are inextricably linked in this work, and when the cautionary refrain repeats in French, 'Beaulte sans bonte ne vaut rien' (Beauty without goodness is worth nothing), the translation

Figure 19.3 *Here foloweth a lytell treatyse on the Beaute of Women . . .* (London: R. Fawkes, c. 1525). STC 1696, title page.[14]

joins a wider medieval philosophical debate. That debate, which draws its medieval energy from Augustine's *De Doctrina Christiana*, is not about women but rather about the connections between inner being and surface appearance, between signs and essences, *res et verba*. Many of the translations on women and gender, if not philosophical in this sense, are dialectical and serious, taking their cue from the literature surrounding the late-medieval French *querelle des femmes. An interlocucyon betwixt a man and a woman* actually takes the form of such a debate and gives the woman the longer part and the last word.[15] Another notable point is the eager English uptake of the work of Christine de Pizan, founder of the *querelle* and respondent to the misogynies in French romance and in the work of Mathéolus. Several of Christine's works were printed in English translation before appearing in French print.

This particular segment of the corpus, the translations of material on gender, challenges us to see early modern French and English discourses on gender as distinct, when our tendency may be to lump them together under 'socio-cultural context' rubrics. The translations show quite precisely what France had to offer England where discourses on gender are concerned, and what parts of the available discourses English printers saw and responded to: not only a set of romance vocabularies, already available to certain sectors of the English reading public, but a well-developed body of satiric misogyny and misogamy. Perhaps most interesting here are translations of the protofeminist works of Christine de Pizan without any translations at all of her opponents in the *querelle des femmes*. (Although Chaucer's translation of the *Roman de la Rose* is printed regularly, nothing from Pierre Col, Jean de Montreuil, Jean Gerson, or other *querelle*-rs makes it into early English print.) On the one hand, the translations show us a lopsided, univocal, protofeminist uptake of the *querelle*, and on the other, an uptake of anti-marital and misogynist satires countering the many idealizing romance translations. In their specifics, as in the case of the *Beaute of Women* woodcut and of Copland's additions to the *Hye Way*, the translations reveal specific slants on the material. And in these broader patterns of uptake, the translations challenge us to specify, to *préciser*, what we mean by 'early modern gender poetry', to ask where and when and for whom such works were made widely available.

Alongside the large verse uptake of French works on gender is a large uptake of explicitly religious material. Many of the poems are translated French prayers, rosaries, ten commandments, and other devotional verses, often in printed *horae* or prayerbooks or alongside religious prose, some of that also translated from French. Pilgrimages of the soul, pilgrimages of the life of man, visions of the devil in hell, a versified life of Saint Alban and Saint Amphabel, and an *ars moriendi* (*The crafte to lyue and to dye well translated out of frensshe*) either include or are made entirely of verses translated from French. Andrew Chertsey translated the very popular *Ordinaire des Chrétiens* into the religious omnibus of prayers, sacraments, articles of faith, and more, the *Ordynarye of Crystyanyte*. Chertsey, a prolific and passionately committed religious translator, also versified an elaborated ten commandments, *The floure of the commaundementes of god translated out of Frensshe*. This last differs from Robert Copland's 'The .x. commaundements', translations of 'Vng seul dieu tu adoreras', found in at least five shepherds calendars and at least nine books of hours.[16] (It also differs from translations of the French 'ten commandments of the devil'.) The ten commandments made a popular topic. Calvin, for instance, wrote sermons on them, and the finer points of difference in these translations should keep literary-theologians busy for years. We may have here an example of translation's role in fuelling a minor sub-genre.

Chertsey also translated from French verse on the seven sins, works of mercy, articles of faith, Biblical captions, and a *Lucidary*. He translated and revised significantly the *passyon of our lorde Iesu Chryst*. Copland's verse prologue to this *Passion* praises Chertsey's skill and lists his other works. The religious translations do sometimes feature this sort of visible literary-historical consciousness, something we more usually associate with secular works. Anthony Marcourt's *A Declaration of the Masse . . . translated newly out of French into English*, the long title of which claims it was done in Geneva, carries the false publication data 'Wittenberge: H. Lufte', but was published in two editions of 1547 in London by John Day. Many of these religious translations invite a comparatist theology, a reconsideration of the categories – e.g. 'Catholic', 'Protestant' and 'Huguenot' – since the contexts surrounding the imprint so heavily inflect the translation itself.

In another sense, this is also true of *The true and lyuely historyke purtreatures of the woll bible*, more easily understood as 'the true and lively historical portraitures of the whole Bible'.[17] This imprint is Frenchman Peter Derendel's translation of Claude Paradin's *Quadrins historiques de la Bible*, a kind of religious emblem book in which 108 biblical scenes are captioned with descriptive, analytic, or (usually) didactic quatrains. Derendel's long, lucid translator's prologue amounts to a defence of the contemplative use of images against charges of idolatry. In a familial metaphor for translation that I have not seen widely used in the Renaissance, Derendel says to his dedicatee, the English ambassador Pikeling:

> I have thought it mete to endeuer myself to translate the argument of eche
> figure in Englishe meter, being likewise putte in six other languages, to
> the entent that the countre, wherin I had been nourished and brought up,
> shulde in no wise remain bastard allone, his tonge kipping her place
> among other[s] . . .

Here is a rare case of openly expressed affection between the two nations and a view of translation as part of diplomacy. Derendel's translation, with its goal of interpretive parity among sibling versions and its implicit theory of translation as a defence against idolatry, asks for a rethinking of the whole relation between image and text.

As suggestive of potential controversy as these religious titles are, they do not record the truly widespread verses scattered through English liturgies, primers and books of hours. Religious verse translated from French appears in at least fifty-four books of hours, liturgies and other such imprints that I can find in preliminary searching, not to mention religious verses in the many shepherds calendars. However, not a single translated French poem appears in the twenty-seven editions of The Prymer, Set Foorth by the Kynges maiestie and his Clergie, to be taught lerned and read: and none other to be used throughout all his dominions.[18] The conspicuous absence in the official Tudor primer of the French-derived verse so widespread elsewhere may indicate that, despite their prevalence, their seeming ubiquitousness, the verses translated from French were not innocent and were not so fully absorbed as to be uncontroversial. What does it mean to translate devotional verse – really a kind of applied doctrine – from France both before and after Henry VIII's break with Rome, when French religious discourses were also undergoing change, though with different reasons and at a different pace? Again, translation raises questions that would not otherwise be so visible. This material should be of real interest to scholars writing the history of the Reformation in England and may challenge us to write that history cross-culturally.

The third thematic segment of the corpus contains translations that bring anti-court critiques and moral verse about wealth and power to English print. Alain Chartier's Curial, translated by William Caxton in prose and verse, is printed in 1483, reprinted in 1484, and finally revised by Francis Segar in 1549 with the title A briefe declaration of the great, and innumerable myseries . . . in courtes ryall. In this work, court life brings 'nothing but shame, ruine, and destruction'. The translations of the Curial are printed at very sensitive moments for the critique of power in England, years of sedition and rebellion.[19] Caxton himself may have been involved in the rebellion of 1483 (Gill 1997). In June of 1483, his collaborator, patron and fellow translator of French verse, Anthony Woodville, Earl Rivers, was murdered while trying to protect his nephews, the young princes, sons of Edward IV, from Richard III. Later, at Bosworth field in 1485, Henry VII would restore stability and a pro-poetry Tudor court culture, complete with a French poet laureate (orator regis Bernard André was tutor to Prince Arthur and the future Henry VIII; see Carlson 1991a, 1991b). But 'court' (Valois) and 'court' (Tudor) were not identical or even seamlessly similar sites, despite the many ties of marriage, trade and diplomacy between them. Chartier's poem was created in France in the early 1400s, during the truly terrible latter years of the Hundred Years' War, when dukes of Burgundy were murdering Valois princes and when Armagnacs plotted for the throne. English translators and printers, not once but twice, during the rebellions of 1483–84 and 1549, found new relevance in the moral critique of Alain Chartier, a French poet who died circa 1430.[20] Such translations give English printers a French template for speaking truth to power, but they also drive home the uncomfortable point that The Other Is Us. They make it impossible, in other words, for English readers either to be smugly insular or to be nostalgic about an idealized past, as the fictional and romance translations sometimes encourage readers to be. Since translation here equates three sets of ills having very different historical contexts, it asks for a nearly counterintuitive study of similarity between, rather than difference between, widely distant historical contexts. And it poses the problem of corrupt power as transnational, even transhistorical.

Luckily for the translators, critiques of court are often safely general, included in other advisory wisdom about the use of power, such as Christine de Pizan's advice translated as the *Morale Prouerbes of Cristyne*. Caxton's printing of her opening lines illustrates how Woodville's translation subtly emphasizes English national virtue.[21] *The Morale Prouerbes of Cristyne* advises the rich to be more sympathetic to the poor and warns the powerful to be just. Such advice seems to be easily naturalized into English verse, and common tropes against court life show up consistently through the period (e.g. Wyatt's 'Circa regna tonat' or 'Mine Own John Poins', or Raleigh's 'The Lie'). In Andrew Cadiou's translation, *The Porteous of noblenes translatid out of Franch in scottis* (Edinburgh, Chepman and Myllar, 1508), each section is a numbered noble virtue: 'the tenth vertu in a nobill man is larges' and 'the xi vertu in a nobill man is clenlynes'. Generosity, cleanliness, perseverance, courage, faith; the general virtues are all here. But the translator addresses nobles directly at the end of the work: 'Nobles report your matynis in this buke/And wysely luk ye be not contrefeit'. This imprint also recalls the strong, lasting connections between Scotland and France during the period, connections felt by the English to be threatening. Alastair Fowler reminds me about the French court at Edinburgh during the regency of Marie de Guise, a situation that produced real anxiety in England. Any specific poem, critique or advice aimed at court life will have to engage with a readership's understanding of current events, so it makes sense that these verses are more often general than specific. With translations, however, we can gauge the generality or specificity of a work by comparison not only with its own historical contexts but by reading its foreign sources and their contexts in parallel with the work in question.

Certain exemplary works here, like the historical-romance translation *Kynge Appolon of Thyre* or some of the wisdom translation in *The history of kyng Boccus and Sydracke*, also contain implicit comment on court life, and casting the net loosely would permit us to connect all this verse with advice-to-princes and even courtesy book literature, under the predominant idea 'didactic'. A few such poems treat *fortuna*, but not in the line of Petrarch's *De Remediis*. Thomas More's translation of a short French poem, 'Fortune perverse', as well as the French poem itself, is included in *The Boke of the fayre Gentylwoman . . . Lady Fortune* (c. 1540). Roger Bieston's *The Bayte and Snare of Fortune* comes from Claude Platin's *Débat de l'homme et de l'argent*.[22] While it does tangentially treat fortune in the humanist or classical sense of *fortuna*, it is really a medieval debate poem about the problems of earning, keeping and morally managing a 'fortune' or wealth. The punning English title reflects its slant on the question. Like estates satires and other translated social satires (for instance the well-studied *Ship of Fools* or the little-known *Hye Way to the Spittal Hous*), the *Bayte and Snare of Fortune* includes nobles in its broader critiques. (Sometimes the publishing history leaves a trace of the way such critiques were contextualized for readers: the French original of the *Hye Way of the Spittal Hous* was actually printed together with an advice-to-princes book.)[23] Copland, the printer-translator of the *Hye Way*, adds a direct plea to the powerful and rich that is not found in the French version: 'I pray all yow, which haue ynough with grace/ For the loue of god, to do your charyte/ And fro the poore, neuer turne your face'. Here, the moral-didactic translations flirt with a transnational, transhistorical critique of wealth – not quite an Internationalism *avant la lettre*, but they invite consideration of shared ground between old-Christian and new-Socialist ideologies.

A fourth subset of this corpus is made up of practical or everyday verse, what I am loosely calling 'low-georgic' translations. Not Virgilian or even Hesiodic georgic, this poetry is designed to guide and order the daily lives of readers. These verses appear in shepherds' calendars, books of husbandry, proverb books, and the like. At the upper or less practical end of 'low georgic' would fit some of the verse in *King Boccus and Sydrach*, in the *Morale Prouerbes of Cristyne*, or in *The boke of wysdome, folowynge the auctorities of auncyent Phylosophers Dyuidynge and spekyng of vyces and vertues translated out of Frenche*. The speaker of this last work, whose stated goal in translating the *Chapelet des Vertus* is to instruct on 'how a man ought to govern hym selfe as well of the tonge as of wytte and understandynge', cites Aristotle and other high authorities on Prudence; the translator's prologue has the literary conventions and aspirations of a medieval dream vision poem. At the lower or more practical end of 'low georgic' are many short translations like our commonplace mnemonic 'Thirty days hath September', found in four editions of *A goodly prymer in Englysshe*. Mnemonics for saints' days or ember days and verse captions to woodcut illustrations are further examples. Several printings of Fitzherbert's *Boke of husbandry*, or *Newe tracte or treatyse moost profytable for all husbande men*, include common verse from French about horses. 'The sayenge of the frenche man' is quoted first in French and immediately restated in English:

> Mort de langue et de eschine, [f]ount maladyes saunce medicine. The mournynge of the tonge, and of the chyne, are diseases without remedye or medicyne. And ferther he sayth, Gardes bien que il soyt cler de vieu, que tout trauayle ne soit perdue. Be wel aware that he be clere of syght, lest all thy travayll or iourney be lost or nyght.[24]

The French and English verses are not set as poetry in any of the extant imprints of this work I have seen but rather are fully incorporated into the prose, just as short verse tended, I suspect, to be more fully integrated into everyday lives than it is now. Healthy-horse verses certainly raise questions about the 'poetic' or the 'literary' as we now conceive it. The eye may not find these as couplets, set in the prose as they are, but the ear does, and the translation draws extra attention to the difference. One poem on the ages of man is longer – forty-eight lines – and appears in at least thirty-one imprints between 1527 and 1556. 'Called I am Ianuarye the colde' (couplets) and 'The fyrst is prymetyme' (rhyme royal) each translate French verses on the seasons. Such 'low georgic' items had proven best-sellers on the continent, so the economic risk of making such imprints must have seemed small. Parisian printer Antoine Vérard himself may have set the sweeping English fashion for shepherd's calendars (or at least may have given other printers something to improve). Figure 19.4 shows a page from Vérard's rather badly translated and produced English *Kalendayr of the shyppars . . . wyth syndry [sic] addycyons new adjowstyt*, which he published in Paris in 1503, apparently seeing a niche for himself in the young English market. Relatively little of the extensive criticism of Spenser's *Shepheardes Calender* reads in terms of this deep bicultural background to that poem – another specific challenge of translation.

Relations were not always so advantage-filled as Vérard's cross-cultural enterprises, nor as cordial as Derendel's irenic translation. Occasionally one sees in the low georgic imprints a resistance to things French (and Scottish), or a bow to English national sensibilities. The low-georgic compendium *Le Debat de lhiver et de leste* includes verses on the state of humankind, on the characteristics of the professions, on the

Figure 19.4 *The Kalendayr of Shyppars* (Paris: Vérard, 1503), STC 22407, pages 2 and 4, Douce Fragm.d.10.[25]

benefits of rising early and eating moderately, on how to choose a good horse, and more. The anonymous translator of this imprint as the *Debate and stryfe betwene Somer and wynter* makes one telling change to his source text. A French *dixain* lists what appear to be the fine qualities of natives of each nation or region: 'Larges de Francoys/ Et Loyaute d'Anglois . . .' (generosity of the French, loyalty of the English . . .), and so on. The enumerated national traits build in nine parallel lines, only to be deflated in line ten: they're all worthless. In English, the positive catalogue and deflating twist are the same, but the disloyal Englishman of the original is translated into a disloyal Scotsman, alone in a long list of (un)kind Picards, (dis)honest Normans, (un)trustworthy Burgundians. 'Largess of the French men/Loyalte of the scottis men/ . . . All is not worth a poynte of leather'. The translator anticipated his audience's prejudices or perhaps felt a certain 'loyaute d'Anglois' himself. The variety and reach of the low-georgic translations makes one wonder what it means for English readers to absorb so much common wisdom from a country toward which it professed enmity and displayed complex mixtures of desire and disgust.

All four thematic subsets of the corpus, taken together, have implications for a history of English poetics. With so many common couplets floating around, did the low georgics, for instance, give a head start to the latter-century epigram shift? Moreover, the 'high-culture' position we assume for poetry now seems not to have fully solidified yet; the low georgics imply that verse may have been much more a part of everyday lives than it is now. How and when do certain genres take on a 'non-literary' valence and decorum, even as the categories of literary and non-literary, poetic and non-poetic, verse and prose, were solidifying? Formally, couplets predominate in the whole corpus; here, we might reopen questions about the development of the pentameter couplet after Chaucer. There are also many rhyme royal stanzas, Monk's Tale stanzas, and *abab* quatrains. These stanzaic forms, especially rhyme royal, tended to be used to translate more formal content, such as prologues, debates, authorial defences, or colophon flourishes, even when the French sources were in prose or in other forms. The distribution of these forms around content is not perfectly patterned, but it does suggest that by 1500, stanzas were seen as more formal and paratextual vehicles while the shorter forms (couplets and a few triplets) were starting to be used in mainly two ways – first as mnemonics, inscriptions or woodcut captions, and proverbs; and second, in long series of couplet narratives. The translations illuminate what might not be so clear otherwise: already a post-medieval pattern of usage of verse forms was beginning to show in the translators' choices, although this is emergent rather than perfected.

There are some interesting formal experiments in the translations as well, and these tend to challenge our literary period and movement categories. For example, Robert Copland picks up one of the favourite devices of the *rhétoriqueurs*, the *acrostiche* or anagram poem. He translates Pierre Gringore's authorial acrostic, a crossed-rhyme *huitain* from the *Complainte de trop tard marié*, into a two-stanza rhyme royal acrostic on his own name that bears almost no resemblance to the content of the French.[26] Gringore's

> Gouuerner [debuez] la maison
> Renger vos gens vostre famille
> Iouyeusement et par raison
> Noyses euiter et castille
> Gentement faire vostre estille
> Ordonnez voz cas promtement
> Rigueur a battre estre habille
> Espoir fait viure longuement

[Govern and order your house, kin, and family joyfully and reasonably; avoid disputes and quarrels; make your manner gentle; take care of things promptly; be capable of strong punishments; hope makes for a long life.]

becomes Copland's

> Rychenes in youth with good gouernaunce
> Often helpeth age whan youth is gone his gate
> Both yonge and olde must haur theyr sustenaunce
> Euer in this worlde soo fekyll and rethrograte
> Ryght as an ampte the which all gate
> Trusseth and caryeth for his lyues fode
> Eny thynge that which hym semeth to be good
> Crysten folke ought for to haue
> Open hertes vnto god almyght
> Puttynge in theyr mynde thyr soule to saue
> Lernynge to come vnto the eternall lyght
> And kepe well theyr maryage and trouth plyght
> Notynge alway of theyr last ende
> Durynge theyr lyues how they the tyme spende.

Copland also creates another authorial acrostic when he translates a companion poem, the *Complainte de trop tost marié*. That poem is not by Gringore and has no French acrostic, but Copland adds to it a disingenuously witty Monk's Tale stanza acrostic likewise based on his own name. The first acrostic shows his willingness to ignore content in order to translate a formal poetic device, and the second shows his ability to create original instances of the device. In this sense Copland's experiment is typical of the early printers' raids on French literature, especially of their literary pretensions and skills. But note that English readers only unevenly welcomed the loot that the raiding translators brought home. Whereas in France the rhétoriqueurs enjoyed a century-long vogue and were formative in some ways of Pléiade habits (formative even of their rejection of the rhétoriqueurs' formal excesses), in England such devices and methods, while available, would not find a real vogue in England until the age of Euphuism nearly a century later, and then not in the same way or to the same degree. The early formal experiments in translation – failures, in a way – nevertheless highlight the two nations' diverging literary histories and sensibilities.

Conclusions

Once one reads past the high canon's editorially sanitized selections, the early decades of print seem frankly and excitingly strange, variable, even chaotic, and so inextricably bound up with translation as to make single or simple accounts unlikely. Translations so un-Wyattesque, so absolutely un-Surreyan, challenge not only the predominating account of English Renaissance poetry's Petrarchan origins, but also a venerable model of literary history, the translatio studii. In this model, texts are passed from one (higher, older) culture to another (lesser, younger), usually through the good offices of appropriately servile translators. Sallust's classic formulation of it, 'Ita imperium semper ad optumum [sic] quemque a minus bono transfertur' (Bellum catilinae 2.6), permits the connection between a transfer of learning and the transfer of empire. This is the stuff Tudor myths are made on, and the stuff of which Tudor poets and humanists so frequently remind their patrons. The dominant model assumes that literary change is largely linear and teleological, a matter of influence. Literary change does often work in a linear way – poets do read and respond to poets – and there may indeed prove to be traditional 'influence' at work in this corpus. But so much of the translated verse is anonymous or unattributed that it probably won't support a Bloomian or author-to-author approach to poetics. The lack of lyric poetry in early English print and the lack of a single-author-poetic-book or 'Works' model, both of which had thrived since the earliest days of print in France, also counter the idea of linear influence. Furthermore, the corpus shows evidence of simultaneous or nearly simultaneous poetic translation among multiple languages. The Dutch, French and English translations of The Ship of Fools, like the Apollonius of Tyre stories or some works of Diego de San Pedro, appearing in Spanish, French and English versions more or less simultaneously, exemplify a vernacular cosmopolitanism that is dynamic and absorptive and in which reciprocity and mutuality among language versions seem at least as important as linearity from one to another.[27] Sometimes, 'El original es infiel a la traducción', as Jorge Luis Borges said of the novel Vathek (Borges 1974/2002), implying that a translation may take on an independent life and that translations can be viewed 'backwards' as well as from the usual direction. So temporal sequence, one of the most fixed of all critical and cognitive categories, is not the only and may not always be the best guide to literary analysis, as certain of these translations suggest.

G.H. Tucker reminds us that the intertextuality that matters is 'not so much . . . the scattered bones of individual sources as the suggestive skeleton of a once living cultural context' (1990:4). In light of the French-derived verse of the early phases of English printing, the history of Renaissance verse would seem to involve much more than a chain of authorial influence, more than canonical dominoes tumbling northward in the line of the translatio studii. These translations invite us to develop more inclusive, more comprehensive explanations of textual transmission and transformation and new models of literary change.

We might do this in any number of ways. The high variability of the corpus and the apparent randomness of particular literary appropriations might lead us to consider chaos theory, a model of change derived from non-linear dynamics, a subfield of physics. Or, a recent theory of cultural change derived from cognitive linguistics (with roots in Darwin) that may be useful in thinking of translation and literary history is 'meme theory'. More useful still, disease-tracking and ecological models of change would hold that environmental factors must support the spread of any disease, trend or organism. Derived from disease-tracking models in epidemiology, Malcolm Gladwell's tipping point theory, really a sociological and economic model, explains that trends arise, or do not, according to the actions of trend agents, whom he calls Connectors, Mavens and Salespersons, and those small groups who communicate and sustain the trends (Gladwell 2000). If their actions conjoin, accelerate and reach a critical population, a trend reaches its tipping point and spreads widely. 'Stickiness', or the quality of the trend that makes it appealing to a given population, and 'contagiousness', the ease and speed with which it takes over in that population, are two factors Gladwell studies that measure the interaction of a trend with its contexts. Certainly, in this model, the Mavens/translators would be bringing something new to the system, and the Connectors/printers would have the multiple social contacts for whom they put the new material in easily receivable terms and congenial (i.e., printed texts presented in a certain way); a printer-translator would fill both roles, as well as the persuasive Salesperson role, in the process. The stickiness and contagiousness of any given work might be gauged by, say, the memorability of a poem's lines, the flexibility of its rhyme schemes, or the effectiveness of an imprint's mise-en-page. There's more to tipping point theory than this, of course, but Gladwell's concept gives us another way to think about the canon: editors, readers, bookstore owners, and even professors negotiate a work's contexts as agents of literary change on whom authors depend for textual survival.

Such a model describes literary change in general terms, but it may also have more direct explanatory force in particular cases. For example, the *Quinze joyes de mariage*, an anti-marital satire, is first translated into English verse as *The Fyftene Joyes of Maryage* in 1509. By the end of the century it is controversial enough to be censored and burned, and then to be retranslated and reissued dozens of times over the following several centuries. This printing history indicates a sustained early-modern appropriation of French misogamy. Yet the very same themes and attitudes – indeed, some of the same phrasing – when translated from the *Farce du Pasté* by John Heywood as *Johan Johan and his Wife Tyb*, played at Henry VIII's court, and printed by William Rastell in 1533, otherwise made no splash, hardly even a drip, in English. Both French items were hugely popular in France, but only one translation became popular in England. Author-to-author influence models will not explain this, nor will evaluative or aesthetic models: Heywood's translation is more skillful by nearly any standard. Dynamic or non-linear models of change, however, address coteries, contexts, timing, and agents of transmission. Tipping point theory, for instance, would hold that the *Fyftene Joyes of Maryage* readership of 1509 was sufficient to assure a second and many subsequent printings, and thus an ever-expanding series of trend agents and social networks. The contextual 'buzz' of its censorship in 1599 may also have helped its later popularity. On the other hand, John Heywood would seem to have been an excellent potential Maven for his *Johan Johan*, introducing its satirical tropes to the Henrician court. But despite the higher social status of its potential Connectors and Salespersons (a court audience and printer William Rastell), its private, less favourable performance environment and a restricted single printing did not allow the play enough contagiousness to reach its 'tipping point' and catch on. (And the mix of its anti-marital genre and its timing, in 1533, the year of Anne Boleyn's pregnancy and marriage to Henry VIII, might not have made for ideal 'stickiness'.)

Dynamic models have explanatory force for early modern literary history, even outside the corpus I've identified. For instance, while author-to-author influence explains a lot about imitations of Petrarchan verse, the 'butterfly effect' borrowed from non-linear dynamics (in which a small change in initial conditions results in very large later developments) might also help explain the particular rage for Petrarchism and sonnet sequences in the 1590s. Just a few translations by Wyatt and Surrey in the 1540s, really only a butterfly in Tokyo compared with the actual practice of translators in print, had the effect of the hurricane of sonnet sequences a half-century later. Or, the general environment for sonnets had been long conditioned as favourable by Tottel's miscellany (1557), but particular receptors of the 'sonnet sequence' meme were not fully open until the 1580s. Or, although the *Hekatompathia* was printed in 1581, the tipping point for the English sonnet sequence, *Astrophil and Stella* (1591), can be explained by the particular social groups and powerful Mavens and Connectors acting after Sidney's death. Such models help us think of coteries, contexts and interactive agents over time, outside the usual categories.

Another way – a most useful way, I think – to answer the epistemological challenge of these translations is to read this large corpus in terms of what Karlheinz Stierle (1996) sees as 'perhaps the most important aspect of what we call "Renaissance" ': the 'co-presence of cultures'. This notion aligns well with what Mary Louise Pratt has called contact zones, 'social spaces where disparate cultures meet, clash, and grapple with each other' (Pratt 1992:4). A contact perspective is dynamic, asking 'how subjects are constituted in and by their relations to each other' (ibid.:7). Although Pratt generally discusses contact zones in terms of the asymmetrical relations of colonialism, it is not much of a stretch to read English literature as 'post-colonial' in a certain sense. A former colony of France (which after the Norman Conquest imposed laws, language, servitudes and cultural forms on England, many of which endure even today), England continued to struggle toward an assertive and successful nationhood of its own. This ongoing appropriation takes place between two cultures that had been as one since 1066 and were in the final years of separation after the Hundred Years War. One can see these (and other) translations as traces of cultural systems in a long process of individuation. Contact, in Pratt's view, involves a struggle 'for self-determination, that is, significant control over the terms and conditions under which [the colonized] will develop their relations with the nation-state' (Pratt 1996:3) – how England will, in other words, produce itself separately from France, and, where this corpus is concerned, how English poetry will produce itself separately from French literature. It is a very long and uneven process: Henry V asserted English as the language of government in 1415, but the law French of Littleton's *Tenures* was not put in English until the 1520s. The continuing Tudor claims to the French throne, protracted warfare and diplomacy between England and France, imitation (and mockery) of French fashion, art and architecture, apprentice risings against foreigners, and national flash points such as the marriage of Mary Tudor to Louis XII or the rival displays at the Field of the Cloth of Gold – such historical background to the verse indicates that France had long been, and arguably continues to be, under England's skin in ways that Italy simply was not. And as David Wallace reminds me, England was under France's skin, as well, continuing to hold Calais between 1348 and 1558, and trying intermittently, with varying success, to expand that territory; chroniclers even complained of the English 'colonizers' there.[28]

Indeed one finds hybridity or *métissage* between these two cultures. The rather bizarre profusion of this corpus, with its multiplicity of forms and genres, its variety of themes, its experiments in poetics, seems a literary analogue to so-called 'contact languages' like pidgins and creoles. Linguists think of these as liminal, chaotic languages, with more fluid than fixed structures (Pratt 1996:6). In terms of literary history, we can see the explosion of early printed translations from French as actively improvisational, as one last intensive part of the long post-colonial negotiations of English identity. Often the struggle for individuation appears in particular features of a translation: the visibility of titles noted above; the retention of French names, place-names, allusions, and even phrases left in French, like the refrain line 'Beaute sans bonte ne vaut rien' or the title *Lamant mal traicte de samye*; the French speaker identifications, 'La Femme' and 'L'homme' in the *Interlocucyon*; Fitzherbert's retention of the French horse-buying mnemonic alongside his English version; the woodcuts; the layouts; right down to the very typefaces. These and many other visible residues testify to Stierle's 'co-presence of cultures' and to a process of transculturation at work.[29]

From this view, it's not only the predominance of numbers but their dynamic potential within the cultural context that makes the verse translations from French compelling. I would propose the early printers' houses as non-literal contact zones that function in the history of English poetics much as early modern colonial contact zones or eighteenth-century Habermasian 'public spheres' do: dangerous, exciting, newly-open but conflicted spaces where experiments happen and opportunities for change abound. This unread, little-studied literary engagement – taking place at a crucial moment in the history of English poetics, in the wake of a stunning new technology – can teach us a great deal. The translations, for instance, challenge the many critics following Richard Helgerson's *Forms of Nationhood* (1992) to account for the foundational, constitutive alterity of early modern poetry.[30] Certainly, if we are serious about 'always historicizing', we will not choose monolingual approaches to relentlessly polyglot Renaissance texts and an intensely bicultural (really, multi-cultural) Renaissance world. Properly explored and understood, the new-old corpus promises to change the way we think about textual transformation in the Renaissance, about early modern intercultural and intertextual relations, and about the development of English identity and poetics.

The broader challenge for the critic exemplified here – the challenge of translation – is to read not in comfortable, relatively static epistemes but to read across national, 'movement', and period categories and to think instead in terms of polysystems. This means treating translations (and all texts) as dynamic rather than static: to watch them as moving creations against moving cultural backgrounds.[31] Translations may serve, as Margaret Ferguson says, 'as a theory of history, as a hermeneutic tool, and as a linguistic practice' (1984:25), or, among other things, as agents of change, irenic time-travellers, reconnecting divided worlds. And they usually do, if we watch them in motion, challenge the critical and scholarly stories we tell each other.

Notes

1   All translations are mine unless otherwise noted. Early imprints can be located via the STC or *Short Title Catalogue of Books Printed in England, Scotland and Ireland and of English Books Printed Abroad 1475–1640* (London 1926; rev. ed. Katherine Pantzer, London: Bibliographical Society, 1976–1991) or the on-line catalogue of the Bibliothèque nationale de France

<www.bnf.fr>. This essay describes parts of my larger study of the entire corpus. See also Coldiron (2004).

2   For instance, although the syllable-counts in a French poem and its English translation may be ten, a *décasyllabe* is not a pentameter and has different effects, a different history. Once aware of this, we can compare each metre's respective relation to its history and to its effects, rather than one to the other. Such questions multiply at every level, and some will be more relevant than others for any given translation pair.

3   For a cogent review of the naming debates in literary studies, see Marcus (1992); for the historian's view, see Grafton (1998); for an interrogation, see Coldiron (2000), 145–190. Whatever we call it, 'the Renaissance is a primal scene of European historiography to which we seem bound to return out of fascination or denial', as Starn (1998:122) puts it.

4   Caxton's first press was in Bruges before he came to Westminster. On the Burgundian influence, see Armstrong (1983), Kipling (1977), and Munro (1972). Robert Copland's experiments in poetry included many translations from French, most edited by Mary C. Erler in Copland (1993). French-born Richard Pynson was King's printer to Henry VIII. Wynkyn de Worde translated and printed many items from French. For a superior, detailed survey of the evolution of French-born printing between Caxton and Pynson, see Boffey (2000).

5   From *The Hye Way to the Spittal Hous* (London: Copland, *c.* 1536); this image is taken from the Early English Books Online database of images, although it is freely and widely available on microfilm (STC 5732); the extant printed copy is held at the Huntington Library.

6   This image is reproduced by permission of the Huntington Library, San Marino, California. Image published with permission of ProQuest Information and Learning Company. Further reproduction is prohibited without permission.

7   Neatly countering an older view represented by Sanders (1951).

8   Figure 19.2, title cut from Alain Chartier, *Les Demandes d'amours avecque les responses* (s.l.: s.n., s.d.), but probably before 1500; Bibliothèque nationale de France, numerisé, No. FRBNF37286581, reproduced from <gallica.bnf.fr> with permission.

9   The two strains, of course, are not unrelated in origins (troubadours, *stilnovisti*) or in effects; Laura/Beatrice, the *donna* types, and courtly ladies are cousins.

10   As Anne Lake Prescott points out, verse we now call sexist was not then intended or thought of as woman-hating: misogynist-then and misogynist-now are two different things (private correspondence, 2001). Misogamous or anti-marriage poems, too, may include misogyny, and/or may include what we now think of as sexism. But there is also misogamous verse that is not particularly anti-feminist.

11   Like so many words on both sides of the corpus, the meanings of these have changed. Drab: OED *sb* r, dirty and untidy woman. Slut: OED *sb* 1, a woman of dirty, slovenly, or untidy habits. Callet: OED *sb* 1, a lewd woman. Over time 'drab' and 'slut' take on connotations of promiscuity, and 'callet' comes to imply 'scold'.

12   Sometimes French misogyny enters English in translations of works not ostensibly concerned with women. For example, *The sayings or prouerbs of king Salomon, with the answers of Marcolphus tra[n]slated out of Frenche to englysshe* (London: R. Pynson for R. Wyer, *c.* 1529) undercuts most of Solomon's general philosophical points of wisdom with Marcolphus's bawdy misogynist (and misanthropist) pronouncements:

> Solomon:
> Men accompte them as wyse as fooles
> That the burnyng coles
> In theyr bosomes will hyde;
> Marcolphus:
> For a foole he is tolde
> That wasteth all his golde
> To clothe a hoores syde.

13   R. Fawkes, *c.* 1525; another edition is printed by Wyer, *c.* 1540. This image is taken from the widely available microfilm copy of Fawkes's imprint, STC 1696.

14   This image is reproduced by permission of the Huntington Library. San Marino, California. Image published with permission of ProQuest Information and Learning Company. Further reproduction is prohibited without permission.

15   *Here begynneth an interlocucyon, with an argument, betwixt a man and a woman*, . . . (London: de Worde, c. 1525), translating Guillaume Alexis, *Le Debat de lomme et de la fenime* (Paris: Trepperel, n.d., and Paris: 1520); but composed c. 1460.

16   Calendars, STC numbers 22409, 22409.5, 22410, 22411, 22412; hours, STC numbers 15935, 15937, 15938, 15938.5, 15939, 15962, 15986.3, 15992, 15993.

17   Lyon: J. de Tournes, 1553. The French version is also printed by Tournes in 1553.

18   London: R. Grafton, 1545; with many subsequent editions.

19   In France, these moments are not as tense, though Louis XI died and Louis XII succeeded to the French throne in 1483. In England, however, Edward IV died in 1483 and Richard III claimed the throne and (probably) murdered the princes in the Tower. Woodville, translator of French verse and patron of early English printing, was 'the noblest and most accomplished victim of Richard III' (DNB). The *Calendar of State Papers (Domestic Series) of the Reigns of Edward VI, Mary, Elizabeth and James I* (London, Longman, Brown, Green, Longmans, & Roberts; [etc., etc.] 1856–72) shows that 1549 was also a terrible year of uprisings, rebellions, treason, sedition, and the calling of nobles to court to support the monarch, Edward VI. Francis Segar, the translator, is not named, and the details are beyond the scope of this essay, but the entries for the months June through November, especially, give an indication of court intrigue as a serious problem for the realm; Segar's translation is timely.

20   Likewise, Fabyan's *Chronicles* include short, scornful translated verses against the early-fourteenth-century duke Phillip of Valois (STC 10659, 10650, 10651, 10652, dated 1516 to 1542).

21   Westminster: Caxton, 1478; reprinted with minor revisions in *The Boke of Fame* (London: Pynson, 1526). When compared with the French original, the first couplet shows a concern for nationhood that resonates with the rest of the translation's implicit critiques of court. The English begins:

> [T]he grete vertus of oure elders notable
> Ofte to remember is thing profitable

Unremarkable, by itself, but Christine's French version, found in BL Harley 4431, a manuscript owned by Woodville, begins:

> Les bonnes meurs et les sages notable [*sic*]
> Rementeuoir souuent sont proufitable [*sic*]

Roughly, Christine begins by saying that good morals or manners and notable wise people are profitable often to remember. Woodville, on the other hand, says that it is a profitable thing often to remember the great *virtues* (not 'meurs', morals-manners) of (not 'et', and our (not just any) notable *elders* (not 'sages'). Woodville adds an awkward extra syllable to these lines, but more significantly, adds a possessive genealogy of virtue. The translation changes mean that these are not just any sages but our own elders, whose virtues, not only whose wisdom, we (English) readers naturally inherit. Woodville opens with a familial implication, a rhetorical 'we' that places the new English reader not in a cosmopolitan, aristocratic coterie but as the obedient child of a tradition, about to receive instruction in 'our' heritage of virtue (a heritage 'englished', despite the high French visibility of the printed title). Woodville's claim to the Frenchwoman's advice as 'oure' heritage recalls England's claims to the French crown and to French lands, claims Woodville himself sought to enforce in several overseas campaigns. With their presentation and pronouns, Woodville and Caxton 'english' its instruction for good, absorbing its wisdom into 'our English elders' virtues'.

22   *The Bayte and Snare of Fortune* (London: Wayland, 1556); Platin's *Débat de l'homme et de l'argent* (Paris: Jehan Sainct Denys, n.d.; and 1529) may itself be a translation of the anonymous *Contrasto del denaro e dell' uomo*.

23   Robert de Balsac, *[La] Nef des princes et des batailles de noblesse: avec aultres enseignments utilz et profitables* . . . *Item plus le regime d'ung jeune prince et les prouerbes des princes et aultres petis livres* . . . (Lyon: G. Balsarin, 1502).

24   London: Berthelet, 1533, fol. 49; London: Wayland, 1556, fol. xxxiv.

25   Reproduced with permission from the Bodleian Library, University of Oxford. Image

26   Gringore, *Complainte de trop tard marié* (Paris: [P. Le Dru?], 1505: Paris: [A. Lotrian?, *c.* 1527]).

27   Diego de San Pedro's *Carcel de Amour* as *Chasteau d'antour* or *Castle of Love*. Some of the early Renaissance Dido literature, ultimately derived from Latin (the *Heroides* or the *Aeneid*), makes its way into French, English and Italian versions without a neat genealogical order. The *Ship of Fools* also has Latin versions, some possibly back-translations.

28   Private correspondence, 2002; and Wallace's MLA presentation, December 2002. Whether these are two nations trying to colonize one another, I cannot say, though the desire for domination and appropriation that Pratt's contact zone model entails is surely there. Johannes Fabricius speaks of the French pox (syphilis) as early as 1520, and trade resentments (of French textiles and of French apprentices taking English jobs) are a commonplace. Not all things French are welcome imports, in short.

29   Transculturation is ethnographers' term for the process by which subordinated groups select and invent from materials transmitted to them by a dominant or metropolitan culture. The Englishness of early modern France seems less compelling to me, though I know of no comprehensive study of it.

30   Pratt's model, furthermore, makes central the relationality of meaning; see Pratt (1993:88).

31   Many scholars do: Stierle, Pratt, Braden, Greene, Wallace, Prescott, and others. I sketch a way in Coldiron (2001).

Chapter 20

Indra Levy

ENGENDERED BY TRANSLATION: MODERN JAPANESE LITERATURE, VERNACULAR STYLE, AND THE WESTERNESQUE *FEMME FATALE*

EDITOR'S INTRODUCTION

Futabatei's translation work carved out an important space for innovation within the field of modern Japanese literature, paradoxically demonstrating the stunning innovations made possible by what, from the perspective of the conventional English discourse on translation, would amount to the slavish imitation of the foreign text.

THE MEIJI PERIOD USHERED IN AN ERA of translations from Western languages that would have a decisive impact on all forms of Japanese literary production, and that were characterized by the use of *kanbun-kundokutai*, a system of rendering written Chinese into Japanized pronunciations, grammatical and syntactic patterns. As the preferred language of translation, it facilitated the acquisition of new social customs and forms of knowledge, but within the context of the novel, the transformative potential of translation into *kanbun-kundokutai* was substantially limited to facilitating the transference of exotic narrative content (essentially stories about the West), without the encumbrance of the aesthetic demands and stylistic conventions of classical Japanese prose.

Against this background, Levy charts Futabatei Shimei's dual career as translator and novelist to demonstrate the importance of the innovative language and style of translation he initiated. Futabatei's attempt to translate the original text as an indivisible unit of linguistic form and narrative content necessitated the creation of a new target language. The language that he created in Japanese is known as *genbun-itchi*, a term that broadly refers to the vernacular but that emphasizes the relationship between speech and writing. Levy demonstrates with extensive examples the specificities of the new language he created and the new gender archetype he introduced, and examines his legacy and impact on the Naturalists. His creation and successful deployment of the *genbun-itchi* style was to constitute the very foundation of the modern Japanese novel. The form of literature he produced using this style was so new as to ultimately create a radical divide between modern Japanese fiction and all that preceded it.

Futabatei believed in the language of truth as an absolute value that demanded nothing less than a complete pledge of allegiance. He sought meaning, rather than purely aesthetic value, in fiction. In the context of the Japanese vernacularization movement, truth was a universal value that demands articulation in the colloquial tongue. Later in his career, Futabatei began to harbour serious doubts about literature as a vehicle of truth. These doubts eventually led him to abandon writing his own novels and producing literary translations for almost an entire decade.

Follow-up questions for discussion

- Levy notes that during a period in Japanese history when literary translators exercised considerable freedom in altering the content and formal characteristics of source texts, 'Futabatei's pious attitude toward the original text could only be described as original in itself. And indeed, it was what enabled, even compelled him to create a new literary language for Japanese'. Consider the dynamics of literal or close translation as opposed to various forms of adaptation in different contexts. Is 'piety' towards the source text necessarily innovative in itself? Is innovation a function of formal features within the text, a function of the context in which experimentation takes place, or both?

- Responding to criticism directed at literary studies that emphasize foreign influences and hence trivialize the importance of local literature, Yoshihiro (2005:145) argues that 'the introduction of foreign cultures is inevitably selective and never lacks initiative, . . . it is not merely a passive operation. The originality of translators and transmitters of texts should be examined and duly recognized, even when their chief mission is the "faithful" introduction of foreign cultures to their audiences'. Consider some of the ways in which the creative work of translators, whatever strategy they adopt, may be given more visibility in the discipline, and the methods and perspectives that provide potential avenues for studying this creativity systematically. Useful references to consult include Boase-Beier and Holman (1999), Baker (2000), Scott (2006), Boase-Beier (2007) and Munday (2008).

- Levy explains that we normally think of translation as 'a process of transference between two discrete and already established languages', whereas Futabatei 'used this process to create a new language in Japanese'. Consider some of the implications of this statement. For instance, are there other instances in which translation participated in the creation of new languages (as well as scripts) in various parts of the world? To what extent can we think of any source or target language as 'discrete' and 'established'? What role does translation play in extending and blurring the boundaries of any language?

Recommended further reading

Cockerill, Hiroko (2006) *Style and Narrative in Translation: The Contribution of Futabatei Shimei*, Manchester: St. Jerome.

Twitchell-Waas, Jeffrey (2001) 'Ghostly Effects: Orientalist Translation in Pound and Yasusada Text', *Asian Journal of Social Science* 29(2): 234–48.

Wakabayashi, Judy (2005) 'The Reconceptionization of Translation from Chinese in 18th century Japan', in Eva Hung (ed.) *Translation and Cultural Change*, Amsterdam: John Benjamins, 121–45.

Wickeri, Janice (1995) 'The Union Version of the Bible and the New Literature in China', *The Translator* 1(2): 129–52.

Yoshihiro, Ohasawa (2005) 'Amalgamation of Literariness: Translations as a Means of Introducing European Literary Techniques to Modern Japan', in Eva Hung and Judy Wakabayashi (eds) *Asian Translation Traditions*, Manchester: St. Jerome, 135–51.

THE HISTORY OF MODERN JAPANESE literature begins with translation in more than one sense. First, we have the translation of the nineteenth-century European concept of 'literature' into the Chinese compound *bungaku* – not a neologism in itself, but the investment of a completely new meaning in an old and fairly recondite term. Tracing it as far back as *The Analects*, the word *bungaku* 文学 originally referred to the study of written documents, and its meaning later evolved to include the study of rhetoric and the Confucian classics. It was not until the early Meiji period that it came to signify 'literature' in the nineteenth-century European sense, as a category of the arts that included poetry, drama and fiction. This reorganization of knowledge marks a watershed in the social history of fiction, raising the novel from its lowly status as frivolous entertainment to the high culture of civilized nations (Isoda 1991).[1] In tandem with the introduction of this new concept, the Meiji period ushered in an era of translations from Western languages that would have a decisive impact on all forms of Japanese literary production.

The onset of the Meiji era saw Kanagaki Robun, a professionally trained writer of the popular fiction of the Edo period known as *gesaku*, struggling to keep up with the rapid changes of 'enlightenment and civilization'. Robun's combination of formal training as a *gesaku* writer and lack of training in foreign languages was to become a serious handicap in the new literary (or rather *newly literary*) world of the Meiji period. *Seiyô dôchû hizakurige* (1870–76) and *Aguranabe* (1871–73), two of Robun's final efforts to maintain his old trade, duly reflect Meiji Japan's signature turn towards the West. The former tells a comic tale of two Yokohama merchants who travel to the West; the latter comprises a series of vignettes about the patrons of a beef restaurant in Tokyo. Although Robun studied up for the composition of these works by reading Fukuzawa Yukichi's best-selling accounts of contemporary conditions in Europe, his formal training had only prepared him to project the profound new changes taking place through the irretrievably outdated lenses of *gesaku* language. It was a flippant comic language that could not resist reducing the West to a series of *dajare* puns:

ゆきの普魯西もさて亜米利加も馬車で通ふて英吉利。僕
はこれほど葡萄牙。きみはいつでも仏蘭西か。浮世の希臘
と只印度、床を土耳其のひとつ夜着。埃及こちらへ寄
らしやんせ。支那／＼と取りすがり。魯西亜の見える恋
のみちハアトツチリトン

Snow **fall/Prussia** too regardless **rain/America** too carriage by travel
Yuki no **purosha** mo sate **amerika** mo basha de kayôte

*go/England. I these days **am smitten/Portugal.** You always*
ingirisu. Boku wa kore hodo **horutogaru**. Kimi wa itsu de mo

*reject/France? Floating world's **duty/Greece** just **once/India**, bed*
furansu ka. Ukiyo no **girisha** to tada **indo**, toko wo

*lay/Turkey of one nightwear. A **little/Egypt** this way please come.*
toruko no hitotsu yogi. **Ejiputo** kochira e irashanse.

*Coquettish/China cling. **Russia/?** visible amour's path*
Shinashina to torisugari. **Roshia** no mieru koi no michi . . .[2]

In this indomitable effort to assimilate Western place names to the language of *gesaku*, most of the double entendres (indicated in bold print above) stretch homophonic associations far beyond their usual limits. Here is the closest approximation I could manage in English:

> Snow may Prussiapitate and American on rain, but I shall be travelEngland by carriage. These days I am in Port-du-gal. Will you never Francy me? Hinduty to the floating world, just once she aGreece Turkish me for a night. Please come a teeniEgyptian in my direction. Sino-ously cuddling up, Russian down the path of amour.

While this almost intoxicated, nonsensical flippancy might have provided a welcome palliative for the merchant classes within the staid Tokugawa hierarchical system, the sobering effects of the social upheaval occasioned by the threat of Western hegemony proved less conducive to the enjoyment of pure verbal play.

The end of the self-proclaimed *gesaku* was undoubtedly hastened by the work of literary translation. In 1877 (Meiji 10), Niwa Jun'ichirô published his epoch-making translation of Bulwer-Lytton's *Ernest Maltravers* – a novel which, though certainly not in itself of great literary merit, offered the reader a compelling story and a more intimate sense, however fictional, of the daily lives and sensibilities of Westerners. A sensation in its time, Niwa's *Karyû shunwa* (A spring tale of flowers and willows) set an important standard for novel-writing in Japan for the remainder of the Meiji teens. According to Itô Sei, one of the most important contributing factors to the popularity of *Karyû shunwa* was that Niwa wrote it in *kanbun-kundokutai*, a Japanese permutation of literary Chinese (ibid.:162–63).[3] While Robun was working in the *gesaku* language of commoners, Niwa wrote in the language of the educated élite. His translation of a modern English novel into literary Chinese helped to establish a new audience for the genre.

The flood of political novels and translations written in *kanbun-kundokutai* that followed in the wake of Niwa's *Karyû shunwa* provide ample evidence of its wide-ranging impact. (Even Tsubouchi Shôyô's translation of Sir Walter Scott's *Bride of Lammermoor* into the rhythmic Japanese style of *gabuntai*, published three years later, follows the precedent set by Niwa in its Chinese title of *Shunpû jôwa*.) This is the second sense in which the history of modern Japanese literature began with translation. As one commentator remarks, 'For the Japanese novel, the period from the publication of *Karyû shunwa* in Meiji 10 to that of Futabatei Shimei's *Ukigumo* in Meiji 20 brought forth so many translations as to suggest a dearth of compositional power in Japanese literary circles at the time' (Tokuda Shûsei 1914/1982:13).[4] Clearly, the popularity of Chinese diction and written style in the Meiji teens was not the manifestation of some Japanese preoccupation with China, but rather with a particular style of translating the civilization and enlightenment of the 'West' that marked its exotic prestige by means of the semi-foreign *lingua franca* of Chinese.[5] Indeed, the entire vocabulary of 'Western civilization' was translated into Chinese compounds (*kango*), from *bunmei* (civilization) and *bungaku* to *sokuhatsu* (the simplified coiffure of the Western-style bun) and *butôkai* (dance ball). As the preferred language of translation, Chinese surely facilitated the acquisition of new social customs, technologies of learning, and the profound reorganization of knowledge by which Japan sought entrance into the exclusive and powerful club of modern nations. Yet within the context of the novel itself, the transformative potential of translation into *kanbun-kundokutai* was substantially limited to the sphere of narrative content.

First, let us examine the language of fiction established in Niwa's *Karyû shunwa*. In his commentary on this work, Kimura Ki selects the following passages for comparison:

[*Ernest Maltravers*]
'You work at the factories, I suppose?' he said.
'I do, sir. Bad times.'

[*Karyû shunwa*]

客問フテ曰ク子、日ニ近傍ノ製造所ニ行キ以テ生活ノ途ヲ立ツルヤ。曰ク誠ニ然リ。然レドモ方今製造所盛ナラズ。僕大ニ之ヲ憂フ。

[back-translation of *Karyû shunwa*]

Quoth the guest, querying, Dost thou go to the proximate factory everyday to earn a subsistence? Quoth, Verily I do. However, recently production is not prolific. I am greatly distressed by this. (Kimura 1972:395–96)

There is no parallel to *kanbun-kuzushi* in the history of English letters, and this gap has made a parody of my attempt to convey the highfalutin language of Niwa's text. It is not my intention here to suggest that Niwa's translation would seem as ridiculous to his contemporary Japanese audience as the above English rendition will surely seem to mine; Niwa was writing in a well-established idiom that was quite familiar to the educated classes of 1870s Japan, to whom a more literal, 'vernacular' translation may have seemed ridiculous indeed. What the above retranslation should make immediately clear is the inability of the *kanbun-kundokutai* style to approximate the pedestrian tone of Bulwer-Lytton's vernacular English. While *kanbun-kundokutai* provided a suitable medium for the translation of European concepts into 'Japanese' in ways that we have already noted above, this is its most obvious drawback.

In the translation of novels, what *kanbun-kundokutai* did facilitate was the transference of exotic narrative content (i.e. stories about the West) unencumbered by the aesthetic demands and stylistic conventions of classical Japanese prose. In her study of Futabatei, Marleigh Grayer Ryan sums up the conditions of literary translation in the early Meiji period as follows (1965:100):

[The translator] was forced to choose between two equally unsatisfactory styles: the cold, terse, extremely difficult intellectual language of *kanbun-chô* [*kanbun-kundokutai*] and the poetic, allusive, flowing *gabuntai* [classical Japanese prose]. The vogue which *kanbun-chô* enjoyed in the mid-1880s stemmed from the fact that readers considered this style to be more suited to Western writing than the flowery *gabuntai*. The images and metaphors of *gabuntai* were so intimately linked with past Japanese literature that they seemed singularly inappropriate to foreign fiction. The wealth of associations conjured up by the mention of a familiar image or even word drawn from traditional Japanese literary writing was likely to destroy the atmosphere of a foreign work. Such images and vocabulary had to be abandoned to forestall the possibility of irrelevant associations with past literature, but substitutions were hard to discover.

The preference for *kanbun-kundokutai* in the translation of Western literatures is also surely related to the fact that this style originated as a language of translation. Neither 'Chinese' nor 'Japanese' in the strict sense, the Japanese practices of reading and writing known as *kanbun-kundokutai* grew out of the tradition of rendering written Chinese into Japanized pronunciations, grammatical and syntactical patterns. As a language of interlineal translation between Chinese and Japanese, *kanbun-kundokutai* was an interlingual *écriture par excellence*. Its greater malleability as a language of translation can be seen, for instance, in its capacity for maintaining gender (and class) neutrality in the translation of English dialogue – aside from the use of the gender-specific first-person pronouns *boku* (male) and *warawa* (female), in Niwa's translation Maltravers and his *amour* Alice 'speak' the same stilted language. Had Niwa rendered his translation in spoken Japanese, such gender parity would have been read as a clear mark of the lower classes.[6]

While Niwa's *kanbun-kundokutai* style was able to provide the reader with fairly straightforward access to the essential elements of the foreign story, *gabuntai*, a language of poetic allusion rather than expository prose, had powerful demands of its own. Ryan (1965:43) provides an illuminating glimpse of the results:

> . . . Tsubouchi translated Scott's 'had, by her frequent rambles, learned to know each lane, alley, dingle, or bushy dell' as

> > . . . koko kashiko to shôyô shi,
> > Sansui no ki o saguritareba
> > Keikyoku no ato o uzumetaru nobe no komichi,
> > Matsukaze no hibiki ni wasuru tagitsuse wa iu mo sara nari,
> > Kaigan arasoitachi,
> > Rôboku outsu taru yûkoku no sumizumi made,
> > Nabete eshirazaru wa nakarikeri. . . .

> > [Wandering here and there
> > exploring the wonders of mountain and river,
> > of paths through fields filled with brambles,
> > or the waterfall echoing in the wind through the pines,
> > every corner of the warring cliffs and ravines thick with ancient
> >   trees –
> > there was none unknown to her. . . .][7]

The broad divergence between the texts will surely strike the reader as gross embellishment on Shôyô's part. Yet it is not necessarily arbitrary. Rather, the poetic elaboration of Scott's descriptive prose reveals the kind of judgement call that inevitably occurs when the translator places primary authority in the conventions of the target language instead of the original text. In the case of *gabuntai*, the nature of that judgement call is simply more obvious than in *kanbun-kundokutai* (or modern English, for that matter).

The creation of a new literary language

Futabatei Shimei's dual career as translator and novelist presents us with the third sense in which modern Japanese literature began with translation. Futabatei's long-standing status as a progenitor of Japanese literary modernity derives primarily from his creation and successful deployment of the *genbun-itchi* style that was to become the very foundation of the modern Japanese novel. He was the first to attempt to translate a modern Western vernacular text into vernacular Japanese, and one of the first to try his hand at writing original fiction in vernacular Japanese. Significantly, his earliest efforts at literary translation predate his work as a novelist, though they were never published and the manuscripts have been lost. By 1886, he had translated a work by Nikolai Gogol (title unknown), and by March of the same year he had translated part of Ivan Turgenev's *Fathers and Children*. From Tsubouchi Shôyô's recollections of these translations, we know that both of them were written in a vernacular style. *Ukigumo* was published in installments over a two-year period from July 1887 through August 1889. In the meantime, Futabatei also débuted as a literary translator with the serialized publication of *Aibiki* (Turgenev's 'The Rendezvous' from *A Sportsman's Notebook*).[8] As this chronology itself suggests, Futabatei's creation of a vernacular Japanese literary language was inextricably tied to the process of translation.

Although in the English context we customarily consider translation to be a process of transference between two discrete and already established languages, Futabatei in fact used this process to create a new language in Japanese. It is in this sense that his translations from modern Russian literature constitute truly original innovations. If the age of literary translation and political novels precipitated by the success of *Karyû shunwa* effectively outmoded the comic *gesaku* reaction to the West, the form of literature presented by Futabatei's *Aibiki* and *Ukigumo* was so new as to ultimately create a radical divide between modern Japanese fiction and all that preceded it. For Futabatei's approach to and practice of translation manifested a new conception of literature itself. Though the effect of his work may not have been immediate, in the long run it proved to be the most incontrovertible: when Japanese Naturalists refer to the *kanbun-kundokutai* fiction they read as youths in the Meiji teens, it is almost always as a trope for their as yet immature conception of literature; by contrast, their glowing recollections of *Aibiki* almost always narrate their awakening to Literature proper (*bungaku* in the modern sense of the term).

As Ryan rightly points out, to undertake literary translation in early Meiji was to first confront a choice between the lesser of two evils. What was the basis upon which Futabatei refused this choice? In an interview, he made the following renowned statement of his personal standard for literary translation:

> Well, in the translation of foreign literature, if you think only of the meaning and place all the weight on it, there is a danger of destroying the

original. I believed that you must imbibe the rhythm of the original and then convey it, so I never disposed of a single comma or period arbitrarily – if there were three commas and one period in the original, then I would also use three commas and one period in the translation in my effort to convey the rhythm of the original. Particularly when I first started to translate, the earnest intent of conveying the rhythm of the original led to a real struggle over the form in which I tried to use the same number of words as the original and not destroy the form, but in reality it did not really turn out as I hoped.[9]

Futabatei's credo for translation serves as an implicit critique of works like *Karyû shunwa* and *Shunpû jôwa*. While Niwa's method of translation placed weight primarily in 'the meaning', Shôyô's placed greater importance on the 'rhythm' of the target language than the original text. At this point, it must be noted that Futabatei's critique of the emphasis on meaning was by no means a defence of 'liberal' translations – he himself strove for the same kind of literalness as did Nabokov in his English translation of Pushkin's *Evgeny Onegin*. This stringent standard, purely self-imposed, created perhaps the single greatest challenge to Futabatei's translations of modern Russian literature. At a time when other literary translators had few inhibitions about altering the content of the translated text and none whatsoever about altering its formal characteristics, Futabatei's pious attitude toward the original text could only be described as original in itself. And indeed, it was what enabled, even compelled him to create a new literary language for Japanese.

Futabatei's standard for translation could not have been based on anything but his understanding of literature itself. Aside from the undeniable differences of style between himself and earlier literary translators that will become apparent shortly, this is where he first departs from all of his predecessors and most of his contemporaries in the production – translation or composition – of Meiji literature. For Futabatei's attitude toward the text to be translated was indeed one of *piety*. With the possible exception of Tsubouchi Shôyô, he was the first of the Meiji literati to treat the novel with the respect customarily reserved for the Chinese classics – ethical philosophy, history, Chinese poetry – that constituted the essential syllabus for élite education in pre-Meiji Japan. Put in terms that would apply to any culture at some point in its development of a modern literature, Futabatei was one of the first in Japan to accord the novel with the respect normally reserved for the language of truth.

In 'Shôsetsu sôron' (Theory of the Novel, 1886), Futabatei defined the novel as follows:

> . . . Art is that which penetrates Ideas by means of emotion.
>
> The two kinds of novels are didactic and mimetic, but for the reasons stated above mimesis is the true essence of the novel . . . Since, from the outset, the novel is that which directly apprehends the necessary affective state (Idea) of the varied multiplicity of phenomena (Form) manifest in this world, in order to convey this apprehension to people it must be direct. In order to be direct, it must be mimetic. Thus it is evident that mimesis is the true essence of the novel . . . Yet just to proclaim mimesis without defining it leaves room for confusion. To state the very broad outlines, that which is called mimesis borrows real appearances in order to depict empty appearances. As articulated above, none of the phenomena of the real world of appearance are without a necessary Idea, yet the

Idea is obscured by contingent form so that it cannot be understood clearly. Certainly, the phenomena described in the novel are also contingent, but to clearly draw out the essential Idea within these contingent forms by means of verbal locution and plot pattern is the purpose of the mimetic novel. This requires that the writing be alive. If the writing is not alive, then even if there is an Idea it will not be evident. It requires that the plot be suitable to the Idea. If it is not suitable, then the Idea will not be able to develop sufficiently.[10]

While the famously cryptic language of this brief essay precluded all but bewilderment in the reactions of Futabatei's contemporaries, it nevertheless provides us with an important summation of his concept of literature. First, Futabatei defines the novel as a genre that borrows the appearance of reality for the sole purpose of revealing the Idea (truth or meaning) hidden within it. This is a significant departure from the notion of realism developed in Shôyô's *Shôsetsu shinzui* (Essence of the Novel, 1886), which can still be read as an advocacy of mimesis for its own sake, and it forms the basis for Futabatei's ambitious attempt to capture 'the contemporary state of the nation' in *Ukigumo*. Furthermore, he cites both verbal locution and plot construction as the key means for achieving this end. His formulation of the relationship between the calculated use of language and plot to the revelation of Idea within the novel thus lays the basis for his approach to translation: if there is something to be 'translated' from a novel, it is the Idea revealed therein, which is necessarily the product of both language (rhetorical and rhythmic form) and story (narrative content).

Futabatei's attempt to translate the original text as an indivisible unit of linguistic form and narrative content necessitated the creation of a new target language. The language that he created in Japanese is known as *genbun-itchi*, a term that in itself provides an illuminating example of the complexities of the translation process even at the morphemic level. While *genbun-itchi* is the Japanese signifier for the phenomenon of vernacularization seen in European languages, its literal translation back into English is 'the reconciliation of spoken and written languages'. Thus *genbun-itchi* provides a specific gloss for the concept of the vernacular that emphasizes the relationship between speech and writing. (Another possible gloss was provided by the term *zokubun*[*tai*] – literally, 'vulgar written style'.) One of the most intransigent problems with translation is its ability to efface itself by naturalizing to the target language, which is precisely what has happened to the language Futabatei created, as well as the very word *genbun-itchi* by which it has been named.

Despite its origins as a neologism that unhesitatingly and constantly announced its foreign derivation, the term *genbun-itchi* has long since naturalized itself to Japanese, with the consequence that it has been written and thought about *specifically as* 'the reconciliation of speech and writing' for long enough to overshadow its original connection to any broader notion of the vernacular. The sharp focus on spoken Japanese has obscured the importance of translation as both the impetus for the movement and the process by which vernacularization was ultimately realized. It is altogether too easy to lose sight of the simple fact that the call for *genbun-itchi* sprang from an awareness of the vernacular nature of modern Western writing. The seeds of the *genbun-itchi* movement were first planted by scholars of Dutch in the Edo period, who commented that the use of colloquial language in Dutch writing greatly contributed to the spread of education in the Netherlands (Yamamoto 1977:318–19).[11] If, on the surface, the *genbun-itchi* movement was a call to close the gap between colloquial speech and written language, at base it was driven by a desire to achieve parity between Japanese and modern European languages. Thus it was intralingual by definition, but interlingual in motivation. (Karatani Kojin points out that this interlingual motivation forms the basis for vernacularization within the European context as well.)[12] A critique of *genbun-itchi* in modern Japanese literature and history can easily expose the lie of 'the reconciliation of spoken and written language' – for instance, critics have pointed to gender, class and regional biases in the selective 'reconciliation' of spoken and written idioms. Yet such critiques of representation fail to account for a crucial determining factor in the competition between different types of vernacular writing in Japanese: the capacity to approximate not Japanese speech itself, but rather the vernacular languages of modern Europe.

It is no accident that one of the key issues in the development of the *genbun-itchi* style, that of the copular sentence ending, was finally decided in favour of *de aru*, a usage that derived from the established translation for the verb 'to be'. Whereas early novelist practitioners of the new vernacular style in the Meiji period were divided between the use of *da*, *desu*, and *de arimasu*, often vacillating between the three, Ozaki Kôyô's use of *de aru* – beginning with *Ninin nyobo* (1892) – gained wide currency by the Meiji 30s.[13] The most casual form of the verb, *da*, borders on rudeness, being used only in conversations that call for the lowest level of politeness; *desu* and *de arimasu* are more formal. All of them, to differing degrees, therefore bear the mark of the speaker/narrator's relationship to the addressee/reader within the social hierarchy. By contrast, because *de aru* was a form derived from translation, it was able to create a neutrality for the narrative voice in vernacular writing that was not common to the enunciations of spoken Japanese (Yamamoto 1977:316, 332).[14] (We are reminded of the relative gender neutrality made available by *kanbun-kundokutai* as a language of translation.) The point is that it took the intervention of translation, as a primarily intertextual deployment of language, to free Japanese literary language from its bonds to the social, wherein each utterance served to mark the class and gender relations between speaker and auditor.

What set Futabatei's vernacular apart from contemporary rivals in the field was not his superior ability to record spoken Japanese in his writing, but rather his ability to translate the language of modern Russian literature into the diction of spoken Japanese. This decisive difference has been obscured by the anachronistic focus on *genbun-itchi* as the realistic representation of common parlance in prose, or rather, the representation of reality in prose via the language of spoken Japanese. With this distinction in mind, let us now take a look at the language of *Aibiki*, which numerous critics have cited as ultimately more important than *Ukigumo* for the later history of the modern Japanese novel. Compare the opening lines of Futabatei's translation with the English translation by Charles and Natasha Hepburn:

[Hepburns' *Rendezvous*]

> I was sitting in a birch-wood one autumn, about the middle of September. Ever since morning a fine drizzle had been falling, giving way now and again to warm sunshine: it was fluky weather. One moment the sky would be all overcast with puffy white clouds, at another it would suddenly clear in places for a moment, and, through the rift, the azure sky would appear, clear and smiling, like the glance of a brilliant eye. (Turgenev 1922:266)

[Futabatei's *Aibiki*]

秋九月中旬といふころ、一日自分がさる樺の林の中に座
してゐたことが有ツた。今朝から小雨が降りそゝぎ、その晴れ
間にはおりおり生ま暖かな日かげも射して、まことに気
まぐれな空ら合ひ。あわあわしい白ら雲が空ら一面に棚引くかと
思ふと、フトまたあちこち瞬く間雲切れがして、無理に押し分
けたやうな雲間から澄みて怜悧（さか）し気に見える人の眼の如
くに朗かに晴れた蒼空がのぞかれた。

[back-translation of *Aibiki*]

Autumn, around mid-September, I spent all day sitting in the middle of a
certain birch forest. A light rain had been falling since the morning, and
in the breaks between the clouds a warm sun would shine now and then,
truly fickle skies. One moment bubbly white clouds would stretch over
the entire sky, only to give way in the blink of an eye to a break in the
clouds, and between the clouds that seemed to have forced themselves
apart could be glimpsed a bright, clear blue sky, looking like a lucid and
sagacious human eye.[15]

My back-translation of Futabatei's *Aibiki* attempts to follow his own standard for
translation, retaining the syntactical form and verbatim meaning of the source text as
much as possible. Clearly, there are minor discrepancies between the Japanese and
English translations of Turgenev's text, and my back-translation does not approach
the felicity of the Hepburns' English. Nonetheless, the above translations are infinitely
closer to each other in tone and meaning than the passages cited above from Niwa
and Bulwer-Lytton or Shôyô and Scott.

The vernacular style of *Aibiki* is so much closer to contemporary Japanese than
Niwa's *kanbun-kundokutai* and Shôyô's *gabuntai* that it almost seems 'natural'. For
instance, Ryan understandably comments that *Aibiki* 'is presented in such natural
Japanese that it is difficult to believe that this is a translation and not an original story'
(1965:122). Yet this is both an unwitting tribute to the fact that Futabatei's innovation set a lasting standard for modern literary style, and a failure to recognize
the radical departure from 'natural' Japanese that it originally constituted. What was
'unnatural' about Futabatei's translation is not apparent in my back-translation either.
In fact, what was 'unnatural' in *Aibiki* can only be indicated in English in terms of the
degree to which Futabatei's text facilitates translation into English, in expressions
such as 'fickle skies' and similes like 'a lucid and sagacious human eye'.

These are no doubt the kinds of expressions that led Ishibashi Shian, a contemporary reviewer of *Aibiki*, to suggest that Futabatei had purposely embellished
the story's descriptive language to compensate for an uneventful plot. Shian found the
descriptive language of *Aibiki* cloying. As a case in point, he quotes the following line:
小雨が忍びやかに、　怪し気に、　私語するやうにバラバラと降ツて通ツた
(Ishibashi Shian 1888/1993:345). The Hepburns render this line as: 'furtively, slyly,
the finest of drizzles began to spray and whisper through the wood' (Ryan
1965:122). Although unavoidable differences of syntactical arrangement between
the Japanese and English translations create subtle shifts of emphasis, the two versions
are close enough that we may consider them essentially equivalent for our purposes
here. Again, a reading of the Hepburns' text does not give us a concrete sense of what
it was that jarred Shian's linguistic sensibilities. However, anyone educated in the

idioms of classical Japanese and Chinese will immediately recognize why this kind of description struck Shian as excessively overwrought. While the use of this particular kind of personification to describe nature in Western literatures is as old as Homer's 'rosy-fingered dawn', it had little place in the literary lexicons of classical Japanese or Chinese, much less in the figures of everyday speech. Within such a linguistic environment, even a phrase like 'kimagure na soraai' (fickle skies) could not avoid having a novel and bizarre ring.

This is the aspect of *Aibiki* that tends to be obscured by Naturalist homages to Futabatei's translation. For instance, Kanbara Ariake describes his first reaction to *Aibiki* in a way that foregrounds the spokenness of the narration: 'I was taken by the feeling that its rare style of *genbun-itchi*, with its skilful use of the colloquial idiom, was ceaselessly whispering intimately into my ear, which gave rise to both an indescribably pleasant sensation and a desire, somewhere at the bottom of my heart, to rebel against it. I just could not stand being spoken to so familiarly' (Kanbara Ariake 1909/1975:79). To be sure, the lack of distance between narrator and reader is an important aspect of the first-person narration of *Aibiki*, which employs the verbal sentence endings *da* and *-ta* of casual speech and the first-person pronoun *jibun*, as opposed to a more writerly pronoun like *yo*.[16] Yet Kanbara's account elides Futabatei's inherently non-idiomatic use of colloquial diction. Ultimately, I believe that it is this subtly *exotic* stylistic feature, rather than simply the 'naturalistic' descriptions of nature hailed by Kunikida Doppo, Tayama Katai and others, that inspired emulation and adulation by Japanese Naturalist writers.

The kind of personification used throughout Turgenev's story seems so natural in English that few native readers would pause to reflect on the central role played by rhetorical convention in Turgenev's 'naturalistic' description. The literal translation of alien rhetorical conventions is destined to produce the shock of the exotic in the target reader, and it is also a method of translation that demonstrates the true difficulty of separating form and content. If Futabatei had wished to produce a more 'natural' Japanese version of Turgenev's story, he could have reduced the personifying descriptions of nature to a level of semantic content which could then be repackaged in the forms already available to Japanese writing, much as Niwa and Shôyô did. In theory, this approach was certainly one option for Futabatei. Yet as Ishibashi Shian's comments suggest, if Futabatei had reduced 'The Rendezvous' to the core narrative content of a plot, he would have been left with very little to translate. Not only was his method of translation revolutionary, but his choice of text was equally radical. Whereas preceding translations of Western fiction reflected an overwhelming interest in exotic stories about the West, Futabatei chose to translate a work of fiction that conveyed almost no story at all. His interest in this particular work was no doubt related to Turgenev's underlying critique of serfdom, yet his radically formalist translation ultimately foregrounded the very language of the text, rather than any message that might be extracted from the body of the narrative. By manifesting a modern Western literary text in and as language, Futabatei's *Aibiki* definitively exposed the adaptational nature of other literary translations – in other words, their apprehension of modern Western literature as mere content.

The emergence of the Westernesque *femme fatale*

As noted above, Futabatei's approach to translation signalled a new perception of literature itself: his stringent personal standard for translation was driven by a passionate belief in the ability of the vernacular novel to reveal the truth. Needless to say, it was the same passion that inspired Futabatei to write *Ukigumo*. The preface to his début novel makes strategically ironic use of the poetic Japanese style's economic elegance to sum up his impetus for writing a novel in the vernacular:

> In a world where roses bloom on heads and live people become pictures, it is wretched that writing alone should have its teeth stuck in stiff, mildewed gibberish, and drool running from its mouth when it practices inarticulate wordings. Thus it occurred to me that the answer must lie in the union of speech and writing, and little could I restrain myself as the winds of civilization and the fever of reform surge nigh all at once . . .
> (Futabatei Shimei 1971:38)[17]

Here, meaning is compacted into a series of striking images: roses blooming on heads and live people becoming pictures refer to women ornamenting their hair with roses and socialites posing for *tableaux vivants*, while the stiff, mildewed gibberish and inarticulate wordings that plague the 'mouth' of writing refer to the inherited Chinese and Japanese styles, respectively. These images serve as both a critique of the *status quo* and a promise for the future. First, the oblique language by which they conjure up the dramatic changes taking place in Meiji Japan eloquently evokes the disjunction between the inherited literary language and the state of contemporary society. As the influx of Western material culture rapidly changes the face of society, Futabatei suggests, it is only fit that writing too should be reformed according to the Western model. Clearly, the use of oral imagery reinforces the notion that this reform will give writing the easily consumable quality of speech. And finally, the allusions to the Westernesque in women's fashion serve as a subtle yet tantalizing suggestion of what Futabatei's new style will be capable of bringing to Japanese fiction.

This association of a new literary style with a new gender type is further developed in critical ways within the story itself, to which we now turn our attention. Even in the preface we find an important clue as to what connects the Westernesque woman to modern Japanese literary media: the rise of the modern vernacular in Japanese literature is simultaneously conceived as a new turn towards the West, and as a return to the native body of spoken Japanese. Thus, the vernacularization of Japanese literary style known as *genbun-itchi* – literally, 'the reconciliation of spoken and written language', as explained earlier – cannot be fully grasped as an ideology of returning to the native tongue. In fact, the successful deployment of a new vernacular literature could only be achieved by means of *translating* Western vernacular literatures. Although the vernacular style is often discussed in terms of its transparency, it is also, particularly at its inception, characterized by the opaque traces of the foreign. In other words, as a literary style, *genbun-itchi* began as an uneasy coalescence of the native body of speech with the exotic textuality of foreign letters. The narrative of *Ukigumo*, constructed as Futabatei's attempt to portray the 'contemporary state of the nation', can also be read as a dramatization of this linguistic dilemma.

The basic story of *Ukigumo* is a fairly simple one: the protagonist, Utsumi Bunzô, is in love with his cousin Sonoda Osei. Her mother, Omasa, has hinted that she would support their marriage. But when Bunzô loses his job, everyone begins to turn against him. Omasa becomes increasingly hostile toward him and increasingly friendly toward Honda Noboru, his former colleague in the prestigious government bureaucracy. In turn, Osei also seems to shift her affections from Bunzô to Noboru. Things go from bad to worse, and by the end of the novel Bunzô is completely alienated from his surroundings.

Described as a natural born mimic, Osei has a distinct facility for picking up on new trends, and an equal tendency to discard them as soon as something newer comes along. Bunzô, by contrast, is characterized by an unswerving adherence to his own ideals, making him almost completely incapable of adapting to his surroundings. Within the terms of the novel, Osei is a talker, while Bunzô is a thinker – or more precisely, someone who sees everything in terms of written texts. The ever-widening gap between the two, when read as the failed betrothal of speech and writing, emerges as a powerful metanarrative on literary media, one that reveals a great deal more about the essential dilemmas of vernacularization than the expository discourse on *genbun-itchi*.

From the outset, the divide between Bunzô and the other main characters in the novel stems from a conspicuous difference in their relationships to language. Bunzô is constantly hampered by his inability to manipulate spoken language: from the inability to curry favour with his boss that results in his loss of employment; to his inability to verbally mollify Omasa; his frequent reduction to stuttering and speech-lessness in moments of highly charged emotion; and, most importantly, his inability to secure Osei's affections in the face of competition from the silver-tongued Noboru. By sharp contrast, the other characters share an easy facility with the spoken word. Omasa spins out words 'with a will that could turn even a heron into a crow' (p. 94), and Noboru's rise up the bureaucratic ladder is fuelled by 'an inexhaustible wealth of eloquence' (p. 90) when it comes to flattering the boss.

The sharp division between Bunzô and these strategic talkers neatly coincides with class distinctions. Both Omasa and Noboru claim samurai roots, but the narrator casts suspicion on their lineage. As a successful money-lender, Omasa is particularly associated with the merchant class. By contrast, Bunzô's bona fide samurai lineage is described in some detail. His father was a former retainer for the Bakufu – an undesirable résumé in the wake of the Meiji Restoration. Stripped of his social stand-ing and formal occupation, Bunzô's father finds himself at a complete loss for navigat-ing the new world. And his dilemma is constituted in part by the distinction between spoken and written language: 'his mouth weighted down by sayô shikaraba could not suddenly make the sound hei' (p. 45). *Sayô shikaraba* is shorthand for the punctili-ous language of the samurai class. In tone, it stands somewhere between 'such being the case, therefore' and '*ergo sum*'. This Sinified phrase is emblematic of a spoken language that imitated learned writing, the basic foundation for a class that claimed moral and intellectual authority. Firmly anchored to the bedrock of written language, Bunzô's father cannot manipulate the spoken language of commercial negotiations. From the perspective of his class, *hei* – *yessir* or *yes'm* – is an obsequious merchant expression, a vulgar and deceptive performance of servility undertaken in the interest of personal profit. Yet in a world no longer defined by a stable hierarchy, his inability to treat spoken language as the malleable stuff of verbal performance rather than the strictly defined terms of self-representation renders what was once a prized social identity into a deadly economic albatross.

Pinning all of his hopes on his son, Bunzô's father places such a complete emphasis on education that Bunzô's subjection to the written word becomes his most significant patrimony. Bunzô's very name suggests as much: it can be read as shorthand for *bungaku zanmai* (immersion in literature). The fundamental incompatibil-ity between the malleable spoken parlance of social commerce and the inflexible, letter-bound language of ideas serves as the impetus for the entire narrative of *Ukigumo*, a novel distinguished by the fact that almost all of its key events are verbal exchanges. Time and time again, we see Bunzô inundated by the artful words of others; his alienation from their language initiates the internal soliloquy by which he attempts to comprehend the world around him. This almost plotless novel depicts an escalating power struggle between two different approaches to language – the seamless speech of Omasa and Noboru against the mental text Bunzô patches together from their words and the ethical code inscribed in his consciousness.

Osei is the enigmatic hybrid at the centre of this bipolar struggle. Not only is she presumably of mixed class, as the daughter of Omasa and Bunzô's paternal uncle, but her penchant for mimicry assimilates the written diction of Chinese and English to her everyday speech. Indeed, the study of these languages constitutes the core of her secondary education, as well as the catalyst for Bunzô's attraction to her. In the process of tutoring Osei in English, we are told that 'Bunzô began to open up a little, occasionally holding forth on the state of Japanese women, the pros and cons of the Western-style bun, and even the relative merits of social intercourse between men and women' (p. 52) Bunzô's English lessons lead to noticeable changes in Osei's demeanour and appearance, making her seem the perfect student.

> Since the beginning of the summer, when he was asked to teach Osei English, Bunzô began to open up a little, occasionally holding forth on the state of Japanese women, the pros and cons of the Western-style bun, and even the relative merits of social intercourse between men and women, whereupon, lo and behold, Osei – who until now had not given any thought to Bunzô as a man and had bragged in front of him to her heart's content – at some point became reticent in front of Bunzô, took on an air of composure, and seemed to become gentle and feminine. One day, Bunzô was surprised to see that Osei was not wearing her spectacles or scarf as usual, and when he asked about it, she said 'But aren't you the one who said that they are actually harmful to people in good health?' Bunzô smiled in spite of himself, said 'That's an excellent thing,' and smiled again. (pp. 52–53)

Clearly, Bunzô takes great pleasure in hearing Osei repeat his own words. This is the event that solidifies in Bunzô what had been a merely latent attraction to Osei, for it is the first time that she seems to acknowledge him as a man and herself as a woman (in his own image). It is particularly interesting that the first signs of sexual tension between them emerge from within their English lessons.

The degree to which Bunzô's idealization of Osei hinges upon her use of language becomes comically clear in the following passage. Bunzô and Osei are home alone together, and their conversation quickly turns to their relationship. When Osei innocently declares that Bunzô is her newfound confidant, he responds with a faltering attempt to confess his true feelings:

> '. . . but I am utterly incapable of associating with you as a confidant.'
>
> 'Now what is that supposed to mean? Just why can't you associate with me as a confidant?'
>
> 'Why? Because I don't understand you, and you also don't under-stand me, so associating as a confidant is, well . . .'
>
> 'Is that it? But I believe that I understand you very well. You are learned, your conduct is exemplary, you treat your parents with filial piety . . .'
>
> 'That's why I say that you don't understand me. You say that I treat

my parents with filial piety, but I am not a good son. For me . . . there is something more . . . important than parents . . .' stammered Bunzô, hanging his head.

Osei stared at Bunzô with a puzzled look. 'Something more important than parents . . . something . . . more important . . . than parents . . . Oh, there is also something more important to me than parents.'

Bunzô raised his hung head, 'What? You too have that?'

'Yes, I do.'

'Wh-who is it?'

'It's not a person, it is Truth.'

'Truth,' repeated Bunzô with a tremble, biting his lips in a moment of silence, soon after which he suddenly let out with a stunned sigh, 'Ah, you are a chaste one, a pure one . . . What is more important than parents is Truth . . . Ah, you are a pure one.' (pp. 55–58)

Osei's demonstration of fluency in Bunzô's learned language generates the comedy of their exchange. Her grasp of Bunzô's idiom has been based on their English lessons and discussions of abstract social and ethical questions. When Bunzô suddenly blurts out that he is not a 'good son' because he values something more than his parents, Osei recasts his faltering confession into the form of a test question, and then searches for a clever answer: what could be more important than parents or filial piety? Ahah! it must be the new Western ideal of 'truth'.

The word *truth* was a key component of many of the new systems of thought coming in from the West, such as Christianity, philosophy, and science. The set Japanese translation, *shinri* 真 理, carries the weight of written language in a way that is closer to the Latin *veritas*. It is certainly not a term used in casual conversation. Osei never elaborates on what she means by *Truth*, nor is her meaning apparent anywhere in the narrative of *Ukigumo*. In fact, the question of *meaning* has nothing to do with her use of the word here; it is simply a clever way to keep up her end of a conversation that apparently strikes her as highly intellectual. Her enunciation of an absolute value in modern Western thought thus reduces the term to the status of an exotic verbal prop.

This is the constitutive difference between Osei and Bunzô. Osei is not subject to the written word; rather, she manipulates that language to aggrandize her self-image. Her meaningless enunciation of written signs has the virtually alchemical effect of converting the heavy materiality of written signs into the weightless ephemerality of sound. While her language is quintessentially performative, however, Bunzô reads it in the referential mode. To our thoroughly literal-minded protagonist, the word *Truth* is strictly bound to the textual sources that give it meaning. Thus, when she spouts out this word in place of the beloved's name he was expecting to hear, he sees a direct reflection of the speaker's pristine self, instead of his own image inadvertently parodied in her performance.

As he begins the sharp descent into nervous prostration toward the end of the novel, Bunzô's internal language takes on a life of its own. His mind suddenly becomes a playground for foreign words that, like his suspicions, seem to emerge from out of nowhere.

Incessant thinking about the same thing eventually exhausts the human mind, weakening its powers of discernment. Thus while Bunzô was constantly worrying about Osei, at some point his concentration scattered and was unable to focus on a single thing, and at times he would have haphazard thoughts about fragments that were totally unrelated to each other. Once he was lying down with his head cupped in his hands staring at the ceiling, at first thinking this and that about Osei as usual, when he happened to notice the grain of the wood ceiling, and he suddenly had a strange thought. 'Looking at it this way, it looks like marks left by flowing water.' Once this thought occurred to him, he completely forgot about Osei and, continuing to stare even harder at the ceiling, thought 'Depending on one's state of mind, it can even appear to have peaks and valleys. Hm, so that's an optical illusion.' Suddenly recalling the magnificently bearded face of the foreign lecturer who taught Bunzô and the others physics, he simultaneously forgot about the grain of the ceiling. Next, he saw seven or eight students appear before his very eyes, all of whom were his classmates, some with pencils stuck behind their ears, some carrying books, and still others opening the books to read. Upon looking closer, it seemed that Bunzô himself was among them. Now the lecture on *electriciteit* had ended and an exam was to take place, and everyone was gathered around an *electrical machine*; and just as it seemed that they were all arguing about something he could not make out, suddenly the *machine* and the students vanished without a trace like so much smoke, and the wood grain came back into sight. Saying 'Hm, so that's an *optical illusion*,' Bunzô smiled for no reason. 'Speaking of *illusion*, the most interesting book I've ever read is Sully's *Illusions*. I must have finished reading it in two days and a night. How does a person get so smart? He must have an intricately organized brain. . . .' Though there would seem to be no relation between Sully's brain and Osei, at this moment the thought of Osei suddenly pierced his chest, erupting like a gushing water fountain. (pp. 214–15)

In the Japanese orthography, foreign words like *illusion*, *electriciteit* (from the Dutch) and *electrical machine* are rendered phonetically in the *hiragana* of native speech, suggesting the degree to which Bunzô has assimilated them to his own language. That in the midst of his obsession with Osei, Bunzô suddenly recalls the word *illusion* is surely not an entirely 'haphazard' thought. As this stream of associations indicates, the word *illusion* exists in Bunzô's mind as part of the Western lexicon of scientific truth. If the deeply reverberating sound of Truth was Osei's siren song, this sudden musing on *illusions* constitutes Bunzô's unsung refrain.

For Bunzô, there is indeed a most profound connection between Osei and all of the associations attached to the word *illusion*. It is the unsettling proximity between truth and illusion that inhabits the space between languages – not only the ineffable difference-in-sameness of *veritas*, truth and *shinri*, but also that of 真理 and 「真理」 truth and 'truth'. Bunzô's delusions and progressive paralysis constitute the quintessential afflictions of his era: a time of bewildering linguistic flux and interlingual mingling initiated by the shock of Western letters, leading to an urgent search for a national language amidst a heterogeneous mass of regional and class idioms, the sudden shift from a graphic to a phonocentric apprehension of language, and a profound devaluation of Chinese writing (*kanbun*) as the exclusive language of learning simultaneous to the rapid proliferation of Chinese words (*kango*) as the primary medium for translating Western concepts and cultural phenomena.

The language of *Ukigumo* directly reflects both the polyphony of heterogeneous class idioms and the complex polyglossia of Chinese, Western and Japanese letters that constituted the original impetus for and the essential challenges to the vernacularization movement. It is this very linguistic heterogeneity that has placed *Ukigumo* at the beginning of most modern Japanese literary histories; it is what enables critics of essentially antagonistic positions to agree about the text's underlying modernity. Yet Futabatei's first novel is much more than a simple reflection of the polyphonic and polyglossic conditions of his times. Within the battlefield of written and spoken language – or foreign *lingua francae* and the native colloquial – represented by Bunzô's struggle against Omasa and Noboru, what Osei personifies is the bewitching appeal of a language that can alchemically compound all of these differences under the single sign of Truth. In this sense, Osei is both Futabatei's dream, and his nightmare. She spans the gap between writing and speech, between foreign languages and Japanese, with no apparent effort. This was precisely Futabatei's goal as a vernacular writer: as both translator and novelist, he attempted to create a language that would span all of these gaps. Yet given his profound reverence for the Russian novel as a textually fixed language of truth, he must have harboured deep-seated anxieties about the elusive medium of spoken Japanese. Indeed, he must have been haunted by the possibility that writing in the Japanese vernacular would have the same effect as Osei's pronouncement of Truth – a hollow ring that reduces the truth of the modern novel to the status of mere talk.

If Bunzô's final paralysis can be traced to a fundamentally irresolvable conflict between heterogeneous languages, then it seems quite fitting that Futabatei himself – as the person who both sensed and created this crisis in fiction – would meet the same fate as a novelist. By the time he was writing the final section of his début novel, Futabatei had already begun to harbour serious doubts about literature as a vehicle of truth. These doubts proved so consuming that Futabatei would not compose another novel of his own until 1906, and he even abandoned literary translation for almost an entire decade, until 1896. For him, the language of Truth – that of Chinese writing, the criticism of Belinsky, and the fiction of Turgenev, Gogol, Goncharov and Dostoevsky – had constituted an absolute value that demanded nothing less than a complete pledge of allegiance. In the context of modern literature, it stems from the idealist stance that seeks meaning, rather than purely aesthetic value, in fiction. And in the context of the Japanese vernacularization movement, it is a universal value that demands articulation in the colloquial tongue. This was the source of Futabatei's ambivalence as a writer, because it fostered an underlying sense of betrayal when he attempted to render this language in the form of Japanese vernacular fiction, which was also the only viable, if not already established, equivalent he could find.

Though the roots of Futabatei's growing skepticism towards literature were no doubt manifold, his disillusionment with the novel bears a striking resemblance to Bunzô's relationship with Osei. Just as Bunzô had idolized Osei as a bearer of 'Truth', Futabatei had embraced the novel as that which reveals the hidden ideas within the contingent forms of apparent phenomena. Yet once he actually tried to achieve such a revelation in practice, he found himself confronted by a multitude of competing languages – in other words, the contingent forms of language itself. Futabatei may have discovered an idea in the forms of contemporary Japanese society worthy of revelation, but the narrative of *Ukigumo* shows that he had a much less certain relationship with the forms and ideas of language, despite his clear advocacy of the vernacular novel. Language being the very medium of the novel, Futabatei's profound loss of confidence in the ability of fiction to represent truth seems all but inevitable. We might say that in intellectual terms, the vernacular novel was Futabatei's first love, but his early disillusionment with the genre – at least as it was written by himself and others in Japanese – prevented him from taking it on as a proper bride.

Futabatei's legacy

The next generation of radical vernacularists, the Naturalists, grew up with a significantly different set of linguistic contingencies, among which the language of Futabatei's translations would come to occupy a position of central importance. Futabatei's translation work carved out an important space for innovation within the field of modern Japanese literature, paradoxically demonstrating the stunning innovations made possible by what, from the perspective of the conventional English discourse on translation, would amount to the slavish imitation of the foreign text. This lesson was not lost on the next generation of radical vernacularists, the Japanese Naturalists, who spared nothing in their praise of Aibiki. In an age when the vernacular style had already become the lingua franca of Japanese fiction, Tayama Katai (1872–1930) called for a revamping of the vernacular that would jettison its most writerly elements (Tayama Katai 1904/1972). While his essay articulated an apparently simplistic conception of the relationship between language and reality, in practice his model for transparent style was none other than Japanese literary translation. In Katai's words,

> what shocked me even more was Futabatei's translation Aibiki . . . Having been raised on the grandiose magnificence of the Confucian classics, as well as Chinese and Japanese writing, my mind and my mental cultivation were extraordinarily moved by this writing's intricate, strange manner of description. I was flustered by the thought that this was writing. Yet that intricate method of description was also a characteristic of foreign writing, and since I thought the writing of Japan would surely have to progress in that direction, from then on I began to pay attention to the magazines and newspapers. (Tayama Katai 1917/1993:34)

The point of Katai's 'raw description' (the title of his 1904 essay) was not simply to bring writing closer to 'nature', but rather to bring Japanese writing closer to his image of the Western Naturalist model.

It is important to note that the virtually fetishistic embrace of Futabatei's translations by Naturalist writers took place in the absence of any significant appraisal of his work as a novelist. Ukigumo was at best considered to be a surprisingly advanced novel for having been written in 1889. Ironically, however, Japanese Naturalism was the primary heir to this novel's legacy of transposing linguistic anxieties onto the figure of a Westernesque femme fatale.

In a clear effort to put into practice the ideals set forth in his famous 1904 essay, Tayama Katai decided to lay bare his illicit attraction to a young female protegé in the epoch-making 1907 novella Futon (The Quilt). Yet despite his profession of absolute faith in the technical ability, and even the moral and artistic necessity, of the 'raw' vernacular to represent 'nature' (i.e., 'truth'), Katai made his name with a novel that, like Ukigumo, overlaid the pure image and promise of this ideal language with the figure of a duplicitous Westernesque *femme fatale*. Yoshiko, the graduate of a Christian girls' school in Kobe who comes to Tokyo to study the art of writing with the novelist-protagonist Tokio, is idolized by her mentor as the very embodiment of his stylistic ideals: she writes in a fluent, colloquial style unfettered by conventional norms, and even her variety of facial expressions seem to offer a transparent window onto her soul. But in the end, Tokio discovers that Yoshiko has merely manipulated these new techniques of self-expression to dupe him into believing that she is a New Woman, pure of mind and body, in the image of his favourite works of Western literature, when in fact she has betrayed his trust by entering into a physical relationship with a young man. After Tokio discovers her duplicity, she hands him a written apology in which she confesses, 'I am a fallen schoolgirl ... The duties of the new Meiji woman Sensei taught me, I was not putting into practice. In the end, I am still an old woman without the courage to put new ideas into practice' (Tayama Katai 1996:78). Yoshiko's admission of guilt is articulated in a style that Katai had already idealized as the best possible medium for conveying truth. In a manner that harkens back to Futabatei's Osei, this siren of transparent language not only established the paradigm for Japanese Naturalist fiction, but also marked many of its fundamental anxieties.

If we focus solely on the genre of fiction, many of the underlying concerns and contradictions of Japanese Naturalism are easily obscured by the semblance of 'vernacular realism'. Yet on the Japanese stage, Shimamura Hôgetsu's Naturalist theatre gave rise to a new star and cultural icon – Matsui Sumako – whose renowned performances of the heroines of translated European dramas reveal the underlying exoticism of the Naturalist project in ways that are impossible to overlook. Hôgetsu's approach to theatre reform mirrors Katai's rejection of literary artifice in the novel. Hôgetsu found the 'element of exaggeration' in Kabuki aesthetically appalling, asserting that it should 'obviously be replaced by naturalistic facial expressions' (Shimamura Hôgetsu 1906:46). His distaste for Kabuki certainly makes sense when we recognize Naturalism as the demand for radical realism in art. According to him, the aim of a modern Japanese theatre should be the naturalistic representation of life on stage. But his practical execution of this credo on the stage of New Theatre surrounds all of these terms – natural, representation, life – in distinctly non-Naturalistic brackets. In opposition to Kabuki, Hôgetsu's theatre did not present naturalistic stage performances of the realities of Japanese life. Rather, he chose to launch his modernization of the Japanese stage with the production of translated European dramas of the female struggle for selfhood – Henrik Ibsen's *A Doll House* and Hermann Sudermann's *Heimat*. In other words, he sought to reproduce the Naturalist performance of the purported realities of European life in modern European drama.

Hôgetsu served as both translator and director for the epoch-making 1911 Japanese production of Ningyô no ie (A Doll House) that catapulted Matsui Sumako to stardom. Theatre critics enthusiastically hailed her performance of Nora as the first example of natural gender performance on the Japanese stage, which had long been dominated by the practice of female impersonation by male actors. Sumako's delivery of Hôgetsu's translated lines was particularly singled out for praise, and she rapidly developed a reputation for her ability to quickly and perfectly memorize entire scripts – a feat that most of her male contemporaries on the Japanese stage achieved only with the greatest difficulty (Kabuki was a performance-based, rather than script-driven, theatre that had no use for the practice of memorizing scripts verbatim).

If the Westernesque *femme fatale* in modern Japanese literature personifies the dangers of spanning the gap between reading Western literatures and writing in

Japanese, then Matsui Sumako constitutes her stunningly physical manifestation. As an actress she made her name playing the parts of New Women from modern European drama, in the process not only seducing an eager public, but also becoming a living *femme fatale* to Hôgetsu himself. The married director fell in love with his star actress in the middle of their second production – Hôgetsu's translation of *Heimat* – and left his wife, children, and university post in order to start up a new theatre company with her, a public scandal that became fodder for contemporary newspapers and journals. Hôgetsu lost a fatal battle with influenza in November 1918 and Matsui Sumako committed suicide two months later; the posthumous story of their love affair also spawned numerous works of fiction, drama, and film. In the aftermath of their scandalous love affair and premature deaths, many of Hôgetsu's most ardent young admirers would come to look upon Sumako's greatest assets as an actress – her strength of will and body, and her ability to memorize the semi-foreign discourse of translated drama – as the tell-tale signs of her identity as a treacherous *femme atale*. The discourse surrounding these events bears a marked similarity to the narratives of *Ukigumo* and *Futon*: a serious male intellectual falls in love with a dangerous *femme fatale* whose apparent facility with the language of new ideas and emotions familiar from Western texts turns out to be nothing more than a deceptive performance, a cleverly calculated seduction.

What Naturalist criticism proclaimed as 'natural', whether in terms of content or stylistic mode, actual practice revealed to be essentially *exotic*. The entire discourse on Naturalist theatre – from the debates on the actress versus the *onnagata* (the male actor who specializes in female roles, the standard for traditional Japanese theatre) to the enthusiastic embrace of the modern actress and New Theatre by young intellectuals – provides the most conspicuous manifestation of the deeply contradictory relationships between gender representation, translation and literary production at work in modern Japanese literature. First emerging in the development of a vernacular literary style for the modern Japanese novel, these relations were not only reproduced, but actually *embodied*, on the stage of modern Japanese theatre.

What is uncanny about *Ukigumo* is that, in spite of its ostensible ideological underpinnings as a vernacular novel, its narrative ultimately hones in on the dilemma posed by the exotic appeal of the rhetoric of Western realism (Truth), and the phantasms fostered by its siren-like imitation in spoken Japanese. It is almost as if Futabatei had unconsciously predicted the future of *Aibiki*'s Naturalist progeny.

Notes

1   Isoda points out that the introduction of this particular concept of literature in Japan took place at a time when the concept of literature in the European context itself was still in a transitional phase, from 'learning, skill in letters' (Samuel Johnson) to the written arts of poetry, drama and fiction.

2   Quoted in Itô Sei (1953/1994:17). I am indebted to Nakajima Fumi for explicating the puns in this passage. We were unable to determine an alternative meaning for *roshia* (Russia) with any certainty.

3   For a thorough account of the relationship between *kanbun* (the Japanese designation for Chinese writing) and *kanbun-kundokutai*, see Ueda (forthcoming).

4   According to Tsubouchi Shôyô, this work was actually written by Katô Asatori (*Kaki no heta*, in *Shôyô senshû*, Vol. a4, bessatsu 4, Shun'yôdô, 1926, p. 407).

5   Ishii Kendô (1944/1997:82) also documents a boom in spoken *kango*.

6   On the importance of the *bôdoku* style of *kanbun* in enabling modern Japanese narratives that were not inscribed with linguistic markers of class hierarchy, see Kamei (2002).

7   The passage from Shôyô's Shunpû jôwa can be found in Shôyô senshû, bessatsu II, 39. The lines of the original text are not separated as in Ryan's romanized transcription.

8   Aibiki was first published in Kokumin no tomo, Vol. 3, nos. 25 and 27 (July and August 1887).

9   'Yo ga hon'yaku no hyôjun', in Futabatei (1984–1993), vol. 4 (1985:167). Originally published in Seikô (January 1906).

10   'Shōsetsu sōron', in Futabatei (1984–1993), vol. 4 (1985:7–8). Originally published in Chûô gakujutsu zasshi (April 1886).

11   Specifically, Yamamoto cites Ôtsuki Gentaku's Kangaku kaitei (1783) and Ôba Sessai's Yaku waran bungo (1855–57). Genbun-itchi advocate Maejima Hisoka was also a Dutch translator for the Edo Bakufu.

12   Although, of course, there are crucial differences between the Japanese and European situations. In the European context, the movement towards the vernacular was a form of resistance against the hegemony of Latin, a prestige language. In Japan, this kind of vernacularization had already been realized long before the threat of Western hegemony, in response to the hegemony of China and Chinese characters. In this sense, the Japanese parallels to the work of Dante, Luther and Chaucer can already be found in such 'ancient' (classical) works of Japanese literature as the Man'yôshû, Kojiki, Kokinshû and Genji monogatari. By the time Japan confronted the threat of Western hegemony, the vernacular as a 'native or indigenous' idiom had already been well established as a literary language for certain genres such as Japanese poetry (as opposed to the Chinese poetry with which it coexisted), narrative fiction, and nativist studies. Thus the 'native' language of 'Japanese' was already a written language, but it was not the common parlance of contemporary Japan, nor could it function as the written language of modern Japan. Whereas the prestige language of Latin served as a model for vernacular writing in the European context, then, it was the vernacular writing of Europe that served as a model for genbun-itchi.

13   It is worth noting that in Ukigumo, Futabatei often circumvented the final copula altogether, preferring to use the circumlocution of the conjunctive de instead.

14   It has also been suggested that the use of desu was particularly reminiscent of the language of the pleasure quarters. Bimyô himself switched from da to desu while writing for the women's education magazine Iratsume, in what may have been an attempt to appeal to female readers by using a more polite (and also more feminine) form of the vernacular.

15   Futabatei Shimei zenshû, vol. 2:5. All citations are from the first version of Aibiki, as published in Kokumin no tomo.

16   Unlike modern English, both written and spoken Japanese encompass a multiplicity of first-person pronouns. Until Futabatei's Aibiki, jibun had never been an option for the first-person pronoun in writing. First of all, first-person statements in writing, whether in 'Japanese' or 'Chinese', did not necessarily require the use of a first-person pronoun, since the first-person nature of a statement could be articulated by verb form alone. However, in cases that required explicit articulation of a first-person pronoun, the options for writing were generally dominated by 'Chinese' usages such as yo and wagahai for men, and warawa for women. The former two examples, belonging to the lexicon of the learned lingua franca, fall somewhere between I and the royal We in English, while the latter example, which marks the female gender of the enunciator, stands somewhere between 'I, being a mere woman' and 'I, being simply a woman but still an educated woman'. The first-person pronoun jibun derives from the spoken lexicon. In English, the closest approximation for jibun is oneself, in the sense that jibun may be used to refer to the 'self' of the speaker or the 'self' of people in general. As opposed to other options from spoken Japanese such as watakushi, boku or atashi, which can only refer to the enunciator, jibun has a more neutral resonance, as it does not clearly mark the relationship between speaker and addressee in the social hierarchy.

17   All translated quotations from Ukigumo are based on the 1971 annotated edition; only page numbers are given for the quotations that follow. In Japanese, Futabatei's preface roughly follows the traditional 7–5 syllabic pattern of Japanese verse in accordance with the conventions of the gabuntai literary style; my translation attempts to preserve this pattern as much as possible. In addition, the translated quotes presented here attempt, as far as possible, to preserve the balance between Chinese and Japanese diction through the use of Latinate and native English terms, respectively.

PART 9

Translation and war

Chapter 21

Vicente Rafael

TRANSLATION IN WARTIME

EDITOR'S INTRODUCTION

> *Moving between languages and societies, translators are also exiled from both. They are neither native nor foreign, but both at the same time. Their uncanny identity triggers recurring crisis among all sides. It is as if their capacity for mediation endows them with a power to disturb and destabilize far out of proportion to their socially ascribed and officially sanctioned positions. But it is a power that also constitutes their profound vulnerability.*

RAFAEL SETS THE SCENE FOR THE discussion of translation in the context of contemporary wars by drawing in the first instance on a statement made by George W. Bush on the need for translators to shore up national security. He goes on to explore the contradictions and ambivalences inherent in translation, and the consequent suspicion with which both the activity and those who perform it are viewed. Translation is a medium for hearing as well as overhearing what others say. It is an instrument of surveillance that magnifies the alienness of alien speech, and in the context of Western imperialisms it promotes linguistic and social hierarchies. The foreign language of the colonizer comes to exercise considerable social power, surpassing any of the local languages, and those who can function in it are then elevated socially and materially. At the same time, translation can be a tool of empowerment. It can establish connections and contacts across linguistic and other divides, and can therefore enable the formation of new publics. In this sense it is not purely an instrument of imperial power but is a form of power in its own right.

Returning specifically to the topic of current wars in Iraq and elsewhere, Rafael examines the tensions and indeterminacy inherent in the positions that translators and interpreters occupy in this context. This position is mired in a series of intractable and irresolvable contradictions. Despite their role in fighting insurgents, they are also feared as potential insurgents themselves. Just by being who they are, translators find themselves attracting interest and sending out messages beyond their control. They are perceived as alien presences that defy assimilation, at the same time as being recognized as indispensable to the assimilation of aliens. They are 'foreign in a domestic sense', as well as 'domestic in a sense that remains enduringly foreign'. Rather than promote understanding and hospitality, translation in this context thus generates misgivings and misrecognition. Finally, Rafael asks: If translation is like war, is there also a way of reversing this association to say that war is like translation? Wartime decimates our normal mode of thinking. It creates mass disorientation at odds with the temporal rhythms of progress and civilization. It is precisely this disordering effect of war on our notions of space and time that brings it in association with translation: translation scatters meaning, displaces origins and exposes the radical undecidability of references, names and addressees. Translation in a time of war thus intensifies the experience of untranslatability. We remain haunted by the permanent possibility of war just as translation is haunted by untranslatability, both participating in 'the feverish circulation of misrecognition and vengeance from which we can find neither safety nor security, national or otherwise'.

Follow-up questions for discussion

- Rafael describes translation during wartime as an instrument of surveillance, used to 'track and magnify the alienness of alien speech, decoding dangers, containing threats, . . . planning for interventions . . . [and] seeking to put the other in its putative place, apart from the self'. To what extent do you believe this function of translation (and interpreting) is limited to wartime? What are the boundaries of 'wartime'? Would the period of the Cold War fall within the definition of 'wartime'? What forms does this surveillance take, and how is its output exploited by parties other than the translator or interpreter?

- Rafael does not distinguish between different types of translators and interpreters in his discussion of the paradoxes inherent in their position and the suspicion with which they are met on both sides. To what extent can the picture he paints be refined to account for differences in cultural and ethnic backgrounds as they impact on the way translators and interpreters are perceived by primary interlocutors during wartime or in colonial contexts? For example, Niranjana notes that the colonial governor of India, William Jones, and his British administrators found it 'highly dangerous to employ the natives as interpreters, upon whose fidelity they could not depend' (1990:774), and that their remedy for this state of affairs was 'the substitution of British translators for Indian ones' (*ibid.*:775). What further distinctions (other than native subject vs. member of colonial society) may influence the interaction between translators/interpreters and those who rely on their services at times of conflict?

- Apter (2006:22) argues that '[a]s the "enemy" in the so-called war against terror increasingly diffuses its base of operations, and as battle zones remove themselves to Internet networks and the arena of electronic diplomacy, war as such is increasingly defined as a translation war: its formal strategy determined by the ability to translate intelligence'. Consider the various ways in which translation intervenes in today's major conflicts through the Internet and similar technologies – including, for example, Youtube video clips, blogs, dedicated advocacy sites, etc. – beyond (as well as including) 'intelligence' as such.

Recommended further reading

Baker, Mona (2006) *Translation and Conflict: A Narrative Account*, London & New York: Routledge.

Inghilleri, Moira (2008) 'The Ethical Task of the Translator in the Geo-political Arena: From Iraq to Guantánamo Bay', *Translation Studies* 1(2): 212–23.

Levinson, Charles (2006) 'Iraq's "terps" face suspicion from both sides', *Christian Science Monitor*, 17 April. http://www.csmonitor.com/2006/0417/p01s01-woiq.html.

Salama-Carr, Myriam (ed.) (2007) *Translating and Interpreting Conflict*, Amsterdam: Rodopi.

A DDRESSING A GATHERING OF UNIVERSITY presidents attending a conference at the State Department on 5 January 2006, President George W. Bush spoke about the country's dire need for translators to shore up national security. He promised to spend $114 million to expand the teaching of so-called critical languages such as Arabic, Farsi, Chinese, and so forth, at the university as well as K-12 levels as part of a new federal programme called the National Security Language Initiative. He illustrated the importance of learning such languages with the following analogy: 'In order to convince people we care about them, we've got to understand their culture and show them we care about their culture. You know, when somebody comes to me and speaks Texan, I know they appreciate Texas culture' (Janofsky 2006).[1]

Bush initially links translation, entailing the learning of a foreign language and culture, with 'care' and 'appreciation'. If I were to learn 'Texan', for example, I would be showing my capacity to defer to his idiom, suppressing my first language in favour of a second, foreign tongue. My deference would be evidence of my ability to recognize and respect his difference and, more generally, to know the difference that the other makes in any speech act. Such knowing is, of course, anything but disinterested, especially when it involves those who have some sort of 'Texan' or some other American idiom as their native language. Such becomes evident in the rest of Bush's remarks: 'When somebody takes time to figure out how to speak Arabic, it means they're interested in somebody else's culture . . . We need intelligence officers who when somebody says something in Arabic or Farsi or Urdu, know what they're talking about'. Here, 'somebody' who 'takes the time to figure out how to speak Arabic' is one who shows 'interest' rather than 'appreciation' in 'somebody's culture'. There is a curious doubling of the word 'somebody' in this passage. The first is one who 'takes time' to learn the other's language – Arabic, Farsi, or Urdu – while the second is one who, we might assume, is a native speaker of such languages. The first acts to know what the second is 'talking about', while the second simply talks. Unlike the 'somebody' who sets aside his or her first language in order to speak 'Texan', and so show appreciation for Texans, this other somebody, for example, 'intelligence officers', learns Arabic or Farsi because he or she is interested only in the content of the other's speech, listening for that 'something' that could be anything, but might also be just the thing from which 'we', as non-Arabic and non-Farsi speakers, need to be protected. In this case, translation occurs not in order to welcome and care for the other but precisely to ensure us that the other stays where it belongs.

Learning to translate thus entails two distinct but related movements. On the one hand, one is required to recognize the singularity of each idiom, for example, Texan or Arabic, that makes one distinct from and irreducible to the other. It is for this very reason that speaking the other's language necessarily means deferring to it, giving it primacy, and thereby keeping one's own out of mind. On the other hand, by promising the transportability and substitutability of one language for another, translation raises the possibility of mastering the language of the other, hearing in it some things that the other him- or herself did not mean or did not intend to be heard. We see, then, how translation looks two ways. It opens up a passage to the other in all its otherness, drawing near what at the same time will always remain far. Faithful to the original, it thus allows for the appreciation of and care for the foreigner whose very foreignness becomes an element of oneself. Translating the other's language, one is transformed, becoming other than oneself. However, translation is also a medium for hearing as well as overhearing what others say even if they did not mean to say it. It is in this sense a kind of instrument of surveillance with which to track and magnify the alienness of alien speech, decoding dangers, containing threats, and planning for interventions. Rather than dwell in the hospitality of the other, translation in this latter sense is unfaithful to the original, seeking to put the other in its putative place, apart from the self.

Bush's view on the learning of foreign languages, however crudely phrased, reflects a certain idea about translation that has a long history. Since the Spanish conquest and religious conversion of the native peoples of the New World and the Pacific, various projects of translation have always accompanied, enabled, and at certain moments disabled the spread of empire.[2] As with the Spanish empire, so with the United States: in both, translation has played the key role of what we might think of as an essential supplement. How so?

Demarcating as it seeks to draw the other near, translation has always had at least a double aspect. First, translation has served historically as an instrument of domination under colonial rule. Speaking the other's language means replacing one's first with a second idiom, investing the second with the primacy that outstrips the first. In a colonial context, the second language, that of the foreign occupier, is usually instituted as the official one, subsuming all other vernaculars. To speak authoritatively and to address state authorities, one must be able to speak up, using this second language in place of one's native speech. Indeed, knowledge of the colonizer's language has often endowed speakers with considerable privileges. By insisting on the inequality of languages, translation tends to promote linguistic hierarchy. Within the context of Western imperialisms and their associated orientalisms, we see how this linguistic hierarchy also generates social hierarchies between those – usually missionaries, colonial officials, and educated élites – who are able to move back and forth between an official and a vernacular, and those – peasants, workers, women, children, the insane, and so on – whose knowledge is restricted to their own. Idealizing the colonizer's speech, empire employs translation as a means for appropriating and reorganizing native languages and their speakers in view of an overarching official language. Translation bound to empire thus imbues a second, foreign language with a social power surpassing any of the local idioms.

There is, however, another aspect to translation that has the potential to lead away from imperial rule. For translation not only erects hierarchy; it can also overcome its distinctions. It does so by establishing connections and contacts across linguistic, social and geographical divides.[3] As such, translation functions as a telecommunicative medium offering the promise of communication at great distances and the prospect of bridging what had seemed unbridgeable. Such a promise makes conceivable all sorts of affiliations, collaborations and even friendships between and among colonizers and colonized, even as it raises the possibility for misunderstanding, misrecognition and conflict. Translation as a technic of promising novel connections can promote the formation of new publics attuned to other modes of publicity that often exceed the borders of the imperial public sphere. Indeed, it is arguably this mediating capacity that makes translation not only a necessary device for linking rulers to ruled – like teletechnologies of all sorts, translation also possesses a certain capacity to reshape the terms of hegemony. We can think of translation, then, as something other than an instrument of imperial power. As the agency of mediation, it is itself a kind of power productive of other modalities of empowerment that comes with crossing and double-crossing differences, linguistic as well as social.

But is there a third possibility? Harnessed into a mere instrument of imperial hegemony or other sorts of power premised on the promise of communication, translation is productive of order and meaning, whether on the register of domination or resistance. Is there a way, though, that translation can also be nonproductive? Can the task of translating result in neither order nor meaning but in an ongoing suspension of both? What happens when translation arrives at its limit, overtaken by the return of that which remains untranslatable?

I'd like to explore this third possibility – of translation giving rise to the untranslatable – by returning to the geopolitical context of George Bush's remarks above, the current US occupation of Iraq. Since the start of the war, a number of news accounts have appeared about the place, at once indispensable and troubling, of Arabic-speaking translators, both Iraqi nationals and Arab American immigrants. From such accounts, it is difficult to infer the social positions of such translators, and as we shall see, it is precisely the indeterminacy of such positions that translation during war makes evident.

Translators are also called interpreters, which is why among the US soldiers they are popularly referred to as 'terps'. Unlike the Americans they work for, interpreters are forced to hide their identities. They often cover their faces with ski masks and sunglasses as they venture outside the military bases and adopt American pseudonyms such as 'Eric' or 'Sally' so as to protect themselves from being singled out for insurgent attacks. At the same time, their identity within the US military remains unsettled and unsettling inasmuch as their presence generates both relief and suspicion among soldiers. Some interpreters earn the military's trust and gratitude, and a handful of the Iraqi nationals are granted asylum to move to the United States. Others who are killed, especially among the very small number of women, are treated with tender regard, often memorialized by US soldiers as 'one of us' (Koopman 2004, Basu 2005, LaFranci 2006).

Still, doubts linger amid reports of some interpreters sending information to the insurgents. As one US soldier puts it, 'These guys [i.e., interpreters] have guts to do what they do. And we'd be nowhere without them. We'd be lost . . . But . . . you always have this fear that they might be leaking op-sec [operational security] stuff. You want to trust them but you're still reserved' (Levinson 2006; see also Wadhams 2006). Given the inability of most American soldiers to speak Arabic, interpreters, as one report puts it, provide 'the public face of the U.S. occupation' (Levinson 2006; see also Tyson 2004). Essential in conducting military operations, they nonetheless are thought to threaten them by leaking information. They mediate the vast gulf that separates soldiers from people, often defusing conflict by being able to decipher, for example, documents that to Americans may look like plans for smuggling weapons but turn out to be in fact no more than sewing patterns (Glionna and Khalil 2005, LaPlante 2005, Brinkley 2004). In this way, they are 'the military's lifeline in communicating with regular Iraqis', as the spokesman for the American Translators Association says (Glionna and Khalil 2005). Yet, despite their essential function in fighting insurgents, they are also feared as potential insurgents themselves. Translators allow Americans to communicate with Iraqis and for this reason are integrated into the ranks, given uniforms and salaries. But their loyalty is always suspect. Interpreters are the only ones searched within the base, especially after every meal, and are forbidden to carry cell phones and cameras, send e-mail, play video games, and as of this writing, even swim in the pool (Levinson 2006). They are subjected to incessant racial insults ('raghead', 'Taliban', and 'hajji' being the most common) and physical harassment at the same time that they are forced to go out of base with neither weapons nor armour to protect themselves (Washburn 2006). Just by being who they are, translators thus find themselves stirring interest and sending out messages beyond what they had originally intended. Without meaning to, they generate meanings outside of their control. In this way, they come across as alien presences that seem to defy assimilation even as they are deemed indispensable to the assimilation of aliens. They are 'foreign in a domestic sense' as much as they are domestic in a sense that remains enduringly foreign.[4]

It is precisely because they are of such great value to the US forces that translators are targeted by insurgents and reviled by most Iraqis. They are accused of being mercenaries, collaborating with the United States to kill other Iraqis, so they face the constant threat of being kidnapped and killed themselves. One Iraqi interpreter with the pseudonym 'Roger' says, 'If you look at our situation it's really risky and kind of horrible . . . Outside the wire, everybody looks at us like we are back-stabbers, like we betrayed our country and our religion, and then inside the wire they look at us like we might be terrorists' (Levinson 2006). Interpreters thus come to literalize that old adage *traduttore, traditore*, at times with tragic results. Recent reports, for example, put the number of slain interpreters at more than two hundred since the start of the war (Washburn 2006, Krane 2005). Moving between languages and societies, translators are also exiled from both. They are neither native nor foreign, but both at the same time. Their uncanny identity triggers recurring crisis among all sides. It is as if their capacity for mediation endows them with a power to disturb and destabilize far out of proportion to their socially ascribed and officially sanctioned positions. But it is a power that also constitutes their profound vulnerability.

These and many other stories about interpreters give us a sense that within the context of the US occupation of Iraq, translation works only too well. That is, it produces effects and relations that are difficult if not impossible to curb. Faced with the translator, both Americans and Iraqis are gripped with the radical uncertainty about the interpreter's loyalty and identity. Translators come across as simultaneously faithful and unfaithful or, more precisely, faithful to their task by being unfaithful to their origins (and on those rare occasions that bear out the fears of the US soldiers, doing the reverse). Rather than promote understanding and hospitality, the work of translation seems to spawn misgivings and misrecognition. In dealing with an interpreter, one is addressed in one's own language – Arabic or English – by an other who also has access to an idiom and culture alien because unavailable to one. Faced with the need to depend on such an other, one responds with ever intensifying suspicions. Such suspicions repeatedly trigger racial insults, often escalating into violence and, in some cases, murder, thereby stoking even more suspicions. Iraqis see in the translator one of their own used against them, a double agent who bears their native language now loaded like a weapon with alien demands. For the US soldier, the indispensability of interpreters is also the source of the latter's duplicity, making them potential insurgents. 'Terps' appear as enemies disguised as friends whose linguistic virtuosity masks their real selves and their true intentions.

The task of the translator is thus mired in a series of intractable and irresolvable contradictions. It begins with the fact that translation itself is a highly volatile act. As the displacement, replacement, transfer and transformation of the original into another language, translation is incapable of fixing meanings across languages. Rather, as with the story of Babel, it consists precisely in the proliferation and confusion of possible meanings and therefore in the impossibility of arriving at a single one. For this reason, it repeatedly brings into crisis the locus of address, the interpretation of signs, the agency of mediation, and the ethics of speech. Hence the impossibility of fully controlling, much less recuperating, its operations and effects. The treachery and treason inherent in translation are the insistent counterpoints to its promise of telecommunication and the just exchange of meaning. In the body of the interpreter, translation reaches its limits. 'Terps', as the uncanny doubles of US soldiers and Iraqi insurgents, are productive neither of meaning nor of domination, but only the circulation of what remains untranslatable. It would seem, then, that in the war on terror, translation is at permanent war with itself, and imperialist and anti-imperialist projects seeking to capitalize on this turmoil do so only at the risk of being ensnared and undone by it.

To conclude, I want to return to the analogical relationship between translation and war, with reference to their shared temporality as suggested by the title of this essay. If translation is like war, is there also a way of reversing this association to say that war is like translation? It is possible I think if we consider that the time of war bears some relationship to the movement of translation that leads not to the privileging of meaning but to emergence of the untranslatable. 'Wartime' spreads what Nietzsche called in the wake of the Franco-Prussian War 'an all consuming fever' that creates a crisis in historical thinking. So much of the way we think about history, certainly in the Westernized parts of our planet since the Enlightenment, is predicated on a notion of time as the succession of events leading toward increasingly more progressive ends. Wartime decimates that mode of thinking. Instead, it creates mass disorientation at odds with the temporal rhythms of progress and civilization. In this way, wartime is what Samuel Weber refers to as 'pure movement'. It is a 'whirlwind that sweeps everything up in its path and yet goes nowhere. As a movement, the whirlwind of war marks time, as it were, inscribing it in a destructive circularity that is both centripetal and centrifugal, wrenching things and people out of their accustomed places, displacing them and with them, all [sense] of place as well. Wartime thus wrecks havoc with traditional conceptions of space and time and with the order they make possible' (Weber 1997:92).[5] It is precisely this dis-ordering effect of war on our notions of space and time that brings it in association with translation that, as we saw, scatters meaning, displaces origins, and exposes the radical undecidability of references, names and addressees. Put differently, trans-lation in a time of war intensifies the experience of untranslatability. It is arguably this stark exposure to translation's limits that we see, for example, in the uncanny body of the Iraqi interpreter. Such a body, now ineradicably part of our own imperial body politic, generates the sense of severe disorientation, sending back to us an interminable scattering of discourses and opinions about the war. Just as civilizational time engenders the permanent possibility of wartime, the time that is out of joint and out of whack, so translation is haunted by untranslatability, the feverish circulation of misrecognition and vengeance from which we can find neither safety nor security, national or otherwise.

Notes

1   For more details on the National Security Language Initiative, see Bureau of Educational and Cultural Affairs, US Department of State, 'National Security Language Initiative', exchanges. state.gov/NSLI/; Dina Powell and Barry Lowenkron, 'Fact Sheet: National Security Language Initiative', Office of the Spokesman, US Department of State, 5 January 2006, www.state.gov/r/pa/ prs/ps/2006/58733.htm; and US Department of Education, 'Press Release: Teaching Language for National Security and Global competitiveness: U.S. Department of Education Fact Sheet', 5 January 2006, www.ed.gov/news/pressreleases/2006/01/ 01052006.html. It is unclear, however, how much of the funding for this programme has actually been released as of the date of this writing. I am grateful to Mary Pratt for referring me to this story on Bush's language initiative.

2   For an extended discussion of the politics of translation in the Spanish empire, see Rafael 1993, 2005).

3   The following argument on translation as a telecommunicative technology draws largely from Rafael (2005).

4   The term 'foreign in a domestic sense' comes from Kaplan (2002).

5   I also owe the reference to Nietzsche to Weber's essay.

Chapter 22

Zrinka Stahuljak

WAR, TRANSLATION, TRANSNATIONALISM:[1] INTERPRETERS IN AND OF THE WAR (CROATIA, 1991–1992)

EDITOR'S INTRODUCTION

> . . . the shock, the violence of an event such as war, cannot be translated or processed without 'shocking' the very structure of its transmission, and especially its claim to neutrality . . . The scandal of war cannot be neutrally translated. It may even be that the war, as an interpreter claimed, should not be neutrally translated, for to do so would be to miss the event itself.

CONTINUING WITH THE THEME OF WAR, Stahuljak offers an extended and wide-ranging account of interpreting in contemporary war zones, using data derived from the war in Croatia in the early 1990s. This unique study is based on interviews conducted during the war with interpreters working for the European Community Monitor Mission (ECMM), and on the author's own personal experience as someone who worked as a volunteer interpreter in the same context. After a relatively brief account of the background to the conflict, which demonstrates the complexity of the issues involved, Stahuljak proceeds to consider the discursive violence to which interpreters are exposed in an armed conflict.

Despite their original motivation to become witnesses for the ECMM (as a patriotic duty), Croatian interpreters understood that as 'professionals' they must accept a form of erasure, at least while interpreting. Thus, interpreters who volunteered to translate in order to testify are denied the very possibility of testimony. The two conditions that characterize much interpreting in war zones, namely the desire to bear witness (what Stahuljak refers to as volunteerism) and the obligation to mediate between the main interlocutors (professional-ism), come into conflict with each other, since the positions of the witness and of the inter-preter are mutually exclusive. Interpreters are torn between the two, and while translating the violence of the war, they themselves become the site of a violent conflict.

Stahuljak distinguishes between conscious manipulation of source material during inter-preting, and other types of intervention that are possible on the frontlines. In the current case, interpreters often went with the same ECMM teams on multiple missions and came to spend time with them outside the interpreting context proper. This gave them an opportunity to 'switch' between bearing witness in their own right, and interpreting for other, 'officially

recognized' witnesses. In other words, they were able to switch from the position of interpreter to the position of interlocutor in unofficial situations, expressing personal opinions outside the translation structure, but within the translation war zone. However, 'switching' became more difficult as the tension between professionalism and volunteerism was
gradually put under additional strain, especially as the interpreters increasingly saw the
European Community as unwilling to act on the basis of physical evidence and testimony that
the ECMM collected, and as unable to stop the continuing war. Especially when they witnessed emotionally charged situations, the structure of address within which they undertook
their interpreting became liable to explode. It was then that interpreters became subjects
speaking in their own voice, that they became witnesses in their very failure to be interpreters. Precisely because 'switching' can and does disrupt the structure of translation, it
reveals the inherent precariousness of the interpreter's 'professional', 'neutral' and 'self-
erasing' stance.

Follow-up questions for discussion

- Stahuljak states that 'translation as mediation is always already an intervention', and
  Baker (2008: 16) similarly suggests that intervention is 'inherent in the act of translation and interpreting, as it is inherent in any act of reporting'. Consider how terms
  such as 'mediation' and 'intervention' are used here, and elsewhere in the literature.
  Are they clearly defined? Are they synonymous with or different from terms such as
  'manipulation', 'appropriation', 'interference', 'liaison', etc? What are the implications, both practical and theoretical, of claims such as Stahuljak's and Baker's?
  What forms of 'intervention' would you advocate or wish to see accommodated within
  a code of ethics for the profession, and under what circumstances?
- The ECMM is shown in this study to have failed to learn from the experience of its
  interpreters; it 'fail[ed] to see in them the war that it came to observe' and in doing so
  was 'already . . . missing the war'. In a different study that does not engage with the
  issue of war, Temple and Edwards (2002) argue for giving interpreters visibility and
  personhood in qualitative, cross-language research, for treating them as key informants
  in their own right rather than as language intermediaries who are merely there to assist
  the researchers. To what extent, and in what contexts, might interpreters be treated as
  active contributors to the interaction in their own right? What are the implications of
  encouraging researchers, parties to a conflict, and other types of primary interlocutors
  to treat them as such? How might a 'recommended' programme of engagement with
  interpreters be drawn up for each type of context?
- Despite insisting on it, the ECMM ultimately acknowledged the interpreters' neutrality as a fiction when they began to suspect the interpreters of being spies and their
  very willingness to volunteer as politically motivated. At the same time, the Croatians
  (their own side) treated them with suspicion: the very fact that they were working for
  a 'politically neutral' organization compromised their loyalty and patriotism. To
  what extent is this pattern of suspicion on both sides typical of interpreting in contemporary war zones (for example, Iraq, Kosovo, Afghanistan), and to what extent is
  it inherent in all situations of (political) conflict? What similar examples might be
  found in colonial and postcolonial history, for instance? And how does this relate to
  current theorizing of the translator's and/or interpreter's positionality (cf. Tymoczko,
  this volume)?

Recommended further reading

Cronin, Michael (2002) 'The Empire Talks Back: Orality, Heteronomy and the Cultural Turn in Interpreting Studies', in Edwin Gentzler and Maria Tymoczko (eds) *Translation and Power*, Boston & Amherst: University of Massachussets Press, 45–62.

Jones, Francis R. (2004) 'Ethics, Aesthetics and Décision: Literary Translating in the Wars of the Yugoslav Succession', *Meta* 49(4): 711–28.

Kahane, Eduardo (2007) 'Interpreters in Conflict Zones: The Limits of Neutrality', *Communicate!* (AIIC's Online Journal), available online: http://www.aiic.net/ViewPage.cfm?page_id=2691

THE CASE OF INTERPRETERS WORKING for the European Community (EC) in the 1991–92 war in Croatia, during the break-up of Yugoslavia, brings together several issues of concern to scholars of translation and interpreting. First, it questions the presumed neutrality of interpreters in order to highlight the constraints inherent in the translation structure within which interpreters have to operate on a daily basis. Based on Felman and Laub (1992:211), I understand wartime translation as a structure within which the interpreter acts as an 'intermediary' between the interviewer and a witness (with 'witness' understood here to encompass an eye-witness, a refugee, an asylum-seeker or any victim of an armed aggression). As intermediaries, interpreters and translators play a vital role in the gathering and transmission of testimonies (Felman and Laub 1992, Barsky 1996, Stahuljak 1999, Jacquemet 2005), but the responsibility to which they respond and on account of which they intervene, and the kinds of structural violence and trauma to which they may be subjected in the process, have only begun to be addressed recently (Inghilleri 2005, Maier 2007, Moeketsi 2007, Tipton 2008).

Secondly, beyond the question of structural constraints, the case of the Croatian interpreters demonstrates that wartime interpreters do not merely lend their voices as interpreters in the conflict but are also agents in it; in this respect, the analysis offered here contributes to studies of interpreter agency and activism. Recent work in translation studies has shown that interpreters in war conflicts, most notably in Iraq, have to grapple with a host of conflictual issues and negotiate their positions in relation to them (Inghilleri 2008a, Kahane 2007, Maier 2007, Palmer 2007). Among the most important of these issues is the question of trust and credibility (Inghilleri 2009, Rafael 2007), but other issues also come up, such as interpreter reflexivity (Tipton 2008), agency (Inghilleri 2005), ethics (Baker 2008, Inghilleri 2008a, 2009), and, most importantly for the case of Croatian interpreters, activism in the context of volunteer interpreting and translation (Baker 2006a, 2006b, 2009, Boéri 2008, Tymoczko 2000, 2007). Activism should not be understood here as necessarily involving a conscious distortion and manipulation of source materials, for as Baker argues, 'we may well find that accuracy acquires an additional value in this context and that much of the "political" work is done through the selection of material to be translated and through various methods of framing the translation' (Baker 2006b:477); this will become clear in some of the examples I analyze later in this article. Ultimately, interpreter activism merely renders visible what is inherent in translation, that is, that interpreters, whether explicitly activist or not, do not occupy neutral, in-between positions, that they do not reside outside cultural or ideological systems.

Finally, while the question of the violence that interpreters perform against witnesses has occasionally been raised in the literature (Jacquemet 2005, Inghilleri 2008a), I wish to consider here the discursive violence to which interpreters themselves are exposed in an armed conflict, in order to further our understanding of issues of political neutrality and allegiance in wartime translation. The interpreter is not a metaphor here for the physical violence of the war conflict. Rather, the relationship between the Croatian interpreters and Western Europe examined in this article highlights the political and active role of translation as a conflicted battle-ground in itself, and demonstrates that translation is constitutive of and critical to the political processes of nation-building and international recognition. In this global context, interpreters, as cultural mediators, are subject to the violence of the Western European discourse of conflict arbitration.

The data analyzed in this article is drawn from an unpublished study of Croatian interpreters by the Croatian social psychologist Ivan Magdalenic. During the 1991–1992 war, Croatian interpreters for the European Community were organized through the Croatian Liaison Office. At the invitation of the main administrator of the Croatian Liaison Office, Magdalenic conducted interviews with them from 11 September to 18 October 1993, but was later dismissed by the Office without explanation (personal communication, 23 September 1996). Although never intended for publication, and used only as one element in the clinical diagnosis, Dr. Magdalenic was willing to share his records of interviews with me in September 1996. The interviews constituted confidential material, and at his request, I have withheld the names of interpreters. They were conducted in Croatian; all translations from Croatian into English in the analysis that follows are mine. The interviews were partly transcribed and partly summarized by Magdalenic, which explains the occasional occurrence of indirect speech in quotations from the interviews. Magdalenic interviewed twenty-five Croatian interpreters, and some were evaluated on two different occasions. Ten were female, ages 19–50, and fifteen were male, ages 18–41. In an attempt to protect their privacy, but still indicate the diversity of their opinions, I have 'coded' them as Interpreter A, Interpreter B, etc.

The interpreters responded to a series of questions in a face-to-face interview with the psychologist (see Appendix: Interpreter Questionnaire). Magdalenic's primary objectives, in his role as clinical psychologist, were to look for the kind of specific trauma that interpreting in and of the war may have produced and to propose an optimal way for dealing with the length of assignments and their potential effects. Each interview was followed by an informal conversation with Magdalenic that was not summarized in the study, but in lieu of which Magdalenic offered his psychological assessment of each subject (personal communication). While clearly designed to identify signs of psychological distress, what emerges from Magdalenic's questions is that apart from talking to each other, the psychologist was the first to provide these interpreters with a space to tell their story. These interviews demonstrate that interpreters are full-fledged participants in the testimonial process, not merely a communication channel, and in the wartime context − as in refugee, asylum and court proceedings − they are under severe pressure to perform accurately and professionally, as well as conform to various norms and live up to (self)-expectations (Inghilleri 2005, Jacquemet 2005, Moeketsi 2007, Tipton 2008, Wadensjö 1998). Finding ways to narrate their experience, as Magdalenic's questions enabled them to, may relieve the pressure and help make sense of the lived experience.

In addition to the accounts provided by Magdalenic's interviewees, some of whom are my former colleagues, I also draw in the following analysis on my own personal experience as someone who has worked as a volunteer interpreter in the same context.[2]

The war in Croatia

The 1991–1992 war in Croatia has been largely occulted, first, by the immensity of the events in Bosnia and Herzegovina (1992–1995) and the role Croatia played in them, along with Serbia, which came to light in the late 1990s and in the early years of the twenty-first century through the work of the International Crimes Tribunal for ex-Yugoslavia (ICTY) in The Hague; and second, by the war conflict and NATO strikes in Kosovo (1998–1999). Given the limitations imposed by my source material, which was gathered in the fall of 1993 by Magdalenic, I restrict my comments in this section of the article to the war in Croatia, outlining the situation as experienced by the interpreters in 1993, without the hindsight of Bosnian events.

The 1991–92 war in Croatia erupted as the result of a conflict over borders between Croatia and Serbia during the break-up of the Socialist Federal Republic of Yugoslavia. The Socialist Federal Republic of Yugoslavia, as its name denotes, was a federation of republics. The republics constituting the Yugoslav federation from 1945 to 1992 were Slovenia, Croatia, Bosnia and Herzegovina, Serbia (with two autonomous provinces of Voïvodina and Kosovo), Montenegro and Macedonia. The 1974 Yugoslav constitution had secured for the republics the right to secede from the federation. However, in the Communist one-party system and for the duration of the Cold War, this kind of self-determination was ideologically and practically inconceivable. The freedom of choice to form or not form a federation with other republics became available only after 1989; multi-party elections were first held in Slovenia and Croatia in the spring of 1990, and then later in other republics of the former Yugoslavia. Initially, a proposal for the confederation of sovereign states, modelled on the European Community, was put forward. After the refusal of the Republic of Serbia and the Republic of Montenegro to form a confederation with other republics that constituted federal Yugoslavia, the Republic of Croatia, along with its western neighbour the Republic of Slovenia, exercised the right to self-determination granted by the Yugoslav constitution and proclaimed independence on 25 June 1991. Independence from federal Yugoslavia was declared following a democratic referendum in which 94% of the Croatian population expressed support for this option in the event that the confederation with other republics was not formed.

Serbia, the republic bordering Croatia to the east, took the position that, in the case of secession, borders between republics were to be reconsidered and renegotiated, because it claimed that all the Serbs of the former Yugoslavia could live only within the national borders of Serbia. In the former federal Yugoslavia, all the Serbs lived in one state in which they constituted the majority. In July 1991, the Yugoslav Army, led by Serbs, mobilized its units and began a strategically developed military campaign on the territory of the former Yugoslav Republic of Croatia, claiming that the Serbian minority in Croatia was now physically and legally 'endangered' and in need of protection from 'secessionist' Croats. The Yugoslav Army dropped the adjective 'national' from its old federal name, Yugoslav National Army, since in the course of the war its commanding chain and soldiers became uniquely of Serbian and

Montenegrin nationality, and all other nationalities either gradually deserted the army or were released from duty at the beginning of the war. From the beginning, and in its entirety, the war took place on the territory of the Republic of Croatia; fourteen cease-fires did not hold as they were violated by the Yugoslav Army. By the time the fifteenth cease-fire took effect (on 3 January 1992) and the independent Republic of Croatia began to gain international recognition (15 January 1992), one third of the Croatian territory was under the occupation of the Yugoslav Army (in three different, non-contiguous areas of Eastern Slavonia, Western Slavonia, and Krajina). The Yugoslav Army and Serbian paramilitary units first made use of the technique of 'ethnic cleansing' in Croatia, soon to become infamous for its use in Bosnia and Herzegovina. The occupied territories were cleansed of the Croat ethnic presence, with the exception of small numbers of elderly people. All non-Serbian minorities were expelled alongside the Croat population. In January 1993, the numbers stood at 330,100 Croatian civilians who were displaced or took refuge elsewhere, 2181 killed, 6762 injured, and 14,805 missing out of the total population of Croatia, which then stood at 4,784,265 (Bulletin 1993). The occupied territories were populated, and in the years to follow, continuously settled, by Serbs coming from Serbia proper and from Bosnia and Herzegovina. The interpreters interviewed in Magdalenic's study, from which the data for this paper is drawn, belonged primarily – but not exclusively – to the Croat population.

This first major armed conflict on European soil since World War II commanded the immediate attention of the European Community. At the time of the conflict, the European Community (EC) had not yet expanded its membership nor changed its name to the European Union (EU). The EC consisted of twelve member countries: Germany, France, United Kingdom, Spain, Portugal, The Netherlands, Belgium, Ireland, Italy, Greece, Denmark and Luxembourg. However, the EC was unable to intervene, for, as long as the borders of Croatia were not internationally recognized, international law could not view the Serbian military invasion as a war between two sovereign countries, but rather as an internal settling of accounts, a civil war. Before adjudicating, the EC wanted to establish the real aggressor in the conflict. In spite of the urgency of the continuing Serbian occupation, as a precondition of Croatia's international recognition the European Community also chose to scrutinize the constitution and the legislature of Croatia in order to verify the status and the rights which the Croatian constitution granted its minorities. According to the 1991 census, there were a number of larger minority groups living in Croatia: Czechs (0.27%), Slovaks (0.46%), Hungarians (0.46%), Italians (0.44%), Muslims (0.90%) and Albanians (0.25%).[3] There were also 2.2% of Yugoslavs in 1991.[4] To this list can be added fifteen other nationalities with a population of fewer than 10,000 declared. Among all the nationalities residing in Croatia, Serbs were the largest minority group (12.15%). In its constitution, drawn before the proclamation of independence, Croatia guaranteed all groups the status of minority, enjoying full rights. Only the Croatian Serbs refused the minority status and questioned the status of Croats as the only constitutional majority (representing 78% of the population at that point). The other minority groups in Croatia did not make similar constitutional claims, nor any claims in the war fought on the Croatian side. Although interpreters working for the Croatian Liaison Office were mostly ethnic Croats, there were also ethnic Serbian, Macedonian and Albanian interpreters, all citizens of Croatia. Magdalenic's interviewees reflect the diversity of the Croatian population, hence the choice of the Croatian (rather than ethnic Croat) label to refer to the interpreters discussed in this article.

In order to facilitate the work of the EC Arbitration Commission as well as to follow the developments and negotiate the conflict on the ground, the European Community set up the European Community Monitor Mission (ECMM) in July 1991, an international task force with direct access to the conflict. The EC adopted what it referred to as a position of neutrality. 'Neutrality' comes from the Latin word *neuter* and stands for 'neither one nor the other, taking neither side, neither active nor passive, intransitive'. The European arbitration in the conflict was thus intended to proceed neutrally, 'taking neither side', and therefore be independent of the two governments in question for information which it transmitted to the EC. Fifteen countries participated in the work of the ECMM: the twelve member countries of the European Community plus Canada, the Czech Republic and Slovakia. ECMM's objective was to achieve peace and bring all war activities in Croatia to a halt. The negotiation of a cease-fire, however, focused on freezing the situation on the battle field while leaving aside the question of enabling the Croatian side to reinstate their borders as they were prior to the outbreak of war. In addition, one of ECMM's tasks was to implement confidence-building measures – in other words, to ensure the protection of the rights of minorities. ECMM's function was thus to neutrally monitor the cease-fire(s) they negotiated and to monitor the respect of minority rights in Croatia. The EC monitors collected testimonies from Croats and Serbs alike, both civilians and military personnel, on and close to the front lines. ECMM needed interpreters who could translate these oral testimonies consecutively into English, the *lingua franca* of the organization, and only occasionally into French and German. Thus the triangular structure of translation was set: the interviewer (an EC monitor), the witness (a Croat or a Serb), and the interpreter, a Croatian national.

Its declared position of neutrality allowed the EC to pose as an unengaged, and thus by definition objective and just arbiter in the conflict, but an arbiter nevertheless. The EC Arbitration Commission in charge of this process took seven months to complete the review. The European Community and several other countries recognized Croatia on 15 January 1992; full international recognition followed on 22 May 1992, when Croatia became a member of the United Nations. Twelve out of the twenty-five interpreters interviewed by Dr. Magdalenic started interpreting during the open conflict in the summer and fall of 1991 and in early 1992 (before the international recognition of Croatia in May 1992), nine began interpreting for the ECMM after May 1992, and four in 1993. It is important to note that notwithstanding the fifteenth cease-fire and the international recognition of Croatia, the state of war continued until 1995, as the Croatian territories remained occupied. Thus, interpreters who joined in 1992 still experienced war conditions on the front lines similar to those at the peak of the conflict in the fall and winter of 1991, and conditions of interpreting on the front lines were occasionally life-threatening. The major change for the interpreters was ECMM's decision in the fall of 1992 to begin paying for interpreter services: seventeen of the twenty-five interpreters interviewed started working as volunteers; eight (Interpreters J, L, M, P, S, V, W, X) joined in the fall of 1992 as paid interpreters.

Wartime translation

Wartime translation began as a purely volunteer, small-scale operation, improvised at first by the Croatian Liaison Office. As the demand grew, so did the number of volunteers. The data gathered from the interviews shows that Croatian interpreters volunteered to translate the war for the ECMM, a politically neutral organization, but their decision to do so was not neutral or disinterested.

Interpreters volunteered out of 'patriotism' (Interpreters B, E, F, G, L, N, R), 'a feeling of responsibility' (Interpreter D), because they 'didn't want to stay on the sidelines' (Interpreter V), because they wanted 'to do something' (Interpreters A, B, E, H, I, K, N, O, S, T, X), 'to help' (Interpreters C, D, M, P, U, Y), by using their highly valued linguistic skills: 'I believe to be doing a useful job', says Interpreter Q, echoed by Interpreter P. For these interpreters, translation is a privileged site in which they can exercise their agency, a weapon that can be used to alert the international community to the Croatian position in the conflict:

> **Interpreter V:** 'An interpreter cannot and should not be just a "transmitter".'

They refuse to be seen as mere linguistic intermediaries, as invisible go-betweens, 'transmitters' without a voice, and instead exercise their agency at a time when Croatia is under attack. They volunteer out of the desire to witness: Interpreter D 'wanted to see for herself what is really happening on the front-lines',[5] as did Interpreter H, with the intention of bearing witness before the ECMM. In the urgency of a war conflict toward which the EC adopted a position of neutrality, without an internal consensus on who is the aggressor and who is the victim, interpreter volunteering was a form of activism, an attempt to persuade individual monitors of the ECMM to take sides, to show them who the real aggressor is. Translation is not a neutral zone, and in this case became a war zone in itself, one in which Croatia can be defended against the aggression of the occupying Serb forces. To translate here is to be at war, to be on a 'mission'. This is also evident in the way the interpreters interviewed here often resort to the use of military terminology: they are a part of a 'civilian army', 'soldier[s]'. They feel the bond of being 'brothers in arms' (Interpreter D). It is not surprising then that many of the volunteer interpreters also call themselves 'veterans' (Interpreters B, L, M, P, S).

But within the structure of translation set up by the EC, interpreters are supposed to function as the conduit of an address between the witness and the EC monitor, an address from which they themselves are excluded. Through the interpreter, the EC monitor and the witness address each other, they become interlocutors. The interpreter, as the third element in the interaction, must remain outside the address; he or she is the 'intermediary' through whom the address can take place. Despite their original motivation to become witnesses for the ECMM, Croatian interpreters appear to respect the existing structure of translation, which does not allow them to be the patriotic, engaged witness that they thought they could be. I wish to underline the difference here between conscious interventions in the translation zone, pre-meditated and intended to manipulate the meaning of the original, and the unconscious alteration or renarration (Baker 2006a) which is always at work in translation – among other things, because of the lack of equivalence between languages and cultures. The interpreters' discourse itself distinguishes between the two: they claim to refrain from manipulating the utterances of the primary interlocutors and take great pride in the accuracy of their translations and their professionalism, as will become clear in the examples that follow.

Some of the interpreting occurred on visits to Serb villages in the remaining free territory of Croatia in order to monitor their status, and very often in tripartite meetings and negotiations between the Croatian military, the Serbian military, and the EC monitors. Here, interpreting clearly involved translating for the enemy party. According to the interpreters interviewed, irrespective of the context, even in cases when the interpreters themselves were personally offended, linguistic neutrality was maintained:

> **Interpreter G:** 'I translated all of her words [insults] calmly.'
> **Interpreter W:** 'One of the monitors was saying bad things about Croatian politics. I did not participate in the debate.'

To translate 'calmly' indicates that the interpreter is focused exclusively on language. On the other hand, not to 'participate in the debate' testifies to an attempt to keep the interpreters' linguistic performance free from political contamination. Interpreters transmit the words of the witness without performing any evaluative or interpretative acts – at least as far as their linguistic output is concerned. Indeed, interpreters persist in translating in the most taxing situations:

> **Interpreter F:** 'It is embarrassing to have to admit that [Croats] did it [that they blew up Serbs' family houses].'
> **Interpreter H:** 'It is unpleasant to translate [Serbian] lies.'
> **Interpreter N:** 'Situations, when one must translate rude comments about [Croatian] interlocutors, are unpleasant.'
> **Interpreter V:** 'It is unpleasant to translate rude comments about the ECMM.'

They translate professionally in the hope that contradictory evidence will lead the EC monitor to see through those 'lies':

> **Interpreter S:** 'When Serbs say that their children are working as "mechanics" on the other side [in the occupied territory], even monitors laugh it away.'

They resist the temptation to manipulate other interlocutors' utterances intentionally and fight the impulse to give their own counter-testimony in the name of the 'truth'. Although they know that a partial and faulty translation could completely alter the meaning in their favour, they insist that they observe the principles of professionalism and accuracy and avoid conscious manipulation:

> **Interpreter O:** 'Translation is a job of responsibility.' (Similar comments are made by Interpreter D.)
> **Interpreter R:** 'I try to maintain objectivity, professionalism . . . Even though I am a volunteer, I am still a professional.'
> **Interpreter T:** 'I take it all as a part of the job.' (Similar comments are made by Interpreter U.)

Because they are 'professionals', interpreters must accept a form of erasure, at least while interpreting. Rather than distortion and inaccuracy, it is their professionalism which is seen as the best testimony to the fact that Croatia has nothing to hide about its treatment of the Serb minority, nothing to do with violating (one of) the cease-fire(s). ECMM's political neutrality is perceived only as a temporary methodological device, necessary only until the EC monitors find the evidence and themselves witness the war, on the front-lines and in the occupied territories, as Serbian territorial expansion. As far as the interpreters are concerned, then, they and the ECMM are working for the common goal of collecting the evidence to determine who the aggressor is in this conflict:

> **Interpreter A:** 'I feel I am a part of the ECMM team.' (Similar comments are made by Interpreter Q.)

For Interpreter A, there is an 'us' – the EC monitors and the interpreters are on the same side.

This self-erasure is a violence that the interpreting structure imposes on inter-preters and that they feel they have to conscientiously respect. In other words, inter-preters who volunteered to translate in order to testify are denied the very possibility of testimony. The two conditions that make interpreting in and of a war possible, the desire to bear witness (volunteerism) and the obligation to mediate linguistically between primary interlocutors (professionalism), come into conflict with each other, since the positions of the witness and of the interpreter are mutually exclusive. The very demand for interpreter activism/intervention from within the structure of translation, contradicted by the structural impossibility of testifying from within, produces an internal conflict in the interpreter to which **Interpreter I**'s personal story testifies:

> 'I wanted to do something because my brothers too were volunteers in the Croatian Army.'

Unlike her brothers, who could be simultaneously volunteers and professionals when they joined the Croatian Army, the interpreter is split between being *either* a profes-sional *or* a volunteer, between the task of translating Croatian and Serbian testimonies professionally and allegiance to Croatia. As **Interpreter C** puts it succinctly:

> 'It is not clear to me whom I have to obey when on a mission – the directions from the [Croatian Liaison] Office or the orders of the head of the [ECMM] team.'

Torn between political allegiance and professionalism, interpreters literally embody the violence of the conflict that they translate for the international community. While translating the violence of the war, they themselves become the site of a violent conflict.

Just how did Croatian interpreters negotiate their position between volunteerism (bearing witness) and professionalism (providing linguistic mediation)? Here, I wish to differentiate between translations which consciously alter elements of the source material and the particularity of the interpreting context on the front-lines, which often provides opportunities for other types of intervention. In the current case, interpreters often went with the same ECMM teams on multiple missions, which lasted anywhere between one day and two weeks. This created suitable conditions for familiarity, with prolonged mutual exposure ultimately serving the interpreters' aim of bearing witness. The interviews show that the interpreters' interventions in the testimonial process constitute a conscious effort to persuade, while simultaneously refraining from altering the original testimonies that they are asked to translate. This attempt to 'persuade' in some respects resembles the kind of political activism that has developed since 2002 (Baker 2006b, in press, Boéri 2008). Rather than changing any aspect of the original testimony, interpreters in this context retain the original testimony intact but supplement it with their own when the opportunity arises. Moreover, the passage between the two is marked, without attempting to pass one for the other. Interpreters act as witnesses when they perform 'switching', as they call it. They 'switch' from the position of 'interpreter' to the position of 'interlocutor' in 'unofficial' situations, 'when personal opinions can be expressed' (**Interpreter P**) – outside the translation structure, but within the translation war zone, during off-hours:

> **Interpreter D:** 'Regardless of the official function, I try to play the role of an unofficial representative of the Republic of Croatia, I explain the situation in this part of the world to the monitors.'
> **Interpreter E:** 'We talk a lot, exchange opinions, I try to influence them.'
> **Interpreter O:** '[There are] unofficial conversations, explanations of the situation, etc.' (Similar comments are made by Interpreter M.)
> **Interpreter V:** 'One needs to have unofficial conversations – that is how mutual trust and respect are built.'

'Switching' even occurs at the monitors' request:

> **Interpreter C:** 'One needs to help introduce the new monitors to the situation here – they even ask for advice.'
> **Interpreter F:** 'Many are poorly informed.'
> **Interpreter Q:** 'There are elements of guided tours, history lessons.'

To translate the war means to testify to the war in their own voice, that is to demonstrate to the EC monitors who is the aggressor and who is the victim. It is an opportunity to elaborate the narrative of one's own culture and history – because for most of the twentieth century Croatia was part of Yugoslavia, its past had been obscured in the communal Yugoslav history. The interpreters represent their country; they are 'ambassador[s]' of Croatia, says **Interpreter D**, just as they hope to make EC monitors 'into unofficial ambassadors of the Republic of Croatia'.

However, 'switching' becomes more difficult as the tension between professionalism and volunteerism in the interpreters' double position is gradually put under additional strain. With time, some interpreters perceive the European Community as unwilling to act politically or militarily on the basis of physical evidence and testimony that the ECMM collected while investigating the nature and progress of the conflict, and as unable to stop the attacks that continued beyond the fifteenth ceasefire, despite international recognition of Croatia. Indeed, the occupation of Croatia not only continued despite international recognition of its sovereignty, but also advanced unhindered, as Croatian territories were resettled. As **Interpreter D** put it (corroborated by Interpreter K), 'our side has more and more difficulty in dealing with the EC missions, it is harder than before'. **Interpreter X** confirms that the '[EC] missions have recently become less popular', an assessment with which interpreter **T** agrees, and **Interpreter O** observes that 'there used to be more enthusiasm'. There is no point in continuing the EC monitor mission, according to **Interpreter F**, since 'monitors have no [other] jurisdiction except monitoring'. Other interpreters express their impatience in similar terms. Often, they find their skills wasted on 'idle talk' (**Interpreter M, Y**), while 'nothing is being done' (**Interpreter M**). **Interpreter U** elaborates:

> 'I often feel useless. For example, I am at [their] disposal for 96 hours (4 days), I translate for 2–3 hours, and the rest of the time I am on stand-by. I spend time in the hotel . . . but that is not why I went on the mission.' (Similar comments are made by Interpreter M.)

It is because of the growing absurdity of this situation in which, despite their professed 'political neutrality', it becomes clear that not to implement and enforce a political decision is in fact to favour the aggressor that interpreters at times experience difficulties, especially when they witness emotionally charged situations:

> **Interpreter A:** 'The most difficult moment took place in a refugee centre when a child died and the refugees accused us [the ECMM]'.
> **Interpreter B:** '[I] saw 10 months old corpses [of Croatian civilians]'.
> **Interpreter D:** 'The most difficult are the stories of [Croatian] refugees and displaced persons.'
> **Interpreter E:** '[I] went into an unmarked minefield with another monitor.'
> **Interpreter G:** 'Six buses with [Croatian] refugees were arriving, and they [the Serbs] were shooting at them, the situation was very tense, and I was hiding with the monitors in a ditch.'
> **Interpreter M:** 'Destroyed Croat villages are particularly difficult to see.'
> **Interpreter N:** 'A meeting with the parents of a child born in the refugee camp was very moving.'
> **Interpreter T:** 'On several occasions, I was at an exhumation (from the well, from the corn field) and at the exchange of corpses, and I translated the identification procedure. It was sickening to look at the corpse taken out of the well.'
> **Interpreter Y:** 'I saw massacred bodies of [Croatian] soldiers and civilians . . . I also watched a village burning at night.'

The stress involved in such situations was exacerbated by the fact that counselling was not provided for the interpreters. Instead, they developed their own internal support system, with the idea of a 'community of veterans' composed of volunteers who worked for the ECMM from an early stage being one such system. At any rate, it was in such highly charged situations that, occasionally, the 'switch' occurred not *outside of* but *within* the structure of translation, in the course of an official interview. Here, instead of simply translating the witness's testimony, the interpreter 'jumps in' and intervenes. **Interpreter J** had to be recalled from duty after '[m]ostly interpreting, although I was explaining to them what was happening there'. **Interpreter B** admits:

> 'I "jump in", it's more than interpreting: conversations with monitors, discussions about everything that is going on, explanation of our [Croatian] situation.'

The structure of address within which interpreting takes place is exploded. Interpreters become subjects speaking in their own voice, no longer mere intermediaries with no personal history. They become witnesses through their intervention, in their very failure to be interpreters. Precisely because 'switching' can at any given moment disrupt the structure, it reveals the inherent precariousness of the interpreter's 'professional', 'neutral' and 'self-erasing' stance.

In acting as witnesses in their own right, interpreters fail to render the testimony of the original witness faithfully. They divert the address to themselves and respond in lieu of the original witness. This disruption is undeniably a violence committed against witnesses and their testimony. However, the parallels that I have drawn out between professionalism, activism and the break-down of the translation structure allow us to distinguish between conscious activism and unconscious disruptions in interpreting. 'Switching' may be considered a form of activism; however, the interpreters' testimony is not part of the recorded, official evidence. They may be interlocutors to the EC monitors but they are still not admitted as official witnesses to the ECMM; the ECMM are not interested in allowing the interpreters to be witnesses, to tell their story. The ECMM do not acknowledge interpreters as 'knowledgeable' interlocutors (Tipton 2008:12). In addition, the structure of testimony conditions the marginality of interpreters – they do not participate in the war in a personal capacity since their interpreting lends voice to someone else. They are interpreters and not witnesses, intermediaries erased from the official history of witnessing. This structural violence and exclusion from the testimonial process create disruptions in particularly challenging situations, but we should not dismiss such interventions on their part as 'distortions', as Felman and Laub do when they argue that 'the interpreter . . . in some ways distorts and screens [the visual/acoustic information] because the translation is not always absolutely accurate' (1992:212). Rather than a contamination of testimony; the type of 'distortion' described here can be read precisely as interpreters' testimony: to themselves and to their task (Stahuljak 2000).

The 'distortion' of translation should be read here, not as 'failure', as the term implies, but as a speech act. At the moment when interpreters do violence to witnesses, they are bearing witness to the violence that was done to them. The violence involved in working within a conflict that is forcibly neutralized becomes audible when translation breaks down. The interpreters' internal conflict between professionalism and volunteerism erupts in the breakdown of 'neutral' translation and demands acknowledgment. The interpreters bear witness to the fact that, as interpreters, they can never testify, politically or structurally – the former undermines their professionalism and the latter disrupts the transmission of the original testimony. Furthermore, their speech act also reveals that they cannot identify from within the structure of translation. Precisely because translation and testimony are mutually exclusive, interpreters can only recognize themselves *outside of* and *apart from* the act of translation. The interpreter 'emerges' from the speech act – it is a moment of self-witnessing, making the fact of there-being-a-translation audible, but it is also an assertion of one's own voice. It constitutes a moment of recognition that the interpreters are not outside of history, culture or ideology, not simply mechanical transmitters or intermediaries, but always within interaction, as witnesses and participants. Their speech act reveals that translation as mediation is always already an intervention (Baker 2008, Inghilleri 2005, Maier 2007, Munday 2007b).

Translation and neutrality

But interpreters' speech act, their attempt to act as witnesses in their own right, is read as a deliberate distortion and therefore political disobedience, a cause for mistrust and a compromise of credibility (Baker 2008, Inghilleri 2009, Rafael 2007). To intervene in the original testimony is a scandalous gesture, because it is perceived as undermining ECMM's proclaimed neutrality:

> **Interpreter C:** 'I told them that it [bringing medication across the border] wouldn't work, but they got angry at me and reported me [to the manager of the Croatian Liaison Office].'
>
> **Interpreter U:** 'The EC monitor strongly reprimanded me for not doing my job as I should.'

The interpreter's speech act as witness reveals the impossibility of neutral transmission beyond the 'neutrality' of the immediate interpreting situation. If the interpreters' intervention is scandalous, it is not so because of compromised trust and credibility, but because it gestures toward the very position taken by the ECMM. In other words, interpreters here are both the figure and the channel for the kind of neutral transmission that the ECMM claims to perform. There is an uncanny similarity between the position of interpreters and the position of the ECMM. Interpreters 'process' an otherwise incomprehensible minor Slavic language into the 'literal meaning of testimonies' (Felman and Laub 1992:213). Likewise, in providing information that is essential for arbitration in and later resolution of the conflict, the ECMM plays the role of an interpreter of a potentially incomprehensible conflict. It engages in translation as historical transmission, as the passing-on of a historical event, the war, which it is trying to make intelligible to the international community. The interpreters' concrete linguistic performance is reiterated in the kind of translation into meaning that the ECMM performs.

As we saw, interpreting requires a neutralization of the interpreter as witness. The ECMM imposes a structural (linguistic) neutrality on the interpreter as part of grounding its own political (historical) neutrality. As a consequence of this enforced linguistic neutrality, the ECMM can claim to provide a neutral and all-inclusive overview of the war. When the issue is observed from all sides because neither side is taken, arbitration can pose as a comprehensive, closed and understandable account of the event of the war. Neutrality can lay claim to justice because it wills itself as all-inclusive. This 'all-inclusive' vision, however, manages to overlook the interpreter, whose role is underestimated even as it gives rise to concerns about 'neutrality':

> **Interpreter D:** 'My Ph.D. degree confuses them [the monitors] – one of them remarked that I could be of more help to my country at my regular job.'
>
> **Interpreter I:** 'Monitors do not have enough appreciation for the interpreters.'

In another example, the ECMM left the selection of interpreters entirely at the discretion of the Croatian Liaison Office. Its neutrality could have been easily compromised from the outset had the Croatian Liaison Office selected only ethnic Croats for interpreters. The ECMM is there to observe the war, yet it manages not to recognize the interpreters' conflicted body and their war efforts. Interpreters are its blind spot: the ECMM denies them the position of a historical witness while at the same time claiming to be all-inclusive. Since interpreters are not outside the war but part of it, the ECMM fails to see in them the war that it came to observe. In this, already, it is missing the war.

But the ECMM is missing the war in yet another way. As we saw, the ECMM 'neutralizes' interpreters in order to ground its own political neutrality. Interpreters must erase themselves, their own history, in order to provide a smooth translation. Translation, where the interpreter remains self-erased throughout, makes itself transparent and performs what Jean-François Lyotard described as the 'dream of a pre-Babel state, of an ideal form of interlinguistic communication in which there is no need for translation. That is every translation's ideal. To render itself useless, impossible even, and to erase the interlinguistic gap which motivates it' (Lyotard 1989:xi). Just as the interpreters erase themselves, make their physical presence transparent, so does the translation erase itself from the testimony that it translates. Born out of an interlinguistic gap, it aims to make us forget this gap. At the moment of the interpreter's intervention, what becomes visible and *audible* is that in translation, because of the gap that motivates it, something always remains inaccessible, untranslatable (Stahuljak 2000, 2004, Rafael 2007). Smooth, transparent, neutral translation, on the other hand, would be an accessible, coherent historical narrative that 'pretends to reduce historical scandals to mere sense and to eliminate the unassimilable shock of history' (Felman and Laub 1992:151). With the self-erasure and neutralization of the interpreter, what is erased and neutralized is the fact that the war is accessed only through translation, through mediation. But the ECMM plays on the notion of the romanticized bridge-builder and neutral transmitter, despite the fact that its neutral position is inherently questionable: the EC is the arbiter in the conflict. As Roland Barthes reminded us, 'le ni-ni tient le discours du maître: il sait, il juge' (the 'neither-nor' holds the master discourse: it knows, it judges), and this 'ni-nisme' (neither-norism) is far from the 'neutral' position that 'ne sait pas' (does not know) (Barthes 2002:115).

This double erasure enacted by neutrality is what the interpreters do not allow the monitors to forget when they resist a smooth translation. Their speech act may bear witness only to a personal truth, to a personal historical conflict. Yet this personal truth partakes of history to the extent that it reminds the EC monitors that their access to the event is indeed mediated, translational, and personal. Secondly, it underscores the fact that, since the medium, that is the interpreter, is not neutral, not outside the history that he or she translates, the ECMM itself is not outside the history it translates, but is part of it. The ECMM's neutrality plays a historical role in the war, it is a form of engagement. Interpreters reveal the violence that ECMM's disavowal of engagement commits, by way of reminding the EC monitors that, even when proclaiming their neutrality, they are not beyond/outside their own or someone else's history but rather active participants in it:

> **Interpreter D:** 'I had political contacts with the English and the French who strongly represented their respective countries' politics, who are unfavourable to us [Croatians].'
> **Interpreter I:** 'Some monitors speak badly of Croatia.'

By 'strongly representing' their countries, the EC monitors do not abandon an active and engaged stand for a neutral stand in relation to the war in Croatia:

> **Interpreter L:** 'Monitors' partiality is disturbing.'
> **Interpreter R:** 'Many are big nationalists, yet they find the same fault with us.'

Likewise, because of their engagement in their own Western narrative, **Interpreter Q** points out that sometimes 'There are minor conflicts with monitors, for instance when they talk of Yugoslavia without the attribute "former" '. That some EC monitors are unaware or unwilling to recognize the official change in the status of Yugoslavia is explained thus:

> **Interpreter I:** 'Most are here only for the money. Some do not know what to ask their interlocutors when on a mission.'
> **Interpreter V:** 'Some are here only for the money, they are completely uninterested.'

Interpreters report a general lack of interest (Interpreters D, I, L, K, V) or information (Interpreters T, X):

> **Interpreter L:** 'Some come thinking there is war in Zagreb, they are not interested to know whether what they hear is true, they take everything literally'.

They are 'uninterested' because they already 'know' all there is to know about the ancient ethnic conflicts in the Yugoslav region:

> **Interpreter D:** 'Many come with prejudice about the "Balkan" people.'
> **Interpreter R:** '[S]ome behave with superiority, look down on us as "wild Balkan" people.'

Others still, says **Interpreter Y**, are here 'for tourism', visits to the Croatian Adriatic coast; **Interpreter R** claims there is more and more of such behaviour. This manner of being above and outside of history causes the ECMM to be violently oblivious to the situation on the front-lines and to their own historical and cultural position in the conflict; while they are taking their time to arbitrate, temporality becomes de-historicized, thereby privileging the law of the stronger. Finally, even when the ECMM participate by not participating, the interpreters' speech act as witnesses in their own right reminds them that their neutral position is not above or outside violence but is itself a violence: neutral transmission requires a violent erasure of interpreters and their history. Hence, the speech act brings into light the fact that transmission occurs through an erasure. Transmission of history erases the traces of the medium of its transmission and of the history of the medium. Paradoxically, neutral historical trans-mission requires that one participate in the fiction of a de-historicized transmission.

The ECMM ultimately acknowledge that the interpreters', and their own, neutral-ity is a fiction when they suspect the interpreters of being spies:

> **Interpreter C:** 'A Czech monitor searched my belongings, looking for spying equipment, and he did the same to another [female] interpreter.'
> **Interpreter D:** 'Some think that we were "assigned" to this job – they consider us to be official representatives of the Republic of Croatia.'
> **Interpreter U:** 'Some of them are intelligence officers, and so they think we are too – one of them invited me to talk as "colleagues." One of the monitors admitted to an interpreter that he searched her personal belong-ings for spying equipment . . . Some monitors think that I moonlight as a spy.'

Interpreter V: 'The most difficult situation is when the team leader mistrusts the interpreter, thinking that, as a Croat, he will be partial.'

While claiming that they, the ECMM, are neutral, the ECMM suspect that the interpreters' very willingness to translate may be, after all, politically motivated. Conversely, the recognition of the interpreter's fictional neutrality undoes ECMM's own neutrality. Yet the ECMM do not question the political, historical motivation behind their own willingness to provide a neutral translation of the war. Consequently, the fiction of a de-historicized, neutral transmission is a violent and even traumatic one. The trauma can be severe and manifest itself not only as an occasional intervention in translation but also as mental illness. One interpreter, himself a refugee, who was taken off duty after suffering from severe psychological stress, was reported to have no longer been able to bear ECMM's neutrality toward the events on the front-lines (reported by **Interpreter F** and **Interpreter S**).

War is a proof of history that is too complex to lend itself to smooth de-historicization. Ultimately, the interpreters' intervention within translation reminds us that the shock, the violence of an event such as war, cannot be translated or processed without 'shocking' the very structure of its transmission, and especially its claim to neutrality. A neutral arbitration wills the catastrophic event of the war to be rendered accessible through a smooth, neutral and all-inclusive narration. It seeks to make complete sense of the war. But translation as speech act alerts us to the fact that war is unassimilable to a smooth, non-disrupted translation. The scandal of war cannot be neutrally translated. It may even be that the war, as an interpreter claimed, should not be neutrally translated, for to do so would be to miss the event itself. What distinguishes this event is that it does not leave room for neutrality, that it 'shocks' one out of any possible neutral stance, precisely because the breakdown of translation is unavoidable: either the interpreter 'jumps in' or a smooth, uninterrupted translation fails to convey the fact that history is passed on in erasure. The only ethical position may then be to disrupt or undermine the 'neutral' arbiter, a practice that Cronin labels '*translation as resistance*' and describes as 'the ways in which originals can be manipulated, invented or substituted, or the status of the original subverted in order to frustrate the intelligence-gathering activities of the Imperial Agent' (2000a:35), or in this case, of an intelligence officer in the skin of an EC monitor.

Interpreter activism: between volunteerism and professionalism

Not only do the ECMM suspect the interpreters of being spies, but Croatia also looks at them with suspicion. Interpreters are left out of the history of the international community because, as volunteers, they are always marked as politically motivated, volunteer-patriots, or even worse: nationalists. They might then at least hope to be recognized as patriots in the history of their country. Instead, they are perceived as 'double agents' (Rafael 2007), with the Croatian side accusing them of treason:

> **Interpreter A:** '[T]he animosity towards monitors is transferred onto the interpreter.'
> **Interpreter D:** 'It affects me that [Croatians] identify us with the monitors, so that sometimes waiters refuse to serve us, children yell or throw stones at us.'

> **Interpreter H:** 'The lack of sympathy towards monitors is partially transferred onto us.'
> **Interpreter I:** 'Sometimes they [Croatians] throw stones at cars.'
> **Interpreter K:** 'Sometimes [Croatians] yell at me for what angers them in monitors.'

The interpreters' linguistic neutrality is misinterpreted as political neutrality. Croatia perceives their professionalism as a neutralization of their political allegiance rather than as a structural responsibility – it misreads their volunteerism as betrayal. For Croatia, interpreters remain anonymous. By definition volunteerism is a gift that is neither documented nor recognized. Paradoxically then, interpreters' patriotism is compromised by their volunteerism, because records that might testify to their participation in the war and their patriotic political allegiance are non-existent.

In addition to the fact that their volunteerism erases them, then, Croatia also refuses to recognize translation as an act of patriotism; already as volunteers, the fact that they are working for a politically neutral organization compromises them. And any remaining patriotic intention to which they could lay claim is definitely jeopardized when this politically neutral organization starts paying interpreters for their work, perhaps in an attempt to develop staff loyalty. In the fall of 1992, the ECMM started to remunerate the interpreters. A number of new interpreters joined in but with a motivation radically different from that of the volunteers:

> **Interpreter I:** 'Most new translators are here for the money, nothing else interests them.'
> **Interpreter N:** 'It is not good that earnings are the only motivation – when on a mission, those try to work the least they can.'
> **Interpreter T:** 'The newcomers are coming only for the money, so the old ones, who are interested in something else, do not have enough work.'

From then on, the interpreters distinguished between those 'who are interested in something else', something other than money, that is the original volunteers or the 'veterans', and the 'newcomers' or, as they were also called, the 'mercenaries' (Interpreters B, S). **Interpreter B** openly expressed his anger, which is 'connected to the change of atmosphere at work', a thought further developed by **Interpreter L**:

> 'The atmosphere has changed since payments started, there is less enthusiasm and more tension, less comraderie than before'.

Interpreters F and N expressed a similar viewpoint concerning tension among interpreters, and **Interpreter M** felt that

> 'Deserving veterans do not get the job often because of them [the newcomers]'.

At the same time, 'mercenaries' complain that 'veterans feel more valuable' (**Interpreter P**). But outside the Croatian Liaison Office, this internal distinction between volunteers and 'mercenaries' collapsed. The work of the 'veterans' was now documented, along with the work of the 'mercenaries', in contracts and ECMM payroll records. Thus, once the 'veterans' started being paid, their previous volunteerism was occulted. This paradox, the fact that the volunteer-interpreters who are the most engaged and active in the war are also the most erased in the history of their country, is the ultimate violence connected with interpreting in and of the war.

The memory of interpreters' volunteerism faded as volunteers were conflated with 'mercenaries':

> **Interpreter Q:** '[s]ome think we [the "veterans"] only work for the money.'

It is within this context that the then Croatian Minister of Education declared that the 'patriotism' of those who worked for international organizations 'is questionable'. That the reference in the Minister's statement was to the issue of money as well as the activity of interpreting was proven by the fact that her words provoked strong public reactions from various associations of interpreters in Croatia, even though her statement did not single them out. Interpreters' 'patriotism is questionable' because they are on the ECMM's payroll. The minister assumed that interpreters were 'only work-[ing] for the money'. And to be paid by an organization whose proclaimed neutrality was perceived as acting against Croatia's interests defined the interpreters' political allegiance as unpatriotic. On the other hand, for the Minister of Education their 'patriotism is questionable' because translation, surely, constituted a betrayal: the interpreters had not compelled the party on the receiving end of translation to take the Croatian side, and its continuing neutrality prohibited it from championing or, at the very least, recognizing the Croatian rights to the recovery of the occupied territories. Failing to convince the ECMM finally compromised the interpreters' patriotism.

For interpreters, on the other hand, this betrayal of Croatia was unavoidable. If Croatia wanted international recognition, its voice had to be heard. In order to achieve this, interpreters had to translate into the language of the organization upon which Croatia's recognition depended, while at the same time wishing to bear witness to the victimization of their country. But interpreters were condemned to treason because of the incommensurability of the positions of interpreter and witness in a war context. Wartime translation is a double bind: the double bind of having to translate in order to convey the urgency of political recognition of Croatia, but failing to voice this imperative themselves, failing to be a witness in their translation. The neutrality inherent in translation bars the interpreters from ever giving full recognition to Croatia in their translation. On the other hand, this neutrality prevents Croatia from recognizing interpreter volunteerism as a form of patriotism – interpreters will always be locked in another time frame: they lose their place in the future because they have been erased in the past. They do not have a place in history when the Minister of Education calls them traitors and the ECMM exclude them as witnesses. Earlier we saw that at least one interpreter suffered a trauma because her patriotism could no longer bear ECMM's neutrality. But at this point, interpreters are exposed to another kind of trauma, that of (historical) non-recognition: non-recognition of their testimonial stance by the ECMM and non-recognition of their patriotism by Croatia. In December 2005, 14 years after their service began, after many appeals and with a centre-right government in power, Croatia recognized the work of some twenty volunteer-interpreters from the Croatian Liaison Office by awarding them a medal of honour for their war efforts. The ceremony, ironically, took place in the offices of the now-defunct Ministry for European Integration (currently part of the Ministry of Foreign Affairs).

The question of interpreter activism thus emerges under a different light when the variable of professionalization (in the sense of paid service) is introduced; in other words, volunteerism may be a more 'acceptable' form of interpreter activism, one that does not lead to situations that demand ethical choices compromised by financial transactions. Baker (2008: 17) argues that 'just because the client is paying doesn't mean they are entitled to more loyalty or respect from the translators – translators . . . should not behave like mercenaries'; but, as we have seen, the fact that the interpreter is being paid by a client does compromise their position in the eyes of others. This is one lesson that the Babels interpreter-activists seem to have learned: 'following the unhappy experience of a two-tier workforce of voluntary and paid interpreters in Florence, Babels now makes the principle of 100 per cent volunteer interpretation and translation a precondition of its involvement' (Hodkinson and Boéri 2004). However, as I argue below, while complicating notions of interpreter allegiance both professionalism and volunteerism nevertheless open up a unique space for interpreter activism.

Translating 'the Balkans': transnational translation

As we saw, translation as a speech act always involves the interpreter as a participant, an 'intervenient being' (Maier 2007). But the assertion of one's voice also transcends the individual and becomes an instance of reverse interpellation at the international level, from the minor, obscure language to the hegemonic, major arbiter in the conflict.[6] The interpreters' activism in the testimonial process testifies to a complex and plural past and resists its hegemonic and univocal representation. 'Switching' is consistent with the need to tell one's story, to emplot one's past and thus to challenge the neutral narrative – which is also the dominant narrative, because the ECMM are the arbiter in the conflict. Translation as speech act also points to the need to histori-cize wartime translation. Interpreters' intervention revealed that, despite ECMM's seeming interest only in the facts of the conflict, these 'facts' are equally part of monitors' own pre-existing narrative about the history of Yugoslavia. If the ECMM do not acknowledge interpreters as 'knowledgeable' interlocutors, it may be because they can only acknowledge them as 'native informants', precisely because of their vision of Western superiority in arbitrating over the fratricidal, tribal ' "wild Balkan" people' (Interpreter R). The Western narrative of ex-Yugoslavia and its wars in the 1990s reifies cultural and religious differences that inevitably produce conflict among indistinguishable and indistinct ethnicities; in return, the 'balkanization of Europe' can only be a violent process of unstoppable and contagious fragmentation spreading throughout Europe and undermining the stability and unity of its nation states (Mestrovic 1994). Translation then is a site, not only of identity formation for a minor culture, but of identity legitimation and resistance to a hegemonic, superior vision of the arbiter: a site for re-framing the Western European master narrative (Baker 2006a) and for recasting the 'Balkan' discourse. The popular catchphrase 'balkanization of Europe' may be understood then, not as a threat to European political stability, but as fragmentation of the hegemonic, master narrative of the 'Balkans'.

During the Yugoslav wars, 'the Balkans' were reduced to Yugoslavia, even though the former Yugoslavia shunned any Balkan labels. The socialist Yugoslavia (1945–1992) was a second version of the country first pieced together in 1918 under the name of the Kingdom of Serbs, Croats and Slovenes, renamed in 1929 as the Kingdom of Yugoslavia. All this was meant to resolve the problem of a region located at the crossroads of the former Austro-Hungarian and Ottoman Empires. But the West spoke, not of the specificity of this Austro-Hungarian-Ottoman hybrid, encompassing the former borderline between the East and the West, but of 'the Balkans', a much larger, and somewhat vague and shifting geo-political unit of South-East Europe that included Albania, Bulgaria, Greece, Romania, and part of Turkey. In speaking of 'the Balkans', the West evoked an immutable, 'Oriental' image of Ottoman legacy, one in which the 'inhabitants do not care to conform to the standards of behavior devised as normative by and for the civilized world' (Todorova 1997:3). This image was first established in the wake of the two Balkan Wars (1912–1913), precursors to WWI, traditionally thought to have been triggered by the murder of Archduke Franz-Ferdinand by a Serbian nationalist, Gavrilo Princip, in Sarajevo. Maria Todorova demonstrated masterfully 'How . . . a geographical appellation [of the Bulgarian mountain range could] be transformed into one of the most powerful pejorative designations in history, international relations, political science, and, nowadays, general intellectual discourse' (1997:7). The term 'Balkan'

> was used alongside other generalizing catchwords, of which 'Oriental' was most often employed, to stand for filth, passivity, unreliability, misogyny, propensity for intrigue, insincerity, opportunism, laziness, superstitiousness, lethargy, sluggishness, inefficiency, incompetent bureaucracy. 'Balkan', while overlapping with 'Oriental', had additional characteristics [such] as cruelty, boorishness, instability, and unpredictability. Both categories were used against the concept of Europe symbolizing cleanliness, order, self-control, strength of character, sense of law, justice, efficient administration. (*ibid.*:119)

In short: civilization was opposed to barbarism. The term 'balkanization', signifying fragmentation into ever-smaller states in the wake of the Balkan wars and WWI, added to the mix the crucial ingredient of violence, incomprehensible to the civilized Westerner. Archaic aspects of culture, including the cultural tradition of the 'warrior ethos', were naturalized as the essence of 'Balkan' behaviour, epitomized by the Yugoslavs; Yugoslavs just couldn't help themselves, and war was the only path to dialogue, since war is the true expression of the 'Balkan' spirit. In essence, nothing had changed since the Middle Ages, an image frozen in time that the Balkans had already embodied in nineteenth-century travel literature.

It is here that interpreter activism can make a difference. It is, first of all, a demand for recognition. It may have taken a war for the minor to become *audible* and to begin to translate the plural history of what was occulted behind the 'Balkan' narrative. While the war appears to confirm it, the audibility of the minor in wartime translation challenges the Western European discourse of 'the Balkans'. Translation balkanizes Europe not because it directly threatens its political stability and unity, but because it undermines and undoes its hegemonic, master narrative. This is the sphere of transnational translation, as defined at the beginning of this article (see footnote 1): interpreters offer an interpretation of politics, history and culture, directed vertically at the hegemonic arbiter. When they intervene as interpreters of culture and history, they challenge the narrative of neutrality at a personal level and resist the oversimplifying and hegemonic Western discourse of Croatia as a barbaric and 'wild Balkan' nation. But they also remind the arbiter not to ignore his or her own inscription in the event. At the same time, a transnational translation agenda horizontalizes and flattens vertical relations, since the minor becomes a partner in interlocution. Regardless of the major or minor status of languages from and into which translation occurs, all parties in a war conflict depend on the efficiency of translation: war democratizes the status of languages and allows for mutual interpenetration of the 'Western' and the 'Balkan'. Transnational translation plays here a major role: translations correct the mutual discursive violence of narratives and shift conflicting discursive loyalties in an ongoing process of negotiation through what Sampson (2006) calls 'cultural translation'.

But interpreters perform yet another kind of translation and negotiation of discursive violence, this time 'at home'. For they do not hesitate to criticize their own fellow citizens and Croatia's civil servants:

> **Interpreter D:** 'Regular folks make a better impression (on the monitors as well) than some extremists among civil servants.'
> **Interpreter F:** 'Certain situations are uncomfortable when our interlocutors talk politics too much, give lessons in history, and such – those things are unpleasant to translate because they annoy monitors.'
> **Interpreter N:** 'Our people occasionally talk too much.'
> **Interpreter Q:** 'Occasionally I feel ashamed by what and how some of our representatives say and speak.'
> **Interpreter T:** 'I am occasionally saddened by the way some of our people behave; by applying primitive politics and unnecessary [reasoning], they are creating a poor impression of Croatia.'
> **Interpreter X:** 'Sometimes the poor impression that some of our rude interlocutors leave on the monitors makes me sad. I think they hurt the image of Croatia.'

The overall feeling of sadness that the interpreters report is matched by their feeling of powerlessness in a situation that surpasses their intermediary position and reminds them of their lack of agency. The ethical responsibility that they assume in becoming interpreters in and of the war puts them in a position which is neither strictly political, nor national, nor entirely 'neutral' or 'objective.' It is this in-between space, the double agency of the interpreters' ethical responsibility that **Interpreter P** struggles to define:

> 'I think [my work] helps the homeland and it also helps in a more general sense.'

The interpreters' relationship to history points in at least two directions – toward the 'homeland', and also 'in a more general sense'. The interpreters' allegiance to their 'homeland' is not absolute then; they are neither patriots nor traitors, and they are both volunteers and professionals. The case of Croatian translators shows that the ethical responsibility of interpreters in and of the war involves another kind of allegiance to history that situates them beyond their political, national, ethnic, gender, religious or linguistic affiliations, but at the same time not exclusively in the realm of the universal, or the all-inclusive, or the neutral – speaking from the local to the transnational.

Indeed, my emphasis on the interpreters' intervention could be taken to imply a universal claim that interpreters have a privileged relationship to history and ethics, a claim that I do not wish to make, much as I believe that translation and interpreting are a means of destabilizing hegemonic, dominant discourses (Baker 2006a, 2006b, 2008, 2009, Cronin 2000a, 2002, Stahuljak 2004, Rafael 2007). Just as translators and interpreters are not in-between (Tymoczko 2003) or outside any event, translation itself cannot be used as a metaphor of pure translatability (Stahuljak 2004) or as a 'bridge' between different cultures (Baker 2005, 2009). Interpreters do not occupy a position of 'elsewhere' that harmonizes or hybridizes contradictory and conflictual positions; rather they are very much inscribed in their specific time and place (geographical and ideological). Likewise, their interventions, even activism, are not to be privileged as the ultimate access to history, since the interpreters themselves are a product of a particular set of intersecting narratives which, while potentially transcending particular ethnic, national, gender, religious or linguistic affiliations, remain local. Their power and impact lie, not in any claim to universality, but in their geographic and temporal location and their ability to pose a local challenge to the discourse of arbitration. Only by speaking from within, as the Croatian interpreters did, by having a position rather than occupying a place on the outside, by identifying 'what makes specific examples of engaged translation effective' (Tymoczko 2000:34) and by formulating an ethics of translation that is 'guided by the nature of the ethical encounter itself' (Inghilleri 2008a:222), that is, by the social and political conditions of the event, can interpreters hope to effect geopolitical and social change, the stated goal of activist interpreting.

APPENDIX: INTERPRETER QUESTIONNAIRE

Interviews were conducted in Croatian between 11 September and 18 October 1993, by Ivan Magdalenic, psychologist, at the premises of the Croatian Liaison Office, Hotel 'I', Zagreb, Croatia. All translations from Croatian into English are provided by the current author.

1. How long have you been working for the Office?
2. What motivated you to join, what are your main motives?
3. How many times have you gone on a fact-finding mission?
4. Where?
5. What is the average length of a mission? What was the length of your longest mission? And the shortest one?
6. With whom did you talk (on our side and on the other)?
7. Generally speaking, what are the impressions left by our interlocutors and by the interlocutors from the other side? Try to describe, without naming, a person from each side who left the best and who left the worst impression on you.
8. What is the impression left by the people for whom you are translating [EC monitors]? Describe, without naming, the most pleasant and the most unpleasant of them.
9. Generally speaking, what do you like best about them [EC monitors] and what bothers you the most? Give an example for each.
10. What duties other than interpreting are assigned to you while on a mission?
11. What do you like best about your job and what do you dislike the most? What is the most burdensome?
12. When on a mission, how do you feel: (a) in general; (b) while interpreting?
13. Have you ever felt that you were in danger while on a mission, whether in the context of a life-threatening situation, particularly unpleasant events, or social situations? Describe the most uncomfortable event you have experienced while on a mission.

14. While on a mission, are you free and able to be alone or to do something of your own choice (except the time reserved for sleep)? Do you have a daily break? If not, do you feel a need to be alone, to have free time and daily breaks?

15. After how many days on a mission do you begin to experience: (a) physical fatigue; (b) psychic fatigue?

16. How do you feel when you return from a mission? How long does this feeling last?

17. In your free time in Zagreb, when you are not at the Office, do you have recurrent thoughts or feelings about what you saw and experienced? Do you dream about it? Do you have nightmares?

18. Do you feel a need to speak with someone about the events experienced on missions? If so, whom do you talk to? Do these conversations bring you relief? Is there an experience about which you don't wish to speak to anyone?

19. Do you feel a need to speak about all of this with a psychologist or a similar specialist? What do you think about the usefulness of collective or group conversations and exchange of impressions among interpreters? Would you have such conversations conditional upon your choice of participants?

20. What would you personally suggest in order to improve your working conditions, that is, to ease the difficulties encountered by you and your colleagues?

21. Are you under the impression that some of your colleagues are not up to the task they are asked to perform? Based on your experience, what kind of selection process of candidates should be implemented? Or should those who show themselves not to be up to the task be discharged?

22. For how long do you intend to continue doing this job? Under what conditions?

23. How do you feel after this conversation? Do you wish to meet again?

Notes

1   By 'transnational' and 'transnationalism' I refer throughout to linkages and networks among people and groups across national boundaries, as opposed to 'international' cooperation among governments and multinational corporations. Transnationalism is an appropriate term to understand circulation within global systems of political, cultural, and economic exchange, which can no longer be contained within a state-centric definition of exchange and communication. Translator and interpreter activism is a transnational undertaking in this sense.

2   The title of the first article I wrote on this topic (Stahuljak 1999) referred to 'translators', reflecting the high value of the term 'translation', when it should have been about 'interpreters', the term that the recent focus on interpreting in translation studies has validated as equal to 'literary translator' in importance and that I now use throughout.

3   One of the peculiarities of the communist ex-Yugoslavia was the denomination of 'Muslim' as an ethnic group. The designation of 'Muslim' as a nationality was intended to strip the term of all religious significance. It was applied to Bosnian Muslims; this explains why Albanians, for instance, who are mostly Muslim, constituted a separate nationality.

4   Along with being able to choose from 'Serb', 'Croat', 'Muslim', 'Hungarian', etc., people identifying with Yugoslavia, rather than with particular ethnic groups which made up the country, could choose the national designation of 'Yugoslav'.

5   As explained earlier, these interviews were partly transcribed and partly summarized by Magdalenic, hence the occasional use of indirect speech.

6   I understand 'minor' here as any group whose culture, language and history have been perceived as inferior and subordinate, whose culture has been ignored or essentialized.

PART 10

Changing landscapes: new media and technologies

Chapter 23

Rita Raley

MACHINE TRANSLATION AND
GLOBAL ENGLISH

EDITOR'S INTRODUCTION

Because machine translation draws our attention to the interrelation of machine languages and natural languages in the context of the global information society, we can more easily identify some of the cultural-linguistic effects of these relations: the emergence of hybrid forms of language, born of the intermixing of natural language and computer code in experimental writing, art and online communication; the controlling and partial excision of the rhetorical element of language; and the privileging of logic and semantics within a 'Basic English'.

Raley's critical discussion of machine translation, which engages in some detail with Warren Weaver's initial proposal as well as later advances, calls on theorists of translation, cross-cultural communication and transnational literary studies to engage with developments in the field. These developments are closely connected with the spread of globalization and the growing hegemony of English, and it is imperative that we begin to consider their effect on the way we use and conceptualize language.

In the wider context of globalization, machine translation gives further impetus to the principles of functionality and utilitarianism. It is embedded in the ideal of a perfect and fully automated translation, and promotes the myth that languages are neutral, that accuracy and functionality are values to be prioritized and pursued as realizable absolutes. It only produces reasonably accurate and functional draft translations when the input is basic, and when both input and output are restricted in terms of style, vocabulary, figurative expression and content. Raley links the impetus for developing machine translation systems with Ogden and Richards' Basic English Project, which set out 'to institute a simplified version of the English language as a benign and neutral means of international communication'. Like the Basic English Project, machine translation is shown to have partly arisen in the first instance to respond to military needs. Weaver's vision of machine translation is informed by cryptography and the techniques used for decoding Nazi messages. It thus assumes that any language is a code that can be cracked by a machine and that the original message can then be revealed, unchanged, in English.

Beyond Weaver and mainstream developments in machine translation, Raley offers some promising examples of practical critiques that produce alternative visions, such as Warren Sack and Sawad Brooks's Internet-based *Translation Map*, and then moves on to consider the impact of new technology on promoting as well as adapting English (or various electronic Englishes) in cyberspace, and the various, complex environments in which the tension between global and local languages is played out. In this dynamic and fluid environment, the English used is not only 'Basic' but also 'broken', and its free adaptation by native and non-native speakers, European and non-European, élite and non-élite users has a range of consequences, including severing the link between language and geophysical space and undermining collective identity, which is constituted by a shared history and language. Beyond English as such, Raley argues that computer-mediated communication impacts our use of language in general, resulting in a minimalist code based on abbreviation, minimalism of expression, taxonomic units of information, and simplified syntax. It is this minimalism and the insistence on a basic form of legibility that must be critically assessed and resisted.

Follow-up questions for discussion

- In her critique of the assumptions and impact of machine translation, Raley makes it clear that she objects specifically to banality and the flattening out of difference and variation. What role does she ascribe to Global English in this process? And how might translators and those who train them resist it?

- In his discussion of the central role that translation played within European imperialism, focusing on the Indian context and the colonial government's strategy for translating scientific and otherwise 'useful' knowledge from English into Indian languages, Dodson (2005:809) explains that 'translational technology, in the form of language grammars and dictionaries, . . . enabled information gathering and the effective communication of commands, as well as the (at least partial) displacement of European dependence upon interlocutors of perceived dubious reliability'. What parallels can you identify between these older, established technologies and institutional agendas in the colonial context, and current agendas and uses of machine translation and other contemporary technologies?

- Cronin (2003:35–36) stresses the need for theoretical questioning of the practice of translation and argues that 'self-reflexive sensitivity to the dangers of misunderstanding, distortion and censorship in translation, present in much contemporary thinking on translation, means that a view of translation as naïve, unmediated, transparent, instrumentalist communication is no longer tenable'. To what extent is Cronin right in asserting that much contemporary theorizing of translation engages critically with the view of translation outlined by Raley and promoted by machine translation? What perspectives does this questioning of transparency adopt, when it is undertaken, and what impact has it had beyond literary translation?

Recommended further reading

Bennett, Karen (2007) 'Epistemicide!: The Tale of a Predatory Discourse', *The Translator* 13(2): 151–69.

Cronin, Michael (2003) *Translation and Globalization*, London & New York: Routledge.

Hartley, Tony (2009) 'Technology and Translation', in Jeremy Munday (ed.) *The Routledge Companion to Translation Studies*, London & New York: Routledge, 106–127.

McDonough, Julie (2006) 'Hiding Difference: On the Localization of Websites', *The Translator* 12(1): 85–103.

Tong, Q.S. (1999) 'The Bathos of Universalism: I.A. Richards and His Basic English', in Lydia H. Liu (ed.) *Tokens of Exchange: The Problem of Translation in Global Circulations*, Durham & London: Duke University Press, 331–54.

A most serious problem, for UNESCO and for the constructive and peaceful future of the planet, is the problem of translation, as it unavoidably affects the communication between peoples . . . I have wondered if it were unthinkable to design a computer which would translate. Even if it would translate only scientific material (where the semantic difficulties are very notably less), and even if it did produce an inelegant (but intelligible) result, it would seem to me worthwhile.

(Weaver 1955:18)

WHEN WARREN WEAVER FOLLOWED UP ON this private letter of March 1947 to Norbert Wiener by circulating a memorandum in July 1949 among two hundred leading mathematicians, scientists, linguists and public policy makers, envisioning in both texts a super-computer that would apply the cryptographic techniques acquired during WWII to all translation – what we can now understand as using codes to decipher codes – he foresaw in principle, and thus materially enabled, the development of machine translation. Out of a clearly stated desire to contribute both to a newly urgent post-war internationalism and to the march of scientific progress, Weaver articulated his vision of computer-automated translation within the biblical paradigm of linguistic division that continues to structure contemporary cultural, literary and philosophical discourse on translation: the Tower of Babel. A machinic method of coping with the 'multiplicity of languages' that 'impedes cultural interchange between the peoples of the earth', deters 'international understanding' and obstructs the exchange of scientific research would thus be a tower of 'Anti-Babel' (Weaver 1955:15). The tower, though, remains secular, for the proposal to use computers essentially to make all militaristic and scientific material potentially open to the world, thereby facilitating necessarily peaceful international relations, is 'not intended to reach to Heaven. But it is hoped that it will build part of the way back to that mythical situation of simplicity and power when men could communicate freely together, and when this contributed so notably to their effectiveness' (Locke and Booth 1955:vii). Weaver's hope, then, was that machine translation – inputting a text from a source language and outputting the same text in a target language, with the basic meaning preserved – would make multilingual texts available and easily accessible to researchers. This suggestion of instant access to flexible data places Weaver's vision in line with Vannevar Bush's coterminous vision of the desktop Memex system that would put accumulated knowledge instantly at hand (see Nyce and Kahn 1991).

The idea of a computer that can understand natural language and thus listen and talk to anyone in real time continues to wield a certain cultural power. Futurist visions of machine translation are, on the one hand, within the scope of science fiction, exemplified by such fictional devices as Douglas Adams's portable automatic translation machine, the 'Babel fish'.[1] But, in the tradition of Vannevar Bush-era Department of Defence and corporate research, machine translation also continues to be associated with governmental, economic and military interests, as it was in President Clinton's State of the Union Address in 2000: 'Soon, researchers will bring us devices that can translate foreign languages as fast as you can speak'. While still within the realm of speculation, Clinton's comment encapsulates the split between what is essentially a matter of theory, realizing the mid-twentieth-century vision of a fully automated and high quality machine translation (FAHQMT), and pragmatic enterprise on a smaller and less ambitious scale.[2] Weaver noted even from the outset that ' "perfect" translation is almost surely unattainable', foreseeing that a true translating machine would require artificial intelligence and the ability of the computer to comprehend not just vocabulary and syntax, but also rhetoric and context (Weaver 1955:22).[3] What exactly constitutes a 'perfect' translation, or even accuracy, quality and meaning, continues to be contested, and there are no definitive answers, either theoretical or practical. Regardless, within the last decade, machine translation has evolved as a significant commercial venture, combining the research of computational linguistics, logical philosophy and computer science (although work within the computer sciences has primarily shifted over to voice recognition and transcription technologies).[4]

At this point, however, the critical humanities need to intervene and bring contemporary critical thought about translation, cross-cultural communication and transnational literary studies to bear on the issue, particularly since we face a possible future when automated translation might very well function in a basic manner for all discourse, including the literary. Despite the fact that no real work is being done to apply machine translation to literary texts, it is already the case that one can run Dante through the *translate now* function on Google or the Babelfish program connected to AltaVista and produce a basic, if inaccurate and strangely fractured translation. Even as a simple means for rough translation of a source original text, the ubiquitous, yet still-emergent, practice of machine translation requires us to consider both its effects on language and its consequences for our evaluative appraisal of language. Further, its functionalist logic requires us to ask how we have come to view the value of language at all: in terms of basic, communicative meaning, or in terms of ambiguity and complexity in the ordinary sense. Does machine translation constitute a new linguistic utilitarianism, in other words, or is it just an extension of the functionalist cultural logic of Global English? Insofar as machine translation really only works to produce reasonably accurate and functional draft translations when the input is basic, and when both input and output are restricted with respect to style, vocabulary, figurative expression and content, we are presented with a renewed utilitarianism; a renewed appreciation for the basic and easily translatable (the non-figurative, the non-literary); and a new economics and pragmatics of language and informatic exchange.

Machine translation does not present us with a new theory of translation in the context of globalization, but rather with a further dimension and renewed rationale for it: that of functionality and performativity. Machine translation brings to our attention in a materially significant manner the ideal of a perfect and fully automated translation from one natural language to another, with both languages considered as neutral and emphasis falling on the process, accuracy and functionality of the exchange. In our current moment, total translatability and equivalence would mean a database with universal data input-output capacity, specifically for multilingual translation, and without the use of a pivot language like English. (Research into universal data – data that is stable and consistent across different platforms and technologies – is one current incarnation of this vision of universality and transparency.)[5] In that machine translation tries to posit a kind of universality and transparency to translation that has come under critique by theorists such as Venuti (1995, 1998b), Spivak (1993) and Liu (1995, 2000), the two discourses need to be linked so that machine translation research can come to terms with contemporary theories of the politics, philosophical basis and cultural specificity of translation practices.

The issues that translation criticism has engaged – the whole body of work on the subject in philosophical, historical, and cultural analysis – are still relevant and necessarily present in this new technological moment. For example, machine translation assumes a fixed position for target and host languages, but as Venuti has argued, the complexity of translation practice in a global context requires our recognizing that 'domestic' and 'foreign' are shifting, variable and mutually constitutive categories (1998b:186–89). Machine translation research also tends to suppose that linguistic knowledge (grammatical rules, idioms) – as opposed to the extra-linguistic – is the basis for all translations, which places it at odds with Spivak's articulation of the critical and ethical pitfalls of privileging grammar over rhetoric. Without listening to the rhetoricity of the language of the Other, which involves an erotics of submission, she argues, one simply imposes a grammatical structure onto the text and effaces its voice and singularity. Following Spivak's critique of the ethnocentricity and 'law of the strongest' that compels the translation of non-European texts into a 'with-it translatese' (1993:182), Venuti has also called for a translation ethics of difference, a respect for 'the foreignness of the foreign text', rather than an 'ethics of sameness that hews to dominant domestic values', domesticating the foreign within state, or standard, language (1998b:188). Liu has similarly theorized translation in terms of cultural contest: 'translation is no longer a neutral event untouched by the contending interests of political and ideological struggles. Instead, it becomes the very site of such struggles where the guest language is forced to encounter the host language, where the irreducible differences between them are fought out, authorities invoked or challenged, ambiguities dissolved or created, and so forth' (1995:26). But in the instance of machine translation, the site of struggle is primarily a site of resolution, of circumventing or smoothing over linguistic difference. Ambiguities are created in the movement from one language to another, certainly, but the rationale of machine translation is to send a signal with a clear, decipherable message. It follows, then, that the primary discursive sites for machine translation are the weather, finance and the news, all of which affect neutrality and require only a functionally basic semantic accuracy.

This is not, however, an essay about the state of the art of machine translation at the end of the twentieth century: it does not aim to give a technical explanation of its procedural intricacies, nor does it explain or evaluate any particular translation system or any particular instance of government sponsorship in detail. Further, this essay will not move into the field of computational linguistics and delve into the differences among a direct, transfer or interlingual approach to machine translation. Rather, it considers the relationship between machine translation and Global English and argues for a homology between the rationale of the former and that of the latter. Because machine translation draws our attention to the interrelation of machine languages and natural languages in the context of the global information society, we can more easily identify some of the cultural-linguistic effects of these relations: the

emergence of hybrid forms of language, born of the intermixing of natural language and computer code in experimental writing, art and online communication;
the controlling and partial excision of the rhetorical element of language; and the
privileging of logic and semantics within a 'Basic English'.[6]

It is not for nothing, then, that Warren Weaver should specifically link his proposal
for machine translation to C. K. Ogden and I. A. Richards' Basic English project, which
endeavoured to institute a simplified version of the English language as a benign and
neutral means of international communication.[7] Basic was engineered to be more economically sound and efficient than 'normal' English, and it provided an institutional
basis for thinking of the English language as a utilitarian, minimalist and economically
sound system that ensured efficiency and precision and attempted to minimize the
messy ambiguities of signification. In Weaver's letters and memo, Basic English is articulated as an analogue for machine translation: 'Such a program involves a presumably
tremendous amount of work in the logical structure of languages before one would be
ready for any mechanization. This must be very closely related to what Ogden and
Richards have already done for English – and perhaps for French and Chinese'
(Weaver 1955:23). The analogy between the two is both literally and conceptually
articulated in Weaver's proposal. Both are thought in terms of functionality, universalism and a fundamental dichotomy between basic meaning and instrumental communicative action, on the one hand, and the poetic, literary or figurative, on the other.

Somewhat in the manner of Ogden and Richards' development and promotion
of Basic English, research into machine translation has historically arisen in partial
response to international military conflicts. For example, an IBM demo in 1954 of a
Russian-English program with a 250-word vocabulary generated quite a bit of
excitement and funding and paralleled other military and intelligence plans for the
development of 'mechanized systems' to facilitate the use of as much international
technological and scientific research as possible.[8] In this respect, machine translation
has a specific cultural history, tied to postwar internationalism, Cold War-era
anxieties and militaristic conflict. The plausibility and rationale of Weaver's vision
of outsourcing translation to the computer stems from cryptography, and specifically from his idea that the techniques used for decoding Nazi messages could be
brought to bear on the development of machine translation. He called this his
'cryptographic-translation idea' in his letter to Norbert Wiener in March 1947
(Weaver 1955:18):

> Also knowing nothing official about, but having guessed and inferred . . .
> [much] about, powerful new mechanized methods in cryptography –
> methods which I believe succeed even when one does not know what
> language has been coded – one naturally wonders if the problem of trans-
> lation could conceivably be treated as a problem in cryptography. When I
> look at an article in Russian, I say: 'This is really written in English, but it
> has been coded in some strange symbols. I will now proceed to decode'.[9]

The 'cryptographic-translation idea' – which was to become the axiomatic principle
for the development of machine translation – holds that 'foreign' languages, in this
case Russian, are to be regarded as codes to be unencrypted. Simply crack the enigmatic code by machinic means, Weaver suggests, and the message will be revealed,
unchanged, in English. Radically diverging, both theoretically and practically, from
linguistic, philosophical and cultural theories of translation, Weaver makes the same
point later in the memo (ibid.:22):[10]

as was expressed in W.W.'s original letter to Wiener, it is very tempting to say that a book written in Chinese is simply a book written in English which was coded into the 'Chinese code.' If we have useful methods for solving almost any cryptographic problem, may it not be that with proper interpretation we already have useful methods for translation?

If it were only possible to unpack the mysterious code, Weaver suggests, it would be possible to retrieve the information stored in the text.[11] No linguistic or even symbolic relationship between the two languages is offered; instead the presumed relations are morphological and conceptual, with English offered as the master, universal, über language. The idea that all texts written in 'foreign' languages are actually written in English, simply encoded in strange and undecipherable symbols, finds a strange, and strangely analogous, articulation in a 1937 Popeye cartoon.[12]

During the course of the animated feature, 'Popeye the Sailor Meets Ali Baba and the Forty Thieves', Popeye and Olive Oyl stop at a café for food while they are on the run from the thieves. Popeye is handed a menu with illegible scratches and scrawls made to approximate a language with a non-phonetic script with vague hieroglyphic elements, a script that signifies the idea of difference rather than referring specifically to an existing language. Upon being handed the menu, Popeye responds, 'I can read readin "but I can't read writin" '. He folds up the menu from the corners in an origami-like fashion, after which the markings on the paper are arranged into English words and read:

Bacon and Eggs
45¢

The riddle, and even moral, of the menu is as follows: all Other languages derive from English as the common source and the master key to all linguistic mythologies. Any semantic puzzle can ultimately be reconfigured so as to render the alien script as the familiar and civilized voice. As English is fashioned as the master code and origin of all other languages, the common source is instead *the* source – the winding and almost indiscernible path of etymological history leads ultimately back 'home', to English, of which all other languages exist merely as altered, debased and inferior versions. To use the terms of the menu itself, they are English, but scrambled. In a curious formulation that almost constitutes a reversal of primitivist skepticism, the 'foreign' character is writing but it is not reading. It is also thematically linked with other instances of puzzle solving – the rubbing of the lamp and the revelation of the password 'Open Sesame' – and so constitutes yet another rewriting of the *Arabian Nights*. What, then, do both Weaver's remarks about Russian or 'Chinese code' and this caricatured representation of English in the midst of a field of linguistic others tell us about the status of non-European scripts, the fears of incomprehensible alterity, and the inherited mythology of English?

They tell us most obviously that non-European languages are mystifying codes that need to be cracked in order to achieve any degree of communicability, and, unlike the lamp or the password, the menu offers a parable of a subject that distinctly refuses to operate within the structures of a 'foreign' code. Popeye, after all, does not learn this code, but instead makes it over into English, which renders the non-European character as an incomprehensible screen that needs to be torn aside in order to access a set of signifiers that will in turn produce meaning. Such a gesture requires a belief in a universal signified, as Alan Melby notes of Weaver's own gesture toward ripping away the screen of foreign code: 'he was suggesting that a text in a human language is the result of encoding the message behind the text. The message is the same for all languages; only the encoding system differs' (1995:17). Further, these particular representations of English serve as a reminder of the structure of difference and the constitution of value, whereby the appreciation of the western emerges in relation to the debasement of the Other. Thus has it been the case, then, that the celebration of the power of English has historically been made possible in part by the denigration and suppression of non-Roman scripts, of minor languages, of other languages with imperialistic force (e.g., French, Hindi, Bengali), and of the hundreds of dialects in use. Specifically, it has also been made possible by the privileging of the phonetic script over the pictorial, that is, by the suppression of the foreign character as not-linguistic and as not-writing. To cite Jacques Derrida's 'The Violence of the Letter', it was 'legitimate not to call by the name of writing those "few dots" and "zigzags" ' precisely because it was the province of writing that was bracketed off, protected and claimed for the West (1976:110).

Weaver's inclusion of his original letter to Norbert Wiener within the memo situates his visionary proposal of machine translation within the context of informatics and cybernetics. So, too, does Weaver's conterminous and institutionally aligned work and Claude Shannon on *The Mathematical Theory of Communication* suggest a relationship between machine translation and information theory: how to consider untranslated characters, after all, but as dots and zigzags, not writing (Shannon and Weaver 1949)? And as mere noise that impedes intelligibility and the transmission of content and therefore needs to be converted to legible signals? His proposal with regard to 'Chinese code', however, was not at core a suggestion that English was the underlying foundation of all language. Rather, his proposal was based on the belief in a kind of common source, or what he termed 'the real but as yet undiscovered universal language', confused and obscured by the tower of Babel (Weaver 1955:23):

> Thus may it be true that the way to translate from Chinese to Arabic, or from Russian to Portuguese, is not to attempt the direct route, shouting from tower to tower. Perhaps the way is to descend, from each language, down to the common base of human communication – the real but as yet undiscovered universal language – and then re-emerge by whatever particular route is convenient.

While the screen code of each language may well be presented as a logical and statistically regular, though complex, puzzle for the present and for the foreseeable future, he imagines a 'real' universal language at the base of all language, the decoding of which was projected into the distant and virtually unimaginable future. Much as in Plato's *Cratylus* and Walter Benjamin's essay on translation, there are two views of language considered here: functional and mystical. While the more direct route for machine translation – from natural language to natural language – was the more immediately pragmatic and instrumentalist, it was the more mystical route down from the tower to the subterranean, cognitive, authentic language that Weaver offered as both 'true' and efficient.

Contemporary artistic and conceptual commentary on Weaver's rationale for machine translation can be found in Warren Sack and Sawad Brooks's (2003) Internet-based *Translation Map*, which critiques Weaver's notion of translation-as-decoding and explores an alternative: translation-as-collaboration. For too long, Sack and Brooks suggest, has Weaver's axiom held sway over the development of machine translation. Their intervention is 'a computer program that can help connect people together over the Internet facilitating a collaborative re-writing process'.[13] Instead of the interface common to Babelfish and related translation programs, which offers a direct and strictly machinic link between, for example, text in English and French, *Translation Map* maintains Weaver's rhetoric of the 'route' and uses an algorithm to look for a path from home country to receiver country, through a country that has both languages in common. A direct route from English to French would thus proceed from England to Canada to France, and, if a direct route were not available, the algorithm would find a mediating language, so moving from English to Luba-Kusai would take one through Egypt in order to arrive in the Congo. In this respect, the project provides a visual map of the dislocated movement from one language to another and strives to preserve opacity and difference rather than transparency and sameness. Instead of ceding the task of translation strictly to the computer, *Translation Map* relies on participants in online forums such as newsgroups to assist with the various translations along the route chosen by the user. Related to Sack's critical and artistic investment in the information architecture of discourse networks, *Translation Map* literalizes the idea of speaking, moving, and gaining proximity, to the Other (see Sack, n.d.). While it is more of a theoretical than a practical intervention into the problem of machine translation, the *Translation Map* project nevertheless makes a striking contribution to the discourse in its emphasis on cross-cultural exchange, human-machine collaboration, ethno-linguistics, multilingualism and a global space that is not dominated by English.

Electronic English

> Programming languages have eroded the monopoly of ordinary language
> and grown into a new hierarchy of their own.
>
> (Kittler 1997:148)

The increasing ubiquity of buttons and icons that direct the user to *translate now* raises an important question with respect to the futures of English in an age of technological communication. Are we going to be (or even are we now) presented with an all-English Internet or one dominated by Multilingual Webmasters, machine translation and character encoding sets such as Unicode™, to the extent that different characters and different language structures clash and intermingle without producing a dominant linguistic order? In other words, do the global circuits of media, commerce and technology promise monolingualism or radical heteroglossia? Will the contemporary story of English be one of imposition or fragmentation? Will it be a neo-imperial English or Englishes that are broken and radically multiple, promising variation and individuality as partial effects of language technologies such as machine translation (see De Landa 1997:253–64)? With this series of questions we have, essentially, a dialectic between the imagined uniform futures of language (with Global English as a precursor) and the radical individualization of information that 'pull' technology will promise, a vision of extreme tailoring and adaptation.

One view of English in a moment of electronic empire holds that the language constitutes a new empire, one severed from territorial, national, regional régimes of power, but irrevocably linked to the structures of capital. The template critical narrative, exemplified by Joe Lockard in a *Bad Subjects* column, is that English is solidifying its power via cyber-English, which is more global, quantitatively and qualitatively more powerful than previous forms; that cyber-English is consolidating its power in light of 'less common' languages; and that economic structures of power are replicated in the linguistic (Lockard 1996). What is being lamented in such a critical account, as an illustrative example, is the suppression and even loss of local, minor languages in the face of an impending cyber-English, the ceding of the polyphony of language difference to the univocal. There is an immediate aurality and visibility of this process of becoming-major, illustratable in one instance through a sampling of the European Radio Network and its EuroMax English program.[14]

There is another dimension to this question of linguistic power and domination. It has not been necessary in the context of this essay to review the differences between those machine translation programs that are hardware-intensive (e.g. Logos and Systran) and those that are designed for use on an individual computer (e.g. Globalink, which comes with translation utilities for Internet communications).[15] Rather, in order to discuss broader issues of language and culture that arise in relation to the practice of machine translation, I have assumed a general equivalence and for the most part bracketed the question of quantitative difference between the two. However, one difference of qualitative significance is that the individual or home systems are primarily based in English and work exclusively with a handful of European languages.[16] Although machine translation partly arises as a response to monolingualism and promises to preserve local or minor languages, it primarily operates around and with English as a pivot language; as the dominant language for computational linguistic and engineering research; and as the basis for assembly, low-level, and high-level programming languages. While English functions as the dominant source and target language in most bidirectional machine translation systems, Russian is at the centre for some, and the additional presence of much translation work on Chinese and Japanese helps to constitute an axis of linguistic-geopolitical power in the late twentieth century.

As a counter-narrative, however, it is important to keep in mind that language politics are not the same everywhere and that a global theory of language domination is not really possible, particularly when EuroMax is counter-balanced by EuroMix. Translation technologies, encompassing translation memory (TM), which is the storage of multilingual versions of the original content, and machine translation, algorithmic, on-the-fly transmissions, must always introduce a bit of uncertainty and multiplicity into the system and complicate the vision of a monolingual Internet. So, while even the briefest surf through Web sites around the world can confirm that 'Global English' is not just a flight of fancy but in fact has a material basis, and it would thus appear that we are presented with the monologism and 'anglophone triumphalism' that are named as features of a 'cyber-English paradigm', we are nevertheless still in a moment in which linguistic sub-cultures can and do operate against the grain (Lockard 1996). It is possible to seek out both global broadcasting of local languages, e.g., Radio Prague, and numerous cultural-linguistic web rings that are quite comfortably centred in local languages that can themselves have a global reach, e.g., a network of Russian émigrés, all of whom are linked through a central server based in Moscow. There are also networks attuned to non-nationalist pan-European interests, such as the European Council's investment in building up a multilingual, regional information and communication infrastructure (Ewers 1995:esp. 18). Major search engines such as AltaVista have European mirrors with multiple language options and are monitored by such publications as Internet Operator Europe. There are significant individual projects as well, such as Odd de Presno's 'Your electronic daily news', which addresses the subject of language use on the Internet and assures browsers that there are alternatives to English (it is published online in English, German and Norwegian).[17] Moreover, in many communication networks linked through central servers based outside the territorial limits of the Anglophone world, English is present in the network of pages only through those basic international words such as radio, TV, video, computer and DVD.

Not only is English 'Basic' in networked media, but it is often, to use the operative term from chat rooms, bulletin boards and web rings, broken. Marked by a convergence of a myriad of native and non-native forms of English, broken English is by no means exclusively European. Broken English is not regional and not really culturally élite, which is to say that it is not the province of the 'new class' of the global technological intelligentsia alone. Its territory, rather, is the network. There are historical and socio-cultural consequences of this passage from regionalism to globalism, however. As the artist Rainer Ganahl notes, the severing of the exclusive and necessary link between language and geophysical space, the making of English into a mobile, 'transit language', comes at a loss for 'collective memory, of an identity that is somehow constituted through a common language and shared history' (Ganahl 2001:29). If we can allow for a stable referent, this non-territorial language is also named by McKenzie Wark as 'netlish', a mode, and nodal site, of writing that emerges 'without being passed through a single editorial standard'.[18] Such a staging of different and imbricated language practices – with all idioms competing for status, primacy and privilege and with every word and phrase subject to rival pronunciations, social accents and inflections – illustrates the linguistic struggles and conflicts inherent to heteroglossia itself. The Global English network, then, essentially encompasses innumerable networks, matrices of speech, communicative and language practices, and it strongly resonates with our prior critical understandings not just of the dialogic, but of intertextuality (Julia Kristeva and Roland Barthes), signifyin(g) (Henry Louis Gates, Jr.) and tactics (Michel de Certeau). This network cannot be understood, in other words, without considering the dynamics of appropriation, adaptation and inhabitation.

Basic English, or a basic English vernacular dialect (also called 'generic', 'plain', and 'world' English within cultural criticism, linguistics and the discourse of governmental and political policy) literally informs the Simplified and Controlled English systems as they are used in machine translation. The many machine translation systems share a few foundational principles: the language in use should ideally limit vocabulary choices (often to specialized lists designed for particular transactions), prohibit the figurative and rely on literal uses of language, restrict words to one meaning and one part of speech, and depend upon a codified set of rules for syntactical formulations.[19] For these reasons, machine translation was from the beginning imagined and developed for technical rather than literary use, for documents in which rhetoric, style and figuration are unnecessary and even undesirable.[20] As Weaver notes in his proposal for a tower of 'Anti-Babel' (Locke and Booth 1955:vii):

> A few stories above ground would not afford, from this new tower, a dramatic far view of great aesthetic value, but it could be very useful for loading trucks with informative content. This, in fact, is the reasonable purpose of this effort. Not to charm or delight, not to contribute to elegance or beauty; but to be of wide service in the work-a-day task of making available the essential content of documents in languages which are foreign to the reader.

From its visionary inception, then, the rationale behind machine translation has depended on a dichotomy between the useful (to 'be of wide service') and the affective (to 'charm and delight'), the basic and the poetic, the literal and the figurative, the functional and the aesthetic. Further, machine translation has been conceived in terms of technicality, use value, the informative and the ideal of direct communication, as Weaver noted from the outset: 'No reasonable person thinks that a machine translation can ever achieve elegance and style. Pushkin need not shudder' (ibid.). As an interesting counter-point, the digital critic Julian Dibbell experimented with the poetic capabilities of Babelfish and likened its output, 'random acts of senseless beauty', to Dadaism, surrealism and the cut-up (Dibbell 2000). In practical terms, however, the rationale articulated by Weaver has meant that the discursive application of machine translation has historically been weather reports, legal documents and informative instructions. And indeed it is the case that an argument for an ontological differentiation between programming languages and natural languages – based on the notion that programming languages are only capable of instructions and incapable of figuration, generating affect and embodying other historical properties of the literary – still predominates in machine translation research.

To suggest a link between Basic English and a mechanized English is not to speak of a philosophical relation between language and technology but of a practical and cultural–historical relation, to note that commonly cited effects of computers on language practices include abbreviated and simplified syntactic forms (Crystal 2001:84–86, 229–31). The United Nations University's Universal Networking Language Programme (an Internet-based software system), for example, supports translation among seventeen languages by converting and deconverting documents into an electronic language structured according to the relations among basic nominal, verbal, adjectival and adverbial concepts.[21] Indeed, Computer-Mediated Communication, as it is termed, is also structured according to certain formal features that emphasize abbreviation, a minimalism of expression, and the basic taxonomic unit of information, such as the list and the short paragraph. More broadly, the globally dominant language now, as the recent VeriSign dispute over the use of Chinese characters in web addresses attests, is a minimalist code that encompasses such practices as the translation of 'foreign' characters into numerical code, the use of emoticons, and the use of abbreviations (CMC, IMHO, BTW, AFAIK, IP, TM, AOL, ASCII, WYSIWYG).[22] That the basic or simplified form of English, featuring imperative verbs in particular, should function as the necessary precondition to the global network of computer and programming languages, which in turn maintain a parallel function and currency, is noted by Friedrich Kittler as already an inevitability (1997:166):

> Johannes Lohmann, the renowned language scholar and Indo-Germanist, already proposed thirty years ago that one look for the historical condition of possibility of programming languages in the simple fact that they exist in English, and furthermore that they exist only in English verbs such as 'Read' and 'Write,' that is, verbs which in distinction to the Latin *amo amas amat* and so forth have shed all conjugation forms. According to Lohmann, these context-free word blocks may well stem from the historically unique confusion of Norman and Saxon in old England, but that is no hindrance to their being translated into context-free mnemonics and ultimately into computer op-code.

For the software and tech industry, Global English is at times considered to be synonymous with 'simplified or controlled English' and likewise presumed to be universally accessible and comprehensible. These qualities enable the literal consideration of Global English (along with French, North American English, Spanish and German) as a separate language for application and server software such as Win-Frame 1.7 and Lotus's SmartSuite Editions™. Global English, for the software and tech industry and the academy alike, is at once encoding language, linguistic standard and educative mechanism.[23] While the tech market falters on the whole, and in yet another instantiation of the new old economy, the English language sector of this market thrives. This market is currently estimated to exceed $15 billion, with the global English Language Training (ELT) market, including ELT publishing, ESL programmes, English-language publishers, and all-purpose 'global providers of lifelong learning information', is estimated around $300 million.[24] Administering the linguistic laws and theoretical norms of Global English now requires such tools as the AOL-partnered Lernout & Hauspie's Intelligent Content Management (ICM) suite of language technologies, which includes CorrectEnglish™ and International ProofReader™, both of which correct spelling, grammar and punctuation errors commonly made by EFL and ESL speakers. As a strenuous test of the Bourdieusean analysis of the decisive role that the educational system plays in the construction, legitimation and management of official languages (Bourdieu 1991:43–65), providers of life-long learning information such as Thomson Learning are expanding their international infrastructures and investing heavily in the ELT product market. Consequentially, Global English can be symbolically marketed as 'an exciting, new, British Multi-media educational product' by Systems Integrated Research and by Learnz Corporation as the language virtually guaranteed to grant access to both Asian and Internet markets (Rubens 1996:3). The supplementary concept for Bourdieu's delineation of the adjudication and regulation of linguistic law by grammarians and teachers must be 'Protocol' (as in TCP/IP) – in other words, standards for the transmission of data based on use.

Standards, whether for character encoding or universal languages of software development, allow for maximal translatability and commensurability among natural languages, machine languages and programs alike. And, because messages must necessarily become numbers before they can reach the targeted recipient, translatability and reproducibility are at the very heart of the language problem for digital technologies now, as they were for Claude Shannon's articulation of a mathematical theory of communication in the mid-twentieth century. Shannon's statement of the fundamental problem of communication remains current: it is 'that of reproducing at one point either exactly or approximately a message selected at another point' (Shannon and Weaver 1949:3). So it is that such character encoding standards as ASCII would come to be depreciated on the basis of their frequent failure to reproduce, in this particular instance because ASCII cannot allow for languages other than the Roman alphabet and it thereby maintains an inherent ethnocentric bias. A much more extensive range of character encoding is allowable with email program extensions such as MIME, and there are now tools such as IntelliScope(R) Language Recognizer, which identifies more than forty languages and codes, including HTML and XML formats. But the major development in the area of universal standards is Unicode, a worldwide character standard designed to support the interchange, processing and display of textual data in almost all of the world's languages by assigning a unique number to every character, including over 28,000 ideographic characters. By using unique numbers, Unicode eliminates the variation between other encoding systems and comes closer to achieving global status than any other language or encoding system that I know. Hence, its slogan: 'When the world wants to talk, it speaks Unicode'.[25] Such a reach as Unicode achieves and such a facility as it maintains can only be attempted by Global English.

To reduce the chance of misfire, to eliminate noise, a networked Global English must necessarily be universally readable, particularly by machines. The context of late twentieth-century iconic or visual communication is apropos here, placing as it does a premium on images that are literally representational, transparent and universally decodable. Even the non-representational, mystificatory, cryptic and abstract are counter-balanced by a readability, by an absorption into a networked system in which, in a conventional sense of signification, they do not need to mean but function, with and for global capital. If we depart from the practical and functional perspective on programming languages in order to consider iconic or visual communication in aesthetic terms, a certain play on the aesthetics of the code and the aesthetics of programming languages does become available.[26] The most complex and widespread programming languages such as COBOL, BASIC, FORTRAN and ALGOL have acronymic names, professional signatures, in and of themselves.[27] But these professional signatures do not entirely matter; the signatures, in fact, communicate something else. Like the @ and Nike symbols, they are transferred into the realm of advertising and thereby become iconic. In other words, the names of the languages play beyond their formal content to an iconic, transactional register. Combining as it does commerce and the iconic, such a register allows for a power that is as manifest as it is abstract.

Computer languages, operative and performative languages that allow computers to function and connect to each other, and presumably context- and value-free when they are at their premium, do approximate and augment natural language in their reliance on injunctive commands such as *read*, *write* and *perform*.[28] They are further linked to Global English by a common investment in universality, neutrality and transmittability. Their transmissible aspects – the means and mechanism of their spread – are homologous. They share, further, a tendency toward what Kittler names as 'monopoly' and 'hierarchy'. He notes (1997:148):

> Programming languages have eroded the monopoly of ordinary language and grown into a new hierarchy of their own. This postmodern Tower of Babel reaches from simple operation codes whose linguistic extension is still a hardware configuration, passing through an assembler whose extension is this very opcode, up to high-level programming languages whose extension is that very assembler.

A numerical character encoder or a microcode, the lowest and most basic level of instructions for directing a microprocessor to perform, essentially allows that tower to stand or, in this case, run. As English becomes computer languages, as it moves into new codes, and becomes in a sense post-English, it both transforms itself and reveals in different guise its instrumental, functional, performative aspects.[29] What allows English to spread in such a particular way, then, is its functionality.

Because the global communicational apparatus insists on a basic legibility for its transmissions, functionality and performativity are the premium values of language technologies and translation systems. Jean-François Lyotard has commented on the ideology of 'communicational "transparency" ' in the context of the post-industrial, telematic and postmodern society (1984:5). This ideology of transparency, for Lyotard, links social progress and the development of knowledge to the unimpeded and instantaneous circulation of messages. For the commercialization and exteriorization of knowledge, communicability is thus not only demanded but fundamentally required. Borrowing the rhetoric of signal and noise from information theory, Lyotard asserts that the technocratic values of efficiency, productivity and performativity go hand in hand with the transmission of easily decodable messages (*ibid.*). This, then, is how we can understand translatability as an educative value, and more concretely, how we can understand the institutional insistence on the value of writing across the curriculum. The insistence on utility has meant that literary and language departments have turned to their most obviously quantifiable mode of instruction and research: composition and literacy. That the notion of literacy requires further revisiting as we consider the relations between reading practices and digital textuality, or the technological substrate of the text, can be illustrated by a link between the mechanized code of machine languages and an updated pasigraphy.[30] Both are artificial universal systems of writing that use a combination of characters and numbers and that are meant to be universally comprehended. But the difference is that achieving an immediate and easy translation between two different languages no longer requires a knowledge of an intermediary language (such as the characters in a universal alphabet). The user in this sense is removed from the high-caste, seemingly rarefied mediating system, which is now the province of a new technical class. Armand Mattelart's importance for this line of argument lies in his highlighting of the utilitarian aspects of communications research and its new technological tools: 'This is true as well for intellectuals, who are more and more in the grip of managerial positivism, a new utilitarianism that stimulates the search for epistemological tools capable of circumscribing the potential zones of conflict and diminishing tensions through technical solutions' (Mattelart 1994:229).[31]

In *The Power of Identity*, the second volume of his trilogy on the Information Age, Manuel Castells asks a basic and yet pivotal question with respect to Catalan identity: Why is language so important? After considering several answers, he turns to 'an additional and more fundamental answer', which resonates strongly for my own questions concerning the conditions of possibility for Global English. Castells's 'fundamental answer' may be 'linked to what language represents, as a system of codes, crystallizing historically a cultural configuration that allows for symbolic sharing without worshipping of icons other than those emerging in everyday life's communication' (Castells 1997:49). Because 'going digital' ultimately means translation into a basic, common, putatively neutral medium for communicating information on a global scale, codes and iconic images are our new universal languages of transaction.[32] These transactional codes are not just binary in composition, but they are all, whether character encoding system, stock market symbols, pager codes, or even iris codes, machine-readable and machine-producible. One point of entry into this problem for me involves institutional modes of value: in other words, what literary and language departments are to do about the hegemony of English, however minimalist, and about the hegemony of codes, not, as Unicode advertising would have it, something to speak, and not, as Ellen Ullman says, 'a text for an academic to read' (Ullman 1997). At least one answer would have to be that we come to consider codes to be, as Kittler notes, 'subject to the same opacity as everyday languages' (1997:166). What is to be resisted, then, is the insistence on immediate and basic legibility. And while I have no stake in legitimating complexity at the expense of simplicity and minimalism, I would argue for the need for the 'appreciation' of the idea of the tower of programming languages (from machine language up to fourth-generation programming languages), since such a layering not only allows for, but fundamentally requires, variation.

As the status and legitimation of knowledge are continually re-engineered, it follows that the global business of language would fundamentally change. The field of machine translation no longer truly debates the question of what constitutes a perfect, totally automated, or even high-quality translation. The issue, rather, is functionality; that is, whether the machine translation system can produce automated output that is sufficiently usable, without human intervention, while still remaining cost-effective and facilitating global financial trade.[33] Both Global English and machine translation abide by the principle of instrumental rationality and exist in the technocratic mode, as Daniel Bell outlines it, whereby 'the ends have become simply efficiency and output' (1973:354). Both operate in the mode 'of production, of program, of "getting things done" ' (ibid.). With Global English as a precursor network and medium of late twentieth-century communication, computer languages maintain a parallel currency and legitimation. Like the reorganization of the oil industry after the influx of digital technologies, the old economy of English studies has itself been made new as the market focus for corporations, governments and schools alike has shifted to functionality and efficiency, and specifically to the means by which information is retrieved, exchanged, and transmitted. Lyotard has explained how the nature of knowledge has fundamentally changed and how the relevance and value of research will increasingly become a matter of translatability into the computer banks: 'We can predict that anything in the constituted body of knowledge that is not translatable in this way will be abandoned and that the direction of new research will be dictated by the possibility of its eventual results being translatable into computer language' (Lyotard 1984:4). English has been able to survive the fundamental changes that have resulted from a reorganization of knowledge and information, then, precisely because it has been amenable to processing as information and to interfusion with informatic codes.

Language technologies are already a significant growth industry, and the market for advanced machine translation programs continues to expand, but this industry's constant and rapid transformation, its unpredictability, and the unpredictability of its consumers, virtually guarantee that contingency will have a great deal to do with the outcomes and futures of English, even in its current operative incarnation. We cannot say with any degree of certainty what the literal and precise order of language would be were the vision of immediate and universal translation realized, except to speak about its becoming-code, its functioning as a code. Neither the narrative of imposition nor the narrative of radical multiplicity and fragmentation can stand. Instead we have to consider language in this context, and specifically the English language, as a basic neutral code operative and operable as a virus, insinuating itself into various networks, with the hosts accepting, not rejecting, the transmission. This is code-switching of a different order.

Notes

1   As a testament to the possibility of converting fiction into concrete instrument, Douglas Adams's translation machine in *The Hitch Hiker's Guide to the Galaxy* (1979), the 'Babel fish', lends its name to Systran's AltaVista program. A further example of recent MT and teletranslation fantasy can be found in Harry Harrison and Marvin Minsky's *The Turing Option* (1993), which describes the office machinery of the future, the 'languaphone' and 'voxfax'.

2   An influential report in 1966 by the National Academy of Sciences' Automated Language Processing Advisory Committee (ALPAC), which concluded that the idea of a fully automatic and perfect machine translation of all texts on any subject was unrealizable, facilitated this

split between theory and pragmatic, localized research. After ALPAC's report advising on the prospects for machine translation (ALPAC 1966), much funding in the US was cancelled and industry attention turned toward more particular and local machine translation projects: computer-based tools for translators (bilingual dictionaries); MT systems with humans doing the post-editing work to clean up the first copy (e.g. SYSTRAN and LOGOS); MT systems capable of working with specific discourses and controlled language output-input (e.g. the basic business message with standard greetings); and MT systems for the unrestricted input of vernacular language (research into this has increased with the widespread use of the Internet).

3   In addition to speech recognition technologies, MT is now also the province of AI research since accurate translation arguably suggests that the computer comprehended the input. Schwarzl (2001:210–223) considers the future use of artificial neural networks to improve MT performance; see also Wilks (1979).

4   The possibility of voice transcription was considered by Vannevar Bush (1945), but he noted that 'our present languages are not especially adapted to this sort of mechanization'. For recent research on teletranslation, voice communication programs, and the automatic translation of the spoken word, see O'Hagan (1996) and O'Hagan and Ashworth (2002).

5   Because there is an absence of a stable data resource that is consistent across different platforms, there is a need for integrated and integratable data. The concept of universal data speaks to the development of data translation schemes that would move disparate data to a common architecture and thereby eliminate disparity.

6   However, it is not a true or equal meeting and encounter between a natural language such as English and a programming language. The compiler-translator works between assembly code and higher-level programming languages, which are themselves based on English, but these higher-level languages are independent of machine code and independent of any one particular computer. A kind of translation must occur from a natural language to these programming languages, since one must decide what kind of output or results one wants before setting down the instructions or input to achieve them.

7   Simpson (1998) addresses the anti-nationalist, 'democratic imperative' of Basic.

8   English-Vietnamese projects in the 1970s would be another example; see Nagao (1989: 17–21).

9   The link Weaver draws between MT and the field of cryptography is also discussed in Melby (1995:16–19), Nagao (1989:19); Henisz-Dostert et al. (1979:10); Hutchins (2000:18–20); Baker (1998:140); and Locke and Booth (1955:2).

10   Notably, Weaver refers to himself in the memo not only in the third person, but in initialized form, such that his name is itself a cipher.

11   Melby also notes: 'Weaver suggests that there is a universal basis for language and that if we could find it, we would be able to use it as an *interlingua*, that is, something which is neutral and in between various languages' (1995:17).

12   'Popeye the Sailor Meets Ali Baba and the Forty Thieves', *70 Years of Popeye*, New York: Winstar Home Entertainment, 2000.

13   Sack and Brooks (*ibid.*), 'How Does it Work?', available at <translationmap.walkerart.org/how.html>. In their project proposal, they state that 'it may be time to critically examine many of the so-called "fixes" of computer science with the same sort of skepticism Ludwig Wittgenstein applied in his examination of the "problems" of philosophy. Many of the "problems" of natural language processing may stem from a badly chosen set of foundational propositions'.

14   For EuroMax and EuroMix, see <www.euromixonline.com/>.

15   See <www.systransoft.com/>. Systran was developed as a Russian-English translating machine in 1973 and has been used at the European Commission in Luxembourg since 1976. LOGOS was developed for English-Vietnamese translations in the 1970s. Also, TAUM MATEO was developed for the translation of basic Canadian weather reports into English (the system was not adaptable for more complex use in the Canadian aviation industry). See Toma (1976), Wheeler (1987), Chesterman and Wagner (2002:115–32), and Nagao (1989:29–31).

16   An illustrative example of a web-based and local translation software platform for documents and emails is Amakai Enterprise; see <www.amikai.com>.

17   Odd de Presno, *The Online World*, Chapter 9: 'Your electronic daily news'; see <http://home.eunet.no/presno/bok/9.html>.

18   McKenzie Wark, 'Netlish – English Language on the Internet', undated article, no longer available on the web. In his extensive catalogue of the impact of the Internet on language, Crystal (2001:90–92) takes a more optimistic view and argues that in fact 'Netspeak' is 'a genuine linguistic variety'. Instead of an absence of standards, Crystal finds spelling and punctuation conventions, such as the use of angle brackets, particular to the medium.

19   Ogden and Richards' Basic project was developed with similar principles. While the primary function of Basic was communicative and not literary, literary translations were used to demonstrate the flexibility and affective power of its limited vocabulary. See Leonara Lockhart's model translation of Leonhard Frank's *Carl and Anna* (London: Kegan Paul & Co., 1930).

20   John Hutchins (1986:3) notes that MT was for a time considered for literary use, but it quickly became oriented toward technical and scientific discourses, in which meaning could be treated as singular and univocal.

21   UNL is an MT system, somewhat like a semantic *Interlingua* in that it uses a conceptual language or code for translation.

22   See Reuters, 'China Blocks VeriSign from Registering Net Names', November 17, 2000, and the VeriSign Character Variant Solution, available at <http://www.verisign.com/information-services/naming-services/internationalized-domain-names/index.html>.

23   Nancy Hoft Consulting, *Case I: Going Global*, <www.world-ready.com/cases/case1.htm>.

24   'Thomson Learning Expands Its Focus on the Global English Language Teaching (ELT) Market; Company Expands Resources to Develop New Products and Services For This Growing Marketplace', PR Newswire, 19 September 2000.

25   *New Scientist* (9 March 1991). The transliteration of major languages into a Roman character and establishing a singular notation system such as Unicode for as many written languages as possible are serious issues for MT. One cannot even enter the murky terrain of lexical relations (matches and mismatches) between, for example, English and Japanese, until both languages are represented by the same code, either with something like Unicode, or by first writing the Japanese characters (Kanji, or *kana* alphabets) into the Roman alphabet so that it can also be rendered in ASCII. Character recognition for Japanese and Chinese is now fairly advanced, as evinced by recognition tools such as Codeguess, Intelliscope (Belgium-based Lernot & Hauspie), and Alis Qué (Canadian Alis Technologies).

26   John Cayley's programmable poetry and algorithmic texts, such as *Indra's Net* and *river-Island*, exemplify the aesthetics of programming languages.

27   COBOL (Common Business Oriented Language); BASIC (Beginner's All-purpose Symbolic Instruction Code); FORTRAN (formula translation and the 'Sanskrit of computer tongues', *Scientific American* 34(3), December 1979); ALGOL (algorithmic language; an international algebraic language).

28   There is a different element of translation within the tower of programming languages, which has an internal variation. Machine code is the language of the machine (binary code, numerical format); assembly code is the next level, with a symbolic representation of instructions, such as abbreviations and mnemonic names, converted to machine code by an assembler. Then there are programming languages, first called auto-codes (low-level programming language), now high-level languages such as BASIC and PASCAL that use a mathematical-like method of notation, are compiled, and are close to English in structure and vocabulary. Programming languages do not require a knowledge of machine code and they are independent of any one particular computer.

29   To a certain extent one can speak in eschatological terms concerning the 'ends of English', as reflective, constituted by, or otherwise bound up with the 'ends of history' and the 'end of man'.

30   The term 'pasigraphy' is based on a Greek root meaning 'writing for all men'.

31   See also Daniel Bell's earlier commentary on intellectuals and the technocratic mode: 'The new technocratic world is one shaped increasingly by engineers and economists, the riders of technology and rationality – a one-dimensional world, in Herbert Marcuse's phrase – if left unchecked' (1966:4).

32   On digitization and the universal language of the binary code, see Hamelink (1994:70–77). On the 'universal digital language', see Castells (1996:2). See also Lyotard on the 'new languages': 'machine languages, the matrices of game theory, new systems of musical notation . . . the language of the genetic code' (1984:40).

33   On the 'functionality of translation', see Venuti (1998b:158).

Chapter 24

Karin Littau

TRANSLATION IN THE AGE OF POSTMODERN PRODUCTION: FROM TEXT TO INTERTEXT TO HYPERTEXT

EDITOR'S INTRODUCTION

> In presenting its readers with a multiplicity of variant translations on the screen, in flaunting before our very eyes the seriality of translation, hypertext confronts its readers with the very impossibility of a definitive translation, and therefore also with the impossibility of the closure of the original; and, by extension, the impossibility of signing a single text with any equally single proper name, since no single proper name can lay exhaustive claim to a proper text.

L IKE RALEY, LITTAU DISCUSSES the impact of new computer technology on the way we conceptualize translation, but rather than machine translation she focuses on the environment and format of the hypertext. This new interface inevitably influences the ways in which we write, read and translate.

The windows environment displays text in such a way as to encourage intertextuality. Hypertext makes it possible to arrange and rearrange text, to disperse fragments of text, insert them into other texts, connect, dis- and interconnect texts as well as images. This new technology has a range of implications, including implications for the concept of an 'original' text. Translation can no longer be understood as the reproduction of a stable, bounded 'original' but has to be reconceptualized as an ongoing rewriting of an already pluralized 'original'. Moreover, because computer technology records and can display the entire production history of a text, and because it can display texts in a variety of formats and layouts, it undermines the traditional hierarchical relationship between 'original' and version(s).

Hypertext has implications for the notion of authorship too. It is no longer the author, translator or reader as such who generates the endless productivity of a text in this environment. The hypertext system reconfigures all these relations and roles: 'the user of hypertext plunders any and every text, every resource; here, all acts of reading, or acts of translation, are collaborative acts of writing, are versionings'. The less reverent approach to 'originality' and to the idea of a continuous, coherent text afforded by the hypertext environment has much to offer users with political stakes and agendas, such as feminist scholars. It enables them, for instance, to read patriarchal texts against the grain, to resist dominant discourses encoded in them, to foreground and exploit contradictory and alternative ideologies, and ultimately to open up new reading positions.

Littau argues that the full implications of the discourse of visibility, which attempts to foreground the voice and interventions of the translator, are only realized in the hypertext environment. First, because the current discourse of visibility locates the translator's explicit intervention mostly outside the text proper – in prefaces, footnotes and critical commentaries – and thus rarely results in 'the kind of postmodern production we see implicit in the works of Borges or Calvino, or those of Barthes or Derrida'. And second, because the print medium of the book allows only a limited use of the kind of visibility that translators like Godard attempt to achieve through the use of bold and italics, for instance. And it is ultimately the translator's visibility in the text, rather than in the discourses surrounding translations, that can effectively destablize traditional notions of originality and authorship.

Follow-up questions for discussion

- Israel (this volume) describes the Bible Society's insistence on having only one standard version of the Bible in each language in nineteenth-century India, and its denunciation of the proliferation of versions as evil. Compare this attitude, including its motivations and assumptions, with the situation that Littau discusses in this article. How might contemporary translators of the Bible and other sacred texts view the hypertext environment and its implications for the control of meaning?

- Coldiron (this volume) suggests that '[i]n general, new media draw on aesthetic techniques of older media; in early film, for instance, the fade-to-black mimics the fall of a theatre curtain, and is thus comprehensible to audiences as a closural signal. Likewise, production values in early print mimic those of manuscript culture in certain ways: typefaces imitate script, woodcuts stand in for (and sometimes copy) illuminations, title pages and colophons extend the conventions of *incipit* and *explicit*, and the larger printed initials we now know as drop caps simulate rubricated initials'. What aspects of the hypertext and similar environments mimic or approximate the techniques of traditional, non-computerized print media? In what ways do they depart from them, and what are the implications of both (mimicry of and departure from print media) for conceptualizations *and* practices of translation?

- Littau argues that the 'virtual presence of all the "versioners" of the text in the hypertext environment, and the virtual presence of all versions, babelizes the scene of writing'. Consider the implications of this scenario for some of the main themes raised by articles in this volume, including voice (Hermans), minority status (Cronin, Jaffe), the 'habitualization of discourse' (Mason), the advocacy of specific textual strategies and formats and what ethical or political force may be attributed to them (Sturrock, Venuti), and the consecrating role of translation (Casanova).

Recommended further reading

Arrojo, Rosemary (1997) 'The "Death" of the Author and the Limits of the Translator's Visibility', in Mary Snell-Hornby, Zuzana Jettmarová and Klaus Kaindl (eds) *Translation as Intercultural Communication*, Amsterdam & Philadelphia: John Benjamins, 21–32.

Davis, Kathleen (2001) *Deconstruction and Translation*, Manchester: St. Jerome.

Hardwick, Lorna (2001) 'Who Owns the Plays? Issues in the Translation and Performance of Greek Drama on the Modern Stage', *Eirene* XXXVII: 23–39.

Scott, Clive (2006) *Translating Rimbaud's Illuminations*, Exeter: University of Exeter Press.

POSTMODERNITY IS DESCRIBED AS A condition of culture where fading and emergent economic, political, social as well as artistic practices 'meet, clash or exist in a modus vivendi' (Hoesterey 1991:x), and where competing discourses, debates and agendas intersect. Translation with its Babel myth and its confusion of languages emerges as a privileged trope for the postmodern, precisely because it, too, is a site where intercultural exchange as well as cultural dislocation takes place, precisely because it, too, is a site where the difficult acknowledgment of the divisions between texts, languages, traditions, cultures and peoples occurs. Not unlike postmodernism then, translation is characterized by in-betweenness: caught as it is between the demands of the source system and that of the target system, the demand to make familiar that which is other and to do justice to the other as other, to mediate meaning and negotiate the very instability of signification, translation is always a hybrid. As such, the translated text flaunts and re-emphasizes the intertextual basis upon the exclusion of which the myth of textual, or authorial, autonomy is founded: always bearing the marks of (at least) two writers, always bearing the traces of other texts and contexts.

Translation in the age of postmodern production can therefore no longer be conceived of as the reproduction of an original, but has become subject to reconceptualization as the re-writing of an already pluralized 'original'; translation is moreover operative in what has become the embodiment (as we shall see, in a very material sense) of Barthes's, Foucault's and Derrida's theories of textuality in the hypertext, where the convergence between postmodern literary theory and computer technology offers new possibilities not merely for the electronic reading and writing of literature, but also for both the practice and theory of translation. Since the windows environment of the computer screen can put on display the multiple variants of a text's translations, this paper will demonstrate how, on the one hand, what remains a call for the translator's visibility in Lawrence Venuti's and Barbara Godard's writings can become a reality in the virtual reality of the hypertext; and how on the other hand, since computer technology can make visible the entire production history of a text, it can literally undermine the hierarchical separation between the so-called main text and its versions, thus redressing the balance between uniqueness and variation, as well as reconfiguring our conceptions of authorship, originality and, as we shall see, of translation. Before turning to the radical possibilities offered by a hypermedia context for translation studies, though, we must first explore the very theories which anticipated the shift from intertext to hypertext.

Whilst a blind acceptance of 'the supremacy of the original' traditionally led, according to Theo Hermans, to a 'study of translation then serv[ing] merely to demonstrate that original's outstanding qualities by highlighting the errors and inadequacies of any number of translations of it' (1985a:8), this has also, of course, perpetuated a sense of the translation's inferiority vis-à-vis its original.[1] To therefore conceive of a text in postmodern terms, that is, as an intertext, a trace of other texts, itself a translation of other texts and fragments of language, is to blur the very distinction between original and translation, and thus to undermine the hierarchical relation between original and translation, between what is deemed primary and unique and what is deemed secondary and second-rate. As Barthes (1977a:146)[2] puts it in this much quoted passage:

> We know now that a text is not a line of words releasing a single 'theological' meaning (the 'message' of the Author-God) but a multi-dimensional space in which a variety of writings, none of them original blend and clash. The text is a tissue of quotations drawn from innumerable centres of culture.

It is in this sense that Barthes can argue that a writer's 'only power is to mix writings', in other words, that a writer 'ought to know that the inner "thing" he thinks to "translate" is itself a ready-formed dictionary' (ibid.). Here, we might also follow through the implications of Barthes's essay 'The Death of the Author' for the role and status of the translator a little further, since it questions a conception of the author as that genius-creator of a unique literary masterpiece,[3] which lies, of course, at the very basis of a 'transcendental and utopian conception of translation as reproducing the original, the whole original and nothing but the original' (Hermans 1985a:9).

When Barthes declares that '[o]nce the Author is removed, the claim to decipher a text becomes quite futile. To give a text an Author is to impose a limit on that text, to furnish it with a final signified, to close writing' (1977a:147), he also claims to have liberated literature from the authority of an all-powerful presence behind the work, a presence which organizes and gives it meaning. Barthes therefore not only shakes the ancient assumption of discovering the real meaning of the text, deposited there for all eternity by the mysterious mind of the great author, but he also redefines the task of the reader. Here, the reader is no longer the discoverer of the author's intentions and meaning, a mere consumer of the work, but is allowed the pleasure of breaking open the text to produce a multitude of different (re)readings, that are in effect rewritings, of it.[4] Barthes's proclamation of the death of the author, with its impending 'birth of the reader', might also be the birth of the translator, in that the translator opens up writing, thus releasing writing from the constraints of a single and univocal reading. In other words, since Barthes refuses 'to assign a "secret", an ultimate meaning' (1977a:147) to the text, he refuses to curtail the proliferation of meaning; and since he has it that a text therefore 'answers not to an interpretation, even a liberal one, but to an explosion, a dissemination' (1977b:159), it follows that a translation cannot be held to inscribe the meaning of the original. For this reader-translator, the text is no longer a sacred source, but a resource which engenders a multiplicity of rereadings. Here, then, the faithful translation died with the author, with our faith in the Author-God.

What is questioned with this shift towards intertextuality is not only the unity and identity of a text, whether a text can have identifiable limits and borders, but also 'the unity and identity of a language, the decidable form of its limits' (Derrida 1985:173), a point that Derrida elaborates when he writes in The Ear of the Other (1982b/1985:100) that translation

> can get everything across except this: the fact that there are, in one linguistic system, perhaps several languages or tongues. Sometimes – I would even say always – several tongues. This is impurity in every

language. This fact would in some way have to threaten every linguistic system's integrity, which . . . presumes the existence of one language and of one translation in the literal sense, that is, as the passage from one language into another. So, if the unity of the linguistic system is not a sure thing, all of this conceptualization around translation (in the so-called proper sense of translation) is threatened.

By deconstructing the concept of translation, Derrida therefore pushes us to 'the almost unthinkable notion', in Peggy Kamuf's words, 'of an originary translation before the possibility of any distinction between original and translation' (Kamuf 1991:242). This rethinking of translation is also encapsulated in Derrida's phrase *plus d'une langue* (1986a:14–15), which plays out two meanings: more than one language; no more of one language. There is no longer one language, because language itself is a multiplicity, already more than one language.

Derrida's *différance* (Derrida 1982a, Derrida and Labarrière 1986) is the very term which signals not the opposition between two terms, be it the opposition between two languages, or two texts, but the shifting relations within each relation, and moreover, within 'each term'. If a text is an intertext, that is, a trace of other texts, itself a translation of other texts, as we have seen, then a text cannot stand in a clear relation of priority to any other, and a text and its translation cannot therefore stand in a clear opposition to each other. For how could there be a clearly demarcated opposition between two elements, if 'each' element in 'itself' multisects with other texts, if 'an' element is already a trace of traces of other texts/translations and so on and so forth. It follows therefore that the (non)relation between text and translation is never stable, since the shifting relations, the tracery with other texts, refuse a simple static binary opposition, and therefore also defer the very possibility of any clearly demarcated borders or distinctions between them. Consequently, to arrive at an opposition between two elements necessarily requires the suppression of the residue, the excess of reference, the sheer proliferation of signification.

Différance is the logic then by which binary oppositions are outmanoeuvred. Since binary oppositions are based on relations of hierarchy, whereby one term in the relation is privileged whilst the other has clearly been subordinated, a deconstructive move must always seek to dislocate the hierarchical structure by instituting a reversal between the elements in the relation (Johnson 1980:x). This moment of reversal is temporary in so far as it must not simply stop with the elevation of the subordinate term, but must render oppositions untenable *per se*. In the context of our discussion of translation this means, of course, that the opposition between original and translation (which has maintained translation as the secondary element in the relation) becomes undone when the original is exposed as that which is already marked by translation, a logic which temporarily illustrates the importance of translation, but then also proceeds, as I argued earlier, to undermine the hierarchical relation between these terms, by having blurred their very distinction. This is also why Barbara Johnson's point that 'the differences between entities . . . are shown to be based on a repression of differences within entities, ways in which an entity differs from itself' (1980:x), bears relevance for our own discussion: the difference between original and translation, which relies on a fixed binary structure, was shown to be based on a repression of a difference within, a difference which inhabits every text, and as such already inhabits the 'original', making the original *différant* to itself. The question therefore as to how to be 'true' to an original, how to translate it right, or how to be faithful to it, becomes untenable if the original is reinscribed as difference within, to follow Johnson's argument, or as that which is already an intertext, to follow Barthes's argument.

The negative valorization of one term as against the other in binary couplets such as original and translation, or author and translator, can also be discerned in other related couplets, such as model/copy, unique/reproducible, single/multiple.[5] The privileged terms in such binary oppositions are accumulated as properties of originality; for what is revered is the model, not the copy; what is valued is the unique and not the reproducible; what is hierarchized is that which is singular and cannot be multiplied. Hence, there emerges another question as regards the vexed issue of the inferior status of translation: how could one possibly value copies, translations, as much as originals, on which they were modelled, because by their very nature, they come in multitudes? To put this differently, we might say that since there is always the possibility of other translated versions of the *same* text, it precludes the existence of a definitive translation, which would render all subsequent translations superfluous. In this sense, the seriality of translation not only pluralizes 'the original', but it *always already* calls into question originality, that is, uniqueness *per se*. In the face of the sheer multiplicity of translated variants, the inherent failure of the closure of their originals is flaunted. Translation in the age of postmodern production is nothing other than the celebration of the many multivalent translated versions of an already 'anoriginal original' (a phrase coined by Benjamin 1989). This shift 'from the one to the many', to borrow Matei Calinescu's (1991) phrase, is also a shift from loss to gain, a shift from an unattainable equivalence to an unstoppable proliferation.

At this point we must also re-examine the aura of the original, and follow up another line of questioning. What is it then that makes us stand in awe before the unique, the authentic, the original? What is it that makes us uncomfortable in the face of the sheer possibility of a multitude of different versions? What or who is it then that perpetuates the myth of original genius? Is it a faith in God the Almighty as our maker, the king as our sovereign, the father as guardian, and the author as Author-God? Is the emphasis on originality, with its return to authorial intention, the organizing principle by which patriarchy seeks to maintain control, seeks to preserve order and stability for fear of multitudes, anarchy, that 'cancerous and dangerous proliferation of significations', which Foucault speaks of in 'What is an Author' (Foucault 1986)? Is the cult of originality, then, the very mechanism by which we seek to ensure the proper *authorization* of the translator? To answer these questions, we must turn to Foucault's analysis of authorship.

The function of the author in Western tradition is regulatory, according to Foucault: not only is the name of the author used 'to group together a certain number of texts, define them, differentiate them from and contrast them to others', thus 'marking off the edges of the text' (*ibid.*:107) in order to delimit 'a certain unity of writing' (*ibid.*:111); but, by setting up the author as a 'genial creator', by making the author 'so different from all other men, and so transcendent with regard to all languages that, as soon as he speaks, meaning begins to proliferate, to proliferate indefinitely' (*ibid.*:118), one has created a dominion or hierarchy for the author which resembles that of a god. Whilst Foucault's essay analyzes the role and status of the author, it also sets into motion an important reversal. In his thesis, the author is

> a certain functional principle by which, in our culture, one limits, excludes, and chooses; in short, by which one impedes the free circulation, the free manipulation, the free composition, decomposition, and recomposition of fiction . . . The author is therefore the ideological figure

by which one marks the manner in which we fear the proliferation of meaning. (ibid.:119)

This is to say, the author is used

to master and control the great proliferation of discourse, in such a way as to relieve its richness of its most dangerous elements; to organise its disorder so as to skate around its most uncontrollable aspects. (Foucault 1972b:228)

It is precisely here that we enshrine the author as the all-powerful depositor of the riches of meanings, that we endow the author with the control of meaning, because we do not wish meaning to go out of his hand, out of hand, and into the hands of the translator(s). To further transpose Foucault's argument to the context of translation, we might argue that the insistence on the 'errors and inadequacies' of any translation, the insistence on loss, and the concentration on its failures, is not only a way of reducing its status to a second-order product – always measured against its first-order model – but constitutes the very attempt to reduce its potential for proliferation. In other words, we have inferiorized translation, we have devalued it, because we fear it, since it is a flaunting manifestation of textuality's most 'uncontrollable aspects', since it is an index of the 'cancerous and dangerous proliferation of significations'. By extension, we have inferiorized the translator, because we fear her or him, since he or she is the very initiator or proliferator of discourses, the multiplier of versions.

Translation theorists/practising translators such as Barbara Godard and Lawrence Venuti, influenced by much of the above, therefore seek to highlight the original text's potential for proliferation, and set out to flaunt the productive and transformative role of the translator in the process of textual transmission, to counteract the self-effacing and invisible position of the translator. While Venuti insists that 'translation is an active production of the text which resembles, but nonetheless transforms, the original', a conviction which leads him to 'formulate a technique of critical reading in which the productive process of translation can become visible' (1986:181), Godard similarly emphasizes the transformative nature of translation as a 'production' rather than a reproduction of the original, involving 'the translator's dual activities of reading and writing' (1990:91). Furthermore, since Venuti's 'critical reading' as a translation strategy 'exposes [the] multiple and divided meanings in the foreign text and displaces it with another set of meanings, equally multiple and divided' (1992a:8), and since Godard's 're/reading and re/writing' (1990:90) foregrounds the text as a 'network of sliding signs' (Godard 1991:9–10) which in translation 'enters yet another network of signifiers to extend its productivity' (ibid.:11), we might return to Barthes (1990) once more, not only because in S/Z he develops the very strategies which Venuti and Godard draw on here, but also because S/Z also serves others as a model of the hypertext, and can therefore, as we shall see, put into practice their arguments on translation in ways hitherto unrealized.

When Barthes argues in S/Z that we only come to appreciate a text's multiplicity when we reread it, this is to say, we only realize that a text is plural because, when we reread it, we can read it again differently, he consequently calls for a strategy of reading which rereads texts 'from the outset' (1990:16). This strategy, which he deploys throughout S/Z and which breaks open the text of Sarrasine into 561 fragments and unleashes its five different voices, 'consists precisely in manhandling the text, interrupting it' (ibid.:15, my emphasis). According to Barbara Johnson, Barthes's reading practice in S/Z therefore leaves Sarrasine 'as heterogeneous and discontinuous as possible', thus avoiding 'the repressiveness of the attempt to dominate the message and force the text into a single and ultimate meaning' (1980:7). This strategy, which shatters the coherence of the text to reveal not 'a 'secret', an ultimate meaning' but a multiplicity of significations, opens up the text as a site for different reading positions.

As a strategy, this offers a great deal to those who have political stakes in the formation of literatures. For example, Barthes has greatly influenced many current approaches to reading and translation by feminist scholars, such as Godard, precisely because his strategies offer a means by which feminists may read the texts of our patriarchal past 'against the grain', that is, may resist the dominant patriarchal discourse within a text. To reread such texts for their contradictory and alternative ideologies, and to therefore also open up new reading positions, proves a useful strategy for the feminist reader in that she may open up a reading position for herself, in that she may not only reclaim a feminist voice to speak on behalf of women from within those texts, but also thereby rewrite those texts from a feminist perspective. As a feminist translator then, Godard advocates such a strategy for translation when she defines it from the very start as a re/reading-cum-re/writing.[6] Echoing Barthes's words from S/Z, she sums up her project, with its emphasis on the necessary shift in the power relations between authors, readers, and translators respectively, in the following terms (1990:94):

> The feminist translator, affirming her critical difference, her delight in interminable re-reading and re-writing, flaunts the signs of her manipulation of the text. *Womanhandling* the text in translation would involve the replacement of the modest and self-effacing translator. Taking her place would be an active participant in the creation of meaning.

Godard's translator is manipulative rather than faithful, assertive rather than subservient, visible rather than transparent. This newly gained visibility of the translator which she describes here, and which she alongside many other Canadian feminist translators practises, by 'immodestly flaunt-[ing] her signature in italics, in footnotes – even in a preface' (*ibid.*), is preceded by a long history of the translator's invisibility, one which Lawrence Venuti has, of course, exposed at great length in his recent work (see Venuti 1995).

Venuti reacts against an Anglo-American translation convention, which he sees as an aesthetic which promotes 'fluency or easy readability' (*ibid.*:187) as the hallmark of a good translation. Against this aesthetic of 'transparency', which demands that the translation reads fluently and thus at least gives the pretence of being (like) the original, against this 'effacement' of the translator's intervention in the process of textual transmission, he adopts a resistancy strategy in translation. Rather than 'domesticating' the foreign text, Venuti – for his own translations of de Angelis' poetry – deploys a strategy of 'abusive fidelity', a notion which he takes from Philip Lewis, and which, 'far from proving more faithful to the Italian texts, in fact abuse[s] them by exploiting their potential for different and incompatible meanings' (Venuti 1991a:16).[7] As this 'unfaithful' translator, he cannot be accused of betraying the original text, because he does not betray its constitutive plurality. What is important about Venuti's approach is that he seeks neither to tame or 'reduce [a text's] polysemantic possibilities to a single interpretation', nor to 'fit everything together in a consistent pattern' (Iser 1974:283, 285).[8] Such an approach would be based on the premise that all texts can be made readable, rendered intelligible and can finally be mastered. Venuti's translation strategy, in this respect, is not unlike J. Hillis Miller's or Paul de Man's (un)readings of the undecidable structures within a text or even a word. Their deconstructive close readings which pay attention to the irreducible heterogeneity *within* texts constitute a kind of resistance to the totalizing tendencies which, in their view, have reigned over the majority of critical practice and theory. Venuti's translator, not unlike the Yale reader, then, seeks out the contradictions, blind spots, in a text, and not unlike the Barthesian reader, breaks open the text. Venuti (1991a:15) sums up this interpretive translation strategy more specifically when he writes that it

> in effect opens up the contradictions in the poem, foregrounds it, and perhaps reveals an aspect of De Angelis's thinking of which he himself was not conscious or which, at any rate, remains unresolved . . . My interpretive translation exceeds the source-language, supplementing it with research that indicates its contradictory origins and thereby puts into question its status as the original, the perfect and self-consistent expression of authorial meaning of which the translation is always the copy, ultimately imperfect in its failure to capture that self-consistency.

What is evident therefore in both Venuti's and Godard's approach is that by flaunting their presence as translators in the target texts, they multi-determine the scene of writing. This is to say, the insertion of the writing voice, be it that of the author, or in this instance, that of the translator into the (translated) text sets into motion an indeterminability, which is not unlike the indeterminability that Jorge Luis Borges performs in his story 'Borges and I', of which the final line reads: 'I did not know which one of us had written this text'.[9]

Postmodern writing, be it in fiction or in criticism, highlights the very conventions which are part of the writing process, makes visible the devices of their own construction. Thus, as Seàn Burke points out, 'the re-entry of the subject into the writing disrupts its claims to objectivity', because 'far from figuring as a function of Cartesian certitude, the author [here, translator] operates as a principle of uncertainty in the text, like the Heisenbergian scientist whose presence invariably disrupts the scientificity of the observation' (1992:172).[10] If this re-entry of the subject into the writing process is also the result of a refutation of the analogy between reality and writing, world and fiction, then it follows that the entry of the translating subject into the translation is a refutation not merely of the convergence between reality and copy, but also of the equivalence between an original and its translated version. Godard's and Venuti's practice of translation can largely be seen to follow from the kind of description that John Barth gives here (1969:128; quoted in Waugh 1992:58):

> Inasmuch as the old analogy between Author and God, novel and world, can no longer be employed unless deliberately as a false analogy, certain things follow: (1) fiction must acknowledge its fictitiousness and metaphoric invalidity or (2) choose to ignore the question or deny its relevance or (3) establish some other, acceptable, relation between itself, its author, its reader.

Since we may add the translator to the third point in Barth's list, it becomes evident how Godard's or Venuti's visible translator is not simply a reassertion of authorship, but, as in Italo Calvino's If on a Winter's Night a Traveller for instance, as Patricia Waugh points out, 'a fictional completion of Barthes's statement: that the death of the author makes possible the birth of the reader' (Waugh 1984:134), or indeed, the birth of the translator; a point Waugh surprisingly leaves out, since Calvino's character-translator Hermes Marana fictionalizes, and flaunts before our very eyes, 'the shady business' (Calvino 1982:142)[11] of translation; a metafictional statement which is far from unimportant in so far as Waugh quotes from, and seems to be reading, William Weaver's English version of this Italian novel. Waugh's phrase that '[t]o write "I" is to discover that the attempt to fix subjectivity in writing erases that subjectivity, constructs a new subject'[12] can nevertheless be applied to the translator, in that Godard and Venuti construct a new translating subject, which confronts the reader with the impossibility of determining with any certitude, which one of them – author or translator – had written the text.

Here, though, we must also hesitate for a moment, since when Godard and Venuti speak of the necessity for the translator's 'self-presentations',[13] in or outside the translated text, this visibility, in practice, occurs mostly outside the (main) text, either in prefaces, footnotes or critical commentaries, and is thus rarely the kind of postmodern production we see implicit in the works of Borges or Calvino, or those of Barthes or Derrida. Whilst Godard to some extent inserts her presence in the main text via typographical means (in italics or bold print, as for example in Picture Theory), the print medium of the book allows only a limited use of this kind of visibility. When Patricia Waugh therefore argues that '[t]he more the author appears, the less he or she exists. The more the author flaunts his or her presence in the novel, the more noticeable is his or her absence outside it' (1984:134), we are left with the sense that the full implications of Godard's and Venuti's arguments are only partially realized, precisely because it is the translator's visibility in the text, rather than his or her visibility in the discourses surrounding translations, that remains the most effective means of destabilizing the authority of the status of the original as that 'perfect and self-consistent expression of authorial meaning', to use Venuti's words once more, in relation to which translation is regarded as 'ultimately imperfect in its failure to capture that self-consistency' (1991a:15).

Derrida (1979),[14] on the other hand, goes some way towards creating a kind of new textuality, which, through typography, can emphasize, and thereby raise questions as regards the linearity of writing, the dé-bordement of the text, the form of the book. Thus, when we read (in) the parallel text(s) of 'Living On. Border Lines' (Derrida 1979), printed in an above and below margin, commenting on and spilling over into each other, that a text is 'no longer a finished corpus of writing, some content enclosed in a book or its margins, but a differential network, a fabric of traces referring endlessly to something other than itself, to other differential traces' (ibid.: 84), Derrida sums up in this statement what his text in effect performs. 'Living On' shares its page with 'Border Lines' (a 'footnote' text), in which Derrida goes 'so far as to write to the translator about the difficulty he is in the act of creating for him' (Johnson 1985:146).[15] In this sense, Derrida not only pushes language to the limits of translatability, thereby emphasizing that meaning is never transparent, and that it is translation which always brings this to light, but also, more importantly, re-marking the border line between translatability/untranslatability on which the translator will have to live, highlighting the site of the translator's difficult but always necessarily transformative interventions.

In directly addressing the translator about the future translation of 'Living On. Border Lines', Derrida flaunts his presence as the writer of it, '[m]y desire to take charge of the Translator's note myself' (1979:77), but also foreshadows the presence of the translator(s). His question therefore, '[h]ow can one sign in translation, in another language' (ibid.:174) not only refers to the impossibility of translating the proper name of the writer, Jacques Derrida, but also indicates the necessary counter-signature of the translator. 'Living On. *Border Lines*' in translation will therefore bear the marks of two signatures, of two writers. Since Derrida questions, both explicitly and implicitly, whether a text can have clearly identifiable borders, or whether a text can bear the clearly identifiable mark of one writer, he is not only scrutinizing textuality, but also interrogating the very form of the apparatus of writing, that is, the physical object of the printed book. As he puts it in *Dissemination* (1981:3):

> the form of the 'book' is now going through a period of general upheaval, and while that form appears less natural, and its history less transparent, than ever, and while one cannot tamper with it without disturbing everything else, the book form alone can no longer settle . . . the case of those writing processes which, in *practically* questioning that form, must also dismantle it.

The very form of Derrida's 'Living On. *Border Lines*'[16] therefore anticipates alternatives to the printed book such as hypertext, which fulfils many of the promises of post-modern theory, 'creat[ing] an almost embarrassingly literal embodiment of a principle that had seemed particularly abstract and difficult when read from the vantage point of print' according to Landow (1992:53). Since hypertext can electronically arrange and rearrange text, since the window environment can disperse fragments of text, insert fragments into other texts, can connect, dis- and interconnect texts, images and fragments thereof, and thus change the ways in which we write, read and translate, it enacts intertextuality *par excellence*. Whilst the conventions of writing, editing and printing a book tend to follow the strictures of a single or a clear reading text rather than the 'work in progress', hypertext, by contrast, works within an environment which can make visible a text's history of production, and can therefore present multivariant versions simultaneously. Forms of traditional textual scholarship are confronted with the necessity for change, partially in response to postmodern theory, and partially reacting to the impact of computer technology;[17] how can we assume translation – its theorization and its practice – to be exempt from such changes?

Precisely because hypertext can call up numerous translations of the foreign text,[18] thus allowing access to the foreign text's history, including its translational history, Godard's and Venuti's call for the visibility of the translator can be translated into, and visualized in, the new electronic medium. In presenting its readers with a multiplicity of variant translations on the screen, in flaunting before our very eyes the seriality of translation, hypertext confronts its readers with the very impossibility of a definitive translation, and therefore also with the impossibility of the closure of the original;[19] and, by extension, the impossibility of signing a single text with any equally single proper name, since no single proper name can lay exhaustive claim to a proper text. Furthermore, the virtual presence of all the writers, be it the foreign author, or the translators, undermines the notion of a univocal authorial voice, and with it, renders untenable the assumption of the 'perfect and self-consistent expression of authorial meaning' (Venuti 1991a:15). It is in this sense that translation in the age of postmodern (electronic) production turns from *the one to the many*, because this virtual presence of all the 'versioners' of the text in the hypertext environment, and the virtual presence of all versions, babelizes the scene of writing.

The reading practice this fosters is never linear, proceeding through a text in a sequence from beginning to middle to end, but always encourages the reader to create a web of connections and direct his or her own pathways, thus making it possible for the reader to interactively engage with, write on, even rewrite any number of texts on the screen. We can envisage, and moreover, will increasingly see at work, an active reader/translator[20] who can assemble a translation-text from a tissue of other translations, 'drawn from' what Barthes has called 'innumerable centres of culture'. Jay David Bolter's argument that 'in the electronic space, where every reading of a text is a realization or indeed a rewriting of the text, to read is to interpret' (1991:165) may be added to our own: *to read is therefore also to translate*, which, in the final instance, allows not only the 'authorized' translator (in the sense that this translator has been commissioned to translate for a printed publication) to 'flaunt . . . the signs of her manipulation of the text' (Godard 1990:94), but also allows the interactive reader-cum-translator at her PC to become 'an active participant in the creation of meaning' (*ibid*.). In short, this reader does not merely read a finished *product* – the translation in printed book form – but takes on an active role in the *process* of meaning production, produces her own translation.

Translation in the age of postmodern production must therefore be understood doubly. On the one hand, postmodern theory's emphasis on the text's productivity, engendering a multiplicity of versions, always frustrating their closure into the 'one original', rendering it impossible to conceive of translation as a duplication, a copy of this 'original', focuses our attention instead on translation as a proliferation function in this process of productivity; on the other hand, translation in the age of electronic postmodern production materializes this productivity within the frame of its own means of production. This is to say, whilst 'within the hypertext environment all writing becomes collaborative writing, doubly so' (Landow 1992:88), translation becomes collaborative writing, multiply so, not merely between author and translator, but between author, translator and reader, for 'in the electronic medium readers cannot avoid writing the text itself, since every choice they make is an act of writing' (Bolter 1991:144). It is at this juncture that there is no need for the kind of visible translator that Godard and Venuti envisage, to counteract the role of translation as a self-effacing and secondary activity, because the hypertext system, not the author, nor the translator, or reader, generates a (foreign) text's productivity endlessly, and reconfigures the once distinct roles attributed to the author, the translator, or reader respectively. Here, the user of hypertext plunders any and every text, every resource; here, all acts of reading, or acts of translation, are collaborative acts of writing, are versionings.

Notes

1   Compare also: 'The art of translation is a subsidiary art and derivative. On this account it has never been granted the dignity of original work, and has suffered too much in the general judgement of letters. This natural underestimation of its value has had the practical effect of lowering the standard demanded . . . neither its importance nor its difficulty has been grasped'. This quotation from Hillaire Belloc (1931) is cited in Bassnett (1980:2). The 'underestimation' analyzed by Belloc is echoed again and again in the writings of critics evaluating translation, as well as translators themselves who internalize a sense of their own inferiority as against their authors, by insisting that as translators they are merely humble servants striving to render the original faithfully. What versions, such as translations, but also adaptations, share is that they are always different from their original sources, a difference

which lays them open to the charge of unfaithfulness, and therefore also to accusations of having betrayed the original, of not measuring up to the original.

2   All subsequent quotations from foreign texts will appear in translation rather than in the original, precisely because the very assumption that unmediated, truthful access to the original can only be gained by quoting in the original language runs counter to the argument in this paper, which seeks to dismantle both the notion of such an unmediated access to original intention, and the notion that translation might constitute an inferiorized version of the original. As Joan Fillmore Hooker aptly points out, '[t]ranslation involves compromises, some fortunate, some unfortunate, some inevitable. But so does original composition' (1983:20).

3   The copyright law underwrites this unrivalled position of the author, by 'defin[ing] translation as a second-order product, an "adaptation" or a "derivative work" based on an "original work of authorship", whose copyright, including the exclusive right "to prepare derivative works" or "adaptations" is vested in the "author" ' Venuti (1992a:2).

4   This is an argument which Barthes, as we shall see, puts forward in S/Z (Barthes 1990).

5   For a description of such couplets, see Krauss (1991).

6   A feminist strategy of translation which Godard also adopts for the translation of women's writing, whilst Suzanne Jill Levine adopts a similar strategy for her translation of male authors such as Cabrera Infante or Manuel Puig. See Levine (1992, particularly p. 83), or her book *The Subversive Scribe: Translating Latin American Fiction* where she 'ponder[s] the feminized translator, traitor: me as self-betrayer fallen under the spell of male discourse, translating books that speak of woman as the often treacherous or betrayed other, as well as subversive scribe, "transcreating" writing that stretches the boundaries of patriarchal discourse' (1991:181).

7   Also compare his point that his 'translation resists the transparent aesthetic of Anglo-American culture which would try to domesticate De Angelis's difficult writing by demanding a fluency strategy' (*ibid.*:10).

8   We may also note here that Venuti's translator, unlike that of Katharina Reiss and Hans J. Vermeer, does not stipulate that 'the received text must be coherent' (Reiss and Vermeer 1984:114); nor does he assume, like Wolfram Wilss, for instance, that 'translatability of a text [can be] guaranteed by the existence of universal categories' (Wilss 1982:49). In other words, Venuti does not share the kind of doctrine which demands that '[i]f we cannot find (or *impose*) this consistency, sooner or later, we will put the text down' (Iser 1974:285, my emphasis).

9   This story, just as much as his 'Pierre Menard, Author of the *Quixote*' in *Labyrinths* (Borges 1970), calls into question received notions of authorship.

10   Burke is referring particularly to the later, mostly autobiographical, works of critical theorists such as, for instance, Barthes's *Roland Barthes by Roland Barthes* (Barthes 1977c).

11   Also compare Sherry Simon's point as regards Marana's 'crime' and 'motive' in the novel: 'His crime: substituting new texts for translations and having them published under the Author's name. The motive: to weaken the Author's powers of seduction over the Reader. If the Reader can no longer be sure whose words she is actually reading, perhaps she will begin to have doubts about the Author and show more interest in the Translator'. Simon therefore concludes that 'Calvino's brilliant parody plays richly on the long history of suspicion surrounding the translator's "undercover" work. The fact that Calvino uses sexual stereotypes to portray the triangular relationship between Author, Reader, and Translator is by no means accidental. There is a strong analogy between the crisis in gender relations evoked in his novel and the contemporary crisis in gender relations. Both women and translators are the "weak" terms in their respective hierarchies, sexual and literary. Both are now challenging the power relationships behind traditional ideas of fidelity' (Homel and Simon 1988:51–52).

12   Waugh refers specifically to *Roland Barthes by Roland Barthes* (Barthes 1977c), which according to her performs Merleau-Ponty's 'I am never at one with myself' and as such blurs, according to Waugh, 'autobiography-as-fiction or fiction as autobiography' (Waugh 1984:135).

13   As Venuti points out, '[s]uch self-presentations will indicate that the language of the translation originates with the translator in a decisive way' (1995:311).

14   Derrida (1986b) is another, and more successful, instance of this new type of textuality, pushing to the limits the very form of the printed book.

15   Johnson goes on to write that Derrida is 'thus figuratively sticking out his tongue – his mother tongue – at the borderline between the translated text and the original' (1985:147).

16   It has often been argued that Barthes's *S/Z* (Barthes 1990) also anticipates hypertext. See for example Landow (1992:66), where he explains that *S/Z* 'comments on the footnote, and all of *S/Z* turns out to be a criticism of the power relation between portions of text'; which is also why Landow has it that '[h]owever self-dramatizing and overheated Barthes's presentation of his method in *S/Z* might appear from the perspective of print, it accurately describes the way an attempt to move beyond print in the direction of hypertextuality disturbs the text and the reading experience as we know them' (ibid.:53).

17   Hans Walter Gabler's new edition of *Ulysses*, for instance, adopts a revolutionary approach to textual editing. As Cohen and Jackson state: '[w]hereas most CEAA/CSE editions discuss textual history in an introduction and then in textual notes comment on variant readings from different versions, Gabler has adopted a *"show"* rather than a *"tell"* posture towards apparatus in his edition of *Ulysses* . . . The form of apparatus, the synopsis, ingeniously *visualizes* in a synchronic axis of the work's existence, *displaying* through an elaborate system of diacritical marks the growth of the "continuous manuscript text" of the novel' (1991:114, my emphasis). Derek Pearsall's model for editing takes this one step further when he suggests a textual edition based on the idea of a loose-leaf binder or facsimile, or 'its electronic equivalent, a series of "windows" on a CRT'. As D. C. Greetham points out further: 'The "play" involved in Pearsall's suggestion . . . inevitably has Derridian overtones, for could it not be argued that if a reader may (re)construct texts through the caprice of a loose-leaf binder (as a means of reflecting what Pearsall calls the 'history of literary taste') so may the same reader manipulate the features of a text according to the whimsy of *his* own history of taste, a form of deconstructive *jeu*, the play in the text that continually defers a fixable meaning or form to that text and instead allows, indeed promotes, an indeterminate, and continually deferred, meaning according to the requirements of *différance?*' Greetham goes on to suggest that '[i]n fact, it may be ironic that it is only a result of the technical advances in the most traditional disciplines – textual scholarship – that the full critical implications of the Derridian *jeu* can be textually demonstrated. Texts may indeed be spliced and erased, they may be reconstituted and grafted onto other texts, marginalized and (en)folded with an electronic ease that would make the worst nightmares of a New Critic confronting poststructuralism come true!' (1991:84–85).

18   For a use of hypertext systems in the study of translation, see, for instance, *CD Word: The Interactive Bible Library*, which stores different versions of the Bible together with the Greek texts, dictionaries and commentaries, as well as Paul D. Kahn's *Chinese Literature* web, which allows access to the different versions of Tu Fu's poetry, including the Chinese text, transcriptions, varying translations, other reference and contextual material. Both systems allow the reader-user to sift through or compare the variant translations, but also draw on commentaries about them; both are therefore designed as an aid to the scholar in giving comprehensive access to materials that would otherwise remain scattered in libraries across the globe, and an aid to students giving easy and readily available access to it over the net. This multi-user format, then, announces a new way not only of reading, writing and translating, as we have already indicated, but also of researching and teaching (Landow 1992:36).

19   It should also be pointed out here that since the texts which the reader can interact with on the computer screen are always versions – that is – copies of a 'primary version' which exist in the memory of the computer, and since it is only when the user saves her or his working version that there is a brief convergence between the text on the screen and the text in the computer memory, that it makes little sense therefore in electronic word processing to hold on to a distinction between model and copy, or primary and secondary (Landow 1992:19).

20   It is only the Internet, rather than the CD ROM (read-only-memory) facility, which allows the user to write on or rewrite texts on the screen.

Chapter 25

Eric Cazdyn

A NEW LINE IN THE GEOMETRY

EDITOR'S INTRODUCTION

*If we view the original and the subtitled version as both belonging to the present tense – every
subtitling of the original as changing the meaning of the original itself – then we will be right
in the thick of a method that stresses the through-and-through dynamic and political nature
of subtitling.*

CAZDYN LOOKS AT CHANGES IN THE technology of subtitling in recent
years, particularly the introduction of the running subtitle in news reporting since 9/11.
The running title we now see repeatedly on our television screens developed to accommodate
an unmanageable surplus of meaning that cannot be contained or communicated within the
traditional format. It does not relate to the broadcaster's text the way a traditional subtitle
relates to what the characters say on the screen: though appearing in the same language (as in
intralingual subtitling), it is not a transcription of the sounds we hear simultaneously coming
out of the screen. Nor does it even necessarily provide further detail on the main item, though
it may cover related topics – allowing us, for instance, to simultaneously listen to news about
casualities at Manhattan's Ground Zero and read about preparations for an ensuing war.
Cazdyn traces the link between this new form of television subtitling and the established
history of film subtitling, focusing in particular on the practices of the *benshi* (in-house
commentators) in early Japanese cinema. At their best, the *benshi* 'approached the type of
translation dreamt of by Benjamin in which the film (original) and *benshi* (translation) were
dynamically related so that every new *benshi* performance would necessarily transform the
film itself'.

From Benjamin and the *benshi*, Cazdyn moves on to examine what he describes as 'the
most notorious act of subtitling' in recent years: the subtitling by the US Defense Department
of a fifty-minute video of Osama bin Laden speaking to associates about the 9/11 bombings.
The video was released by the Bush administration on 13 December 2001 as a smoking gun
that puts beyond doubt Al-Qaeda's responsibility for the attacks. Just as in debates over
literary translation and film subtitling, the debate over the subtitling of this video revolved

around the question of fidelity, of how accurately the content of the original is rendered by the government-employed subtitlers. No attention was paid to the form of subtitling itself, nor to the Pentagon's choice of subtitling over dubbing, for instance. Moreover, the Pentagon's subtitles are treated as coming after the event of the original video, whereas Cazdyn insists that they do not follow the original but are in a dynamic relation with it, and that we must rethink the temporalization of such events and the way in which the subtitles *transform* the original, especially given the technologies now at our disposal.

The running subtitle and the central broadcast content run at different speeds: the central content at the speed of the national, and the running subtitle at the speed of the global. At times of crisis, we find ourselves focusing on both at the same time, trying to flow at both speeds: 'the slower speed of the main broadcast and the faster speed of the running titles: the slower speed of the national and the faster speed of the global'. Unlike the running subtitle on our television screens, the (interlingual) subtitles in the bin Laden video directly related to the main content, and the two realms (the national and the global) remained discrete. But the running subtitle now promises us new and previously unimaginable ways of seeing and living the new global realities, including ways of seeing and living that we cannot yet envisage.

Follow-up questions for discussion

- Nornes (2007:185–86) likens abusive subtitles, which he advocates, to *en face* or interlinear translations in the printed medium (see Sturrock, this volume). Like interlinear translations, abusive subtitles work to maintain the visibility of the original and encourage viewers to 'work off' the original text/image at the same time as they process the subtitles. To what extent does this scenario overlap with the situation Cazdyn describes, where the new practice of running subtitles has taught us to process two streams of information simultaneously? To what extent do both scenarios enact the kind of time and space compression that characterizes globalization (see Cronin 2003)? And how might these developments further impact translation and interpreting practices in future?

- Pérez-González (2006, 2007) describes a number of features that are unique to fansubbing of Japanese animated films (anime), including the use of glosses (similar to footnotes in written translation) and a profusion of titling elements that are placed almost randomly at various points on the screen, outside the traditional default area for subtitles. To what extent do such strategies call on and nurture reading/viewing practices similar to those described by Cazdyn in relation to running subtitles on television? And if running subtitles in the same language locate us simultaneously within national and global contexts and allow us to process a surplus of information at times of crisis, what functions and effects might we attribute to fansubbing strategies?

- Cazdyn suggests that in the case of the bin Laden tape, '[t]he Pentagon chose subtitling over dubbing in order to lend greater authenticity to the original'. Consider this statement critically in the light of existing literature on dubbing and subtitling. What other motivations have been associated with the choice of each form, whether at a national level or at the level of individual films/programmes or types of film/programme?

Recommended further reading

Nornes, Abé Mark (2007) *Cinema Babel: Translating Global Cinema*, Minneapolis & London: University of Minnesota Press.

O'Sullivan, Carol (2007) 'Multilingualism at the Multiplex: A New Audience for Screen Translation?', *Linguistica Antverpiensia* NS6: 81–95.

Pérez-González, Luis (2007) 'Intervention in New Amateur Subtitling Cultures: A Multi-modal Account', *Linguistica Antverpiensia* NS6: 67–80.

Shohat, Ella (2006b) 'The Cinema after Babel: Language, Difference, Power', in *Taboo Memories, Diasporic Voices*, Durham & London: Duke University Press, 106–138.

1

THE MEDIA REPRESENTATIONS OF 9/11 and the previous War in Iraq call to mind the same question we might ask when reading the seemingly endless string of credits following a big-budget Hollywood film: how could so much money, so much talent, so many human and technological resources produce so much mind-numbing mediocrity? But if we can agree with Fredric Jameson that in every dystopian configuration (from the cultural to the political) there is a utopian dimension (a genuinely radical quality that the dystopian requires in order to conduct its ideological work), then we might want to look again at all of the CNN footage, at all of the interviews and updates, at all of the garden-variety montages and exclusive video-phone footage and ask: what, alongside the mainstream media's Disney-lensed, flattened-out production of History, might persist, might flash a new critical spectatorship that can imagine (however unconsciously) a properly historicized detour from today's prevailing parade route?[1]

It is here that a review of the subtitle is in order. In this case the running subtitle, that termite text gnawing right to left on the bottom of the screen. Beginning with the first Gulf War and finding its home following 9/11, this new line in television's geometry is nothing less than one of cinema's classic tropes. It is indeed ironic, however, that in a country like the US whose audience is so averse to foreign films, and whose mainstream core so vehemently detests the subtitle, there would develop such a dependence on the subtitle itself. It is true that the running subtitle has gained ground ever since the stock market has made its way into the middle-class home, requiring that hypnotized half-eyed optic on the cable channel's running ticker – an activity that has replaced the soap opera and detective novel as the dominant main-stream distraction. What is going on with the running subtitle? How is it related to the cinematic subtitle, to foreign film, and the foreignness of film? And how might it hint at a different form of representation, one that not only represents news and events differently but, in its most allegorical and utopian form, one that also opens up the possibility for a different shape of political representation?

2

At moments of crisis, formal limitations become exposed. This is just as true for aesthetic systems as it is for financial and political ones. For example, when the bottom drops out of a currency the arbitrary nature of value is exposed. Likewise, when social uprisings hit a critical mass the limitation of political representation is clear to see. The same general structure is true for the aesthetic system of television. Television's running title comes into being precisely around a crisis, around an unmanageable surplus of meaning impossible to contain within its usual form: the running subtitle is not a transcription of the broadcaster's words, but either provides more detail on the item in question or on a different but nonetheless related item. Such a form is particularly useful when commenting on real-time events. Take, for example, the events of September 11: too much was happening at once, thus opening up the formal possibility of running subtitles – an aesthetic strategy that could better provide multiple, real-time news updates. As with any eruption, danger is involved; the danger that the thing/being as presently configured can no longer manage itself, but must endanger its own existence to remain in existence. The running subtitle flashes (however momentarily and before it is recuperated) television's essential lack: what is presumably full and self-sufficient is essentially lacking and in need; what appears as full presence is in fact organized around an absence that cannot be filled or even acknowledged, only camouflaged and repressed. Dan Rather no longer runs the show. The 'white elephant' quality of broadcast news, that quality that asks you to stare at it and be satisfied by it and only it, has vanished, laying bare all of the props and pulleys, all of the magician's hardware.

In terms of composition, the running subtitle is located on the bottom of the screen. Already this marks a crucial departure from television's compositional dominant, a dominant that I have named the pornographic aesthetic (Cazdyn 2002). The pornographic aesthetic is one in which the active content monopolizes the absolute centrality of the frame to the marginalization of everything else; the body that exists in the centre of the frame (the talking head of the broadcaster, the implosion of buildings, the copulating couple, the advertised product) pushes-out, crowds-out, snuffs-out significant relational elements of the shot. Relations to other elements inside and outside of the frame, relations to history, relations to that abstraction called the relation itself (all of which might be called the negative space of the shot) are out of sight leaving only the phatic positivity of the look-at-me content. The pornographic content relates to what is called positivism in philosophy, that method whereby speculation is shunned and any resort to the negative (in the name of a bad metaphysics) is eschewed in favour of the here-and-now fact.

But the running subtitle challenges the compositional fact of television; it returns the relation to the equation – the relation between text and image, between the margins of the frame and the centre, between the different speeds of information delivery, and between multiple narrative lines. One can now watch and hear the news about casualties at Manhattan's Ground Zero and at the same time read about preparations for an ensuing war. But before moving to what quickly has become the most notorious act of subtitling (the US Defense Department's titling of a fifty-minute video of Osama bin Laden speaking to associates in an Afghanistan cave) and then to the unlikely relation between the running subtitle and current globalization processes, I first want to establish the link between the most recent trend in television subtitling and the already established history of film subtitling. Which, as usual, comes by way of an excursion into literary translation.

3

The debate over literary translation usually centres on the issues of fidelity and freedom. The former designates a strategy that sticks as closely as possible to the text being translated while the latter departs from it as the translator sees fit. The objective of both is to transmit the meaning of the original text into a different language. In 'The Task of the Translator', Walter Benjamin dismantles this debate and questions the priority placed on the transmission of meaning as the *sine qua non* of all translation (Benjamin 1968). By focusing on syntax and a word-for-word translation that is not concerned with comprehensibility, fluency or 'saying the same thing' in a different language, Benjamin envisions the task of the translator as something completely different, as representing the hidden kinship among languages. The task of the translator is not to get as close as possible to the original text but to release or liberate the pre-Babelian 'pure language' (*reine Sprache*) that is imprisoned in the original as well as in the language of the translation. This pure language is not the pristine original that is then defiled by the translation, rather it is a negative category that cannot be attained by any single language but only hinted at by the totality of intentions (of both the original and the translation) supplementing each other. The act of translating then, for Benjamin, is a longing, a promise, a messianic hope for linguistic complementarity. Or, to put this another way: the deadly serious task of the translator lies in the importance placed on the concept of utopia as such – utopia as a critical category in its most tactically disabused and reflexive form.

To speak of utopia in such terms is thus not to suggest the actual possibility of achieving it, but rather to underscore the significance of the strategy, no matter how doomed, of working toward it.[2] The promise of touching the untouchable pure language is what marks the thoroughly dialectical character of Benjamin's preface: to be fully aware of the limitations of translation (Derrida 1985), of the structural impossibilities of language and necessary failure of translation (de Man 1986), while at the same time aware that these limitations are not static and thus occupy within their very logic the possibility of transformation.[3] This pure language is not a destination or even an ultimate beginning, but it is what inspires the task of the translator. By strategically sacralizing such a notion as pure language, Benjamin is effectively able to de-sacralize the original text.

4

Our move from literature to film comes by way of Japan. During the same years in which Benjamin wrote about translation, an exemplary performance of his theory was being worked out in Japan, however different the cultural context. In early Japanese cinemas, from the 1890s to the early 1930s, an in-house commentator named the *benshi* (or *katsuben*) was present.[4] Standing underneath and to the left of the screen, the *benshi* commented on the images as they were being projected. From explanations of the projection process (film stock, the workings of the projector) to sharing gossip about the actors, from providing historical background to translating a Griffith inter-title into Japanese, the *benshi*'s role did not come after the film in some epiphenomenal way but was dynamically included from the outset so that Japanese cinema equalled the sum total of the film plus the *benshi*. The *benshi*, at their best and before subsequent systemic constraints, approached the type of translation dreamt of by Benjamin in which the film (original) and *benshi* (translation) were dynamically related so that every new *benshi* performance would necessarily transform the film itself – producing that something in excess of both, pure language or Cinema. By 1931, however, the possibilities of the *benshi* were snuffed-out by (1) the political right: the military government that enforced a rigid *benshi* licensing system and a terribly unimaginative template for how *benshi* should go about their work, (2) the new cultural left: those who argued that the *benshi* blocked the growth of cinematic art and thus the critical possibilities of the form (such as writer Tanizaki Junichiro and dramatist Osanai Kaoru), and (3) Marlene Dietrich: the Hollywood talkie, with which the *benshi* simply could not compete.

With the end of the *benshi* system came the beginning of subtitles in Japan, in fact Joseph von Sternberg's *Morocco* was one of the very first films subtitled in Japan (Tanaka Junichiro 1980, Nornes 1999). At this early stage of Japanese subtitling, the effects were quite different from twenty, fifty, or even seventy years later. With the *benshi* no longer in the theatre and no longer factored into the film during the production process itself, the spectator now had a less mediated relation to the film. Despite the addition of the new subtitles, spectators could still focus on the lighting, composition, narrative development and acting in ways that had become hard to do after the *benshi* became more heavy-handed by the early thirties. As the subtitle became dominant and the memory of the *benshi* faded by the late thirties and early forties, however, the possibility of something more abstract (what I am calling Cinema, an analogy to Benjamin's pure language) was closed.

It is true, however, that some of the original *benshi* spirit (and some of the original subtitling spirit) persists in current Japanese subtitling. For example, one title of Quentin Tarantino's *Pulp Fiction* explains that the diner is located in a dangerous neighbourhood of the US. Still, the dominant discourse on subtitling has gone the way of literary translation – avoiding criticism of the presumed ontological status of the original while remaining eager to enter into the fidelity versus freedom debate. In this context the debate either tiredly turns on (1) the infidelity of dubbing over the faithfulness of titling, (2) how the subtitles are either carefully faithful or flexibly free in relation to the original dialogue, or (3) how ridiculously inexact the story-distorting subtitles are. What dominates this debate is the idea of the static title at the bottom of the frame (not running on the bottom or popping up throughout the frame), or the subtitle that only translates dialogue (not, say, a prop or, as in *Pulp Fiction*'s case, one that comments, documentary-like on the setting). This old saw of proper subtitling emerged most powerfully in relation to the heated controversy over the bin Laden videotape.

5

Just over two months after the terrorist attacks in the United States (on 13 December 2001), the Bush administration released a video tape of Osama bin Laden speaking about the September 11th bombings, a smoking gun so damning and undeniable, the administration argued, that those still in doubt are clearly questionable themselves – possible collaborators.[5] The video consisted of two scenes: the first a meeting in which bin Laden (surrounded by a group of buoyant comrades) relaxes on pillows and talks to a Saudi sheik in what appears to be a Kandahar safe-house; the second, approximately twelve minutes of downed US helicopter footage. With a low-end video camera mounted on a tripod about waist-high, the camera operator often shifts the length of the lens and can be heard whispering to someone off-camera. No one ever looks directly into the camera and yet everyone seems aware that it is there.

The version released by the Pentagon (with subtitles running up almost half of the frame) divided the two scenes into three parts, leading with the second part of bin Laden's conversation, followed by the helicopter footage, and ending with the beginning of the meeting. Two questions: (1) why did Pentagon officials cut-up the footage, and (2) why did they wait over one month to release the video to the major networks?

The video was re-cut so that the most incontrovertible evidence would be front and centre, such as bin Laden's admission that the hijackers knew that they were on a martyrdom operation. But why not provide only the most relevant scenes? Because then the tape would appear more mediated (edited and cut-up): the Pentagon, in other words, wanted to provide a context, but not one that would obscure the key moments that it wanted to highlight. (And we must remember that the release of the video came on the heels of the Bush Administration's request that broadcasters not air any unauthorized images of bin Laden for fear that he might surreptitiously transmit possible directives to his North American supporters.)[6]

The decision to wait to release the video is connected to this same desire to emphasize the video's authenticity. Bush officials, who explained that they found the video in a private Jalalabad residence, believed that it was shot in Kandahar on 9 November. When asked about the elapsed time of over one month from the day they found the video to the day they released it to the major networks, the administration pointed to the bad audio quality and their desire to employ four outside translators to double-check their own Arabic-to-English subtitles, a precaution needed to answer possible claims that the White House had doctored or provided an inaccurate translation of the video.

Of course these skeptical claims are precisely what followed. On the more conspiratorial level are those who believe the video was 'Forest Gumped' – totally fabricated from stock footage and basic digital video manipulation. Others did not question the authenticity of the footage but argued that the subtlety of the language was reduced, thus assuring bin Laden's culpability. As one skeptic put it,

> The intention was to satisfy the public that it was not biased – Arabic being a language notoriously vague to translate, with concepts rather than one-for-one equivalencies often being the closest that can be attained. It has no future tense at all, which makes conversations about planning something perhaps less distinguishable from discussions about current events and descriptions of things that have already happened. (Irving 2001)

Then there is the running parenthetical commentary that the Pentagon inserted into the dialogue. Revisionist historian David Irving writes, 'The Pentagon transcript subtitles had over-useful interpolations in round brackets, making direct reference to the World Trade Center, the Pentagon, and civilian deaths, and in one instance identifying an Egyptian member of this Islamic mafia referred to in conversation only as Mohammed, as "Mohammed (Atta)" – which might seem a bold step, given the likely number of other Egyptians called Mohammed'.

More specifically, here are the subtitles for one of the most incriminating segments:

> *Osama bin Laden*: (. . . Inaudible . . .) we calculated in advance the number of casualties from the enemy, who would be killed based on the position of the tower. We calculated that the floors that would be hit would be three or four floors. I was the most optimistic of them all.

(. . . Inaudible . . .) due to my experience in this field, I was thinking that the fire from the gas in the plane would melt the iron structure of the building and collapse the area where the plane hit and all the floors above it only. This is all that we had hoped for.

Sheik: Allah be praised.

David Irving skeptically analyzed subtitles this way: 'Suppose Osama's opening remarks were inaudibilized, an audiotape technique that US presidents have long mastered? Suppose the missing phrases were something like, "According to CNN thousands died in the upper floors. Well, that may be so. I'm a trained engineer and we've done the calculations and . . ." '.

So here, as in the debates over literary translation and film subtitling, is the question of fidelity, of how accurately the content of the original is caught by the government-employed subtitlers. But here, too, what gets lost in this debate is the very form of subtitling itself. The Pentagon chose subtitling over dubbing in order to lend greater authenticity to the original. But with so many viewers familiar with the basic concepts of video production, the status of the original itself is called into question. (This skepticism was no doubt heightened when the US considered authorizing a new government department – The Office of Strategic Influence – whose misinformation mandate would include employing such new media morphing techniques.)[7]

There was a similar obsession with content in the video of the Rodney King beating by Los Angeles police officers in 1991. The repetitive viewing and analysis of George Holliday's amateur video footage led to juror confusion over precisely who was assaulting whom. When defence lawyers for the LAPD performed a frame-by-frame analysis for the jury (with the help of noted cinema studies professors), the larger issue of how the very form of the portable video camcorder – that made it possible for the surveyed to turn the technology back on the surveyors – was lost in the minutiae of whether the exact position of Rodney King's arm indicated that he was getting up or stumbling down. The lesson of the Holliday tape is not that a picture (or a frame of a videotape) tells a thousand words, but that it tells a thousand (conflicting) stories. Part of the disappointment over the not-guilty verdict of the trial stemmed from a sense that the new democratic and liberatory dimension of video was done for, that it was no longer a tool for the oppressed. One cannot be caught red-handed on video when those hands could very well be someone else's. And we are now living with the consequences of this with the present dominance of reality TV, a genre in which the political potential of the amateur videographer has been replaced by the value of the free labour he or she gives to the networks by shooting freak footage of baby and pet accidents.[8]

If the King footage flashed the simultaneous radical possibility of the video camera and its ideological recuperation, then the bin Laden footage does the same with video editing and subtitling. The Pentagon's subtitles are understood as coming after the event of the original video, thus burying what is most significant about the subtitles – that they (in a Benjaminian and *benshi*-like fashion) do not follow the original but are in dynamic relation with it. This now prepares us for the allegorical move, one that relates this more de-privileged understanding of the original (in terms of film and video) to the way the original (in this case nation-states) functions during the most recent transformations of the world-system.

6

All subtitles invariably transform the original text. This concept of transformative subtitling seeks to de-link and de-territorialize the subtitled version from the original. At stake is a disruption of the usual temporalization ascribed to the original subtitle trajectory. Transformative subtitling implies that the original is not only what it is, but that it also exceeds itself. The original is part of a dialectical process in which it is at once part of the past, present and future. If we view the original and the subtitled version as both belonging to the present tense – every subtitling of the original as changing the meaning of the original itself – then we will be right in the thick of a method that stresses the through-and-through dynamic and political nature of subtitling.

At stake here is quite a lot since the present state of the world is one in which the inequality of wealth and power is a result of centuries of past events. And for many of us, the way we justify our concerns and make daily life-choices depends upon how we explain this past to ourselves. To say that the past has not ended (and for our present purposes to say this about a pre-titled film or video) is to set this past (film or video) in a space of real vulnerability, perhaps on the order of those conspiracy theorists who deny the original video itself. But this vulnerability is marked not only with danger and doubt, but possibility. To pull up the anchor of the past is not only to risk obscuring a historical explanation of the present moment, but also to enliven the past and stress how the past is not only past but also part of the present and thus integral to shaping the future. Transformative subtitling draws attention to this process. Although this process is always in motion, it becomes dominant when discourses regarding 'origins' are most immediate, such as during the re-fetishization of national origins in Benjamin's Germany and the return to nativist origins in 1930s Japan. It is for this reason that the emerging force of transformative subtitling is manifesting itself at the precise moment when the nation-state is experiencing another important transformation.

We know that since the early 1970s the global economy has been turning into a different moment of capitalist development, symbolized by the flexible accumulation of capital, cybernetic technologies, a global division of labour, transnationalization of business practices, new times and scales, and the weakened decision-making power of the nation-state. To be sure, the nation-state and various nationalisms (on both the discursive and operational levels) are still strong due to the different speeds at which the various levels within the social formation move. In other words, the cultural dimension of nationalism is stronger than the economic dimension. The North American Free Trade Agreement's (NAFTA) controversial Chapter 11 process, whereby companies who feel their investments are in jeopardy by the intervention of foreign governments can sue these governments for compensation, grants a certain transnational – or more specifically non-national – personhood to corporations of which real persons, who must still obey older rules of national subjecthood, can only dream. This relates to one of the common confusions in globalization discourse: the assumption that the global system's political-economic and cultural-ideological dimensions move at the same speed. For this reason, many political and cultural theorists expect to find the rise of global cultural movements and global working-class movements on par with the rise of global corporations. Whereas no one is surprised to learn that a CEO of a transnational corporation may have more power than local or national politicians in the congresses and parliaments around the world, when it comes to national identities and ideologies – the primary unit by which people locate themselves in the world – the nation's stock is still sky high. We still root for our own teams in the Olympics and our own armies in war while the political-economic stakeholders – without any nostalgia – focus on the bottom line.

The unevenness of the different levels of the social formation produces one of the great contradictions of our time: between the persistent power of residual national forms and the emerging influence of transnational ones. The force of this contradiction paralyzes our capacity to exist squarely in either dimension. Rather, we exist dead-centre in the contradiction and must wait for the movement of history (which is based on both our individual acts and its own structural logic) to transform the situation. This contradiction also explains why there are such odd bedfellows in the current political landscape: anarchists and neo-nationalists, Luddites and cyber-nauts all participating in the counter-globalization movements. Yet socio-political limits and contradictions always presuppose aesthetic possibilities and solutions. The aesthetic, in other words, offers a realm within which formal escapes are posed – however much these experiments might never directly engage the problem at hand. And it is here that the unevenness of the new running subtitle can be read allegoric-ally: as a formal attempt (however unconscious) to square the circle of the national/transnational paradox.

There is a disconnection between the running subtitle and the central broadcast content. The subtitle is running ahead of the main content. It is running at a different speed. At the moment of crisis, we found ourselves focusing (with a double-optic that provided lucid insight rather than vertigo) on both the subtitle and the main content. For a brief moment we were flowing at both speeds, the slower speed of the main broadcast and the faster speed of the running titles: the slower speed of the national and the faster speed of the global. The subtitle is to the global as the main content is to the national. What could not be grasped on the social level (this utopian double-optic) was effortlessly experienced on the aesthetic one. With the bin Laden video, even though the subtitles directly connected to the main content, due to the new realities of video editing and the re-valuation of original texts in the name of transformative subtitling, the two realms remain discrete. The running subtitle, this new line in the geometry of the visual, flashes for us hitherto impossible ways of seeing and living the new global realities – ways of seeing and living that are not yet possible at the present moment.

Notes

1   See in particular the final chapter of The Political Unconscious, 'The Dialectic of Utopia and Ideology' (Jameson 1981: 281–99), and Jameson (1979).

2   As Derrida writes in his comments on the Benjamin preface, 'the promise is not nothing, it is not simply marked by what it lacks to be fulfilled. As a promise, translation is already an event, and the decisive signature of a contract. Whether or not it be honoured does not prevent the commitment from taking place and from bequeathing its record. A translation that manages to promise reconciliation, to talk about it, to desire it or make it desirable – such a translation is a rare and notable event' (1985:191).

3   For an interesting analysis of both Derrida and de Man within the context of anthropology, see Rey Chow (1995).

4   For more on the benshi in English see Aaron Gerow (1994). In Japanese, see Yoshida Chleo (1978).

5   'It is preposterous for anybody to think that this tape is doctored', said Donald Rumsfield, adding 'That's just a feeble excuse to provide weak support for an incredibly evil man' (Sales 2001).

6   With major networks buying footage from Al Jazeera TV in Kuwait, the Administration made a public request for all news organizations to consider the public safety issues involved with such transmissions. All major US networks fell in line, as well as the Canadian Broadcast Corporation (CBC).

7   In late February, the office was proposed only to be quickly dumped by Defence Secretary Donald Rumsfield. President Bush proclaimed zero tolerance for lies from US officials.

8   I write about reality culture in my article 'Representation, Reality Culture, and Global Capitalism in Japan' (Cazdyn 2000).

Bibliography

Abd al-Wahhab, Muhammad Fahmy (n.d.) *Al-harakat al-nisa'iyya fi al-sharq wa silatiha bi al-isti'mar wa al-suhyuniyya al-'alamiyya*, no publisher: Dar al-I'tisam.

Adams, Douglas (1979) *The Hitch-Hiker's Guide to the Galaxy*, London: Pan.

Ahmed, Leila (1987) 'Women of Egypt', *The Women's Review of Books* (November): 7–8.

Ahmed, Leila (1994) *Women and Gender in Islam: Historical Roots of a Modern Debate*, New Haven, Connecticut: Yale University Press.

Ainsworth Vaughn, Nancy (1994) 'Is That a Rhetorical Question? Ambiguity and Power in Medical Discourse', *Journal of Linguistic Anthropology* 4: 194–214.

Alba, R. and V. Nee (2003) *Remaking the American Mainstream: Assimilation and Contemporary Immigration*, Cambridge, MA: Harvard University Press.

ALPAC (1966) *Language and Machines: Computers in Translation and Linguistics*, Division of Behavioral Sciences, National Academy of Sciences, National Research Council Publication 1416, Washington: NAS/NRC.

Amireh, Amal (1996) 'Writing the Difference: Feminists' Invention of the Arab Woman', in Bishnupriya Ghosh and Brinda Bose (eds) *Interventions: Feminist Dialogues on Third World Women's Literature and Film*, New York: Garland, 185–211.

Anderson, Benedict (1983) *Imagined Communities: Reflections on the Origin and Spread of Nationalism*, London: Verso.

Angelelli, Claudia (2004) *Re-visiting the Role of the Interpreter: A Study of Conference, Court and Medical Interpreters in Canada, Mexico and the United States*, Amsterdam & Philadelphia: John Benjamins.

Anonymous (1823) 'Review of William Stewart Rose's translation of *Orlando Furioso*', *Quarterly Review* 30 (October): 40–61.

Anonymous (1854) *Contributions Towards a History of Biblical Translation in India*, Calcutta: Calcutta Auxiliary Bible Society.

Anonymous (1869) *Revision of the Tamil Bible: Report of the Proceedings of the Delegates Appointed for the Revision of the Tamil Bible*, Madras, April 27, 1–15.

Anonymous (1889) *An Open Letter to the Churches from their Missionaries in Madras*, Madras: SPCK Press, 1–7.

Anonymous (1899) 'The Revision of the Vernacular Versions', *The Harvest Field: A Missionary Magazine* 10 (Mysore: Wesleyan Press): 136–42.

Anonymous (1989) 'Letter to the Editor', Kyrn 193: 4.

Anonymous (1990) 'Traddutore, traditore?', Kyrn 336: 35.

Anzaldúa, Gloria (1987) Borderlands – La Frontera: The New Mestiza, San Francisco: Spinsters.

Apter, Emily (2001) 'Balkan Babel: Translation Zones, Military Zones', Public Culture 13(1): 65–80.

Apter, Emily (2006) The Translation Zone: A New Comparative Literature, Princeton: Princeton University Press.

Armstrong, C. A. J. (1983) England, France, and Burgundy in the Fifteenth Century, London: Hambledon Press.

Armstrong, Isobel (1996) 'Transparency: Towards a Poetics of Glass in the Nineteenth Century', in Francis Spufford and Jenny Uglow (eds) Cultural Babbage: Technology, Time and Invention, London: Faber & Faber, 123–48.

Arrojo, Rosemary (1997) 'The "Death" of the Author and the Limits of the Translator's Visibility', in Mary Snell-Hornby, Zuzana Jettmarová and Klaus Kaindl (eds) Translation as Intercultural Communication, Amsterdam & Philadelphia: John Benjamins, 21–32.

Asad, Talal (1980) 'Ideology, Class, and the Origin of the Islamic State', Economy and Society 9: 450–73.

Asad, Talal (1983) 'Anthropological Conceptions of Religion: Reflections on Geertz', Man 18: 237–59.

Asad, Talal (ed.) (1973) Anthropology and the Colonial Encounter, London: Ithaca Press.

Asimakoulas, Dimitris (2005) 'Brecht in Dark Times: Translations of His Works under the Greek Junta (1967–1974)', Target 17(1): 93–110.

Atiya, Nayra (1982) Khul-Khaal: Five Egyptian Women Tell Their Stories, Syracuse: Syracuse University Press.

Atsugi Taka (1940a) 'Story-film no yakugo ni tsuite' (On the translation of story-film), Bunka eiga kenkyū 3(4) (April): 118–19.

Atsugi Taka (1940b) 'Kiroku eiga no kyokō – "jijitsu" wa sono mama "shinjitsu" de wa nai' (Fiction in documentary film – 'actuality' as it is not 'truth'), Nihon eiga 5(2) (November).

Atsugi Taka (1960) 'Yakusha no atogaki' (Translator's afterword), in Paul Rotha Dokyumentarii eiga (Documentary Film), trans. Atsugi Taka, Tokyo: Misuzu Shobō, 329–34.

Atsugi Taka (1991) Josei dokyumentarisuto no kaisō (Reminiscences of a female documentarist), Tokyo: Domesu Shuppan.

Atsuka Ueda (forthcoming) 'Sounds, Scripts, and Styles: Kanbun-kundokutai and the National Language Reforms of 1880s Japan', The Review of Japanese Culture and Society.

Austin, J. L. (1975) How to Do Things with Words, 2nd edn, Cambridge: Harvard University Press.

Aziz, Barbara Nimri (1994) 'Unpicked Fruits', in Joanna Kadi (ed.) Food for Our Grandmothers: Writings by Arab-American and Arab-Canadian Feminists, Boston: South End Press, 56–61,

Aziz, Barbara Nimri (1997) 'Al-Dawwara', in Christian McEwan (ed.) Jo's Girls; Tomboy Tales of High Adventure, True Grit, & Real Life, Boston: Beacon Press, 250–56.

Bachmann-Medick, Doris (2009) '1 + 1 = 3? Intercultural Relations as a Third Space', trans. Kate Sturge, in Mona Baker (ed.) Critical Concepts: Translation Studies, Volume II, London & New York: Routledge, 31–45.

Badran, Margo (trans.) (1986) Harem Years: The Memoirs of an Egyptian Feminist, New York: Feminist Press.

Badran, Margo (1988a) 'Badran's Response [to Mervat Hatem's Review of Harem Years]', AMEWS NEWS (Association of Middle Eastern Women's Studies) 2(7).

Badran, Margot (1988b) 'Critical Forum', AMEWS NEWS 2(8): 17–20.

Badran, Margot (1995) Feminists, Islam, and Nation: Gender and the Making of Modern Egypt, Princeton, NJ: Princeton University Press.

Baer, Brian James (2006) 'Literary Translation and the Construction of a Soviet Intelligentsia', *The Massachusetts Review* 47(3): 537–60.

Baker, David W., Ruth M. Parker, Mark V. Williams, Wendy C. Coates and Kathryn Pitkin (1996) 'Use and effectiveness of interpreters in an emergency room department', *Journal of the American Medical Association* 275: 783–88.

Baker, David W., Risa Hayes and Julia Puebla Fortier (1998) 'Interpreter use and satisfaction with interpersonal aspects of care for Spanish-speaking patients', *Medical Care* 36: 1461–70.

Baker, Mona (2000) 'Towards a Methodology for Investigating the Style of a Literary Translator', *Target* 12(2): 241–66.

Baker, Mona (2005) 'Narratives in and of Translation', *SKASE Journal of Translation and Interpretation* 1(1): 4–13. Available from www.skase.sk.

Baker, Mona (2006a) *Translation and Conflict: A Narrative Account*, London & New York: Routledge.

Baker, Mona (2006b) 'Translation and Activism: Emerging Patterns of Narrative Community', *The Massachusetts Review* 47(3): 462–84.

Baker, Mona (2008) 'Ethics of Renarration – Mona Baker is Interviewed by Andrew Chesterman', *Cultus* 1(1): 10–33.

Baker, Mona (2009) 'Resisting State Terror: Theorising Communities of Activist Translators and Interpreters', in Esperança Bielsa Mialet and Chris Hughes (eds) *Globalisation, Political Violence and Translation*, Basingstoke: Palgrave Macmillan, 222–42.

Baker, Mona (ed.) (1998) *Routledge Encyclopedia of Translation Studies*, London: Routledge.

Bal, Mieke (1985) *Narratology: Introduction to the Theory of Narrative*, trans. Christine van Boheemen, Toronto: University of Toronto Press.

Balibar, Etienne (1987) 'La langue de France exercée au pluriel', in G. Vermès and J. Boutet (eds) *France, Pays Multilingue*, Vol. 2, Paris: L'Harmattan, 9–21.

Balibar, Etienne (1991) 'The Nation Form: History and Ideology', in Immanuel Wallerstein and Etienne Balibar (eds) *Race, Nation, Class: Ambiguous Identities*, New York: Routledge, Chapman & Hall, 86–106.

Ballard, Michel (1992) *De Cicéron à Benjamin: traducteurs, traduction, réflexions*, Lille: Presses Universitaires de Lille.

Barrell, John (1991) 'Death on the Nile: Fantasy and the Literature of Tourism 1840–1860', *Essays in Criticism* 41(2): 97–127.

Barret-Ducrocq, François (ed.) (1992) *Traduire l'Europe*, Paris: Payot.

Barry, Iris (1939) 'Review of *Documentary Film*', *Saturday Review*, 12 August.

Barsky, Robert F. (1996) 'The interpreter as intercultural agent in convention refugee hearings', *The Translator* 1(2): 45–64.

Barsky, Robert (2007) 'Activist Translation in an Era of Fictional Law', *TTR* 18(2): 17–48.

Barth, John (1969) *Lost in the Funhouse*, New York & London: Secker & Warburg.

Barthes, Roland (1972) 'Taking Sides', *Critical Essays*, trans. Richard Howard, Evanston, Ill.: Northwestern University Press, 163–70.

Barthes, Roland (1977a) 'The Death of the Author', *Image – Music – Text*, trans. Stephen Heath, London: Fontana, 142–48.

Barthes, Roland (1977b) 'From Work to Text', *Image – Music – Text*, trans. Stephen Heath, London: Fontana, 155–64.

Barthes, Roland (1977c) *Roland Barthes by Roland Barthes*, trans. Richard Miller, London: Macmillan.

Barthes, Roland (1990) *S/Z*, trans. by Richard Miller, Oxford: Blackwell.

Barthes, Roland (2002) *Le Neutre. Cours au Collège de France (1977–1978)*, edited by Eric Marty, Paris: Seuil/IMEC.

Bassnett, Susan (1980/1991) *Translation Studies*, London & New York: Routledge.

Bassnett, Susan and André Lefevere (eds) (1990) *Translation, History and Culture*, London: Printer Publishers.

Bassnett, Susan and Harish Trivedi (1999) *Post-colonial Translation: Theory and Practice*, London & New York: Routledge.

Basu, Moni (2005) 'Iraqi Interpreters Risk Their Lives to Aid GI's', *Cox News Services*, 2 November.

Batchelor, Kathryn (2008) 'Third Spaces, Mimicry and Attention to Ambivalence: Applying Bhabhian Discourse to Translation Theory', *The Translator* 14(1): 51–70.

Batteux, Charles (1997) 'Principles of Translation', trans. John Miller, in Douglas Robinson (ed.) *Western Translation Theory: from Herodotus to Nietzsche*, Manchester: St. Jerome, 195–99.

Bauman, Richard and Charles Briggs (1990) 'Poetics and Performance as Critical Perspectives on Language and Social Life', *Annual Review of Anthropology* 19: 59–88.

Beal, Peter (1990–1997) *Index of English Literary Manuscripts*, 4 vols., London: Mansell.

Beaton, Morven (2007) 'Interpreted Ideologies in Institutional Discourse: The Case of the European Parliament', *The Translator* 13(2): 271–96.

Beattie, John (1964) *Other Cultures*, London: Cohen & West.

Beaugrande, Robert de and Wolfgang Dressler (1981) *Introduction to Text Linguistics*, London: Longman.

Beecroft, Alexander (2008) 'World Literature Without a Hyphen: Towards a Typology of Literary Systems', *New Left Review* 54 (Nov–Dec): 87–100.

Beer, Gillian (1996) *Open Fields: Science in Cultural Encounter*, Oxford: Clarendon.

Beidao (1993) 'La traduction, une révolution silencieuse', *Littératures d'Extrême-Orient au XXe siècle*, Paris: Picquier, 125–131.

Bell, Daniel (1966) *The Intellectual and the University*, New York: The City College.

Bell, Daniel (1973) *The Coming of Post-Industrial Society: A Venture in Social Forecasting*, New York: Penguin Books.

Belloc, Hillaire (1931), *On Translation*, Oxford: The Clarendon Press.

Bendix, Edward H. (1988) 'Metaphorical and Literal Interpretation: Cross-cultural Communication in Medical Settings', *CUNYForum* 13: 1–16.

Benhabib, Seyla (2002) *The Claims of Culture*, Princeton, NJ: Princeton University Press.

Benhabib, Seyla (2004) *The Rights of Others: Aliens, Residents and Citizens*, Cambridge: Cambridge University Press.

Benjamin, Andrew (1989) *Translation and the Nature of Philosophy*, London & New York: Routledge.

Benjamin, Walter (1968/1970) 'The Task of the Translator: An Introduction to the Translation of Baudelaire's *Tableaux Parisiens*', trans. Harry Zohn, in Hannah Arendt (ed.), *Illuminations*, New York: Schocken Books; reprinted in Marcus Bullock and Michael W. Jennings (eds) *Selected Writings of Walter Benjamin, Vol. 1, 1913–1926*, Cambridge, MA & London: Belknap Press, 1996, 253–63.

Benjamin, Walter (1969) *Illuminations*, New York: Schocken.

Benjamin, Walter (1974) *Werke*, I, 1, Frankfurt: Suhrkamp.

Bennett, Karen (2007) 'Epistemicide! The Tale of a Predatory Discourse', *The Translator* 13(2): 151–69.

Bergunder, Michael (2002) 'The "Pure Tamil Movement" and Bible Translation: The Ecumenical Thiruviviliam of 1995', in Judith M. Brown and Robert Eric Frykenberg (eds) *Christians, Cultural Interactions and India's Religious Traditions*, Grand Rapids & Cambridge: William B. Eerdmans; London: Routledge Curzon, 212–31.

Berk-Seligson, Susan (1990) *The Bilingual Courtroom: Court Interpreters in the Judicial Process*, Chicago & London: The University of Chicago Press.

Berman, Antoine (1984) *L'épreuve de l'étranger: Culture et traduction dans l'Allemagne romantique*, Paris: Gallimard.

Berman, Antoine (1985) 'La traduction et la lettre, ou l'auberge du lointain', in *Les Tours de Babel: Essais sur la traduction*, Mauvezin: Trans-Europ-Repress, 31–150.

Berman, Antoine (1992) *The Experience of the Foreign: Culture and Translation in Romantic Germany*, trans. S. Heyvaert, Albany: State University of New York Press.

Berman, Marshall (1983) *All That Is Solid Melts into Air: The Experience of Modernity*, London: Verso.

Bettelheim, Bruno (1983) *Freud and Man's Soul*, London & New York: Chatto & Windus and Knopf.

Blackhall, Leslie J., Sheila T. Murphy, Geyla Frank, Vicki Michel and Stanley Azen (1995) 'Ethnicity and Attitudes Toward Patient Autonomy', *Journal of the American Medical Association* 274: 825.

Blassneck, Marce (1934) *Frankreich als Vermittler English-Deutscher Einfluesse im 17. und 18. Jahrhundert*, Leipzig: Verlag von Bernhard Tauchnitz.

Blommaert, Jan (1996) 'Language Planning as a Discourse on Language and Society: The Linguistic Ideology of a Scholarly Tradition', *Language Problems and Language Planning* 20: 199–222.

Blommaert, Jan (2001) 'Investigating Narrative Inequality: African Asylum Seekers' Stories in Belgium', *Discourse and Society* 12(4): 413–49.

Blommaert, Jan and Jef Verschueren (1992) 'The Role of Language in European Nationalist Ideologies', in Paul Kroskrity, Bambi Schieffelin and Kathryn Woolard (eds) *Language Ideologies*, Special issue of *Pragmatics* 2(3): 355–75.

Boase-Beier, Jean (2007) *Stylistic Approaches to Translation*, Manchester: St. Jerome.

Boase-Beier, Jean and Michael Holman (eds) (1999) *The Practices of Literary Translation: Constraints and Creativity*, Manchester: St. Jerome.

Boéri, Julie (2008) 'A Narrative Account of the Babels vs. Naumann Controversy', *The Translator* 14(1): 21–50.

Boffey, Julia (2000) 'Wynkyn de Worde, Richard Pynson, and the English Printing of Texts Translated from French', in Jennifer Britnell and Richard Britnell (eds) *Vernacular Literature and Current Affairs in the Sixteenth Century*, Aldershot, Hants: Ashgate Press, 171–83.

Bolden, Galina B. (2000) 'Toward Understanding Practices of Medical Interpreting: Interpreters' Involvement in History Taking', *Discourse Studies* 2(4): 387–419.

Boldiszar, Ivan (1979) *Small Countries, Great Literatures?* Budapest: Publishers & Booksellers Association.

Bolter, Jay David (1991) *Writing Space. The Computer, Hypertext, and the History of Writing*, Hove & London: Lawrence Earlbaum.

Bonn, Charles (1985) 'Entre ville et lieu, centre et periphérie: La difficile localisation du roman algérien de langue française', *Peuples Méditerranéens* 30: 185–95.

Boothby, Guy Newell (1899) *Pharos the Egyptian*, Doylestown: Wildside Press, n.d; trans. by Muhammad Lutfi Jum'ah (see Jum'ah 1906a, 1906b).

Borges, Jorge Luis (1970) 'Pierre Menard, Author of the *Quixote*', in *Labyrinths*, Harmondsworth: Penguin.

Borges, Jorge Luis (1974/2002) 'Sobre el "Vathek" de William Beckford', *Obras Completas*; qtd. in the *Oxford Dictionary of Phrase, Saying, and Quotation*, Oxford: Oxford University Press.

Bot, Hanneke (2005) *Dialogue Interpreting in Mental Health*, Amsterdam: Rodopi.

Bourdieu, Pierre (1977) 'The Economics of Linguistic Exchanges', *Social Science and Information* 16: 645–668.

Bourdieu, Pierre (1982) *Ce Que Parler Veut Dire: L'Économie des Échanges linguistiques*, Paris: Fayard.

Bourdieu, Pierre (1990) 'Les conditions sociales de la circulation internationale des idées', *Romanische Zeitschrift für Literaturgeschichte* 1(2): 1–10.

Bourdieu, Pierre (1991) *Language and Symbolic Power*, trans. Gino Raymond and Matthew Adamson, Cambridge: Polity Press.

Bourdieu, Pierre (1992) *Les Règles de l'art*, Paris: Le Seuil.

Bourdieu, Pierre (1996) *The Rules of Art*, trans. Susan Emanuel, Cambridge: Polity Press.

Bourdieu, Pierre and Luc Boltanski (1975) 'Le fétichisme de la langue', *Actes de la Recherche en Sciences Sociales* 1: 2–32.

Boyd, Brian (1990) *Vladimir Nabokov, Vol. 1: The Russian Years*, London: Chatto & Windus.

Boyden, Michael (2006) 'Language Politics, Translation, and American Literary History', *Target* 18(1): 121–37.

Boyer, Henri (1991) *Langues en Conflit: Études sociolinguistiques*, Paris: L'Harmattan.

Branchadell, Albert and Lovell Margaret West (eds) (2005) *Less Translated Languages*, Amsterdam & Philadelphia, John Benjamins.

Brantlinger, Patrick (1988) *Rule of Darkness: British Literature and Imperialism, 1830–1914*, Ithaca & London: Cornell University Press.

Braudel, Fernand (1979) *Civilisation matérielle, économie et capitalisme, Vol. III, Le Temps du monde*, Paris: Armand Colin; trans. by Sian Reynolds as *Civilization and Capitalism, 15th–18th century, Vol. 3, The Perspective of the World*, London: Collins/Fontana Press, 1984.

Briggs, Charles (1988) 'Disorderly Dialogues in Ritual Impositions of Order', *Anthropological Linguistics* 30(3–4): 448–91.

Brinkley, C. Mark (2004) 'Translators' Fears Disrupt Vital Lines of Communication', *Army Times*, 8 December.

Brisset, Annie (1997) 'La Traduction: Modele d'hybridation des cultures?', *Carrefour* 19(1): 51–69.

Brotherston, Gordon (2002) 'Tlaloc Roars. Native America, the West and Literary Translation', in Theo Hermans (ed.) *Crosscultural Transgressions. Research Models in Translation Studies II. Historical and Ideological Issues.* Manchester: St. Jerome Publishing, 165–79.

Browne, George (1859) *The History of the British and Foreign Bible Society: From Its Institution in 1804, to the Close of Jubilee in 1854*, London: British & Foreign Bible Society.

Bruce, D. (1994) 'Translating the Commune: Cultural Politics and the Historical Specificity of the Anarchist Text', *Traduction, Terminologie, Rédaction* 1: 47–76.

Buchanan, Claudius (1811) *Christian Researches in Asia: with Notices of the Translation of the Scriptures into the Oriental Languages*, London: Cadell & Davies.

Bulletin of the Office for Refugees and Displaced Persons (January 1993), Zagreb.

Burke, Seàn (1992) *The Death and Return of the Author*, Edinburgh: University Press.

Bush, Vannevar (1945) 'As We May Think', *The Atlantic Monthly* (July): 95.

Buzelin, Hélène (2005) 'Translation Studies, Ethnography and the Production of Knowledge', in Paul St-Pierre and Prufella C. Kar (eds) *In Translation: Reflections, Refractions, Transformations*, New Delhi: Pencraft International, 25–41.

Calinescu, Matei (1991) 'From the One to the Many. Pluralism in Today's Thought', in Ingeborg Hoesterey (ed.) *Zeitgeist in Babel*, Bloomington & Indianapolis: Indiana University Press, 156–74.

Calvino, Italo (1982) *If on a Winter's Night a Traveller*, trans. William Weaver, London: Picador.

Calzada Pérez, María (ed.) (2003) *Apropos of Ideology: Translation Studies on Ideology – Ideologies in Translation Studies*, Manchester: St. Jerome.

Cameron, Deborah (1995) *Verbal Hygiene*, London: Routledge.

Candido, Antonio (1995) *Littérature et sous-développement. L'endroit et l'envers*, Paris: Anne-Marie Métailié-Unesco.

Canton, William (1904–10) *A History of the British and Foreign Bible Society*, 5 vols, London: J. Murray.

Carens, J. H. (2000) *Culture, citizenship and community*, Oxford: Oxford University Press.

Carlson, David (1991a) 'Royal Tutors in the Reign of Henry VIII', *Sixteenth Century Journal* 22 (Summer): 253–79.

Carlson, David (1991b) 'Reputation and Duplicity: the Texts and Contexts of Thomas More's Epigram on Bernard André', *ELH* 58 (Summer): 261–81.

Cartellieri, Claus (1983) 'The Inescapable Dilemma: Quality and/or Quantity in Interpreting', *Babel* 29: 209–13.

Casanova, Pascale (1999/2004) *La République mondiale des lettres*, Paris: Éditions du Seuil; trans. M. B. Debevoise as *The World Republic of Letters*, Cambridge, Mass.: Harvard University Press.

Casanova, Pascale (2005) 'Literature as a World', *New Left Review* 31 (Jan-Feb): 71–90.

Casanova, Pascale (2007) 'The Ibsen Battle: A Comparative Analysis of the Introduction of Henrik Ibsen in France, England and Ireland', in C. Charle, J. Vincent and J. Winter (eds) *Anglo-French Attitudes. Comparisons and tranfers between English and French intellectuals since the eighteenth century*, Manchester & New York: Manchester University Press.

Casta, Santu (1990) *Principellu*, Ajaccio: Akenaton è Squadra di u Finusellu.

Castells, Manuel (1996) *The Rise of the Network Society*, Cambridge: Blackwell.

Castells, Manuel (1997) *The Power of Identity*, Cambridge: Blackwell.

Catford, J. C. (1965) *A Linguistic Theory of Translation: An Essay in Applied Linguistics*, London: Oxford University Press.

Cazdyn, Eric (2000) 'Representation, Reality Culture, and Global Capitalism in Japan', *South Atlantic Quarterly* 99(4): 903–27.

Cazdyn, Eric (2002) *The Flash of Capital: Film and Geopolitics in Japan*, Durham: Duke University Press.

Cerani, Daniel (1991) 'Interview: A Funtana d'Altea: Un récit de Ghjacumu Thiers', *Le Corse*, 27 July.

Chamberlain, Lori (1992) 'Gender and the Metaphorics of Translation', in Lawrence Venuti (ed.) *Rethinking Translation: Discourse, Subjectivity, Ideology*, London: Routledge, 57–74.

Champion, Timothy (2003) 'Beyond Egyptology: Egypt in 19th and 20th Century Archeology and Anthropology', in Peter Ucko and Timothy Champion (eds) *The Wisdom of Egypt: Changing Visions Through the Ages*, London: UCL Press, 161–85.

Chartier, Roger and Henri-Jean Martin (eds) (1982–86) *Histoire de l'édition française*, Paris: Promodis.

Chatman, Seymour (1978) *Story and Discourse: Narrative Structure in Fiction and Film*, Ithaca-London: Cornell University Press.

Chatman, Seymour (1990) *Coming to Terms: The Rhetoric of Narrative in Fiction and Film*, Ithaca-London: Cornell University Press.

Chesterman, Andrew (1997) *Memes of Translation The Spread of Ideas in Translation Theory*, Amsterdam: John Benjamins.

Chesterman, Andrew (ed.) (1989) *Readings in Translation Theory*, Helsinki: Oy Finn Lectura Ab.

Chesterman, Andrew and Emma Wagner (2002) *Can Theory Help Translators?*, Manchester: St. Jerome.

Cheung, Martha (2005) ' "To Translate" Means "To Exchange"? A New Interpretation of the Earliest Chinese Attempts to Define Translation ("Fanyi")', *Target* 17(1): 27–48.

Childers, Joseph and Gary Hentzi (1995) *The Columbia Dictionary of Modern Literary and Cultural Criticism*, New York: Columbia University Press.

Chow, Rey (1995) *Primitive Passions: Visuality, Sexuality, Ethnography and Contemporary Chinese Cinema*, New York: Columbia University Press.

Cicourel, Aaron V. (1983) 'Language and the structure of belief in medical communication', in Sue Fisher and Alexandra Todd (eds) *The Social Organization of Doctor-Patient Communication*, Washington, DC: Center for Applied Linguistics, 221–40.

Clark, Herbert H. (1992) *Arenas of Language Use*, Chicago: University of Chicago Press/Center for the Study of Language and Information.

Clark, Herbert H. (1996) *Using Language*, Cambridge: Cambridge University Press.

Clifford, J. and G. E. Marcus (eds) (1986) *Writing Culture: The Poetics and Politics of Ethnography*, Berkeley: University of California Press.

Coates, Jennifer (1999) 'Changing Horses: Nabakov and Translation', in Jean Boase-Beier and Michael Holman (eds) *The Practices of Literary Translation: Constraints and Creativity*, Manchester: St. Jerome, 91–108.

Cockerill, Hiroko (2006) *Style and Narrative in Translation: The Contribution of Futabatei Shimei*, Manchester: St. Jerome.

Cohen, Philip and David H. Jackson (1991) 'Notes on Emerging Paradigms in Editorial Theory', in Philip Cohen (ed.) *Devils and Angels: Textual Editing and Literary Theory*, Charlottesville: University Press of Virginia, 103–23.

Coldiron, A. E. B. (2000) 'Translation and Periodization', in *Canon, Period, and the Poetry of Charles of Orleans: Found in Translation*, Ann Arbor: University of Michigan Press, 145–90.

Coldiron, A. E. B. (2001) 'Toward a Comparative New Historicism: Land Tenures and Some Fifteenth-Century Poems', *Comparative Literature* 53(2): 97–116.

Coldiron, A. E. B. (2004) 'A Survey of Verse Translation from French Printed Between Caxton and Tottel', in Ian Frederick Moulton (ed.) *Reading and Literacy in the Middle Ages and Renaissance*, Arizona Studies in Medieval and Renaissance Literature, Vol. 8, Turnhout: Brepols, 63–84.

Cole, P. (2000) Philosophies of Exclusion: Liberal Political Theory and Immigration, Edinburgh: Edinburgh University Press.

Colla, Elliot (2000) *Hooked on Pharaonics: Literature and the Appropriation of Ancient Egypt*, Unpublished PhD Dissertation, University of California, Berkeley.

Conley, J. and W. O'Barr (1998) *Just Words: Law, Language, and Power*, Chicago: University of Chicago Press.

Copland, Robert (1993) *Robert Copland, Poems*, edited by Mary C. Erler, Toronto: University of Toronto Press.

Corbett, John (1998) *Written in the Language of the Scottish Nation: A History of Literary Translation into Scots*, Clevedon: Multilingual Matters.

Coulmas, Florian (ed.) (1997) *The Handbook of Sociolinguistics*, Oxford: Blackwell.

Coutts, Angela (2002) 'The Gendering of Japanese Literature: The Influence of English-Language Translation on Concepts of Canon in the West', *Japan Forum* 14(1): 103–25.

Crick, Joyce (1989) 'Misreading Freud', *Times Higher Education Supplement*, 15 September.

Crick, Malcolm (1976a) *Towards a Semantic Anthropology: Explorations in Language and Meaning*, London: Malaby.

Crick, Malcolm (1976b) *Explorations in Language and Meaning*, London: Malaby.

Crisp, J. (2003) 'Refugees and the Global Politics of Asylum', in Sarah Spencer (ed.) *The Politics of Migration*, Oxford: Blackwell Publishing, 75–87.

Cronin, Michael (1995) 'Altered States: Translation and Minority Languages', TTR 8(1): 85–103.

Cronin, Michael (1996) *Translating Ireland: Translation, Languages, Cultures*, Cork: Cork University Press.

Cronin, Michael (2000a) 'History, Translation, Postcolonialism', in Sherry Simon and Paul St-Pierre (eds) *Changing the Terms: Translating in the Postcolonial Era*, Ottawa: University of Ottawa Press, 33–52.

Cronin, Michael (2000b) *Across the Lines: Travel, Language, Translation*, Cork: Cork University Press.

Cronin, Michael (2002) 'The Empire Talks Back: Orality, Heteronomy and the Cultural Turn in Interpreting Studies', in Edwin Gentzler and Maria Tymoczko (eds) *Translation and Power*, Boston & Amherst: University of Massachussets Press, 45–62.

Cronin, Michael (2003) *Translation and Globalisation*, London: Routledge.

Cronin, Michael (2008) 'Minority', in Mona Baker and Gabriela Saldanha (eds) *Routledge Encyclopedia of Translation Studies*, 2nd edn, London & New York: Routledge, 169–72.

Crowley, Tony (1996) *Language and History: Theories and Texts*, New York: Routledge.

Crystal, David (2001) *Language and the Internet*, Cambridge: Cambridge University Press.

Cunico, Sonia and Jeremy Munday (eds) (2007) *Translation and Ideology. Encounters and Clashes*, special issue of *The Translator* 13(2).

Cunningham, David and Barb Browning (2004) 'The Emergence of Worthy Targets: Official Frames and Deviance Narratives within the FBI', *Sociological Forum* 19(3): 347–69.

Curien, Annie (2001) 'Regards d'écrivains chinois contemporains sur la littérature française du XXe siècle', in Muriel Détrie (ed.) *France-Asie – Un siècle d'échanges littéraires*, Paris: You Feng, 275–84.

Curwen, Peter (1986) *The World Book Industry*, London: Euromonitor Publications.

Daireaux, Max (1930) *Littérature hispano-américaine*, Paris: Kra.

Daly, Nicholas (1999) *Modernism, Romance and the Fin de Siècle: Popular Fiction and British Culture 1880–1914*, Cambridge: Cambridge University Press.

Damrosch, David (2005) 'Death in Translation', in Sandra Bermann and Michael Wood (eds) *Nation, Language, and the Ethics of Translation*, Princeton & Oxford: Princeton University Press, 380–98.

Dan Shen and Xiaoyi Zhou (2006) 'Western Literary Theories in China: Reception, Influence and Resistance', *Comparative Critical Studies* 3(1–2): 139–55.

Daniel, V. (1996) *Charred Lullabies: Chapters in an Anthropology of Violence*, Princeton: Princeton University Press.

Daniel, V. and J. Knudsen (eds) (1995) *Mistrusting Refugees*, Berkeley: University of California Press.

David, Rand A. and Michelle Rhee (1998) 'The Impact of Language as a Barrier to Effective Health Care in an Underserved Urban Hispanic Community', *The Mount Sinai Journal of Medicine* 65: 393–97.

Davidson, Brad (1998) *Interpreting Medical Discourse: A Study of Cross-linguistic Communication in the Hospital Clinic*, PhD Dissertation, Department of Linguistics, Stanford University.

Davidson, Brad (1999) 'Dialogue in Cross-linguistic Medical Interviews: The Interpretation of Interpretive Discourse', *Proceedings from the Sixth Annual Symposium on Language and Society*, Austin.

Davidson, B. (2000) 'The Interpreter as Institutional Gatekeeper', *Journal of Sociolinguistics* 4(3): 379–405.

Davis, Kathleen (2001) *Deconstruction and Translation*, Manchester: St. Jerome Publishing.

Dedalus (1998) 'Diary', *The Sunday Times*, 15 March.

De Landa, Manuel (1997) *A Thousand Years of Nonlinear History*, New York: Zone Books.

Deleuze, Gilles and Félix Guattari (1975) *Kafka: Pour une littérature mineure*, Paris: Minuit.

Delisle, Jean and Judith Woodsworth (eds) (1995) *Translators Through History*, Amsterdam & Philadelphia: John Benjamins.

de Man, Paul (1986) 'Conclusions: Walter Benjamin's "The Task of the Translator" ', in *The Resistance to Theory*, Minneapolis: University of Minnesota Press, 73–105.

Derrida, Jacques (1967) *La Voix et le Phénomène*, Paris: Presses Universitaires de France.

Derrida, Jacques (1972) *Positions*, Paris: Minuit.

Derrida, Jacques (1976) *Of Grammatology*, trans. Gayatri Spivak, Baltimore: Johns Hopkins University Press.

Derrida, Jacques (1978) *Edmund Husserl's 'Origin of Geometry': An Introduction*, trans. John P. Leavey, Jr, Stony Brook, New York: Harvester.

Derrida, Jacques (1979) 'Living On/Borderlines', trans. James Hulbert, in *Deconstruction and Criticism*, New York: Continuum, 75–176.

Derrida, Jacques (1981) *Dissemination*, trans. Barbara Johnson, London: Athlone.

Derrida, Jacques (1982a) 'Différance', in *Margins of Philosophy*, trans. Alan Bass, Hemel Hempstead: Harvester Wheatsheaf, 1–27.

Derrida, Jacques (1982b/1985) *The Ear of the Other. Otobiography, Transference, Translation*, trans. Peggy Kamuf, Lincoln & London: University of Nebraska Press.

Derrida, Jacques (1985) 'Des Tours de Babel', trans. Joseph Graham, in Joseph Graham (ed.) *Difference in Translation*, Ithaca & London: Cornell University Press, 165–248; French original in Appendix to same volume, 209–248.

Derrida, Jacques (1986a) *Mémoires for Paul de Man*, New York: Columbia University Press.

Derrida, Jacques (1986b) *Glas*, trans. John P. Leavey, Jr and Richard Rand, Lincoln: University of Nebraska Press.

Derrida, Jacques (1991) *Between the Blinds: A Derrida Reader*, Peggy Kamuf (ed.), New York: Harvester Wheatsheaf.

Derrida, Jacques (1992) *Acts of Literature*, Derek Attridge (ed.), New York & London: Routledge.

Derrida, Jacque and Pierre-Jean Labarrière (1986) *Altérités*, Paris: Osiris.

Descartes, René (1968) *Discourse on Method and the Meditations*, trans. F.E. Sutcliffe, Harmonds-worth: Penguin.

de Swaan, Abram (1993) 'The Emergent World Language System', *International Political Science Review* 14(3): 219–26.

de Swaan, Abram (1995) 'The Sociological Study of the Transnational Society', Amsterdam School for Social Science Research, Papers in Progress, No. 46.

de Swaan, Abram (2001) *Words of the World: The Global Language System*, Cambridge: Polity Press.

de Waard, Jan and Eugene A. Nida (1986) *From One Language to Another: Functional Equivalence in Bible Translating*, Nashville: Thomas Nelson.

Dibb, Ashton (1873) 'The Tamil Book and its Story', *The Church Missionary Intelligencer: A Monthly Journal of Missionary Information*, New Series 9: 111–23.

Dibbell, Julian (2000) 'After Babelfish', FEED (July 26), available at <http://www.juliandibbell.com/texts/feed_babelfish.html>.

DiGiacomo, Susan M. (1999) 'Language Ideological Debates in an Olympic City: Barcelona 1992–1996', in Jan Blommaert (ed.) *Language Ideological Debates*, Berlin & New York: Mouton de Gruyter, 105–42.

van Dijk, Teun A. (1993) 'Principles of Critical Discourse Analysis', *Discourse and Society* 4: 249–85.

Diriker, Ebru (2003/2005) 'Presenting Simultaneous Interpreting: Discourse of the Turk-ish Media, 1988–2003', originally published in *The Interpreter's Newsletter*; revised version published in *Communicate*, the webzine of AIIC. (Available online: http://www.aiic.net/ViewPage.cfm/page1742.htm).

Diriker, Ebru (2004) *De-/Re-Contextualizing Conference Interpreting: Interpreters in the Ivory Tower?*, Amsterdam & Philadelphia: John Benjamins.

Dirkx, Paul (1995) 'Paris and Amsterdam as Translational Go-Betweens: The Evolution of Literary Translation in Belgium after World War II', in Peter Jansen and Clem Robyns (eds) *Selected Papers of the CERA Research Seminars in Translation Studies*, Leuven: CETRA, 9–24.

Dodson, Michael S. (2005) 'Translating Science, Translating Empire: The Power of Language in Colonial North India', *Society for Comparative Study of Society and History*, 809–35.

Donnelly, J. (2003) *Universal human rights in theory and practice*, 2nd edn, Ithaca, NY: Cornell University Press.

Douglas, Mary (1966) *Purity and Danger*, London: Routledge & Kegan Paul.

Doyle, M. W. (1997) *Ways of War and Peace: Realism, Liberalism and Socialism*, New York: Norton.

D'Souza, Dinesh (1995) *The End of Racism: Principles for a Multiracial Society*, New York: Free Press.

Dudley, C.S. (1821) *An Analysis of the System of the Bible Society, throughout its Various Parts: Including a Sketch of the Origin and Results of Auxiliary and Branch Societies and Bible Associations: With Hints for Their Better Regulation*, London: R. Watts.

Dummett, M. (1981) 'Objections to Chomsky', *London Review of Books* (September 3–16): 5–6.

Dutrait, Noël (2001) 'L'irrésistible poids du réel dans la fiction chinoise contemporaine', in Annie Curien and Jin Siyan (eds) *Littérature chinoise – Le passé et l'écriture contemporaine*, Paris : Maison des sciences de l'homme, 35–44.

Eagleton, Terry (1983) *Literary Theory*, Oxford: Oxford University Press.

Ebden, Philip, Arvind Bhatt, Oliver J. Carey and Brian Harrison (1988) 'The bilingual consultation', *The Lancet* 1988: 347.

Edwards, Alicia Betsey (1995) *The Practice of Court Interpreting*, Amsterdam: John Benjamins.

Eichenbaum, Boris (1965) 'La théorie de la "méthode formelle" ', *Théorie de la littérature – Textes des formalistes russes réunis, présentés et traduits par Tzvetan Todorov*, Paris: Le Seuil.

Eichenbaum, Boris (2001) 'The Theory of Formal Method', in Vincent B. Leitch (ed.) *The Norton Anthology of Theory and Criticism*, New York & London: Norton.

Elliot, Carl (1999) *A Philosophical Disease: Bioethics, Culture, and Identity*, New York: Routledge.

Erzinger, Sharry (1991) 'Communication between Spanish-speaking Patients and their Doctors in Medical Encounters', *Culture, Medicine, and Psychiatry* 15: 91–110.

Evans, Frank (1939) 'How the Film Can Help Democracy', *Evening Chronicle* (Newcastle upon Tyne), 12 May.

Evans-Pritchard, Edward E. (1956) *Nuer Religion*, Oxford: Clarendon Press.

Even-Zohar, Itamar (1978) 'The Position of Translated Literature within the Literary Polysystem', in James Holmes, Jose Lambert and Raymond Van den Broeck (eds) *Literature and Translation: New Perspectives in Literary Studies*, Leuven: Acco, 117–27.

Even-Zohar, Itamar (1990) *Polysystem Studies*, Tel Aviv: The Porter Institute for Poetics and Semiotics, and Durham: Duke University Press. Special issue of *Poetics Today*, 11(1).

Ewers, Andy (1995) *The European Internet: An Update*, London: British Library Research and Development Department, 1995.

Fagan, Brian (2004) *The Rape of the Nile: Tomb Robbers, Tourists and Archeologists in Egypt*, Boulder: Westview Press.

Fairclough, Norman (1995) *Critical Discourse Analysis: the Critical Study of Language*, London: Longman.

Fawcett, Peter (1997) 'Macerated Malraux: A Study of *La Voile royale* in Translation', in Karl Simms (ed.) *Translating Sensitive Texts: Linguistic Aspects*, Amsterdam & Atlanta: Rodopi, 247–65.

Felman, Shoshana and Dori Laub (1992) *Testimony. Crisis of Witnessing in Literature, Psychoanalysis and History*, New York & London: Routledge.

Ferguson, Margaret (1984) ' "The Afflatus of Ruin": Meditations on Rome by Du Bellay, Spenser, and Stevens', in Annabel Patterson (ed.) *Roman Images*, Baltimore: Johns Hopkins University Press, 23–50.

Findlay, Bill (2004) *Frae Ither Tongues: Essays on Modern Translations into Scots*, Clevedon: Multilingual Matters.

Firth, Raymond (1966) 'Twins, Birds and Vegetables', *Man* 1: 1–17.

Fisher, Walter R. (1987) *Human Communication as Narration: Toward a Philosophy of Reason, Value, and Action*, Columbia, South Carolina: University of South Carolina Press. Reprinted 1989.

Folkart, Barbara (1991) *Le conflit des énonciations: Traduction et discours rapporté*, Candiac: Les Éditions Balzac.

Forsythe, D. P. (2000) *Human Rights in International Relations*, Cambridge: Cambridge University Press.

Foucault, Michel (1963/1973) *The Birth of the Clinic: An Archaeology of Medical Perception*, New York: Vintage Books.

Foucault, Michel (1971) L'Ordre du discourse, Paris: Gallimard.

Foucault, Michel (1972a/1981) 'The Order of Discourse', in R. Young (ed.) Untying the Text: A Post-Structuralist Reader, London & New York: Routledge & Kegan, 108–38.

Foucault, Michel (1972b) 'The Discourse on Language', in The Archeology of Knowledge, trans. A. M. Sheridan Smith, New York: Pantheon Books.

Foucault, Michel (1979) The History of Sexuality, Vol. 1, London: Allen Lane.

Foucault, Michel (1986) 'What is an Author', trans. V. Harari Josu, in Paul Rabinow (ed.) The Foucault Reader, London: Penguin, 101–20.

Fowler, Roger (1991) 'Critical Linguistics', in Kirsten Malmkjær (ed.) The Linguistics Encyclopedia, London & New York: Routledge, 89–93.

Franchi, Jean Joseph (1989a) Knock, Ajaccio: Editions La Marge.

Franchi, Jean Joseph (1989b) 'Editorial: Lingua Corsa', Kyrn 210: 45.

Frankel, Richard (1990) 'Talking in Interviews: A Dispreference for Patient-initiated Questions in Physician-patient Encounters', in George Psathas (ed.) Interaction Competence, Lanham, Maryland: University Press of America, 231–62.

Frere, John Hookman (1820) 'Review of Thomas Mitchell's translation of The Comedies of Aristophanes', Quarterly Review 23 (July): 474–505.

Freud, Sigmund (1960) The Psychopathology of Everyday Life, trans. Alan Tyson, James Strachey (ed.), New York: Norton.

Freud, Sigmund (1961) Beyond the Pleasure Principle, trans. James Strachey, New York: Norton.

Friedman, Susan Stanford (2006) 'Periodizing Modernism: Postcolonial Modernities and the Space/Time Borders of Modernist Studies', Modernism/Modernity 13(3): 425–443.

Furet, François (1995) Le passé d'une illusion. Essai sur l'idée communiste au XXè siècle, Paris: Robert Laffont/Calmann-Lévy.

Fusina, Jacques (1989a) 'Preface to U Stringagliulu di Sigolu, by Lisandrina Grimaldi', Bastia: Scola Corsa.

Fusina, Jacques (1989b) 'Editorial: Lingua Corsa', Kyrn 203.

Futabatei Shimei (1971) Futabatei Shimei shû, edited by Hata Yūzō and Yasui Ryōhei, Nihon kindai bungaku taikei 4, Tokyo: Kadokawa shoten.

Futabatei Shimei (1984–1993) Futabatei Shimei zenshû, 8 vols, Tokyo: Chikuma shobô.

Gal, Susan (1989) 'Language and Political Economy', Annual Review of Anthropology 18: 345–67.

Ganahl, Rainer (2001) 'Free Markets: Language, Commodification, and Art', Public Culture 31(1): 23–38.

Ganne, Valérie and Marc Minon (1992) 'Géographie de la traduction', in F. Barret-Ducrocq (ed.) Traduire l'Europe, Paris : Payot, 55–95.

Garavini, Fausta (1988) 'Quelle langue pour la prose d'oc contemporaine?', Lengas 24: 33–88.

Geary, James (1997) 'Speaking in Tongues', Time, 7 July, 38–44.

Geddes, A. and A. Favell (eds) (1999) The Politics of Belonging: Migrants and Minorities in Contemporary Europe, Aldershot: Ashgate.

Gee, James Paul (1990) Social Linguistics and Literacies: Ideology in Discourses, London: Falmer Press.

Gellner, Ernest (1959) Words and Things, London: Gollancz.

Gellner, Ernest (1969) Saints of the Atlas, London: Weidenfeld and Nicolson.

Gellner, Ernest (1970) 'Concepts and Society', in B. R. Wilson (ed.) Rationality, Oxford: Basil Blackwell, 18–49.

Genette, Gérard (1983) Nouveau discours du récit, Paris: Seuil.

Genette, Gérard (1991) Fiction et diction, Paris: Seuil.

Gentile, L. (2002) 'New Asylum Regimes or a World without Asylum? The Myth of International Protection', in Danièle Joly (ed.) Global Changes in Asylum Regimes, Houndmills, Basingstoke: Palgrave Macmillan, 38–47.

Gentzler, Edwin (1993) *Contemporary Translation Theories*, London: Routledge.

Gentzler, Edwin (1996) 'Translation, Counter-Culture and *The Fifties* in the USA', in Román Álvarez and M. Carmen-África Vidal (eds) *Translation, Power, Subversion*, Clevedon: Multilingual Matters, 116–37.

Gentzler, Edwin (2002) 'Translation, Poststructuralism, and Power', in Maria Tymoczko and Edwin Gentzler (eds) *Translation and Power*, Amherst and Boston: University of Massachusetts Press, 195–218.

Gentzler, Edwin and Maria Tymoczko (eds) (2002) *Translation and Power*, Amherst, Mass.: University of Massachusetts Press.

Gerow, Aaran (1994) 'The Benshi's New Face: Defining Cinema in Taisho Japan', *Iconics* 3: 69–86.

Ghawaji, Wahby Sulaiman (1982) *Al-mar'a al-muslima*, Beirut: Mu'assassat al-Risala.

Gibb, H.A.R. (1982) *Studies on the Civilization of Islam*, Stanford J. Shaw and William R. Polk (eds), New Jersey: Princeton University Press.

Giddens, Anthony (1979) *Central Problems in Social Theory: Action, Structure, and Contradiction in Social Analysis*, Berkeley & Los Angeles: University of California Press.

Gill, Louise (1997) 'William Caxton and the Rebellion of 1483', *English Historical Review* (February): 105–18.

Ginsberg, C., V. Martin, Dennis Andrulis, Yoku Shaw-Taylor and C. McGregor (1995) *Interpretation and Translation Services in Health Care: A Survey of U.S. Public and Private Teaching Hospitals*, Washington, DC: National Public Health and Hospital Institute.

Gladwell, Malcolm (2000) *The Tipping Point: How Little Things Can Make a Big Difference*, Boston: Little Brown.

Glass, Charles (2006) 'Cyber-Jihad', *London Review of Books* 28(5): 14–18.

Glionna, John M. and Ashraf Khalil (2005) ' "Combat Linguists" Battle on Two Fronts', *Los Angeles Times*, 5 June.

Gluckman, Max (1973) 'The State of Anthropology', *Times Literary Supplement* 3 August: 905.

Gobard, Henri (1976) *L'Aliénation linguistique*, Paris: Flammarion.

Godard, Barbara (1990) 'Theorizing Feminist Discourse/Translation', in Susan Bassnett & André Lefevere (eds) *Translation, History and Culture*, London & New York: Pinter Publishers, 87–96.

Godard, Barbara (1991) 'Preface', *Picture Theory*, by Nicole Brossard, trans. Barbara Goddard, Montreal: Guernica, 7–11.

Goethe, Johann Wolfgang von (1819) 'Übersetzungen', *Noten und Abhandlungen zu besserem Verständnis des West-östlichen Divans*, Vol. 2 of *Werke*, Hamburger Ausgabe.

Goffman, Erving (1974/1986) *Frame Analysis: An Essay on the Organization of Experience*, Boston: Northeastern University Press.

Goffman, Erving (1981) *Forms of Talk*, Philadelphia: University of Pennsylvania Press, 124–59.

Gombrowicz, Witold (1968) *Journal Paris-Berlin – 1963–1964*, Vol. 3a, trans. A. Kosko, Paris: Christian Bourgois.

Gonda Yasunosuke (1931) *Minshūgorakuron* (On Popular Entertainment), Tokyo: Ganshōdō Shoten.

Goodwin, M.J. (1990) *He-Said-She-Said: Talk as Social Organization Among Black Children*, Bloomington: Indiana University Press.

Gordon, Neve (2002) 'Zionism, Translation and the Politics of Erasure', *Political Studies* 50: 811–28.

Graeber, Wilhelm (1991) 'German Translators of English Fiction and Their French Mediators', in Harald Kittel and Armin Paul Frank (eds) *Interculturality and the Historical Study of Literary Translators*, Berlin: Erich Schmidt Verlag, 5–16.

Grafton, Anthony (1998) 'The Revival of Antiquity: A Fan's Notes and Recent Work', *American Historical Review* 103(1): 118–21.

Greenfield, William (1830) *A Defence of the Serampore Mahratta Version of the New Testament in Reply to The Animadversions of an Anonymous Writer in The Asiatic Journal for September 1829*, London: printed for Samuel Bagster.

Greetham, D.C. (1991) 'The Manifestation and Accommodation of Theory in Textual Editing', in Philip Cohen (ed.) *Devils and Angels. Textual Editing and Literary Theory*, Charlottesville: University Press of Virginia, 78–102.

Gregory, Derek (2004) 'Scripting Egypt: Orientalism and the Cultures of Travel', in James Duncan and Derek Gregory (eds) *Writes of Passage: Reading Travel Writing*, London: Routledge, 114–49.

Gregory, Lady Augusta (1910) *The Kiltartan Molière*, Dublin: Maunsel.

Gregory, Lady Augusta (1928) *Three Last Plays*, London & New York: Putnam.

Greimas, A. J. (1982) *Semiotics and Language: An Analytical Dictionary*, Bloomington: Indiana University Press.

Grillo, Ralph D. (1989) 'Dominant Languages: Language and Hierarchy in Britain and France', Cambridge: Cambridge University Press.

Grimaldi, Lisandrina (1989) *U Stringagliulu di Sigolu*, Bastia: Scola Corsa.

Grogan, Tom (1997) 'Role of the Internet in the Implementation of a Global Localisation Process', *Localisation Resources Centre Yearbook*, Dublin: University College Dublin, 51–59.

Guerin, Wilfred (1992) *A Handbook of Critical Approaches to Literature*, New York: Oxford University Press.

Gulliford, Rev. H. (1898) 'Bible Revision with Special Reference to Tamil. A Symposium', *The Harvest Field* 9 (Mysore: Wesleyan Press): 361–71, 440–56.

Gupta, Akhil (1990) 'Translation and the Politics of Writing', Unpublished Paper, American Anthropological Association Annual Meeting, New Orleans.

Gupta, Akhil and James Ferguson (eds) (1997) *Culture Power Place: Explorations in Critical Anthropology*, Durham: Duke University Press.

Gutt, Ernest-A. (2000) *Translation and Relevance: Cognition and Context*, Manchester: St. Jerome.

Gwegen, Jorj (1975) *La langue bretonne face à ses oppresseurs*, Quimper: Nature et Bretagne.

Haffner, Linda (1992) 'Translation is Not Enough: Interpreting in a Medical Setting', in *Cross Cultural Medicine – A Decade Later*, Special Issue of *The Western Journal of Medicine* 157: 255–59.

Haggard, Rider (1887) *She*, London: Longmans, Green.

Haggard, Rider (1981) 'The Trade in the Dead', in *The Best Short Stories of Rider Haggard*, London: Michael Joseph, 141–47.

Hale, Sandra (2004) *The Discourse of Court Interpreting: Discourse Practices of the Law, the Witness and the Interpreter*, Amsterdam: John Benjamins.

Hale, Terry (2008) 'Publishing Strategies', in Mona Baker and Gabriela Saldanha (eds) *Routledge Encyclopedia of Translation Studies*, 2nd edn, London & New York: Routledge, 217–22.

Hall, E.T. (1997) 'The Local and the Global: Globalization and Ethnicity', in A. D. King (ed.) *Culture, Globalization, and the World-System: Contemporary Conditions for the Representation of Identity*, Minneapolis: University of Minneapolis Press.

Hall, John R., Mary Jo Neitz and Marshall Battani (2003) *Sociology on Culture*, London & New York: Routledge.

Halliday, Michael (1978) *Language as Social Semiotic*, London: Edward Arnold.

Halliday, Michael and Ruqaiya Hasan (1976) *Cohesion in English*, London: Longman.

Hamelink, Cees J. (1994) *Trends in World Communication*, Penang: Southbound and Third World Network.

Handler, Richard (1988) *Nationalism and the Politics of Culture in Quebec*, Madison: University of Wisconsin Press.

Hannerz, Ulf (1992) *Cultural Complexity: Studies in the Social Organization of Meaning*, New York: Columbia University Press.

Hannerz, Ulf (1996) *Transnational Connections*, London: Routledge.

Hannerz, Ulf (1997) 'Scenarios for Peripheral Cultures', in Anthony D. King (ed.) *Culture, Globalization, and the World-System: Contemporary Conditions for the Representation of Identity*, Minneapolis: University of Minneapolis Press, 107–28.

Hardwick, Lorna (2001) 'Who Owns the Plays? Issues in the Translation and Performance of Greek Drama on the Modern Stage', *Eirene* 37: 23–39.

Harris, Brian (1990) 'Norms in Interpretation', *Target* 2(1): 115–119.

Harrison, Harry and Marvin Minsky (1993) *The Turing Option*, London: ROC.

Hartley, Tony (2009) 'Technology and Translation', in Jeremy Munday (ed.) *The Routledge Companion to Translation Studies*, London & New York: Routledge, 106–27.

Harvey, David (1989) *The Condition of Postmodernity*, Oxford: Blackwell.

Harvey, Keith (1998) 'Translating Camp Talk. Gay Identities and Cultural Transfer', *The Translator* 4(2): 295–320.

Harvey, Keith (2003a) *Intercultural Movements. American Gay in French Translation*, Manchester: St. Jerome.

Harvey, Keith (2003b) ' "Events" and "Horizons": Reading Ideology in the "Bindings" of Translations', in María Calzada Pérez (ed) *Apropos of Ideology – Translation Studies on Ideology – Ideologies in Translation Studies*, Manchester: St. Jerome Publishing, 43–69.

Hasanayn, Ahmad Tahir (1983) *Dawr al-shamiyyin al-muhajirin ila misr fil-nahdah al-adabiyyah al-hadithah* [The Role of Syrian Immigrés in the Modern Literary Nahdah in Egypt], Damascus: Dar al-Wathbah.

Hatem, Mervat (1988) 'Feminist Analysis and the Subjection World of Women', *AMEWS NEWS* (Association of Middle East Women's Studies) 2(6): 7–9.

Hatim, Basil (1991) 'The Pragmatics of Argumentation in Arabic: The Rise and Fall of a Text Type', *Text* 11(2): 189–99.

Hatim, Basil (1997) *Communication across Cultures: Translation Theory and Contrastive Text Linguistics*, Exeter: University of Exeter Press.

Hatim, Basil (2001) *Teaching and Researching Translation*, London: Longman.

Hatim, Basil and Ian Mason (1990) *Discourse and the Translator*, London: Longman.

Hatim, Basil and Ian Mason (1991) 'Coping with Ideology in Professional Translating', *Interface: Journal of Applied Linguistics* 6(1): 23–32.

Hatim, Basil and Ian Mason (1997) *The Translator as Communicator*, London & New York: Routledge.

Hedayat, Sadegh (1953) *La Chouette aveugle*, trans. R. Lescot, Paris: José Corti.

Heilbron, Johan (1995) 'Nederlandse vertalingen wereldwijd', in Johan Heilbron, Wouter de Nooy and Wilma Tichelaar (eds) *Waarin een klein land*, Amsterdam: Prometheus, 206–52.

Heilbron, Johan and Gisèle Sapiro (2007) 'Outline for a Sociology of Translation: Current Issues and Future Prospects', in Michaela Wolf and Alexandra Fukari (eds) *Constructing a Sociology of Translation*, Amsterdam & Philadelphia: John Benjamins, 93–107.

Hein, Norbert and Ruth Wodak (1987) 'Medical Interviews in Internal Medicine: Some Results of an Empirical Investigation', *Text* 7: 37–65.

Heinich, Nathalie (1984) 'Les traducteurs littéraires: l'art et la profession', *Revue française de sociologie* 25: 264–80.

Held, D. (2002) 'Law of States, Law of Peoples', *Legal Theory* 8: 1–44.

Held, D., A. McGrew, D. Goldblatt and J. Perraton (1999) *Global Transformations*, Cambridge: Polity Press.

Helgerson, Richard (1992) *Forms of Nationhood: The Elizabethan Writing of England*, Chicago: University of Chicago Press.

Henisz-Dostert, Bozena, R. Ross Macdonald and Michael Zarechnak (1979) *Machine Translation*, The Hague: Mouton Publishers.

Hermans, Theo (1985a) 'Introduction: Translation Studies and a New Paradigm', in Theo Hermans (ed.) *The Manipulation of Literature*, London: Croom Helm, 7–15.

Hermans, Theo (ed.) (1985b) *The Manipulation of Literature*, London: Croom Helm.

Hermans, Theo (1999) *Translation in Systems. Descriptive and System-oriented Approaches Explained*, Manchester: St. Jerome Publishing.

Hermans, Theo (2000) 'Self-reference, Self-reflection and Re-entering Translation', in D. de Geest, O. de Graef, D. Delabastita, K. Geldof, R. Ghesquiere and J. Lambert (eds) *Links for the Site of Literary Theory: Essays in Honour of Hendrik van Gorp*, Leuven: Leuven University Press.

Hermans, Theo (2007) *The Conference of the Tongues*, Manchester: St. Jerome.

Hewitt, William E. (1995) *Court Interpretation*, Williamsburg, Virginia: National Center for State Courts.

Hill, J. and J. Irvine (eds) (1992) *Responsibility and Evidence in Oral Discourse*, Cambridge: Cambridge University Press.

Hirsch, S. (1998) *Pronouncing and Persevering: Gender and the Discourse of Disputing in an African Islamic Court*, Chicago: University of Chicago Press.

Hobsbawm, Eric J. (1990) *Nations and Nationalism since 1780: Programme, Myth, Reality*, New York: Cambridge University Press.

Hodkinson, Stuart and Julie Boéri (2004) 'Social Forums after London: The Politics of Language', *Red Pepper*, http://www.redpepper.org.uk/article267.html, consulted 29 April 2008.

Hoesterey, Ingeborg (ed.) (1991) 'Introduction', *Zeitgeist in Babel*, Bloomington & Indianapolis: Indiana University Press.

Hoey, Michael (2005) *Lexical Priming: A New Theory of Words and Language*, London and New York: Routledge.

Hoffman, Eva (1989) *Lost in Translation*, New York: Penguin.

Hollander, J. (1959) 'Versions, Interpretations and Performances', in R. A. Bower (ed.) *On Translation*, Cambridge, Mass.: Harvard University Press, 205–31.

Holmes, James S. (1988) *Translated! Papers on Literary Translation and Translation Studies*, Amsterdam: Rodopi.

Holmes, James S. (1994) *Translated! Papers on Literary Translation and Translation Studies* (2nd edn), Amsterdam: Rodopi.

Holmes, James, José Lambert and Raymond Van den Broeck (eds) (1978) *Literature and Translation, New Perspectives in Literary Studies*, Louvain: Acco.

Homel, David and Sherry Simon (eds) (1988) *Mapping Literature: The Arts and Politics of Translation*, Montreal: Vehicule Press.

Hooker, Joan Fillmore (1983) *T. S. Eliot Poems in French Translation. Pierre Leyris and Others*, Ann Arbor: University of Michigan Press.

Hooper, J.M.S. (ed.) (1957) *Greek New Testament Terms in Indian Languages (A Comparative Word List)*, Bangalore: The Bible Society of India & Ceylon.

House, Juliane (2006) 'Text and Context in Translation', *Journal of Pragmatics* 38(3): 338–58.

Howe, Irving (1999) *Le Monde de nos Pères*, trans. C. Bloc-Rodot and H. Michaud, Paris: Michalon.

Humboldt, Wilhelm (1992) 'From Introduction to His Translation of *Agamemnon*', trans. Sharon Sloan, in Rainer Schulte and John Biguenet (eds) *Theories of Translation*, Chicago & London: The University of Chicago Press, 55–59.

Humboldt, Wilhelm (2000) *Sur la traduction. Partie centrale de l'Introduction à l'Agamemnon*, trans. D. Thouard, Paris: Le Seuil.

Huntington, Samuel (1993) 'The Clash of Civilizations', *Foreign Affairs* 72(3): 22–49.

Huntington, Samuel (1996) *The Clash of Civilizations and the Remaking of World Order*, New York: Touchstone.

Huntington, Samuel (1998) *Sidam Al Hadarat wa I'adat Son' Al-Nizam Al 'Alami* (The Clash of Civilizations and the Remaking of World Order), trans. Tal'at Al-Shayib, Cairo: Sutur.

Huntington, Samuel (1999) *Sidam Al Hadarat wa I'adat Bina' Al-Nizam Al 'Alami* (The Clash of Civilizations and the Rebuilding of World Order), trans. Malik Obeid Abu Shuhaya and Mahmoud Mohammed Khalaf, Benghazi: Al-Dar Al-Jamahiriyya lilnashr wa-ltawzee' wa-li'laan.

Hutcheon, Linda (2002) 'Rethinking the National Model', in Linda Hutcheon and Mario J. Valdes (eds) *Rethinking Literary History: A Dialogue on Theory*, Oxford University Press, 3–49.

Hutchins, W. John (2000) *Early Years in Machine Translation: Memoirs and Biographies of Pioneers*, Amsterdam: John Benjamins.

Hutchins, John (ed.) (1986) *Machine Translation: Past, Present, Future*, Chichester, West Sussex: Ellis Horwood.

Hymes, Dell (1972) 'Models of the Interaction of Language and Social Life', in John J. Gumperz and Dell Hymes (eds) *Directions in Sociolinguistics: The Ethnography of Communication*, New York: Holt, Rinehart and Winston, 35–71.

Imamura Taihei (1952) *Eiga riron nyūmon* (Introduction to Film Theory), Tokyo: Itagaki Shoten.

Inghilleri, Moira (2005) 'Mediating Zones of Uncertainty: Interpreter Agency, the Interpreting Habitus and Political Asylum Adjudication', *The Translator* 11(1): 69–85.

Inghilleri, Moira (2008a) 'The Ethical Task of the Translator in the Geo-political Arena: From Iraq to Guantánamo Bay', *Translation Studies* 1(1): 212–23.

Inghilleri, Moira (2008b) 'Asylum', in Mona Baker and Gabriela Saldanha (eds) *Routledge Encyclopedia of Translation Studies*, 2nd edn, London & New York, 10–13.

Inghilleri, Moira (2009) 'Translators in War Zones', in Esperança Bielsa Mialet and Chris Hughes (eds) *Globalisation, Political Violence and Translation*, Basingstoke: Palgrave Macmillan, 207–21.

Irving, David (2001) 'Controversial Historian David Irving on the bin Laden Tape', available at http://www.rense.com/general18/ckk.htm.

Iser, Wolfgang (1974) 'The Reading Process: A Phenomenological Approach', in *The Implied Reader*, Baltimore: The Johns Hopkins University Press, 274–94.

Iser, Wolfgang (1980) 'The Reading Process: A Phenomenological Approach', in Jane Tompkins (ed.) *Reader Response Criticism: From Formalism to Post-Structuralism*, Baltimore: Johns Hopkins University Press, 50–69.

Iser, Wolfgang (1995) 'On Translatability: Variables of Interpretation', *The European English Messenger* 4(2): 30–38.

Ishibashi Shian (1888/1993) 'Aibiki o yonde', in *Futabatei Shimei zenshū bessatsu*, 345 (Chikuma shobō, 1993).

Ishii Kendô (1944/1997) Meiji jibutsu kigen (Daiichihen Jinji-bu), Chikuma shobō.

Isoda Kôichi (1991) 'Yakugo "bungaku" no tanjô', *Rokumeikan no keifu* (Kôdansha bungei bunko): 7–40.

Itô Sei (1953/1994) *Nihon bundan shi 1 Kaika no hitobito*, Kôdansha bungei bunko.

Jackson, R. (2005) *Classical Modern Thought on International Relations: From Anarchy to Cosmopolis*, Houndmills, Basingstoke: Palgrave Macmillan.

Jacobson, D. (1996) *Rights Across Borders: Immigration and the Decline of Citizenship*, Baltimore, Md.: Johns Hopkins University Press.

Jacquemet, M. (1996) *Credibility in Court: Communicative Practices in the Camorra's Trials*, Cambridge: Cambridge University Press.

Jacquemet, Marco (2005) 'The Registration Interview: Restricting Refugees' Narrative Performances', in Mike Baynham and Anna De Fina (eds) *Dislocations/Relocations: Narratives of Displacement*, Manchester: St Jerome Publishing, 197–220.

Jakobson, Roman (1921) La Poésie moderne russe, equisse 1, Prague.

Jakobson, Roman (1959) 'On Linguistic Aspects of Translation', in R. A. Brower (ed.) On Translation, Cambridge: Harvard University Press, 232–39.

Jameson, Fredric (1979) 'Reification and Utopia in Mass Culture', Social Text 1: 130–48.

Jameson, Fredric (1981) The Political Unconscious: Narrative as a Socially Symbolic Act, Ithaca: Cornell University Press.

Jameson, Fredric (1992) Signatures of the Visible, New York: Routledge.

Janofsky, Michael (2006) 'Bush Proposes Broader Language Training', New York Times, 6 January.

Jauss, Hans Robert (1982) Toward an Aesthetic of Reception, trans. Timothy Bahti, Minneapolis, Minnesota: University of Minnesota Press.

Johnson, Barbara (1980) The Critical Difference: Essays in Contemporary Rhetoric of Reading, Baltimore: Johns Hopkins University Press.

Johnson, Barbara (1985) 'Taking Fidelity Philosophically', in Joseph F. Graham (ed.) Difference in Translation, Ithaca, New York: Cornell University Press, 142–48.

Johnson, Samuel (1759) The Idler, Nos. 68–69, London.

Johnson, Samuel (1927) History of Rasselas, Prince of Abyssinia, Oxford: Clarendon Press.

Joly, D. (1996) Haven or Hell? Asylum Policies and Refugees in Europe, Houndmills, Basingstoke: Macmillan Press.

Joly, D. (ed.) (2002) Global Changes in Asylum Regimes, Houndmills, Basingstoke: Palgrave Macmillan.

Jones, Francis R. (2004) 'Ethics, Aesthetics and Decision: Literary Translating in the Wars of the Yugoslav Succession', Meta 49(4): 711–28.

Jones, J.P. (1895) 'The Need of a Revision of the Tamil Bible', The Harvest Field: A Missionary Magazine 6: 41–51.

Joppke, C. (1998) Challenge to the Nation State: Immigration in Western Europe and the United States, Oxford: Oxford University Press.

Jordan, B. and F. Düvell (2003) Migration: The Boundaries of Equality and Justice, Cambridge: Polity Press.

Joyce, James (1971) Ulysses, Harmondsworth: Penguin.

Joyce, James (1995) 'Ulysse: note sur l'histoire du texte', Oeuvres complètes, Vol. 2, Paris: Gallimard, 1030–33.

Juhel, Denis (1982) Bilinguisme et traduction au Canada: role sociolinguistique du traducteur, Quebec: International Center for Research on Bilingualism.

Jum'ah, Muhammad Lutfi (1906a) 'Riwayat al-sahir al-khalid' [The Immortal Magician], Musamarat al-sha'b (40 pp.); trans. Guy Newell Boothby (1906) Pharos the Egyptian, Doylestown: Wildside Press, n.d.

Jum'ah, Muhammad Lutfi (1906b) 'Riwayat al-intiqam al-ha'il' [Colossal Revenge], Musamarat al-sha'b (41 pp.); trans. Guy Newell Boothby (1906) Pharos the Egyptian, Doylestown: Wildside Press, n.d.

Jum'ah, Rabih Lutfi (1991) Muhammad Lutfi Jum'ah wa ha'ula' al-a'lam 1900–1950 [Muhammad Lutfi Jum'ah and the Great Men of His Day], Cairo: Dar Wazzan.

Kadi, Joanna (1994) Food for Our Grandmothers: Writings by Arab-American and Arab-Canadian Feminists, Boston: South End Press.

Kadish, Doris and Françoise Massardier-Kenney (eds) (1994) Translating Slavery. Gender and Race in French Women's Writing, 1783–1823, Kent, Ohio: Kent State University Press.

Kahane, Eduardo (2007) 'Interpreters in Conflict Zones: The Limits of Neutrality', Communicate! (AIIC's Online Journal), available online: http://www.aiic.net/ViewPage.cfm?page_id=2691.

Kahf, Mohja (1999) Western Representations of the Muslim Woman: From Termagant to Odalisque, Austin: University of Texas Press.

Kamei Fumio (1940) 'Bunka eiga geppyō' (Monthly Culture Film Criticism), *Nihon eiga* 5(12) (December): 24–26.

Kamei Fumio, Akimoto Takeshi, Ueno Kōzō, Ishimoto Tōkichi and Tanaka Yoshiji (1940) 'Nihon bunka eiga no shoki kara kyō o kataru zadankai' (Zadankai to talk about Japanese culture films from the early period to today), *Bunka eiga kenkyū* 3(2) (February): 16–27.

Kamei Hideo (2002) *Transformations of Sensibility*, trans. and edited by Michael Bourdaghs, Ann Arbor: Center for Japanese Studies, The University of Michigan.

Kamuf, Peggy (ed.) (1991) *A Derrida Reader: Between the Blinds*, Hemel Hempstead: Harvester.

Kanbara Ariake (1909/1975) ' "Aibiki" ni tsuite', in *Futabatei Shimei*, edited by Tsubouchi Shōyō and Uchida Roan (Ekifūsha); reprinted Tokyo: Kindai bungakukan, 1975, 79–83.

Kang, Ji-Hae (2007) 'Recontextualization of News Discourse: A Case Study of Translation of News Discourse on North Korea', *The Translator* 13(2): 219–42.

Kant, I. (1957) *Perpetual Peace*, Lewis White Beck (ed.), New York: The Bobbs-Merrill Company. First published 1795.

Kaplan, Amy (2002) *The Anarchy of Empire in the Making of U.S. Culture*, Cambridge, Mass.: Harvard University Press.

Katan, David (1999, 2004) *Translating Cultures*, Manchester: St. Jerome Publishing (2nd edn).

Katz, Jerrold J. (1978) 'Effability and Translation', in F. Guenthner and M. Guenthner-Reutter (eds) *Meaning and Translation*, London: Duckworth, 191–234.

Kaufert, Joseph M. and William W. Koolage (1984) 'Role Conflict Among "Culture Brokers": The Experience of Native Canadian Medical Interpreters', *Social Science and Medicine* 18: 283–86.

Keenaghan, Eric (1998) 'Jack Spicer's Pricks and Cocksuckers. Translating Gay Desire into Visibility', *The Translator* 4(2): 273–94.

Kelly, Louis (1979) *The True Interpreter: A History of Translation Theory and Practice in the West*, Oxford: Basil Blackwell.

Khleif, Bud (1980) *Language, Ethnicity and Education in Wales*, New York: Mouton.

Kiberd, Declan (1995) *Inventing Ireland: The Literature of the Modern Nation*, London: Jonathan Cape.

Kiernan, Victor (1991) 'Languages and Conquerors', in Peter Burke and Roy Porter (eds) *Language, Self, and Society: A Social History of Language*, Cambridge: Polity Press, 191–210.

Kimura Ki (ed.) (1972) 'Kaidai', in *Meiji hon'yaku bungaku shū*, Meiji bungaku zenshû 7 (Chikuma shobô), 395–410.

King, Anthony D. (ed.) (1997) *Culture, Globalization, and the World-System: Contemporary Conditions for the Representation of Identity*, Minneapolis: University of Minneapolis Press.

Kipling, Gordon (1977) *The Triumph of Honour: Burgundian Origins of the Elizabethan Renaissance*, Leiden: Leiden University Press.

Kittler, Friedrich (1997) *Literature, Media, Information Systems: Essays by Friedrich A. Kittler*, edited by John Johnston, Amsterdam: G&B Arts International.

Kleinman, Arthur (1988) *The Illness Narratives: Suffering, Healing, and the Human Condition*, Harper Collins: Basic Books.

Kloos, Ulrike (1992) *Niederlandbild und deutsche Germanistik 1800–1933*, Amsterdam: Rodopi.

Klor de Alva, J. Jorge (1989) 'Language, Politics and Translation: Colonial Discourse and Classic Nahuatl in New Spain', in Rosanna Warren (ed.) *The Art of Translation*, Boston: Northeastern University Press, 140–58.

Knudsen, J. (1995) 'When Trust is on Trial: Negotiating Refugees Narratives', in V. Daniel and J. Knudsen (eds) *Mistrusting Refugees*, Berkeley: University of California Press, 13–35.

Koopman, John (2004) 'Interpreter's Death Rattles Troops', *San Francisco Chronicle*, 1 August.

Koppell, J. G. S. (2000) 'No "There" There', *Atlantic Monthly*, August: 16–18.

Korpel, L.G. (1992) *Over het nut en de wijze der vertalingen. Nederlandse vertaalreflectie in een Westeuropees kader (1750–1920)*, Amsterdam: Rodopi.

Kramer, J. (2003) 'Refugee: An Afghan Woman Who Fled Tyranny on Her Own', *New Yorker*, January 20: 64–73.

Krane, Jim (2005) 'Translators Dying by the Dozens in Most Dangerous Civilian Jobs in Iraq', *Associated Press*, 21 May.

Krauss, Rosalind (1991) 'The Originality of the Avant-Garde', in Ingeborg Hoesterey (ed.) *Zeitgeist in Babel*, Bloomington & Indianapolis: Indiana University Press, 66–84.

Kress, Gunther (1985/1988) *Linguistic Processes in Sociocultural Practice*, Victoria & Oxford: Deakin University Press & Oxford University Press.

Kristal, Efraín (2002) 'Considering Coldly . . . A Response to Franco Moretti', *New Left Review* 15 (May–June): 61–74.

Kubota Tatsuo (1940a) *Bunka eiga no hōhōron* (The Methodology of the Culture Film), Kyoto: Daiichi Geibunsha.

Kubota Tatsuo (1940b) 'Gekiteki yōso to kirokuteki yōso' (Theatrical elements and documentary elements), *Bunka eiga kenkyū* 3(10) (October): 575–76.

Kuwano Shigeru (1941) 'Kuwano Shigeru', *Bunka eiga* 1(6) (June).

Kuwano Shigeru (1973) *Dokyumentarii no sekai – sōzōryoku to hōhōron* (The World of Documentary – Creative Power and Methodology), Tokyo: Simul Shuppankai.

Ladmiral, Jean-René (1979) *Traduire: théorèmes pour la traduction*, Paris: Payot.

Lady (1939) 'Documentary Film', 3 August.

LaFranci, Howard (2006) 'Remembering Allan: A Tribute to Jimm Carroll's Interpreter', *Christian Science Monitor*, 6 March.

Lai, John T. P. (2007) 'Institutional Patronage: The Religious Tract Society and the Translation of Christian Tracts in Nineteenth-Century China', *The Translator* 13(1): 39–61.

Laine, Elizabeth (1939) 'About Documentary Films', *Transcript* (Boston), 10 June.

Lakoff, G. and M. Johnson (1980) *Metaphors We Live By*, Chicago: University of Chicago Press.

Landow, George P. (1992) *Hypertext. The Convergence of Contemporary Critical Theory and Technology*, Baltimore: The Johns Hopkins University Press.

Lane-Mercier, Gillian (1997) 'Translating the Untranslatable: The Translator's Aesthetic, Ideological and Political Responsibility', *Target* 9(1): 43–68.

LaPlante, Matthew D. (2005) 'Speaking the Language; A Vital Skill; Interpreters in High Demand in Iraq', *Salt Lake Tribune*, 13 October 13.

Laqueur, Thomas (2006) 'Why the Margins Matter: Occultism and the Making of Modernity', *Modern Intellectual History* 3(1): 111–35.

Larbaud, Valery (1936) *Ce vice impuni, la lecture. Domaine anglais*, Paris: Gallimard.

Lawrence, Bruce (ed.) and James Howarth (trans.) (2005) *Messages to the World: The Statements of Osama Bin Laden*, London & New York: Verso.

Lazreg, Marnia (1990) 'Feminism and Difference: The Perils of Writing as a Woman on Women in Algeria', in Evelyn Fox Keller and Marianne Hirsch (eds) *Conflicts in Feminism*, New York: Routledge, 326–48.

Leach, Edmund R. (1954) *Political Systems of Highland Burma*, London: G. Bell & Sons.

Leach, Edmund R. (1973) 'Ourselves and Others', *Times Literary Supplement*, 6 July: 771–72.

Leerssen, Joep (1996) *Mere Irish and Fíor-Ghael*, Cork: Cork University Press.

Lefevere, André (1977) *Translating Literature: The German Tradition from Luther to Rosenzweig*, Amsterdam: Van Gorcum.

Lefevere, André (1985) 'Why Waste our Time on Rewrites? The Trouble with Interpretation and the Role of Rewriting in an Alternative Paradigm', in Theo Hermans (ed.) *The Manipulation of Literature: Studies in Literary Translation*, London: Croom Helm, 215–43.

Lefevere, André (1990) 'Translation: Its Genealogy in the West', in Susan Bassnett and André Lefevre (eds) *Translation, History and Culture*, London: Pinter Publishers, 14–28.

Lefevere, André (1992a) *Translation, Rewriting, and the Manipulation of Literary Fame*, London: Routledge.

Lefevere, André (ed.) (1992b) *Translation, History, Culture: A Sourcebook*, London: Routledge.

Lefevere, André and Susan Bassnett (1990) 'Proust's Grandmother and the Thousand and One Nights', in Susan Bassnett and André Lefevre (eds) *Translation, History and Culture*, London: Pinter Publishers, 1–13.

León Portilla, Miguel (1990a) 'Tiene la Historia un Destino?', *El Correo de la UNESCO* (April), Paris: UNESCO.

León Portilla, Miguel (1990b) 'History or Destiny?' *The UNESCO Courier* (April), Paris: UNESCO.

Leuven-Zwart, Kitty van (1990) 'Translation and Original; Similarities and Dissimilarities II', *Target* 2: 69–96.

Levine, Suzanne Jill (1991) *The Subversive Scribe: Translating Latin American Fiction*. St Paul, Minnesota: Graywolf Press.

Levine, Suzanne Jill (1992) 'Translation as (Sub)version', in Lawrence Venuti (ed.) *Rethinking Translation*, London: Routledge, 75–85.

Levinson, Charles (2006) 'Iraq's "Terps" Face Suspicions on Both Sides', *Christian Science Monitor*, 17 April, www.csmonitor.com/2006/0417/p01s01-woiq.html.

Lewis, Philip E. (1985) 'The Measure of Translation Effects', in Joseph Graham (ed.) *Difference in Translation*, Ithaca, NY: Cornell University Press, 31–62.

Lianeri, Aleka (2002) 'Translation and the Ideology of Culture: Reappraising Schleiermacher's Theory of Translation', *Current Writing: Text and Reception in Southern Africa* 14(2): 2–18.

Lienhardt, Godfrey (1954) 'Modes of Thought', in E. E. Evans-Pritchard (ed.) *The Institutions of Primitive Society*, Oxford: Basil Blackwell, 95–107.

Littau, Karin (1993) 'Intertextuality and Translation: *The Waste Land* in French and German', in Catriona Picken (ed.) *Translation – the Vital Link*, London: Chamelon Press, 63–69.

Liu, Lydia (1995) *Translingual Practice: Literature, National Culture, and Translated Modernity—China, 1900–1937*, Stanford: Stanford University Press.

Liu, Lydia (ed.) (2000) *Tokens of Exchange: The Problem of Translation in Global Circulations*, Durham, NC: Duke University Press.

Lockard, Joe (1996) 'Resisting Cyber-English', *Bad Subjects* 24: 1–14. Available at <http://bad.eserver.org/issues/1996/24/lockard.html>.

Locke, W. N. and A. D. Booth (eds) (1955) *Machine Translation of Languages: Fourteen Essays*, Cambridge: MIT Press.

Lockman, Zachary (1994) 'Imagining the Working Class: Culture, Nationalism, and Class Formation in Egypt, 1899–1914', *Poetics Today* 15(2): 157–90.

Lüdi, Georges (1992) 'French as a Pluricentric Language', in Michael Clyne (ed.) *Pluricentric Languages*, Berlin: Mouton de Gruyter, 149–77.

Luhmann, N. (1995) *Social Systems*, trans. by J. Bednarz Jr and D. Baecker, Stanford: Stanford University Press.

Lupton, Carter (2003) 'Mummymania for the Masses – Is Egyptology Cursed by the Mummy's Curse?', in Sally MacDonald and Michael Rice (eds) *Consuming Ancient Egypt*, London: UCL Press, 23–45.

Luria, A. R. and F. I. Yudovich (1971) *Speech and the Development of Mental Processes in the Child*, London: Penguin Books.

Lyotard, Jean-Francois (1984) *The Postmodern Condition: A Report on Knowledge*, trans. Geoff Bennington and Brian Massumi, Minneapolis: University of Minnesota Press.

Lyotard, Jean-François (1989) 'Foreward', in Andrew Benjamin (ed.) *The Lyotard Reader*, Oxford: Blackwell Publishers, vi–xiv.

Magdalenic, Ivan (1993) 'Interviews with Interpreters from the Croatian Liaison Office', Unpublished Paper.

Maier, Carol (2007) 'The Translator as an Intervenient Being', in Jeremy Munday (ed.) *Translation as Intervention*, New York: Continuum, 1–17.

Makino Mamoru (1978) 'Kiroku eiga no rironteki dōkō o otte 41' (Pursuing the theoretical movement of documentary film 41), *Unitsūshin*, 19 June.

Malcolm, J. (1982) *Psychoanalysis: The Impossible Profession*, London: Pan Books.

Malinowski, Bronislaw (1935) *Coral Gardens and their Magic*, Vol. II, London: G. Allen & Unwin.

Malkki, L. (1995) 'Refugees and Exiles', *Annual Review of Anthropology* 24: 495–523.

Marcos, Luis R. and Manuel Trujillo (1984) 'Culture, language, and communicative behavior: The psychiatric examination of Spanish-Americans', in Richard P. Durán (ed.) *Latino Language and Communicative Behavior*, New Jersey: Ablex Publishing, 187–94.

Marcus, Leigh (1992) 'Renaissance/Early Modern Studies', in Stephen Greenblatt and Giles Gunn (eds) *Redrawing the Boundaries*, New York: MLA, 49–62.

Mari, Petru (1986) *Scritti d'Altrò*, Bastia: Stamperia Sammarcelli.

Martinez, Deborah, Elizabeth A. Lenoe and Jennifer Sternback de Medina (1985) 'Language as a Barrier to Health Care', in Lucia Elias-Olivares (ed.) *Spanish Language Use and Public Life in the United States*, Berlin: Walter de Gruyter, 153–64.

Martyn, Henry (1811) *Christian India; or an Appeal on Behalf of 900,000 Christians in India, who want the Bible: A Sermon Preached at Calcutta on Tuesday, January 1, 1811 for Promoting the Objects of the British and Foreign Bible Society*, Calcutta: n.p.

Maryns, K. (2006) *The Asylum Speaker: Language in the Belgian Asylum Procedure*, Manchester: St Jerome Publishing.

Mason, Ian (2004) 'Conduits, Mediators, Spokespersons: Investigating Translator/Interpreter Behavior', in Christina Schäffner (ed.) *Translation Research and Interpreting Research*, Clevedon: Multilingual Matters Ltd, 89–97.

Mason, Ian (2009a) 'Translator Moves and Reader Response: the Impact of Discoursal Shifts in Translation', in Monika Klein-Kuhle and Michael Schwarzer (eds) *Translationswissenschaftliches Kolloquium I*, Bern: Peter Lang, 55–71.

Mason, Ian (2009b) 'Role, Positioning and Discourse in Face to Face Interpreting', in Raquel de Pedro Ricoy, Isabelle A. Perez and Christine W. L. Wilson (eds) *Interpreting and Translating in Public Service Settings: Policy, Practice, Pedagogy*, Manchester: St Jerome, 52–73.

Mason, Ian (ed.) (1999) *Dialogue Interpreting*, Special issue of *The Translator* 5(2).

Mattei, Francescu (1971) *Febre Maligne*, Ajaccio: Cyrnos et Méditerranée.

Mattelart, Armand (1994) *Mapping World Communication: War, Progress, Culture*, Minneapolis: University of Minnesota Press.

May, Steven (1981) 'Tudor Aristocrats and the Mythical Stigma of Print', *Renaissance Papers* 1980: 11–18.

McDonald, Maryon (1989) *We Are Not French*, London: Routledge.

McDonough, Julie (2006) 'Hiding Difference: On the Localization of Websites', *The Translator* 12(1): 85–103.

McKee, Rachel (2004) 'Interpreting as a Tool for Empowerment of the New Zealand Deaf Community', in Sabine Fenton (ed.) *For Better or For Worse: Translation as a Tool for Change in the South Pacific*, Manchester: St. Jerome Publishing, 89–132.

Mehrez, Samia (1992) 'Translation and the Postcolonial Experience: The Francophone North African Text', in Lawrence Venuti (ed.) *Rethinking Translation: Discourse, Subjectivity, Ideology*, London: Routledge, 120–38.

Melby, Alan K. (with C. Terry Warner) (1995) *The Possibility of Language: A Discussion of the Nature of Language, with Implications for Human and Machine Translation*, Amsterdam: John Benjamins.

Mélitz, Jacques (1998) 'English-Language Dominance, Literature and Welfare', Paris:

CREST, Document de Travail No. 9832. Also published as Discussion Paper 2055, London: Centre for Economic Policy Research, 1999.

Merlini, Raffaela and Roberta Favaron (2005) 'Examining the "Voice of Interpreting" in Speech Pathology', *Interpreting* 7(2): 263–302.

Meschonnic, Henri (1973) *Pour la poétique II, Poétique de la traduction*, Paris: Gallimard.

Meschonnic, Henri (1999) *Poétique du traduire*, Lagrasse-Verdier.

Mestrovic, Stjepan G. (1994) *The Balkanization of the West: The Confluence of Postmodernism and Postcommunism*, London & New York: Routledge.

Metzger, Melanie (1999) *Sign Language Interpreting: Deconstructing the Myth of Neutrality*, Washington, DC: Gallaudet University Press.

Meylaerts, Reine (2007) ' "La Belgique vivra-t-elle?": Language and Translation Ideological Debates in Belgium (1919–1940)', *The Translator* 13(2): 297–319.

Mignolo, Walter (2002) 'Rethinking the Colonial Model', in Linda Hutcheon and Mario J. Valdes (eds) *Rethinking Literary History: A Dialogue on Theory*, Oxford University Press, 155–93.

Mikkelson, Holly (1998) 'Towards a Redefinition of the Role of the Court Interpreter', *Interpreting* 3: 21–45.

Mishler, Elliot G. (1984) *The Discourse of Medicine: Dialectics of Medical Interviews*, New Jersey: Ablex Publishing.

Mitchell, Timothy (1988) *Colonising Egypt*, Berkeley: University of California Press.

Moeketsi, Rosemary M. H. (2007) 'Intervention in Court Interpreting: South Africa', in Jeremy Munday (ed.) *Translation as Intervention*, New York: Continuum, 97–117.

Mohanty, Chandra Talpade (1991) 'Under Western Eyes: Feminist Scholarship and Colonial Discourse', in Ann Russo Talpade and Lourdes Torres (eds) *Third World Women and the Politics of Feminism*, Bloomington: Indiana University Press, 51–80.

Monius, Anne E. (2001) *Imagining a Place for Buddhism: Literary Culture and Religious Community in Tamil-Speaking South India*, Oxford: Oxford University Press.

Moretti, Franco (2000) 'Conjectures on World Literature', *New Left Review* 1 (Jan–Feb): 54–68.

Moretti, Franco (2003) 'More Conjectures', *New Left Review* 20 (Mar–Apr): 73–81.

Mossop, Brian (1998) 'What is a Translating Translator Doing', *Target* 10(2): 231–66.

Multatuli (1927) *Max Havelaar or the Coffee Sales of the Netherlands Trading Company*, trans. W. Siebenhaar, introduction by D.H. Lawrence, New York: A.A. Knopf.

Multatuli (1949) *Max Havelaar of de koffij-veilingen der Nederlandsche Handel-maatschappij*, G. Stuiveling (ed.), Amsterdam: Van Oorschot.

Multatuli (1968) *Max Havelaar*, trans. Mme Roland Garros, Paris: Editions universitaires.

Multatuli (1975) *Max Havelaar o las subastas de café de la Compañía Comercial Holandesa*, trans. Francisco Carrasquer, Barcelona: Frontera.

Multatuli (1987) *Max Havelaar or the Coffee Auctions of the Dutch Trading Company*, trans. Roy Edwards, Harmondsworth: Penguin.

Multatuli (1992) *Max Havelaar of de koffiveilingen der Nederlandsche Handelmaatschappy* (2 vols), A. Kets-Vree (ed.), Assen & Maastricht: Van Gorcum.

Munday, Jeremy (2001) *Introducing Translation Studies. Theories and Applications*, London & New York: Routledge.

Munday, Jeremy (2002) 'Systems in Translation. A Systemic Model for Descriptive Translation Studies', in Theo Hermans (ed.) *Crosscultural Transgressions. Research Models in Translation Studies II. Historical and Ideological Issues*. Manchester: St. Jerome Publishing, 76–92.

Munday, Jeremy (2007a) 'Translation and Ideology: A Textual Approach', *The Translator* 13(2): 195–217.

Munday, Jeremy (ed.) (2007b) *Translation as Intervention*, New York: Continuum.

Munday, Jeremy (2008) *Style and Ideology in Translation*, London & New York: Routledge.

Munro, John H. A. (1972) *Wool Cloth, and Gold: the Struggle for Bullion in Anglo-Burgundian Trade 1340–1478*, Brussels: Editions de l'Université de Bruxelles.

Murdoch, John (1876) *Renderings of Scriptural Terms in the Principal Languages of India*, Madras: Christian Vernacular Education Society.

Nagao, Makoto (1989) *Machine Translation: How Far Can It Go?*, trans. Norman D. Cook, New York: Oxford University Press.

Needham, Rodney (1972) *Belief, Language, and Experience*, Oxford: Basil Blackwell.

Newmark, Peter (1991) *About Translation*, Clevedon: Multilingual Matters.

Nic Eoin, Máirín and Liam Mac Mathúna (eds) (1997) *Ar Thóir an Fhocail Chruinn: Iriseoirí, Téarmeolaithe agus Fadhbanna an Aistriúcháin*, Dublin: Coiscéim.

Nida, Eugene A. (1952) *God's World in Man's Language*, New York: Harper & Brothers.

Nida, Eugene A. (1954/1975) *Customs and Cultures: Anthropology for Christian Missions*, South Pasadena, CA: William Carey Library.

Nida, Eugene A. (1964) *Toward a Science of Translating, with Special Reference to Principles and Procedures Involved in Bible Translating*, Leiden: Brill.

Nida, Eugene A. and Charles Taber (1969) *The Theory and Practice of Translation*, Leiden: E.J. Brill.

Niranjana, Tesjawini (1990) 'Translation, Colonialism and Rise of English', *Economic and Political Weekly*, 14 April, 773–79.

Niranjana, Tejaswini (1992) *Siting Translation: History, Post-Structuralism. and the Colonial Context*, Berkeley: University of California Press.

Niranjana, Tejaswini (1994) 'Colonialism and the Politics of Translation', in Alfred Arteaga (ed.) *An Other Tongue: Nation and Ethnicity in the Linguistic Borderlands*, Durham, NC: Duke University Press, 35–52.

Nkashama, Pius Ngandu (1992) *Littératures et écritures en langues africaines*, Paris: L'Harmattan.

Nornes, Abé Markus (1999) 'For an Abusive Subtitling', *Film Quarterly* 52(3): 17–34.

Nornes, Abé Mark (2007) *Cinema Babel: Translating Global Cinema*, Minneapolis & London: University of Minnesota Press.

Nyce, James M. and Paul Kahn (eds) (1991) *From Memex to Hypertext: Vannevar Bush and the Mind's Machine*, London: Academic Press.

O'Barr, W. (1982) *Linguistic Evidence: Language, Power, and Strategy in Courtroom*, New York: Academic Press.

O'Brien, Flann (1973) *The Poor Mouth*, trans. Patrick Power, London: Picador.

O Fearaíl, Pádraig (1975) *The Story of Conradh na Gaeilge*, Dublin: Clódhanna Teo.

O'Hagan, Minako (1996) *The Coming Industry of Teletranslation*, Clevedon: Multilingual Matters.

O'Hagan, Minako and David Ashworth (2002) *Translation-Mediated Communication in a Digital World*, Clevedon: Multilingual Matters.

Okamoto Masao (1996) *Bunka eiga jidai + Jūjiya eigabu no hitobito* (The Era of Culture Film and the People of Jūjiya's Film Unit), Tokyo: Unitsūshin.

Oksaar, E. (1978) 'Interference, Bilingualism and Interactional Competence', in L. Grähs, G. Korlén and B. Malmberg (eds) *Theory and Practice of Translation*, Bern: Peter Lang.

Okuda Shinkichi (1943) *Eiga bunkenshi* (The History of Film Literature), Tokyo: Dai Nippon Eiga Kyōkai.

Ó Ruairc, Maolmhaodhóg (1996) *Dúchas na Gaeilge*, Dublin: Cois Life.

O'Sullivan, Carol (2007) 'Multilingualism at the Multiplex: A New Audience for Screen Translation?', *Linguistica Antverpiensia* NS6: 81–95.

O'Sullivan, Emer (1998) 'Ireland and the World of Children's Books: The Aspect of Translation', *Translation Ireland* 12(1): 4–6.

Oz-Salzberger, Fania (1995) *Translating the Enlightenment: Scottish Civic Discourse in Eighteenth-Century Germany*, Oxford: Oxford University Press/Clarendon Press.

Palmer, Jerry (2007) 'Interpreting and Translation for Western Media in Iraq', in Myriam

Salama-Carr (ed.) *Translating and Interpreting Conflict*, Amsterdam & New York: Rodopi, 13–28.

Palmer, Jerry and Victoria Fontan (2007) ' "Our Ears and Our Eyes". Journalists and Fixers in Iraq', *Journalism* 8(1): 5–24.

Papastergiadis, N. (2000) *The Turbulence of Migration*, Cambridge: Polity Press.

Parmentier, R. J. (1993) 'The Political Function of Reported Speech: A Belauan Example', in J. A. Lucy (ed.) *Reflexive Language: Reported Speech and Metapragmatics*, Cambridge: Cambridge University Press.

Paul, Anthony (1990) 'Dutch Literature and the Translation Barrier', in B. Westerweel and T. D'Haen (eds) *Something Understood: Studies in Anglo-Dutch Translation*, Amsterdam: Rodopi.

Pérez González, Luis (2006) 'Fansubbing Anime: Insights into the "Butterfly Effect" of Globalisation on Audiovisual Translation', *Perspectives: Studies in Translatology* 14(4): 260–77.

Pérez-González, Luis (2007) 'Intervention in New Amateur Subtitling Cultures: A Multimodal Account', *Linguistica Antverpiensia* NS6: 67–80.

Pergnier, Maurice (1989) *Les anglicismes*, Paris: PUF.

Peterson, Derek R. (2004) *Creative Writing: Translation, Bookkeeping, and the Work of Imagination in Colonial Kenya*, Portsmouth, NH: Heinemann.

Phillips, Russel S., Mary Beth Hamel, Joan M. Teno, Paul Bellamy, Steven K. Broste, Robert M. Califf, Humberto Vidaillet, Roger B. Davis, Lawrence H. Muhlbaier, Alfred F. Conners, Joanne Lynne and Lee Goldman (1996) 'Race, Resource Use, and Survival in Seriously Ill Hospitalized Adults', *Journal of General Internal Medicine* 11: 387–96.

Pick, Daniel (1996) *Faces of Degeneration: A European Disorder, 1848–1918*, Cambridge: Cambridge University Press.

Pöchhacker, Franz (2004) *Introducing Interpreting Studies*, London & New York: Routledge.

Pocock, David (1961) *Social Anthropology*, London & New York: Sheed & Ward.

Polezzi, Loredana (2000) 'Reflections of Things Past: Building Italy through the Mirror of Translation', *New Comparison* 29: 27–47.

Pöllabauer, Sonja (2004) 'Interpreting in Asylum Hearings: Issues of Role, Responsibility and Power', *Interpreting* 6(2): 143–80.

Poor, Glen (1996) 'Localising *Windows* and *Office '95*': A Sim-Ship Strategy', *Software Localisation* 1(1): 1–2.

Porter, Bernard (1982) 'The Edwardians and their Empire', in Donald Read (ed.) *Edwardian England*, London & Canberra: Croon Helm, 128–44.

Portes, A. (1997) 'Immigration Theory for a New Century: Some Problems and Opportunities', *International Migration Review* 31(4): 799–825.

Pratt, Mary Louise (1992) *Imperial Eyes. Travel Writing and Transculturation*, London & New York: Routledge.

Pratt, Mary Louise (1993) 'Criticism in the Contact Zone: Decentering Community and Nation', in Steven M. Bell, Albert H. Le May and Leonard Orr (eds) *Critical Theory, Cultural Politics, and the Latin American Narrative*, Notre Dame & London: University of Notre Dame Press, 83–102.

Pratt, Mary Louise (1996) *Apocalypse in the Andes: Contact Zones and the Struggle for Interpretive Power*, Washington, DC: IDB Cultural Center.

Prince, Ellen (1981) 'Toward a taxonomy of given-new information', in Peter Cole (ed.) *Radical Pragmatics*, New York: Academic Press, 223–55.

Putsch, Robert W. III. (1985) 'Cross Cultural Communication: The Special Case of Interpreters in Health Care', *Journal of the American Medical Association* 254: 3344–48.

Pym, Anthony (1992) *Translation and Text Transfer: An Essay on the Principles of Intercultural Communication*, Frankfurt am Main: Peter Lang.

Pym, Anthony (1998) *Method in Translation History*, Manchester: St. Jerome.

ul-Qais, Imra (1994) 'Mu'allaqa', in Ahmad bin Amin al-Shanqiti and Fayez Tarhini, (eds) *Sharh al Mu'allaqat al'Ashr wa Akhbar Shu'ara'i-him*, Beirut: Dar al-Kitab al-'Arabi, 25–33.

Quine, Willard van Orman (1959) 'Meaning and Translation', in Reuben A. Brower (ed.) *On Translation*, New York: Oxford University Press, 148–72.

Quine, Willard van Orman (1960) *Word and Object*, Cambridge MA: MIT Press.

Quine, Willard van Orman (1963) 'Two Dogmas of Empiricism', in *From a Logical Point of View*, New York: Harvard University Press.

Quinlan, Maurice J. (1941) *Victorian Prelude: A History of English Manners, 1780–1830*, New York: Columbia University Press.

Rabassa, Gregory (1984) 'If This be Treason: Translation and its Possibilities', in William Frawley (ed.) *Translation: Literary, Linguistic and Philosophical Perspectives*, Newark: University of Delaware Press, 21–29.

Rafael, Vicente (1988) *Contracting Colonialism: Translation and Christian Conversion Under Early Spanish Rule*, Ithaca: Cornell University Press.

Rafael, Vicente (1993) *Contracting Colonialism: Translation and Christian Conversion in Tagalog Society under Early Spanish Rule*, Durham & London: Duke University Press.

Rafael, Vicente (2005) *The Promise of the Foreign: Nationalism and the Technics of Translation in the Spanish Philippines*, Durham, NC: Duke University Press.

Rafael, Vicente L. (2007) 'Translation in Wartime', *Public Culture* 19(2): 239–46.

Raghib, Nabil (1988) *Huda Sha'rawi wa 'Asr al Tanwir*, Cairo: al-Hay'a al-Masriyya al-'Amma li al-Kutub.

Rastegar, Kamran (2007) 'Literary Modernity between Arabic and Persian Prose: Jurji Zaydan's Riwayat in Persian Translation', *Comparative Critical Studies* 4(3): 359–78.

Reid, Donald Malcolm (1975) *The Odyssey of Farah Antun: A Syrian Christian's Quest for Secularism*, Minneapolis: Bibliotheca Islamica.

Reid, Donald Malcom (2002) *Whose Pharaohs? Archeology, Museums and Egyptian National Identity from Napoleon to World War I*, Berkeley: University of California Press.

Reiss, Katharina and Hans J. Vermeer (1984) *Grundlegung einer allgemeinen Translationstheorie*, Tübingen: Niemeyer.

Reitz, J. G. (2003) 'Immigration and Canadian Nation-building in the Transition to a Knowledge Economy', in Wayne A. Cornelius, Peter L. Martin, James F. Hollifield and Takeyuki Tsuda (eds) *Controlling Immigration: A Global Perspective*, 2nd edn, Stanford, CA: Stanford University Press, 97–133.

Rener, Frederick M. (1989) *Interpretatio: Language and Translation From Cicero to Tyler*, Amsterdam/Atlanta: Rodopi.

Reynolds, Siân (1991) 'Shadowland Gospels', *Times Higher Education Supplement*, 29 November.

Ricard, Alain (1995) *Littératures d'Afrique noire. Des langues aux livres*, Paris : CNRS-Kartala.

Rice, Michael and Sally MacDonald (2003) 'Tea with a Mummy: The Consumer's View of Egypt's Immemorial Appeal', in Sally MacDonald and Michael Rice (eds) *Consuming Ancient Egypt*, London: UCL Press, 1–22.

Rimmon-Kenan, Shlomith (1983) *Narrative Fiction: Contemporary Poetics*, London & New York: Methuen.

Ringler, William A., Jr (1988) *Bibliography and Index of English Verse Printed 1476–1558*, London & New York: Mansell Press.

Robins, Lynne S. and Frederic M. Wolf. (1988) 'Confrontation and Politeness Strategies in Physician-patient Interactions', *Social Science Medicine* 27: 217–221.

Robinson, Douglas (1997a) *Translation and Empire*, Manchester: St Jerome.

Robinson, Douglas (ed.) (1997b) *Western Translation Theory: from Herodotus to Nietzsche*, Manchester: St. Jerome.

Rochiccioli, Natale (1982) *Cavalleria Paesana*, Paris: ERTI-LECERF.

Rodriguez, Richard (1982) *Hunger of Memory*, Boston: David R. Godine.

Rose, Gillian (1992) *The Broken Middle: Out of Our Ancient Society*, Oxford: Blackwell.

Rotha, Paul (1935) *Documentary Film*, London: Faber & Faber.

Rotha, Paul (1938) *Bunka eigaron* (Culture Film), trans. Atsugi Taka, Kyoto: Daiichi Geibunsha.

Rotha, Paul (1939a) 'Bunka eigaron josetsu' (Introduction to *Bunka eigaron*), trans. Ueno Ichirō, *Eiga kenkyū* 1: 54–84.

Rotha, Paul (1939b) 'Dokyumentarii no jyakuha to sono shiteki kōsatsu' (Various groups in documentary and their historical thought), trans. Ueno Ichirō, *Eiga kenkyū* 2: 50–85.

Rotha, Paul (1960) *Dokyumentarii eiga* (Documentary film), revised and expanded edition, trans. Atsugi Taka, Tokyo: Misuzu Shobō; reprinted 1976; 1995 reprint published by Miraisha.

Roy, Cynthia (1999) *Interpreting as a Discourse Process* (Oxford Studies in Sociolinguistics), New York: Oxford University Press.

Rubens, Paul (1996) 'Say it in Global English', *New Zealand Infotech Weekly* (29 July): 3.

Rushdie, Salman (1991) *Imaginary Homelands: Essays and Criticism 1981–1991*, London: Granta Books & Penguin; trans. by A. Chatelin as *Patries imaginaires – Essais et critiques*, Paris: Christian Bourgois, 1993.

Ryan, Marleigh Grayer (1965) *Japan's First Modern Novel: UKIGUMO*, New York: Columbia University Press.

Sack, Warren (n.d.) 'Conversation Map: A Content-Based Usernet Newsgroup Browser'. Available at http://web.media.mit.edu/~lieber/IUI/Sack/Sack.html

Sack, Warren and Sawad Brooks (2003) *Translation Map*, Walker Art Center Online Exhibition: *Translocations*, February, available at <translationmap.walkerart.org>.

Said, Edward (1979) *Orientalism*, New York: Vintage Books.

Said, Edward (1989) 'Representing the Colonized: Anthropology's Interlocutors', *Critical Inquiry* 15: 205–25.

Said, Edward (1991) 'Traveling Theory', in *The World, the Text and the Critic*, New York: Vintage, 226–47.

Said, Edward (1994) 'Traveling Theory Reconsidered', in *Reflections on Exile and Other Essays*, Cambridge, Mass.: Harvard University Press, 436–52.

Sajdi, Dana (2009) 'Print and Its Discontents: A Case for Pre-Print Journalism and Other Sundry Print Matters', in Samah Selim (ed.) *Nation and Translation in the Middle East*, Special Issue of *The Translator* 15(1): 105–38.

Sakai, Naoki (1997) 'The Subject of Translation/the Subject in Transit', from the Introduction to *Translation and Subjectivity: On 'Japan' and Cultural Nationalism*, Minneapolis & London: University of Minnesota Press, 11–17.

Salama-Carr, Myriam (ed.) (2007) *Translating and Interpreting Conflict*, Amsterdam: Rodopi.

Sales, Leigh (2001) 'White House defends authenticity of latest Osama video tape', available at http://www.abc.net.au/am/stories/s441284.htm.

Salmon, W. C. (1998) *Causality and Explanation*, New York: Oxford University Press.

Sampson, Fiona (2006) 'Heidegger and the Aporia: Translation and Cultural Authenticity', *Critical Review of International Social and Political Philosophy* 9(4): 527–39.

Samuelsson, Kurt (1961) *Religion and Economic Action*, London: Heinemann.

Sánchez, Dolores (2007) 'The Truth about Sexual Difference: Scientific Discourse and Cultural Transfer', in Sonia Cunico and Jeremy Munday (eds) *Translation and Ideology. Encounters and Clashes*. Special Issue of *The Translator* 13(2): 171–94.

Sanders, J. W. (1951) 'The Stigma of Print: A Note on the Social Bases of Elizabethan Poetry', *Essays in Criticism* 1: 139–64.

Santarelli, Paule (1989) 'Traddutore, traditore?', *Kyrn* 200: 21–22.

Sarangi, Srikant and Stefaan Stembrouk (1996) *Language, Bureaucracy, and Social Control*, London & New York: Longman.

Sapiro, Gisèle (2008) 'Translation and the Field of Publishing', *Translation Studies* 1(2): 154–66.

Schaffer, Kay and Xianlin Song (2006) 'Writing beyond the Wall: Translation, Cross-cultural Exchange and Chan Ran's *A Private Life*', *Journal of Multidisciplinary International Studies* 3(2). Available online at http://epress.lib.uts.edu.au/ojs/index.php/portal/article/view/155/341.

Schäffner, Christina (2003) 'Third Ways and New Centres. Ideological Unity or Difference?', in María Calzada Pérez (ed.) *Apropos of Ideology. Translation Studies on Ideology – Ideologies in Translation Studies*, Manchester: St. Jerome Publishing, 23–41.

Schegloff, Emanuel (1992) 'On Talk and its Institutional Occasions', in Paul Drew and John Heritage (eds) *Talk at Work: Interaction in Institutional Settings*, Cambridge: Cambridge University Press, 101–36.

Schenkeveld, Maria A. (1991) *Dutch Literature in the Age of Rembrandt*, Amsterdam: John Benjamins.

Scheppele, Kim Lane (1989) 'Telling Stories', *Michigan Law Review* 87: 2073–98.

Schiavi, Giuliana (1996) 'There Is Always a Teller in a Tale', *Target* 8(1): 1–21.

Schlegel, A.W. (1964) *Geschichte der klassischen Literatur*, Stuttgart: Kohlhammer.

Schleiermacher, Friedrich (1813/1977) 'On the Different Methods of Translating', in André Lefevere (ed. and trans.) *Translating Literature: The German Tradition from Luther to Rosensweig*, Assen: Van Gorcum, 67–89.

Schleiermacher, Friedrich (1813/1992) 'On the Different Methods of Translating', trans. Waltraud Bartscht, in Rainer Schulte and John Biguenet (eds) *Theories of Translation*, Chicago & London: The University of Chicago Press, 36–54.

Schleiermacher, Friedrich (1999) *Über die verschiedenen Methoden des Übersetzens – Des différentes méthodes du traduire*, trans. Antoine Berman, Paris: Le Seuil.

Schoneveld, W. (1983) *Intertraffic of the Mind: Studies in Seventeenth-Century Anglo-Dutch Translation*, Leiden: E.J. Brill.

Schott, Thomas (1991) 'The World Scientific Community: Globality and Globalisation', *Minerva* 29: 440–62.

Schuck, P. H. (1998) *Citizens, Strangers and In-betweens*, Boulder, Col.: Westview Press.

Schulte, Rainer and John Biguenet (eds) (1992) *Theories of Translation: An Anthology of Essays from Dryden to Derrida*, Chicago: University of Chicago Press.

Schwarzl, Anja (2001) *The (Im)Possibilities of Machine Translation*, Frankfurt: Peter Lang.

Scott, Clive (2006) *Translating Rimbaud's Illuminations*, Exeter: University of Exeter Press.

Searle, J. R. (1969) *Speech Acts: An Essay in the Philosophy of Language*, Cambridge: Cambridge University Press.

Segers, Winibert (1994) 'Derrida's onvertaalbaarheidsweb', in Raymond van den Broeck (ed.) *Bouwen aan Babel: Zes opstellen over onvertaalbaarheid*, Antwerpen-Harmelen: Fantom, 89–100.

Sekino Yoshio (1940a) '*Kyō made no eiga to ashita no eiga (1)*' (Film till now and the films of tomorrow [1]), *Bunka eiga kenkyū* 3(2) (February): 8–11.

Sekino Yoshio (1940b) '*Kyō made no eiga to ashita no eiga (2)*' (Film till now and the films of tomorrow [2]), *Bunka eiga kenkyū* 3(3) (March): 58–60.

Sekino Yoshio (1940c) '*Kyō made no eiga to ashita no eiga (3)*' (Film till now and the films of tomorrow [3]), *Bunka eiga kenkyū* 3(4) (April): 109–12.

Sekino Yoshio (1940d) '*Kyō made no eiga to ashita no eiga (4)*' (Film till now and the films of tomorrow [4]), *Bunka eiga kenkyū* 3(5) (May): 176–79.

Sekino Yoshio (1940e) 'Dokyumentariiron kentō no tame ni (1)' (For an investigation into documentary theory [1]), *Bunka eiga kenkyū* 3(6) (June): 236–39.

Sekino Yoshio (1940f) 'Dokyumentariiron kentō no tame ni (2)' (For an investigation into documentary theory [2]), *Bunka eiga kenkyū* 3(7) (July): 304–307.

Sekino Yoshio (1940g) 'Dokyumentariiron kentō no tame ni (3)' (For an investigation into documentary theory [3]), *Bunka eiga kenkyū* 3(10) (October): 563–67.

Sekino Yoshio (1940h) 'Pōru Rūta: dokyumentarii eiga no sonogo no shinten 1' (Paul Rotha: documentary film and progress since then 1), *Nihon eiga* 5(7) (July): 22–29.

Sekino Yoshio (1940i) 'Pōru Rūta: dokyumentarii eiga no sonogo no shinten 2' (Paul Rotha: documentary film and progress since then 2), *Nihon eiga* 5(8) (August): 68–73.

Sekino Yoshio (1940j) 'Pōru Rūta: dokyumentarii eiga no sonogo no shinten 3' (Paul Rotha: documentary film and progress since then 3), *Nihon eiga* 5(10) (October): 72–77.

Sekino Yoshio (1942) *Eiga kyōiku no riron* (Theory of Film Education), Tokyo: Shōgakkan.

Selim, Samah (2004a) *The Novel and the Rural Imaginary in Egypt 1880–1986*, London: Routledge-Curzon.

Selim, Samah (2004b) 'The *Nahda*, Popular Fiction and the Politics of Translation', *MIT Electronic Journal of Middle East Studies* 4: 70–89.

Shamma, Tarek (2009) *Translation and the Manipulation of Difference: Arabic Literature in Nineteenth-Century England*, Manchester: St. Jerome.

Shannon, Claude E. and Warren Weaver (1949) *The Mathematical Theory of Communication*, Urbana: University of Illinois Press.

Sha'rawi, Huda (1981) *Mudhakkirati*, Cairo: Dar al-Hilal.

Shimamura Hôgetsu (1906) 'Shinkyû engeki no zento', Interview in *Shumi* 1(6): 46–54.

Shirai Shigeru (1988) 'Kameraman jinsei' (Cameraman life), in Iwamoto Kenji and Saiki Tomonori (eds) *Kinema no seishun* (Japanese Cinema in Its Youth), Tokyo: Libroport.

Shohat, Ella (2006a) 'The "Postcolonial" in Translation: Reading Edward Said between English and Hebrew', in *Taboo Memories, Diasporic Voices*, Durham and London: Duke University Press, 359–84.

Shohat, Ella (2006b) 'The Cinema after Babel: Language, Difference, Power', in *Taboo Memories, Diasporic Voices*, Durham & London: Duke University Press, 106–38.

Shuy, Roger (1976) 'The Medical Interview: Problems in Communication', *Primary Care* 3: 365–86.

Simmel, Georg (1997) 'On the Psychology of Money', in David Frisby and Mike Featherstone (eds) *Simmel on Culture*, London: Sage, 233–43.

Simms, Norman (1983) 'Three Types of "Touchy" Translation', *Pacific Quarterly Moana* 8(2): 48–58.

Simon, Sherry (1996) *Gender in Translation*, London & New York: Routledge.

Simpson, David (1998) 'Prospects for Global English: Back to BASIC?', *The Yale Journal of Criticism* 11(1): 304, 306.

Simpson, Paul (1993) *Language, Ideology and Point of View*, London & New York: Routledge.

Smith, Michael. (1974) 'English Translations and Imitations of Italian Madrigal Verse', *Journal of European Studies* 4(2): 164–77.

Snell-Hornby, Mary (1988) *Translation Studies: An Integrated Approach*, Philadelphia: John Benjamins.

Somers, Margaret (1992) 'Narrativity, Narrative Identity, and Social Action: Rethinking English Working-Class Formation', *Social Science History* 16(4): 591–630.

Somers, Margaret (1994) 'The Narrative Construction of Identity: A Relational and Network Approach', *Theory and Society* 23(5): 605–49.

Somers, Margaret (1997) 'Deconstructing and Reconstructing Class Formation Theory: Narrativity, Relational Analysis, and Social Theory', in John R. Hall (ed.) *Reworking Class*, Ithaca & London: Cornell University Press, 73–105.

Somers, Margaret R. and Gloria D. Gibson (1994) 'Reclaiming the Epistemological

"Other": Narrative and the Social Constitution of Identity', in Craig Calhoun (ed) *Social Theory and the Politics of Identity*, Oxford UK & Cambridge USA: Blackwell, 37–99.

Sophocles (1973) *Antigone*, trans. R. E. Braun, New York: Oxford University Press.

Sophocles (1999) *Antigone*, M. Griffith (ed.), Cambridge: Cambridge University Press.

Sorá, Gustavo (1998) 'Francfort: la foire d'empoigne', *Liber* 34: 2–3.

Sötemann, A.L. (1972) *De structuur van de 'Max Havelaar'*, Groningen: Wolters-Noordhoff.

Soysal, Y. N. (1994) *Limits of citizenship: Migrants and postnational membership in Europe*, Chicago, Ill.: University of Chicago Press.

Spenser, Edmund (1970) *A View of the Present State of Ireland*, Oxford: Clarendon.

Sperber, Dan and Deirdre Wilson (1995) *Relevance: Communication and Cognition*, 2nd edn, Oxford: Blackwell.

Spivak, Gayatri (1992) 'The Politics of Translation', in M. Barrett and A. Phillips (eds) *Destabilizing Theory*, Oxford: Polity Press, 177–200.

Spivak, Gayatri (1993) 'The Politics of Translation', *Outside in the Teaching Machine*, New York: Methuen, 179–200.

St. André, James (2004) ' "But do They have a Notion of Justice?": Staunton's 1810 Translation of the Great Qing Code', *The Translator* 10(1): 1–31.

Stahuljak, Zrinka (1999) 'The Violence of Neutrality: Translators in and of the War (Croatia, 1991–92)', *College Literature* 26(1): 34–51.

Stahuljak, Zrinka (2000) 'Violent Distortions: Bearing Witness to the Task of Wartime Translators', *TTR* 13(1): 37–51.

Stahuljak, Zrinka (2004) 'An Epistemology of Tension: Translation and Multiculturalism', *The Translator* 10(1): 33–57.

Stangerup, Henrik (1987) *Le séducteur*, trans. E. Eydoux, Paris: Mazarine.

Starn, Randolph (1998) 'Renaissance Redux', *American Historical Review* 103(1): 122–24.

Statham, P. (2003) 'Understanding Anti-asylum Rhetoric: Restrictive Politics or Racist Publics?', in Sarah Spencer (ed.) *The Politics of Migration*, Oxford: Blackwell Publishing, 163–77.

Steenmeijer, Maarten (1989) *De Spaanse en Spaans-Amerikaanse literatuur in Nederland 1946–1985*, Muiderberg: Coutinho.

Steiner, George (1975) *After Babel: Aspects of Language and Translation*, London & New York: Oxford University Press.

Steiner, George (1979) 'The Retreat from the Word', in *Language and Silence: Essays 1958–1966*, London: Peregrine, 31–56.

Steiner, T. R. (1975) *English Translation Theory, 1650–1800*, Assen: Van Gorcum.

Stierle, Karlheinz (1996) 'Translatio studii and Renaissance', in Wolfgang Iser and Sanford Budick (eds) *The Translatability of Cultures*, Stanford University Press, 55–66.

Stoker, Bram (1993) *Dracula*, London: Everyman.

Stone, Lawrence (1977) *The Family, Sex and Marriage in England, 1500–1800*, New York: Harper & Row.

Strich, F. (1946) *Goethe und die Weltliteratur*, Berne: Francke Verlag.

Stubbs, Michael (1997) 'Whorf's Children: Critical Comments on Critical Discourse Analysis', in Ann Ryan and Alison Wray (eds) *Evolving Models of Language. Papers from the Annual Meeting of the British Association for Applied Linguistics, Swansea 1996*, Clevedon: BAAL/Multilingual Matters, 100–116.

Sturge, Kate (1997) 'Translation Strategies in Ethnography', *The Translator* 3(1): 21–38.

Sturge, Kate (2007) *Representing Others: Translation, Ethnography and the Museum*, Manchester: St. Jerome.

Sturge, Kate (2008) 'Cultural Translation', in Mona Baker and Gabriela Saldanha (eds) *Routledge Encyclopedia of Translation Studies*, London & New York: Routledge, 2nd edn, 67–70.

Sugirtharajah, R.S. (2001) *The Bible and the Third World: Precolonial, Colonial and Postcolonial Encounters*, Cambridge: Cambridge University Press.

Susam-Sarajeva, Şebnem (2003) 'Multiple-entry Visa to Travelling Theory', *Target* 15(1): 1–36.

Suzuki Kiyomatsu (1941) *Eiga kyōikuron* (On Film Education), Tokyo: Shikai Shobō.

Swedberg, Richard (1994) 'Markets as Social Structures', in Neil Smelser and Richard Swedberg (eds) *The Handbook of Economic Sociology*, Princeton, NJ & New York: Princeton University Press & Russell Sage Foundation, 255–82.

Tachibana, Hidehiro (2000) '*Les Chants de Maldoror* et le modernisme japonais – autour de Daigaku Horiguchi', *Lautréamont au Japon ou Les Chants de Maldoror et la culture d'après-guerre*, *Cahiers Lautréamont*, livraison LII and LIII (1st semester): 18–42.

Takagiba Tsutomu (1940a) 'Kyokō no riron – Tsumura Hideo-shi no "Pōru Rūta hihan'o yomu" ' (Theory of Fiction – Reading Tsumura Hideo's 'Paul Rotha criticism'), *Bunka eiga kenkyū* 3(1): 525–28.

Takagiba Tsutomu (1940b) 'Dokyumentarii firumu no oboegaki' (A memo on *Documentary Film*), *Bunka eiga kenkyū* 3(4) (April): 112–13.

Takagiba Tsutomu (1940c) 'Eiga no honshitsu ni kan suru ronmo' (Discussion regarding the essence of cinema), *Bunka eiga kenkyū* 3(10) (October): 577–80.

al-Tamawi, Ahmad Husayn (1993) *Muhammad Lutfi jum'ah fi mawkib al-haya wal-adab* [Muhammad Lutfi Jum'ah: A Literary Biography], Cairo: 'Alam al-kutub.

Tanaka Junichiro (1980) *Nihon eiga hattatsu-shi II*, Tokyo: Chuokoron-sha.

Tanikawa Yoshio (1990) *Dokyumentarii eiga no genten – sono shisō to hōhō* (The Origins of Documentary Film – Its Thought and Method), 3d edn, Tokyo: Futosha.

Tannen, Deborah and Cynthia Wallat (1993) 'Interactive Frames and Knowledge Schemas in Interaction: Examples from a Medical Examination/Interview', in Deborah Tannen (ed.) *Framing in Discourse*, New York: Oxford University Press, 57–76.

Taslitz, A. (1999) *Rape and the Culture of the Courtroom*, New York: New York University Press.

Tayama Katai (1904/1972) 'Rokotsu naru byōsha' (Raw description), in *Kindai hyōron shū* I, Nihon kindai hungaku taikei 57, Kadokawa shoten, 1972, 198–200.

Tayama Katai (1917/1993) *Tôkyô no sanjûnen*, Tokyo: Iwanami shoten.

Tayama Katai (1996) *Futon Jûeimon no saigo*, Tokyo: Shinchô bunko.

Tedlock, Dennis (1989) 'The Translator: Or, Why the Crocodile was not Disillusioned', in Rosanna Warren (ed.) *The Art of Translation*, Boston: Northeastern University Press, 159–74.

Temple, Bogusia and Rosalind Edwards (2002) 'Interpreters/translators and Cross-language Research: Reflexivity and Border Crossings', *International Journal of Qualitative Methods* 1(2). Available online at http://www.ualberta.ca/~iiqm/backissues/1_2Final/html/temple.html.

Thamkins, Theresa (1995) 'Culture Influences Patients' Desire to hear Unfavorable Diagnosis', *Asian Medical News*: October.

Thompson, John B. (1984) *Studies in the Theory of Ideology*, Berkeley: University of California Press.

Times (1939) 'Documentary Film', 11 August.

Tipton, Rebecca (2008) 'Reflexivity and the Social Construction of Identity in Interpreter-Mediated Asylum Interviews', *The Translator* 14(1): 1–19.

Todorova, Maria (1997) *Imagining the Balkans*, New York & Oxford: Oxford University Press.

Tokuda Shûsei (1914/1982) *Meiji shôsetsu bunshô hensen shi*, Bungaku fukyû kai. Reprint Nihon tosho sentaa.

Toma, Peter (1976) 'An Operational Machine Translation System', in Richard W. Brislin (ed.) *Translation: Applications and Research*, New York: Gardner Press, 247–59.

Tong, Q.S. (1999) 'The Bathos of Universalism: I. A. Richards and His Basic English', in

Lydia H. Liu (ed.) *Tokens of Exchange: The Problem of Translation in Global Circulations*, Durham & London: Duke University Press, 331–54.

Toury, Gideon (1980) *In Search of a Theory of Translation*, Tel Aviv: Porter Institute.

Toury, Gideon (1995) *Descriptive Translation Studies and Beyond*, Amsterdam: John Benjamins.

Tsumura Hideo (1939) 'Pōru Rūta no eigaron hihan—sono cho "Documentary Film" ni tsuite' (Criticism of Paul Rotha's film theory – on that writer's *Documentary Film*), *Shineiga* 9(12).

T.S.W. (1875) 'The Name of our Lord in Hindi and Urdu', *The Indian Evangelical Review: A Quarterly Journal of Missionary Thought and Effort* 2(8): 493–503.

Tucker, G. H. (1990) *The Poet's Odyssey*, Oxford: Clarendon.

Turgenev, Ivan (1922) *A Sportsman's Notebook*, trans. Charles and Natasha Hepburn, London: Everyman's Library.

Twitchell-Waas, Jeffrey (2001) 'Ghostly Effects: Orientalist Translation in Pound and Yasusada Text', *Asian Journal of Social Science* 29(2): 234–48.

Tymoczko, Maria (1986) 'Translation as a Force for Literary Revolution in the Twelfth-Century Shift from Epic to Romance', *New Comparison* 1: 1–16.

Tymoczko, Maria (1990) 'Translation in Oral Tradition as a Touchstone for Translation Theory and Practice', in Susan Bassnett and André Lefevere (eds) *Translation, History and Culture*, London: Pinter, 46–55.

Tymoczko, Maria (1999) *Translation in a Postcolonial Context: Early Irish Literature in English Translation*, Manchester: St. Jerome.

Tymoczko, Maria (2000) 'Translation and Political Engagement. Activism, Social Change and the Role of Translation in Geopolitical Shifts', *The Translator* 6(1): 23–47.

Tymoczko, Maria (2003) 'Ideology and the Position of the Translator. In What Sense is a Translator "In Between"?', in María Calzada Pérez (ed.) *Apropos of Ideology*, Manchester: St. Jerome, 181–205.

Tymoczko, Maria (2006) 'Reconceptualizing Translation Theory: Integrating Non-Western Thought about Translation', in Theo Hermans (ed.) *Translating Others*, Vol. 1, Manchester: St. Jerome, 13–32.

Tymoczko, Maria (2007) *Enlarging Translation, Empowering Translators*, Manchester: St. Jerome.

Tyson, Ann Scott (2004) 'Always in Hiding, an Iraqi Interpreter's Anguished Life', *Christian Science Monitor*, 15 September.

Tytler, Alexander Fraser, Lord Woodhouselee (1791/1907) *Essays on the Principles of Translation*, London.

Ueda, Atsuko (forthcoming) 'Sounds, Scripts, and Styles: *Kanbun-kundokutai* and the National Language Reforms of 1880s Japan', *The Review of Japanese Culture and Society*.

Ueno Ichirō (1939) 'Eikoku no bunka eiga' (British culture film), *Eiga kenkyū* 1: 146–61.

Ueno Kōzō (1940a) 'Eiga ni okeru geijutsu to kagaku – bunka eigaron no kisoteki mondai 1' (Art and science in cinema – the fundamental problem for culture film theory 1), *Nihon eiga* 5(2) (February): 24–35.

Ueno Kōzō (1940b) 'Eiga ni okeru geijutsu to kagaku – bunka eigaron no kisoteki mondai 2' (Art and science in cinema – the fundamental problem for culture film theory 2), *Nihon eiga* 5(3) (March): 25–35.

Ullman, Ellen (1997) 'Elegance and Entropy: Ellen Ullman Talks with Scott Rosenberg About What Makes Programmers Tick', *Salon Magazine* (9 October). Available at http://archive.salon.com/21st/feature/1997/10/09interview.html.

Unesco (1965–85) *Statistical Yearbook*, Paris: Unesco.

Urla, Jacqueline (1987) *Being Basque, Speaking Basque: The Politics of Language and Identity in the Basque Country*, PhD dissertation, University of California, Berkeley.

Urla, Jacqueline (1988) 'Ethnic Protest and Social Planning: A Look at Basque Language Revival', *Cultural Anthropology* 3: 379–94.

Urry, John and Scott Lash (1994) *Economies of Signs and Space*, London: Sage.

Valéry, Paul (1960) 'La Liberté de l'Esprit', *Regards sur le Monde Actuel, Œuvres*, Vol. II, Paris: Gallimard.

van Bottenburg, Maarten (1994) *Verborgen competitie: over de uiteenlopende populariteit van sporten*, Amsterdam: Bert Bakker.

van Hoof, Henri (1991) *Histoire de la traduction en Occident*, Paris: Duculot.

van Noesel, Marion and Ans Janssen (1985) *De Nederlandse literatuur in Franse vertaling*, Utrecht: Frans en Occitaans Instituut.

Vanderauwera, Ria (1985) *Dutch Novels Translated into English*. Amsterdam: Rodopi.

Varende, Yves (2000) 'Dickson-Holmes. Le clone retour à son modèle' (Dickson-Holmes: The Clone Returns to His Origins), *Le Rocambole*, Special Issue: 'Stratégies de traduction', 11(winter): 85–94.

Vasquez, Carmen and Rafael A. Javier (1991) 'The Problem with Interpreters: Communicating with Spanish-speaking Patients', *Hospital and Community Psychiatry* 42: 163–65.

Venuti, Lawrence (1986) 'The Translator's Invisibility', *Criticism* 28(2): 179–212.

Venuti, Lawrence (1991a) 'Simpatico', *SubStance* 65: 3–21.

Venuti, Lawrence (1992a) 'Introduction', in Lawrence Venuti (ed.) *Rethinking Translation*, London: Routledge, 1–17.

Venuti, Lawrence (1992b) 'Genealogies of Translation Theory: Schleiermacher', *TTR: Traduction, Terminologie, Rédaction* 4(2): 125–50.

Venuti, Lawrence (1993) 'Translation as Cultural Politics: Regimes of Domestication in English', *Textual Practice* 7: 208–223.

Venuti, Lawrence (1995) *The Translator's Invisibility*, London & New York: Routledge.

Venuti, Lawrence (1998a) 'Introduction', *Translation and Minority*, Special issue of *The Translator* 4(2): 135–44.

Venuti, Lawrence (1998b) *The Scandals of Translation: Towards an Ethics of Difference*, London & New York: Routledge.

Venuti, Lawrence (2000) 'Translation, Community, Utopia', in Lawrence Venuti (ed.) *The Translation Studies Reader*, London & New York: Routledge, 468–88.

Venuti, Lawrence (2008) *The Translator's Invisibility: A History of Translation*, 2nd revd edn, London: Routledge.

Vermeer, Hans J. (1997) 'Translation and the "Meme" ', *Target* 9(1): 155–66.

Vološinov, V. N. (1971) 'Reported Speech', trans. L. Matejka and I. R. Titunik, in L. Matejka and K. Pomorska (eds) *Readings in Russian Poetics: Formalist and Structuralist Views*, Cambridge: MIT Press.

von Flotow, Luise (1997) *Translation and Gender. Translating in the 'Era of Feminism'*, Manchester: St. Jerome Publishing.

von Flotow, Luise (ed.) (2000) *Translation and Ideology*. Special Issue of TTR (Traduction, Terminologie, Rédaction) 13(1).

Von Stackelberg, Jürgen (1984) *Uebersetzungen aus zweiter Hand: Rezeptionsvorgaege in der europaeischen Literatur vom 14. bis 18. Jahrhundert*, Berlin & New York: Walter de Gruyter.

Wadensjö, Cecilia (1998) *Interpreting as Interaction* (Language in social life series), London & New York: Longman.

Wadhams, Nick (2006) 'Iraqi Interpreters Face Death Threats from Countrymen, Alienation from U.S. Troops', *Associated Press*, 23 January.

Waisman, Sergio (2005) *Borges and Translation: the Irreverence of the Periphery*, Lewisburg: Bucknell University Press.

Waitzkin, Howard (1983) *The Second Sickness: Contradictions of Capitalist Health Care*, New York & London: The Free Press.

Waitzkin, Howard (1991) *The Politics of Medical Encounters: How Patients and Doctors Deal with Social Problems*, New Haven & London: Yale University Press.

Wakabayashi, Judy (2005) 'The Reconceptionization of Translation from Chinese in

18th-century Japan', in Eva Hung (ed.) *Translation and Cultural Change*, Amsterdam: John Benjamins, 121–45.

Wallerstein, Immanuel (1991) *Geopolitics and Geoculture: Essays on the Changing World-System*, Cambridge & Paris: Cambridge University Press & Éditions de la Maison des Sciences de l'Homme.

Walzer, M. (1983) *Spheres of Justice: A Defence of Pluralism and Equality*, New York: Basic Books.

Washburn, David (2006) 'Dangerous Work of Contractors in Iraq', *San Diego Union-Tribune*, 22 November.

Watts, Richard (2000) 'Translating Culture: Reading the Paratexts of Aimé Césaire's *Cahier d'un retour au pays natal*', TTR 13(2): 29–46.

Waugh, Patricia (1984) *Metafiction*, London: Methuen.

Waugh, Patricia (1992) *Practising Postmodernism/Reading Modernism*, London: Edward Arnold.

Weaver, Charlotte Ann (1982) *Role Evolution of Language Translators in a Major Medical Center*, PhD Dissertation: University of California at San Francisco.

Weaver, Warren (1955) 'Translation', in W. N. Locke and A. D. Booth (eds) *Machine Translation of Languages: Fourteen Essays*, Cambridge: MIT Press.

Weber, Samuel (1997) 'Wartime', in Hent de Vries and Samuel Weber (eds) *Violence, Identity, and Self-Determination*, Stanford, CA: Stanford University Press.

Weinstein, Brian (1990) 'Language Policy and Political Development: An Overview', in Brian Weinstein (ed.) *Language Policy and Political Development*, Norwood, Ablex, 1–22.

Weitbrecht, H.U. (1900) *The Urdu New Testament: A History of Its Languages and Its Versions*, Bible House Papers 3. London: The British and Foreign Bible Society.

Weitbrecht, H.U. (1903) 'The Madras Missionary Conferences of December, 1902', *The Church Missionary Intelligencer: A Journal of Missionary Information* 54 (New Series, 28): 485–96.

Wenger (1876) 'The Work of A Biblical Translator in India', *The Indian Evangelical Review: A Quarterly Journal of Missionary Thought and Effort* 4(13) (Bombay: Education Society's Press): 1–21.

West, Candace (1984) *Routine Complications: Troubles with Talk between Doctors and Patients*, Bloomington: Indiana University Press.

West, Candace and Richard Frankel (1991) 'Miscommunication in Medicine', in Nikolas Coupland, Howard Giles and John Wiemann (eds) *'Miscommunication' and Problematic Talk*, Newbury Park: Sage, 166–94.

Wheeler, Peter J. (1987) 'Systran', in Margaret King (ed.) *Machine Translation Today: The State of the Art*, Edinburgh: Edinburgh University Press, 192–208.

Whitebrook, Maureen (2001) *Identity, Narrative and Politics*, London & New York: Routledge.

Wickeri, Janice (1995) 'The Union Version of the Bible and the New Literature in China', *The Translator* 1(2): 129–52.

Wilks, Yorick (1979) 'Machine Translation and Artificial Intelligence', in Barbara M. Snell (ed.) *Translating and the Computer*, Amsterdam: North Holland Publishing, 27–43.

Wilss, Wolfram (1982) *The Science of Translation*, Tübingen: Gunther Narr.

Wittgenstein, Ludwig (1953) *Philosophical Investigations*, Oxford: Blackwell.

Wodak, Ruth (1996) *Disorders of Discourse*, London & New York: Longman.

Wollstonecraft, Mary (1992) *A Vindication of the Rights of Woman*, London & New York: Penguin Books.

Woloshin, Steven, Nina A. Bickell, Lisa M. Schwartz, Francesca Gany and Gilbert Welch (1995) 'Language Barriers in Medicine in the United States', *Journal of the American Medical Association* 273: 724–28.

Woolard, Kathryn (1989) *Double Talk: Bilingualism and the Politics of Ethnicity in Catalonia*, Stanford, CA: Stanford University Press.

Wurm, Stephen A. (1996) *Atlas of the World's Languages in Danger of Disappearing*, Paris: UNESCO Publishing/Pacific Linguistics.

Yamada Hideyoshi (1940) *Eiga kokusaku no zenshin* (The Progress of National Film Policy), Tokyo: Koseisho.

Yamamoto Masahide (1977) 'Genbun-itchi-tai', in *Buntai*, Iwanami kôza Nihongo 10 (Iwanami shoten), 311–48.

Yoashida Chleo (1978) *Mo hitotsu no eiga-shi: katsuben no jidai*, Tokyo: Jiji Tsushin-sha.

Yoshihiro, Ohasawa (2005) 'Amalgamation of Literariness: Translations as a Means of Introducing European Literary Techniques to Modern Japan', in Eva Hung and Judy Wakabayashi (eds) *Asian Translation Traditions*, Manchester: St. Jerome, 135–51.

Zemka, Sue (1991) 'The Holy Book of Empire: Translations of the British and Foreign Bible Society', in Jonathan Arac and Harriet Ritvo (eds) *Macropolitics of Nineteenth Century Literature: Nationalism, Exoticism, Imperialism*, Philadelphia: University of Pennsylvania Press.

Zhang Longxi (1998) 'Western Theory and Chinese Reality', Chapter 5 of *Mighty Opposites: From Dichotomies to Difference in the Comparative Study of China*, Stanford, CA: Stanford University Press, 1998), 151–83.

Name index

Page numbers in bold denote author contributions

Subject index